THE
CLASSICAL GREEK
READER

THE

CLASSICAL GREEK
READER

EDITED BY
KENNETH J. ATCHITY

ASSOCIATE EDITOR,
ROSEMARY MCKENNA

Oxford University Press
New York   Oxford

Oxford University Press

Oxford   New York

Athens   Auckland   Bangkok   Bogotá   Bombay
Buenos Aires   Calcutta   Cape Town   Dar es Salaam   Delhi
Florence   Hong Kong   Istanbul   Karachi
Kuala Lumpur   Madras   Madrid   Melbourne
Mexico City   Nairobi   Paris   Singapore
Taipei   Tokyo   Toronto   Warsaw

and associated companies in

Berlin   Ibadan

First published in 1996 by Henry Holt and Company, Inc.,
115 West 18th Street, New York, New York 10011

First issued as an Oxford University Press paperback, 1998

Oxford is a registered trademark of Oxford University Press

Library of Congress Cataloging-in-Publication Data
The classical Greek reader / edited by Kenneth J. Atchity ;
associate editor, Rosemary McKenna.
p.   cm.
Includes bibliographical references and index.
ISBN 0-19-512303-4 (pbk.)
1. Greek language—Readers. 2. Greece—Civilization—Problems,
exercises, etc.   I. Atchity, Kenneth J.   II. McKenna, Rosemary.
PA260.C57   1998
488.6'421—dc21   98-12978

1 3 5 7 9 10 8 6 4 2

Printed in the United States of America
on acid-free paper

in memory of
Robert Fitzgerald,
Richmond Lattimore, and
Cedric Whitman

CONTENTS

PART TWO

Classical

PART THREE

Postclassical

Preface

*T*his book seeks to present the widest possible perspective on the Greek classical period, from its roots in the Homeric epics to its echoes in the histories of Plutarch and romances of Heliodorus. Its purpose is to provide today's reader with direct access to the voices that shaped the classical Greek spirit.

Students in literature, history, political science, art history, psychology, women's studies, and anthropology may find here sufficient documentation to provoke further explorations of the magnificent outpouring of human expression associated with the Greeks before and after their capture by the Roman Empire.

The collection is admittedly biased, especially in favor of the positive and the patriarchal. The time saw more than its share of warfare, misogyny, racism, slavery, and epidemics. Though all the ills of human nature are represented in classical Greek history, its legacy to us has taken, through two and a half millennia, the shape of our highest and most noble aspirations. Female readers may wonder at the paucity of women in this anthology, and indeed they should. Despite the importance of powerful women such as Helen, Klytaimnestra, Penelope, Medea, and Antigone in early Greek myth, classical Greece was a primarily masculine culture. In Sparta, women served in the military, and were treated as equals in some regards. But in Athens, with the exception of influential courtesans, women were more or less seen and not heard. Ironically, Athens' principal deity was a goddess, Athena, after whom the city was named because she bestowed the olive on it for food, light, warmth, and oil. Athena is not a woman's woman, but a man's woman. She has no mother, born full-bodied from the forehead of Zeus; no spouses, and no children. She was created by men to legitimize patriarchy, and to buffet it against its fear of reversion to a previous matriarchal dominance that may have existed in pre-Mycenaean Minoan civilization. Just as the editors of the Hebrew Bible edited its variants to produce a consistent, monotheistic worldview, the patriarchal writers of classical Greece rewrote the myths they inherited to portray the world they preferred. Despite the brilliant and respected Sappho, as well as Tecmessa, Korinna, and Erinna, classical Greece was male-dominated. Even that so little of these women's writings survive further underlines this reality.

Yet the magnificent achievements of Greece merit its being presented in its own image. Loose chronological arrangement allows the reader to set out on an odyssey from the islands off the coast of Asia Minor that gave birth to the Homeric epics after the fall of Troy in the twelfth century B.C. to the decadence of Greece under Alexander, then under the Roman Empire. Presenting these encounters in order makes it possible to observe the development of important themes, concerns, and motifs. The index and glossary make it possible to focus on a particular interest. Each encounter is given perspective with its own introduction so that readers unfamiliar with the period can just as easily dip in and out of this anthology serendipitously.

Students of the classical Greece—mathematics, astronomy, literature, art history, ethics, political science, philosophy, history, psychology, history of religion—will find here my favorite texts from courses like "The Greek Mind" and "Comp. Lit. 101: Classical Survey" without the frustration of having their selection limited by the academic calendar. The selections can be used as steppingstones to deeper investigations. The themes, images, and characteristics discussed in the General Introduction can be used to map individual routes through the texts here reprinted.

I have selected both contemporary and older translations based on availability and verisimilitude, fully acknowledging that nothing can equal direct experience with the Greek text which I had the privilege of encountering for the first time in my Jesuit high school classes. One of my Yale mentors, Thomas G. Bergin, wrote to me a year after his retirement from teaching that he had now turned to doing something he'd waited his whole life to do: reading Homer's *Odyssey,* for the first time, in the original, teaching himself Homeric Greek as he went. If you haven't learned Greek, it's never too late! In our age of overstimulated minds, its brilliant clarity will restore your confidence in the western mind's foundations.

As a predecessor anthologist explains, "there is a regrettable amount of caprice in the transliteration of Greek names," and I've chosen to do nothing here to undo the chaos that two thousand years of usage has inflicted on us. As much as possible, I've tried to follow "Greek" spellings without distracting today's reader. For example, the god of healing can be spelled in English in any number of ways: Asclepius (Roman version), Asklepios (closest to the Greek), or Asclepios (version used here). The problem began with the Romans, who gave their own names to Greek authors; Terpandros, for example, became Terpander, Demokritos, Democritus. The British preferred the Romanized names, though many twentieth-century scholars have chosen to go back toward the original. For example, Richmond Lattimore, great translator of Homer's epics and of the Greek tragedians, prefers *Achilleus* to the more familiar *Achilles*. Familiarity to the American ear has been my ultimate criterion in the names employed in the introductory essays. The glossary and index help the reader conform the variant spellings that appear in the excerpts. With names such as Apollonius, Orpheus, Euclid, or Galen, I've simply retained the spelling that most Americans would recognize.

Since the dating of many events in classical Greece is still uncertain and contradictory, I've generally followed a consensus of scholarly opinion; or given my own estimate.

I am grateful to Kenneth Wright, my editor, his assistant Kevin Ohe, and Sandra Watt, my reference agent, for the suggestion that I undertake this anthology; and to my Greek mentors and associates at Georgetown, Yale, Harvard, and Occidental College, especially E. J. Barber, Kenneth Cavander, Robert Fitzgerald, David Glidden, Marcia Homiak, Scott Littleton, Adam Parry, Jr., R. J. Schork, Erich Segal, Joseph Russo, Cedric Whitman, and Robert Young, S.J., who nurtured my love and admiration for this remarkable outpouring of excellence. This book's advisory board have been invaluable sources of general perspective and particular suggestions. I am especially grateful to Willis Barnstone, for allowing me to use freely his vibrant and impeccable translations of the lyric poets.

I also wish to thank the following:

Rosemary McKenna, for her research, suggestions, copyright consulting, and commentary. Harmony Wu for research. Chi-Li Wong for her patient assistance in putting the manuscript together. My students at Occidental College. Art Resource for allowing reproduction of the images from its excellent collections.

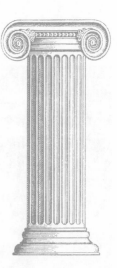

INTRODUCTION

One of the most magical moments of my life was witnessing the "rosy-fingered dawn" from the highest hill of the Cycladic island of Naxos. I'd received an award from the Graves Foundation to spend the summer in Greece exploring aspects of the Homeric epics. A recurrent formula in the *Odyssey*, "and when rosy-fingered dawn appeared," had long intrigued me because it was hard for me to envision the metaphor's basis in observation, though I knew Homer's language was characteristically concrete. I determined to watch the dawn, and when I arrived on Naxos and spied the hill, knew I had discovered the perfect observation point.

I awoke at 3 A.M. and climbed to the top of the hill, having scouted the path the day before so I could find it in the dark. It was very dark, but somehow I made it up the twisted path, hampered from time to time by the undergrowth and by my vivid imagination of unpropitiated Harpies rooting in the eerie darkness for a stray man to offer to their insatiable matriarchal appetites.

I sat in the clearing on the hilltop, and waited in the preternatural stillness so unlike the noisiness of the harshly sunny summer days that had greeted me when I'd left Piraeus. The first signal to break the stillness was the muffled, uncertain barking of dogs. I remember being surprised by the dogs, since I'd fully expected crowing cocks. Within moments, the barking awakened cows, whose lowing soon mingled with the baaing of a goat. At last, the cocks trumpeted their belated annunciations.

I fixed my gaze on the eastern horizon and saw the first glimpse of light, which indeed illuminated in pink a hand-like spread of perpendicular cirrus clouds that for a few vivid instants were the only expressions of the new day. Then, like a brightly polished brass coin, the first sliver of sun

"Ruins of Apollo's temple on Naxos"

"Helen, from a white-figure vase"

showed itself and obliterated the effect. As the disk lifted itself above the horizon, it reminded me of the scene in Book 19 of the *Iliad*, where Thetis nearly blinds Achilles' Myrmidon troops by showing them the magnificent shield the god Hephaestos has forged for her heroic but doomed son.

I had seen rosy-fingered dawn with my own eyes, and suddenly understood that the epithet must have arisen from a weaving metaphor. Dawn, the weaver, with her nimble fingers weaves the new day as Penelope wove and re-wove Laertes' burial shroud to keep the suitors at bay while she awaited Odysseus' return. After having read and translated the *Odyssey* from the age of fourteen, I had finally proved the validity of the emotions evoked by the beautiful words. Nearly 3,500 years ago, a poet had sung them not only because they were beautiful but also because they painted the world of glorious deeds accomplished by the sons and daughters of gods who slept with mortals.

Moments like this recurred as I made my way from one side of the Aegean to the other:

- remembering Helen's diminished role in the *Odyssey*, when Telemachos meets her restored to her husband Menelaos' court, when I found the feather of a hawk in the ruins of her temple above Sparta—where she was once worshiped as a goddess.
- receiving a flower on Paros from a tiny village girl, who handed it to me saying nothing but welcome writ large in her dark eyes, and marveling that the fundamental institution of *xeinia*, guest-friendship, was as alive in Greece today as it was in Homer's time.
- sitting in the *choregos'* stone chair at the ancient theater at the foot of the Acropolis, imagining how it felt, when, in 468, the festival's tragedies had been mounted and the audience spoken its criticism, to wait for the ballots to be counted—and to learn that Sophocles had defeated Aeschlyus.
- distrusting my map-using abilities, and turning back to Sparta to ask directions again to the ancient agora—only to find that I had, in fact, found it and that it was nothing but stubbles of stone among the pines; and the chilling feeling to recall Thucydides' warning that nothing monumental would remain to tell the world of Sparta's greatness.
- standing in the ruins of Knossos' sister-city Phaistos, on Crete, where Minos' brother Rhadamanthys ruled—Rhadamanthys who had, by the time Homer sang of him, already receded so much into legend that Homer identified him as the "judge of the dead" in the underworld.

The feelings I experienced on these marvelous occasions are, ultimately, impossible to verbalize. But they are evoked each time I open the pages of an ancient Greek text, where the brilliant clarity of that sunlit experience shines through the well-wrought words. In the Greek mind, articulation and reality are so nearly equivalent that, as André Gide put it, "for the poet, as for God, the word becomes the world." Edith Hamilton summarized the Greek achievement: "They wanted to know what things are and what things mean." And, like the endless days under the unforgiving sun, their thirst for knowledge was a constant.

Remote from today's world? Perhaps. But ask what these words have in common:

triangle	criticism	cosmopolitan
cosmos	nuclear	logical

physical	cosmetics	statistics
crisis	synthesis	geography
technology	atom	politics
dichotomy	erotic	calculate
circle	psychology	energy
enthusiasm	theory	analysis
ellipse	cybernetics	Pentagon

Only a sampling of Greek words that shape our routine life today. Is that sufficient motive to become familiar with Greek thought? I don't know. Perhaps in this day of "relevancy" we need to find more direct parallels (yet another Greek word) between our time and the past before we take the past seriously. Certainly if Aristophanes were alive as the twentieth century draws to a close he'd find no lack of subject matter for his satirical comedies. Euripides would find common ground with Quentin Tarantino, and Plato, although attracted by their similar beliefs, would take Deepak Chopra to task for his sophist tendencies. If Solon, Demosthenes, and Pericles were alive, the dearth of worthy leadership in American politics would become even more painfully obvious by contrast to their civic zeal and fierce personal integrity.

Maps can reveal the vastness and geographical complexity of the world known as "ancient Greece," stretching from Sicily in the west to Asia Minor in the east, and from mountainous Macedon in the north to the massive island of Crete that forms its southern boundary. But what *is* Greece, I wondered, as I sailed back and forth through the Ionian, Aegean, and Thracian Seas. I observed today's Greeks on these ships, as much at home as Americans are on land, rolling easily with the waves as though to undulations of their racial unconsciousness. Greece—peninsulas, archipelagoes, mainlands, isthmuses, and islands—seemed more like a concept than a country. How could the people from Corcyra, in the northern Ionian Sea off the coast of Epirus, possibly have anything in common with the natives of Sappho's Lesbos, an island of Asia Minor that's closer to Troy than to Mycenae or even to Athens? Then, as happens occasionally in life, I recognized the answer that had been all the while, through every voyage, directly before my eyes. The words were emblazoned on the seal of Greece mounted in every ship's lounge: "The sea unites us." The very force that separates others brings the Greeks together.

Generally when we speak of "the Greek mind" we refer specifically to the Athenian mind of the fourth and fifth centuries B.C. Athens of this "golden age" witnessed the culmination of Greek civilization, liberated by a richly organized language made possible by the relatively new discovery of an alphabetical system for recording thought and expression. The poet Howard Nemerov asked, "Who put the alphabet in alphabetical order?" The answer is the Greeks. The Phoenicians may lay claim to originating signs that became known as the alphabet (*alpha, beta,* etc.), but it was the Greeks who transformed them into a system of twenty-four signs without individual significance that could be used to transcribe the vowels and consonants of words in a permanent record. The literary explosion that began in the eighth and seventh centuries B.C. as a result is equaled only by that following Gutenberg's printing press. Both the Babylonians and the Egyptians, we know from their prodigious constructions, understood the Pythagorean theorem; but it remained for the Greek Pythagoras to put it down on paper. Writing not only recorded, but caused a continuous outpouring of expression that flows through the millennia to our own shores like an enormous river of emotion, thought, and spiritual awareness.

In its Aeolian, Dorian, Ionian, Boeotian, and Attic dialects, Greek developed thanks to the invention of writing from a mythic language that could express abstractions only indirectly into a logical language from which all subsequent western culture inherited its fundamental methodologies. The word *logos* itself is a prime example, beginning its history as a word charged with religious power, and referring to the word of wisdom and truth. By the time of Aristotle, *logos* had lost its philosophical connotations and had come to mean the "study of" something: biology, the study of life; zoology, the study of animal forms; and theology, the study of God.

For better or worse, the Greeks brought western civilization from *mythos* to *logos*, out of the mythic and into the logical way in which we face life today. The mythic representation of reality, canonized in Homer's *Iliad* and *Odyssey*, presents a heroic universe in which the gods are real forces, and a man is born into his character depending on his relationship to them and to other men. Sophocles' observation, "A man's character is his fate," means one thing in the Homeric world, another in the golden age of Athens. In Homer's world, the seed of Achilles' doom is contained in the golden apple brought to the wedding feast of his father and mother. Since his personal ability to evade that fate is relatively limited, the issue is only how he will behave while he awaits it. Like Oedipus, Achilles is defined entirely by his birthright. By Sophocles' time, character was redefined. Human action was no longer regarded as being entirely futile against the capriciousness of the gods; the gods themselves were questionable—and man was the questioner. Even the Homeric poems show signs of this new rational, postmythic consciousness, as when Achilles asks questions that no one can answer: "Why *have* the Achaians come here to fight with the Trojans? Is it really because of this woman?" His questions go unanswered because, though the rhapsodes who sang them might have been capable of rational speculation, the heroic world was not. Its language could not say, "Achilles changed his mind." Instead: "Ares moved in his [Achilles'] shaggy breast, and his arm went to his sword." Agamemnon insults Achilles, he later explains, because the god Até came upon him, as he came once upon even Zeus himself. The Homeric gods are mythic representations of what the logical age would call "elements of the psyche." By perfecting the tool of written language the Greeks brought us from myth to religion to philosophy to science.

Linguistic analysis leads to explanation, and to heightened understanding. The Greeks analyzed everything from the heavens to the self, from the minutiae of zoology to the nature of the ultimate reality (what Plato called "the really real"). Their accomplishments span the width and depth of human experience:

- **The city-state.** Renaissance Florence, and its sister city-states throughout Europe, modeled itself consciously on classical Athens, Sparta, Thebes, Corinth, and other Greek towns where "nationalism" was alway secondary to urban loyalty. Because each city was centered on its marketplace and temples, inhabitants gathered regularly to deal with matters of common interest. The synergies created by this daily physical interaction of statesmen and philosophers, shopkeepers and historians, dramatists and scientists go far to explain the cultural explosion of the golden age. So fierce was the Greek citizen's loyalty to his city-state that ostracism—being exiled from the city for life—was considered worse than death.

- **Democracy.** The term itself named after the *demes* (or tribes) of Athens, democracy was practiced in a purer form there than at any subsequent time in history. True, participatory government, where citizens gathered daily in the agora and the various senates to steer the ship of state, was made possible by slavery and excluded women. Yet the form created by the Athenians remains today the ideal that has freed slaves and liberated repressed minorities in nations where its principles have been applied.

- **Jurisprudence.** At the end of the *Odyssey* the goddess Athena propitiates the enraged families of the suitors slain by an avenging Odysseus, stopping what might otherwise have become an endless vendetta. In the *Oresteia* of Aeschylus she creates a twelve-man jury and the principle of "innocent, until proved guilty," with the bias in favor of the defendant, when she breaks the jury's deadlock with her own vote in favor of the matricide Orestes. From the litigation reforms of Solon to the constitution of Athens presided over by Pericles, western civilization can trace its system of justice, via the Roman Empire, to those developed by the classical Greeks.

- **Mystery cults.** Beneath the controlled and rational façade of patriarchal classical Greece lay a seething understructure of primitive, chaotic, unassimilated energy that took expression in the cults of Eleusis, Aphrodite, Dionysius, Pythagoras, and Orpheus, among others. These secret societies, alternately condoned and condemned by the powers that be, created an esoteric literature and oral tradition that finds expression today in groups such as the Masons, the Rosicrucians, the goddess branch of feminism, or wicca. The concept of mystery lies in wait at the heart of the greatest Greek dramas, as when Oedipus discovers that evil is not, as he'd expected, a problem to be solved but an irreducible mystery.

- **Reason.** The primary instrument of western civilization owes its birthright to the Greek philosophers and scientists who refined and perfected it.

- **Systematic analysis and the scientific method.** After a long evolution from the Ionian cosmographers to his master Plato, Aristotle perfected observation and classification based on analysis, and set the stage for theory based on observation, which remains today's standard for scientific thought.

Nearly all categories of western expression can be traced to Greek origins:

- **Epic poetry.**   The Homeric *Iliad* and *Odyssey* have inspired all subsequent epic poems in the west, from Apollonius' romantic *Argonautica* and the Roman Virgil's imperial *Aeneid* to Torquato Tasso's *Jerusalem Delivered* and Stephen Vincent Benét's *John Brown's Body*. As the supreme expression of poetry, the epic is distinguished by its universal scope and its focus on heroic man engaging in an impossible quest fully understanding the possibility of defeat. The epic is also the grandfather of such "epic novels" as Miguel de Cervantes' *Don Quixote de la Mancha* and Herman Melville's *Moby Dick*.

- **Lyric.**   The spread of writing by the late seventh century B.C. allowed Greek poets to examine and express the microcosm in a form that might be considered the epic's opposite. The precise and poignant lyrics of Alkman, Archilochos, Sappho, and Theognis provide glimpses into the heart and humor, mind and manners of their authors, from Praxilla's love for cucumbers to Simonides' eloquent tribute to the Spartans who died at Thermopylae.

- **Music.**   Whether strictly defined as "tonal art" or generally applied to all the arts and sciences, music played a dominant role in every aspect of Greek thought and expression—from Pan's pipes to Apollo's lyre and the flute-playing courtesans of Athens, from the lyrics celebrating Olympic victories to the choruses of tragedy and comedy. The Pythagoreans believed that the cosmos was generated out of music, and that the ultimate reality is primal sound. Plato speculated on the impact of various modes of music upon soul and human emotions.

- **Mathematics.**   Strongly allied with music, early Greek mathematics was not so much inventive as it was transcriptive. Many of the principles enunciated by Hippocrates, Pythagoras, Euclid, Zeno, and Eudoxos, including the definition of π and the Pythagorean theorem, had been discovered already by the Egyptians and Babylonians (the latter inventing algebra, numbers, and proof); but the Greeks take credit for recording them and refining them. Their mathematical prowess in trigonometry, integral calculus, geometry, and logic was particularly remarkable considering they accomplished it without the concept of zero, and without negative numbers.

- **Physical sciences.**   After a rocky start (Thales' belief that the earth was a disk floating on water), pre- and postclassical Greek physicists, from Anaximander to Archimedes, went on to posit early forms of unified field theory; and to define:

  - atomic theory;
  - electricity;
  - the relationship between space, time, and matter;
  - a spherical earth spinning on its axis;

- a way of measuring the circumference of the earth;
- and theories of both a heliocentric and a geocentric explanation of planetary and stellar motion.

Along the way, they invented the water clock, the pendulum, open-heart surgery, and interacting gimbals. Preferring the intellectual challenges of investigation and theory over practical application, the Greeks either invented or refined all the physical sciences known to us today—including astronomy, biology, botany, medicine, physics (also nuclear physics), and zoology.

- **Drama.**   The social importance of the theater to ancient Greece can't be overstated. The annual dramatic festivals were a major focal point of communal reorganization, where the mythic values that held the city-state to a unanimous course of action were regularly reinvoked, reinterpreted, and readjusted to fit the needs of the day. For the duration of the festival, the participants and the audience, aided by mild intoxicants, shared a single, collective mind (similar to the experience of a twentieth-century rock concert).

  - **Tragedy.**   Whether it sprang full-blown from epic, or began as hero worship at the tombs of fallen warriors, Greek tragedy, celebrated at the Great Dionysian Festival, is defined by Aristotle as "an imitation of an action that is serious, complete, and of a certain magnitude; in language embellished with each kind of artistic ornament, the several kinds being found in separate parts of the play; in the form of action, not of narration; through pity and fear effecting the proper purgation of these emotions." Aristotle would say that people go to see horror films not to learn how to commit horrors but to purge themselves of the emotions the films provide. When you leave the theater, you say to yourself, "I thought I had problems!" Greek tragedy places the hero at the brink of the abyss and allows us to observe how he behaves. It confronts death and absurdity, recognizing them as the final measures of a man's life: "Count no man happy until he is dead. The ending tells all." (Sophocles) In tragedy every moment is eternity.
  - **Comedy.**   In Greek comedy, staged at the annual Lenaia festival also presided over by the spirit of Dionysius, eternity is no more than the moment at hand. If tragedy, examining beginnings, middles, and ends, was linear, comedy is cyclical. Both Old and New Comedy present an initial problem followed by humorous complications and resolutions plotted to lead to a wedding (gamos). Greek comedy, satirically didactic and intensely celebratory of the fleeting and the perennial craziness, agonies, and joys of life, pretends that death does not exist; and ends happily, with renewal. Whether Aristophanes' social commentary or Menander's comedies of manners, the social function of Greek comedy was to remind the au-

dience to keep life in perspective and to reinvigorate the communal spirit through shared laughter.

- **Art and architecture.** Serenity, strength, simplicity, symmetry—the characteristics of preclassical Greek art—evolved rapidly in the two hundred years before the golden age into a compelling dynamism that makes the statues appear as if they were about to move, their musculature so perfectly delineated that it conveys the sense of strain that accompanies action. The faces sculpted by Phidias and Praxiteles reflect serenity and confident self-awareness, echoing contemporary written expression. Mastery of harmony and proportion, concealing the applied geometry beneath the architect's idealistic vision, made even the most massive temples, such as the Parthenon, seem graceful, almost ephemeral.

- **Philosophy.** Every realm of Greek expression is influenced by breakthrough definitions in philosophy and metaphysics. Greek philosophy (literally, "love of wisdom") was dedicated to discerning the truth, not for practical reasons but as the proper occupation of the human mind, whose origins lay in the direction of its natural yearnings for knowledge. Oedipus pursues the truth even when he sees it leading to his own ruin, because he believes that pursuit is his human duty. From the cosmographer Thales, by way of Socrates, Plato, and Aristotle, to Epicurus, the Greeks developed idealism, realism, Stoicism, Skepticism, and Epicureanism, and provided the foundation for our very way of thinking. They formulated and sought to answer questions such as:

"Parthenon, interior view"

- What is real?
- What is the meaning of life?
- What is fate?
- What is happiness?
- How should a man best conduct his life?
- Is perfection possible?
- What is good?
- What is virtue?

And, in so doing, opened a dialogue continued by western philosophers through the ages.

- **Ethics.**   Defining happiness as "an activity of the soul's highest faculty in conformity with virtue," Aristotle went on to clarify Plato's speculations on ethics by classifying vice and virtue in relation to both their origins in the soul and their purposes in society. Basing their ethics on pursuit of the "highest good," Socrates, Plato, and Aristotle considered their approach superior to that of sophists such as Protagoras, Gorgias, Prodicus, and Antiphon, who taught socially effective behavior.

- **Political science.**   The science of the city (*polis*) was defined as a separate study by Plato and Aristotle. Plato saw, based on his belief in the absolute ideal, that the value of laws lies in compromising between the ideal and the real, setting a standard by which the ideal might influence the real without diminishing its practicality. His concept of the "body politic" would be transformed by Catholic theology into the doctrine of the "Mystical Body of Christ." In his *Politics* Aristotle defines man as a "political animal," recognizing that civilization requires rules and standard values that would be irrelevant to a hermit.

- **History.**   Aware of the importance of writing, Herodotus undertook to describe the Persian War but decided to start a little earlier, with the entire history of the world up to the war's outbreak. His rambling, digressive, all-inclusive, indiscrimate storytelling set the stage for his successor Thucydides, the first scientific historian and the first to discriminate between political ideology and political fact, in his record of the Peloponnesian War. His didactic purpose and method of presenting contrary viewpoints set a timeless standard of objective viewpoint and evenhanded procedure for western historians.

- **Psychology.**   Freudian theories of the "Oedipus" and "Elektra" complexes find their roots in Greek tragedy. Freud's concept of "day residue" as reflected in dreams can be traced to Aristotle. And Aristotle's *De Anima* (On the Soul) is in fact the first psychological treatise to be conscious of itself as such.

From the time of Empedocles and Heraclitus, Greek thinkers believed that progress results from the creative interaction of opposites, arising from the dynamic tension between them. Out of chaos comes forward-moving order. The Greeks, as expressed in the great tragedies of Aeschylus, Sophocles, and Euripides, understood that the most defining conflicts in human life come from the opposition not of right and wrong, but of two rights. In *Antigone* both Antigone and Creon are right. The result is tragedy. The selections gathered here reveal the major paradoxical patterns of classical Greek thought:

- **Universal knowledge versus self-knowledge.**   No subject is too small, each morsel is worth a comment by Athenaeus; nor is any too large. The same mind deals with both the trivial, as when Aristotle discusses the Pythagoreans' belief that beans contain the soul of the dead, and the immense, as when the same philosopher speculates on the motion of the heavenly spheres. The Greeks believed, in fact, that the microcosm and the macrocosm are formally related, so that the behavior of *atomoi* ("atoms," the term coined by Democritus and Leucippus) resembles structurally the motion of stars and planets. The part reflects the whole, the whole is shaped by the parts. Knowledge of others, then, must begin at home. Inscribed above the portals of the oracle at Delphi, the words "Know thyself" became Socrates' inspiration. He recognized that without self-knowledge man is incapable of truly knowing anything beyond himself. The psyche of the individual reflects the organization of the body politic, just as morality was thought of as the individual face of politics and politics as the public face of morality. The economy of the household and of the commonwealth are essentially identical.

- **Monism versus dualism.** Is the cosmos (the term the Greeks invented to describe all of visible reality, whether it is visible or not) organized essentially around a single underlying principle (Thales called it *water*, Anaximenes *air*)? Or is it, instead, made up of the dynamic tension referred to by Empedocles and Heraclitus—the two Strifes, whose interaction creates progress in the form of life? At one extreme, the Atomists posited an infinite pluralism of discrete worlds whose ceaseless movement shapes our reality. At the other, Plato's belief in the priority of the "really real," though this distinction of ideals from appearances borrows from dualism, led to a monistic worldview that would later become part and parcel of Thomas Aquinas' orthodox summation of Christian doctrine. Plato's insistence on the "oneness" of the Prime Mover gave Aquinas the language he needed to describe the Catholic God.

- **The two Strifes.** Hesiod was the first on record to distinguish explicitly between Good Strife and Bad Strife, one who "builds up evil war, and works all kinds of evil for man, and slaughter" and the other who "is natural, and kind" and necessary for man's growth. Both Strifes are prefigured in Homer's *Iliad* (in the law court and embattled city shown on the shield forged by Hephaestos for Achilles). The Greeks were the first to recognize that strife is an integral part of life, and to prefer the healthy kinds of stress over those that are destructive to the self or to the state. The Olympic games, by providing a peaceful forum for discharging rivalries among the Greek city-states, lessened tensions that had done such damage in the Peloponnesian War. The arbitration for a blood price, depicted on Homer's shield, foreshadows Solon's new laws for Athens and classical Greek revolutions in legal procedure. The Greeks recognized competition as the engine of creative progress, whether in the dialectic method of reasoning through examining opposing theses, or in the elaborate staging of the annual Lenaea and Great Dionysian Festivals.

- **Being versus not-Being.** Which of the two truly exists, and which is an illusion? It is highly characteristic of the classical Greeks to have worried about this, an argument taken up fiercely by Zeno, Heraclitus, Parmenides, and Empedocles, as well as by Plato and Aristotle. If only Being exists, and not-Being does not truly exist, then change, which we perceive through our senses, must be an illusion. If not-Being alone exists, and Being is only an idea, then the world is trapped in temporality. If both Being and not-Being exist, in which direction is the universe heading?—a question still asked by nuclear astronomers. Along the way these "cosmographers," as they called themselves, defined and redefined concepts such as illusion, appearance, reality, truth, opinion, and change.

- **Idealism versus realism.**   Beginning by distinguishing the word from the concept it depicted (a particular chair, for example, as opposed to *chairness*), Plato came to believe that the "real" world of appearances portrayed to us by our senses isn't worth our trust and affection compared to the invisible "really real" world of absolute Ideas that exist unchanging through all eternity and that our souls experience directly before they become clouded by occupying our bodies. Philosophy's goal, through questioning, is to find our way back to the ideal. As the founder of western idealism, Plato's dialogues sought to define the perfect education, the perfect commonwealth, the perfect good. By contrast, his student Aristotle believed that the ultimate formal quality of the world could be found in the precise classification and analysis of *things*. He was, by comparison, a realist, though his theory of Forms borrows from his master's idealism. Every time we question the distinction between appearance and reality, we return to this classic Greek debate.

- **Homocentric versus theocentric.**   As God stood at the center of the ancient Hebrew world, man stood at the center for the Greeks. Even in Homer, Longinus pointed out, "the gods have become men, and the men gods," because the editors of these ancient epics were already moving away from the nature religion ascribed to by their heroes. Odysseus, offered immortality by Calypso, rejects it in favor of human imperfection. He loves being mortal, and he knows how to be. The hero Prometheus, at the risk of eternal punishment, steals fire from Zeus to bring to mortals, so strong is his admiration for the human spirit. Epicurus believed that the gods exist but are irrelevant. Xenophanes (tr. Willis Barnstone) expressed his skepticism this way:

> *Our gods have flat noses and black skins,*
> *say the Ethiopians. The Tracians say our gods*
> *have red hair and hazel eyes.*

Socrates would die to defend his insistence on preferring "the god within" to the murky and chaotic voices of the "state's gods." The gods' behavior was too unpredictable. They could not, in their imperviousness to the pain experienced by mortals, be understood, used as models, or trusted.

- **Measure versus chaos.**   Inheriting a mythic system that accepted the simultaneous existence of absolute opposites and managed to build a heroic lifestyle around the chaos, the early philosophers rejected the notion of chaos and set about to measure everything imaginable, from reality to the atom, from mind to matter, from the nature of virtue to the genealogy and domiciles of the gods. The sophist Protagoras made the most eloquent statement about the drive to analyze and measure: "Man is the measure of all things. Of things that are, that they are; and of things that are not, that they are not." Man, not the divine, was the great measurer. All significance is created by his mere attention, and without it the tree in the forest falls without meaning. Man is somehow defined not only by his ability to measure but just as much by his need to measure and, consequently, his endless need to find things to measure. The verb *krittein*, to examine, giving rise to criticism, became the order of the day. "The unexamined life," Socrates announced, "is not worth living."

Measurement and analysis as the first step to understanding and self-awareness are integral parts of the modern western psyche. The search for measure led to:

- **Moderation versus excess.**   The "golden mean" became the principle of ideal behavior, as the midpoint between two extremes. The lyric poet Theognis writes: "Try for nothing excessive. The middle way is best./In this way . . . virtue is won." Whether practiced by the mystics like Pythagoras or the hardheaded Aristotelians, "nothing to excess" became a rallying cry for the well-lived life. "Balance," "proportion" *harmonia* characterized achievements in literature, art, and architecture as well as in political science, ethics, and psychology. When this standard gave way to the decadent self-interests of Alexandrian times, Hellenistic civilization had become a weak reflection of its Hellenic model. It wasn't Circe who turned Odysseus' men into pigs; they did it to themselves, by eating too much.

- **Dialectical reasoning versus intuition.**   The Greeks invented the dialectic, the process of human reasoning by which statement (or *thesis*) leads to counter-statement (*antithesis*), until a balanced midpoint, *synthesis*, is reached. Yet each new synthesis, in turn, breeds an antithesis—and so on ad infinitum, as thought or argument or invention progress through this methodology of point and counterpoint. So effective was this process as a method for learning that Plato spent much of his life defending it as the only way to achieve knowledge of the ultimate reality. But a lifetime of analysis frustrated him, and in his last dialogues, *The Sophist* and *Theatetus*, he turned back to his poetic and mythic roots and declared that intuition was an essential part of the philosopher's metaphysical arsenal. Plato, who had banished the poets, was himself an outstanding poet. It was the mystical Pythagoras, after all, who had influenced Plato's doctrine of reincarnation. Aristotle, observing his master's evolution, would make this remarkable statement in his *Poetics*: "Poetry is more truly scientific, or philosophical, than history because history shows us only those things that were or are, while poetry shows us what should be, or ought to be."

- **Hero versus "Protean" man.** The contrast between adamant Achilles and "many-minded" Odysseus indicated the evolution from a heroic age of behavioral models based on universally accepted orthodox values and the postheroic, classical age, where men become conscious of the constancy of change in human experience; and of the need to change themselves to deal adequately with life. Proteus, the shape-shifter, is the sea god who will tell the truth if you can hold on to him until he reveals his true nature. Versatile Odysseus, the prototypical "man for all seasons," whose version of the truth depends on whom he's talking to, becomes the first spokesman for modern "moral relativity." Opposed to him is Socrates, the heroic *eiron*, whose occupation as social gadfly becomes a death sentence he glady accepts. The citizen's ability to master more than one activity is another facet of the Protean aspect of classical Greece. Sophocles was not only a playwright and producer, but also a general and an ambassador, living proof of Pericles' boast that Athenians were "capable . . . of the utmost dexterity and grace in the widest range of activities."

- **Individual versus community.** In every realm of human expression, the Greeks weighed both sides of the issue of individual rights versus the greater good of the community. In Sophocles' *Antigone*, the heroine dies to defend her right to bury her brother; King Creon feels compelled by his communal role to order the death of his niece even though it leads to the death of his son. The paradox is shown at its most tragic in Sophocles' *Oedipus the King*, where the needs of the individual, at the outset, appear to be identical with those of the community. When Oedipus discovers that he himself is the criminal jeopardizing the well-being of Thebes, he is hopelessly conflicted. Plato's *Republic* extends the paradigm of part versus whole to define the relationship between the individual "members" and the "body politic." He and Aristotle insisted that offending members be cut off to preserve the life of the body. Socrates chooses to die in his own fashion rather than to live in the fashion of those he condemns.

- **Dionysian versus Apollonian.** As Friedrich Nietzsche observed, Greek thought was polarized by the chaotic, earthbound values associated with the frenzy of the wine-god, the "ecstatic artist," Dionysius; and the cool, spiritual intellect of the sun god, the "dream artist," Apollo. In Euripides' *The Bacchae*, Dionysius represents the uncontrollable eruption of nature in individuals and cities, the life-force incarnate, the force

"Achilles and Aias playing dice, black-figure vase"

that through the green fuse drives the flower. No matter how civilized man becomes, his inherent wildness can never be entirely repressed. Dionysian rituals, expressed in the satyr plays that concluded the annual tragic festival, induce a state of ecstasy, a kind of possession by the raw life-force. The drunken Herakles, in Euripides' *Alcestis*, exemplifies the Dionysian force when he urges King Admetus to break his Apollonian vows and take a new woman to his bed to restore his kingdom's life-force. Nietzsche calls the Apollonian a "slave morality," binding its adherent to the needs of others. Only the Dionysian morality is truly free, for all its primitive and anarchic repercussions.

- **Reason versus the irrational.** Another way of expressing the Dionysian-Apollonian paradigm is in terms of the opposing forces, reason and irrationality. Oedipus, the most reasonable of men, bases his entire approach to Thebes' dilemma on an irrational foundation over which his brilliant powers of analysis have absolutely no control. E. R. Dodds, in *The Greeks and the Irrational*, indicates that for all their celebrated achievements of reasoning the Greeks were never unaware of the irrational, intuitive forces in life. Annual festivals such as the *Aphrodisia* loosed the irrational urges so closely restricted during the balance of the year by the rules of the *polis*. Dream temples, where patients came to incubate dream-cures to physical and psychological problems, were part of the same culture that held dreams to be nothing more than indigestion caused by eating cucumbers or zucchini too close to retiring (Aristotle, *On Dreams*, which posits a skeletal theory of what Sigmund Freud later referred to as "day residue"). Euripides in his most disturbing retellings of the ancient matriarchal myths may even suggest that reason is only one of the many masks of Unreason, that order may be nothing more than an accidental manifestation of chaos, symmetry a random occurrence in the ceaseless cycle of asymmetric, irrational reality.

- **Memory versus reason.** As they moved from an oral culture that passed its values from generation to generation through the epic cycle to a literate culture that held data in a mode of stability that allowed revisiting and the birth of analysis, the Greeks were torn between memory and reason as sovereigns of man's intellectual development. Plato reconciled the conflict in his "theory of recollection," which showed that the exercise of reason depends on memory, and that the exercise of memory is given productive direction by reason.

- **Cyclical versus linear.** Before the patriarchal Greek culture, the Mediterranean was dominated by matriarchal societies that based their worldview on the cyclically recurring seasons. Their sense of time and space was quite different from the linear classifications achieved by the Greeks. Scott Littleton supposes that the volcanic explosions on the island of Thera (modern Santorini) that destroyed Minoan culture also introduced linearity into Mediterranean man's view of the cosmos. These were definite, catastrophic events that marked clear-cut "befores" and "afters" in ways that could not be explained by the old cosmologies and theologies. The river god Poseidon, associated with tidal waves and earthquakes and Thera, was gradually replaced in Mycenaean and preclassical Greece by the sky god Zeus, whose orderly plan for the universe the Greeks clung to in the hopes that catastrophes would not repeat themselves.

These and other issues provided substance to the achievements of classical Greek civilization as echoed in the selections that follow. What distinguishes Greek thought is the flow between defined extremes, an exact human metaphor for the geography of ancient Greece with its harsh shores along its life-providing, unifying seas. The flow is communication, between opposites that are set apart so that the connection between them can be examined in detail. Understanding comes only when the right questions are asked. The Greeks gave us our way of asking questions. The questions they asked resound in our own century:

- "Should man pursue truth despite the ruin that pursuit might unleash?"
- "Should the individual's rights be protected at whatever cost to the community?"
- "Does the community have the right to destroy the offending individual?"

Rising above all issues expressed by these voices from ancient Greece is the concept of harmony, which evolved as these paradoxes were defined and dealt with. The ideal man holds the middle way between all opposites, taking from both sides what his character requires to face the slings and arrows of outrageous fortune.

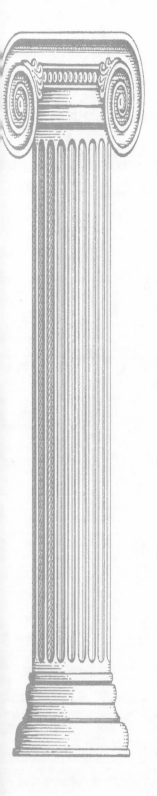

PART ONE

Preclassical

HOMER
The Iliad

*O*ne of the great ironies of western literature is that the first of its mighty epic poems, the *Iliad,* attributed by the Greeks to the blind bard Homer, is arguably its finest. The narrative forcefulness of this poem is based on the purity and precision of its vision of a world inhabited by human beings but too often visited by gods who cannot keep themselves from mingling with mortal affairs. If you read the gods as personifications of the psychological forces at work within the minds of men, you will understand that the epic's worldview is not so different from our own. When Achilles draws his sword in anger, Ares has moved within him. Agamemnon, possessed by Até (Blindness), insults the chief warrior of his own army.

- Codified sometime between the seventh and fifth centuries B.C., the story told in this poem of some 22,000 hexameters was transmitted to classical Greece by an oral tradition dating back to the thirteenth century B.C., when the matrilineal Minoan domination of the Aegean was giving way to that of the patriarchal, mainland Mycenaeans (whose primary courts were located on the Peloponnesus, at Mycenae, Tiryns, and Sparta). "Homer" may simply have been the most famous of generations of singers who preserved these heroic tales from court to court, century to century. The rhapsodes' mnemonic abilities were served by the elegant and powerful simplicity of the hexameters in which their cyclic songs were composed. The content of the *Iliad* and the *Odyssey* was both didactic and encyclopedic (long before such abstract terms had been coined), embodying the entire scope of the myth by which the Greeks explained, in a time before rational explanation itself was invented, everything in the world and beyond the world, all of life and death.

Despite the popular misconception that the *Iliad* is the story of the Trojan War, the poem, instead, is focused tightly on the repercussions of the quarrel between the mightiest Greek hero, Achilles, and the Commander in Chief of the Greek confederation against Troy, Agamemnon. Helen, the purported cause of the war, though the historian Herodotus had his doubts about her historical role in this pan-

Aegean crusade, was the wife of Agamemnon's brother, Menelaos of Sparta. She was abducted to Troy at the instigation of Aphrodite, by Paris, the Trojan.

Agamemnon's insult to Achilles' honor, detailed in Book 1 of the *Iliad,* leads the son of the goddess Thetis and mortal Peleus to sulk in his tents, refusing to fight. As a result the Trojans, led by King Priam's son Hektor, begin to turn the tide of the war in their favor. To prevent this from happening, Patroklos, Achilles' best friend, begs to borrow the armor of Achilles. When Achilles agrees, Patroklos wears his friend's armor into battle—and is slain by Hektor. Now Achilles, in the depths of his grief, is motivated, by vengeance, to carry on the fight against the Trojans.

- Yet Achilles cannot go back into battle to avenge Patroklos without armor. Thetis remedies the situation by arriving at the Olympian smithy of Hephaestos, the artisan-god, and begging him to make magical armor for her son. The lame smith-god grumbles that no one can save Achilles from the death that is fated for him, but at least he can die gloriously with armor worthy of his heroic nature. The passage that follows, in Richmond Lattimore's accurate and compelling translation, is from Book 18. In the comprehensiveness and arrangement of the scenes Hephaestos depicts on Achilles' new shield, we get an overview of the symmetry and exuberance of classical Greek thought. Aristotle, in his *Poetics,* credited Homer for "himself being nowhere in his work, his characters everywhere," and commended him for beginning "in the middle of things." Note the air of urgency, authority, and precision that characterizes this language that had not yet become dominated by logic and syntax.

The shield of Achilles is the primary metaphor of *The Iliad.* The "meaning" of this magnificent metaphor is clear. Indeed, because both Achilles and the forger of the shield know full well that he will die despite its power, the shield functions purely and only as a metaphor: As he carries it before him into battle, the scenes depicted on the surface of Achilles' new, divine shield will remind all those who see them on the plain before Troy, and who hear of the shield when the epic is sung or read in ages to come, of the peaceful orderliness, including the settlement of disputes by arbitration, that is the alternative to war.

"Gold headdress from Mycenae"

. . . Thetis of the silver feet came to the house
of Hephaistos,
imperishable, starry, and shining among the
immortals,
built in bronze for himself by the god of the
dragging footsteps.
She found him sweating as he turned here and
there to his bellows
busily, since he was working on twenty
tripods
which were to stand against the wall of his
strong-founded dwelling.
And he had set golden wheels underneath the
base of each one
so that of their own motion they could wheel
into the immortal
gathering, and return to his house: a wonder
to look at.
These were so far finished, but the elaborate
ear handles
were not yet on. He was forging these, and
beating the chains out.
As he was at work on this in his craftsmanship
and his cunning

meanwhile the goddess Thetis the silver-
footed drew near him.
Charis of the shining veil saw her as she came
forward,
she, the lovely goddess the renowned strong-
armed one had married.
She came, and caught her hand and called her
by name and spoke to her:
"Why is it, Thetis of the light robes, you have
come to our house now?
We honor you and love you; but you have not
come much before this.
But come in with me, so I may put
entertainment before you."
She spoke, and, shining among divinities,
led the way forward
and made Thetis sit down in a chair that was
wrought elaborately
and splendid with silver nails, and under it
was a footstool.
She called to Hephaistos the renowned smith
and spoke a word to him:
"Hephaistos, come this way; here is Thetis,
who has need of you."
Hearing her the renowned smith of the
strong arms answered her:
"Then there is a goddess we honor and
respect in our house.
She saved me when I suffered much at the
time of my great fall
through the will of my own brazen-faced
mother, who wanted
to hide me, for being lame. Then my soul
would have taken much suffering
had not Eurynome and Thetis caught me and
held me,

Eurynome, daughter of Ocean, whose stream
    bends back in a circle.
With them I worked nine years as a smith,
    and wrought many intricate
things; pins that bend back, curved clasps,
    cups, necklaces, working
there in the hollow of the cave, and the
    stream of Ocean around us
went on forever with its foam and its murmur.
    No other
among the gods or among mortal men knew
    about us
except Eurynome and Thetis. They knew,
    since they saved me.
Now she has come into our house; so I must
    by all means
do everything to give recompense to lovely-
    haired Thetis
for my life. Therefore set out before her fair
    entertainment
while I am putting away my bellows and all
    my instruments."
    He spoke, and took the huge blower off
    from the block of the anvil
limping; and yet his shrunken legs moved
    lightly beneath him.
He set the bellows away from the fire, and
    gathered and put away
all the tools with which he worked in a silver
    strongbox.
Then with a sponge he wiped clean his
    forehead, and both hands,
and his massive neck and hairy chest, and put
    on a tunic,
and took up a heavy stick in his hand, and
    went to the doorway
limping. And in support of their master
    moved his attendants.

These are golden, and in appearance like
    living young women.
There is intelligence in their hearts, and there
    is speech in them
and strength, and from the immortal gods
    they have learned how to do things.
These stirred nimbly in support of their
    master, and moving
near to where Thetis sat in her shining chair,
    Hephaistos
caught her by the hand and called her by
    name and spoke a word to her:
"Why is it, Thetis of the light robes, you have
    come to our house now?
We honor you and love you; but you have not
    come much before this.
Speak forth what is in your mind. My heart is
    urgent to do it
if I can, and if it is a thing that can be
    accomplished."
    Then in turn Thetis answered him, letting
    the tears fall:
"Hephaistos, is there among all the goddesses
    on Olympos
one who in her heart has endured so many
    grim sorrows
as the griefs Zeus, son of Kronos, has given
    me beyond others?
Of all the other sisters of the sea he gave me
    to a mortal,
to Peleus, Aiakos' son, and I had to endure
    mortal marriage
though much against my will. And now he,
    broken by mournful
old age, lies away in his halls. Yet I have other
    troubles.
For since he has given me a son to bear and to
    raise up

conspicuous among heroes, and he shot up
like a young tree,
I nurtured him, like a tree grown in the pride
of the orchard.
I sent him away in the curved ships to the
land of Ilion
to fight with the Trojans; but I shall never
again receive him
won home again to his country and into the
house of Peleus.
Yet while I see him live and he looks on the
sunlight, he has
sorrows, and though I go to him I can do
nothing to help him.
And the girl the sons of the Achaians chose
out for his honor
powerful Agamemnon took her away again out
of his hands.
For her his heart has been wasting in sorrow;
but meanwhile the Trojans
pinned the Achaians against their grounded
ships, and would not
let them win outside, and the elders of the
Argives entreated
my son, and named the many glorious gifts
they would give him.
But at that time he refused himself to fight
the death from them;
nevertheless he put his own armor upon
Patroklos
and sent him into the fighting, and gave many
men to go with him.
All day they fought about the Skaian Gates,
and on that day
they would have stormed the city, if only
Phoibos Apollo
had not killed the fighting son of Menoitios
there in the first ranks

after he had wrought much damage, and given
the glory to Hektor.
Therefore now I come to your knees; so might
you be willing
to give me for my short-lived son a shield and
a helmet
and two beautiful greaves fitted with clasps
for the ankles
and a corselet. What he had was lost with his
steadfast companion
when the Trojans killed him. Now my son lies
on the ground, heart sorrowing."
Hearing her the renowned smith of the
strong arms answered her:
"Do not fear. Let not these things be a
thought in your mind.
And I wish that I could hide him away from
death and its sorrow
at that time when his hard fate comes upon
him, as surely
as there shall be fine armor for him, such as
another
man out of many men shall wonder at, when
he looks on it.
So he spoke, and left her there, and went
to his bellows.
He turned these toward the fire and gave
them their orders for working.
And the bellows, all twenty of them, blew on
the crucibles,
from all directions blasting forth wind to blow
the flames high
now as he hurried to be at this place and now
at another,
wherever Hephaistos might wish them to
blow, and the work went forward.
He cast on the fire bronze which is weariless,
and tin with it

and valuable gold, and silver, and thereafter
set forth
upon its standard the great anvil, and gripped
in one hand
the ponderous hammer, while in the other he
grasped the pincers.
　First of all he forged a shield that was huge
and heavy,
elaborating it about, and threw around it a
shining
triple rim that glittered, and the shield strap
was cast of silver.
There were five folds composing the shield
itself, and upon it
he elaborated many things in his skill and
craftsmanship.
　He made the earth upon it, and the sky,
and the sea's water,
and the tireless sun, and the moon waxing
into her fullness,
and on it all the constellations that festoon
the heavens,
the Pleiades and the Hyades and the strength
of Orion
and the Bear, whom men give also the name
of the Wagon,
who turns about in a fixed place and looks at
Orion
and she alone is never plunged in the wash of
the Ocean.
　On it he wrought in all their beauty two
cities of mortal
men. And there were marriages in one, and
festivals.
They were leading the brides along the city
from their maiden chambers
under the flaring of torches, and the loud
bride song was arising.

The young men followed the circles of the
dance, and among them
the flutes and lyres kept up their clamor as in
the meantime
the women standing each at the door of her
court admired them.
The people were assembled in the market
place, where a quarrel
had arisen, and two men were disputing over
the blood price
for a man who had been killed. One man
promised full restitution
in a public statement, but the other refused
and would accept nothing.
Both then made for an arbitrator, to have a
decision;
and people were speaking up on either side, to
help both men.
But the heralds kept the people in hand, as
meanwhile the elders
were in session on benches of polished stone
in the sacred circle
and held in their hands the staves of the
heralds who lift their voices.
The two men rushed before these, and took
turns speaking their cases,
and between them lay on the ground two
talents of gold, to be given
to that judge who in this case spoke the
straightest opinion.
　But around the other city were lying two
forces of armed men
shining in their war gear. For one side counsel
was divided
whether to storm and sack, or share between
both sides the property
and all the possessions the lovely citadel held
hard within it.

But the city's people were not giving way, and
    armed for an ambush.
Their beloved wives and their little children
    stood on the rampart
to hold it, and with them the men with age
    upon them, but meanwhile
the others went out. And Ares led them, and
    Pallas Athene.
These were gold, both, and golden raiment
    upon them, and they were
beautiful and huge in their armor, being
    divinities,
and conspicuous from afar, but the people
    around them were smaller.
These, when they were come to the place that
    was set for their ambush,
in a river, where there was a watering place for
    all animals,
there they sat down in place shrouding
    themselves in the bright bronze.
But apart from these were sitting two men to
    watch for the rest of them
and waiting until they could see the sheep and
    the shambling cattle,
who appeared presently, and two herdsmen
    went along with them
playing happily on pipes, and took no thought
    of the treachery.
Those others saw them, and made a rush, and
    quickly thereafter
cut off on both sides the herds of cattle and
    the beautiful
flocks of shining sheep, and killed the
    shepherds upon them.
But the other army, as soon as they heard the
    uproar arising
from the cattle, as they sat in their councils,
    suddenly mounted

behind their light-foot horses, and went after,
    and soon overtook them.
These stood their ground and fought a battle
    by the banks of the river,
and they were making casts at each other with
    their spears bronze-headed;
and Hate was there with Confusion among
    them, and Death the destructive;
she was holding a live man with a new wound,
    and another
one unhurt, and dragged a dead man by the
    feet through the carnage.
The clothing upon her shoulders showed
    strong red with the men's blood.
All closed together like living men and fought
    with each other
and dragged away from each other the corpses
    of those who had fallen.
    He made upon it a soft field, the pride of
    the tilled land,
wide and triple-plowed, with many plowmen
    upon it
who wheeled their teams at the turn and
    drove them in either direction.
And as these making their turn would reach
    the end-strip of the field,
a man would come up to them at this point
    and hand them a flagon
of honey-sweet wine, and they would turn
    again to the furrows
in their haste to come again to the end-strip
    of the deep field.
The earth darkened behind them and looked
    like earth that has been plowed
though it was gold. Such was the wonder of
    the shield's forging.
    He made on it the precinct of a king,
    where the laborers

were reaping, with the sharp reaping hooks in
    their hands. Of the cut swathes
some fell along the lines of reaping, one after
    another,
while the sheaf-binders caught up others and
    tied them with bind-ropes.
There were three sheaf-binders who stood by,
    and behind them
were children picking up the cut swathes, and
    filled their arms with them
and carried and gave them always; and by
    them the king in silence
and holding his staff stood near the line of the
    reapers, happily.
And apart and under a tree the heralds made a
    feast ready
and trimmed a great ox they had slaughtered.
    Meanwhile the women
scattered, for the workmen to eat, abundant
    white barley.
    He made on it a great vineyard heavy with
    clusters,
lovely and in gold, but the grapes upon it were
    darkened
and the vines themselves stood out through
    poles of silver. About them
he made a field-ditch of dark metal, and drove
    all around this
a fence of tin; and there was only one path to
    the vineyard,
and along it ran the grape-bearers for the
    vineyard's stripping.
Young girls and young men, in all their
    lighthearted innocence,
carried the kind, sweet fruit away in their
    woven baskets,
and in their midst a youth with a singing lyre
    played charmingly

upon it for them, and sang the beautiful song
    for Linos
in a light voice, and they followed him, and
    with singing and whistling
and light dance-steps of their feet kept time
    to the music.
    He made upon it a herd of horn-straight
    oxen. The cattle
were wrought of gold and of tin, and thronged
    in speed and with lowing
out of the dung of the farmyard to a pasturing
    place by a sounding
river, and beside the moving field of a reed
    bed.
The herdsmen were of gold who went along
    with the cattle,
four of them, and nine dogs shifting their feet
    followed them.
But among the foremost of the cattle two
    formidable lions
had caught hold of a bellowing bull, and he
    with loud lowings
was dragged away, as the dogs and the young
    men went in pursuit of him.
But the two lions, breaking open the hide of
    the great ox,
gulped the black blood and the inward guts, as
    meanwhile the herdsmen
were in the act of setting and urging the quick
    dogs on them.
But they, before they could get their teeth in,
    turned back from the lions,
but would come and take their stand very
    close, and bayed, and kept clear.
    And the renowned smith of the strong
    arms made on it a meadow
large and in a lovely valley for the glimmering
    sheepflocks,

with dwelling places upon it, and covered
shelters, and sheepfolds.
And the renowned smith of the strong
arms made elaborate on it
a dancing floor, like that which once in the
wide spaces of Knosos
Daidalos built for Ariadne of the lovely
tresses.
And there were young men on it and young
girls, sought for their beauty
with gifts of oxen, dancing, and holding hands
at the wrist. These
wore, the maidens long light robes, but the
men wore tunics
of finespun work and shining softly, touched
with olive oil.
And the girls wore fair garlands on their heads,
while the young men
carried golden knives that hung from sword-
belts of silver.
At whiles on their understanding feet they
would run very lightly,
as when a potter crouching makes trial of his
wheel, holding
it close in his hands, to see if it will run
smooth. At another
time they would form rows, and run, rows
crossing each other.

And around the lovely chorus of dancers stood
a great multitude
happily watching, while among the dancers
two acrobats
led the measures of song and dance revolving
among them.
He made on it the great strength of the
Ocean River
which ran around the uttermost rim of the
shield's strong structure.
Then after he had wrought this shield,
which was huge and heavy,
he wrought for him a corselet brighter than
fire in its shining,
and wrought him a helmet, massive and
fitting close to his temples,
lovely and intricate work, and laid a gold top-
ridge along it,
and out of pliable tin wrought him leg-armor.
Thereafter
when the renowned smith of the strong arms
had finished the armor
he lifted it and laid it before the mother of
Achilleus.
And she like a hawk came sweeping down
from the snows of Olympos
and carried with her the shining armor, the
gift of Hephaistos. . . .

The Odyssey

$\mathcal{C}$omparing the second great Homeric epic to the *Iliad,* the postclassical Greek critic Longinus called the more romantic *Odyssey* an aging Homer's setting sun: "The grandeur is still there, but not the intensity." Yet intensity is replaced with psychological nuance that makes the *Odyssey,* in contrast with its heroic predecessor, compellingly modern. In this great tale of the return of the Trojan hero Odysseus to his beloved island Ithaka, entirely new aesthetic and moral value systems reveal themselves: the aesthetic of individualism, and the relativity of morals. Under the patronage of the artisan goddess Athena, Odysseus fights, or talks his way, through a sea of troubles, many of them of his own making. Even his name, etymologically, means suffering. In the proem of the epic, he is called *polutropos,* "many-turning," indicating the poem's understanding of his Protean nature. Unlike the steadfast Hektor or the stubborn Achilles of the *Iliad,* Odysseus is a man for all seasons, who is as different as each new occasion demands.

- When, in the passage excerpted here, Athena herself asks him his identity, he promises to tell her the truth—then weaves her such an elaborate tale that she laughs and commends him for being more like her than any other mortal. The relativity of truth to the individual's perception of the world and his place in it is a new element in Greek thought, but one that will be of monumental importance. Socrates chose to die in its defense, and Aristotle left Athens rather than submit to a monolithic view of reality.
- Using the *Odyssey* as example, Aristotle distinguishes between two kinds of discourse: "the strictly true" (realistic) and the "intentionally fallacious" (metaphorical) argument. The realistic *Iliad* provides a narrative that attempts to fix the "facts of the story" into a consistent pattern; no sub-story in the *Iliad* directly contradicts any other. The *Odyssey,* in contrast, is indeed, as Longinus also noted, preoccupied with narrative in and for itself. It is filled with twice-told tales—variations on a theme, the "consistent truth" of which must be understood metaphorically. The hero of the epic is like the god Proteus, who shifts shapes constantly and must be held firmly with intuition if his true nature is to be understood.
- Two women succeed in piercing through Odysseus' dodges and recognizing him for what and who he is: Athena, the goddess, his patroness; and Penelope, the faithful wife, whose wiles are, psychologically and rhetorically, her husband's match. Both women represent the "new female," supporting the patriarchy that had become all-powerful by the time the Homeric poems were codified in more or less their present form. Opposed to Penelope are two other women in the *Odyssey:* Helen, whose self-determination caused the Trojan War; and Klytaimnestra, who took a lover in King Agamemnon's absence, then, with him, slew the king

upon his return. Along the way, the *Odyssey* examines other women men must encounter and deal with: the seductress Circe, enchanting Calypso, youthful Nausicaa—all temptations that Odysseus first tastes, then escapes from, in his determination to return to Penelope and the patriarchal kingdom of Ithaka.

- In Book 13 that return is accomplished at long last by agency of the preternatural navigators, the Phaiakians. The language is rich with resonance of rebirth. Delivered from the womblike ship that wafts him easily across the waters, Odysseus is awakened from a deep sleep to find himself on a "strange land" covered in mist. Ironically, the "strange land" is the island he knows the very best—the Ithaka he has been seeking for twenty years. Seated beneath its sacred olive tree, mortal and immortal, the individualist hero and the goddess of wisdom plot the restoration of his patriarchal rule.

When on the East the sheer bright star arose
that tells of coming Dawn, the ship made landfall
and came up islandward in the dim of night.
Phorkys, the old sea baron, has a cove
here in the realm of Ithaka; two points
of high rock, breaking sharply, hunch around it,
making a haven from the plunging surf
that gales at sea roll shoreward. Deep inside,
at mooring range, good ships can ride unmoored.
There, on the inmost shore, an olive tree
throws wide its boughs over the bay; nearby
a cave of dusky light is hidden
for those immortal girls, the Naiadês.
Within are winebowls hollowed in the rock
and amphorai; bees bring their honey here;
and there are looms of stone, great looms, whereon
the weaving nymphs make tissues, richly dyed

as the deep sea is; and clear springs in the cavern
flow forever. Of two entrances,
one on the north allows descent of mortals,
but beings out of light alone, the undying,
can pass by the south slit; no men come there.
   This cove the sailors knew. Here they drew in,
and the ship ran half her keel's length up the shore,
she had such way on her from those great oarsmen.
Then from their benches forward on dry ground
they disembarked. They hoisted up Odysseus
unruffled on his bed, under his cover,
handing him overside still fast asleep,
to lay him on the sand; and they unloaded
all those gifts the princes of Phaiákia
gave him, when by Athena's heart and will
he won his passage home. They bore this treasure
off the beach, and piled it close around

"Victorious Athene"

the roots of the olive tree, that no one passing
should steal Odysseus' gear before he woke.
That done, they pulled away on the homeward
　　track.
　　But now the god that shakes the islands,
　　brooding
over old threats of his against Odysseus,
approached Lord Zeus to learn his will. Said
　　he:
"Father of gods, will the bright immortals ever
pay me respect again, if mortals do not?—
Phaiákians, too, my own blood kin?

　　　　　　　　　　　　　　　I thought
Odysseus should in time regain his homeland;
I had no mind to rob him of that day—
no, no; you promised it, being so inclined;
only I thought he should be made to suffer
all the way.

　　　　　　　　　But now these islanders

have shipped him homeward, sleeping soft,
　　and put him
on Ithaka, with gifts untold
of bronze and gold, and fine cloth to his
　　shoulder.
Never from Troy had he borne off such booty
if he had got home safe with all his share."
　　Then Zeus who drives the stormcloud
　　answered, sighing:
"God of horizons, making earth's underbeam
tremble, why do you grumble so?
The immortal gods show you no less esteem,
and the rough consequence would make them
　　slow
to let barbs fly at their eldest and most noble.
But if some mortal captain, overcome
by his own pride of strength, cuts or defies you,
are you not always free to take reprisal?
Act as your wrath requires and as you will."
　　Now said Poseidon, god of earthquake:
　　　　　　　　　　　　　　　　　"Aye,
god of the stormy sky, I should have taken
vengeance, as you say, and on my own;
but I respect, and would avoid, your anger.
The sleek Phaiákian cutter, even now,
has carried out her mission and glides home
over the misty sea. Let me impale her,
end her voyage, and end all ocean-crossing
with passengers, then heave a mass of
　　mountain
in a ring around the city."
　　Now Zeus who drives the stormcloud said
　　benignly:
"Here is how I should do it, little brother:
when all who watch upon the wall have
　　caught
sight of the ship, let her be turned to stone—
an island like a ship, just off the bay.

Mortals may gape at that for generations!
But throw no mountain round the sea port
   city."
   When he heard this, Poseidon, god of
   earthquake,
departed for Skhería, where the Phaiákians
are born and dwell. Their ocean-going ship
he saw already near, heading for harbor;
so up behind her swam the island-shaker
and struck her into stone, rooted in stone, at
   one
blow of his palm,
               then took to the open sea.
Those famous ship handlers, the Phaiákians,
gazed at each other, murmuring in wonder;
you could have heard one say:
               "Now who in thunder
has anchored, moored that ship in the seaway,
when everyone could see her making harbor?"
   The god had wrought a charm beyond
   their thought.
But soon Alkínoös made them hush, and told
   them:
"This present doom upon the ship—on me—
my father prophesied in the olden time.
If we gave safe conveyance to all passengers
we should incur Poseidon's wrath, he said,
whereby one day a fair ship, manned by
   Phaiákians,
would come to grief at the god's hands; and
   great
mountains would hide our city from the sea.
So my old father forecast.
               Use your eyes:
these things are even now being brought to
   pass.
Let all here abide by my decree:
               We make

an end henceforth of taking, in our ships,
castaways who may land upon Skhería;
and twelve choice bulls we dedicate at once
to Lord Poseidon, praying him of his mercy
not to heave up a mountain round our city."
   In fearful awe they led the bulls to
   sacrifice
and stood about the altar stone, those
   captains,
peers of Phaiákia, led by their king in prayer
to Lord Poseidon.
             Meanwhile, on his island,
his father's shore, that kingly man, Odysseus,
awoke, but could not tell what land it was
after so many years away; moreover,
Pallas Athena, Zeus's daughter, poured
a gray mist all around him, hiding him
from common sight—for she had things to
   tell him
and wished no one to know him, wife or
   townsmen,
before the suitors paid up for their crimes.
   The landscape then looked strange,
   unearthly strange
to the Lord Odysseus: paths by hill and shore,
glimpses of harbors, cliffs, and summer trees.
He stood up, rubbed his eyes, gazed at his
   homeland,
and swore, slapping his thighs with both his
   palms,
then cried aloud:
             "What am I in for now?
Whose country have I come to this time?
   Rough
savages and outlaws, are they, or
godfearing people, friendly to castaways?
Where shall I take these things? Where take
   myself,

with no guide, no directions? These should be
still in Phaiákian hands, and I uncumbered,
free to find some other openhearted
prince who might be kind and give me
            passage.
I have no notion where to store this treasure;
first-comer's trove it is, if I leave it here.

    My lords and captains of Phaiákia
were not those decent men they seemed, not
            honorable,
landing me in this unknown country—no,
by god, they swore to take me home to Ithaka
and did not! Zeus attend to their reward,
Zeus, patron of petitioners, who holds
all other mortals under his eye; he takes
payment from betrayers!

                        I'll be busy.
I can look through my gear. I shouldn't
            wonder
if they pulled out with part of it on board."

    He made a tally of his shining pile—
tripods, cauldrons, cloaks, and gold—and
            found
he lacked nothing at all.

                    And then he wept,
despairing, for his own land, trudging down
beside the endless wash of the wide, wide sea,
weary and desolate as the sea. But soon
Athena came to him from the nearby air,
putting a young man's figure on—a shepherd,
like a king's son, all delicately made.
She wore a cloak, in two folds off her
            shoulders,
and sandals bound upon her shining feet.
A hunting lance lay in her hands.

                        At sight of her
Odysseus took heart, and he went forward
to greet the lad, speaking out fair and clear:

"Friend, you are the first man I've laid eyes
            on
here in this cove. Greetings. Do not feel
alarmed or hostile, coming across me; only
receive me into safety with my stores.
Touching your knees I ask it, as I might
ask grace of a god.

                        O sir, advise me,
what is this land and realm, who are the
            people?
Is it an island all distinct, or part
of the fertile mainland, sloping to the sea?"
    To this gray-eyed Athena answered:
                        "Stranger,
you must come from the other end of
            nowhere,
else you are a great booby, having to ask
what place this is. It is no nameless country.
Why, everyone has heard of it, the nations
over on the dawn side, toward the sun,
and westerners in cloudy lands of evening.
No one would use this ground for training
            horses,
it is too broken, has no breadth of meadow;
but there is nothing meager about the soil,
the yield of grain is wondrous, and wine, too,
with drenching rains and dewfall.

                        There's good pasture
for oxen and for goats, all kinds of timber,
and water all year long in the cattle ponds.
For these blessings, friend, the name of Ithaka
has made its way even as far as Troy—
and they say Troy lies far beyond Akhaia."
    Now Lord Odysseus, the long-enduring,
laughed in his heart, hearing his land
            described
by Pallas Athena, daughter of Zeus who rules
the veering stormwind; and he answered her

with ready speech—not that he told the truth,
but, just as she did, held back what he knew,
weighing within himself at every step
what he made up to serve his turn.

                                   Said he:
"Far away in Krete I learned of Ithaka—
in that broad island over the great ocean.
And here I am now, come myself to Ithaka!
Here is my fortune with me. I left my sons
an equal part, when I shipped out. I killed
Orsílokhos, the courier, son of Idómeneus.
This man could beat the best cross country
     runners
in Krete, but he desired to take away
my Trojan plunder, all I had fought and bled
     for,
cutting through ranks in war and the cruel
     sea.
Confiscation is what he planned; he knew
I had not cared to win his father's favor
as a staff officer in the field at Troy,
but led my own command.

                              I acted: I
hit him with a spearcast from a roadside
as he came down from the open country.
   Murky
night shrouded all heaven and the stars.
I made that ambush with one man at arms.
We were unseen. I took his life in secret,
finished him off with my sharp sword. That
     night
I found asylum on a ship off shore
skippered by gentlemen of Phoinikia; I gave
all they could wish, out of my store of plunder,
for passage, and for landing me at Pylos
or Elis Town, where the Epeioi are in power.
Contrary winds carried them willy-nilly
past that coast; they had no wish to cheat me,

but we were blown off course.

                              Here, then, by night
we came, and made this haven by hard
     rowing.
All famished, but too tired to think of food,
each man dropped in his tracks after the
     landing,
and I slept hard, being wearied out. Before
I woke today, they put my things ashore
on the sand here beside me where I lay,
then reimbarked for Sidon, that great city.
Now they are far at sea, while I am left
forsaken here."

                       At this the gray-eyed goddess
Athena smiled, and gave him a caress,
her looks being changed now, so she seemed a
     woman,
tall and beautiful and no doubt skilled
at weaving splendid things. She answered
     briskly:
"Whoever gets around you must be sharp
and guileful as a snake; even a god
might bow to you in ways of dissimulation.
You! You chameleon!
Bottomless bag of tricks! Here in your own
     country
would you not give your stratagems a rest
or stop spellbinding for an instant?
You play a part as if it were your own tough
     skin.
No more of this, though. Two of a kind, we
     are,
contrivers, both. Of all men now alive
you are the best in plots and storytelling.
My own fame is for wisdom among the gods—
deceptions, too.

                       Would even you have guessed
that I am Pallas Athena, daughter of Zeus,

I that am always with you in times of trial,
a shield to you in battle, I who made
the Phaiákians befriend you, to a man?
Now I am here again to counsel with you—
but first to put away those gifts the Phaiákians
gave you at departure—I planned it so.
Then I can tell you of the gall and wormwood
it is your lot to drink in your own hall.
Patience, iron patience, you must show;
so give it out to neither man nor woman
that you are back from wandering. Be silent
under all injuries, even blows from men."

　　His mind ranging far, Odysseus answered:
"Can mortal man be sure of you on sight,
even a sage, O mistress of disguises?
Once you were fond of me—I am sure of
　　　that—
years ago, when we Akhaians made
war, in our generation, upon Troy.
But after we had sacked the shrines of Priam
and put to sea, God scattered the Akhaians;
I never saw you after that, never
knew you aboard with me, to act as shield
in grievous times—not till you gave me
　　　comfort
in the rich hinterland of the Phaiákians
and were yourself my guide into that city.

　　Hear me now in your father's name, for I
cannot believe that I have come to Ithaka.
It is some other land. You made that speech
only to mock me, and to take me in.
Have I come back in truth to my home
　　　island?"

　　To this the gray-eyed goddess Athena
　　　answered:
"Always the same detachment! That is why
I cannot fail you, in your evil fortune,
coolheaded, quick, well-spoken as you are!

Would not another wandering man, in joy,
make haste home to his wife and children?
　　Not
you, not yet. Before you hear their story
you will have proof about your wife.

　　　　　　　　I tell you,
she still sits where you left her, and her days
and nights go by forlorn, in lonely weeping.
For my part, never had I despaired; I felt
sure of your coming home, though all your
　　men
should perish; but I never cared to fight
Poseidon, Father's brother, in his baleful
rage with you for taking his son's eye.

　　Now I shall make you see the shape of
　　　Ithaka.
Here is the cove the sea lord Phorkys owns,
there is the olive spreading out her leaves
over the inner bay, and there the cavern
dusky and lovely, hallowed by the feet
of those immortal girls, the Naiadês—
the same wide cave under whose vault you
　　came
to honor them with hekatombs—and there
Mount Neion, with his forest on his back!"

　　She had dispelled the mist, so all the
　　　island
stood out clearly. Then indeed Odysseus'
heart stirred with joy. He kissed the earth,
and lifting up his hands prayed to the
　　nymphs:
"O slim shy Naiadês, young maids of Zeus,
I had not thought to see you ever again!

　　　　　　　O listen smiling
to my gentle prayers, and we'll make offering
plentiful as in the old time, granted I
live, granted my son grows tall, by favor
of great Athena, Zeus's daughter,

who gives the winning fighter his reward!"

The gray-eyed goddess said directly:

> "Courage;
and let the future trouble you no more.
We go to make a cache now, in the cave,
to keep your treasure hid. Then we'll consider
how best the present action may unfold."

The goddess turned and entered the dim
    cave,
exploring it for crannies, while Odysseus
carried up all the gold, the fire-hard bronze,
and well-made clothing the Phaiákians gave
    him.
Pallas Athena, daughter of Zeus the storm
    king,
placed them, and shut the cave mouth with a
    stone,
and under the old gray olive tree those two
sat down to work the suitors death and woe.
Gray-eyed Athena was the first to speak,
    saying:

> Son of Laërtês and the gods of old,
Odysseus, master of land ways and sea ways,
put your mind on a way to reach and strike
a crowd of brazen upstarts.

> > Three long years
they have played master in your house: three
    years
trying to win your lovely lady, making
gifts as though betrothed. And she? Forever
grieving for you, missing your return,
she has allowed them all to hope, and sent
messengers with promises to each—
though her true thoughts are fixed elsewhere."

> > At this
the man of ranging mind, Odysseus, cried:

> "So hard beset! An end like Agamémnon's
might very likely have been mine, a bad end,
bleeding to death in my own hall. You
    forestalled it,
goddess, by telling me how the land lies.
Weave me a way to pay them back! And you,
    too,
take your place with me, breathe valor in me
the way you did that night when we Akhaians
unbound the bright veil from the brow of
    Troy!
O gray-eyed one, fire my heart and brace me!
I'll take on fighting men three hundred strong
if you fight at my back, immortal lady!"

The gray-eyed goddess Athena answered
    him:

> "No fear but I shall be there; you'll go forward
under my arm when the crux comes at last.
And I foresee your vast floor stained with
    blood,
spattered with brains of this or that tall suitor
who fed upon your cattle.

> > Now, for a while,
I shall transform you; not a soul will know
    you,
the clear skin of your arms and legs shriveled,
your chestnut hair all gone, your body dressed
in sacking that a man would gag to see,
and the two eyes, that were so brilliant,
    dirtied—
contemptible, you shall seem to your enemies,
as to the wife and son you left behind.

> But join the swineherd first—the overseer
of all your swine, a good soul now as ever,
devoted to Penélopê and your son.
He will be found near Raven's Rock and the
    well
of Arethousa, where the swine are pastured,
rooting for acorns to their hearts' content,
drinking the dark still water. Boarflesh grows

pink and fat on that fresh diet. There
stay with him, and question him, while I
am off to the great beauty's land of Sparta,
to call your son Telémakhos home again—
for you should know, he went to the wide land
of Lakedaimon, Meneláos' country,
to learn if there were news of you abroad."

Odysseus answered:

        "Why not tell him, knowing
my whole history, as you do? Must he
traverse the barren sea, he too, and live
in pain, while others feed on what is his?"

At this the gray-eyed goddess Athena said:
"No need for anguish on that lad's account.
I sent him off myself, to make his name
in foreign parts—no hardship in the bargain,
taking his ease in Meneláos' mansion,
lapped in gold.

        The young bucks here, I know,
lie in wait for him in a cutter, bent
on murdering him before he reaches home.

I rather doubt they will. Cold earth instead
will take in her embrace a man or two
of those who fed so long on what is his."

Speaking no more, she touched him with
    her wand,
shriveled the clear skin of his arms and legs,
made all his hair fall out, cast over him
the wrinkled hide of an old man, and bleared
both his eyes, that were so bright. Then she
clapped an old tunic, a foul cloak, upon him,
tattered, filthy, stained by greasy smoke,
and over that a mangy big buckskin.
A staff she gave him, and a leaky knapsack
with no strap but a loop of string.

               Now then,
their colloquy at an end, they went their
    ways—
Athena toward illustrious Lakedaimon
far over sea, to join Odysseus' son.

HESIOD (FL. CA. 700 B.C.)
Theogony

𝒰nlike Homeric epic, with its powerful dramatization based on character and events, the epic poetry of Boeotia was intent on compiling useful and/or interesting information. The first such classifier
whose work survives, Hesiod, tells us that the Muses called him as he was tending sheep on Mt. Helicon, to sing about the generations of the gods: Ouranos' castration by Kronos, and the overthrow of
Kronos and the Titans by Zeus' Olympian gods.

- We know very little about Hesiod's life. His father retired from the sea to move from Cyme in Aeolia to Boeotian Ascra; Hesiod won a tripod in a funeral song contest at Chalcis; he and his brother Perses were at odds over their inheritance; he was murdered at Oeneon in Locris; his bones, at the command of the oracle of Delphi, were laid to rest in the marketplace of Orchomenus.

- The work known since ancient times as the *Theogony* serves the patriarchal classical Greeks by providing, in verse catalog, a more or less orderly account of the succession of Zeus against the backdrop of the genealogy of the gods. It also surveys the most important myths, including the story of Prometheus and a description of Tartarus, and became the foundation for all subsequent Greek mythography. Stylistically the *Theogony* is unremarkable, yet the section known as "the battle of the gods" resonates with a powerful enthusiasm that influenced later writers, including John Milton (*Paradise Lost*). In providing this catalog of nearly 300 deities descended from Chaos and Earth, Hesiod also laid the foundation for the rational approach to philosophy that characterized the "preSocratics" as well as Socrates, Plato, and Aristotle themselves.

Let us begin our singing
   from the Helikonian Muses
who possess the great and holy mountain
   of Helikon
and dance there on soft feet
   by the dark blue water
of the spring, and by the altar
   of the powerful son of Kronos;
who wash their tender bodies in the waters
   of Permessos
or Hippokrene, spring of the Horse,
   or holy Olmeios,
and on the high places of Helikon
   have ordered their dances
which are handsome and beguiling,
   and light are the feet they move on.
From there they rise, and put a veiling
   of deep mist upon them,
and walk in the night, singing
   in sweet voices, and celebrating
Zeus, the holder of the aegis, and Hera,
   his lady
of Argos, who treads on golden sandals,
   and singing also
Athene the gray-eyed, daughter of Zeus
   of the aegis,
Phoibos Apollo, and Artemis
   of the showering arrows,
Poseidon who encircles the earth in his arms
   and shakes it,
stately Themis, and Aphrodite
   of the fluttering eyelids,
Hebe of the golden wreath, beautiful Dione,
Leto and Iapetos and devious-devising
     Kronos,
Eos, the dawn, great Helios,

and shining Selene,
Gaia, the earth, and great Okeanos,
    and dark Night,
and all the holy rest of the everlasting
    immortals.
And it was they who once taught Hesiod
    his splendid singing
as he was shepherding his lambs
    on holy Helikon,
and these were the first words of all
    the goddesses spoke to me,
the Muses of Olympia, daughters of Zeus
    of the aegis:
"You shepherds of the wilderness, poor fools,
    nothing but bellies,
we know how to say many false things
    that seem like true sayings,
but we know also how to speak the truth
    when we wish to."
    So they spoke, these mistresses of words,
    daughters of great Zeus,
and they broke off and handed me a staff
    of strong-growing
olive shoot, a wonderful thing;
    they breathed a voice into me,
and power to sing the story of things
    of the future, and things past.
They told me to sing the race
    of the blessed gods everlasting,
but always to put themselves
    at the beginning and end of my singing . . .

Come you then, let us begin from the Muses,
    who by their singing
delight the great mind of Zeus, their father,
    who lives on Olympos,
as they tell of what is, and what is to be,
    and what was before now

with harmonious voices, and the sound
    that comes sweet from their mouths
never falters, and all the mansion of Zeus
    the father
of the deep thunder is joyful
    in the light voice of the goddesses
that scatters through it, and the peaks
    of snowy Olympos re-echo
and the homes of the immortals, and they
    in divine utterance
sing first the glory of the majestic race
    of immortals
from its beginning, those born
    to wide Ouranos and Gaia,
and the gods who were born to these in turn,
    the givers of blessings.
Then next they sing of Zeus, the father
    of gods and of mortals,
and they begin this strain and end
    this strain singing of him,
how greatly he surpasses all gods,
    and in might is the strongest.
And then again the Olympian Muses,
    daughters of aegis-
wearing Zeus, delight his mind that dwells
    on Olympos
by singing the race of human kind,
    and the powerful Giants.
    Mnemosyne, queen of the Eleutherian
     hills,
    bore them
in Pieria, when she had lain
    with the Kronian Father;
they bring forgetfulness of sorrows,
    and rest from anxieties.
For nine nights Zeus of the counsels
    lay with her, going
up into her sacred bed, far away

from the other immortals.
But when it was a year,
    after the seasons' turning
and the months had waned away, and many
        days
    were accomplished,
she bore her nine daughters, concordant
    of heart, and singing
is all the thought that is in them,
    and no care troubles their spirits.
She bore them a little way off
    from the highest snowy summit
of Olympos; there are their shining
    dancing places, their handsome
houses, and the Graces and Desire live there
    beside them
in festivity; lovely is the voice
    that issues from their lips
as they sing of all the laws and all
    the gracious customs
of the immortals, and glorify them
    with their sweet voices.
At that time, glorying in their power
    of song, they went to Olympos
in immortal music, and all the black earth
    re-echoed to them
as they sang, and the lovely beat
    of their footsteps sprang beneath them
as they hastened to their father, to him
    who is King in the heaven,
who holds in his own hands the thunder
    and the flamy lightning,
who overpowered and put down
    his father Kronos, and ordained
to the immortals all rights that are theirs,
    and defined their stations.
    All these things the Muses who have
    their homes on Olympos

sang then, and they are nine daughters
    whose father is great Zeus:
Kleio and Euterpe, Thaleia and Melpomene,
Terpsichore and Erato, Polymnia and Ourania,
with Kalliope, who of all holds
    the highest position.
For it is she who attends
    on the respected barons.
And when on one of these kingly nobles,
    at the time of his birth,
the daughters of great Zeus cast their eyes
    and bestow their favors,
upon his speech they make a distillation
    of sweetness . . . blessed
    is that one whom the Muses
love, for the voice of his mouth runs
    and is sweet, and even
when a man has sorrow fresh
    in the troublement of his spirit
and is struck to wonder over the grief
    in his heart, the singer,
the servant of the Muses singing
    the glories of ancient
men, and the blessed gods
    who have their homes on Olympos,
makes him presently forget his cares,
    he no longer remembers
sorrow, for the gifts of the goddesses
    soon turn his thoughts elsewhere.

Hail, then, children of Zeus:
    grant me lovely singing.

Now sound out the holy stock
    of the everlasting immortals
who came into being out of Gaia
    and starry Ouranos
and gloomy Night, whom Pontos, the salt sea,

brought to maturity;
and tell, how at the first the gods
   and the earth were begotten
and rivers, and the boundless sea,
   raging in its swell,
the blazing stars, and the wide sky above all,
   tell of
the gods, bestowers of blessings,
   who were begotten of all these,
and how they divided their riches
   and distributed their privileges,
and how they first took possession
   of many-folded Olympos,
tell me all this, you Muses
   who have your homes on Olympos,
from the beginning, and tell who was first
   to come forth among them.
    First of all there came Chaos,
   and after him came
Gaia of the broad breast,
   to be the unshakable foundation
of all the immortals who keep the crests
   of snowy Olympos,
and Tartaros the foggy in the pit
   of the wide-wayed earth,
and Eros, who is love, handsomest among all
   the immortals,
who breaks the limbs' strength,
   who in all gods, in all human beings
overpowers the intelligence in the breast,
   and all their shrewd planning.
From Chaos was born Erebos, the dark,
   and black Night,
and from Night again Aither and Hemera,
   the day, were begotten,
for she lay in love with Erebos
   and conceived and bore these two.
But Gaia's first born was one

who matched her every dimension,
Ouranos, the starry sky,
   to cover her all over,
to be an unshakable standing-place
   for the blessed immortals.
Then she brought forth the tall Hills,
   those wild haunts that are beloved
by the goddess Nymphs who live on the hills
   and in their forests.
Without any sweet act of love
   she produced the barren
sea, Pontos, seething in his fury of waves,
   and after this
she lay with Ouranos, and bore him
   deep-swirling Okeanos
the ocean-stream . . .
   And still other children were born
   to Gaia and Ouranos,
three sons, big and powerful, so great
   they could never be told of,
Kottos, Briareos, and Gyes,
   overmastering children.
Each had a hundred intolerably strong arms
   bursting
out of his shoulders,
   and on the shoulders of each grew fifty
heads, above their massive bodies;
   irresistible
and staunch strength matched the appearance
   of their big bodies,
and of all children ever born
   to Gaia and Ouranos
these were the most terrible,
   and they hated their father
from the beginning, and every time each one
   was beginning
to come out, he would push them back again,
   deep inside Gaia,

and would not let them into the light,
   and Ouranos exulted
in his wicked work; but great Gaia
   groaned within for pressure
of pain; and then she thought of an evil,
   treacherous attack.
Presently creating the element of gray flint
she made of it a great sickle,
   and explained it to her own children,
and spoke, in the disturbance of her heart,
   to encourage them:
     "My sons, born to me of a criminal father,
   if you are willing
to obey me, we can punish your father
   for the brutal treatment
he put upon you, for he was first to think
   of shameful dealing."
So she spoke, but fear took hold of all,
   nor did one of them
speak, but then great devious-devising Kronos
   took courage
and spoke in return,
   and gave his gracious mother an answer:
"My mother, I will promise to undertake
   to accomplish
this act, and for our father,
   him of the evil name, I care
nothing, for he was the first
   to think of shameful dealing."
   So he spoke, and giant Gaia
   rejoiced greatly in her heart
and took and hid him in a secret ambush,
   and put into his hands
the sickle, edged like teeth, and told him
   all her treachery.
And huge Ouranos came on
   bringing night with him, and desiring
love he embraced Gaia and lay over her

stretched out
complete, and from his hiding place his son
   reached with his left hand
and seized him, and holding in his right
   the enormous sickle
with its long blade edged like teeth,
   he swung it sharply,
and lopped the members of his own father,
   and threw them behind him
to fall where they would,
   but they were not lost away when they were
     flung
from his hand, but all the bloody drops
   that went splashing from them
were taken in by Gaia, the earth,
   and with the turning of the seasons
she brought forth the powerful Furies
   and the tall Giants
shining in their armor
   and holding long spears in their hands;
and the nymphs they call, on boundless earth,
   the Nymphs of the Ash Trees.
But the members themselves, when Kronos
   had lopped them with the flint,
he threw from the mainland
   into the great wash of the sea water
and they drifted a great while
   on the open sea, and there spread
a circle of white foam
   from the immortal flesh, and in it
grew a girl, whose course first took her
   to holy Kythera,
and from there she afterward made her way
   to sea-washed Cyprus
and stepped ashore, a modest lovely Goddess,
   and about her
light and slender feet the grass grew,
   and the gods call her

Aphrodite, and men do too,
    and the aphro-foam-born
goddess, and garlanded Kythereia,
    because from the seafoam
she grew, and Kythereia because she had gone
    to Kythera,
and Kyprogeneia, because she came forth
    from wave-washed Cyprus,
and Philommedea, because she appeared
    from *medea*, members.
And Eros went with her, and handsome
     Himeros
    attended her
when first she was born, and when she joined
    the immortal community,
and here is the privilege she was given
    and holds from the beginning,
and which is the part she plays among men
    and the gods immortal:
the whispering together of girls,
    the smiles and deceptions,
the delight, and the sweetnesses of love,
    and the flattery . . .
Then Zeus the cloud-gatherer
    in great vexation said to him:
"Son of Iapetos, versed in planning
    beyond all others,
old friend, so after all you did not forget
    your treachery."
    So Zeus, who knows imperishable
     counsels,
    spoke in his anger,
and ever remembering this deception
    thereafter, he would not
give the force of weariless fire
    to the ash-tree people,
not to people who inhabit the earth
    and are mortal,

no, but the strong son of Iapetos
    outwitted him
and stole the far-seen glory
    of weariless fire, hiding it
in the hollow fennel stalk;
    this bit deep into the feeling
of Zeus who thunders on high,
    and it galled the heart inside him
when he saw the far-seen glory of fire
    among mortal people,
and next, for the price of the fire,
    he made an evil thing for mankind.
For the renowned smith of the strong arms
    took earth, and molded it,
through Zeus's plans, into the likeness
    of a modest young girl,
and the goddess gray-eyed Athene
    dressed her and decked her
in silverish clothing, and over her head
    she held, with her hands,
an intricately wrought veil in place,
    a wonder to look at,
and over this on her head
    she placed a wreath of gold, one
that the very renowned smith
    of the strong arms had fashioned
working it out with his hands,
    as a favor to Zeus the father.
On this had been done much intricate work,
    a wonder to look at:
wild animals, such as the mainland
    and the sea also produce
in numbers, and he put many on,
    the imitations of living
things, that have voices, wonderful,
    and it flashed in its beauty.
    But when, to replace good,
    he had made this beautiful evil

thing, he led her out
    where the rest of the gods and mortals
were, in the pride and glory
    that the gray-eyed daughter of a great
father had given; wonder
    seized both immortals and mortals
as they gazed on this sheer deception,
    more than mortals can deal with.
For from her originates the breed
    of female women,
and they live with mortal men,
    and are a great sorrow to them,
and hateful poverty they will not share,
    but only luxury.
As when, inside the overarching hives,
    the honeybees
feed their drones (and these are accomplished
    in doing no good,
while the bees, all day long
    until the sun goes down
do their daily hard work
    and set the white combs in order,
and the drones, spending their time
    inside the hollow skeps,
garner the hard work of others
    into their own bellies),
so Zeus of the high thunder established
    women,

for mortal
men an evil thing,
    and they are accomplished in bringing
hard labors.
                And Zeus made, in place
    of the good, yet another evil.
For whoever, escaping marriage
    and the sorrowful things women do,
is unwilling to marry, must come then
    to a mournful old age
bereft of one to look after it,
    and in need of livelihood
lives on, and when he dies
    the widow-inheritors divide up
what he has. While if the way of marriage
    befalls one
and he gets himself a good wife,
    one with ways suited to him,
even so through his lifetime the evil remains,
    balancing
the good, and he whose luck
    is to have cantankerous children
lives keeping inside him discomfort
    which will not leave him
in heart and mind; and for this evil
    there is no healing.
    So it is not possible to hide
    from the mind of Zeus, nor escape it . . .

Works and Days

*T*he first "Farmer's Almanac" in western history, Hesiod's *Works and Days* is a remarkable work in Ionian-Boeotian dialect, offering advice on everything from avoiding the evils of women (the story of Pandora's box) to when, in the cycle of the moon, to plant soybeans. The *Works and Days* is a verse catalog of observations about ritual, etiquette, fishing, navigation, husbandry, and household improvement. Along the way, we learn of Hesiod's anger at his younger brother Perses, who defrauded him of his rightful inheritance by bribing the estate judge. Perses obviously does not share Hesiod's hatred for dishonesty and idleness, nor his puritanical love for hard work and effective time management. "If you put a little upon a little," Hesiod scolds his brother, "soon it will become a lot." Perses preferred the lawsuit approach to instant riches.

- Events of everyday life, fables, myth, and commonsense proverbs mingle to give the *Works and Days* an easy familiarity and vivid texture, bringing us a wide-ranging perspective on grassroots peasant existence in preclassical rural Greece. Hesiod's endless personal trials resemble those of the Hebrew Bible's Job. His grumpy, Calvinistic, curmudgeon's personality makes him sound like the ancestor of Shakespeare's Polonius (in *Hamlet*). He distrusts men in general and women in particular, and shows a delightfully self-conscious sense of the entire world on his shoulders. Hesiod is the first person we know of to have recorded the myth of the "ages of man" and the principle of the golden rule. His account of the two kinds of Strife, Good and Bad, is an important philosophical reference point for later thinkers and resembles the modern distinction between good stress and bad stress. Good strife (competition) is constructive, a blessing, containing aggression and competition within a predetermined structure like the Olympic games or the arbitration depicted on Hephaestos' shield for Achilles. War is the curse of Bad Strife (discord), destructive to the fabric of society. Bad Strife, *Eris,* is the one who, excluded from the wedding feast of Thetis and Peleus, dropped the golden apple inscribed "To the Fairest" in its midst to provoke Hera, Athena, and Aphrodite into starting the Trojan War.

Muses, who from Pieria give glory through
      singing,
come to me, tell of Zeus, your own father,
   sing his praises, through whose will
mortal men are named in speech or remain
      unspoken.
Men are renowned or remain unsung
   as great Zeus wills it.
For lightly he makes strong,
   and lightly brings strength to confusion,
lightly diminishes the great man,
   uplifts the obscure one,
lightly the crooked man he straightens,
   withers the proud man,
he, Zeus, of the towering thunders,
   whose house is highest.

Hear me, see me, Zeus: hearken:
   direct your decrees in righteousness.
To you, Perses, I would describe
   the true way of existence.

It was never true that there was only one kind
   of strife. There have always
been two on earth. There is one
   you could like when you understand her.
The other is hateful. The two Strifes
   have separate natures.
There is one Strife who builds up evil war,
   and slaughter.
She is harsh; no man loves her, but under
      compulsion
and by will of the immortals men
   promote this rough Strife.
But the other one was born
   the elder daughter of black Night.

The son of Kronos, who sits on high and
   dwells in the bright air,
set her in the roots of the earth and among
      men;
   she is far kinder.
She pushes the shiftless man to work,
   for all his laziness.
A man looks at his neighbor, who is rich:
   then he too
wants work; for the rich man presses on with
   his plowing and planting
and the ordering of his state.
   So the neighbor envies the neighbor
who presses on toward wealth. Such Strife
   is a good friend to mortals.
Then potter is potter's enemy, and
      craftsman is craftman's
rival; tramp is jealous of tramp,
   and singer of singer.
         So you, Perses, put all this firmly away
   in your heart,
nor let that Strife who loves mischief
   keep you from working
as you listen at the meeting place
   to see what you can make of
the quarrels. The time comes short for
      litigations
   and lawsuits,
too short, unless there is a year's living
   laid away inside
for you, the stuff that the earth yields,
   the pride of Demeter.
When you have got a full burden of that,
   you can push your lawsuits,
scheming for other men's goods, yet you
   shall not be given another chance

to do so. No, come, let us finally settle
   our quarrel
with straight decisions, which are from Zeus,
   and are the fairest.
Now once before we divided our inheritance,
   but you seized
the greater part and made off with it,
   gratifying those barons
who eat bribes, who are willing
   to give out such a decision.
Fools all! who never learned
   how much better than the whole the half is,
nor how much good there is
   in living on mallow and asphodel.
For the gods have hidden and keep hidden
   what could be men's livelihood.
It could have been that easily
   in one day you could work out
enough to keep you for a year,
   with no more working.
Soon you could have hung up your steering oar
   in the smoke of the fireplace,
and the work the oxen and patient mules do
   would be abolished,
but Zeus in the anger of his heart hid it away
because the devious-minded Prometheus had
   cheated him;
and therefore Zeus thought up dismal sorrows
   for mankind.
He hid fire; but Prometheus, the powerful son
   of Iapetos,
stole it again from Zeus of the counsels,
   to give to mortals.
He hid it out of the sight of Zeus
   who delights in thunder
in the hollow fennel stalk. In anger
   the cloud-gatherer spoke to him:

"Son of Iapetos, deviser of crafts beyond all
   others,
you are happy that you stole the fire,
   and outwitted my thinking;
but it will be a great sorrow to you,
   and to men who come after.
As the price of fire I will give them an evil,
   and all men shall fondle
this, their evil, close to their hearts,
   and take delight in it."
   So spoke the father of gods and mortals;
   and laughed out loud.
He told glorious Hephaistos to make haste,
   and plaster
earth with water, and to infuse it with a
   human voice
and vigor, and make the face
   like the immortal goddesses,
the bewitching features of a young girl;
   meanwhile Athene
was to teach her her skills, and how
   to do the intricate weaving,
while Aphrodite was to mist her head
   in golden endearment
and the cruelty of desire and longings
   that wear out the body,
but to Hermes, the guide, the slayer of Argos,
   he gave instructions
to put in her the mind of a hussy,
   and a treacherous nature.
So Zeus spoke. And all obeyed Lord Zeus,
   the son of Kronos.
The renowned strong smith modeled her
    figure of earth,
   in the likeness
of a decorous young girl, as the son of Kronos
   had wished it.

The goddess gray-eyed Athene dressed and
    arrayed her;
   the Graces,
who are goddesses, and hallowed Persuasion
   put necklaces
of gold upon her body, while the Seasons,
   with glorious tresses,
put upon her head a coronal of spring flowers,
[and Pallas Athene put all decor upon her
    body].
But into her heart Hermes, the guide,
   the slayer of Argos,
put lies, and wheedling words
   of falsehood, and a treacherous nature,
made her as Zeus of the deep thunder wished,
   and he, the gods' herald,
put a voice inside her, and gave her
   the name of woman,
Pandora, because all the gods
   who have their homes on Olympos
had given her each a gift, to be a sorrow to
   men
who eat bread. Now when he had done
   with this sheer, impossible
deception, the Father sent the gods' fleet
   messenger,
   Hermes,
to Epimetheus, bringing her, a gift,
   nor did Epimetheus
remember to think how Prometheus had told
   him never
to accept a gift from Olympian Zeus,
   but always to send it
back, for fear it might prove
   to be an evil for mankind.
He took the evil, and only perceived it
   when he possessed her.

Since before this time the races of men
   had been living on earth
free from all evils, free from laborious work,
   and free from
all wearing sicknesses that bring
   their fates down on men
[for men grow old suddenly
   in the midst of misfortune];
but the woman, with her hands lifting away
    the lid
from the great jar,
scattered its contents, and her design
   was sad troubles for mankind.
Hope was the only spirit that stayed there
   in the unbreakable
closure of the jar, under its rim,
   and could not fly forth
abroad, for the lid of the great jar
   closed down first and contained her;
this was by the will of cloud-gathering Zeus
   of the aegis;
but there are other troubles by thousands
   that hover about men,
for the earth is full of evil things,
   and the sea is full of them;
there are sicknesses that come to men by day,
   while in the night
moving of themselves they haunt us,
   bringing sorrow to mortals,
and silently, for Zeus of the counsels
   took the voice out of them.

So there is no way to avoid what Zeus has
   intended.

Or if you will, I will outline it for you
   in a different story,

well and knowledgeably—store it up
  in your understanding—
the beginnings of things, which were the same
    for gods
    as for mortals.

In the beginning, the immortals
  who have their homes on Olympos
created the golden generation of mortal
    people.
These lived in Kronos' time, when he
  was the king in heaven.
They lived as if they were gods,
  their hearts free from all sorrow,
by themselves, and without hard work or pain;
  no miserable
old age came their way; their hands, their feet,
  did not alter.
They took their pleasure in festivals,
  and lived without troubles.
When they died, it was as if they fell asleep.
  All goods
were theirs. The fruitful grainland
  yielded its harvest to them
of its own accord; this was great and
    abundant,
  while they at their pleasure
quietly looked after their works,
  in the midst of good things
[prosperous in flocks, on friendly terms
  with the blessed immortals].

  Now that the earth has gathered over this
    generation,
these are called pure and blessed spirits;
  they live upon earth,
and are good, they watch over mortal men
  and defend them from evil;

they keep watch over lawsuits and hard
    dealings;
  they mantle
themselves in dark mist
  and wander all over the country;
they bestow wealth; for this right
  as of kings was given them.
  Next after these the dwellers upon
    Olympos created
a second generation, of silver, far worse
  than the other.
They were not like the golden ones either in
    shape
  or spirit.
A child was a child for a hundred years,
  looked after and playing
by his gracious mother, kept at home,
  a complete booby.
But when it came time for them to grow up
  and gain full measure,
they lived for only a poor short time;
  by their own foolishness
they had troubles, for they were not able
  to keep away from
reckless crime against each other,
  nor would they worship
the gods, nor do sacrifice on the sacred altars
  of the blessed ones,
which is the right thing among the customs of
    men,
  and therefore
Zeus, son of Kronos, in anger engulfed them,
  for they paid no due
honors to the blessed gods who live on
    Olympos.

  But when the earth had gathered over this
    generation

also—and they too are called blessed spirits
   by men, though under
the ground, and secondary, but still
   they have their due worship—
then Zeus the father created the third
     generation
   of mortals,
the age of bronze. They were not like
   the generation of silver.
They came from ash spears. They were terrible
   and strong, and the ghastly
action of Ares was theirs, and violence.
   They ate no bread,
but maintained an indomitable and
     adamantine spirit.
None could come near them; their strength
     was big,
   and from their shoulders
the arms grew irresistible on their ponderous
     bodies.
The weapons of these men were bronze,
   of bronze their houses,
and they worked as bronzesmiths. There was
     not yet
   any black iron.
Yet even these, destroyed beneath the hands
   of each other,
went down into the moldering domain of cold
     Hades;
nameless . . .

I mean you well, Perses, you great idiot,
   and I will tell you.
Look, badness is easy to have, you can take it
   by handfuls
without effort. The road that way is smooth
   and starts here beside you.

But between us and virtue the immortals have
     put
   what will make us
sweat. The road to virtue is long
   and goes steep uphill,
hard climbing at first, but the last of it,
   when you get to the summit
(if you get there) is easy going after the hard
     part.

That man is all-best who himself works out
   every problem
and solves it, seeing what will be best late
   and in the end.
That man, too, is admirable who follows one
   who speaks well.
He who cannot see the truth for himself, nor,
   hearing it from others,
store it away in his mind, that man
   is utterly useless.
As for you, remember what I keep telling you
   over and over:
work, O Perses, illustrious-born, work on,
   so that Famine
will avoid you, and august and garlanded
     Demeter
   will be your friend, and fill your barn
   with substance of living;
Famine is the unworking man's most constant
   companion.
Gods and men alike resent that man who,
   without work
himself, lives the life of the stingless drones,
who without working eat away the substance
   of the honeybees'
hard work; your desire, then, should be
   to put your works in order

so that your barns may be stocked with all
    livelihood in its season.
It is from work that men grow rich and own
      flocks
   and herds;
by work, too, they become much better
      friends
   of the immortals.
[and to men too, for they hate the people
    who do not labor].
Work is no disgrace; the disgrace is in not
     working;
and if you do work, the lazy man will soon
     begin
   to be envious
as you grow rich, for with riches go nobility
    and honor.
It is best to work, at whatever you have a
     talent
   for doing,
without turning your greedy thought toward
     what
   some other man
possesses, but take care of your own
     livelihood,
   as I advise you. . . .

First of all, get yourself an ox for plowing,
    and a woman—
for work, not to marry—one who can plow
    with the oxen,

and get all necessary gear in your house
    in good order,
lest you have to ask someone else, and he
     deny you,
   and you go
short, and the season pass you by, and your
     work
   be undone.
Do not put off until tomorrow and the day
    after.
A man does not fill his barn by shirking his
    labors
or putting them off; it is keeping at it that
     gets
   the work done.
The putter-off of work is the man who
     wrestles
   with disaster.
  At the time when the force of the cruel
     sun
   diminishes,
and the sultriness and the heat, when
     powerful Zeus
   brings on
the rains of autumn, and the feel of a man's
     body
   changes
and he goes much lighter, for at this time
    the star Seirios
goes only a little over the heads
    of hard-fated mankind . . .

ANONYMOUS

Homeric Hymns (ca. 700 B.C.): Hymn to Aphrodite

*O*ne of the most remarkable collections of the preclassical era includes thirty-three paeans to the gods and heroes in the dactylic hexameter of Homer's *Iliad* and *Odyssey,* composed by anonymous rhapsodes. Known as the Homeric Hymns, they celebrate, among others, Gaia and Dionysius, Artemis and Hermes, Poseidon, Zeus, and Apollo. The hymns may have been composed as preludes to the singing of the *Iliad* and *Odyssey,* honoring the god of a particular township or on his or her special feast day.

- Throughout the Homeric Hymns, the relationship between men and gods, whether described heroically or comically, is resoundingly personal and dynamic, dreadful and glorious. Here we learn of rituals and epithets, how the gods and goddesses were worshiped and addressed by men. While Homer anticipates, in the comic and skeptical depth of his mythic psychology, the logical era where gods become embodiments of human emotions and motivations, these hymns offer the mirror image of a mythic way of life that is unquestioning of the gods' reality and their impact on human affairs:

  - Demeter's grief for the loss of her daughter Persephone to Hades, the god of the underworld, explains the winter's loss of crops. The goddess is in her annual mourning.
  - Apollo's birth and founding of the oracle at Delphi.
  - The miracle-working Dionysius dazzles his captors until they leap into the sea and become dolphins.
  - Hermes' thievery is a reminder of his anomalous role among the gods, as one who oversees the borders between nations and exchanges between people in his multiple roles as thief, trickster, magician, salesman, seducer, bargainer, comedian, and escort of souls from one life to another.

- One of the most powerful of the collection, the *Hymn to Aphrodite,* celebrates the mysterious power of the Cyprian, Cytherean goddess of erotic love and procreation. The hymn details her love for the mortal Anchises, by whom she bore Aeneas, hero of Troy and legendary (according to the Romans) founder of Rome. When wolves, bears, lions, and panthers follow Aphrodite to her trysting place and themselves lie down in pairs to copulate, we see the goddess' origins in Britomartis, the ancient Mesopotamian goddess of the animals. Aphrodite, as a manifestation of the "great Mother," is a reminder of earlier matriarchal Mediter-ranean cultures, such as that of the Minoans on Crete, that predated Mycenaean hegemony and the birth of the "classical era." The herdsman Anchises' terror at her soliciting his sexual attention on Mt. Ida is therefore not at all surprising, representing the anxiety of a newly solidified patriarchy that still recalls a time when a new king is chosen and must die for the sake of ritual fertility each year after enjoying the bed of the queen. When laughter-loving Aphrodite arrays herself with ointments and gold, what mere mortal can resist her? Her charms and her lies both evoke male potency and render men powerless. When Zeus, the "father of gods and men," himself a victim of her wiles, punishes Aphrodite for her lack of sexual restraint, the taming hand of the patriarchy comes into play, which chose as its principal goddess the motherless, childless, sexless Athena.

Ah Muse,
tell me about the things that Aphrodite
does, the golden one, the Cyprian one,
she who awakens a pleasant yearning in
gods, she who subdues the race of mortal
men, and the birds of Zeus, and all the
many animals that the land nourishes,
and the sea nourishes. The works of
the beautifully crowned Cytherean are
the concern of all of these.

But there are three minds that she is
unable to persuade, unable, that is,
to seduce: there is the daughter of Zeus
who carries the aegis, Athena with her
gleaming eyes. She doesn't like the things
that Aphrodite does, the things that the
golden one does. Wars are what she likes,
and the work of Ares: fights and battles
are what she likes. And she concerns herself
with the decorative arts: she was the first
to teach the workingmen of earth how to
make great chariots, and how to make their
chariots

inwrought with bronze. And she's the one who
teaches soft-skinned young ladies the
decorative arts, she puts it in the mind of
each one.

"Aphrodite of Milos"

The second one
that Aphrodite, lover of laughter, cannot
subdue in love is noisy Artemis with her
golden arrows. She likes her bow, and she
likes murdering animals on mountains.
She likes lyres and dances, women's thrilling
screams and shady woods, and she likes the
cities of just men.

And third,
the things that Aphrodite does are not
pleasing to that venerable virgin, Hestia,
whom Cronos in his craftiness first gave
birth to (and also last—thanks to Zeus
who carries the aegis), the lady that
Poseidon and Apollo were both after. She
didn't want them, she refused them firmly.
And she swore a great oath on it, one that
was fulfilled, touching the head of father
Zeus who carries the aegis, that she would
be a virgin every day, a divine goddess.
And father Zeus gave her a beautiful
privilege instead of a wedding-gift: he has
her sit in the center of the house to receive
the best in offerings. In all the temples
of the gods she is honored, and among all
mortals she is a venerated goddess.

These are the three
minds that she is unable to persuade, that
is, to seduce. But nobody else, none of the
blessed gods, no mortal man, no one else can
ever escape Aphrodite. She even leads astray
the mind of Zeus himself, the lover of
     lightning,
the greatest of all, the one who receives the
greatest honor. And when she wants to, she
can deceive that sage heart of his easily,

and make even him mate with mortal women,
hiding from Hera, his sister and wife, she
who maintains the finest beauty among the
immortal goddesses, she whom Cronos in his
craftiness and mother Rheia bore to be
glorious, she whom Zeus, with his endless
concerns, has made his respected and trusted
wife.

But Zeus
put in Aphrodite's heart in turn a pleasant
yearning to mate with a mortal man, so that,
immediately, she would not be able to resist
a mortal man's bed, and boast some day to
all the gods that she, Aphrodite, lover of
laughter, with a sweet smile had mated the
gods with mortal women and they bore mortal
sons to immortal gods, and that she mated
goddesses with mortal men.

And it was for Anchises
therefore that he put in her heart a
pleasant longing, who at the time was
grazing his cattle on the mountain heights
of Ida, with its many springs, his body
very much like a god. And when she saw
him, Aphrodite, lover of laughter, she
loved him, and a terrifying desire seized
her heart.

She went away
to Cyprus, and entered her fragrant
temple at Paphos, where she has a precinct
and a fragrant altar. After going inside
she closed the bright doors, and the
Graces gave her a bath, they oiled her
with sacred olive-oil, the kind that the
gods always have on, that pleasant ambrosia

that she was perfumed with. Having put on
all her beautiful
clothing, and having ornamented herself
in gold, Aphrodite, lover of laughter,
hurried away to Troy, leaving sweet-smelling
Cyprus, quickly cutting a path through
the clouds high up.

And she came to Ida
with its many springs, the mother of
animals. She went right up the mountain
to the sheepfolds. Behind her moved gray
wolves, fawning on her, and bright-eyed
lions, bears, and quick, insatiable panthers.
When she saw them she felt joy in her
heart, and she put longing in their breasts,
and immediately they all went into the
shade of the valley in twos to sleep
with each other.

She herself
went to the huts, which were well-made.
She found him in the huts, left
all alone, alone from all the others,
the hero Anchises, who had beauty from
the gods. The others had followed their
cattle into the grasslands, all of them,
except him, he was in the huts,
left all alone, alone from all the others,
walking around here and there, playing on
his lyre thrillingly.

She stood in front of him—
Aphrodite, the daughter of Zeus—in the
form and size of a young virgin, lest
he recognize her, lest he be frightened
in his eyes. Anchises saw her and he
marveled at her, he was astonished by

her form, and size, and by her expensive
clothes. She wore a robe that was brighter
than a fire-flash, and she had on spiral
ringlets, and bright ornaments,
and necklaces around her delicate neck
that were very beautiful, and lovely, and
golden, and finely wrought, shining like
the moon on her delicate breasts, and
astonishing. Love gripped Anchises, and he
spoke these words to her:

"Hello, great lady,
you must be one of the gods coming to visit
my house here, Artemis or Leto or the golden
Aphrodite or noble Themis or bright-eyes
    Athena—
or you're one of the Graces coming to visit me
here, who hang around with the gods and are
    called
immortal—or you're one of the nymphs who
    live
in beautiful groves—
or you're one of the nymphs who live on
this beautiful mountain here, the source
of rivers and grassy meadows. I'll build
an altar to you, on some high spot that
can be seen from all around, I'll offer
beautiful sacrifices to you in every season.
And in the goodness of your heart, make me
into a magnificent man among the Trojans!
Make my descendants flourish later on!
Let me live well for a long time, seeing
the light of the sun, rich among my people!
Let me attain the threshold of old age!"

And Aphrodite,
the daughter of Zeus, replied to him:
"Anchises, the most splendid man who lives

on the earth, I'm not at all a goddess.
Why do you take me for one of the
     immortals?
On the contrary, I'm a mortal, and the mother
who bore me was just a woman. My father's
famous name is Otreus—perhaps you've heard
of him—he rules over all of Phrygia with
its great walls. And I know your language as
     well
as I know my own. The nurse who brought me
     up
in our palace was Trojan. She took care of me
from the moment I was a tiny child, right out
     of
the arms of my dear mother. That's why I
     know
your language as well as I know my own.
Argeiphontes with his golden wand has just
snatched me from the dances of noisy Artemis
with her golden arrows. We were playing,
many of us nymphs and well-endowed
     virgins,
and a huge crowd started to circle around us.
That's when Hermes with his golden wand
snatched me away. He brought me over
many lands plowed by mortal men, many that
belonged to nobody, many that were
     untouched,
where man-eating animals roam in shaded
valleys. It seemed that my feet would never
     touch
earth again, the source of life.

     He told me
that in the bed of Anchises I would be called
a lawful wife, and that I would bear you
splendid babies. And when he had pointed
     this

out, and told me, the powerful Hermes went
     back
to the race of immortals. But I've come to
     you,
and strong was the force that brought me.
I beg you, in the name of Zeus and your noble
parents—for surely no bad people could have
produced such a person as you—take me,
virgin that I am, ignorant of love-making
as I am, and present me to your father
and your good mother and to your brothers,
born from the same stock as you. I won't be
a daughter-in-law unfitting for them, but very
     fitting.
Send a messenger immediately to the
     Phrygians
with their fast horses to tell my father
and my worried mother. And they'll send
     back
gold and plenty of woven garments, and you,
you receive these splendid things as a dowry.
And after you've done these things, prepare a
pleasant wedding-feast, so liked by mortal
     men
and by the immortal gods."

     Saying this,
the goddess filled his heart with a sweet
longing. And love seized Anchises, and he
     spoke
these words:

     "If you really are
a mortal, and the mother that bore you
really was a woman, and if Otreus is in fact
the famous name of your father, as you say,
and if you do really come here through the
     will

of the immortal guide, Hermes, then you will
be
called my wife for all time. No one, no god,
no mortal man will stop me right here and
now
from making love to you immediately. Even if
the great Archer Apollo himself should fire
groaning
arrows from his silver bow—why I would even
consent to disappear into the house of Hades
after mounting your bed, lady, you who look
so much like a goddess."
          And saying this
he took her hand. Aphrodite, smiling, turned
her head and advanced, with her beautiful
eyes lowered,
toward his bed, which was well laid-out, and
where
soft garments were strewn about for the
prince.
Upon it were the skins of bears and roaring
lions, which he had himself killed in the high
mountains. When they had climbed into the
bed that
was so well-made, he first of all took off the
bright
ornaments from her body, brooches and spiral
ringlets
and flower-like necklaces. He took off her
beautiful
clothes and removed her girdle and put them
on a
silver chair, he, Anchises! And then, by the
will
and fate of the gods, he slept, a mortal, with
an
immortal goddess. And he didn't even know
it.

          At that moment,
when shepherds turn back their cattle to the
stable,
and their sturdy sheep from flowering
meadows,
at that moment she put a deep and pleasant
sleep
over Anchises, and then she dressed herself
in her beautiful clothes. And after she put on
all her things, the divine goddess then stood up
in the tent, and her head touched its well-
made
top, and from her cheeks shone an ambrosial
beauty,
just as it is on the crowned Cytherean. She
woke him
from his sleep and she spoke a word with him:

          "Get up,
son of Dardanus! Why do you sleep such a
deep sleep?
And tell me if I appear to you now to be the
same
as when you first saw me with your eyes?"

          So she spoke.
He did what she said and came out of his
sleep
very rapidly. But when he saw her neck and
the
beautiful eyes of Aphrodite, he was scared,
and
he turned his eyes away to the side. Then he
covered his own beautiful face with his cloak,
and begging her, he spoke these words:

          "Right then
when I first saw you with my eyes, goddess,

I knew you were divine. But you didn't speak
 honestly
to me. Now at your knees I implore you, in
 the name of
Zeus who carries the aegis, don't permit me to
 live
impotent among men from now on. Pity me.
 For a man
who sleeps with immortal goddesses loses his
potency."

 Aphrodite,
the daughter of Zeus, then replied:

 "Anchises,
most glorious of mortal men, cheer up!

Don't scare yourself out of your senses
so much! You have nothing terrible to fear
from me, nor from the other gods, because
the gods love you. You will have a fine son,
who will rule among the Trojans, and
 children
will be born forever to his children.
And his name shall be called Aeneas,
because the anguish that has come to me
is so terrible, since I let myself sleep
with a mortal man. And those mortal men
who in beauty and form come nearest
to the gods will always be from your stock. . . .

ARCHILOCHOS (FL. 650 B.C.)

Lyrics

From the Cycladic island of Paros, the iambic and elegiac poet "first sergeant" Archilochos was the son of Telesikles and the slave Enipo. Most of what we know about him is derived from his own work. Clement of Alexandria credits him with inventing the iamb. Pindar blamed Archilochos' poverty on his cantankerousness.

- About the time of the full eclipse of the sun of 648 B.C., Archilochos had an affair with Neobule, daughter of the nobleman Lycambes. According to legend, Lycambes broke his daughter's engagement with the poet when he learned of Archilochos' illegitimate birth. When Archilochos responded with a bombardment of abusive verse about Neobule's virtue, Lycambes, in despair, hanged Neobule, his other daughters—and himself.

Surly and churlish, the Charles Bukowski of his time, Archilochos was banned in Sparta for his coarse language. He fought, possibly as a mercenary, in Thasos and Thrace, and boasts of leaving his shield behind in battle. Ironically, he died in battle, slain by Calondas, from nearby Naxos, who was for the rest of his life cursed by the oracle of Delphi for killing a great servant of the Muses—considered by many second only to Homer. Meanwhile, legend tells us, the inscription on Archilochos' monument on Paros warned: "Keep moving, passerby—or you'll stir up the wasps."

- The father of satire, Archilochos sang about wine and war in a time dominated poetically by the heroic Homeric epics, and found a voice for himself that could not have been in greater contrast with the *Iliad*'s aristocratic idealization and objectivity. Taking his cue instead from the *Odyssey*'s relatively subjective view of life and action, he wrote of his own faults and foibles and those of others, his gaze focusing firmly on what *is*, not what *ought to be.* Unlike other Greek lyric poets, Archilochos seems to have had no patron—not surprising, considering his refusal to kowtow to anyone. Richmond Lattimore calls him the earliest amateur poet. Though none of his poems have survived intact, even the fragments portray him clearly.
- Known in his own time as a genius for metrical inventiveness and wide-ranging subject matter, Archilochos sees the world with a questioning eye and lampoons—betrayed friendship, the fickleness of fame, the manipulativeness of lovers—with precise observation and vivid tongue. Meleager called him "a thistle with graceful leaves." He writes in a vibrant Ionic vernacular, weaving his lyric from homespun images, folk tales, animal fables, and the language of the trenches to express his irritation and indignation with life. He saw no glory in war. Archilochos' poems were the models for Horace's *Epodes.*

THASOS AND SICILY

              This wheatless island
stands like a donkey's back. It bristles
with a tangle of wild woodland.
              Oh,
there is no country so beautiful,
no sensual earth that keys my passion
as these plains around the river Siris.

THE DOUBLECROSS

Let brawling waves beat his ship
against the shore, and have the mop-haired
  Thracians

take him naked at Salmydessos,
and he will suffer a thousand calamities
as he chews the bread of slaves.
His body will stiffen in freezing surf
as he wrestles with slimy seaweed,
and his teeth will rattle like a helpless dog,
flopped on his belly in the surge,
puking out the brine. Let me watch him
    grovel
in mud—for the wrong he did me:
as a traitor he trampled on our good faith,
he who was once my comrade.

PAROS FIGS
Say goodbye to the island Paros,
farewell to its figs and the seafaring life.

AN ECLIPSE OF THE SUN
Nothing in the world can surprise me now. Nothing
is impossible or too wonderful, for Zeus, father
of the Olympians, has turned midday into black night
by shielding light from the blossoming sun,
and now dark terror hangs over mankind.
Anything may happen, so do not be amazed if beasts
on dry land seek pasture with dolphins in the ocean, and those beasts who loved sunny hills
love crashing seawaves more than the warm mainland.

ON THE MALE ORGAN
Feeble now are the muscles in my mushroom.

PROVERB FOR A GREAT SCOUNDREL
The fox knows many tricks,
the hedgehog only one. A good one.

ON HIS SHIELD
Well, what if some barbaric Thracian glories
in the perfect shield I left under a bush?
I was sorry to leave it—but I saved my skin.
Does it matter? O hell, I'll buy a better one.

MY KIND OF GENERAL
I don't like a general
who towers over the troops,
lordly with elegant locks
and trim mustachios.
Give me a stumpy soldier
glaringly bowlegged,
yet rockfirm on his feet,
and in his heart a giant.

ON THE DAUGHTER OF LYKAMBES
I pray for one gift: that I might merely touch
Neoboule's hand.

LOVE
I live here miserable and broken with desire,
pierced through to the bones by the bitterness
of this god-given painful love.

"Hermes, by Praxiteles." By permission of Art Resource.

O comrade, this passion makes my limbs limp
and tramples over me.

THIRST

I want to fight you
just as when I am thirsty I want to drink.

MODERATION

O my soul, my soul—you are mutilated
    helplessly
by this blade of sorrow. Yet rise and bare your
    chest,
face those who would attack you, be strong,
    give no ground.
And if you defeat them, do not brag like a
    loudmouth,
nor, if they beat you, run home and lie down
    to cry.
Keep some measure in your joy—or in your
    sadness during
crisis—that you may understand man's up-
    and-down life.

DEATH

When dead no man finds respect or glory
    from men
of his town. Rather, we hope while alive for
    some
favor from the living. The dead are always
    scorned.

". . . but if you're in a hurry and can't wait for
    me
there's another girl in our house who's quite
    ready
to marry, a pretty girl, just right for you."
That was what she said, but I can talk too.

"Daughter of dear Amphimedo," I said,
"(a fine woman she was—pity she's dead)
there are plenty of kinds of pretty play
young men and girls can know and not go all
    the way
—something like that will do. As for marrying,
we'll talk about that again when your
    mourning
is folded away, god willing. But now
I'll be good, I promise—I do know how.
Don't be hard, darling. Truly I'll stay
out on the garden-grass, not force the doorway
—just try. But as for that sister of yours,
someone else can have her. The bloom's
    gone—she's coarse
—the charm too (she had it)—now she's on
    heat
the whole time, can't keep away from it—
damn her, don't let anyone saddle me with
    that.
With a wife like she is I shouldn't half
give the nice neighbors a belly-laugh.
You're all right, darling. You're simple and
    straight
—she takes her meat off anyone's plate.
I'd be afraid if I married her
my children would be like the bitch's litter
—born blind, and several months too early."
But I'd talked enough. I laid the girl
down among the flowers. A soft cloak spread,
my arm round her neck, I comforted
her fear. The fawn soon ceased to flee.
Over her breasts my hands moved gently,
the new-formed girlhood she bared for me;
over all her body, the young skin bare,
I spilt my white force, just touching her yellow
    hair.

THALES OF MILETUS (624–546 B.C.)
Water

*T*he first of the "Ionian physicists" and considered to be one of the Seven Sages, Thales was a mathematician and natural philosopher. He was first to pose the question, "What is the basic physical substance of the universe?" His answer: "Water."

- Miletus in Asia Minor, no doubt because it was a center for east-west trade, importing thought as well as goods from Crete, Egypt, and Babylonia, was the cradle of western scientific speculation, the birthplace not only of Thales, but also of Anaximander and Anaximenes.

- Herodotus relates that Thales predicted the solar eclipse of May 25, 585 B.C., in the rule of Alyattes, king of Lydia, and that he visited Egypt and used Egyptian geometry to measure the height of the pyramids and predict the flooding of the Nile. He is credited with changing the course of the river Halys for Croesus, and of amassing great wealth by speculation in olive oil and leasing oil presses.

- The move from a mythological portrait of reality to a logical philosophy based on analysis and reason begins with Thales' assumption that all existence can be understood by reference to a single generative principle that may or may not be visible and apparent. Although he believed that the earth was a flat disc floating on water, Thales also believed that life is indistinguishable from matter, and that every material particle is alive. The world, he said, is constantly changing but indestructible. Humans, animals, and plants have immortal souls: "All things are full of gods." Aristotle considered Thales the founder of physical science. Nothing that he wrote survives.

TERPANDROS (FL. 645 B.C.)

Lyrics

*T*hough it is not certain that the fragments credited to Terpandros (or Terpander) are genuine, they are certainly "Terpandrean," based on the reputation of this lyric musician from Antissa, in Lesbos. In his own lifetime, much of which he spent in Sparta, Terpandros was compared with Homer, whose words he set to music in both the Aeolian and Dorian dialects. He is also credited with perfecting the choral lyric, and with reintroducing the seven-string lyre to the Greek world. According to the *Suda Lexicon*, "The Spartans were fighting among themselves and sent to Lesbos for the musician Terpandros; he came and made their minds tranquil and stopped the quarrel. After that whenever the Spartans listened to a musician, they would say, 'He is not the equal of the poet of Lesbos.'" (tr. Barnstone)

HYMN TO ZEUS
Zeus, inceptor of all,
of all things the commander,
Zeus, I bring you this gift:
the beginning of song.

TO APOLLO AND THE MUSES
Let us pour a libation
to the Muses, daughters

of Memory, and to Leto's
son, their lord Apollo.

SPARTA
The Muse sings brilliantly and
spears of young men flower.
Justice, defender of brave works,
goes down the street of light.

ALKMAN (FL. 630 B.C.)
Lyrics

Although it is not clear where Alkman was born, he lived his productive life as a lyric poet in Sparta, where he arrived as a slave from Lydian Sardis only to be freed for his talent. He is known for his choral odes, written to be sung by choruses of young men and maidens in an artificial language mixing Aeolic and Dorian in a fashion recalling Homer. Some credit him with the invention of love songs, though none of his love songs survive. Instead, what we have of Alkman celebrates festivals and feasts. His imagery is sharp, his meters simple, his style sparse and pointed. Antipatros of Thessalonika wrote his epitaph (tr. Barnstone):

> Do not judge the man by his gravestone. The tomb you see is small but it holds the bones of a great man. For know that this is Alkman, supreme artist of the Lakonian lyre, who commanded the nine Muses. And twin continents dispute whether he is of Lydia or Lakonia, for the mothers of a singer are many.

ARS POETICA
I know the tunes
of every bird,

but I, Alkman, found my words and song
in the tongue
of the strident partridge.

ON A POETESS
Aphrodite commands and love rains
upon my body and melts my heart

for Megalostrata to whom the sweet
Muse gave the gift of poetry. O
happy girl of the goldenrod hair!

ALKMAN'S SUPPER
Get him that enormous caldron on the tripod
so he can bloat his stomach with every food.
It is cool but soon will boil with good soup
which gobbler Alkman likes sparkling hot,
especially in the cold season of the solstice.
The glutton Alkman abstains from fancy
    dishes
but like the demos eats a plain massive meal.

THE FOUR SEASONS
Three seasons were created: summer
and winter and a third in autumn,
and even a fourth—the spring—

when the fields are heavy with crops
and a glutton still goes hungry.

THE JOURNEY
Narrow is our way of life
and necessity is pitiless.

I AM OLD
O girls of honey-sweet voices, my limbs are
    weak.

They will not bear me. I wish, ah, I wish I
    were
a carefree kingfisher flying over flowering foam
with the halcyons—sea-blue holy birds of
    spring.

CALM SEA
The calm sea falls dumbly
on the shore
among a tangle of seaweed.

ALCAEUS (FL. 590 B.C.)

Lyrics

Born on Lesbos, in Mytilene, the aristocratic lyric poet Alcaeus reports that he lost his shield in the battle against Athens at Sigeion. From his boyhood, when his brothers Antimenidas and Cicis, aided by Pittakos, overthrew the tyrant Melanchros, he spent much of his life embroiled in civil wars on Lesbos, sometimes as a mercenary. His poetry, much of it written from exile in Pyrrha, reflects the violent political turmoil of his life. The Roman rhetorician Quintilian wrote that Alcaeus "is rightly awarded the golden quill in that part of his work where he assails tyrants; his ethical value is also great; his style is concise, magnificent, exact, very much like Homer's; but he stoops to humor and love when better suited for higher themes." (tr. Barnstone)

- Extroverted and aggressive, better at hating than loving, Alcaeus lived, drank hard, and wrote primarily of wine, women, and war. The god Bacchus, he says, provides men with drink as solace against a life of hardship: "Let us drink. Why wait for the lighting of the lamps? Night is a hair's breadth away." Although no complete poem of his survives, the Alexandrians collected ten volumes of his work. Alcaeus writes in the Lesbian Aeolic dialect. His metrical virtuosity is equaled only by the variety of his interests—from translations of Hesiod, to rowdy drinking songs, to comments on female beauty contests, romantic monologues, fiery political diatribes, and hymns to the gods. His greatest contribution is making the lyric entirely personal, an influence still at work among the twentieth century's "confessional poets."

WINTER EVENING

Zeus rumbles and a mammoth winter of
    snow
pours from the sky; agile rivers are ice.

Damn the winter cold! Pile up the burning
    logs
and water the great flagons of red wine;
place feather pillows by your head, and drink.

Let us not brood about hard times. Bakchos,
our solace is in *you* and your red wines:
our medicine of grape. Drink deeply, drink.

SUMMER STAR

Wash your gullet with wine for the Dog-Star
    returns
with the heat of summer searing a thirsting
    earth.
Cicadas cry softly under high leaves, and pour
    down
shrill song incessantly from under their wings.
The artichoke blooms, and women are warm
    and wanton—
but men turn lean and limp for the burning
    Dog-Star parches their brains and knees.

WHY WAIT FOR THE LIGHTING OF
THE LAMPS?

Let us drink. Why wait for the lighting of the
    lamps?
Night is a hair's breadth away. Take down the
    great goblets
from the shelf, dear friend, for the son of
    Semele and Zeus
gave us wine to forget our pains. Mix two
    parts water, one wine,
and let us empty the dripping cups—urgently.

DRINK, SONG, AND SHIPS

Why water more wine in the great bowl?
Why do you drown your gullet in grape?
I cannot let you spill out your life
on song and drink. Let us go to sea,

and not let the wintry calm of morning
slip by as a drunken sleep. Had we
boarded at dawn, seized rudder and spun
the flapping cross-jack into the wind,

we would be happy now, happy as swimming
in grape. But you draped a lazy arm
on my shoulder, saying: "Sir, a pillow,
your singing does not lead me to ships."

COSTUME

But let them hang braided garlands
of yellow dill around our necks,
and drape strands of redolent myrrh
across our breasts.

ON HIS BROTHER'S HOMECOMING

You have come home from the ends of the
    earth,
Antimenidas, my dear brother; come
with a gold and ivory handle to your sword.
You fought alongside the Babylonians
and your prowess saved them from
    annihilation
when you battled and cut down a warrior
    giant
who was almost eight feet tall.

THE LYRE

Daughter of the rock and the gray sea,
    you fill all hearts
with triumph, tortoise shell of the sea.

BIRDS

What birds are these
wildgeese—flying from precincts where the
earth
and oceans end—
with their enormous wings and speckled
throats?

ON MONEY

Aristodemos wasn't lying
when he said one day in Sparta,

"Money is the man; and a poor man
can be neither good nor honorable."

THINGS OF WAR

The great house glitters with bronze. War has
patterned the roof with shining helmets,
their horsehair plumes waving in wind,
headdress of fighting men. And pegs
are concealed under bright greaves of brass
which block the iron-tipped arrows. Many
fresh-linen corslets are hanging and hollow
shields are heaped about the floor,
and standing in rows are swords of Chalkidian
steel, belt-knives and warriors' kilts.
We cannot forget our arms and armor when
soon our dreadful duties begin.

WALLS AND THE CITY

Not homes with beautiful roofs,
nor walls of permanent stone,
nor canals and piers for ships

make the city—but men of strength.

Not stone and timber, nor skill
of carpenter—but men brave

who will handle sword and spear.

With these you have: city and walls.

A NATION AT SEA

I can't tell you which way the gale has turned
for waves crash in from west and east, and we
are tossed and driven between, our black ship
laboring under the giant storm.

The sea washes across the decks and maststep
and dark daylight already shows through long
rents
in the sails. Even the halyards slacken as
windward waves coil above the hull.

What sore labor to bail the water we've
shipped!
Let us raise bulwarks and ride out the storm,
heeding my words: "Let each man now be
famous."
Yet base cowards betray the state.

TO THE MYTILENIANS

The local tyrant
rants and blusters and you are silenced
like a school of frightened neophytes
confronting the dead in holy rituals.

But I tell you, O citizens of Lesbos,
rise up and quench the smoldering logs
before their flames climb and consume you all
in total fire!

EARTHQUAKE

The tyrant's craze for absolute power will soon
demolish his country; already the earth
trembles.

TO THE BASEBORN TYRANT

I say this to him too: he is a strident
lute who would like to be heard at a party
of the well-born people of Lesbos. Better
had he chosen to drink with the filthy herd.
He married a daughter from the ancient
race of Atreus; now let him offend our people
as he did the former tyrant Myrsilos,
until the Wargod makes us revolt. We must
forget our anger and cease these pitiful
clashes between brothers. Only a god
could have maddened our people into war
and so give Pittakos his bit of glory.

TO HIS FRIEND MELANIPPOS

Drink and be drunk with me, Melanippos. Do
   you
think when you have crossed the great fuming
   river,
you will ever return from Hell to see the clean
bright light of the sun? Do not strive for wild
   hopes.

Even the son of Aiolos, King Sisyphos, wisest
   of men,
thought he had eluded death. But for all his
   brains

Fate made him recross Acheron, and the son
   of Kronos
assigned him a terrible trial below the dark
   earth.

Come, I beg you not to brood about these
   hopeless
matters while we are young. We will suffer
   what must

be suffered. When the wind is waiting in the
   north,
a good captain will not swing into the open
   sea.

SOLON (640–560 B.C.)
Lyrics and Law Codes

*O*ne of the "Seven Sages," his very name synonymous with wisdom, Solon was the first Athenian poet and a legendary lawmaker and statesman. His knowledge, as impressive as his wisdom, was gleaned from travels in Asia Minor and Egypt, and throughout Greece. Son of Execestides and a distant relative of the tyrant Pisistratus, Solon was a noble merchant, of modest means because of his father's business excesses.

- In a time of economic unrest and volatile social instability, with the lower classes on the verge of revolution against their virtual enslavement by the upper classes, Solon was chosen *ar-*

chon, and was called upon because of his diplomatic skills and charisma to propose new legislation. His "great reform" of 594–593 B.C., a brilliantly effective compromise between an oligarchy based on wealth (timocracy) and a democracy, encompassed agriculture, law, and the constitution of Athens, laying a foundation for the city's classical renaissance in all areas of thought and expression. The high points of Solon's reform, and of his new constitution of Athens, include:

- Repealing Draco's harsh criminal code, leaving only its regulations concerning homicide.
- The *Seisachtheia,* "shaking off of burdens," to give immediate relief to debtors—who were losing their lands, and being sold into slavery—by canceling all burdens, public and private, that were secured by personal liberty or land ownership. Our modern bankruptcy laws find their source in this ordinance.
- To facilitate Athens' trade with her Greek sister states, "Attic" standards of coinage, weights, and measures were adopted based on the silver standard, and made uniform with the Euboic standard in use in other parts of Greece.
- Immigrant craftsmen were granted citizenship, to encourage the growth of commerce and trade.
- Agricultural exports, except for olive oil, were prohibited.
- The constitution divided the populace into four classes, sorted by wealth:

1. *Pentakosiomedimnoi,* who earned at least 500 *medimnoi* (750 bushels) of corn or *metretoe* of wine or oil yearly;
2. *Hippeis,* "knights," whose income was a minimum of 150 *medimnoi;*
3. *Zeugitai* (owners of a "yoke" of oxen), enjoying a minimum of 150 *medimnoi;*
4. *Thetes* ("workers"), with a yearly income of less than 150 *medimnoi.*

Only the first class could elect the *archon* of Athens. The top three classes could vote for the most responsible public offices, and were subject to taxation. The *thetes* could vote in general assembly for lesser officials and for new law, and were not taxed. Military service was also linked to class, with the *thetes* able to serve only as ordinary seamen or infantry.

- Trial by jury, in which even the *thetes* were allowed to participate as jurors, was instituted.
- The victors in the Olympian and Isthmian games were rewarded.
- The *boule,* or "council of 400," one hundred from each of the four tribes of Athens, was instituted as the principal consultative body to carry on the legislative decisions of the general assembly.

- The *Areopagus,* consisting only of those who had served as *archon,* was established as the principal administrative body.
- Public officials served without pay.

Despite the effectiveness of the new constitution, the tyrant Pisistratus seized power in Athens and abolished it in 560 B.C., two years before Solon's death.

- Solon's iambic and elegiac poetry expressed his views on current politics and explained his political positions and actions—and the moral concerns that governed them. His noble and authoritative voice, inspiring patriotism and belief in the excellence of the human spirit, comes through clearly even in translation.

ELEGIACS

1, *SALAMIS*

Myself as herald from lovely Salamis I come, having fashioned an ordered array of words, a poem instead of a speech.

Verily on that day may I change my fatherland, and be a man of Pholegandros or Sikinos rather than an Athenian; for soon would talk like this arise among men—"Here comes an Attic fellow, one of the Salamis-betrayers."

Let us go to Salamis, that we may do battle for the lovely island, and fling off our bitter disgrace.

2

If on our city ruin comes, it will never be by the dispensation of Zeus and the purpose of the blessed immortal gods, so powerful is our great-hearted guardian, born of mighty sire, Pallas Athene, who holds over it her hands. It is the people themselves who in their folly seek to destroy our great city, prompted by desire for wealth; and their leaders, unjust of heart, for whom awaits the suffering of many woes, the fruit of their great arrogance, since they know not how to check their greed, and to enjoy with order and sobriety the pleasures set before them at the feast. . . . They have wealth through their following of unjust works and ways. . . . Neither the sacred treasure nor that of the state do they spare in any wise, but they steal, each in his own corner, like men pillaging. They take no heed of the holy foundations of Justice, who in silence marks what happens and what has been, and who in course of time comes without fail to exact the penalty. Behold, there is coming now upon the whole state an injury that cannot be avoided; she has fallen swiftly into the evil of servitude, which awakens civil strife and war from their sleep— war that destroys many men in the bloom of their youth. By the work of the disaffected, swiftly our lovely city is being worn away, in those gatherings which are dear to unjust men.

Such are the ills that are rife within our state; while of the poor great numbers are journeying to foreign lands, sold into slavery, and bound with shameful fetters. [They bear perforce the accursed yoke of slavery.] Thus the public ill comes home to every single man, and no longer do his courtyard gates avail to hold it back; high though the wall be, it leaps over, and finds him out unfailingly, even though in his flight he be hid in the farthest corner of his chamber.

These are the lessons which my heart bids me teach the Athenians, how that lawlessness brings innumerable ills to the state, but obedience to the law shows forth all things in order and harmony and at the same time sets shackles on the unjust. It smooths what is rough, checks greed, dims arrogance, withers the opening blooms of ruinous folly, makes straight the crooked judgment, tames the deeds of insolence, puts a stop to the works of civil dissension, and ends the wrath of bitter strife. Under its rule all things among mankind are sane and wise.

3

To the people I have given just as much power as suffices, neither taking away from their due nor offering more; while for those who had power and were honored for wealth I have taken thought likewise, that they should suffer nothing unseemly. I stand with strong shield flung around both parties, and have allowed neither to win an unjust victory.

4, 5

The people will best follow its leaders if it be neither given undue liberty nor unduly op-

"Interior, Temple of Hera, Paestum"

pressed; for excess bears arrogance, whenever great prosperity attends on men whose minds are not well balanced.

6

In great undertakings it is hard to please all.

7

From the cloud comes the violent snow- and hail-storm, and the thunder springs from the lightning-flash; so from the men of rank comes ruin to the state, and the people through their ignorance fall into the servitude of rule by one man. When a man has risen too high, it is not easy to check him after; now is the time to take heed of everything.

8

As for my madness, a little time shall make its nature plain to the citizens, yea, plain indeed, when truth comes forth into public view.

9, 10

If you have grievous sufferings through your own wrongheadedness, charge not the gods with having assigned you this lot. You yourselves have raised up these men by giving means of protection, and it is through this that you have gained the evil of servitude. Each separate man of you walks with the tread of a fox, but in the mass you have the brain of an idiot; for you look to the tongue and the words of a wheedler, and never turn your eyes to the deed as it is being done.

11

Through the winds is the sea stirred to wrath; but if none disturb it, it is of all things the mildest.

12

Ye glorious children of Memory and Olympian Zeus, Muses of Pieria, hear me as I pray. Grant me from the blessed gods prosperity, and from all mankind the possession ever of good repute; and that I may thus be a delight to my friends, and an affliction to my foes, by the first revered, by the others beheld with dread. Wealth I do desire to possess, but to gain it unjustly I have no wish; without fail in after-time comes retribution. The wealth that the gods give stays with a man firmplanted from bottommost foundation to summit; whereas that which men pursue through arrogance comes not in orderly wise, but, under constraint of unjust deeds, against her will she follows; and swiftly is ruin mingled therewith. The beginning, as of a fire, arises from little; negligible at first, in its end it is without remedy; the works of men's arrogance have no long life. Zeus watches over the end of all things; and all at once, like a wind, that suddenly scatters the clouds, a wind of spring, that having stirred the deeps of the many-billowed unhar-

vested sea, and razed the fair works of husbandry over the wheat-bearing earth, reaches the abode of the gods, the lofty sky, and makes it bright again to behold; and the sun in his might shines fair over the rich earth, and no longer is any cloud to be seen—such is the retribution of Zeus. Not over single happenings, like a mortal, does he show himself swift to wrath; yet no man who has a sinful heart escapes his eye forever; in the end without fail he is brought to light. But one man pays the penalty straightway, another at a later time; and if the offenders themselves escape, and the fate of the gods in its oncoming alight not on them, yet it comes without fail at another time; the innocent pay for those deeds, either the children or the generations that come after. We mortals, good and bad alike, think thus—each one has a good opinion of himself, before he comes to grief; then at once he begins to lament; but up to that moment in gaping folly we gloat over our vain hopes. The man who is crushed by cruel disease sets his thought on the hope of becoming well. [Another who is a coward thinks himself a brave man, and the uncomely man thinks himself handsome.] The needy man, whom the works of poverty constrain, thinks that he will assuredly win great wealth. One man spends his effort in one direction, another in another. One wanders over the sea, home of fishes, striving to bring back gain in ships, borne along by the fierce winds, having no mercy on his life. Another, one of those whose business is with curved plows, cleaves the earth rich in trees, doing service throughout the year. Another, skilled in the works of Athene and Hephaistos the able craftsman, collects a living by means of his two hands. Another, trained in the gifts of the Olympian Muses, has knowledge of lovely poesy's measure. Another the Lord Apollo, worker from afar, has appointed to be a seer, and he, if he be one whom the gods accompany, discerns the distant evil coming upon a man; yet that which is fated assuredly neither omen of bird nor of victim shall avert. Others, who follow the profession of Paion, god of medicines, are physicians; and for their work, too, no certain issue is set; often from a slight pain comes great suffering, nor can anyone relieve it by the giving of soothing medicines; again, when a man is afflicted with disease fell and fierce, by a touch of his hands at once the physician makes him whole. Verily, Fate brings to mortals both evil and good; the gifts of the immortal gods may not be declined. In every kind of activity there is risk, and no man can tell, when a thing is beginning, what way it is destined to take. One man, trying to do his work well, falls unexpectedly into great and bitter ruin; to another who blunders in his work the god grants good luck in everything, to save him from his folly. In wealth no limit is set up within man's view; those of us who now have the largest fortune are doubling our efforts; what amount would satisfy the greed of all? Gain is granted to mankind by the immortals; but from it arises disastrous Folly, and when Zeus sends her to exact retribution, she comes now to this man, now to that.

13

No mortal is blest with happiness; wretched are all human souls on whom the sun looks down.

14

For many unworthy men are rich, while good men are poor; but we will not barter with them our worth for their wealth, since the one stands ever unshaken, whereas riches pass now into one man's hands, now into another's.

15

It is very difficult to discern that hidden measure of wisdom which alone contains the ends of all things.

IAMBIC TETRAMETERS

28, *TO PHOKOS*

If I spared my native land, and did not defile and dishonor my good repute by laying hands on a tyranny of cruel violence, I feel no shame at all; for in this way I believe that I shall win a greater triumph—over all mankind.

29

"Solon is not gifted by nature with depth of wit and shrewdness; for when the god was offering him boons, of his own accord he declined them. He made his cast and his catch, but dumbfounded he failed to draw in the big net, falling short alike in pluck and wits. If I could get the mastery, and seize boundless wealth and the lordship of Athens for one single day, I would be willing afterwards to be flayed for a wineskin, and let my family be obliterated."

30, 31

Those who came as pillagers had lavish hopes; every man of them believed he would light on a great fortune, and that I, though I coaxed so smoothly, would soon reveal a harsh purpose. Vain were their imaginings then, and now in their anger against me they all eye me askance as if I were an enemy. It is undeserved; for that which I promised I have fulfilled, by heaven's aid; and other things I undertook, not without success. To achieve aught by violence of tyranny is not to my mind; nor that the unworthy should have an equal share with the good in the rich soil of my native land.

. . . Whereas I, before the people had attained to any of the things for the sake of which they had drawn my chariot, brought it to a standstill. A witness I have who will support this claim full well in the tribunal of Time— the mighty mother of the Olympian deities, black Earth, from whose bosom once I drew out the pillars everywhere implanted; and she who was formerly enslaved is now free. Many men I restored to Athens, their native city divinely-founded, men who justly or unjustly had been sold abroad, and others who through pressure of need had gone into exile, and who through wanderings far and wide no longer spoke the Attic tongue. Those here at home who were reduced to shameful slavery, and trembled at the caprices of their masters, I made free. These things I wrought by main strength, fashioning that blend of force and justice that is law, and I went through to the close as I had promised, and ordinances for noble and base alike I wrote, fitting a rule of jurisdiction straight and true to every man. Had another, a villainous and covetous man, grasped the goad as I did, he would not have held the people back. Had I complied with the wishes of my opponents then, or at a later time

with the designs of the other party against them, this city would have been bereaved of many sons. Wherefore I stood at bay, defending myself on every side, like a wolf among a pack of hounds.

32A

The people—if I must utter my rebuke publicly—would never in their dreams have beheld the boons which they now hold; while those of higher rank and greater power would all commend me and seek my friendship.

32B

For if another man [had held this office] he would not have checked the people, nor have stopped before he had stirred up the milk and extracted its fatness. But I took my stand like a boundary-stone in the debatable land between the two parties.

LYRICS

Watch guardedly every man, lest he have a sword hidden in his breast while he accosts you with bright countenance, and lest his tongue utter words of double meaning from a black soul.

TEN AGES IN THE LIFE OF MAN

A boy who is still a child grows baby teeth
    and loses them all in seven years.
When God makes him fourteen, the signs of
    maturity begin to shine on his body.
In the third seven, limbs growing, chin
     bearded,
    his skin acquires the color of manhood.
In the fourth age a man is at a peak in
    strength—a sign in man of excellence.

The time is ripe in the fifth for a young man
  to think of marriage and of offspring.
In the sixth the mind of man is trained in all
  things; he doesn't try the impossible.
In the seventh and eighth, that is, fourteen
    years,
  he speaks most eloquently in his life.

He can still do much in the ninth but his
    speech
  and thought are discernibly less keen;
and if he makes the full measure of ten
    sevens,
  when death comes, it will not come too
    soon.

SAPPHO (FL. 580 B.C.)

Lyrics

*B*orn in Eresos of the aristocratic Skamandronymos and Kleïs, and a citizen of Mytilene, in Lesbos, Sappho (or Psappho) is one of the finest of the great Greek lyric poets. She spent time in Sicily, in political exile, was married to Kerkylos, a wealthy man from Andros, and had a daughter whom she named after her mother. Along with Alcaeus, who also lived in Mytilene, she is credited with creating the subjective lyric—a form more in vogue than ever in the twentieth century. Most of the nine books of her poetry were destroyed by early Christian fundamentalists, disapproving of their content.

- Although some of her surviving poems make it clear that she experienced heterosexual love, Sappho's most delicate and resonant lyrics detail her feelings for the aristocratic girls, including Atthis and Anactoria, who were her companions and lovers. Her control over this group was compared, in classical times, to Socrates and his followers in the Athenian agora.
- Of the fragments that survive, only her prayer to Aphrodite appears to be complete. The gracefully melodious poems in the Aeolic dialect deal with her family, her friends, her religious feelings, and her erotic urges and impulses. Her selection of details is one of the greatest joys of her craft, along with the authoritative sculpting by which she juxtaposes her selections. Her lyrics, ranging in diction from the colloquial to the highly formal, display the entire spectrum of human emotion, which they express with a delicacy, poignancy, precision, and intensity unequaled by her contemporaries and imitated by the Roman love lyricist Catullus.
- In contrast to Plato, Sappho regarded love not as a destructive obsession, but as the ultimate personal fulfillment. But Plato admired her poetry, and wrote of her, "Some say nine Muses—

but count again./Behold the tenth: Sappho of Lesbos." (tr. Barnstone) Strabo, in his geography, comments: "In all the centuries since history began we know of no woman who in any true sense can be said to rival her as a poet." (tr. Barnstone) Her sense of herself resonates today as radiantly as it must have in her own time.

HYMN TO APHRODITE

Star-throned, incorruptible Aphrodite,
Child of Zeus, wile-weaving, I supplicate thee,
Tame me not with pangs of the heart, dread
    mistress,
    Nay, nor with anguish.

But come thou, if erst in the days departed
Thou didst lend thine ear to my lamentation,
And from afar, the house of thy sire deserting,
    Camest with golden

Car yoked: thee thy beautiful sparrows hurried
Swift with multitudinous pinions fluttering
O'er black earth, adown from the height of
    heaven
    Through middle ether:

Quickly journeyed they; and, O thou, blest
    Lady,
Smiled at me with brow of undying luster,
Asked me what new grief at my heart lay,
    wherefore
    Now I had called thee.

What I fain would have to assuage the
    torment
Of my frenzied soul. "And whom now, to
    please thee,
Must persuasion lure to thy love, and who now,
    Sappho, hath wronged thee?

"Yea, for though she flies, she shall quickly
    chase thee;
Yea, though gifts she spurns, she shall soon
    bestow them;
Yea, though now she loves not, she soon shall
    love thee,
    Yea, though she will not!"

Come, come now too! Come, and from heavy
    heartache
Free my soul, and all that my longing yearns to
Have done, do thou; be thou for me thyself
    too
    Help in the battle!

125, ALONE
The moon and Pleiades
are set. Midnight,
and time spins away.
I lie in bed, alone.

128, SEIZURE
To me he seems like a god
as he sits facing you and
hears you near as you speak
softly and laugh

in a sweet echo that jolts
the heart in my ribs. For now
as I look at you my voice
is empty and

can say nothing as my tongue
cracks and slender fire is quick
under my skin. My eyes are dead
to light, my ears

pound, and sweat pours over me.
I convulse, greener than grass,
and feel my mind slip as I
go close to death,

yet, being poor, must suffer
everything.

133, FULL MOON
The glow and beauty of the stars
are nothing near the splendid moon
when in her roundness she burns silver
about the world.

134, THEN
In gold sandals
dawn like a thief
fell upon me.

135, THE CRICKET
When sun dazzles the earth
with straight-falling flames,
a cricket rubs its wings
scraping up a shrill song.

139, CEREMONY
Now the earth with many flowers
puts on her spring embroidery.

141, TO ATTHIS
Though in Sardis now,
she thinks of us constantly

"Girl at her toilet, Lemnos, terra-cotta figurine."
Photograph by Erich Lessing. The Louvre, Paris.
By permission of Art Resource.

and of the life we shared.
She saw you as a goddess
and above all your dancing gave her deep joy.

Now she shines among Lydian women like
the rose-fingered moon
rising after sundown, erasing all

stars around her, and pouring light equally
across the salt sea
and over densely flowered fields

lucent under dew. Her light spreads
on roses and tender thyme
and the blooming honey-lotus.

Often while she wanders she remembers you, gentle Atthis,
and desire eats away at her heart

for us to come.

142, A LETTER
"Sappho, if you do not come out,
I swear, I will love you no more.

O rise and free your lovely strength
from the bed and shine upon us.
Lift off your Chian nightgown, and

like a pure lily by a spring,
bathe in the water. Our Kleïs
will bring a saffron blouse and violet

tunic from your chest. We will place
a clean mantle on you, and crown
your hair with flowers. So come, darling,

with your beauty that maddens us,
and you, Praxinoa, roast the nuts
for our breakfast. One of the gods

is good to us, for on this day
Sappho, most beautiful of women,
will come with us to the white city

of Mytilene, like a mother
among her daughters." Dearest Atthis,
can you now forget all those days?

143, TO HER FRIEND
Honestly I wish I were dead!
Although she too cried bitterly

when she left, and said to me,
"Ah, what a nightmare it is now.
Sappho, I swear I go unwillingly."

And I answered, "Go, and be happy.
But remember me, for surely you
know how we worshiped you. If not,

then I want to remind you of all
the exquisite days
we two shared; how

you took garlands of violets
and roses, and when by my side
you tied them round you in soft bands,

and you took many flowers
and flung them in loops
about your sapling throat,

how the air was rich in a scent
of queenly spices made of myrrh
you rubbed smoothly on your limbs,

and on soft beds, gently, your desire
for delicate young women
was satisfied,

and how there was no dance and no
holy shrine
we two did not share,

no sound,
no
grove."

144, TO ATTHIS
Love—bittersweet, irrepressible—
loosens my limbs and I tremble.

Yet, Atthis, you despise my being.
To chase Andromeda, you leave me.

165, SLEEP
May you find sleep on
a soft girlfriend's breast.

168, THE VIRGIN
Like a sweet apple reddening on the high
tip of the topmost branch and forgotten
by the pickers—no, beyond their reach.

Like a hyacinth crushed in the mountains
by shepherds; lying trampled on the earth
yet blooming purple.

172, WEDDING SONG

Groom, we virgins at your door
will pass the night singing of the love
between you and your bride. Her limbs
are like violets.

Wake and call out the young men,
your friends, and you can walk the streets
and we shall sleep less tonight than
the bright nightingale.

176, AFTER THE CEREMONY

Happy groom, the wedding took place
and the woman you prayed for is yours.

Now her charming face is warm with love.

My bride, your body is a joy,
your eyes soft as honey,
and love pours its light
on your perfect features.

Using all her skill Aphrodite
honored you.

182, ONE NIGHT

All the while, believe me, I prayed
our night would last twice as long.

185, LOSS

Virginity, virginity, when you leave me,
where do you go?

I am gone and never come back to you.
I never return.

186, REMORSE

Do I still long
for my virginity?

188, TO HERSELF

It's no easy thing to rival a goddess
for the beauty of her figure
or be more than Adonis.

Aphrodite poured nectar with her own hands
from a gold vial. Then Peitho . . .
was at the shrine at Geraistos.

Darling,
I will go to you.

189, HOMECOMING

You came. And you did well to come.
I longed for you and you brought fire
to my heart, which burns high for you.

Welcome, darling, be blessed three times
for all the hours of our separation.

200, TO A HANDSOME MAN

If you love me, stand and gaze at me candidly,
let the grace in your eyes pour forth.

202, APPEARANCES

A handsome man now looks handsome.
A good man will soon take on beauty.

226, WEATHERCOCKS

Those whom I treated kindly
especially injure me now.

238, THE LAUREL TREE

You lay in wait
behind a laurel tree,

and everything
was pleasant:

you a woman
wanderer like me.

I barely heard you,
my darling;

you came in your
trim garments,

and suddenly: beauty
of your garments.

253, OLD AGE

Of course I am downcast and tremble
with pity for my state
when old age and wrinkles cover me,

when Eros flies about
and I pursue the glorious young.
Pick up your lyre

and sing to us of her who wears
violets on her breasts. Sing especially
of her who is wandering.

254, TO HER DAUGHTER WHEN SAPPHO WAS DYING

It would be wrong for us. It is not right
for mourning to enter a home of poetry.

256, SOMEONE, I TELL YOU

Someone, I tell you,
will remember us.

[We are oppressed by
fears of oblivion

yet are always saved
by judgment of good men.

Therefore, I tell you,
stand upright for me.]

258, EROS

Now in my
Heart I
see clearly

A beautiful
face
shining,

etched
by love.

624, I SAY

You would want
few
to be carried away.
Sweeter.
You yourself know
but someone forgot.

Some might say
I will love
as long as there is breath
in me.
I'll care.
I say I've been a firm friend.

Things grievous,
bitter,
but know
I will love.

STESICHOROS (FL. 580 B.C.)

Lyrics

*S*tesichoros of Mataurus (real name: Teisias; Stesichoros means "master of the chorus") was a lyric poet who, writing in Doric, preferred lengthy narrative forms based on the myths of Thebes and of Troy. Quintilian called him the Homer of lyric poets. He was supposedly struck blind for his blasphemous poems about Helen, who in Sparta was considered a goddess. It was Stesichoros, allegedly, who invented the story of Athena born full-bodied from the forehead of Zeus. His choral lyrics were highly regarded for their noble conception and dignified execution, treating epic themes in a lyric fashion. Of the twenty-six books of his poems collected in Alexandria, only twenty or so survive.

ON THE ILIAD
The white-horsed myth.

RECANTATION TO HELEN
I spoke nonsense and I begin again:

The story is not true.
You never sailed on a benched ship.
You never entered the city of Troy.

ON KLYTAIMNESTRA
> *Foreseeing the end of*
> *the Aigisthos line.*

She dreamed that a serpent appeared
> with blood-dripping scales,
and from his belly stepped a king
> from the ancient dynasty
of Pleisthenes and Agamemnon.

ON SONG AND LAMENT
Apollo loves happy play and cadenced singing
but he leaves groans and mourning to Hades.

Yet how futile even to weep for the dead—
for when dead, a man's glory dies among men.

SEASON OF SONG
Forget the wars.
It is time to sing.
Take out the flute from Phrygia
and recall the songs of our blond Graces.

Clamor of babbling swallows:
it is already spring.

ANACREON (FL. 540 B.C.)
Lyrics

Anacreon, son of Scythinus, of Teos, is the last great lyric poet of Ionian Asia Minor. He is known primarily for his banquet songs (in fact, Francis Scott Key's "The Star-Spangled Banner" was written to the melody of a drinking song in Anacreon's honor) and satirical verse written under the shadow of the Persian Empire.

- When the Persians attacked Teos in 540 B.C., Anacreon and his fellow countrymen fled to colonize Thracian Abdera. The tyrant Polycrates invited him to his court on Samos to teach his son music. But the Persians pursued Anacreon to Samos, and when Polycrates was killed in 522 B.C. the poet was conveyed by a fifty-oared ship to Athens to become the protégé of Hipparchus and friend of the poet Simonides. When Hipparchus was assassinated in 514 B.C., Anacreon fled to Thessaly, where he continued to hobnob with royalty until the newly democratic Athenians insisted that he bring his music back to entertain them. Attic red-figure vases show young men dancing wildly around the lyre-playing Anacreon. After he died, choking on a raisin, his statue was displayed on the Acropolis.

- Anacreon wrote metrically straightforward songs of wine, women, and old age, though he was also outstanding in satire and recognized for the elegance of his elegies. Beneath their superficial playfulness, his poems reflect a refined artfulness and ironic sensitivity so often characteristic of a declining culture. As much as moderation makes philosophical sense, he can't escape the attractions of intoxication's oblivion. Talk of sexual prowess seems safer and more satisfying than the deed itself, romantic looks more seductive than the pain that inevitably results from consummation. At his most lyric, Anacreon's insatiable thirst for life and intense appreciation of the moment command our attention: "Who can speak about tomorrow? I care only for today." His critical self-awareness, and wry detachment from the diminishing life he reflects on compel us to him across the millennia.

Horns to bulls wise Nature lends;
Horses she with hoofs defends;
Hares with nimble feet relieves;
Dreadful teeth to lions gives;
Fishes learn through streams to slide;
Birds through yielding air to glide;
Men with courage she supplies;
But to women these denies.
What then gives she? Beauty, this
Both their arms and armor is:
She, that can this weapon use,
Fire and sword with ease subdues.

Downward was the wheeling Bear
Driven by the Waggoner:
Men by powerful sleep opprest,
Gave their busy troubles rest;
Love, in this still depth of night,
Lately at my house did light;
Where, perceiving all fast lock'd,
At the door he boldly knock'd.
"Who's that," said I, "that does keep
Such a noise and breaks my sleep?"
"Ope," saith Love, "for pity hear;
'Tis a child, thou need'st not fear,
Wet and weary, from his way
Led by this dark night astray."
With compassion this I heard;
Light I struck, the door unbarr'd,
Where a little boy appears,
Who wings, bow, and quiver bears;
Near the fire I made him stand,
With my own I chaf'd his hand,
And with kindly busy care
Wrung the chill drops from his hair.
When well warm'd he was, and dry,
"Now," saith he, " 'tis time to try

If my bow no hurt did get,
For methinks the string is wet."
With that, drawing it, a dart
He let fly that pierc'd my heart;
Leaping then, and laughing said,
"Come, my friend, with me be glad;
For my bow thou seest is sound
Since thy heart has got a wound."

Roses (Love's delight) let's join
To the red-cheek'd God of Wine;
Roses crown us, while we laugh,
And the juice of Autumn quaff!
Roses of all flowers the king,
Roses the fresh pride o' th' Spring,
Joy of every deity.
Love, when with the Graces he
For the ball himself disposes,
Crowns his golden hair with roses.
Circling then with these our brow,
We'll to Bacchus' temple go:
There some willing beauty lead,
And a youthful measure tread.

Now will I a lover be;
Love himself commanded me.
Full at first of stubborn pride,
To submit my soul denied;
He his quiver takes and bow,
Bids defiance, forth I go,
Arm'd with spear and shield, we meet;
On he charges, I retreat:
Till perceiving in the fight
He had wasted every flight,
Into me, with fury hot,
Like a dart himself he shot,
And my cold heart melts; my shield

Useless, no defense could yield;
For what boots an outward screen
When, alas, the fight's within!

Chattering swallow! what shall we,
Shall we do to punish thee?
Shall we clip thy wings, or cut
Tereus-like thy shrill tongue out?
Who Rhodantha driv'st away
From my dreams by break of day.

I care not for Gyges' sway,
Or the Lydian scepter weigh;
Nor am covetous of gold,
Nor with envy kings behold;
All my care is to prepare
Fragrant unguents for my hair;
All my care is where to get
Roses for a coronet;
All my care is for to-day;
What's to-morrow who can say?
Come then, let us drink and dice,
And to Bacchus sacrifice,
Ere death come and take us off,
Crying, Hold! th' hast drunk enough.

All thy skill if thou collect,
Make a cup as I direct:
Roses climbing o'er the brim,
Yet must seem in wine to swim;
Faces too there should be there,
None that frowns or wrinkles wear;
But the sprightly son of Jove,
With the beauteous Queen of Love;
There, beneath a pleasant shade,
By a vine's wide branches made,
Must the Loves, their arms laid by,
Keep the Graces company;

And the bright-hair'd god of day
With a youthful bevy play.

Fruitful earth drinks up the rain;
Trees from earth drink that again;
The sea drinks the air, the sun
Drinks the sea, and him the moon.
Is it reason then, d'ye think,
I should thirst when all else drink?

On my knees do I entreat thee, O Pheraean
Goddess golden-helmed, of wild beasts
    huntress,
Come with all thy train of nymphs Pelasgian
  To Lethe's whirlpools.

Daughter of Zeus, swift slayer of the
    mountain
Deer, view propitiously this suffering city:
Cheer thy stricken people; no barbarous
    citizens
  Crave thy divine aid.

O Eros, conqueror of hearts, with whom
  Disport the blue-eyed nymphs and Cypris
    fair:
With eyes uplift to Ida's leafy gloom
  I breathe to thee a prayer.

The maid for whom I glow thy power defies.
  Her snow-cold bosom melt with thy fond
    fire;
That she moved by my importunities
  May grant my heart's desire.

My jowl's gone gray, gone bare my head,
My teeth are old, and fair youth fled:
Sweet life has but a span to go,

And oftentime I cry me woe
For fear of what Death has for me;
Dire's his dark hold, and rough will be
The road thither; but worst of all,
Once down, I'm down beyond recall.

Boy, bring the jug; I want a wet;
    Five parts wine, and water ten:
I mean to play the toper; yet
    Topers can be gentlemen.

Let's give this barbarous boozing up,
    This clamorous after-dinner clatter,
And take a mild and modest cup
    'Twixt pretty songs on themes that matter.

I crave not Amalthaea's horn;
    O'er Arganthonius' domain
    Long weary years I'd scorn to reign,
And be with cares of kingcraft worn.
    One little hour of wine-bred bliss
    To me indeed much better is.

Thracian filly, tell me why
You look askance when I come nigh,
And flee unkind, as though I knew
Nought of how to manage you?

Should it please me, truth to tell,
I could bridle you right well,
And take and ride you hand on rein
Up the course and down again;

And if instead you graze your fill
And frisk it in the meadow still,
'Tis but because a man like me
Knows how long to leave you free.

Eros, the blond god of lovers,
strikes me with a purple ball
and asks me to play with a girl
    wearing colorful sandals;

but the girl is from beautiful
Lesbos, and scorns my white hair,
and turning her back runs gaping
    behind another girl.

O sweet boy like a girl,
I see you though you will not look my way.
You are unaware that you handle the reins
    of my soul.

Here lies Timokritos: soldier: valiant in battle.
Arês spares not the brave man, but the coward.

Love once among the roses
Perceived a bee reposing,
And wondered what the beast was,
And touched it, so it stung him.
Sorely his finger smarted,
And bitterly he greeted,
And wrung his hands together;
And half he ran, half fluttered
To Cytherea's bosom,
Unto his fair, sweet mother.
Loud sobbed he, "Ai! ai! mother
Olola! I am murdered!
Olola! it has killed me!
A small brown snake with winglets,
Which men the honey-bee call,
Bit me!" But Cytherea
Said, laughing, "Ah, my baby,
If bees' stings hurt so sorely,
Bethink thee what the smart is
Of those, Love, whom thou piercest."

YOUTH DECAYS

Golden hues of youth are fled;
Hoary locks deform my head.
Bloomy graces, dalliance gay,
All the flowers of life decay.
Withering age begins to trace
Sad memorials o'er my face:
Time has shed its sweetest bloom,
All the future must be gloom!
This awakes my hourly sighing;
Dreary is the thought of dying!
Pluto's is a dark abode,
Sad the journey, sad the road:
And, the gloomy travel o'er,
Ah! we can return no more!

TAKE THE CASH, AND LET THE CREDIT GO

Rich in bliss, I proudly scorn
The stream of Amalthea's horn!
Nor should I ask to call the throne
Of the Tartessian prince my own;
To totter through his train of years,
The victim of declining fears.
One little hour of joy for me
Is worthy a dull eternity.

SIMONIDES (CA. 560–CA. 468 B.C.)

Lyrics

*B*orn in Iulis on Ceos, the diversely talented lyricist and epigrammatist Simonides spent time in Athens in the household of the tyrant Hipparchus, and was later a supporter of Themistocles and friend of Pausanias. Later in life, he moved to Sicily where he became influential in the court of Hieron. Though he was criticized for being the first to accept compensation for his poetry, the patronage did not affect its artistic excellence and craftsmanlike quality.

- His epigrams and elegies commemorated the great victories of the Persian War. His funeral songs were noted for their poignant dignity, leading the Roman Quintilian to admire him for being the greatest poet at expressing pathos, and Catullus to coin the phrase, "sadder than tears shed by Simonides." He won fifty-six poetic contests.
- He developed the victory song from brief poems of welcome into full-blown choral compositions. His humor set him apart from his chief rival, Pindar. Simonides said, "Poetry is painting with words." His epitaph for the men who fell at Thermopylae defeated all contenders, including Aeschylus. Aristotle reports that Simonides, asked whether it was better to become wise or rich, replied: "To become wealthy. For I see the wise sitting on the doorsteps of the rich." (tr. Barnstone)

FOR THE SPARTANS KILLED AT THERMOPYLAE
Tell them in Lackedaimon, passerby,
That here, true to their command, we lie.

When, in the carved chest,
The winds that blew and waves in wild unrest
Struck her with fear, she, not with cheeks
    unwet,
Her arms of love round Perseus set,
  And said: O child, what grief is mine!
But you slumber, and your baby breast
Is sunk in rest,
Here in the cheerless brass-bound bark,
Tossed amid starless night and pitchy dark.
  Now do you heed the crashing brine
Of waves that wash above your curls so deep,
Nor the shrill winds that sweep,
Lapped in your purple robe's embrace,
Fair little face!
But if this dread were dreadful too to you,
Then would you lend your listening ear to me;
Therefore I cry, Sleep, babe, and sea be still,
And slumber our unmeasured ill!
  Oh, may some change of fate, lord Zeus,
    from you
Descend, our woes to end!
But if this prayer, too overbold, offend
Your justice, yet be merciful to me!

Of those who died at Thermopylae glorious is the fate and fair the doom; their grave is an altar; instead of lamentation, they have endless fame; their dirge is a chant of praise. Such winding-sheet as theirs no rust, no, nor all-conquering time, shall bring to naught. But this sepulcher of brave men hath taken for its habitant the glory of Hellas. Leonidas is wit-ness, Sparta's king, who hath left a mighty crown of valor and undying fame.

GORGIPPUS' EPITAPH
A poor man, not a Croesus, here lies dead,
  And small the sepulcher befitting me:
Gorgippus I, who knew no marriage-bed,
  Before I wed pale Persephone.

TO FLEE IS DEATH
O dearest Sparta, we are those that strove
For fair Thyrea; we, three hundred, fought
Equally matched, the sons of Inachus.
Where first our feet we planted, there we
    stood,
And turning back no glance, unshaken died.
The honored shield of bold Othryadas,
In blood upon it written, bears these words:
"Thyrea is Sparta's, mighty Zeus!"
And if one Argive has escaped from death,
A son of craven Adrastus he must be;
Since for the sons of Sparta, not to die,
Nay, but to flee, is death.

ON THE LAKEDAIMONIANS FALLEN AT PLATAIA
These men left an altar of glory on their land,
  shining in all weather,
when they were enveloped by the black mists
  of death.
but although they died
they are not dead, for their courage raises
  them in glory
from the rooms of Hell.

ON THOSE WHO DIED AT THERMOPYLAI

Through their extraordinary courage, the wide
farmlands of Tegea
Their tomb is an altar on which stand our
     bowls of remembrance
and the wine of our praise.
Neither mold and worms, nor time
which destroys all things, will blacken their
     deaths.
The shrine of these brave men
has found its guardian
in the glory of Greece. Leonidas, the Spartan
     king,
lives in the great ornament he left behind
of unending fame and virtue.

GRAVE BY THE WATER

We were slaughtered in a Dirphian gully, and
     our graves,
   near Euripos, were paid for by our nation.
Justice. For in confronting the cruel clouds of
     war,
   we gave away our years of lovely youth.

ARETE

Virtue lives on a high rock
painful to climb and guarded by
a band of pure and evasive nymphs.
No mortal may look upon her
unless sweat pours from his body
and he climbs the summit of manliness.

CROSSING THE GULF OF CORINTH

All these victors from the Tyrrhenian wars
were on their way to Apollo at Delphi
with their first plunder
when they found their grave
on one night, in one ship, in one deep sea.

THE ATHENIAN VANGUARD

Athenian sons demolished the Persian army
and saved their country from painful slavery.

SOCIAL DICTUM

The city is the teacher of the man.

A MODEST GRAVE

Sir, you are not looking at the tomb
of some great Lydian king,
for being poor my gravestone is small,
yet still too much for me.

ON THE GIRL GORGO

As she lay dying in her dear mother's arms,
Gorgo wept and whispered her last words:

"Stay with my father,
and on a better day bear a second daughter
who will care for you when you are old."

ENCIRCLED WOMAN

I am possessed by the fierce noise
all around me
of the purple, tormented sea.

HUMAN BANKRUPTCY

I who lie here, Brotachos of Gortyn, was born
     in Krete,
and I did not come here for death but weighty
     business.

SACRED HEALTH

Not even lucid wisdom
will give you joy
when sacred health is gone.

FLUX
If you are a simple mortal, do not speak
of tomorrow or how long this man may be
among the happy, for change comes suddenly
like the shifting flight of a dragonfly.

ACCOMPLISHMENTS
Without the gods
a man or city can do nothing.

Only God knows everything, and man
suffers for what he does.

There is no evil
man may not expect, and soon
God wipes away the few things
he may have done.

ANAXIMANDER (FL. 560 B.C.)
Fragments from "On Nature," gleaned from Aristotle, Galen, Hippocrates, and others

Anaximander, son of Praxiades of Miletus, was the first western astronomer to invent a consistent cosmology and to write a philosophical treatise. He is said to have been a student of Thales, lived in Samos at the court of the tyrant Polycrates, and may have led the Milesian colony into Apollonia.

- Although only what follows has survived of his writings, he appears, in distinction from his fellow "Ionian cosmologists," to have believed that the universe was not reducible to a single element. Instead it is unlimited, a kind of primeval chaos out of which infinite worlds are generated, each defined by a harmony of opposites, and back into which all eventually return.
- Anaximander studied geography, evolution, and astronomy. He noted that land life had risen from the sea; mapped the world; constructed a celestial globe; invented the sundial, and theorized about the orbits of the planets.

1. The first principle of all other things is infinite. . . . From this the heavens and the worlds in them arise.

2. This first principle is eternal and does not grow old, and it surrounds all the worlds.

3. Motion is eternal, and as a result of it the heavens arise.

4. "Immortal" and "indestructible" surround all and direct all.

5. [To that they return when they are destroyed] of necessity; for . . . they suffer punishment and give satisfaction to one another for injustice.

6. Existing opposites are separated from the unity.

7. Things come into being [not] by change in the nature of the element, but by the separation of the opposites which the eternal motion causes.

8. The earth is a heavenly body, controlled by no other power, and keeping its position because it is the same distance from all things; the form of it is curved, cylindrical like a stone column; it has two faces: One of these is the ground beneath our feet, and the other is opposite to it.

9. The stars are a circle of fire, separated from the fire about the world, and surrounded by air. There are certain breathing-holes like the holes of a flute through which we see the stars; so that when the holes are stopped up, there are eclipses.

10. The moon is sometimes full and sometimes in other phases as these holes are stopped up or open.

11. The circle of the sun is twenty-seven times that of the moon, and the sun is higher than the moon, but the circles of the fixed stars are lower.

12. Animals come into being through vapors raised by the sun.

13. Man, however, came into being from another animal, namely the fish, for at first he was like a fish.

14. Winds are due to a separation of the lightest vapors and the motion of the masses of these vapors; and moisture comes from the vapor raised by the sun from them; and lightning occurs when a wind falls upon clouds and separates them.

15. The soul is like air in its nature.

ANAXIMENES (FL. CA. 545 B.C.)

Air

*A*naximenes, the third Ionian physicist, replaced Thales' "water" with "air" as the underlying principle of creation. A student of Anaximander, he chose to explain the varied consistency of matter in terms of degrees of condensation and rarefaction. At its lightest, air is fire. At its most evenly diffuse, air is the atmosphere and sky. As it becomes heavier, it becomes visible: as clouds, as water, then as solid matter. What others saw as qualitative differences among the things of creation, he considered a matter of quantity. He saw air as containing life, and therefore as the principle that associated the material world with the transcendent divine. The breath breathed by living beings is one and the same as their souls and the "unifying air" of the universe itself.

1. Air is the one, movable, infinite first principle of all things.
2. Air is the nearest to an immaterial thing; for since we are generated in the flow of air, it is necessary that it should be infinite and abundant, because it is never exhausted.
3. The breadth of the earth is the reason why it remains where it is.
4. The earth was wet, and when it dried it broke apart, and ... earthquakes are due to the breaking and falling of hills; accordingly, earthquakes occur in droughts, and in rainy seasons also; they occur in drought, as has been said, because the earth dries and breaks apart, and it also crumbles when it is wet through with waters.
5. We should not neglect either cold or heat in *being* but should regard them as common experiences of matter which are incident to its changes. . . . The compressed and the condensed state of matter is cold, while the rarefied and relaxed state of it is heat. . . . It is not strange that men breathe hot and cold out of the mouth; for the breath is cooled as it is compressed and condensed by the lips, but when the mouth is relaxed, it comes out warm by reason of its rarefaction.
6. Air differs in rarity and in density as

the nature of things is different; when very attenuated it becomes fire, when more condensed wind, and then cloud, and when still more condensed water and earth and stone, and all other things are composed of these. . . . Motion [is] eternal, and by this changes are produced.

7. And the form of air is as follows: When it is of a very even consistency, it is imperceptible to vision, but it becomes evident as the result of cold or heat or moisture, or when it is moved. It is always in motion; for things would not change as they do unless it were in motion. It has a different appearance when it is made more dense or thinner; when it is expanded into a thinner state it becomes fire, and again winds are condensed air, and air becomes cloud by compression, and water when it is compressed further, and earth and finally stones as it is more condensed. So that generation is controlled by the opposites, heat and cold. And the broad earth is supported on air; similarly the sun and the moon and all the rest of the stars, being fiery bodies, are supported on air by their breadth. And stars are made of earth, since exhalations arise from this, and these being attenuated become fire, and of this fire when it is raised to the heaven the stars are con-

stituted. There are also bodies of an earthy nature in the place occupied by the stars, and carried along with them in their motion. . . . The stars do not move under the earth, as others have supposed, but around the earth, just as a cap is moved about the head. . . . The stars do not give forth heat because they are so far away. Winds are produced when the air that has been attenuated is set in motion; and when it comes together and is yet further condensed, clouds are produced, and so it changes into water. And hail is formed when the water descending from the clouds is frozen; and snow, when these being yet more filled with moisture become frozen; and lightning, when clouds are separated by violence of the winds; for when they are separated, the flash is bright and like fire. And a rainbow is produced when the sun's rays fall on compressed air; and earthquakes are produced when the earth is changed yet more by heating and cooling.

8. Air is the first principle of things, for from this all things arise and into this they are all resolved again. As our soul which is air . . . holds us together, so wind and air encompass the whole world.

9. The soul is like air in its nature.

THEOGNIS (FL. 540 B.C.)
Lyrics

*T*heognis was from Megara, in Sicily, a member of the landowning oligarchy. Because his class was under siege from populist forces, he was forced to flee and spent much of his life in exile longing for his homeland. Theognis is considered the greatest of the "gnomic" elegists.

- Theognis wrote ardently about the decline of his proud social class from the onslaught of democratic elements he disdained. He eloquently celebrated his volatile affections for a man named Kyrnos, son of Polypas. The collection that survives under his name includes love songs and drinking songs, as well as proverbs, preludes, hymns, and epitaphs. Most of the poems seem to have been composed for banquet performances.
- Theognis is interesting today for the extremity of his conservatism, praising the aristocracy for its courage and condemning plebeians as uniformly evil; the terms "good guys" and "bad guys" may claim their origins in his verse. He especially celebrates athletic lovemaking and occasional moderation; and laments:

  - intermarriage among social classes or generations,
  - the force of money as a moral pollutant,
  - the blessed brevity of human life, and
  - the miseries of poverty: "The poor man can do or say nothing / worthwhile. Even his mouth is gagged."

- Theognis remains compelling for vividly expressing his personal despair, anxiety, and cynicism about the human condition. He is the master of bitterness. Greek anthologist Stobaios tells us that Theognis "is concerned with no other matter than the virtues and vices of man, and his poetry is a study of man just as a treatise on horsemanship written by an expert horseman studies horses." (tr. Barnstone)

SHADOWS

Fools and children you are, mankind! You
    mourn
      the dead and not the dying flower of youth.

EUGENICS

In breeding donkeys, rams or horses, we seek
    out
      the thoroughbred to get a good strain,
my Kyrnos. Yet now the noblest man will
    marry
      the lowest daughter of a base family,
if only she brings in money. And a lady
    will share her bed with a foul rich man,
preferring gold to pedigree. Money is all.
    Good breed with bad and race is lost
to riches. Don't wonder our city's blood is
    polluted
      when noble men will couple with upstarts.

LIBERATION

Death, friend Kyrnos, is better to the poor
    than a life cursed with painful poverty.

POVERTY

Nothing destroys a good man quicker than
    poverty:
      not malarial fever, Kyrnos, nor old age.
Better to hurl oneself into the abysmal sea
    or over a blunt cliff—than be a victim
of poverty. The poor man can do or say
    nothing
      worthwhile. Even his mouth is gagged.

A LOOSE VESSEL

A ripe young wife and an old husband
make a very sad conjunction.

She is like a ship. Her wild rudder
doesn't respond to him.
Her anchors don't hold.
Often she slips her moorings altogether
to enter at night in another port.

TO KYRNOS, A REPROACH

I gave you wings to fly looming high and easy
    over unboarded sea and the entire earth.
At every meal and banquet you will be present
    on the lips of guests. Graceful young men
will sing of you in limpid lovely notes
    to the clean piping of the flutes.
When you go under the dark vaults of earth
    to the mournful chambers of sad Hell,
even when you lie dead you will not lose
    your glory. Your name will be recalled
among men always, Kyrnos. You will wheel
    high
      over the mainland and Greek islands
and cross the unharvested sea pulsing with
    fish,
      not by horse but carried to those who love
    you
in the gifts of Muses capped in violet flowers.
    You will be like a song to the living
as long as there is sun, earth. Yet you ignore
    me
      and trick me as if I were a child.

A SEAMAN'S SORROW

I heard the sharp cry of the bird, O son of
    Polypas,
      who came to men with the message to plow
in good season; and it wounded my heart
    black
      that others own my flowering lands,

and not for me are mules dragging the curved
   plow,
  now, in my exile, on the wretched sea.

WORDS OF A BEARDED MAN RECLINING ON A COUCH

O beautiful boy, I crave you more than any
   man.
  Stand where you are and hear my few
   words.

GOOD WILL WASTED

I knew it before and know it better now:
  don't wait for thanks from the lower classes.

HIS FAIRNESS

I will blame no enemy who is a good man
  nor praise a friend who may be vile.

THE ATHLETE

Blessed is the man who knows how to make
   love
  as one wrestles in a gym,
and then goes home happy to sleep the day
  with a delicious young boy.

GOOD AND EVIL

Easier to make bad out of good than good out
   of bad.
  Don't try to teach me. I am too old to learn.

A CITY IN TRAVAIL

Kyrnos, the city is pregnant, and I fear it will
   bear
  a man who will clean up our outrageous
   pride.
The people are still well behaved, but the
   leaders
  plunge along a course of vile corruption.

AESOP (D. 564 B.C.?)

Fables

*A*esop shares with Homer almost total "anonymity in all but name." The fables ascribed to him from ancient times suggest that he was, like the brothers Grimm, an editor and compiler. The typical Greek fable has animal characters and a clear moral statement.

- Nothing is known for certain of Aesop's life except that he may have been a Thracian slave on Samos, and may have lived during the reign of the pharaoh Amasis. Legend has it that he was a humpback, a stammerer, and a kind of court jester. But unproved legend also says that Homer was blind. In both cases, the affliction may have been symbolic: Homer's blindness, for the clarity of his vision; Aesop's stammering, for the fluidity and earthy temper of the fables.

- Although the fables survive because of their surface humor, the tradition of "instructive satire" is already well under way in these stories about human behavior thinly disguised as animal. Recalling Hesiod's down-to-earth practicality, they are cautionary tales serving the purpose of social order. For the modern reader, the "morals" will be as interesting as their stories—that often seem, by modern standards, unrelated to them.

A lion, wandering on the beach, saw a dolphin swimming in the sea, and urged him to an alliance, saying it is right to be friendly and helpful to one another, "for you are (king) of the animals of the sea, and I of those of the land." The dolphin agreed with him gladly. The lion, after a long time, fighting against the fierce bull, invited the dolphin to help. But the dolphin resolved that he did not want to leave the sea, and the lion called him a traitor. But the dolphin, replying, said, "But can you blame me?"

A crow sat in a tree holding in his beak a piece of meat that he had stolen. A fox who saw him determined to get the meat. It stood under the tree and began to tell the crow what a beautiful big bird he was. He ought to be king of all the birds, the fox said; and he would undoubtedly have been made king, if only he had a voice as well. The crow was so anxious to prove that he *had* a voice, that he dropped the meat and croaked for all he was worth. Up ran the fox, snapped up the meat, and said to him: "If you added brains to all your other qualifications, you would make an ideal king."

An old lion, who was too weak to hunt or fight for his food, decided that he must get it by his wits. He lay down in a cave, pretending to be ill, and whenever any animals came to visit him, he seized them and ate them. When many had perished in this way, a fox who had seen through the trick came and stood at a distance from the cave, and inquired how he was. "Bad," the lion answered, and asked why he did not come in. "I would have come in," said the fox, "but I saw a lot of tracks going in and none coming out."

¶A wise man recognizes danger signals in time to avoid injury.

A lion and a bear began fighting over a fawn that they had found, and mauled each other so badly that they lost consciousness and lay half-dead. A fox who passed by, seeing them incapacitated and the fawn lying between them, picked it up and threaded his way out from among them. Unable to get up, they said: "A grievous fate is ours—to undergo all this suffering for the benefit of a fox."

¶People have good reason to be distressed when they see the fruits of their own labors borne away by chance comers.

A lion, a donkey, and a fox formed a partnership and went out hunting. When they had taken a quantity of game the lion told the donkey to share it out. The donkey divided it into three equal parts and bade the lion choose one—at which the lion leapt at him in a fury and devoured him. Then he told the fox to divide it. The fox collected nearly all of it into one pile, leaving only a few trifles for himself, and told the lion to make his choice. The lion asked who taught him to share things in that way. "What happened to the donkey," he answered.

¶We learn wisdom by seeing the misfortunes of others.

A wolf, seeing a lamb drinking from a river, wanted to find a specious pretext for devouring him. He stood higher up the stream and accused the lamb of muddying the water so that he could not drink. The lamb said that he drank only with the tip of his tongue, and that in any case he was standing lower down the river, and could not possibly disturb the water higher up. When this excuse failed him the wolf said: "Well, last year you insulted my father." "I wasn't even born then," replied the lamb. "You are good at finding answers," said the wolf, "but I'm going to eat you all the same."

"*Beehive tomb, Mycenae*"

¶When a man is determined to get his knife into someone, he will turn a deaf ear to any plea, however just.

A wolf who had swallowed a bone went about looking for someone to relieve him of it. Meeting a heron, he offered it a fee to remove the bone. The heron put its head down his throat, pulled out the bone and then claimed the promised reward. "Are you not content, my friend," said the wolf, "to have got your head safe and sound out of a wolf's mouth, but you must demand a fee as well?"

¶When one does a bad man a service, the only recompense one can hope for is that he will not add injury to ingratitude.

A shepherd took a newborn wolf cub that he had found and brought him up with his dogs till he was full grown. Whenever a sheep was stolen by another wolf, this one joined with the dogs in pursuit. And if the dogs had to return without catching the marauder, he went on till he overtook him, and then—like the wolf he was—shared the plunder with him. Sometimes, too, when there had been no robbery, he secretly killed a sheep himself and shared it with the dogs, until in the end the shepherd guessed what was going on and hanged him on a tree.

¶A vicious nature will never make a good man.

Wandering in a lonely place as the sun went down, a wolf noticed the long shadow cast by his body. "Fancy a big fellow like me being afraid of a lion!" he said. "Why, I must be thirty yards long! I'll make myself king and rule all the animals, every single one of them." But for all his boasting, a strong lion caught him and sat down to devour him. Too late, he regretted his mistake. "Conceit," he wailed, "has helped to bring about my ruin."

A wild boar was standing against a tree and whetting his tusks. A fox asked why he sharpened them when no huntsman was pursuing him and no danger threatened. "I have a reason for doing so," he replied. "If danger overtakes me, I shall not have time then to sharpen them, but they will be all ready for use."

¶Do not wait till danger is at hand to make your preparations.

A field mouse invited a friend who lived in a town house to dine with him in the country. The other accepted with alacrity; but when he found that the fare consisted only of barley and other corn, he said to his host: "Let me tell you, my friend, you live like an ant. But I have an abundance of good things to eat, and if you will come home with me you shall share them all." So the two of them went off at once; and when his friend showed him peas and beans, bread, dates, cheese, honey, and fruit, the astonished field mouse congratulated him heartily and cursed his own lot. They were about to begin their meal when the door suddenly opened, and the timid creatures were so scared by the sound that they scuttled into chinks. When they had returned and were just going to take some dried figs, they saw someone else come into the room to fetch something, and once more they jumped to take cover in their holes. At this the field mouse decided that he did not care if he had to go hungry. "Good-bye, my friend," he said with a groan. "You may eat your fill and enjoy yourself. But

your good cheer costs you dear in danger and fear. I would rather gnaw my poor meals of barley and corn without being afraid or having to watch anyone out of the corner of my eye."

¶A simple life with peace and quiet is better than faring luxuriously and being tortured by fear.

A mouse ran over the body of a sleeping lion. Waking up, the lion seized the mouse and was minded to eat him. But when the mouse begged to be released, promising to repay the lion if he would spare him, the lion laughed and let him go. Not long afterward the mouse's gratitude was the means of saving the lion's life. Being captured by hunters, he was tied by a rope to a tree. The mouse heard his groans, and running to the spot freed him by gnawing through the rope. "You laughed at me the other day," he said, "because you did not expect me to repay your kindness. Now you see that even mice are grateful."

¶A change of fortune can make the strongest man need a weaker man's help.

A snake and a weasel started fighting together in the house where they lived, instead of killing the mice as both of them were in the habit of doing. When the mice saw them at it they came walking out of their holes. The sight of the mice put an end to the battle; for the combatants at once turned to attack their old enemies.

¶The same thing is seen in politics. When people mix themselves up in the quarrels of rival demagogues, they find, too late, that both parties unite to destroy them.

Zeus was entertaining all the animals at his wedding feast. Only the tortoise stayed away, and

Zeus could not think why. So next day he asked him why he did not come with the others. "There's no place like home," he replied—an answer which angered Zeus so much that he made him carry his own house about on his back.

¶Many men would rather have plain fare at home than live on the fat of the land in other people's houses.

A tortoise asked an eagle to teach him to fly. The eagle pointed out that he was ill-adapted by nature for flight, but the tortoise only importuned him the more. So the eagle, taking him up in his talons, bore him to a great height and let him go. He fell at the foot of some rocks and was dashed to pieces.

¶A spirit of rivalry will often make men disregard the advice of wiser heads, with fatal results for themselves.

Some thieves, on breaking into a house, found nothing in it but a cock, which they picked up and took away. They were about to sacrifice him, when he begged to be spared on the plea that he rendered men a useful service by waking them before daybreak to start their work. "All the more reason for killing you," was the reply; "for by waking *them* you stop *us* from stealing."

¶What benefits honest men is the rogue's worst handicap.

The bees grudged their honey to men because they regarded it as their own property. So they went to Zeus and prayed him to grant them the power of stinging to death anyone who approached their combs. Zeus was so angry with them for their ill-nature that he condemned them not only to lose their stings whenever they used them on anyone, but to forfeit their lives as well.

¶This fable is an apt censure of people who indulge their ill will even at the cost of injury to themselves.

There was a shepherd who was fond of playing practical jokes. He would drive his flock some distance from the village and then shout to the villagers for help, saying that wolves had attacked his sheep. Two or three times the inhabitants came rushing out in alarm—and then went back with the shepherd laughing at them. Eventually, however, some wolves really came. They got between the shepherd and his flock and he called the neighbors to aid him. But they thought he was up to his usual trick and did not bother their heads about him. So he lost his sheep.

¶A scaremonger gains nothing by raising false alarms. He merely makes people disbelieve him when he does speak the truth.

A bald man who wore a wig was riding one day, when a puff of wind blew the wig off, at which the bystanders guffawed. Reining in his horse, he said: "It is not surprising that I cannot keep hair which is not mine on my head, since its proper owner, on whose head it grew, could not keep it there."

¶Let no man be cast down by the accidents which befall him. What Nature did not give us at our birth can never be a permanent possession. Naked we came into the world, and naked shall we leave it.

PYTHAGORAS (FL. 530 B.C.)
The Golden Verses

One of the most influential of the preSocratic mathematician-philosophers is also the most elusive when it comes to our knowledge of his life. He was the son of Mnesarchos, and was expelled from his native Samos by the tyrant Polycrates. He may have been the student of Creophilus and of Pherecydes of Syros. He traveled to Babylon and Egypt, where he studied the mysticism of Asia Minor and the East. He finally settled in Croton, in southern Italy, in 531–529, where he attracted such a large number of followers that they soon controlled the city.

- The Pythagoreans, centered in Magna Graecia, were a semimystical scientific cult honoring Apollo and claiming Pythagoras, whom they called Apollo Hyperboreus, "who lived at the end of the earth" as their founder. They were similar to the Orphics. Women as well as men, generally from among the wealthiest citizens of Croton, were admitted to this "300 Club" as "initiates" if they would ascribe to these principles:

  - To lead a chaste and devout life
  - To avoid extremes
  - To accept death without fear
  - To pledge loyalty to one another
  - To protect the secrets of the cult
  - To unite in supporting chastity and morality
  - To practice silence, for centering the mind
  - To practice self-examination
  - To abstain from eating flesh
  - To promote harmony in the commonwealth

Like modern Rosicrucians or Masons, Pythagoreans recognized one another when they met abroad by using a secret sign. They shared Pythagoras' belief in the transmigration of souls, and honored his claim to have "past-life regression" as the source of his knowledge—a doctrine influential in the formation of Plato's theory of "remembered" ideas. Pythagoras, the ancestor of present-day channelers, claimed that he had been, among others, Euphorbus, the son of Panthoiis, in the Trojan War.

Supposedly Pythagoras also condemned eating beans which, he said, contained the souls of the dead. The theory of transmigration (or "metempsychosis") held that all life progresses from its basest animal form to its highest expression, the gods, and that humans should aspire upward by focusing on spiritual rather than material goods. Pythagoreans also believed in the kinship of all living beings, and, to purify the spirit, practiced abstinence similar to that of the East Indian Jains and the Provençal Catharists.

In an upheaval led by Cylon against the society's exclusiveness, Pythagoras and his 300 charter followers may have perished when the house of Milo, where they were assembled, was set on fire. Another account says he fled to Metapontum, where he died in a hunger strike in 504 B.C. At this point the repression of the Pythagoreans was under way throughout Magna Graecia, and the club was forced underground.

- Pythagoras is the first man to have called himself a lover of wisdom (philosopher), basing his way of life on a study of nature that became a religion. He was the first to use the word "cosmos" to describe the world. Like the other Milesian philosophers, he aimed to relate all knowledge about the universe and its contents to a single orderly principle. He recognized that the earth is spherical, and that it is one of many planets orbiting from east to west: the "central fire." He is also credited with discovering the theory of musical intervals (including the ratio between the length of a string and the musical note it produced); and with believing that the universe was generated from numbers—that its basic structure is mathematical. The term "music of" or "harmony of" the "spheres" dates back to Pythagoras' theories. He believed that the universe's orderliness results from its *harmonia,* or "being in tune," and that the human soul must strive to imitate the harmony. We cannot hear the harmony because our ears have been dulled by the illusory world of sensory perception; but by purifying and attuning our minds we may be able to hear the omnipresent sound that generates the universe.

- Pythagoras is the first in history to study all aspects of numbers systematically. He may also have discovered the "Pythagorean theorem," that the square of the hypotenuse of a right-angled triangle is equal to the sum of the squares of the other two sides:

$$a^2 + b^2 = c^2$$

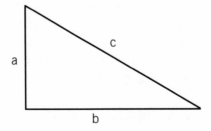

He divided men into those who sought knowledge, those who sought fame, and those who sought riches. Although it is generally believed that the Golden Verses were not by his own hand, they certainly reflect his beliefs.

First honor the immortal gods, as they are established and ordained by the Law.

Honor the Oath, with all religious devotion.

Next honor the heroes, full of goodness and light.

Honor likewise the terrestrial demons, rendering to them the worship that is lawfully due them.

Honor also your father and mother, and near relatives.

As for the rest of mankind, make those your friends who distinguish themselves in virtue.

Give ear to a (Pythagorean) comrade's lightest word; avoid being irked by his incidental faults.

Above all, have respect for yourself.

Accustom yourself not to perform actions except as governed by reason.

Reflect always that it is ordained by destiny that all men must die.

Reflect that the goods of fortune are uncertain, and that as they are acquired so they may likewise be lost.

Do not neglect the health of your body: give it drink and meat in due measure, and give it such exercises as it needs.

Accustom yourself to a way of living that is neat and tasteful but without luxury.

Avoid all that will stir envy.

After going to bed do not allow sleep to close your eyelids until you have first examined all your actions of the day, asking yourself: Wherein have I done amiss? What have I omitted that ought to have been done? If you find on reflection that you have done anything amiss, be severe with yourself; if you have done anything good, rejoice.

Never put your hand to any undertaking until you have first prayed to the gods that you may accomplish what you are about to attempt.

When you have made this habit (of prayer to the gods) familiar to yourself, then you will know the constitution of the immortal gods and of men.

XENOPHANES (CA. 570–CA. 455 B.C.)
On Nature and Lyrics

*B*orn the son of Dexias, in Colophon, in Ionia, Asia Minor, Xenophanes left his city before the attacking Persians. After traveling widely throughout the Greek world, he began teaching philosophy in Sicily, both in Catania and at the court of Hieron in Syracuse. He died an old man of nearly one hundred in Elea, in southern Italy.

- Xenophanes was a prolific poet, writing on a variety of subjects, including a long hexameter poem on the founding of Elea. He systematized his philosophical thoughts in the form of "rhapsodies," which he recited Homeric-style in public. Espousing what has become known as "Eleatic pantheism," he attacked Homer's representation of the gods as being anthropomorphic: "If horses or cattle had hands and could draw, they would draw the gods like horses and cattle." He held that, instead, God was a self-sufficient entity whose form could not be determined by mere mortals.
- He envisions God as "the one and the all," unmoved and unmoving, eternal and undivided, from whom the universe is generated, and with whom the universe is identical. In his *Lives of the Philosophers,* Diogenes Laertes wrote:

Xenophanes says . . . the essence of god is spherical, in no way
resembling man. He is all eyes and all ears but does not breathe.
He is in his totality mind and thinking, and is eternal.
Xenophanes was the first to have declared that all that exists is
transitory and destructible, and that the soul is breath or spirit. (tr. Barnstone)

---

1. God is one, supreme among gods and men, and not like mortals in body or in mind.
2. The whole [of god] sees, the whole perceives, the whole hears.
3. But without effort he sets in motion all things by mind and thought.
4. It [*i.e.,* being] always abides in the same place, not moved at all, nor is it fitting that it should move from one place to another.
5. But mortals suppose that the gods are born (as they themselves are), and that they wear man's clothing and have human voice and body.
6. But if cattle or lions had hands, so as

to paint with their hands and produce works of art as men do, they would paint their gods and give them bodies in form like their own—horses like horses, cattle like cattle.

7. Homer and Hesiod attributed to the gods all things which are disreputable and worthy of blame when done by men; and they told of them many lawless deeds, stealing, adultery, and deception of each other.

8. For all things come from earth, and all things end by becoming earth.

9. For we are all sprung from earth and water.

10. All things that come into being and grow are earth and water.

11. The sea is the source of water and the source of wind; for neither would blasts of wind arise in the clouds and blow out from within them, except for the great sea, nor would the streams of rivers nor the rainwater in the sky exist but for the sea; but the great sea is the begetter of clouds and winds and rivers.

12. This upper limit of earth at our feet is visible and touches the air, but below it reaches to infinity.

13. She whom men call Iris (rainbow), this also is by nature cloud, violet and red and pale green to behold.

14. Accordingly there has not been a man, nor will there be, who knows distinctly what I say about the gods or in regard to all things, for even if one chances for the most part to say

what is true, still he would not know; but everyone thinks he knows.

15. These things have seemed to me to resemble the truth.

16. In the beginning the gods did not at all reveal all things clearly to mortals, but by searching men in the course of time find them out better.

17. The following are fit topics for conversation for men reclining on a soft couch by the fire in the winter season, when after a meal they are drinking sweet wine and eating a little pulse: Who are you, and what is your family? What is your age, my friend? How old were you when the Medes invaded this land?

. . . .

19. But if one wins a victory by swiftness of foot, or in the pentathlon, where the grove of Zeus lies by Pisas' stream at Olympia, or as a wrestler, or in painful boxing, or in that severe contest called the pancration, he would be more glorious in the eyes of the citizens, he would win a front seat at assemblies, and would be entertained by the city at the public table, and he would receive a gift which would be a keepsake for him. If he won by means of horses he would get all these things although he did not deserve them, as I deserve them, for our wisdom is better than the strength of men or of horses. This is indeed a very wrong custom, nor is it right to prefer strength to excellent wisdom. For

if there should be in the city a man
good at boxing, or in the pentathlon, or in wrestling, or in swiftness of foot, which is honored more
than strength (among the contests
men enter into at the games), the
city would not on that account be
any better governed. Small joy
would it be to any city in this case if
a citizen conquers at the games on
the banks of the Pisas, for this does
not fill with wealth its secret chambers.

BANQUET DECORUM

Now the floor is scrubbed clean, our hands are
washed
and cups are dry. A boy loops garlands
in our hair. Another passes round a phial
of redolent balsam. The mixing bowl
is bubbling with good cheer, and more
fragrant wine
stands potent in the earthen jars.
Incense floats a holy perfume through the
room.
Water is cold, crystal, sweet.
Golden bread is set near on a princely table
loaded down with cheese and rich honey.
The altar in the center is submerged in flowers
and the house vibrates with fun and
singing.

Gracious men should first sing praises to God
with proper stories and pure words.
After the libation when we pray for strength
to act with rectitude (our first concern),

there is no sin in drinking all one can
and still get home without a servant—
unless too old. We commend the man who
shows
good memory after drink; who seeks virtue
and not to harangue us with the ancient
myths
of noisy wars of Titans, Giants,
Centaurs. These things are worth nothing.
The good
lies in our reverence for the gods.

PYTHAGORAS AND THE TRANSMIGRATED SOUL

One day a dog was being thrashed in the
street,
and behold, Pythagoras, philosopher of
spirits,
was walking by.
His heart was in his mouth
for the poor pup.
"Stop! Stop!" he cried.
"Don't beat him any more.
This is my dear friend's soul.
I recognize the voice when I hear him bark."

KNOWLEDGE

The gods did not enrich man
with a knowledge of all things
from the beginning of life.
Yet man seeks, and in time
invents what may be better.

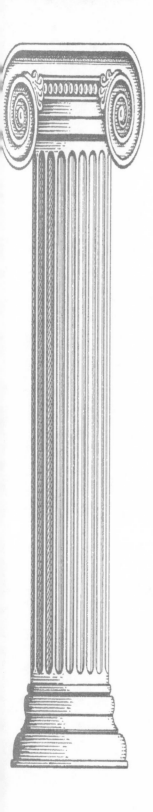

PART TWO

Classical

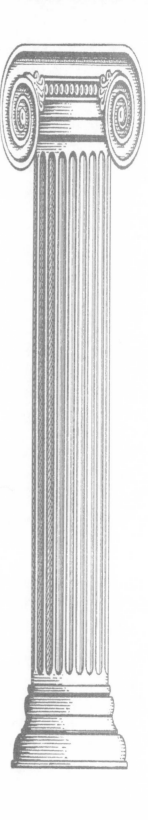

Pindar (518–442/438 B.C.)
Olympian Ode 2

⌇━✛━⌇

*B*orn in Boeotian Cynoscephalae, near Thebes, Pindar was the son of Cleodice and Daiphantos of the noble family of Aegeidae, who, along with his flute-playing uncle Scopelinus, gave him his first instruction in music before sending him to Athens to complete his education. He was the greatest and most prolific of the aristocratic choral lyric poets, living most of his life, and buried, in Thebes.

- No doubt influenced by his education in Athens under dithyrambist Lasos of Hermione, the Boeotians Myrtis and Korinna, the musician Agathocles and Apollodorus, and perhaps even the tragedian Aeschylus, Pindar chose to write in a sacred poetic language, mingling Homer's Ionic dialect with flavors of Dorian and Aeolian. Pindar, whose works included hymns, dancing songs, drinking songs, paeans, dithyrambs, odes, encomia, and threnodies, was honored in his lifetime both for his art and his piety by monarchs and tyrants from Macedon to Syracuse in Sicily as well as by the citizens of Greek democracies and city-states from Athens to Tenedos. Pausanias tells us the story that as a young man, Pindar fell asleep on the side of a road, and awakened to discover that the bees had placed honey on his lips. Pindar was granted his own position at Apollo's shrine at Delphi, and was the poet laureate of Hieron of Syracuse from 476 to 472 B.C.
- Four books of Pindar's victory odes come down to us, celebrating the winners in the Greek national contests. They were written for patrons and sung by a chorus, either at the site of the games or at the winner's victory party. Like all his odes, the one selected here from the eight Olympian victory songs is characteristic for its oligarchic piety. It also provokes unique insight into Orphic beliefs in life after death. Instead of celebrating the winner's personal prowess or the details of the particular contest, which was considered unworthy of poetic celebration, Pindar exalts aspects of his family and his birthplace, offering instant mythologizing for the new hero with sublime gravity and thanks to the gods. Like his fellow Boeotian Hesiod, Pindar is convinced of the divine inspiration of his poetic vocation and speaks with unabashed straightforwardness. But unlike Hesiod's, Pindar's work is noted for its harmony of thought, elegance of expression, and highly polished meter. He has been called a "prophet

of Herakles," because his celebrations of Olympic victors evoke the mythic hero who bravely embraces toils sent to him by the gods. Though the aristocracy whose values molded Pindar was fading from power, their favorite son created a heroic memory worthy of their highest aspirations. When Alexander the Great destroyed the city of Thebes, he spared Pindar's house and family.

Songs, lords of the lyre,
   what god, what hero, what man
      shall we celebrate?
Pisa belongs to Zeus.
   Herakles founded the Olympian Games,
    first fruits of war.
   And Theron must be proclaimed
for his chariot victory—
              Theron, true host of strangers,
bulwark of Akragas, exalter of his city,
   noblest scion of noble ancestors

who suffered much
   to win their sacred home
    by the river, and they became
the light of Sicily,
   their fated course
    bringing wealth and honor
to match their inborn greatness.
But O Kronian son of Rhea,
         lord of Olympos' throne,
of Alpheos' crossing and the greatest of
   contests:
   moved by my song, preserve their native
land to them

and their posterity.
       What has been done

with justice or without
not even time the father of all
can undo.
   But with good luck
oblivion may come, for malignant pain
perishes in noble joy, confounded

whenever a fate from the gods
   raises
    happiness on high.
So the royal daughters of Kadmos
   suffered greatly,
    but their sorrows
    fell before mightier blessings.
Long-haired Semela, dying
           in the thunder-roar,
lives among the Olympians, beloved of Pallas
   and Zeus
   and ever beloved of Dionysos, her son,
and they say that in the sea
   with the daughters of Nereus
    for all time
imperishable life embraces Ino.
   Truly, mortals have no way
    of knowing the bounds of death,
    nor even whether we shall finish
a day, a sun's child,
        with cheer unblemished.

The shifting tides of good and evil
    beat incessantly upon mankind.

Thus the fate that guards the ancestral
    fortune
of these men, bringing them happiness
    secured
by the gods,
        has also sent them affliction, sure
to abate in its turn,
           from the moment
Laios' tragic son, crossing his father's path,
killed him
      and fulfilled the oracle spoken of
      old at Pytho.

And sharp-eyed Erinys saw and slew
   his warlike children
     at each other's hands.
Yet Thersandros survived
   fallen Polyneikes and won honor
     in youthful contests
   and the brunt of war, a scion of aid
to the house of Adrastos;
         and his seed lives on
in Theron, son of Ainesidamos, who deserves
    to enjoy the lyre and the song of praise.

For he himself took the prize at Olympia,
   while at Pytho and Isthmos too
    kindred Graces brought his brother,
paired with him in destiny, garlands
   for the four horses driven
    twelve times around the post.
  A man forgets the strain of contending
when he triumphs.

"Discus-thrower, by Miron." Copyright Archivi Alinari, 1989. By permission of Art Resource.

        And wealth, uplifted by
        nobility,
gives scope for actions of every kind,
    kindling the heart with zeal for
    achievement,
a star far-seen, a man's truest beacon-light.
And if, possessing it, one knows what must
   befall—
that of those who die here, the arrogant
are punished without delay,
       for someone under the earth
weighs transgressions in this realm of Zeus,
and there is iron compulsion in his word.

But with equal nights
   and equal days,
      possessing the sun forever,
the noble enjoy an easy existence, troubling
   neither earth nor the sea's waters
     in might of hand
    for an empty living,
but with the gods they honored, all
               who delighted in
               oath-keeping
abide free of affliction, while the others
   go through pain not to be looked at.

And those who have endured
   three times in either realm
    to keep their souls untainted
by any injustice, travel
   Zeus' road to the tower of Kronos,
    where ocean-born breezes blow around
   the island of the blest
and sprays of gold flower
              from the earth and
              from the sea—
with these they wreathe their hands
   and crown their heads,

obeying the high decrees of Rhadamanthys,
who sits, a ready companion, beside
the great Father, consort of Rhea throned on
   high.
Among them dwell the heroes Peleus and
   Kadmos
and Achilleus, whom Thetis, moving Zeus'
   heart with prayer,
brought to their company, her son
who smote Hektor to the ground, Troy's
   invincible, unyielding bastion,

and consigned to death
Kyknos and Memnon, child of the Dawn.
   There are in my quiver
    many swift arrows, striking
   to the wise, but the crowd need
    interpreters.
The man of discernment
              knows much by
             nature.
Let those who have acquired their knowledge
   chatter in vain, unruly jackdaws bickering

at the majestic eagle of Zeus.
   It is time we took aim, my heart:
    whom are we hitting
again, letting fly
   the arrows of glory
    from the string of gentle thoughts?
   Aiming at you, Akragas,
I swear with true mind,
             no city in a hundred
            years
has reared a man more liberal in thought
   or lavish of hand

than Theron.
      But praise falls in with surfeit
and is muted, not in justice
but because of boisterous men, whose noise
would obscure beauty,
           for sands cannot be
           counted,
and how many joys
this man has brought his fellows,
        who can say?

KORINNA (FL. 510 B.C.)

Lyric Fragments

To the Romans Korinna was synonymous with excellence. We know only that she was Boeotian, born at Tanagra, daughter of Acheloodoros and Hippokrateia, nicknamed "the fly," and was probably an elder contemporary of Pindar. She wrote the "clean water" of her verses to be sung by a chorus of women on mythological subjects, including Athena of the war shield. Many of her surviving lyrics were discovered on papyrus only in the twentieth century.

- Korinna took her stories, like the "Seven against Thebes," "the Contest of Helicon and Cithaeron," and the "Return of Orion" from Boeotian mythology, and may have been Pindar's mentor as she herself was the "pupil" of Myrtis, whom she celebrates for rivaling Pindar. Legend has it that she beat him in a number of contests, and, Plutarch tells us, scolded him for poor taste. Although Korinna was renowned for her beauty, the defeated Pindar, according to Aelianus, called her "a pig."
- She used mythology as a seasoning in her verse, and recommended that Pindar do the same. Pausanias reports that when Pindar showed her a poem that introduced nearly the whole scope of Theban mythology, she responded: "We should sow with the hand, not with the whole sack."

ON HERSELF
I Korinna am here to sing the courage
of heroes and heroines in old myths.
To daughters of Tanagra in white robes,
I sing. And all the city is delighted
with the clean water of my plaintive voice.

THE CONTEST OF HELIKON AND KITHAIRON
Kithairon sang of cunning Kronos
and sacred Rheia who stole her son
Zeus, mighty among immortals.

Then the Muses asked the gods to put
their ballot stones in the urn of
gold. All stood up and Kithairon won

the greater part. Hermes shouted loud,
at once proclaiming sweet victory.
The gods adorned his brow with flowers,

and Kithairon rejoiced. But Helikon
was stunned with bitter rage, and tore
a massive boulder from the mountain;

insanely he shouted and lobbed the rock
down on thousands of mortals below.

HERMES

When he sailed into the harbor
his ship became a snorting horse.
Hermes ravished the white city
while the wind like a nightingale
sang with his whirling war-axe.

ROUT OF THE ERETRIAN FLEET

For you alone, Tanagra,
Hermes came to fight
with his naked fists.

ON MYRTIS

Although I was her pupil,

Even I reproach Myrtis
of the crystalline voice.

"Bronze hands with bracelets, Taranto." Archivi
Alinari, copyright 1989. By permission of Art Resource.

She was a mere woman poet,
yet she challenged Pindar.

ON HERSELF

Will you sleep forever? There was a time,
Korinna, when you were not a loafer.

AESCHYLUS (525–456 B.C.)
The Eumenides

At the conclusion of Homer's *Odyssey* (Book 24), the goddess Athena appears to put a stop to the vendetta between the relatives of Penelope's unwelcome suitors and the forces of the returned king Odysseus, their slayer. So, too, in the tragedian Aeschylus' *The Eumenides* (part of the *Oresteia,* model for Eugene O'Neill's *Mourning Becomes Electra*), Athena puts an end to the vicious cycle of revenge that has found its latest victim in the hapless Orestes. Aeschylus, born in Eleusis, in Attica, of a noble family, fought at the battle of Marathon (490 B.C.), and traveled twice to Sicily at the request of Hieron. He died in Sicily, at Gela. He was the first great tragedian after the legendary Thespis, and was credited with introducing the second actor, which brought realistic dialogue to the drama. Of the ninety plays he wrote, his most important surviving ones include:

- *Seven Against Thebes,* about the sons of Oedipus squabbling over their patrimony— later to inspire *Seven Brides for Seven Brothers, The Seven Samurai,* and *The Magnificent Seven*
- *The Persians,* glorifying the Greek victory at Salamis
- *Prometheus Bound*

- In *The Eumenides,* Orestes throws himself at the mercy of Athena after being hounded from Mycenae, where, in obedience to the command of the patriarchal Apollo (whose epithets include "Phoebus" and "Loxias"), he had avenged the murder of his father Agamemnon by slaying his mother. The story is a domestic tragedy, but since the domicile involved is the royal household, all society is involved in the story's outcome. Queen Klytaimnestra had killed Agamemnon, "like an ox at the manger," upon his triumphant return from the Trojan War. She herself was avenging Agamemnon's sacrifice of their daughter Iphigeneia at the outset of the war. Meanwhile she had taken her husband's cousin Aegisthus as her lover and stand-in consort. Together they slew Agamemnon, from her viewpoint to protect Orestes and his sister Elektra.
- Apollo's command to Orestes followed the highest law of the patriarchy, that the patricide— in this case, the regicide—must surely die. Yet the moment Orestes, dutiful to both the god and his father's memory, overcomes any personal compunctions based on love for his mother to carry out the patriarchal order, he finds himself in trouble with the Furies, female daughters of female Night, who persecute him for being a matricide.

- The bewildered and exhausted hero makes his way to the Areopagus of patriarchal Athens ("Ares' hill" near the Acropolis, the site of the ancient criminal court), wisely presided over by the goddess who has no mother, Athena. The issue Aeschylus brings into dramatic focus with Orestes' plight is the conflict between the ancient, earthy, blood-based, savage power of matrilineal society that predated Mycenaean and classical Athenian society and the more recently secured, orderly, law-based patriarchy, whose nightmares evoked earlier times when men were controlled by matriarchs. Athena's role in the play is to exorcise these nightmares, supporting Apollo's astonishing definition of parenthood as primarily a male value.

- Aeschylus' nearness to the choral origins of tragedy throws light on the feature that modern readers find most difficult—his language. His use of language was all his own. No other poet goes so far as he in the use of strange compound words, in piling adjective upon adjective, in the creation of metaphors that cram the force of a whole Homeric simile into a single phrase. Metaphor is his natural speech. But his language belongs to the choral ode, and resembles Pindar more than Homer. As he adapted this highly charged style to the needs of language, in his later plays Aeschylus melds them with his underlying themes and conforms them with his characters' development. Powerful and majestic figures must speak in a fashion suited to their strength and stature. He is also important for having introduced dramatic conventions that have been used ever since: imaginary scenes, flashbacks, messengers' reports.

- *The Eumenides* is the third play in the trilogy known as the *Oresteia* (first staged at the Great Dionysian Festival in 458 B.C.). The first two plays, *The Agamemnon* and *The Libation Bearers,* dramatize Agamemnon's return from Troy, his death at the hands of his wife and her lover Aegisthus, and Orestes' coming of age, encounter with Apollo, and subsequent return to take his vengeance with the help of his sister Elektra.

- After listening to the arguments of the Furies (the prosecutors) and Apollo (Orestes' advocate), the twelve-member jury casts its secret ballot. The vote is tied. Athena therefore judges in favor of Orestes. He is declared immune from his crime. He is not "innocent," but he is "not guilty." Athena's decision about how Orestes will be judged resembles the "innocent, until proven guilty" trial by jury in use today, with the benefit of the doubt going to the defendant. Athena's reason for this rule is not the presumption of innocence but her contention that, all things being equal, patriarchal values should prevail.

- Athena transforms the anger of the matriarchal Furies (the Chorus) by granting them their own temple and priestly service on the Acropolis. Henceforth, they shall be known in Athens not as the Dark Furies, but as the Blessed Spirits (Eumenides). The demonic forces of female power have been transformed into guardian angels, whose job it is to help grateful men.

"Gold death mask of Agamemnon, from Mycenae"

. . . *Chorus*   Examine him then yourself.
Decide it, and be fair.

Athene   You would turn over authority in this
case to me?

Chorus   By all means. Your father's degree,
and yours, deserve as much.

Athene   Your turn, stranger. What will you
say in answer? Speak,
tell me your country and your birth, what has
befallen
you, then defend yourself against the anger of
these;
if it was confidence in the right that made you
sit
to keep this image near my hearth, a
supplicant
in the tradition of Ixion, sacrosanct.
Give me an answer which is plain to
understand.

Orestes   Lady Athene, first I will take the
difficult thought
away that lies in these last words you spoke. I
am
no supplicant, nor was it because I had a stain
upon my hand that I sat at your image. I
will give you a strong proof that what I say is
true.
It is the law that the man of the bloody hand
must speak
no word until, by action of one who can
cleanse,
blood from a young victim has washed his
blood away.
Long since, at the homes of others, I have
been absolved
thus, both by running waters and by victims
slain.
I count this scruple now out of the way. Learn
next
with no delay where I am from. I am of Argos
and it is to my honor that you ask the name
of my father, Agamemnon, lord of seafarers,
and your companion when you made the
Trojan city
of Ilium no city any more. He died
without honor when he came home. It was my
mother
of the dark heart, who entangled him in subtle
gyves
and cut him down. The bath is witness to his
death.
I was an exile in the time before this. I came
back
and killed the woman who gave me birth. I
plead guilty.

My father was dear, and this was vengeance
    for his blood.
Apollo shares responsibility for this.
He counterspurred my heart and told me of
    pains to come
if I should fail to act against the guilty ones.
This is my case. Decide if it be right or
    wrong.
I am in your hands. Where my fate falls, I
    shall accept.

Athene   The matter is too big for any mortal
    man
who thinks he can judge it. Even I have not
    the right
to analyse cases of murder where wrath's edge
is sharp, and all the more since you have
    come, and clung
a clean and innocent supplicant, against my
    doors.
You bring no harm to my city. I respect your
    rights.
Yet these, too, have their work. We cannot
    brush them aside,
and if this action so runs that they fail to
    win,
the venom of their resolution will return
to infect the soil, and sicken all my land to
    death.
Here is dilemma. Whether I let them stay or
    drive
them off, it is a hard course and will hurt.
    Then, since
the burden of the case is here, and rests on
    me,
I shall select judges of manslaughter, and
    swear

them in, establish a court into all time to
    come.

Litigants, call your witnesses, have ready your
    proofs
as evidence under bond to keep this case
    secure.
I will pick the finest of my citizens, and come
back. They shall swear to make no judgment
    that is not
just, and make clear where in this action the
    truth lies.

                                (Exit.)

Chorus   Here is overthrow of all
the young laws, if the claim
of this matricide shall stand
good, his crime be sustained.
Should this be, every man will find a way
to act at his own caprice;
over and over again in time
to come, parents shall await
the deathstroke at their children's hands.
We are the Angry Ones. But we
shall watch no more over works
of men, and so act. We shall
let loose indiscriminate death.
Man shall learn from man's lot, forejudge
the evils of his neighbor's case,
see respite and windfall in storm:
pathetic prophet who consoles
with strengthless cures, in vain.

Nevermore let one who feels
the stroke of accident, uplift
his voice and make outcry, thus:
"Oh Justice!

Throned powers of the Furies, help!"
Such might be the pitiful cry
of some father, of the stricken
mother, their appeal. Now
the House of Justice has collapsed.

There are times when fear is good.
It must keep its watchful place
at the heart's controls. There is
advantage
in the wisdom won from pain.
Should the city, should the man
rear a heart that nowhere goes
in fear, how shall such a one
any more respect the right? . . .

Vengeance will be upon you.
The all is bigger than you.
Let man see this and take
care, to mother and father,
and to the guest
in the gates welcomed, give all rights
that befall their position.

The man who does right, free-willed, without
    constraint
shall not lose happiness
nor be wiped out with all his generation.
But the transgressor, I tell you, the bold man
who brings in confusion of goods unrightly
    won,
at long last and perforce, when ship toils
under tempest must strike his sail
in the wreck of his rigging.

He calls on those who hear not, caught inside
the hard wrestle of water.

The spirit laughs at the hothearted man,
the man who said "never to me," watches him
pinned in distress, unable to run free of the
    crests.
He had good luck in his life. Now
he smashes it on the reef of Right
and drowns, unwept and forgotten.
(*Athene reenters, guiding twelve citizens chosen
as jurors and attended by a herald. Other
citizens follow.*)

Athene   Herald, make proclamation and hold
    in the host
assembled. Let the stabbing voice of the
    Etruscan
trumpet, blown to the full with mortal wind,
    crash out
its high call to all the assembled populace.
For in the filling of this senatorial ground
it is best for all the city to be silent and learn
the measures I have laid down into the rest of
    time.
So too these litigants, that their case be fairly
    tried.
    (*Trumpet call. All take their places. Enter
Apollo.*)

Chorus   My lord Apollo, rule within your
    own domain.
What in this matter has to do with you?
    Declare.

Apollo   I come to testify. This man, by
    observed law,
came to me as suppliant, took his place by
    hearth and hall,

and it was I who cleaned him of the stain of
    blood.
I have also come to help him win his case. I
    bear
responsibility for his mother's murder.

(To Athene.)
You

who know the rules, initiate the trial. Preside.

Athene (to the Furies)   I declare the trial
    opened. Yours is the first word.
For it must justly be the pursuer who speaks
    first
and opens the case, and makes plain what the
    action is.

Chorus   We are many, but we shall cut it
    short. You, then,
word against word answer our charges one by
    one.
Say first, did you kill your mother or did you
    not?

Orestes   Yes, I killed her. There shall be no
    denial of that.

Chorus   There are three falls in the match
    and one has gone to us.

Orestes   So you say. But you have not even
    thrown your man.

Chorus   So. Then how did you kill her? You
    are bound to say.

Orestes   I do. With drawn sword in my hand
    I cut her throat.

Chorus   By whose persuasion and advice did
    you do this?

Orestes   By order of this god, here. So he
    testifies.

Chorus   The Prophet guided you into this
    matricide?

Orestes   Yes. I have never complained of this.
    I do not now.

Chorus   When sentence seizes you, you will
    talk a different way.

Orestes   I have no fear. My father will aid me
    from the grave.

Chorus   Kill your mother, then put trust in a
    corpse! Trust on.

Orestes   Yes. She was dirtied twice over with
    disgrace.

Chorus   Tell me how, and explain it to the
    judges here.

Orestes   She murdered her husband, and
    thereby my father too.

Chorus   Of this stain, death has set her free.
    But you still live.

Orestes   When she lived, why did you not
    descend and drive her out?

Chorus   The man she killed was not of blood
    congenital.

Orestes   But am I then involved with my
    mother by blood-bond?

Chorus   Murderer, yes. How else could she
    have nursed you beneath her heart? Do
    you forswear your mother's intimate
    blood?

Orestes   Yours to bear witness now, Apollo,
    and expound
the case for me, if I was right to cut her down.
I will not deny I did this thing, because I did
do it. But was the bloodshed right or not?
    Decide
and answer. As you answer, I shall state my
    case.

Apollo   To you, established by Athene in
    your power,
I shall speak justly. I am a prophet, I shall not
lie. Never, for man, woman, nor city, from my
    throne
of prophecy have I spoken a word, except
that which Zeus, father of Olympians, might
    command.
This is justice. Recognize then how great its
    strength.
I tell you, follow our father's will. For not
    even
the oath that binds you is more strong than
    Zeus is strong.

Chorus   Then Zeus, as you say, authorized
    the oracle
to this Orestes, stating he could wreak the
    death

of his father on his mother, and it would have
    no force?

Apollo   It is not the same thing for a man of
    blood to die
honored with the king's staff given by the
    hand of god,
and that by means of a woman, not with the
    far cast
of fierce arrows, as an Amazon might have
    done,
but in a way that you shall hear, O Pallas and
    you
who sit in state to judge this action by your
    vote.
He had come home from his campaigning. He
    had done
better than worse, in the eyes of a fair judge.
    She lay
in wait for him. It was the bath. When he was
    at
its edge, she hooded the robe on him, and in
    the blind
and complex toils tangled her man, and
    chopped him down.
There is the story of the death of a great man,
solemn in all men's sight, lord of the host of
    ships.
I have called the woman what she was, so that
    the people
whose duty it is to try this case may be
    inflamed.

Chorus   Zeus, by your story, gives first place
    to the father's death.
Yet Zeus himself shackled elder Cronus, his
    own

father. Is this not contradiction? I testify,
judges, that this is being said in your hearing.

Apollo   You foul animals, from whom the
        gods turn in disgust,
Zeus could undo shackles, such hurt can be
        made good,
and there is every kind of way to get out. But
        once
the dust has drained down all a man's blood,
        once the man
has died, there is no raising of him up again.
This is a thing for which my father never
        made
curative spells. All other states, without effort
of hard breath, he can completely rearrange.

Chorus   See what it means to force acquittal
        of this man.
He has spilled his mother's blood upon the
        ground. Shall he
then be at home in Argos in his father's
        house?
What altars of the community shall he use? Is
        there
a brotherhood's lustration that will let him
        in?

Apollo   I will tell you, and I will answer
        correctly. Watch.
The mother is no parent of that which is
        called
her child, but only nurse of the new-planted
        seed
that grows. The parent is he who mounts. A
        stranger she
preserves a stranger's seed, if no god interfere.

I will show you proof of what I have explained.
        There can
be a father without any mother. There she
        stands,
the living witness, daughter of Olympian
        Zeus,
she who was never fostered in the dark of the
        womb
yet such a child as no goddess could bring to
        birth.
In all else, Pallas, as I best may understand,
I shall make great your city and its populace.
So I have brought this man to sit beside the
        hearth
of your house, to be your true friend for the
        rest of time,
so you shall win him, goddess, to fight by your
        side,
and among men to come this shall stand a
        strong bond
that his and your own people's children shall
        be friends.

Athene   Shall I assume that enough has now
        been said, and tell
the judges to render what they believe a true
        verdict?

Chorus   Every arrow we had has been shot
        now. We wait
on their decision, to see how the case has
        gone.

Athene   So then. How shall I act correctly in
        your eyes?

Apollo   You have heard what you have heard,
        and as you cast your votes,

good friends, respect in your hearts the oath
that you have sworn.

Athene   If it please you, men of Attica, hear
my decree
now, on this first case of bloodletting I have
judged.
For Aegeus' population, this forevermore
shall be the ground where justices deliberate.
Here is the Hill of Ares, here the Amazons
encamped and built their shelters when they
came in arms
for spite of Theseus, here they piled their rival
towers
to rise, new city, and dare his city long ago,
and slew their beasts for Ares. So this rock is
named
from then the Hill of Ares. Here the reverence
of citizens, their fear and kindred do-no-wrong
shall hold by day and in the blessing of night
alike
all while the people do not muddy their own
laws
with foul infusions. But if bright water you
stain
with mud, you nevermore will find it fit to
drink.
No anarchy, no rule of a single master. Thus
I advise my citizens to govern and to grace,
and not to cast fear utterly from your city.
What
man who fears nothing at all is ever righteous?
Such
be your just terrors, and you may deserve and
have
salvation for your citadel, your land's defense,
such as is nowhere else found among men,
neither

among the Scythians, nor the land that Pelops
held.
I establish this tribunal. It shall be untouched
by money-making, grave but quick to wrath,
watchful
to protect those who sleep, a sentry on the
land.

These words I have unreeled are for my
citizens,
advice into the future. All must stand upright
now, take each man his ballot in his hand,
think on
his oath, and make his judgment. For my word
is said.

Chorus   I give you counsel by no means to
disregard
this company. We can be a weight to crush
your land.

Apollo   I speak too. I command you to fear,
and not   /
make void the yield of oracles from Zeus and
me.

Chorus   You honor bloody actions where you
have no right.
The oracles you give shall be no longer clean.

Apollo   My father's purposes are twisted
then. For he
was appealed to by Ixion, the first murderer.

Chorus   Talk! But for my part, if I do not win
the case,
I shall come back to this land and it will feel
my weight.

Apollo   Neither among the elder nor the
    younger gods
have you consideration. I shall win this
    suit. . . .

Athene   It is my task to render final
    judgment here.
This is a ballot for Orestes I shall cast.
There is no mother anywhere who gave me
    birth,
and, but for marriage, I am always for the
    male

with all my heart, and strongly on my father's
    side.
So, in a case where the wife has killed her
    husband, lord
of the house, her death shall not mean most
    to me. And if
the other votes are even, then Orestes wins.
You of the jurymen who have this duty
    assigned,
shake out the ballots from the vessels, with all
    speed. . .

PERICLES (CA. 495–CA. 429 B.C.)
Funeral Oration (from Thucydides)

*T*he "father of his country," Pericles is probably more responsible than any other individual for the flowering of Athenian democracy and the height of classical Greek culture. He was the son of the Alcmaeonid Agariste and Xanthippus, who, though ostracized in 484 B.C., returned to Athens to command its army at the battle of Mycale in 479 B.C. Pericles studied under the musician Damon and the philosophers Zeno and Anaxagoras.

- When warfare among the Greek states ended in the truce of 451 B.C., Pericles, who had risen to leadership, set out to consolidate Athens' political and cultural primacy, which had profited from Sparta's withdrawal from the war against Persia and the Greek confederation's transfer of its treasury from Delos to Athens. He oversaw the construction of the Parthenon, commissioning Phidias to create the gold and ivory statue of Athena.
- His reign saw demonstrations of Athenian naval might, an enhancement of the importance of the Eleusinian mysteries, an expansion of the Panathenaean festival. But he was not able to hold the Peloponnesian War at bay, and spent the last part of his rule trying to hold the Athenian army together against Spartan inroads. The funeral speech he delivered over the

Athenians who fell during the first campaign of the war was reported by the historian Thucydides. In this manifesto of the high point of classical Greek culture, Pericles' ideal of Athenian life, for which these men had fallen—and of the central importance of Athens as the intellectual beacon of all Greece—is nowhere else more clearly envisioned and enunciated.

In the same winter the Athenians gave a funeral at the public cost to those who had first fallen in this war. It was a custom of their ancestors, and the manner of it is as follows. Three days before the ceremony, the bones of the dead are laid out in a tent which has been erected; and their friends bring to their relatives such offerings as they please. In the funeral procession cypress coffins are borne in cars, one for each tribe, the bones of the deceased being placed in the coffin of their tribe. Among these is carried one empty bier decked for the missing, that is, for those whose bodies could not be recovered. Any citizen or stranger who pleases joins in the procession, and the female relatives are there to wail at the burial. The dead are laid in the public sepulchre in the most beautiful suburb of the city, in which those who fall in war are always buried; with the exception of those slain at Marathon, who for their singular and extraordinary valor were interred on the spot where they fell. After the bodies have been laid in the earth, a man chosen by the state, of approved wisdom and eminent reputation, pronounces over them an appropriate panegyric, after which all retire. Such is the manner of the burying; and throughout the whole war, whenever the occasion arose, the established custom was observed. Meanwhile these were the first that had

fallen, and Pericles, son of Xanthippus, was chosen to pronounce their eulogium. When the proper time arrived, he advanced from the sepulchre to an elevated platform in order to be heard by as many of the crowd as possible, and spoke as follows . . .

. . . "I shall begin with our ancestors: It is both just and proper that they should have the honor of the first mention on an occasion like the present. They dwelt in the country without break in the succession from generation to generation, and handed it down free to the present time by their valor. And if our more remote ancestors deserve praise, much more do our own fathers, who added to their inheritance the empire which we now possess, and spared no pains to be able to leave their acquisitions to us of the present generation. Lastly, there are few parts of our dominions that have not been augmented by those of us here, who are still more or less in the vigor of life; while the mother country has been furnished by us with everything that can enable her to depend on her own resources whether for war or for peace. That part of our history which tells of the military achievements which gave us our several possessions, or of the ready valor with which either we or our fathers stemmed the tide of Hellenic or foreign aggression, is a theme too familiar to my hearers for me to dilate on, and I shall

"Parthenon, on the Acropolis of Athens"

therefore pass it by. But what was the road by which we reached our position, what the form of government under which our greatness grew, what the national habits out of which it sprang? These are questions which I may try to solve before I proceed to my panegyric upon these men; since I think this to be a subject upon which on the present occasion a speaker may properly dwell, and to which the whole assemblage, whether citizens or foreigners, may listen with advantage.

"Our constitution does not copy the laws of neighboring states; we are rather a pattern to others than imitators ourselves. Its administration favors the many instead of the few; this is why it is called a democracy. If we look to the laws, they afford equal justice to all in their private differences; if to social standing, advancement in public life falls to reputation for capacity, class considerations not being allowed to interfere with merit; nor again does poverty

bar the way: If a man is able to serve the state, he is not hindered by the obscurity of his condition. The freedom which we enjoy in our government extends also to our ordinary life. There, far from exercising a jealous surveillance over each other, we do not feel called upon to be angry with our neighbor for doing what he likes, or even to indulge in those injurious looks which cannot fail to be offensive, although they inflict no positive penalty. But all this ease in our private relations does not make us lawless as citizens. Against this fear is our chief safeguard, teaching us to obey the magistrates and the laws, particularly such as regard the protection of the injured, whether they are actually on the statute book, or belong to that code which, although unwritten, yet cannot be broken without acknowledged disgrace.

"Further, we provide plenty of means for the mind to refresh itself from business. We celebrate games and sacrifices all the year round, and the elegance of our private establishments forms a daily source of pleasure and helps to banish the spleen; while the magnitude of our city draws the produce of the world into our harbor, so that to the Athenian the fruits of other countries are as familiar a luxury as those of his own.

"If we turn to our military policy, there also we differ from our antagonists. We throw open our city to the world, and never by alien acts exclude foreigners from any opportunity of learning or observing, although the eyes of an enemy may occasionally profit by our liberality; trusting less in system and policy than to the native spirit of our citizens; while in education, where our rivals from their very cradles by a painful discipline seek after manliness, at Athens we live exactly as we please, and yet are just as ready to encounter every legitimate danger. In proof of this it may be noticed that the Lacedaemonians do not invade our country alone, but bring with them all their confederates; while we Athenians advance unsupported into the territory of a neighbor, and fighting upon a foreign soil usually vanquish with ease men who are defending their homes. Our united force was never yet encountered by any enemy, because we have at once to attend to our marine and to despatch our citizens by land upon a hundred different services; so that, wherever they engage with some such fraction of our strength, a success against a detachment is magnified into a victory over the nation, and a defeat into a reverse suffered at the hands of our entire people. And yet if with habits not of labor but of ease, and courage not of art but of nature, we are still willing to encounter danger, we have the double advantage of escap-

ing the experience of hardships in anticipation and of facing them in the hour of need as fearlessly as those who are never free from them.

"Nor are these the only points in which our city is worthy of admiration. We cultivate refinement without extravagance and knowledge without effeminacy; wealth we employ more for use than for show, and place the real disgrace of poverty not in owning to the fact but in declining the struggle against it. Our public men have, besides politics, their private affairs to attend to, and our ordinary citizens, though occupied with the pursuits of industry, are still fair judges of public matters; for, unlike any other nation, regarding him who takes no part in these duties not as unambitious but as useless, we Athenians are able to judge at all events if we cannot originate, and instead of looking on discussion as a stumbling-block in the way of action, we think it an indispensable preliminary to any wise action at all. Again, in our enterprises we present the singular spectacle of daring and deliberation, each carried to its highest point, and both united in the same persons; although usually decision is the fruit of ignorance, hesitation of reflection. But the palm of courage will surely be adjudged most justly to those who best know the difference between hardship and pleasure and yet are never tempted to shrink from danger. In generosity we are equally singular, acquiring our friends by conferring, not by receiving, favors. Yet, of course, the doer of the favor is the firmer friend of the two, in order by continued kindness to keep the recipient in his debt; while the debtor feels less keenly from the very consciousness that the return he makes will be a payment, not a free gift. And it is only the Athenians who, fearless of consequences, confer their benefits not from calculations of expediency, but in the confidence of liberality.

"In short, I say that as a city we are the school of Hellas; while I doubt if the world can produce a man, who where he has only himself to depend upon, is equal to so many emergencies, and graced by so happy a versatility, as the Athenian. And that this is no mere boast thrown out for the occasion, but plain matter of fact, the power of the state acquired by these habits proves. For Athens alone of her contemporaries is found when tested to be greater than her reputation, and alone gives no occasion to her assailants to blush at the antagonists by whom they have been worsted, or to her subjects to question her title by merit to rule. Rather, the admiration of the present and succeeding ages will be ours, since we have not left our power without witness, but have shown it by mighty proofs; and far from needing a Homer for our panegyrist, or other of his craft whose verses might charm for the moment only for the impression which they gave to melt at the touch of fact, we have forced every sea and land to be the highway of our daring, and everywhere, whether for evil or for good, have left imperishable monuments behind us. Such is the Athens for which these men, in the assertion of their resolve not to lose her, nobly fought and died; and well may every one of their survivors be ready to suffer in her cause.

"Indeed if I have dwelt at some length upon the character of our country, it has been to show that our stake in the struggle is not the same as theirs who have no such blessings to lose, and also that the panegyric of the men over whom I am now speaking might be by definite proofs established. That panegyric is now in a great measure complete; for the Athens that I have celebrated is only what the heroism of these and their like have made her, men whose fame, unlike that of most Hellenes, will be found to be only commensurate with their deserts. And if a test of worth be wanted, it is to be found in their closing scene, and this not only in the cases in which it set the final seal upon their merit, but also in those in which it gave the first intimation of their having any. For there is justice in the claim that steadfastness in his country's battles should be as a cloak to cover a man's other imperfections; since the good action has blotted out the bad, and his merit as a citizen more than outweighed his demerits as an individual. But none of these allowed either wealth with its prospect of future enjoyment to unnerve his spirit, or poverty with its hope of a day of freedom and riches to tempt him to shrink from danger. No, holding that vengeance upon their enemies was more to be desired than any personal blessings, and reckoning this to be the most glorious of hazards, they joyfully determined to accept the risk, to make sure of their vengeance and to let their wishes wait; and while committing to hope the uncertainty of final success, in the business before them they thought fit to act boldly and trust in themselves. Thus choosing to die resisting, rather than to live submitting, they fled only from dishonor, but met danger face to face, and after one brief moment, while at the summit of their fortune, escaped, not from their fear, but from their glory.

"So died these men as became Athenians. . . ."

HERACLITUS (FL. CA. 500 B.C.)
On Nature

he philosopher Heraclitus (called "the obscure") was born in Ephesus in Ionia, the son of Blyson, under Persian rule, and wrote in Ionic. We know little else about his life. He appears to have been of truculent disposition, and not pleased when democratic forces won supremacy after the defeat of the Persians. He withdrew to his aristocratic country estate and, like Montaigne, gave himself to his studies.

- Socrates was not the first to complain of Heraclitus' obscurity, associated with his terse, pithy, and often hopelessly enigmatic oracular style. He was no doubt influenced by East Indian thought, believing that the key to understanding the workings of nature lay in understanding the self, that the microcosm reflected the formal qualities of the macrocosm. His *On Nature,* the oldest known Greek prose, was published, at his request, only after his death. He wanted to think, but did not want to be bothered. His book was divided into three parts: "Concerning the All," "Politics," and "Theology."

- Where Thales argued that the underlying element is water, Heraclitus believed that the basic element of which the universe is composed is fire. He considered change, or "flux," to be the most important principle in understanding the physical universe: "All things flow." Modern theories of entropy are remarkably similar to Heraclitus' insights. Change is generated by ceaseless opposition: of dark and light, love and strife, sickness and health, pain and pleasure. Out of this dualistic opposition is derived a unified stability: "The way up and the way down are the same." As Lewis A. Richards puts it, "His fascinating thesis is that there is harmony in opposition, that harmony does exist in tension, and that rest and stability are merely the temporary equilibrium of opposite, striving forces." Twentieth-century nuclear and astrophysicists have corroborated Heraclitus' intuition about the illusory nature of both stability and change. In total contrast to Platonic "absolutism," Heraclitus posits a reality in which all values, individual and cosmic, are relative—foreshadowing Albert Einstein by 2,500 years. His belief that *change* (or Strife) is a good thing, pushing the envelope of Hesiod's distinction between the two Strifes, is the cutting edge of twentieth-century existential and entrepreneurial wisdom. He felt that the highest good in human experience is the development of the mind. The questions Heraclitus raised, as listed by Richards, are ones we are still working on:

  - How should an individual live his life?
  - How is knowledge assimilated?

- To what extent should man depend upon reason?
- What is faith?
- How much can man know?
- What is justice?
- What is the meaning of life?
- What is the underlying principle of things?

---

1. Not on my authority, but on that of truth, it is wise for you to accept the fact that all things are one.
2. Those who hear without the power to understand are like deaf men; the proverb holds true of them: "Present, they are absent."
3. Eyes and ears are bad witnesses for men, since their souls lack understanding.
4. If you do not hope, you will not find that which is not hoped for; since it is difficult to discover and impossible to attain.
5. Seekers for gold dig much earth, and find little gold.
6. Controversy.
7. Nature loves to hide.
8. What can be seen, heard, and learned, this I prize.
9. Eyes are more exact witnesses than ears.
10. Much learning does not teach one to have understanding. . . .
11. No one of all whose discourses I have heard has arrived at this result: the recognition that wisdom is apart from all other things.
12. Wisdom is one thing . . . it is willing
and it is unwilling to be called by the name Zeus.
13. This order, the same for all things, no one of gods or men has made, but it always was, and is, and ever shall be, an ever-living fire, kindling according to fixed measure, and extinguished according to fixed measure.
14. The transformations of fire are, first of all, sea; and of the sea one half is earth, and the other half is lightning flash.
15. All things are exchanged for fire, and fire for all things; as wares are exchanged for gold, and gold for wares.
16. [The earth] is poured out as sea, and measures the same amount as existed before it became earth.
17. Want and satiety.
18. Fire lives in the death of earth, and air lives in the death of fire; water lives in the death of air, and earth in that of water.
19. Fire coming upon all things will test them, and lay hold of them.
20. The sun will not overstep his bounds; if he does, the Erinnyes, allies of justice, will find him out.
21. Hesiod is the teacher of all men;

they suppose that his knowledge was very extensive, when in fact he did not know night and day, for they are one.

22. God is day and night, winter and summer, war and peace, satiety and hunger; but he assumes different forms, just as when incense is mingled with incense; everyone gives him the name he pleases.

23. If all things should become smoke, then perception would be by the nostrils.

24. Souls smell in Hades.

25. Cool things become warm, the warm grows cool; the wet dries, the parched becomes wet.

26. It scatters and brings together; it approaches and departs.

27. You could not step twice in the same river; for other and yet other waters are ever flowing on.

28. Heraclitus blamed Homer for saying, "Would that Strife might perish from among gods and men!" For then, he said, all things would pass away.

29. War is father of all and king of all; and some he made gods and some men, some slaves and some free.

30. Men do not understand how that which draws apart agrees with itself; harmony lies in the bending back, as for instance of the bow and the lyre.

31. Opposition unites. From what draws apart results the most beautiful harmony. All things take place by strife.

32. Men who desire wisdom must be learners of very many things.

33. For woolcarders the straight and the crooked path are one and the same.

34. Good and bad are the same.

35. Thou shouldst unite things whole and things not whole, that which tends to unite and that which tends to separate, the harmonious and the discordant; from all things arises the one, and from the one all things.

36. All the things we see when awake are death, and all the things we see when asleep are sleep.

37. The name of the bow is life, but its work is death.

38. For to souls it is death to become water, and for water it is death to become earth; but water is formed from earth, and from water, soul.

39. Upward, downward, the way is one and the same.

40. The limits of the soul you could not discover, though traversing every path.

41. Life and death, and waking and sleeping, and youth and old age, are the same; for the latter change and are the former, and the former change back to the latter.

42. Lifetime is a child playing draughts; the kingdom is a child's.

43. I inquired of myself.

44. In the same rivers we step and we do not step; we are and we are not.

45. It is weariness to toil at the same things, and to be subject to them.

46. Changing it finds rest.

47. Even a potion separates into its ingredients when it is not stirred.

48. Understanding is common to all. It is necessary for those who speak with intelligence to hold fast to the common element of all, as a city holds fast to law, and much more strongly. For all human laws are nourished by one which is divine and it has power so much as it will; and it suffices for all things and more than suffices.

49. And though reason is common, most people live as though they had an understanding peculiar to themselves.

50. They that are awake have one world in common, but of the sleeping each turns aside into a world of his own.

51. It is not good for men to have whatever they want. Disease makes health sweet and good; hunger, satiety; toil, rest.

52. It is hard to contend with passion; for whatever it desires to get it buys at the cost of soul.

53. It is better to conceal stupidity, but it is an effort in time of relaxation and over the wine.

54. It is better to conceal ignorance than to put it forth into the midst.

55. One day is equal to every other.

56. Character is a man's guardian divinity.

57. All things are full of souls and of divine spirits.

58. False opinion of progress is the stoppage of progress.

59. Their education is a second sun to those that have been educated.

60. The . . . shortest way to glory was to become good.

PARMENIDES (FL. 470 B.C.)

On Nature

*P*armenides, a native of Elea in southern Italy, was among the most important of the preSocratic philosophers, and one of the founders of the study of metaphysics. On a trip to Athens when he was sixty-five, he supposedly met and discussed philosophy with Socrates himself.

- Born of a well-known, affluent family, Parmenides was influenced by Pythagoras. Like his teacher Xenophanes, Parmenides wrote poetry. He was also a legislator, admired for the justness of his laws by his fellow citizens. His simple concept that truth and illusion, reality and

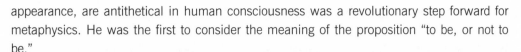

appearance, are antithetical in human consciousness was a revolutionary step forward for metaphysics. He was the first to consider the meaning of the proposition "to be, or not to be."

- Parmenides' *On Nature* is a didactic poem in hexameters, divided into three parts:

  - The *proem,* describing a mystic chariot ride into the world of dreams where he encounters a goddess who expounds the "two ways" to him;
  - The *way of truth,* which starting with the proposition *It is,* expounds logically on its ramifications and portrays reality as perfectly harmonious, unique, ungenerated, unmoving, indivisible, imperishable, infinite, and spherical. Yet this isn't how things appear to us, therefore our senses, by which we perceive, must be erroneous and characteristic of
  - *The way of opinion:* This section describes the illusory, phenomenal world of apparent multiplicity, presided over by Light and Dark, in which nonphilosophers, trapped by their senses, live their transitory existence believing in the reality of change.

Parmenides believed that true knowledge could be found only in the logical, unifying "way of truth," and that therefore men had to look beyond their senses to perceive the ultimate, unchangeable reality. His belief that only existence *is* truly real, and that nonexistence (chaos and change) *is not* truly real, provided the foundation for Plato's theory of ideas and Aristotle's refinement of it in his theory of forms—and, in the Christian era, for Thomas Aquinas' summary principles of Catholic theology.

THE REAL

Come now, I will tell thee—and do thou hearken to my saying and carry it away—the only two ways of search that can be thought of. The first, namely, that *It is,* and that it is impossible for it not to be, is the way of belief, for truth is its companion. The other, namely, that *It is not,* and that it must needs not be—that, I tell thee, is a path that none can learn of at all. For thou canst not know what is not—that is impossible—nor utter it; for it is the same thing that can be thought and that can be.

2. It needs must be that what can be spoken and thought *is;* for it is possible for it to be, and it is not possible for what is nothing to be. This is what I bid thee ponder. I hold thee back from this first way of inquiry, and from this other also, upon which mortals knowing naught wander two-faced; for helplessness guides the wandering thought in their breasts, so that they are borne along stupefied like men deaf and blind. Undiscerning crowds, who hold that it is and is not the same and not the same, and all things travel in opposite directions!

3. For this shall never be proved, that the

things that are not are; and do thou restrain thy thought from this way of inquiry.

4. One path only is left for us to speak of, namely, that *It is*. In this path are very many tokens that what is is uncreated, and indestructible; for it is complete, immovable, and without end. Nor was it ever, nor will it be; for now *it is*, all at once, a continuous one. For what kind of origin for it wilt thou look for? In what way and from what source could it have drawn its increase? . . . I shall not let thee say nor think that it came from what is not; for it can neither be thought nor uttered that anything is not. And, if it came from nothing, what need could have made it arise later rather than sooner? Therefore must it either be altogether or be not at all. Nor will the force of truth suffer aught to arise besides itself from that which is not. Wherefore, Justice doth not loose her fetters and let anything come into being or pass away, but holds it fast. Our judgment thereon depends on this: *"Is it or is it not?"* Surely it is adjudged, as it needs must be, that we are to set aside the one way as unthinkable and nameless (for it is no true way), and that the other path is real and true. How, then, can what *is* be going to be in the future? Or how could it come into being? If it came into being, it is not; nor is it if it is going to be in the future. Thus is becoming extinguished and passing away not to be heard of.

Nor is it divisible, since it is all alike, and there is no more of it in one place than in another, to hinder it from holding together, nor less of it, but everything is full of what is.

Wherefore it is wholly continuous; for what is, is in contract with what is.

Moreover, it is immovable in the bonds of mighty chains, without beginning and without end; since coming into being and passing away have been driven afar, and true belief has cast them away. It is the same, and it rests in the self-same place, abiding in itself. And thus it remaineth constant in its place; for hard necessity keeps it in the bonds of the limit that holds it fast on every side. Wherefore it is not permitted to what is to be infinite; for it is in need of nothing; while, if it were infinite, it would stand in need of everything.

The thing that can be thought and that for the sake of which the thought exists is the same; for you cannot find thought without something that is, as to which it is uttered. And there is not, and never shall be, anything besides what is, since fate has chained it so as to be whole and immovable. Wherefore all these things are but names which mortals have given, believing them to be true—coming into being and passing away, being and not being, change of place and alteration of bright color.

Since, then, it has a furthest limit, it is complete on every side, like the mass of a rounded sphere, equally poised from the center in every direction; for it cannot be greater or smaller in one place than in another. For there is nothing that could keep it from reaching out equally, nor can anything that is to be more here and less there than what is, since it is all inviolable. For the point from which it is equal in every direction tends equally to the limits.

TELESILLA (FL. 500 B.C.)
Lyric Fragments

Only tiny fragments remain of Telesilla, a poet of Argos who wrote hymns to Apollo and Artemis for women.

She is credited by Pausanias, in his *Description of Greece,* and Plutarch, in his *Feminine Virtue,* with assembling an army of Argive women to thwart an attack by Kleomenes, king of Sparta. Pausanias also notes that her statue, showing her eyes focused on a helmet, and books at her feet, graced the Temple of Aphrodite in Argos. According to legend, she dedicated herself to the Muses because they brought her health.

REFUGE FROM RAPE
O Artemis and your virgin girls,
come to us. Run swiftly
to escape the hunter Alpheus.

SONG TO APOLLO
O the sun-loving Apollo!

EMPEDOCLES (CA. 493–CA. 433 B.C.)
Fragments and *On Nature*

Empedocles was born in Agrigento (then known as Acragas), in Sicily, and though his family were wealthy aristocrats his ideals were egalitarian. Meton, his father, was instrumental in the overthrow of the tyrant Thrasydaeus. He was a mystic, a natural scientist, a historian of medicine, and a statesman, as well as a philosopher; and he committed his theories to writing.

• When his democratic party was overthrown, after their success in 471 B.C., Empedocles traveled throughout Greece and Italy, and lived for a while in the Peloponnesus. Legend has it that he ended his life by jumping into the crater of the active volcano Etna—an event memorialized poetically in Matthew Arnold's "Empedocles on Etna."

- In Orphic hexameters, as powerful as Homer's, Empedocles argued that the cosmos, which he believed to be spherical, is comprised of four primary and irreducible elements—fire, air, earth, and water—the varying configurations of which are determined by the endless interaction between Love and Strife (concentration or attraction, and abandonment or repulsion). His belief in the unity of all things has been attributed to the influence of Parmenides. We are able to perceive things, Empedocles argued, because our pores receive particle "emanations" from them. Like Pythagoras, he believed in transmigration and purification to escape from its 30,000-year cycle; and, like Anaxagoras, in the equivalence between the individual's thought and the mind of the universe. He influenced particularly Aristotle, who considered Empedocles the inventor of rhetoric, and the Roman Lucretius.

When Strife has reached the very bottom of the seething mass, and love assumes her station in the center of the ball, then everything begins to come together, and to form one whole—not instantaneously, but different substances come forth, according to a steady process of development. Now, when these elements are mingling, countless kinds of things issue from their union. Much, however, remains unmixed, in opposition to the mingling elements, and malignant Strife still holds within his grasp. For he has not yet withdrawn himself altogether to the extremities of the globe; but part of his limbs still remain within its bounds, and part have passed beyond. As Strife, however, step by step, retreats, mild and innocent love pursues him with her force divine; things which had been immortal instantly assume mortality; the simple elements become confused by interchange of influence. When these are mingled, then the countless kinds of mortal beings issue forth, furnished with every sort of form—a wonder to behold.

BOOK I.

1. And do thou hear me, Pausanias, son of wise Anchites.

2. For scant means of acquiring knowledge are scattered among the members of the body; and many are the evils that break in to blunt the edge of studious thought. And gazing on a little portion of life that is not life, swift to meet their fate, they rise and are borne away like smoke, persuaded only of that on which each one chances as he is driven this way and that, but the whole he vainly boasts he has found. Thus these things are neither seen nor heard distinctly by men, nor comprehended by the mind. And thou, now that thou hast withdrawn hither, shalt learn no more than what mortal mind has seen.

11. But, ye gods, avert the madness of those men from my tongue, and from lips that are holy cause a pure stream to flow. And thee I pray, much-wooed white-armed maiden Muse, in what things it is right for beings of a day to hear, do thou, and Piety, driving obedient car, conduct me on. Nor yet shall the flowers of honor well esteemed compel me to pluck them from mortal hands, on condition that I speak boldly more than is holy and only then sit on the heights of wisdom.

19. But come, examine by every means each thing how it is clear, neither putting greater faith in anything seen than in what is heard, nor in a thundering sound more than in the clear assertions of the tongue, nor keep from trusting any of the other members in which there lies means of knowledge, but know each thing in the way in which it is clear.

24. Cures for evils whatever there are, and protection against old age shalt thou

"Theater at Taormina, Sicily, with Mt. Aetna in the background." Copyright *Archivi Alinari, 1989. By permission of Art Resource.*

learn, since for thee alone will I accomplish all these things. Thou shalt break the power of untiring gales which rising against the earth blow down the crops and destroy them; and, again, whenever thou wilt, thou shalt bring their blasts back; and thou shalt bring seasonable drought out of dark storm for men, and out of summer drought thou shalt bring streams pouring down from heaven to nurture the trees; and thou shalt lead out of Hades the spirit of a man that is dead.

33. Hear first the four roots of all things: bright Zeus, life-giving Hera (air), and Aidoneus (earth), and Nestis who moistens the springs of men with her tears.

36. And a second thing I will tell thee: There is no origination of anything that is mortal, nor yet any end in baneful death; but only mixture and separation of what is mixed, but men call this "origination."

40. But when light is mingled with air in human form, or in form like the race of wild beasts or of plants or of birds, then men say that these things have come into being; and when they are separated, they call them evil fate; this is the established practice, and I myself also call it so in accordance with the custom.

45. Fools! for they have no far-reaching studious thoughts who think that what was not before comes into being or that anything dies and perishes utterly.

48. For from what does not exist at all it is impossible that anything come into being, and it is neither possible nor perceivable that being should perish completely; for things will always stand wherever one in each case shall put them.

60. Twofold is the truth I shall speak; for at one time there grew to be one alone out of many, and at another time, however, it separated so that there were many out of the one. Twofold is the coming into being, twofold the passing away, of perishable things; for the latter (*i.e.*, passing away) the combining of all things both begets and destroys, and the former (*i.e.*, coming into being), which was nurtured again out of parts that were being separated, is itself scattered.

66. And these (elements) never cease changing place continually, now being all united by Love into one, now each borne apart by the hatred engendered of Strife, until they are brought together in the unity of the all, and become subject to it. Thus inasmuch as one has been wont to arise out of many and again with the separation of the one the many arise, so things are continually coming into being and there is no fixed age for them; and farther, inasmuch as they (the elements) never cease changing place continually, so they always exist within an immovable circle.

74. But come, hear my words, for truly learning causes the mind to grow. For as I said before in declaring the ends of my words: Twofold is the truth I shall speak; for at one time there grew to be the one alone out of many, and at another time

it separated so that there were many out of the one; fire and water and earth and boundless height of air, and baneful Strife apart from these, balancing each of them, and Love among them, their equal in length and breadth.

81. Upon her do thou gaze with thy mind, nor yet sit dazed in thine eyes; for she is wont to be implanted in men's members, and through her they have thoughts of love and accomplish deeds of union, and call her by the names of Delight, and Aphrodite; no mortal man has discerned her with them (the elements) as she moves on her way. But do thou listen to the undeceiving course of my words. . . .

87. For these (elements) are equal, all of them, and of like ancient race; and one holds one office, another another, and each has his own nature. . . . For nothing is added to them, nor yet does anything pass away from them; for if they were continually perishing they would no longer exist. . . . Neither is any part of this all empty, nor overfull. For how should anything cause this all to increase, and whence should it come? And whither should they (the elements) perish, since no place is empty of them? And in their turn they prevail as the cycle comes round, and they disappear before each other, and they increase each in its allotted turn. But these (elements) are the same; and penetrating through each other they become one thing in one place and another in another, while ever they remain alike (*i.e.*, the same).

96. But come, gaze on the things that bear farther witness to my former words, if in what was said before there be anything defective in form. Behold the sun, warm and bright on all sides, and whatever is immortal and is bathed in its bright ray, and behold the raincloud, dark and cold on all sides; from the earth there proceed the foundations of things and solid bodies. In Strife all things are, endued with form and separate from each other, but they come together in Love and are desired by each other.

104. For from these (elements) come all things that are or have been or shall be; from these there grew up trees and men and women, wild beasts and birds and water-nourished fishes, and the very gods, long-lived, highest in honor.

110. For they two (Love and Strife) were before and shall be, nor yet, I think, will there ever be an unutterably long time without them both.

121. And as when painters are preparing elaborate votive offerings—men well taught by wisdom in their art—they take many-colored pigments to work with, and blend together harmoniously more of one and less of another till they produce likenesses of all things; so let not error overcome thy mind to make thee think there is any other source of mortal things that have likewise come into distinct existence in unspeakable numbers; but know these (elements), for thou didst hear from a god the account of them.

ANAXAGORAS (CA. 500–CA. 428 B.C.)
On Nature

The son of Hegesiboulos, of a wealthy family in Anatolia (Asia Minor), in Klazomenae, this Ionian philosopher lived in Athens as a resident alien for thirty years beginning in 480 B.C., where he was an associate of Pericles. Pericles defended him when the Athenians condemned him for claiming that the sun was a stone somewhat larger than the Peloponnesus.

- Despite being exonerated in Athens, Anaxagoras retired to Lampsacus to found a school. He believed that matter is infinitely divisible into what he called *spermata* ("the seeds of things"); and that the universe as we experience it was generated out of the unifying Reason or Mind (*nous*) which, by rotating upon itself, separated out material opposites. Each material being lives because the *nous* within it directs its energies. He is also credited with discovering the true cause of eclipses.
- The first philosopher of classical Athens, and therefore influential on both Plato and Aristotle, Anaxagoras is noted for positing a spiritual source for material reality, and for honoring the primacy of *logos* over *mythos*. He denied the reality of birth and death, preferring to refer to them as "mingling" and "unmingling." Anaxagoras was a dualist, believing that "being is not not-being."

All things were together, infinite both in number and in smallness; for the small also was infinite. And when they were all together, nothing was clear and distinct because of their smallness; for air and ether comprehended all things, both being infinite; for these are present in everything, and are greatest both as to number and as to greatness.

For air and ether are separated from the surrounding mass; and the surrounding (mass) is infinite in quantity.

But before these were separated, when all things were together, not even was any color clear and distinct; for the mixture of all things prevented it, the mixture of the moist and the dry, of the warm and the cold, and of the bright and the dark (since much earth was present), and of germs infinite in number, in no way like each other; for none of the other things at all resembles the one the other.

And since these things are so, it is necessary to think that in all the objects that are compound there existed many things of all sorts, and germs of all objects, having all sorts of forms and colors and tastes.

And men were constituted, and the other animals, as many as have life. And the men have inhabited cities and works constructed as among us, and they have sun and moon and other things as among us; and the earth brings forth for them many things of all sorts, of which they carry the most serviceable into the house and use them. These things then I have said concerning the separation, that not only among us would the separation take place, but elsewhere too.

So these things rotate and are separated by force and swiftness. And the swiftness produces force; and their swiftness is in no way like the swiftness of the things now existing among men, but it is certainly many times as swift.

When they are thus distinguished, it is necessary to recognize that they all become no fewer and no more. For it is impossible that more than all should exist, but all are always equal.

In all things there is a portion of everything except mind; and there are things in which there is mind also.

Other things include a portion of everything, but mind is infinite and self-powerful and mixed with nothing, but it exists alone itself by itself. For if it were

not by itself, but were mixed with anything else, it would include parts of all things, if it were mixed with anything; for a portion of everything exists in everything, as has been said by me before, and things mingled with it would prevent it from having power over anything in the same way that it does now that it is alone by itself. For it is the most rarefied of all things and the purest, and it has all knowledge in regard to everything and the greatest power; over all that has life, both greater and less, mind rules. And mind ruled the rotation of the whole, so that it set it in rotation in the beginning. First it began the rotation from a small beginning, then more and more was included in the motion, and yet more will be included. Both the mixed and the separated and distinct, all things mind recognized. And whatever things were to be, and whatever things were, as many as are now, and whatever things shall be, all these mind arranged in order; and it arranged that rotation, according to which now rotate stars and sun and moon and air and ether, now that they are separated. Rotation itself caused the separation, and the dense is separated from the rare, the warm from the cold, the bright from the dark, the dry from the moist. And there are many portions of many things. Nothing is absolutely separated nor distinct, one thing from another, except mind. All mind is of like character, both the greater and the smaller. But nothing different is like anything else, but in whatever object there are the most, each single object is and was most distinctly these things.

And when mind began to set things in motion, there was separation from everything that was in motion, and however much mind set in motion, all this was made distinct. The rotation of the things that were moved and made distinct caused them to be yet more distinct.

The dense, the moist, the cold, the dark, collected there where now is the earth; the rare, the warm, the dry, the bright, departed toward the farther part of the ether.

Earth is condensed out of these things that are separated. For water is separated from the clouds, and earth from the water; and from the earth stones are condensed by cold; and these are separated farther from water.

But mind, as it always has been, especially now also is where all other things are, in the surrounding mass, and in the things that were separated, and in the things that are being separated.

Things in the one universe are not divided from each other, nor yet are they cut off with an axe, neither hot from cold, nor cold from hot.

For neither is there a least of what is small, but there is always a less. For being is not non-being. But there is always a greater than what is great. And it is equal to the small in number; but with reference to itself each thing is both small and great.

And since the portions of the great and the small are equal in number, thus also all things would be in everything. Nor yet is it possible for them to exist apart, but all things include a portion of everything. Since it is not possible for the least to exist, nothing could be separated, nor yet could it come into being of itself, but as they were in the beginning so they are now, all things together. And there are many things in all things, and of those that are separated there are things equal in number in the greater and the lesser.

The Greeks do not rightly use the terms "coming into being" and "perishing." For nothing comes into being nor yet does anything perish, but there is mixture and separation of things that are. So they would do right in calling the coming into being "mixture," and the perishing "separation."

For how could hair come from what is not hair? Or flesh from what is not flesh?

PROTAGORAS (CA. 485–CA. 415 B.C.)
Fragments

Although he wrote the books *On Truth* and *On the Gods,* Protagoras will forever be associated with the only surviving fragment of his thought—which characterizes the classical Greek "renaissance" of individualism.

- Born in Abdera, in Thrace, Protagoras was the first to lead the career of a popular and financially successful sophist, lecturing, primarily on grammar and rhetoric but also on morality and politics, for forty years throughout Greece, but especially in Athens and Sicily. He was appointed magistrate of Thurii, in Italy, in recognition of his fame. Plato, who named a dialogue after Protagoras, considered him to be Socrates' rival.
- Protagoras based his philosophy of excellence in daily living on the subjectivity of knowledge, despising mathematics and science and considering theology a waste of time. Influenced by Heraclitus, Protagoras applied his cosmic laws to human nature. Though Pericles was his patron, Protagoras, in 415 B.C., was exiled from Athens because of his view of the gods, and subsequently his books were publicly burned.

Man is the measure of all things; of things that are, that they are, and of things that are not, that they are not.

Of the gods I know nothing, whether they exist or do not exist: nor what they are like in form.

SOPHOCLES (CA. 495–405 B.C.)

Antigone

*T*he second great classical Greek playwright, Sophocles, was born in Athens, in the deme of Colonus, the son of the aristocratic munitions manufacturer Sophillus. His education emphasized music and gymnastics, and Sophocles became renowned for his performances on the *cithara* as well as for his acting. He was also active in public life, and served as a general in the fleet led by Pericles against Samos in 440 B.C. Sophocles continued his military service during the Peloponnesian War, also accepting an appointment as a priest of Asclepios, the god he honored for giving him his characteristic good health. Sophocles' son Iophon, by his Athenian wife Nikostrate, was also known as a tragic poet though none of his works survive. At Sophocles' death the Spartan general declared a truce to allow his burial in the family plot.

- At the age of twenty-seven, in 468 B.C., he was awarded the prize for tragedy over his elder, Aeschylus. Sophocles composed nearly 130 plays, nearly all of them about mythic subjects, and winning the first or second prize twenty-four times. Seven of his plays have survived:

  - *Aias*
  - *Antigone*
  - *The Women of Trachis*
  - *Oedipus the King*
  - *Elektra*
  - *Philoktetes*
  - *Oedipus at Colonus*

Sophocles' innovations for the theater included:

- introducing a third actor; and, in his later plays, a fourth; thereby enhancing the importance of dialogue as action.
- increasing the chorus from twelve to fifteen and developing its role as an emotional counterpoint to the primary action, while at the same time subordinating it to the central importance of the characters.

- introducing painted scenery.
- structuring his plays around dramatic action arising from character motivation, a particularly striking achievement since the stories he told were well known to his audiences.
- adding dramatic details to the accepted myth, including unexpected reversals; he believed that complications increase emotional intensity.
- developing irony into an art form, having his characters say things with meaning beyond what they themselves can presently comprehend.

- With Sophocles, drama became a study of character, turning inward upon the principal actors instead of reaching outward and elsewhere to the past or to the gods. *Oedipus the King* begins with the plague in Thebes, but by the end it is all Oedipus. The past affects his heroes, but it is their pain Sophocles dramatizes. At the same time that the focus is on the hero, the emphasis is philosophical. Sophocles' interest was in human nature at its most challenged. "I paint men as they should be," he is quoted as saying, "while my rival Euripides paints them as they are." The playwright challenges his audiences to contemplate the existential absurdity of good people being punished for unintentional, or even well-intentioned, acts. Oedipus had no idea it was his father he slew, nor that he was sleeping with his mother. Antigone wanted only to do the right thing in burying her brother Polyneices.
- As the characters through their dialogue acquired flesh and blood, the chorus was also affected by the change. Sophocles' chorus was always on a different level of reality from that of the actors. Not only had they fewer verses to sing than before, but their vitality dwindled as that of the characters increased. Songs shared between the chorus and one of the actors often replaced choral odes in his later plays. The odes themselves, some of the finest in all Greek poetry, are always relevant to the action.
- *Antigone,* performed in 440 B.C., focuses on the eternally compelling dilemma of individual conscience versus the collective will. Considered from the viewpoint of individualism, Antigone is the play's heroine. But considering the situation from that of the commonwealth, Creon is the pivotal character who must make the harsh decision of enforcing royal authority over her personal rebellion; for her civil disobedience he condemns her to death. When he finally relents, she has ended her own life; and his son, Antigone's suitor Haemon, has committed suicide. Creon is led away, broken by his tragic fate, himself a metaphor for the impossible choices faced by the tragic hero.
- Balancing philosophical inquiry into the values of life against human nobility in the face of their uncertainty, Sophocles brought classical Greek drama to perfection. Although *Oedipus the King* is the most familiar of his plays, influencing the underpinnings of twentieth-century psychology, *Antigone* is more truly a drama of character and is therefore more typically Sophoclean.

...Creon This girl—a prisoner! How and where didst thou take her?

Guard She was burying the man. Thou knowest all.

Creon Dost thou understand? Dost thou speak aright thy words?

Guard Yea, I saw her burying the corpse thou didst forbid. Is my meaning plain and clear?

Creon But how was she seen? How taken in the act?

Guard Why, thus it happened: When we reached the spot—under the spell of those dread threats of thine—we swept away all the dust which covered the corpse, and carefully bared the clammy body, and then sat down on the hill-top, to windward, drawing aside that no stench from it should strike us. Each kept his neighbor on the alert with noisy threatenings, should one be careless of this task.

Thus went it for some time, until the sun's

"Great Dionysian theater of Athens, at the foot of the Acropolis"

bright orb stood in midheaven and there was burning heat. Then on a sudden a whirlwind lifted from the ground a storm of dust, an evil reaching high as heaven, and covered the plain, marring all the foliage of its woods, and the wide air was completely filled therewith. Our eyes close shut, we bore that scourge from the gods.

And when, after a long while, this storm had passed, the maid was seen; and she wailed aloud with the shrill cry of a bird in sorrow, even as when, in the empty nest, it sees the bed stripped of its young. So she too, seeing the corpse bare, broke forth into lamentation, and loudly cursed those who had done the deed. And straightway she brings thirsty dust in her hands, and from a shapely jar of bronze, raised high, with three libations, crowns the dead.

At that sight we rushed forward, and at once closed upon the maid, who was no whit dismayed. Both the past and the present doings we laid to her charge, and nothing did she deny—at once to my joy and my grief. For to have escaped from ills one's self is a great joy; but to bring one's friends to ill is fraught with grief. However, all such things are of less account to me than mine own safety.

Creon Thou there—thou bending to the ground thy face—dost confess or deny this deed?

Antigone I confess it; I make no denial.

Creon (*To Guard*) Thou mayst betake thyself whither thou wilt, free and clear of a heavy charge.

(Exit Guard.)

(To Antigone) But as for thee, tell me—not at length, but in brief—didst thou know an edict had forbidden this?

Antigone   I knew it. Could I fail to know? It was plain.

Creon   And didst thou really dare to transgress this law?

Antigone   Yes, for in my eyes it was not Zeus who published that edict; nor yet did Justice, who dwells with the gods below, ordain such laws among men; nor did I think thy edicts of such force that the unwritten ever-abiding statutes of God thou, a mortal man, couldst override. For not of today or yesterday, but for eternity is their life, and no one knows the hour of their birth. Not through fear of any will of man could I take Heaven's punishment for breaking these. I must die—that I well knew—how could I not know?—even without thy proclamation. But if I must die before my time, I count it a gain. For whoso lives, as I do, amid many evils, how can he fail to find in death a gain? So for me to meet this doom is a grief of no account; but when my mother's son was dead, if I had suffered him to be an unburied corpse, for that I should have grieved. For this I grieve not. And if my present course seems to thee a foolish one, it may be that a fool is charging me with folly.

Chorus   'Tis clear that the maid is the passionate child of a passionate father. She knows not how to yield to evils.

Creon   But know that spirits over-stubborn most often fall. 'Tis the strongest iron, tempered to hardness in the fire, that thou mayst oftenest see snapped and broken. By a tiny curb I know that high-mettled steeds are made submissive. One may not be proud of spirit, who is his neighbor's slave. This girl had knowledge of insolence, even when she transgressed the laws established; and, after that, lo! another insult, to vaunt of this and gloat o'er the deed. Surely I am no longer man, but she is the man, if without penalty this victory be put to her credit. Nay, be she my sister's child or nearer to my blood than any who worship our household Zeus, she and her kin shall not escape a woeful doom; for indeed I charge that other equally with the plotting of this burial.

And now summon her—for I saw her within even now raving and dispossessed of reason. 'Tis often thus—the mind is convicted of guilt before the act, when in the dark men are planning evil deeds. Yet this, too, I hate, when one who hath been caught in treason then seeks to glorify his crime.

Antigone   Wouldst thou do more than take and kill me?

Creon   No more. Having that, I have all.

Antigone   Why, then, dost thou delay? In thy words I find no pleasure—nor may I ever find it—and, in like manner, mine are displeasing to thee. And yet, whence could I have won nobler renown, than by giving burial to mine own brother? All here would agree that this was well, did not fear lock their lips. But royalty, amid all its blessings, may also do and say what it will.

Creon   Thou alone of these Cadmeans holdest this view.

Antigone   These, too, hold it, but, through fear of thee, they curb their tongues.

Creon   And art thou not ashamed, if thou thinkest otherwise than they?

Antigone   Nay; 'tis nothing shameful to show piety to a brother.

Creon   Was not he, too, a brother, who fell on the other side?

Antigone   A brother sprung from one mother and one father.

Creon   How, then, dost thou render a favor he must count impious?

Antigone   He that is dead will not testify thus.

Creon   He will, if thou showest him but the same honor thou showest the wicked.

Antigone   'Twas not his slave that died; 'twas his brother.

Creon   But in wasting this land; while that other was its champion.

Antigone   For all that, Hades demands these laws.

Creon   Yet the good should not win like portion with the base.

Antigone   Who knows if in the world below this seem not righteous?

Creon   Never is a foe a friend—no, not in death.

Antigone   Not in their hates, but in their loves would I join.

Creon   Go, then, to the world below and love them, if thou must. But while I live, no woman shall rule me.

Chorus   Lo, here forth from the doors comes Ismene, shedding tears of sisterly love; a cloud on her brow lowers over her flushed face, and bedews her lovely cheek.

Creon   Thou, too, who lurking in my house like a viper, hast secretly been draining my life-blood—and I knew not that I was harboring two pests to rise against my throne. Come, tell me now, wilt thou say that thou, too, hadst a part in this burial, or wilt thou deny on oath all knowledge?

Ismene   I have done the deed—if she concurs—and I bear with her the burden of the charge.

Antigone   Nay, Justice will not suffer thee to do this; for thou wouldst naught of the deed, nor did I share it with thee.

Ismene   Yet, in thy ills, I am not ashamed to be thy fellow-voyager on this troubled sea.

Antigone   Whose was the deed, Hades knows and those below. I love not a friend who loves in words alone.

Ismene   Nay, sister, refuse me not the boon of dying with thee and honoring the dead.

Antigone   Die not thou with me, nor make thine own what thou didst not touch. 'Tis enough that I die.

Ismene   But what life is dear to me, bereft of thee?

Antigone   Ask Creon; 'tis for him thou carest.

Ismene   Why pain me thus, when thou hast naught to gain?

Antigone   Nay, if I mock thee, 'tis with pain I mock.

Ismene   How can I serve thee even now?

Antigone   Save thyself; I begrudge not thy escape.

Ismene   Ah, wretched me! Am I not to share thy fate?

Antigone   No, thou didst choose to live, I to die.

Ismene   Yet my warning words were not unspoken.

Antigone   To some thou seemedst wise; to others, I.

Ismene   And yet the offense is the same for us both.

Antigone   Take heart; thou livest; but my life has long been dead, that I might serve the dead.

Creon   Of these two girls, the one, look you, hath but lately shown herself a fool; the other hath ever been such.

Ismene   Aye, Sire, for the mind one hath by nature abides not with the wretched, but wanders afield.

Creon   As did thine, when thou chosest to act basely with the base.

Ismene   But what life is bearable for me, bereft of her?

Creon   Speak not of "her"; she lives no more.

Ismene   But wilt thou slay the betrothed of thine own son?

Creon   Aye, there are other fields that may be plowed.

Ismene   But never such a union as linked him to her.

Creon   I loathe an evil wife for son of mine.

Antigone   O, Haemon, beloved! How thy father wrongs thee!

Creon   Thou dost but vex me—thou and thy marriage.

Chorus   Wilt thou indeed rob thy son of this maid?

Creon   'Tis Death that shall put a stop to these nuptials for me.

Chorus   'Tis fixed, it seems, that she must die.

Creon   Aye, fixed for thee and for me. *(To Attendants)* No more delays, servants, but lead them in! From now on they must be women, and not roam at large; for even the bold would fain flee, when they see Death now drawing near their life.

(Exeunt Attendants, with Antigone and Ismene.). . .

. . .ANAPAESTS

But lo, here is Haemon, thy last, thy youngest son. Is it in grief for the fate of the maid, Antigone, that he comes—of her that should have been his bride, and wroth that he is foiled in his marriage?

Creon   Soon shall we know, better than seers could tell us. My son, can it be that, hearing of the final doom of thy promised bride, thou art come in rage against thy father? Or am I loved of thee, whate'er I do?

Haemon   Father, I am thine; and thou, in thy wisdom, dost direct my mind aright, that I should follow. By me no marriage shall be deemed a prize of greater worth than thy good guidance.

Creon   Aye, son, so should thy mind be fixed, that thy father's will should rule in all things. 'Tis for this men pray to become the parents of dutiful children in their homes, that these may requite their father's foe with evil, and honor his friend even as he doth. But, if one begets unprofitable children, what wilt thou say that he hath sown, save troubles for himself and great cause for mocking for his foes?

Then do not thou, my son, at pleasure's bidding, lose thy wit for a woman's sake, knowing that this is but a chilling thing to clasp in one's arms—an evil woman to share one's bed in his home. For what wound could be more grievous than a loved one that is false? Nay, spurn her, and as though she were thy foe, let this girl fare to the house of Hades, to find a husband there. For, since I have found her, alone of all the city, openly disobedient, I will not make myself a liar to the state—I will slay her.

So let her call on Zeus, the god of kinship. For if I am to rear those of mine own kin to be unruly, surely I shall find others such. He who in his own household is a worthy man will be found righteous in the state as well. But if one transgresses, or violates the laws, or thinks to dictate to those in rule, he shall have no praise from me. No, whomsoever the city may appoint him must all obey, in things small and great, in things just and unjust. And he who thus obeys would, I am sure, prove a good ruler, as he proves a good subject, and in the storm of spears would stand his ground where stationed, a trusty and stalwart comrade.

But disobedience is the greatest of ills. This ruins cities; this wastes homes; this breaks allied ranks that they flee in rout; but of those who prosper, the most owe their safety to obedience. Therefore must support be rendered to the cause of law and order, and we must in no wise be worsted by a woman. Better, if fall we must, to fall by the hand of a man; so shall we not be called weaker than womankind.

Chorus To us, unless through age we are bereft of wit, thou seemest to say with reason what thou sayest.

Haemon Father, the gods plant reason in men, which of all possessions is the highest. Now in what respect thou speakest not aright, I could not say, nor may I ever seek to say.

And yet it might be that another, too, is right. In any case it is my natural part to watch, on thy behalf, all that men say, or do, or find to blame. For thine eye brings fear to the citizen, lest he speak words such as thou wouldst be displeased to hear; yet I may hear these sayings in the dark—even the wailing of the city for this maid. "Of all womankind," 'tis said, "she least deserves her fate—a death most shameful for deeds most glorious. She, when her own brother had fallen amid bloodshed, would not leave him unburied to be torn by savage dogs, or any bird—is not she worthy of golden honor?" Such is the dark rumor that goes its secret way.

For me, my father, nothing I have is more precious than thy welfare. For what is greater glory for children than a thriving father's fair name, or for a father than his son's? Bear not, then, one belief only in thy heart, that what thou sayest, and naught else, is right. For whoso thinks that he alone is wise, or that in tongue or mind he excels all others—such an one, when laid open, is found empty.

Nay, though a man be wise, 'tis no shame for him to learn much and not be over-firm. Beside the wintry torrents thou seest how many trees bend down and save their very twigs; but those that stand unyielding, perish root and branch. So he who draws his vessel's sheet taut and slackens not, capsizes his boat and thenceforth sails with upturned benches. Nay, abate thy wrath and suffer thyself to change. For if I, the younger, may proffer an opinion, I deem it far best that by nature man should in all respects abound in wisdom; but failing that—and the balance is not wont so to incline—'tis well, also, to learn from those who counsel aright.

HERODOTUS (CA. 485–CA. 425 B.C.)
The History

*B*orn in Dorian Halicarnassus, in Caria, Asia Minor, Herodotus, son of Lyxes and Dryo, was forced to flee from his homeland by the tyrant Lygdamis. After a sojourn on Samos, he lived for years in Athens, friend to Sophocles and Pericles. He signed up as a colonist to Thurii, in southern Italy, where he completed his writings after traveling throughout the length and breadth of the known world. He reports his observations on North Africa, southern Russia, Egypt, Mesopotamia, and Scythia, on the Black Sea. Known as the "father of history," his public recitations inspired the young Thucydides to become a historian.

- His *History of the Persian Wars* is not only the story of the military and naval conflict between the Greeks and the Persians leading up to Xerxes' invasion of Greece, but is also a comprehensive survey of the world as the Greeks knew it in all its richness of religions and societies, political systems and mythologies. The *History* is the first major work in prose, its Ionic style combining the authority of epic with qualities later associated with the novel. In Herodotus' mind, the historian's duty is to report what he sees and hears without judging, allowing his reader to make final selections regarding what and what not to believe. His prejudice was clearly in favor of the "personal" motivation of history, ascribing the initiation and outcome of events primarily to the personalities of those involved in them. He believes that human life is governed by Providence, and that men bring the wrath of the gods down upon themselves when their behavior is morally excessive.
- Unlike Thucydides, Herodotus writes a rambling and digression-filled narrative. He has also been called the "father of anthropology" because he is fascinated with all the details of the cultures he observed. His is an inherent sense of drama that makes for compelling reading; and an appreciation for beauty and goodness wherever he finds them. What might seem, to the impatient and to the worshipers of objectivity, to be his vices, are precisely Herodotus' virtues. The digressions and "footnotes," as well as the admittedly subjective lens through which he observes and reflects, provide the most enjoyable and memorable passages of the nine books. Without them we would be deprived of knowledge of the folklore and customs of the nations surrounding the Greek world in antiquity.

BOOK VII—THERMOPYLAE. HERE THE SPARTANS, UNDER LEONIDAS, MADE THEIR MEMORABLE STAND AGAINST THE PERSIANS, IN 480 B.C.

King Xerxes pitched his camp in the region of Malis called Trachinia, while on their side the Greeks occupied the straits. These straits the Greeks in general call Thermopylae (the Hot Gates); but the natives, and those who dwell in the neighborhood, called them Pylae (the Gates). Here then the two armies took their stand; the one master of all the region lying north of Trachis, the other of the country extending

"Delphi, from the theater"

southward of that place to the verge of the continent.

The Greeks who at this spot awaited the coming of Xerxes were the following: From Sparta, 300 men-at-arms; from Arcadia, 1,000; Tegeans and Mantineans, 500 of each people; 120 Orchomenians, from the Arcadian Orchomenus; and 1,000 from other cities: from Corinth, 400 men: from Phlius, 200; and from Mycenae, eighty. Such was the number from the Peloponnese. There were also present, from Boeotia, 700 Thespians and 400 Thebans.

Besides these troops, the Locrians of Opus and the Phocians had obeyed the call of their countrymen, and sent, the former all the force they had, the latter 1,000 men. For envoys had gone from the Greeks at Thermopylae among the Locrians and Phocians, to call on them for assistance, and to say, "They were themselves but the vanguard of the host, sent to precede the main body, which might every day be expected to follow them. The sea was in good keeping, watched by the Athenians, the Aeginetans, and the rest of the fleet. There was no cause why they should fear; for after all the invader was not a god but a man; and there never had been, and never would be, a man who was not liable to misfortunes from the very day of his birth, and those greater in proportion to his own greatness. The assailant therefore, being only a mortal, must needs fall from his glory." Thus urged, the Locrians and the Phocians had come with their troops to Trachis.

The various nations had each captains of their own under whom they served; but the one to whom all especially looked up, and who had the command of the entire force, was the Lacedaemonian, Leonidas. Now Leonidas was the son of Anaxandridas, who was the son of Leo, who was the son of Eurycratidas, who was the son of Naxander, who was the son of Eurycrates, who was the son of Polydorus, who was the son of Alcamenes, who was the son of Tele-cles, who was the son of Archelaus, who was the son of Agesilaus, who was the son of Doryssus, who was the son of Labotas, who was the son of Echestratus, who was the son of Agis, who was the son of Eurysthenes, who was the son of Aristodemus, who was the son of Aristom-achus, who was the son of Cleodaeus, who was the son of Hyllus, who was the son of Heracles.

Leonidas had come to be king of Sparta quite unexpectedly. Having two elder brothers, Cleomenes and Dorieus, he had no thought of ever mounting the throne. However, when Cleomenes died without male offspring, as Dorieus was likewise deceased, having perished in Sicily, the crown fell to Leonidas, who was older than Cleombrotus, the youngest of the sons of Anaxandridas, and, moreover, was mar-ried to the daughter of Cleomenes. He had now come to Thermopylae, accompanied by the 300 men which the law assigned him, whom he had himself chosen from among the citizens, and who were all of them fathers with sons living. On his way he had taken the troops from Thebes, whose number I have already mentioned, and who were under the command of Leontiades the son of Eurymachus. The rea-son why he made a point of taking troops from Thebes and Thebes only, was that the Thebans were strongly suspected of being well inclined to the Medes. Leonidas therefore called on them to come with him to the war, wishing to see whether they would comply with his de-mand, or openly refuse, and disclaim the Greek alliance. They, however, though their wishes leaned the other way, nevertheless sent the men.

The force with Leonidas was sent forward by the Spartans in advance of their main body, that the sight of them might encourage the al-lies to fight, and hinder them from going over to the Medes, as it was likely they might have done had they seen Sparta backward. They in-tended presently, when they had celebrated the Carneian festival, which was what now kept them at home, to leave a garrison in Sparta, and hasten in full force to join the army. The rest of the allies also intended to act similarly; for it happened that the Olympic festival fell exactly at this same period. None of them looked to see the contest at Thermopylae de-cided so speedily; wherefore they were content to send forward a mere advanced guard. Such accordingly were the intentions of the allies.

The Greek forces at Thermopylae, when the Persian army drew near to the entrance of the pass, were seized with fear, and a council was held to consider about a retreat. It was the wish of the Peloponnesians generally that the army should fall back upon the Peloponnese, and there guard the Isthmus. But Leonidas, who saw with what indignation the Phocians and Locrians heard of this plan, gave his voice for remaining where they were, while they sent en-voys to the several cities to ask for help, since they were too few to make a stand against an army like that of the Medes.

While this debate was going on, Xerxes sent a mounted spy to observe the Greeks, and note how many they were, and what they were doing. He had heard, before he came out of Thessaly, that a few men were assembled at this place, and that at their head were certain Lacedaemonians, under Leonidas, a descendant of Heracles. The horseman rode up to the camp, and looked about him, but did not see the whole army; for such as were on the further side of the wall (which had been rebuilt and was now carefully guarded) it was not possible for him to behold; but he observed those on the outside, who were encamped in front of the rampart. It chanced that at this time the Lacedaemonians held the outer guard, and were seen by the spy, some of them engaged in gymnastic exercises, others combing their long hair. At this the spy greatly marveled, but he counted their number, and when he had taken accurate note of everything, he rode back quietly; for no one pursued after him, or paid any heed to his visit. So he returned, and told Xerxes all that he had seen.

Upon this, Xerxes, who had no means of surmising the truth—namely, that the Spartans were preparing to do or die manfully—but thought it laughable that they should be engaged in such employments, sent and called to his presence Demaratus the son of Ariston, who still remained with the army. When he appeared, Xerxes told him all that he had heard, and questioned him concerning the news, since he was anxious to understand the meaning of such behavior on the part of the Spartans. Then Demaratus said, "I spoke to you, O King, concerning these men long since, when we had just begun our march upon Greece; you, however, only laughed at my words, when I told you of all this, which I saw would come to pass. Earnestly do I struggle at all times, to speak the truth to you, sire; and now listen to it once more. These men have come to dispute the pass with us, and it is for this that they are now making ready. It is their custom, when they are about to hazard their lives, to adorn their heads with care. Be assured, however, that if you can subdue the men who are here and the Lacedaemonians who remain in Sparta, there is no other nation in all the world which will venture to lift a hand in their defense. You have now to deal with the first kingdom and town in Greece, and with the bravest men."

Then Xerxes, to whom what Demaratus said seemed altogether to surpass belief, asked further, "How was it possible for so small an army to contend with his?"

"Oh King," Demaratus answered, "let me be treated as a liar, if matters fall not out as I say."

But Xerxes was not persuaded any the more. Four whole days he suffered to go by, expecting that the Greeks would run away. When, however, he found on the fifth that they were not gone, thinking that their firm stand was mere impudence and recklessness, he grew wroth, and sent against them the Medes and Cissians, with orders to take them alive and bring them into his presence. Then the Medes rushed forward and charged the Greeks, but fell in vast numbers: others however took the places of the slain, and would not be beaten off, though they suffered terrible losses. In this way it became clear to all, and especially to the king, that though he had plenty of combatants, he had but very few warriors. The struggle, however, continued during the whole day.

Then the Medes, having met so rough a reception, withdrew from the fight; and their place was taken by the band of Persians under Hydarnes, whom the king called his Immortals: they, it was thought, would soon finish the business. But when they joined battle with the Greeks, it was with no better success than the Median detachment—things went much as before—the two armies fighting in a narrow space, and the barbarians using shorter spears than the Greeks, and having no advantage from their numbers. The Lacedaemonians fought in a way worthy of note, and showed themselves far more skillful in fight than their adversaries, often turning their backs, and making as though they were all flying away, on which the barbarians would rush after them with much noise and shouting, when the Spartans at their approach would wheel round and face their pursuers, in this way destroying vast numbers of the enemy. Some Spartans likewise fell in these encounters, but only a very few. At last the Persians, finding that all their efforts to gain the pass availed nothing, and that whether they attacked by divisions or in any other way, it was to no purpose, withdrew to their own quarters.

During these assaults, it is said that Xerxes, who was watching the battle, thrice leaped from the throne on which he sat, in terror for his army.

Next day the combat was renewed, but with no better success on the part of the barbarians. The Greeks were so few that the barbarians hoped to find them disabled, by reason of their wounds, from offering any further resistance; and so they once more attacked them. But the Greeks were drawn up in detachments according to their cities, and bore the brunt of the battle in turns, all except the Phocians, who had been stationed on the mountain to guard

the pathway. So when the Persians found no difference between that day and the preceding, they again retired to their quarters.

Now, as the king was at a loss, and knew not how he should deal with the emergency, Ephialtes, the son of Eurydemus, a man of Malis, came to him and was admitted to a conference. Stirred by the hope of receiving a rich reward at the king's hands, he had come to tell him of the pathway which led across the mountain to Thermopylae; by which disclosure he brought destruction on the band of Greeks who had there withstood the barbarians. This Ephialtes afterwards, from fear of the Lacedaemonians, fled into Thessaly; and during his exile, in an assembly of the Amphictyons held at Pylae, a price was set upon his head by the Pylagorae. When some time had gone by, he returned from exile, and went to Anticyra, where he was slain by Athenades, a native of Trachis. Athenades did not slay him for his treachery, but for another reason, which I shall mention in a later part of my history: yet still the Lacedaemonians honored him none the less. Thus did then Ephialtes perish a long time afterwards.

Besides this there is another story told, which I do not at all believe, that Onetas the son of Phanagoras, a native of Carystus, and Corydallus, a man of Anticyra, were the persons who spoke on this matter to the king, and took the Persians across the mountain. One may guess which story is true, from the fact that the deputies of the Greeks, the Pylagorae, who must have had the best means of ascertaining the truth, did not offer the reward for the heads of Onetas and Corydallus, but for that of Ephialtes of Trachis; and again from the flight of Ephialtes, which we know to have been on this account. Onetas, I allow, although he was not a Malian, might have been acquainted with the path, if he had lived much in that part of the country; but as Ephialtes was the person who actually led the Persians around the mountain by the pathway, I leave his name on record as that of the man who did the deed.

Great was the joy of Xerxes on this occasion; and as he approved highly of the enterprise which Ephialtes undertook to accomplish, he forthwith sent upon the errand Hydarnes, and the Persians under him. The troops left the camp about the time of the lighting of the lamps. The pathway along which they went was first discovered by the Malians of these parts, who soon afterwards led the Thessalians by it to attack the Phocians, at the time when the Phocians fortified the pass with a wall, and so put themselves under covert from danger. And ever since, the path has always been put to an ill use by the Malians.

The course which it takes is the following: Beginning at the Asopus, where the stream flows through the cleft in the hills, it runs along the ridge of the mountain (which is called, like the pathway over it, Anopaea), and ends at the city of Alpenus—the first Locrian town as you come from Malis—by the stone called Black-buttock and the seats of the Cercopians. Here it is as narrow as at any other point.

The Persians took this path, and crossing the Asopus, continued their march through the whole of the night, having the mountains of Oeta on their right hand, and on their left those of Trachis. At dawn of day they found themselves close to the summit. Now the hill was guarded, as I have already said, by 1,000 Phocian men-at-arms, who were placed there to defend the pathway, and at the same time to secure their own country. They had been given the guard of the mountain path, while the other Greeks defended the pass below, because they had volunteered for the service, and had pledged themselves to Leonidas to maintain the post.

The ascent of the Persians became known to the Phocians in the following manner: During all the time that they were making their way up, the Greeks remained unconscious of it, inasmuch as the whole mountain was covered with groves of oak; but it happened that the air was very still, and the leaves which the Persians stirred with their feet made, as it was likely they would, a loud rustling, whereupon the Phocians jumped up and flew to seize their arms. In a moment the barbarians came in sight, and perceiving men arming themselves, were greatly amazed; for they had fallen in with an enemy when they expected no opposition. Hydarnes, alarmed at the sight, and fearing lest the Phocians might be Lacedaemonians, inquired of Ephialtes to what nation these troops belonged. Ephialtes told him the exact truth, whereupon he arrayed his Persians for battle. The Phocians, galled by the showers of arrows to which they were exposed, and imagining themselves the special object of the Persian attack, fled hastily to the crest of the mountain, and there made ready to meet death; but while their mistake continued, the Persians, with Ephialtes and Hydarnes, not thinking it worth their while to delay on account of the Phocians, passed on and descended the mountain with all possible speed.

The Greeks at Thermopylae received the

first warning of the destruction which the dawn would bring on them from the seer Megistias, who read their fate in the victims as he was sacrificing. After this deserters came in, and brought the news that the Persians were marching round by the hills: it was still night when these men arrived. Last of all, scouts came running down from the heights, and brought in the same accounts, when the day was just beginning to break. Then the Greeks held a council to consider what they should do, and here opinions were divided: some were strong against quitting their post, while others contended to the contrary. So when the council had broken up, part of the troops departed and went their ways homeward to their several states; part, however, resolved to remain, and stand by Leonidas to the last.

It is said that Leonidas himself sent away the troops who departed, because he tendered their safety, but thought it unseemly that either he or his Spartans should quit the post which they had been especially sent to guard. For my own part, I incline to think that Leonidas gave the order, because he perceived the allies to be out of heart and unwilling to encounter the danger to which his own mind was made up. He therefore commanded them to retreat, but said that he himself could not draw back with honor; knowing that, if he stayed, glory awaited him, and that Sparta in that case would not lose her prosperity. For when the Spartans, at the very beginning of the war, sent to consult the oracle concerning it, the answer which they received from the priestess was that either Sparta must be overthrown by the barbarians, or one of her kings must perish. The prophecy was delivered in hexameter verse, and ran thus:

Oh! ye men who dwell in the streets of broad
    Lacedaemon,
Either your glorious town shall be sacked by
    the children of Perseus
Or, in exchange, must all through the whole
    Laconian country
Mourn for the loss of a king, descendant of
    great Heracles.
He cannot be withstood by the courage of
    bulls or of lions,
Strive as they may; he is mighty as Zeus; there
    is nought that shall stay him
Till he have got for his prey your king, or your
    glorious city.

The remembrance of this answer, I think, and the wish to secure the whole glory for the Spartans, caused Leonidas to send the allies away. This is more likely than that they quarreled with him, and took their departure in such unruly fashion.

To me it seems no small argument in favor of this view, that the seer also who accompanied the army, Megistias, the Acarnanian, said to have been of the blood of Melampus, and the same who was led by the appearance of the victims to warn the Greeks of the danger which threatened them, received orders to retire (as it is certain he did) from Leonidas, that he might escape the coming destruction. Megistias, however, though bidden to depart, refused, and stayed with the army; but he had an only son present with the expedition, whom he now sent away.

So the allies, when Leonidas ordered them to retire, obeyed him and forthwith departed. Only the Thespians and the Thebans remained with the Spartans; and of these the Thebans were kept back by Leonidas as hostages, very much against their will. The Thespians, on the contrary, stayed entirely of their own accord, refusing to retreat, and declaring that they would not forsake Leonidas and his followers. So they abode with the Spartans, and died with them. Their leader was Demophilus, the son of Diadromes.

At sunrise Xerxes made libations, after which he waited until the time when the marketplace is wont to fill, and then began his advance. Ephialtes had instructed him thus, as the descent of the mountain is much quicker, and the distance much shorter, than the way around the hills, and the ascent. So the barbarians under Xerxes began to draw nigh; and the Greeks under Leonidas, as they now went forth determined to die, advanced much further than on previous days, until they reached the more open portion of the pass. Hitherto they had held their station within the wall, and from this had gone forth to fight at the point where the pass was the narrowest. Now they joined battle beyond the defile, and carried slaughter among the barbarians, who fell in heaps. Behind them the captains of the squadrons, armed with whips, urged their men forward with continual blows. Many were thrust into the sea, and there perished; no one heeded the dying. For the Greeks, reckless of their own safety and desperate, since they knew that, as the mountain had been crossed, their destruction was nigh at hand, exerted themselves with the most furious valor against the barbarians.

By this time the spears of the greater number were all shivered, and with their swords they hewed down the ranks of the Persians; and here, as they strove, Leonidas fell fighting bravely, together with many other famous Spartans, whose names I have taken care to learn on account of their great worthiness, as indeed I have those of all the 300. There fell too at the same time very many famous Persians: among them, two sons of Darius, Abrocomes and Hyperanthes, his children by Phratagune, the daughter of Artanes. Artanes was brother of King Darius, being a son of Hystaspes, the son of Arsames; and when he gave his daughter to the king, he made him heir likewise of all his substance; for she was his only child.

Thus two brothers of Xerxes here fought and fell. And now there arose a fierce struggle between the Persians and the Lacedaemonians over the body of Leonidas, in which the Greeks four times drove back the enemy, and at last by their great bravery succeeded in bearing off the body. This combat was scarcely ended when the Persians with Ephialtes approached; and the Greeks, informed that they drew nigh, made a change in the manner of their fighting. Drawing back into the narrowest part of the pass, and retreating even behind the cross wall, they posted themselves upon a hillock, where they stood all drawn up together in one close body, except only the Thebans. The hillock whereof I speak is at the entrance of the straits, where the stone lion stands which was set up in honor of Leonidas. Here they defended themselves to the last, such as still had swords using them, and the others resisting with their hands and teeth; till the barbarians, who in part had pulled down the wall and attacked them in front, in part had gone round and now encircled them upon every side, overwhelmed and buried the remnant left beneath showers of missile weapons.

Thus nobly did the whole body of Lacedaemonians and Thespians behave, but nevertheless one man is said to have distinguished himself above all the rest, to wit, Dieneces the Spartan. A speech which he made before the Greeks engaged the Medes remains on record. One of the Trachinians told him, "Such was the number of the barbarians, than when they shot forth their arrows the sun would be darkened by their multitude." Dieneces, not at all frightened at these words, but making light of the Median numbers, answered, "Our Trachinian friend brings us excellent tidings. If the Medes darken the sun, we shall have our fight in the shade." Other sayings too of a like nature are said to have been left on record by this same person.

Next to him two brothers, Lacedaemonians, are reputed to have made themselves conspicuous: they were named Alpheus and Maro, and were the sons of Orsiphantus. There was also a Thespian who gained greater glory than any of his countrymen: he was a man called Dithyrambus, the son of Harmatidas.

The slain were buried where they fell; and in their honor, nor less in honor of those who died before Leonidas sent the allies away, an inscription was set up which said:

Here did four thousand men from Pelops' land
Against three hundred myriads bravely stand.

This was in honor of all. Another was for the Spartans alone:

Go, stranger, and to Lacedaemon tell
That here, obeying her behests, we fell.

This was for the Lacedaemonians. The seer had the following:

The great Megistias' tomb you here may view,
Whom slew the Medes, fresh from Spercheius'
fords.
Well the wise seer the coming death foreknew,
Yet scorned he to forsake his Spartan lords.

These inscriptions, and the pillars likewise, were all set up by the Amphictyons, except that in honor of Megistias, which was inscribed to him (on account of their sworn friendship) by Simonides, the son of Leoprepes.

ZENO (FL. 450 B.C.)
On Motion

*K*nown as "Zeno of Elea" because he was born, the son of Teleutagoras, in that city of southern Italy, Zeno studied with Parmenides and went to Athens with him in 450 B.C. Plato referred to him as "Parmenides' son" because the two men were inseparable. Strabo considered him a Pythagorean.

- Zeno's writings, of which only fragments survive, defend his master's argument that only "an unchangeable one" exists—against philosophers believing in multiplicity and pluralism. His defense is primarily based on examples dealing with motion, space, and arithmetic magnitude.
- He is remembered primarily for his "paradigms," dealing with motion:

  - Achilles and the tortoise, as Aristotle records Zeno's argument: "The slow runner will never be overtaken by the swiftest, for it is necessary that the pursuer should first reach the point from which the pursued started, so that necessarily the slower is always somewhat in advance."
  - An arrow going from point a to point b. An arrow can never get from point a to point b, as Simplicius records Zeno's argument: "The arrow which is moving forward is at every present moment in a space equal to itself, accordingly it is in a space equal to itself in all time; but that which is in a space equal to itself in the present moment is not in motion. Accordingly it is in a state of rest, since it is not moved in the present moment, and that which is not moving is at rest, since everything is either in motion or at rest. So the arrow which is moving forward is at rest while it is moving forward, in every moment of its motion."
  - A man crossing a stadium can never actually cross the stadium. First, he would have to get halfway there; but before that, a quarter of the way there; but before that, an eighth, etc., ad infinitum. Therefore he can never get from a to b. His motion is an illusion, for the same reasoning. The Roman response to this paradigm of Zeno's: *"Solvitur ambulando"* (the problem is "solved by walking").

1. If any one explains . . . the *one*, what it is, [he] can tell him what things are.
2. What is is not increased by receiving additions, or decreased as parts are taken away.
3. A man who affirms multiplicity naturally falls into contradictions.
4. If there are many things, these are both great and small—great enough to be infinite in size, and small enough to be nothing in size. . . . that what has neither greatness nor thickness nor bulk could not ever be.
5. Nothing has any greatness because each thing of the many is identical with itself and is one.
6. If anything were added to another being, it could not make it any greater; for since greatness does not exist, it is impossible to increase the greatness of a thing by adding to it. So that which is added would be nothing. If when something is taken away that which is left is no less, and if it becomes no greater by receiving additions, evidently that which has been added or taken away is nothing.
7. If there is a multiplicity of things, it is necessary that these should be just as many as exist, not more nor fewer. If there are just as many as there are, then the number would be finite. If there is a multiplicity at all, the number is infinite, for there are always others between any two, and yet others between each pair of these. So the number of things is infinite.
8. If being did not have magnitude, it would not exist at all . . . if anything exists, it is necessary that each thing should have some magnitude and thickness, and that one part of it should be separated from another. The same argument applies to the thing that precedes this. That also will have magnitude and will have something before it. The same may be said of each thing once for all, for there will be no such thing as last, nor will one thing differ from another. So if there is a multiplicity of things, it is necessary that these should be great and small—small enough not to have any magnitude, and great enough to be infinite.
9. If there is such a thing as place, it will be in something, for all being is in something, and that which is in something is in some place. Then this place will be in a place, and so on indefinitely. Accordingly there is no such thing as place.
10. The earth does not move, and . . . space is void of content. . . . That which is moved is moved in the place in which it is, or in the place in which it is not; it is neither moved in the place in which it is, nor in the place in which it is not; accordingly it is not moved at all.
11. The one is universal . . . it exists alone, eternal, and unlimited.
12. The all is unmoved.

EURIPIDES (480–405 B.C.)
Alcestis

The third of the great Athenian dramatists, Euripides was educated in gymnastics and philosophy and once served as a priest at Phyla. He was a close friend of Socrates, and an associate of Anaxagoras, Protagoras, and the sophist Prodicos as well. For most of his productive life, he wrote in relative seclusion in Salamis, where, on the day of a great naval battle, he was born the son of the taverner Mnesarchides and the herbalist Cleito. He was married twice, first to Choerile, then to Melito. He died in the Macedonian court of Archelaus at Pella.

Euripides first competed in the Dionysian festival in 455 B.C., winning his first prize for tragedy in 441 B.C. at the age of forty-three. Although he won only four prizes, his ninety-two plays became even more popular than those of Aeschylus and Sophocles. In retrospect, we consider them to be the most modern, in their psychological insight and sensitivity to the feminine principle. Nineteen of his plays survived.

- Euripides' favorite theme is the moral repercussions of human relationships, with particular interest in the emotional and psychological reactions of passionate women. He wrote, as translator Paul Roche puts it, about "war, women, and God." His most important plays include *Medea, Hippolytus, Ion, The Trojan Women, The Suppliant Women, Elektra, Iphigeneia at Aulis,* and *The Bacchae.*
- Reflecting a time when intellectual interest was focused on the nature of man rather than of the divine, Euripides takes liberties with the established myth in order to pursue his psychological explorations of character. Even the gods are presented with human motivations. Aristotle, in his *Poetics,* considered him to be the most tragic of the tragic dramatists. He was also the most sentimental. Unlike the lyric language of Aeschylus and the philosophical ritual of Sophocles, the language of Euripides is realistic and deceptively commonplace—though able to rise to heights of emotion through its jarring asymmetries and chaotic forms.
- The naturalistic idiom of prose proved highly suitable to Euripides' greater emphasis on actual dialogue between actors, adding both subtlety and clarity to his dialogue. Euripides' men, as they grapple with the stuff of their very being, exist as center points in a profound tension between life and death, and between the disorder of life with its necessary earthly limits and an assumed order of universal necessity that decrees that life continue even though men die in an inexorable but invisible pattern. This inherent ambivalence in human existence strikes the keynote to Euripides' portrayal of man's inescapable irrationality.

- The earliest of his surviving plays is *Alcestis*. Its hero, King Admetus, is given the chance to postpone his death if he can find someone to die in his place. His wife, Queen Alcestis, volunteers. Her dying request, which Admetus must swear to on their children: that he will never marry again. What feels like a triumph for Admetus quickly turns to gloom and despair—not only for the king himself, whose life after her death seems not worth living, but also for his kingdom, which suffers from his loss of vitality. Royal marriage is necessary for happy kingdoms. Into the mix comes Herakles, who arrives as a guest and in a state of Dionysian intoxication convinces Admetus to go on living by taking the hand of a "veiled woman" he claims is Alcestis. Rather than a story about the resurrection of Alcestis, this subtle play is about the need for the living to go on living and to "let the dead bury their dead." It is a hybrid of comedy and tragedy, for though the premise is tragic, it ends, like Old Comedy, with a *gamos* (marriage) which restores happiness to the previously moribund kingdom.

FOURTH EPISODE

Admetus Oh, my return to my home is return to lament
Oh, the emptiness left in unwelcoming rooms!
Go where? Be where? What say? What not?
I wish I were dead.
What doom-laden womb, what mother produced me?
I yearn for the shades. I lust after phantoms.
Theirs are the homes I crave to indwell.
The joy in my eyes is a light gone dim.
The joy in the tread of my feet is gone.
Death has cleft from me half my life:
Traded to Hades.

CHORAL DIALOGUE

Chorus Enter, enter into your home's retreat.

STROPHE 1

Admetus Aiai!

Chorus You've suffered enough to make you cry.

Admetus Weep. Aiai!

Chorus I understand. I know the ordeal.

Admetus Heave. Aiai!

Chorus It is no help to her below.

Admetus Grieve. Aiai!

Chorus To miss forever the face of your beloved
Is bitter indeed.

Admetus The mere recall of it batters my
  heart.
What greater pain can any man face
Than suffer the loss of a faithful wife?
I wish I had never married or lived
Inside this house with her I loved.
I covet the ones who never wed:
The childless ones—their single life
Only a measured grief begets.
The ills of children, the nuptial bed
Scattered by death, are all regrets
Compared to lives that can be led
Single and with no child instead.

Chorus Fate, fate, ineluctable fate!

ANTI-STROPHE 1

Admetus Aiai!

Chorus Your lamentation has no limit.

Admetus Cry. Aiai!

Chorus It is a bitter load to bear, but . . .

Admetus Heave. Aiai!

"Theater of Herod, Athens"

Chorus Bear up, you're not the first to
   lose . . .

Admetus Grieve. Aiai!

Chorus A wife. Disaster strikes in many a
   guise
At other mortals and in other ways.

Admetus The long sorrow, love's lost lament
For those under the ground . . .
Why did you hold me back from the leap
Into the grave that gaped,
There to lie dead with her
Who has no human peer?
Hades would then have been able to take
Two devoted souls, not one,
To cross the land of the nether lake.

STROPHE 2

Chorus There was in my own
Family a man whose only son
Died in his home:
A youth well worth his tears.
Yet *he* measured his grief, this childless man,
Although his locks had turned
White and he had gone
Far into life.

Admetus [*unable to proceed into the house*]
   This palace, my
   home, how shall I go in?
How shall I dwell with luck's reverse:
Everything changed, everything worse?
Once by torchlight, wedding songs ringing,
Holding her hand, I went in.
And after us came the revelers singing,

Cheering my dead one, cheering me.
A beautiful couple, that we were
And seen to be
Noble and rich.
But now instead of the wedding march
and glittering clothes, you send me in
Vested in dark
To a lonely, dismal, empty couch.

ANTI-STROPHE 2

Chorus To shatter your bliss
This unrehearsable sorrow struck.
Nevertheless
It saved your life and soul.
Your consort has gone, deserted her love.
Is this so strange? Many a man
Death has divided from his spouse.

Admetus Friends, my wife's fate is happier
   than mine,
I think, although it might not seem to be:
for now no pain shall ever touch her—
a thousand worries she has stopped with glory.
But I, who have not title to be living,
have overstepped my mark and must drag out
a bitter life . . . I realize it now.
   How shall I bear to go into my empty home?
   Whom shall I greet inside? By whom be
      welcomed?
   Which way to look?
   The wilderness in there shall drive me out:
the empty bed, her favorite seats, their very
      sight;
the floors unswept throughout the house;
then the children clinging to my lap and
      crying
for their mother.

And the servants all in tears
for that tender queen this house has lost.
   Thus will it be at home,
but in the world outside . . . ah!
Young unmarried women with weddings in
    their eyes
will frighten me away—
buzzing around in female swarms . . .
No, I shall not be able to brave the sight
of my wife's compeers.
   And those who have no time for me
will seize their chance and say:
   "Look, the cheap coward
alive and well, who ran away from death:
so small he got his wife to die instead . . .
Is he a man, do you think? He execrates his
    parents
but could not die himself."
   Yes, that's the charming reputation I shall
    earn,
on top of all my sorrows.
   Tell me, dear friends,
is there any point in going on—
with such a reputation, such a record?

THIRD CHORAL ODE

[*The Chorus sings of implacable Necessity and
the impossibility of raising the dead. And yet Alcestis' choice was beautiful*]

STROPHE 1

High as the Muses I
Have sung and searched the sky
Where great ideas lie
But never have found as yet
A greater thing than fate.
Nor any drug in Thrace
Listed or engraved

By Orpheus; not his voice,
Nor what Apollo gave
Asclepius and his race.
No anodyne that can
Cure the fate of man.

ANTI-STROPHE 1

Necessity alone
Although she is divine
Is approached by none
Through effigy or shrine.
She heeds no sacrifice.
O Mistress, do not move
To make me less alive,
For even mighty Zeus
Needs you to fulfill
His work and so his will.
Chalybian steel
Is far less hard, for she'll
Bend to none or feel
Soft for us.

STROPHE 2

And now in the vice of her grip,
Admetus, she has you fast.
Bear it, for never will weeping
Raise the gone from the dead.
Even the children of gods
Death fades into his shades.
Loved she was among us
Loved will she be though dead.
The noblest woman you could
Harness to your bed.

ANTI-STROPHE 2

Never think of her tomb as the same
As the mounds of the dead gone by
But more like a shrine of the gods

And a pilgrim's place to pray.
Climbing the path that winds
A passerby will say:
"Here lies she who saved
Her consort. Now is she
A hallowed spirit. I
Salute you, Lady, bless us."
Thus will pilgrims cry.

Leader   Ah! here comes Alcmena's son,
 Admetus.
It looks as though he's making for your home.
[*Enter Heracles, leading a woman heavily
 veiled*]

EXODUS OR DENOUEMENT

Heracles   One should be candid with a
 friend, Admetus:
 not keep grudges buried deep inside.
 Coming upon you in your hour of sorrow
I might have thought to share it like a friend.
 Why then did you never tell me
the body that you had to bury was your wife's?
 You made me at home and welcomed me
as if the one you mourned were just a far-off
 friend.
 I went and wreathed my head quite merrily
and tossed libations to the gods—
all in a stricken house.
  [*wagging his finger*]
 That was reprehensible of you . . .
  reprehensible . . .
but I shall not tax you with it
seeing how great your present sufferings are.
 Well, what I've come back to tell you is:
take this woman and keep her for me please,

till I return here with the Thracian steeds,
having done Diomédes in—the Bistonians'
 king.
 If I fail to come back safe and sound,
she is yours to fetch and carry in your home.
 She came into my hands through much
  hard work.
 It was a local public contest
organized by people that I met:
a real test of strength for athletes.
 That's her origin. I took her as a prize.
The winners in the lighter heats led horses off,
 but in the major events—boxing and
  wrestling—
 the prize was cattle. A woman was thrown
 in.
 To decline such a splendid offering, once
  I'd won it,
seemed to me a shame.
 So, as I was saying,
I put this woman in your care.
 She isn't something I just grabbed:
I won her with my sweat and blood.
 In time, perhaps, you too will come to
  thank me.

Admetus   It was not to snub you, Heracles,
or antagonize you in the least,
that I hid my poor wife's fate from you,
but had you taken off and gone to stay with
 someone else,
it would have only added one anguish to
 another.
 There were tears enough for the hurt I *had*.
 As to this woman, I beg you, sir,
if it is remotely possible,
ask some other Thessalian—

one who hasn't had to face what I have—
to take care of her
     You have many friends in Pherae.
     Don't bring home my grief to me:
I could not view her in the house and keep
          from tears.
     I am sick to the heart, weighted down with
          sorrow,
do not make me sicker.
     Where, moreover, in my house
could a young woman properly be lodged . . .
for young she seems to be, from her pretty
          style and dress.
     Will the men's wing suit her for a home—
and she remain untouched lodging with young
          men?
For it is not easy, Heracles, to check a young
          man in his prime.
     I am only thinking of you.
     Or am I to intrude her into my dead wife's
          room,
lodge her there?
     But how could I? . . . Give her my own
          wife's bed?
     I recoil from the double blame that might
          bring:
the charge first from some citizen
that I was being unfaithful to the one who
          saved me,
falling into bed with another woman, and a
          young one too;
then from the deceased herself—
who so merits my adoration . . .
     Oh, I must be circumspect!
[*He turns toward the veiled figure with a start
          . . . and a deep sigh*]
     Young lady, whoever you are,

know you have the build and figure of
          Alcestis.
[*He breaks away*]
     By the gods! take the woman from my sight.
     Don't trample on a man that's down.
     For when I look at her, I'm looking at my
          wife, it seems:
my soul is in a turmoil; tears prick into my
          eyes.
     Stricken to the heart, at last I taste
the full peculiar bitterness of my fate.

Leader   There's nothing good about your lot
          that I can say.
     Heaven's visitations we must shoulder as we
          may.

Heracles   I wish I had the power
to march your consort from the mansions
          underground
back into the light, and do a kindness to you.

Admetus   I'm well aware you would. There is
          no way, however.
The dead once dead never come to light.

Heracles   Do not overshoot the mark. Take
          things quietly.

Admetus   And *that* is easier said than done.

Heracles   What good is there in endless
          grief?

Admetus   None, I know. It is a love compels
          me.

Heracles   Yes, love for the dead compels our
tears.

Admetus   Oh, she has ruined me more than I
can utter!

Heracles   You've lost a perfect wife: there's
no denying.

Admetus   So perfect, I'll not enjoy this life
again.

Heracles   Time softens things. Now your
grief is young.

Admetus   Time, you say. If only time spelled
death!

Heracles   A new bride could change all that:
the love of a woman. . . .

HIPPOCRATES (469–399 B.C.)
The Physician's Oath

Hippocrates was born on the island of Cos into the priestly temple family of Asclepiadae, whose service to the god of healing Asclepios was to preserve medical information and traditions. He was in Athens during the Peloponnesian War, where he studied with the sophists Gorgias and Prodicos, as well as with Democritus of Abdera. He died in Larissa in Thessaly.

- Like most important figures of the classical period, Hippocrates was philosophically minded, believing that a philosophical physician was godlike. One of his most famous proverbs was: "Life is brief, the craft is mighty, opportunity is fleeting, experiment perilous, judgment critical." The vigorous pursuit of both practical and theoretical knowledge was his lifelong ambition. He believed that in order to understand the parts of the body the physician must understand the whole as a functional organism. Specialized knowledge of the parts will never accomplish a satisfactory diagnosis or prognosis. Trusting in philosophical cause and effect, Hippocrates looked to natural instead of divine sources to explain sickness and disease.

- Hippocrates' instructions to his medical students are still pronounced in one form or another by today's physicians.

I swear by Apollo the physician, and Aesculapius, and Health, and All-heal, and all the gods and goddesses, that, according to my ability and judgment, I will keep this Oath and this stipulation—to reckon him who taught me this Art equally dear to me as my parents, to share my substance with him, and relieve his necessities if required; to look upon his offspring in the same footing as my own brothers, and to teach them this art, if they shall wish to learn it, without fee or stipulation; and that by precept, lecture, and every other mode of instruction, I will impart a knowledge of the Art to my own sons, and those of my teachers, and to disciples bound by a stipulation and oath according to the law of medicine, but to none others. I will follow that system of regimen which, according to my ability and judgment, I consider for the benefit of my patients, and abstain from whatever is deleterious and mischievous. I will give no deadly medicine to any one if asked, nor suggest any such counsel; and in like manner I will not give to a woman a pessary to produce abortion. With purity and with holiness I will pass my life and practice my Art. I will not cut persons laboring under the stone, but will leave this to be done by men who are practitioners of this work. Into whatever houses I enter, I will go into them for the benefit of the sick, and will abstain from every voluntary act of mischief and corruption; and, further, from the seduction of females or males, of freemen and slaves. Whatever, in connection with my professional practice or not, in connection with it, I see or hear, in the life of men, which ought not to be spoken of abroad, I will not divulge, as reckoning that all such should be kept secret.

"Lead pipe, Paestum, Magna Graecia"

While I continue to keep this Oath unviolated, may it be granted to me to enjoy life and the practice of the art, respected by all men, in all times! But should I trespass and violate this Oath, may the reverse be my lot!

- As the founder of modern scientific medicine and the most famous doctor of classical Greece, Hippocrates was associated generically with over seventy works in the Attic and Ionian dialects, though it is now believed that many of them were written by his sons and grandsons and that few of them are definitely by him. Their subject matter includes health and disease, epidemics, surgery, pharmacology, dietetics, therapeutics, prognostics, ethnography, medical ethics, and the history of medicine; and the diseases dealt with include mumps, epilepsy, heart disease, cancer, and malaria. The Hippocratic Airs, Waters, and Places was the first extensive commentary in western thought on the influence of climate and living conditions on health, intellectual accomplishment, and attitude.

ON AIRS, WATERS, AND PLACES

Whoever wishes to investigate medicine properly, should proceed thus: in the first place to consider the seasons of the year, and what effects each of them produces (for they are not at all alike, but differ much from themselves in regard to their changes). Then the winds, the hot and the cold, especially such as are common to all countries, and then such as are peculiar to each locality. We must also consider the qualities of the waters, for as they differ from one another in taste and weight, so also do they differ much in their qualities. In the same manner, when one comes into a city to which he is a stranger, he ought to consider its situation, how it lies as to the winds and the rising of the sun; for its influence is not the same whether it lies to the north or the south, to the rising or to the setting sun. These things one ought to consider most attentively, and concerning the waters which the inhabitants use, whether they be marshy and soft, or hard, and running from elevated and rocky situations, and then if saltish and unfit for cooking; and the ground, whether it be naked and deficient in water, or wooded and well watered, and whether it lies in a hollow, confined situation, or is elevated and cold; and the mode in which the inhabitants live, and what are their pursuits, whether they are fond of drinking and eating to excess, and given to indolence, or are fond of exercise and labor, and not given to excess in eating and drinking.

2. From these things he must proceed to investigate everything else. For if one knows all these things well, or at least the greater part of them, he cannot miss knowing, when he comes into a strange city, either the diseases peculiar to the place, or the particular nature of common diseases, so that he will not be in doubt as to the treatment of the diseases, or commit mistakes, as is likely to be the case provided one had not previously considered these matters. And in particular, as the season and the year advances, he can tell what epidemic diseases will attack the city, either in summer or in winter, and what each individual will be in danger of experiencing from the change of regimen. For knowing the changes of the seasons, the risings and settings of the stars, how each of them takes place, he will be able to know beforehand what sort of a year is going to ensue. Having made these investigations, and knowing beforehand the seasons, such a one must be acquainted with each particular, and must succeed in the preservation of health, and be by no means unsuccessful in the practice of his art. And if it shall be thought that these things belong rather to meteorology, it will be admitted, on second thoughts, that astronomy contributes not a little, but a very great deal, indeed, to medicine. For with the seasons the digestive organs of men undergo a change.

3. But how each of the aforementioned things should be investigated and explained, I will now declare in a clear manner. A city that is exposed to hot winds (these are between the wintry rising, and the wintry setting of the sun), and to which these are peculiar, but which is sheltered from the north winds; in such a city the waters will be plenteous and saltish, and as they run from an elevated

source, they are necessarily hot in summer, and cold in winter; the heads of the inhabitants are of a humid and pituitous constitution, and their bellies subject to frequent disorders, owing to the phlegm running down from the head; the forms of their bodies, for the most part, are rather flabby; they do not eat nor drink much; drinking wine in particular, and more especially if carried to intoxication, is oppressive to them; and the following diseases are peculiar to the district: In the first place, the women are sickly and subject to excessive menstruation; then many are unfruitful from disease, and not from nature, and they have frequent miscarriages; infants are subject to attacks of convulsions and asthma, which they consider to be connected with infancy, and hold to be a sacred disease [epilepsy]. The men are subject to attacks of dysentery, diarrhea, hepialus, chronic fevers in winter, of epinyctis, frequently, and of hemorrhoids about the anus. Pleurisies, peripneumonies, ardent fevers, and whatever diseases are reckoned acute, do not often occur, for such diseases are not apt to prevail where the bowels are loose. Ophthalmies occur of a humid character, but not of a serious nature, and of short duration, unless they attack epidemically from the change of the seasons. And when they pass their fiftieth year, defluxions supervening from the brain, render them paralytic when exposed suddenly to strokes of the sun, or to cold. These diseases are endemic to them, and, moreover, if any epidemic disease connected with the change of the seasons, prevail, they are also liable to it.

4. But the following is the condition of cities which have the opposite exposure, namely, to cold winds, between the summer settings and the summer risings of the sun, and to which these winds are peculiar, and which are sheltered from the south and the hot breezes. In the first place the waters are, for the most part, hard and cold. The men must necessarily be well braced and slender, and they must have the discharges downwards of the alimentary canal hard, and of difficult evacuation, while those upwards are more fluid, and rather bilious than pituitous. Their heads are sound and hard, and they are liable to burstings [of vessels?] for the most part. The diseases which prevail epidemically with them, are pleurisies, and those which are called acute diseases. This must be the case when the bowels are bound; and from any causes, many become affected with suppurations in the lungs, the cause of which is the tension of the body, and hardness of the bowels; for their dryness and the coldness of the water dispose them to ruptures [of vessels?]. Such constitutions must be given to excess of eating, but not of drinking; for it is not possible to be gourmands and drunkards at the same time. Ophthalmies, too, at length supervene; these being of a hard and violent nature, and soon ending in rupture of the eyes; persons under thirty years of age are liable to severe bleedings at the nose in summer; attacks of epilepsy are rare but severe. Such people are likely to be rather long-lived; their ulcers are not attended with serious discharges, nor of a malignant character; in disposition they are rather ferocious than gentle. The diseases I have mentioned are peculiar to the men, and besides they are liable to any common complaint which may be prevailing from the changes of the seasons. But the women, in the first place, are of a hard consti-

tution, from the waters being hard, indigestible, and cold; and their menstrual discharges are not regular, but in small quantity, and painful. Then they have difficult parturition, but are not very subject to abortions. And when they do bring forth children, they are unable to nurse them; for the hardness and indigestible nature of the water puts away their milk. Phthisis frequently supervenes after childbirth, for the efforts of it frequently bring on ruptures and strains. Children while still little are subject to dropsies in the testicle, which disappear as they grow older; in such a town they are late in attaining manhood. It is, as I have now stated, with regard to hot and cold winds and cities thus exposed.

5. Cities that are exposed to winds between the summer and the winter risings of the sun, and those the opposite to them, have the following characters: Those which lie to the rising of the sun are all likely to be more healthy than such as are turned to the north, or those exposed to the hot winds, even if there should not be a furlong between them. In the first place, both the heat and cold are more moderate. Then such waters as flow to the rising sun, must necessarily be clear, fragrant, soft, and delightful to drink, in such a city. For the sun in rising and shining upon them purifies them, by dispelling the vapors which generally prevail in the morning. The persons of the inhabitants are, for the most part, well colored and blooming, unless some disease counteract. The inhabitants have clear voices, and in temper and intellect are superior to those which are exposed to the north, and all the productions of the country in like manner are better. A city so situated resembles the spring as to moderation between heat and cold, and the diseases are few in number, and of a feeble kind, and bear a resemblance to the diseases which prevail in regions exposed to hot winds. The women there are very prolific, and have easy deliveries. Thus it is with regard to them.

6. But such cities as lie to the west, and which are sheltered from winds blowing from the east, and which the hot winds and the cold winds of the north scarcely touch, must necessarily be in a very unhealthy situation: In the first place the waters are not clear, the cause of which is, because the mist prevails commonly in the morning, and it is mixed up with the water and destroys its clearness, for the sun does not shine upon the water until he be considerably raised above the horizon. And in summer, cold breezes from the east blow and dews fall; and in the latter part of the day the setting sun particularly scorches the inhabitants, and therefore they are pale and enfeebled, and are partly subject to all the foresaid diseases, but no one is peculiar to them. Their voices are rough and hoarse owing to the state of the air, which in such a situation is generally impure and unwholesome, for they have not the northern winds to purify it; and these winds they have are of a very humid character, such being the nature of the evening breezes. Such a situation of a city bears a great resemblance to autumn as regards the changes of the day, inasmuch as the difference between morning and evening is great. So it is with regard to the winds that are conducive to health, or the contrary. . . .

THUCYDIDES (471/455–CA. 399 B.C.)
The Peloponnesian War

$\mathcal{S}$on of the Athenian Olorus, the historian Thucydides was distantly related on his paternal side to a king of Thrace, and owned property there. He was educated by the sophists Antiphon and Gorgias, and also studied with Anaxagoras. Thucydides is said to have been so moved by Herodotus' reading history at the Olympian Games that he wept with admiration and vowed to become a historian. Though his family were conservative democrats, Thucydides himself enthusiastically supported the tyrant Pericles. Assassinated upon his return to Athens, Thucydides was buried in the family vault of Cimon, the Athenian statesman and general who was also his relative.

- As an Athenian commander, Thucydides arrived hours too late to defend the colony of Amphipolis, on the Thracian coast, against the Spartans under Brasidas. He was tried for treason, and exiled, for this failure; and did not return to Athens until after the Peloponnesian War. He spent this time in Thrace, where he owned gold mines, as well as in the Peloponnesus and Sicily. Ironically, this banishment allowed him, with newfound objectivity, to record, analyze, and study the clash between Sparta and Athens, the two greatest powers of the Greek world.
- His eight-book history of that war aims at providing posterity with an accurate record of the conflict between Sparta and Athens, but he died before he could carry it through the conquest of Athens in 404 B.C. Xenophon and Theopompus completed his work.
- Having foreseen that the conflict would be a mighty and prolonged one, Thucydides began collecting material from the very beginning. His approach to history was more methodical and logical than that of the rambling Herodotus, whose work ends where Thucydides' begins. He has been called the father of philosophical history. In addition to filtering one eyewitness account against another, Thucydides "filled in" the speeches given by the generals on both sides by imagining their emotions and political motivations. This impartial "historical method," far from being considered fanciful, was regarded by Aristotle as being more scientific and philosophical than merely recording known facts. Because of Thucydides' exiled position, he was able to gather observations from both sides of the battle lines. His style—direct, concise, vivid, serious, and straightforward, refraining from personal opinion, not drawing attention to itself but serving the story it tells—is highly accessible to the contemporary reader.

BOOK I, *CHAPTER I*

THE STATE OF GREECE FROM THE EARLIEST
TIMES TO THE COMMENCEMENT OF THE
PELOPONNESIAN WAR

. . . Now Mycenae may have been a small place, and many of the towns of that age may appear comparatively insignificant, but no exact observer would therefore feel justified in rejecting the estimate given by the poets and by tradition of the magnitude of the armament. For I suppose if Lacedaemon were to become desolate, and the temples and the foundations of the public buildings were left, that as time went on there would be a strong disposition with posterity to refuse to accept her fame as a true exponent of her power. And yet they occupy two-fifths of Peloponnese and lead the whole, not to speak of their numerous allies without. Still, as the city is neither built in a compact form nor adorned with magnificent temples and public edifices, but composed of villages after the old fashion of Hellas, there would be an impression of inadequacy. Whereas, if Athens were to suffer the same misfortune, I suppose that any inference from the appearance presented to the eye would make her power to have been twice as great as it is. We have therefore no right to be skeptical, nor to content ourselves with an inspection of a town to the exclusion of a consideration of its power; but we may safely conclude that the armament in question surpassed all before it, as it fell short of modern efforts; if we can here also accept the testimony of Homer's poems, in which, without allowing for the exaggeration which a poet would feel himself licensed to em-

"Temple of Zeus, Athens"

ploy, we can see that it was far from equaling ours. He has represented it as consisting of 1,200 vessels; the Boeotian complement of each ship being 120 men, that of the ships of Philoctetes fifty. By this, I conceive, he meant to convey the maximum and the minimum complement; at any rate he does not specify the amount of any others in his catalog of the ships. That they were all rowers as well as warriors we see from his account of the ships of Philoctetes, in which all the men at the oar are bowmen. Now it is improbable that many supernumeraries sailed if we except the kings and high officers; especially as they had to cross the open sea with munitions of war, in ships, moreover, that had no decks, but were equipped in the old piratical fashion. So that if we strike the average of the largest and smallest ships, the number of those who sailed will appear inconsiderable, representing, as they did, the whole force of Hellas. And this was due not so much to scarcity of men as of money. Difficulty of subsistence made the invaders reduce the numbers of the army to a point at which it might live on the country during the prosecution of the war. Even after the victory they obtained on their arrival—and a victory there must have been, or the fortifications of the naval camp could never have been built—there is no indication of their whole force having been employed; on the contrary, they seem to have turned to cultivation of the Chersonese and to piracy from want of supplies. This was what really enabled the Trojans to keep the field for ten years against them; the dispersion of the enemy making them always a match for the detachment left behind. If they had brought plenty of supplies with them, and had persevered in the war without scattering for piracy and agriculture, they would have easily defeated the Trojans in the field; since they could hold their own against them with the division on service. In short, if they had stuck to the siege, the capture of Troy would have cost them less time and less trouble. But as want of money proved the weakness of earlier expeditions, so from the same cause even the one in question, more famous than its predecessors, may be pronounced on the evidence of what it effected to have been inferior to its renown and to the current opinion about it formed under the tuition of the poets.

Even after the Trojan war Hellas was still engaged in removing and settling, and thus could not attain to the quiet which must precede growth. The late return of the Hellenes from Ilium caused many revolutions, and factions ensued almost everywhere; and it was the citizens thus driven into exile who founded the cities. Sixty years after the capture of Ilium the modern Boeotians were driven out of Arne by the Thessalians, and settled in the present Boeotia, the former Cadmeis; though there was a division of them there before, some of whom joined the expedition to Ilium. Twenty years later the Dorians and the Heraclids became masters of Peloponnese; so that much had to be done and many years had to elapse before Hellas could attain to a durable tranquility undisturbed by removals, and could begin to send out colonies, as Athens did to Ionia and most of the islands, and the Peloponnesians to most of Italy and Sicily and some places in the rest of Hellas. All these places were founded subsequently to the war with Troy.

But as the power of Hellas grew, and the acquisition of wealth became more an object, the revenues of the states increasing, tyrannies were by their means established almost everywhere—the old form of government being hereditary monarchy with definite prerogatives—and Hellas began to fit out fleets and apply herself more closely to the sea. It is said that the Corinthians were the first to approach the modern style of naval architecture, and that Corinth was the first place in Hellas where galleys were built; and we have Ameinocles, a Corinthian shipwright, making four ships for the Samians. Dating from the end of this war, it is nearly 300 years ago that Ameinocles went to Samos. Again, the earliest seafight in history was between the Corinthians and Corcyraeans; this was about 260 years ago, dating from the same time. Planted on an isthmus, Corinth had from time out of mind been a commercial emporium; as formerly almost all communication between the Hellenes within and without Peloponnese was carried on overland, and the Corinthian territory was the highway through which it traveled. She had consequently great money resources, as is shown by the epithet "wealthy" bestowed by the old poets on the place, and this enabled her, when traffic by sea became more common, to procure her navy and put down piracy; and as she could offer a mart for both branches of the trade, she acquired for herself all the power which a large revenue affords. Subsequently the Ionians attained to great naval strength in the reign of Cyrus, the first king of the Persians, and of his son Cambyses, and while they were at war with the former commanded for a while the Ionian sea. Polycrates also, the tyrant of Samos, had a powerful navy in the reign of Cambyses with which he reduced many of the islands, and among them Rhenea, which he consecrated to the Delian Apollo. About this time also the Phocaeans, while they were founding Marseilles, defeated the Carthaginians in a sea-fight. These were the most powerful navies. And even these, although so many generations had elapsed since the Trojan war, seem to have been principally composed of the old fifty-oars and long-boats, and to have counted few galleys among their ranks. Indeed it was only shortly before the Persian war and the death of Darius, the successor of Cambyses, that the Sicilian tyrants and the Corcyaeans acquired any large number of galleys. For after these there were no navies of any account in Hellas till the expedition of Xerxes; Aegina, Athens, and others may have possessed a few vessels, but they were principally fifty-oars. It was quite at the end of this period that the war with Aegina and the prospect of the barbarian invasion enabled Themistocles to persuade the Athenians to build the fleet with which they fought at Salamis; and even these vessels had not complete decks.

The navies, then, of the Hellenes during the period we have traversed were what I have described. All their insignificance did not prevent their being an element of the greatest power to those who cultivated them, alike in revenue and in dominion. They were the means by which the islands were reached and reduced, those of the smallest area falling the easiest prey. Wars by land there were none, none at least by which power was acquired; we have the usual border contests, but of distant expeditions with conquest for object we hear nothing among the Hellenes. There was no union of subject cities around a great state, no spontaneous combination of equals for confederate expeditions; what fighting there was consisted merely of local warfare between rival neighbors. The nearest approach to a coalition took place in the old war between Chalcis and Eretria; this was a quarrel in which the rest of the Hellenic name did to some extent take sides.

Various, too, were the obstacles which the national growth encountered in various localities. The power of the Ionians was advancing with rapid strides, when it came into collision with Persia, under King Cyrus, who, after having dethroned Croesus and overrun everything between the Halys and the sea, stopped not till he had reduced the cities of the coast; the islands being only left to be subdued by Darius and the Phoenician navy. Again, wherever there were tyrants, their habit of providing simply for themselves, of looking solely to their personal comfort and family aggrandisement, made safety the great aim of their policy, and prevented anything great proceeding from them;

though they would each have their affairs with their immediate neighbors. All this is only true of the mother country, for in Sicily they attained to very great power. Thus for a long time everywhere in Hellas do we find causes which make the states alike incapable of combination for great and national ends, or of any vigorous action of their own.

But at last a time came when the tyrants of Athens and the far older tyrannies of the rest of Hellas were, with the exception of those in Sicily, once and for all put down by Lacedaemon; for this city, though after the settlement of the Dorians, its present inhabitants, it suffered from factions for an unparalleled length of time, still at a very early period obtained good laws, and enjoyed a freedom from tyrants which was unbroken; it has possessed the same form of government for more than 400 years, reckoning to the end of the late war, and has thus been in a position to arrange the affairs of the other states. Not many years after the deposition of the tyrants, the battle of Marathon was fought between the Medes and the Athenians. Ten years afterward the barbarian returned with the armada for the subjugation of Hellas. In the face of this great danger the command of the confederate Hellenes was assumed by the Lacedaemonians in virtue of their superior power; and the Athenians having made up their minds to abandon their city, broke up their homes, threw themselves into their ships, and became a naval people. This coalition, after repulsing the barbarian, soon afterward split into two sections, which included the Hellenes who had revolted from the king, as well as those who had aided him in the war. At the head of the one stood Athens, at the head of the other Lacedaemon, one of the first naval, the other the first military power in Hellas. For a short time the league held together, till the Lacedaemonians and Athenians quarreled, and made war upon each other with their allies, a duel into which all the Hellenes sooner or later were drawn, though some might at first remain neutral. So that the whole period from the Median war to this, with some peaceful intervals, was spent by each power in war, either with its rival, or with its own revolted allies, and consequently afforded them constant practice in military matters, and that experience which is learned in the school of danger.

The policy of Lacedaemon was not to exact tribute from her allies, but merely to secure their subservience to her interests by establishing oligarchies among them; Athens, on the contrary, had by degrees deprived hers of their ships, and imposed instead contributions in money on all except Chios and Lesbos. Both found their resources for this war separately to exceed the sum of their strength when the alliance flourished intact.

Having now given the result of my inquiries into early times, I grant that there will be a difficulty in believing every particular detail. The way that most men deal with traditions, even traditions of their own country, is to receive them all alike as they are delivered, without applying any critical test whatever. The general Athenian public fancy that Hipparchus was tyrant when he fell by the hands of Harmodius and Aristogiton; not knowing that Hippias, the eldest of the sons of Pisistratus, was really supreme, and that Hipparchus and Thessalus were his brothers; and that Harmodius and

Aristogiton suspecting, on the very day, nay at the very moment fixed on for the deed, that information had been conveyed to Hippias by their accomplices, concluded that he had been warned, and did not attack him, yet, not liking to be apprehended and risk their lives for nothing, fell upon Hipparchus near the temple of the daughters of Leos, and slew him as he was arranging the Panathenaic procession.

There are many other unfounded ideas current among the rest of the Hellenes, even on matters of contemporary history which have not been obscured by time. For instance, there is the notion that the Lacedaemonian kings have two votes each, the fact being that they have only one; and that there is a company of Pitane, there being simply no such thing. So little pains do the vulgar take in the investigation of truth, accepting readily the first story that comes to hand. On the whole, however, the conclusions I have drawn from the proofs quoted may, I believe, safely be relied on. Assuredly they will not be disturbed either by the lays of a poet displaying the exaggeration of his craft, or by the compositions of the chroniclers that are attractive at truth's expense; the subjects they treat of being out of the reach of evidence, and time having robbed most of them of historical value by enthroning them in the region of legend. Turning from these, we can rest satisfied with having proceeded upon the clearest data, and having arrived at conclusions as exact as can be expected in matters of such antiquity. To come to this war; despite the known disposition of the actors in a struggle to overrate its importance, and when it is over to return to their admiration of earlier events, yet an examination of the facts will show that it was much greater than the wars which preceded it.

With reference to the speeches in this history, some were delivered before the war began, others while it was going on; some I heard myself, others I got from various quarters; it was in all cases difficult to carry them word for word in one's memory, so my habit has been to make the speakers say what was in my opinion demanded of them by the various occasions, of course adhering as closely as possible to the general sense of what they really said. And with reference to the narrative of events, far from permitting myself to derive it from the first source that came to hand, I did not even trust my own impressions, but it rests partly on what I saw myself, partly on what others saw for me, the accuracy of the report being always tried by the most severe and detailed tests possible. My conclusions have cost me some labor from the want of coincidence between accounts of the same occurrences by different eye-witnesses, arising sometimes from imperfect memory, sometimes from undue partiality for one side or the other. The absence of romance in my history will, I fear, detract somewhat from its interest; but if it be judged useful by those inquirers who desire an exact knowledge of the past as an aid to the interpretation of the future, which in the course of human things must resemble if it does not reflect it, I shall be content. In fine, I have written my work, not as an essay which is to win the applause of the moment, but as a possession for all time.

The Median war, the greatest achievement of past times, yet found a speedy decision in two actions by sea and two by land. The Peloponnesian war was prolonged to an immense length, and long as it was it was short without parallel for the misfortunes that it brought upon Hellas. Never had so many cities been taken and laid desolate, here by the barbarians, here by the parties contending (the old inhabitants being sometimes removed to make room for others); never was there so much banishing and blood-shedding, now on the field of battle, now in the strife of action. Old stories of occurrences handed down by tradition, but scantily confirmed by experience, suddenly ceased to be incredible; there were earthquakes of unparalleled extent and violence; eclipses of the sun occurred with a frequency unrecorded in previous history; there were great droughts in sundry places and consequent famines, and that most calamitous and awfully fatal visitation, the plague. All this came upon them with the late war, which was begun by the Athenians and Peloponnesians by the dissolution of the thirty years' truce made after the conquest of Euboea. To the question why they broke the treaty, I answer by placing first an account of their grounds of complaint and points of difference, that no one may ever have to ask the immediate cause which plunged the Hellenes into a war of such magnitude. The real cause I consider to be the one which was formally most kept out of sight. The growth of the power of Athens, and the alarm which this inspired in Lacedaemon, made war inevitable. Still it is well to give the grounds alleged by either side, which led to the dissolution of the treaty and the breaking out of the war.

SOCRATES (469–399 B.C.)

Speech to the Athenians (from Plato's Apology)

Socrates was born in Athens, the son of the stonecutter Sophroniscus and the midwife Phaenarete. Early in life, after studying the natural scientists Anaxagoras and Archelaus, he dedicated himself to the vocation of moral philosophy, seeking to improve himself and his associates. He fought in the Peloponnesian war, saving the general Alcibiades' life at Potidaea, and was commended for bravery in action. He married a woman named Xanthippe, who led him to the observation: "Go ahead and marry. If you find a good wife, you'll be happy. If not, you'll be a philosopher." His ascetic way of life made him more or less immune to her constant haranguing. He achieved peace of mind by subjecting every passion to reason, practicing stoicism before Stoicism became a school of thought. He hated the sophists because he felt they had no loyalty to anything but argument for its own sake.

- Socrates taught through the dialectical method, by which he led his students, whom he called *sunontes* (associates), to knowledge by continually asking them to answer questions. After being told by the oracle at Delphi that no man was wiser than he, Socrates set out to disprove the oracle by ascertaining the wisdom of his contemporaries. He learned the truth of the oracle, for while he himself knew he knew nothing, he discovered the leaders of Athens knew nothing but thought they knew. "In this particular," he said, "I seemed to have the better of them." As he conducted his dialogues with a growing number of associates in the Athenian agora, Socrates quickly earned the reputation of a gadfly, whose persistent questions led him to conflict with the Athenian authorities. He questioned everything, from the accepted wisdom about military strategy and political rectitude to the very existence of the gods. For his belief that his behavior was governed by an "internal god," which he called his *daemon,* the Athenians condemned him to exile or death. He chose death, accepting hemlock rather than exile, because, he said, death was preferable to living in ignorance. Socrates' *daemon* is the predecessor for the modern concept of conscience. His twentieth-century avatar is Mahatma Gandhi. His associates included Alcibiades (the leader of the democratic forces), and Critias (leader of the oligarchy).
- The inspiration for the first great expression of philosophy in western civilization never wrote a word. Yet Socrates' words have been memorialized by his two famous students, the philosopher Plato and the historian Xenophon. His method of teaching, to challenge authority at every turn, is both the foundation and the greatest paradox of western education to this day. Its influence can be heard in Albert Einstein's complaint, "The penalty fate has given me for my hatred of authority is making me one."

. . . Someone will say: And are you not ashamed, Socrates, of a course of life which is likely to bring you to an untimely end? To him I may fairly answer: There you are mistaken: A man who is good for anything ought not to calculate the chance of living or dying; he ought to consider in doing anything he is doing right or wrong—acting the part of a good man or of a bad. Whereas, upon your view, the heroes who fell at Troy were not good for much and the son of Thetis above all, who altogether despised danger in comparison with disgrace; and when he was so eager to slay Hector, his god-dess mother said to him that if he avenged his companion Patroclus, and slew Hector, he would die himself. "Fate," she said, in these or the like words, "waits for you next after Hector"; he, receiving this warning, utterly despised danger and death, and instead of fearing them, feared rather to live in dishonor, and not to avenge his friend. "Let me die forthwith," he replies, "and be avenged of my enemy, rather than abide here by the beaked ships, a laughingstock and a burden on the earth." Had Achilles any thought of death and danger? For wherever a man's place is, whether the place which he has chosen or that in which he has been placed by a commander, there he ought to remain in the hour of danger; he should not think of death or of anything but of disgrace. And this, O men of Athens, is a true saying.

Strange, indeed, would be my conduct, O men of Athens, if I who, when I was ordered by the generals whom you chose to command me at Potidaea and Amphipolis and Delium, remained where they placed me, like any other man, facing death—if now, when, as I conceive and imagine, God orders me to fulfill the philosopher's mission of searching into myself and other men, I were to desert my post through fear of death, or any other fear; that would indeed be strange, and I might justly be arraigned in court for denying the existence of the gods, if I disobeyed the oracle because I was afraid of death, fancying that I was wise when I was not wise. For the fear of death is indeed the pretense of wisdom, and not real wisdom, being a pretense of knowing the unknown; and no one knows whether death, which men in their fear apprehend to be the greatest evil, may not be the greatest good. Is not this ignorance of a disgraceful sort, the ignorance which is the conceit that a man knows what he does not know? And in this respect only I believe myself to differ from men in general, and may perhaps claim to be wiser than they are: that whereas I know but little of the world below, I do not suppose that I know; but I do know that injustice and disobedience to a better, whether God or man, is evil and dishonorable, and I will never fear or avoid a possible good rather than a certain evil. And therefore if you let me go now, and are not convinced by Anytus, who said that since I had been prosecuted I must be put to death (or if

not that I ought never to have been prosecuted at all); and that if I escape now, your sons will all be utterly ruined by listening to my words—if you say to me, Socrates, this time we will not mind Anytus, and you shall be let off, but upon one condition, that you are not to enquire and speculate in this way anymore, and that if you are caught doing so again you shall die; if this was the condition on which you let me go, I should reply: Men of Athens, I honor and love you; but I shall obey God rather than you, and while I have life and strength I shall never cease from the practice and teaching of philosophy, exhorting anyone whom I meet and saying to him after my manner: You, my friend, a citizen of the great and mighty and wise city of Athens, are you not ashamed of heaping up the greatest amount of money and honor and reputation, and caring so little about wisdom and truth and the greatest improvement of the soul, which you never regard or heed at all? and if the person with whom I am arguing, says: Yes, but I do care; then I do not leave him or let him go at once; but I proceed to interrogate and examine and cross-examine him, and if I think that he has no virtue in him, but only says that he has, I

"Agora of Athens"

reproach him with undervaluing the greater, and overvaluing the less. And I shall repeat the same words to every one whom I meet, young and old, citizen and alien, but especially to the citizens inasmuch as they are my brethren. For know that this is the command of God; and believe that no greater good has ever happened in the state than my service to the God. For I do nothing but go about persuading you all, old and young alike, not to take thought for your persons or your properties, but first and chiefly to care about the greatest improvement of the soul. I tell you that virtue is not given by money, but that from virtue comes money and every other good of man, public as well as private. This is my teaching, and if this is the doctrine which corrupts the youth, I am a mischievous person. But if anyone says that this is not my teaching, he is speaking an untruth. Wherefore, O men of Athens, I say to you, do as Anytus bids or not as Anytus bids, and either acquit me or not; but whichever you do, understand that I shall never alter my ways, not even if I have to die many times. . . .

There are many reasons why I am not grieved, O men of Athens, at the vote of condemnation. I expected it, and am only surprised that the votes are so nearly equal; for I had thought that the majority against me would have been far larger; but now, had thirty votes gone over the other side, I should have been acquitted. And I may say, I think, that I have escaped Meletus. I may say more; for without the assistance of Anytus and Lycon, anyone may see that he would not have had a fifth part of the votes, as the law requires, in which case he would have incurred a fine of a thousand drachmae.

And so he proposes death as the penalty. And what shall I propose on my part, O men of Athens? Clearly that which is my due. And what is my due? What return shall be made to the man who has never had the wit to be idle during his whole life; but has been careless of what the many care for—wealth, and family interests, and military offices, and speaking in the assembly, and magistracies, and plots, and parties. Reflecting that I was really too honest a man to be a politician and live, I did not go where I could do no good to you or to myself; but where I could do the greatest good privately to every one of you, thither I went, and sought to persuade every man among you that he must look to himself, and seek virtue and wisdom before he looks to his private interests, and look to the state before he looks to the interests of the state; and that this should be the order which he observes in all his actions. What shall be done to such an one? Doubtless some good thing. O men of Athens, if he has his reward; and the good should be of a kind suitable to him. What would be a reward suitable to a poor man who is your benefactor, and who desires leisure that he may instruct you? There can be no reward so fitting as maintenance in the Prytaneum, O men of Athens, a reward which he deserves far more than the citizen who has won the prize at Olympia in the horse or chariot race, whether the chariots were drawn by two horses or by many. For I am in want, and he has enough; and he only gives you the appearance of happiness, and I give you the reality. And if I am to estimate the penalty fairly, I should say that maintenance in the Prytaneum is the just return.

Perhaps you think that I am braving you in

what I am saying now, as in what I said before about the tears and prayers. But this is not so. I speak rather because I am convinced that I never intentionally wronged any one, although I cannot convince you—the time has been too short; if there were a law at Athens, as there is in other cities, that a capital cause should not be decided in one day, then I believe that I should have convinced you. But I cannot in a moment refute great slanders; and, as I am convinced that I never wronged another, I will assuredly not wrong myself. I will not say of myself that I deserve any evil, or propose any penalty. Why should I?

Because I am afraid of the penalty of death which Meletus proposes? When I do not know whether death is a good or an evil, why should I propose a penalty which would certainly be an evil? Shall I say imprisonment? And why should I live in prison, and be the slave of the magistrates of the year—of the Eleven? Or shall the penalty be a fine, and imprisonment until the fine is paid? There is the same objection. I should have to lie in prison, for money I have none, and cannot pay. And if I say exile (and this may possibly be the penalty which you will affix) I must be blinded by the love of life, if I am so irrational as to expect that when you, who are my own citizens, cannot endure my discourses and words, and have found them so grievous and odious that you will have no more of them, others are likely to endure me. No indeed, men of Athens, that is not very likely. And what a life should I lead, at my age, wandering from city to city, ever changing my place of exile, and always being driven out! For I am quite sure that wherever I go, there, as here, the young men will flock to me; and if I drive them away, their elders will drive me out at their request; and if I let them come, fathers and friends will drive me out for their sakes.

Some one will say: Yes, Socrates, but cannot you hold your tongue, and then you may go into a foreign city, and no one will interfere with you? Now I have great difficulty in making you understand my answer to this. For if I tell you that to do as you say would be a disobedience to the God, and therefore that I cannot hold my tongue, you will not believe that I am serious; and if I say again that daily to discourse about virtue, and of those other things about which you hear me examining myself and others, is the greatest good of man, and that the unexamined life is not worth living, you are still less likely to believe me. Yet I say what is true, although a thing of which it is hard for me to persuade you. Also, I have never been accustomed to think that I deserve to suffer any harm. Had I money I might have estimated the offense at what I was able to pay, and not have been much the worse. But I have none, and therefore I must ask you to proportion the fine to my means. Well, perhaps I could afford a mina, and therefore I propose that penalty: Plato, Crito, Critobulus, and Apollodorus, my friends here, bid me say thirty minae, and they will be the sureties. Let thirty minae be the penalty; for which sum they will be ample security to you. . . .

Not much time will be gained, O Athenians, in return for the evil name which you will get from the detractors of the city, who will say that you killed Socrates, a wise man; for they will call me wise, even although I am not wise, when they want to reproach you. If you had waited a little while, your desire would have been fulfilled in the course of nature. For I am far advanced in years, as you may perceive, and not far from death. I am speaking now not to all of you, but only to those who have condemned me to death. And I have another thing to say to them: You think that I was convicted because I have no words of the sort which would have procured my acquittal—I mean, if I had thought fit to leave nothing undone or unsaid. Not so; the deficiency which led to my conviction was not of words—certainly not. But I had not the boldness or impudence or inclination to address you as you would have liked me to do, weeping and wailing and lamenting, and saying and doing many things which you have been accustomed to hear from others, and which, as I maintain, are unworthy of me. I thought at the time that I ought not to do anything common or mean when in danger: nor do I now repent of the style of my defense; I would rather die having spoken after my manner, than speak in your manner and live. For neither in war nor yet at law ought I or any man to use every way of escaping death. Often in battle there can be no doubt that if a man will throw away his arms, and fall on his knees before his pursuers, he may escape death; and in other dangers there are other ways of escaping death, if a man is willing to say and do anything. The difficulty, my friends, is not to avoid death, but to avoid unrighteousness; for that runs faster than death. I am old and move slowly, and the slower runner has overtaken me, and my accusers are keen and quick, and the faster runner, who is unrighteousness, has overtaken them. And now I depart hence condemned by you to suffer the penalty of death; they too go

their ways condemned by the truth to suffer the penalty of villainy and wrong; and I must abide by my award—let them abide by theirs. I suppose that these things may be regarded as fated, and I think that they are well.

And now, O men who have condemned me, I would fain prophesy to you; for I am about to die, and in the hour of death men are gifted with prophetic power. And I prophesy to you who are my murderers, that immediately after my departure punishment far heavier than you have inflicted on me will surely await you. Me you have killed because you wanted to escape the accuser, and not to give an account of your lives. But that will not be as you suppose: far otherwise. For I say that there will be more accusers of you than there are now; accusers whom hitherto I have restrained: and as they are younger they will be more inconsiderate with you, and you will be more offended at them. If you think that by killing men you can prevent someone from censuring your evil lives, you are mistaken; that is not a way of escape which is either possible or honorable; the easiest and the noblest way is not to be disabling others, but to be improving yourselves. This is the prophecy which I utter before my departure to the judges who have condemned me.

Friends, who would have acquitted me, I would like also to talk with you about the thing which has come to pass, while the magistrates are busy, and before I go to the place at which I must die. Stay then a little, for we may as well talk with one another, while there is time. You are my friends, and I should like to show you the meaning of this event which has happened to me. O my judges—for you I may truly call judges—I should like to tell you of a wonderful circumstance. Hitherto the divine faculty of which the internal oracle is the source has constantly been in the habit of opposing me even about trifles, if I was going to make a slip or error in any matter; and now as you see there has come upon me that which may be thought, and is generally believed to be, the last and worst evil. But the oracle made no sign of opposition, either when I was leaving my house in the morning, or when I was on my way to the court, or while I was speaking, at anything which I was going to say; and yet I have often been stopped in the middle of a speech, but now in nothing I either said or did touching the matter in hand has the oracle opposed me. What do I take to be the explanation of this silence? I will tell you. It is an intimation that what has happened to me is a good, and that those of us who think that death is an evil are in error. For the customary sign would surely have opposed me had I been going to evil and not to good.

Let us reflect in another way, and we shall see that there is great reason to hope that death is a good; for one of two things—either death is a state of nothingness and utter unconsciousness, or, as men say, there is a change and migration of the soul from this world to another. Now if you suppose that there is no consciousness, but a sleep like the sleep of him who is undisturbed even by dreams, death will be an unspeakable gain. For if a person were to select the night in which his sleep was undisturbed even by dreams, and were to compare with this the other days and nights of his life, and then were to tell us how many days and nights he had passed in the course of his life

better and more pleasantly than this one, I think that any man, I will not say a private man, but even the great king will not find many such days or nights, when compared with the others. Now if death be of such a nature, I say that to die is gain; for eternity is then only a single night. But if death is the journey to another place, and there, as men say, all the dead abide, what good, O my friends and judges, can be greater than this? If indeed when the pilgrim arrives in the world below, he is delivered from the professors of justice in this world, and finds the true judges who are said to give judgment there, Minos and Rhadamanthus and Aeacus and Triptolemus, and other sons of God who were righteous in their own life, that pilgrimage will be worth making. What would not a man give if he might converse with Orpheus and Musaeus and Hesiod and Homer? Nay, if this be true, let me die again and again. I myself, too, shall have a wonderful interest in there meeting and conversing with Palamedes, and Ajax the son of Telamon, and any other ancient hero who has suffered death through an unjust judgment; and there will be no small pleasure, as I think, in comparing my own sufferings with theirs. Above all, I shall then be able to continue my search into true and false knowledge; as in this world, so also in the next; and I shall find out who is wise, and who pretends to be wise, and is not. What would not a man give, O judges, to be able to examine the leader of the great Trojan expedition; or Odysseus or Sisyphus, or numberless others, men and women too! What infinite delight would there be in conversing with them and asking them questions! In another world they do not put a man to death for asking questions: assuredly not. For besides being happier than we are, they will be immortal, if what is said is true.

Wherefore, O judges, be of good cheer about death, and know of a certainty, that no evil can happen to a good man, either in life or after death. He and his are not neglected by the gods; nor has my own approaching end happened by mere chance. But I see clearly that the time had arrived when it was better for me to die and be released from trouble; wherefore the oracle gave no sign. For which reason, also, I am not angry with my condemners, or with my accusers; they have done me no harm, although they did not mean to do me any good; and for this I may gently blame them.

Still I have a favor to ask of them. When my sons are grown up, I would ask you, O my friends, to punish them; and I would have you trouble them, as I have troubled you, if they seem to care about riches, or anything, more than about virtue; or if they pretend to be something when they are really nothing, then reprove them, as I have reproved you, for not caring about that for which they ought to care, and thinking that they are something when they are really nothing. And if you do this, both I and my sons will have received justice at your hands.

The hour of departure has arrived, and we go our ways—I to die, and you to live. Which is better God only knows.

Praxilla (fl. 451 b.c.)

Lyrics

First century A.D. epigrammist Antipater of Thessalonika defined the canon of women poets: "These are the divine-voiced women that Helicon fed with song, Helicon and Macedonian Pieria's rock: Praxilla; Moero; Anyte, the female Homer; Sappho, glory of the Lesbian women with lovely tresses; Erinna; renowned Telesilla; and you Corinna, who sang the martial shield of Athena; Nossis, the tender-voiced, and dulcet-toned Myrtis—all craftswomen of eternal pages. Great Heaven gave birth to nine Muses and Earth to these nine, the deathless delight of mortals" (from Fantham, Foley, *et al*). Born in Argolid Sicyon, on the Gulf of Corinth, Praxilla wrote dithyrambs, drinking songs, and hymns. Tatian, in his *Against the Greeks,* and Zenobios accused her of writing nonsense because she put cucumbers on a par with the sun and the moon in her lyric list of Adonis' favorite things.

OF THE SENSUAL WORLD
Most beautiful of things I leave is sunlight;
then come glazing stars and the moon's face;
then ripe cucumbers and apples and pears.

APPEARANCE
You gaze at me teasingly through the window:
a virgin face—and below—a woman's thighs.

ACHILLES
(You understood their words)

but they never reached the heart
buried in your chest.

THE COWARD
Under cover
a coward will strike from any side.
I warn you, friend:
watch out for his sting.
Under every rock is a lurking scorpion.

ARISTOPHANES (CA. 450–CA. 388 B.C.)
Lysistrata

*T*he greatest of the Greek comic dramatists lived in the Athens of Pericles during the Peloponnesian War. He was the son of Philippus of Egypt or Rhodes. According to Plato's *Symposium,* he was good friends with Socrates and the general Alcibiades. He wrote forty plays, averaging one a year, of which we have eleven nearly complete—the only surviving examples of Old Comedy. They include *The Acharrnians, The Knights, The Clouds, The Wasps, The Peace, The Birds, Lysistrata,* and *The Frogs.* He won only three prizes in his lifetime, perhaps because he took no part in the production of his plays; and was not as popular as Cratinus and Eupolis (neither of whose works survive).

The statesman Cleon tried to question his citizenship, no doubt riled by Aristophanes' unrestrained invective. Aristophanes' dialogue is brilliantly realistic, incorporating echoes from rhetoric, law, tragedy, lyric, and religion. His humor ranges effectively across an astonishing number of channels, from the broadest slapstick to the most sophisticated wit. He attacked the urbane leaders and philosophical and literary movements of his time as inferior to those of the golden, simpler, more agrarian past he imagined and associated with Marathon. Plato said Aristophanes divided his time between Dionysius (wine-drinking) and Aphrodite (love-making). He was widely admired for his integrity, and Plato also wrote of him, "When looking for an inviolable sanctuary, / the Graces found the soul of Aristophanes." (tr. Barnstone)

- Though his plays were filled with fantastic situations, and exuberant obscenities, Aristophanes constructed them around a mordant and outrageously inventive satire, lambasting the follies of the human, political, and military situations he observed. His plays were structured in six parts:

  1. *Prologos* (Prologue), in which the protagonist conceives an absurd idea.
  2. *Parodos,* when the chorus enters to let the audience know that they've gotten wind of the idea.
  3. *Agon,* where the protagonist defends his idea against the chorus's or the antagonist's arguments. Then the pros and cons of the idea are put to every possible dramatic variation.
  4. *Parabasis,* when the chorus sings an ode to the audience, usually communicating the poet's opinions on matters unrelated to the story.
  5. *Episodes* and *Stasima,* where the idea is put to work in a variety of situations.
  6. *Exodos,* where the chorus comments on the idea's success or defeat.

- *Lysistrata,* performed for the first time in 411 B.C., reflects, hilariously and profanely, the imminent fall of Athens to the Spartans. Only a year earlier, the Athenians had learned of the destruction of their fleet at Syracuse. The fear and outrage of the citizens of Athens is reflected in Aristophanes' fable about the women of the various provinces of Greece. Led by Athenian Lysistrata (her name means, literally, "disbander of armies") they stage a "sex strike"—to force the men to reevaluate the war—and take over the Acropolis. The strike creates the ridiculous image of Greek men walking around with two "spears" under their clothing, each spear in direct conflict with the other. Although considered an anti-war play off and on for centuries, in fact *Lysistrata* is an anti-peace play, satirizing the absurdity of peace efforts. The play, the last he wrote on a purely political theme, features choruses of men and of women.

...Myrrhiné Oh dear! what a scatterbrain I am; if I haven't gone and brought Rhodian perfumes!

Cinesias Never mind, dearest, let it go now.

Myrrhiné You don't really *mean* that.

(*She goes.*)

Cinesias Damn the man who invented perfumes!

Myrrhiné (*coming back with another flask*) Here, take this bottle.

Cinesias I have a better one all ready for you, darling. Come, you provoking creature, to bed with you, and don't bring another thing.

"Throne of the priest of Dionysius, Great Theater of Athens"

Myrrhiné Coming, coming; I'm just slipping off my shoes. Dear boy, will you vote for peace?

Cinesias I'll think about it. (*Myrrhiné runs away.*) I'm a dead man, she is killing me! She has gone, and left me in torment! (*In tragic style*) I must have someone to lay, I must! Ah me! the loveliest of women has choused and cheated me. Poor little lad, how am I to give you what you want so badly? Where is Cynalopex? quick, man, get him a nurse, do!

Leader of Chorus of Old Men Poor, miserable wretch, balked in your amorousness! what tortures are yours! Ah! you fill me with pity. Could any man's back and loins stand such a strain. He stands stiff and rigid, and there's never a wench to help him!

Cinesias Ye gods in heaven, what pains I suffer!

Leader of Chorus of Old Men Well, there it is; it's her doing, that abandoned hussy!

Cinesias No, no! rather say that sweetest, dearest darling.

(*He departs.*)

Leader of Chorus of Old Men That dearest darling? no, no, that hussy, say I! Zeus, thou god of the skies, canst not let loose a hurricane, to sweep them all up into the air, and whirl them round, then drop them down crash! and impale them on the point of this man's tool!
(*A Spartan Herald enters; he shows signs of being in the same condition as Cinesias.*)

Herald Say, where shall I find the Senate and the Prytanes? I am bearer of despatches.

(*An Athenian Magistrate enters.*)

Magistrate Are you a man or a Priapus?

Herald (*with an effort at officiousness*) Don't be stupid! I am a herald, of course, I swear I am, and I come from Sparta about making peace.

Magistrate (*pointing*) But look, you are hiding a lance under your clothes, surely.

Herald (*embarrassed*) No, nothing of the sort.

Magistrate Then why do you turn away like that, and hold your cloak out from your body? Have you got swellings in the groin from your journey?

Herald By the twin brethren! the man's an old maniac.

Magistrate But you've got an erection! You lewd fellow!

Herald I tell you no! but enough of this foolery.

Magistrate *(pointing)* Well, what is it you have *there* then?

Herald A Lacedaemonian "skytalé."

Magistrate Oh, indeed, a "skytalé," is it? Well, well, speak out frankly; I know all about these matters. How are things going at Sparta now?

Herald Why, everything is turned upside down at Sparta; and all the allies have erections. We simply must have Pellené.

Magistrate What is the reason of it all? Is it the god Pan's doing?

Herald No, it's all the work of Lampito and the women who are acting at her instigation; they have kicked the men out from between their thighs.

Magistrate But what are you doing about it?

Herald We are at our wits' end; we walk bent double, just as if we were carrying lanterns in a wind. The jades have sworn we shall not so much as touch them till we have all agreed to conclude peace.

Magistrate Ah! I see now, it's a *general* conspiracy embracing all Greece. Go back to Sparta and bid them send envoys plenipotentiary to treat for peace. I will urge our Senators myself to name plenipotentiaries from us; and

to persuade them, why, I will show them my own tool.

Herald What could be better? I fly at your command.

> *(They go out in opposite directions.)*

Leader of Chorus of Old Men No wild beast is there, no flame of fire, more fierce and untamable than woman; the leopard is less savage and shameless.

Leader of Chorus of Women And yet you dare to make war upon me, wretch, when you might have me for your most faithful friend and ally.

Leader of Chorus of Old Men Never, never can my hatred cease towards women.

Leader of Chorus of Women Well, suit yourself. Still I cannot bear to leave you all naked as you are; folks would laugh at you. Come, I am going to put this tunic on you.

Leader of Chorus of Old Men You are right, upon my word! it was only in my confounded fit of rage that I took it off.

Leader of Chorus of Women Now at any rate you look like a man, and they won't make fun of you. Ah! if you had not offended me so badly, I would take out that nasty insect you have in your eye for you.

Leader of Chorus of Old Men Ah! so that's what was annoying me so! Look, here's a ring, just remove the insect, and show it to me. By

Zeus! it has been hurting my eye for a long time now.

Leader of Chorus of Women   Well, I agree, though your manners are not over and above pleasant. Oh! what a huge great gnat! just look! It's from Tricorythus, for sure.

Leader of Chorus of Old Men   A thousand thanks! the creature was digging a regular well in my eye; now that it's gone, my tears can flow freely.

Leader of Chorus of Women   I will wipe them for you—bad, naughty man though you are. Now, just one kiss.

Leader of Chorus of Old Men   A kiss? certainly not!

Leader of Chorus of Women   Just one, whether you like it or not.

Leader of Chorus of Old Men   Oh! those confounded women! how they do cajole us! How true the saying: " 'Tis impossible to live with the baggages, impossible to live without 'em!" Come, let us agree for the future not to regard each other any more as enemies; and to clinch the bargain, let us sing a choric song.

Combined Chorus of Women and Old Men (*singing*) We desire, Athenians, to speak ill of no man; but on the contrary to say much good of everyone, and to do the like. We have had enough of misfortunes and calamities. If there is any man or woman who wants a bit of money—two or three minas or so; well, our purse is full. If only peace is concluded, the borrower will not

have to pay back. Also I'm inviting to supper a few Carystian friends, who are excellently well qualified. I have still a drop of good soup left, and a young porker I'm going to kill, and the flesh will be sweet and tender. I shall expect you at my house today; but first away to the baths with you, you and your children; then come all of you, ask no one's leave, but walk straight up, as if you were at home; never fear, the door will be . . . shut in your faces!

Leader of Chorus of Old Men   Ah! here come the envoys from Sparta with their long flowing beards; why, you would think they wore pigsties between their thighs. (*Enter the Laconian Envoys afflicted like their herald.*) Hail to you, first of all, Laconians; then tell us how you fare.

Laconian Envoy   No need for many words; you can see what a state we are in.

Leader of Chorus of Old Men   Alas! the situation grows more and more strained! the intensity of the thing is simply frightful.

Laconian Envoy   It's beyond belief. But to work! summon your Commissioners, and let us patch up the best peace we may.

Leader of Chorus of Old Men   Ah! our men too, like wrestlers in the arena, cannot endure a rag over their bellies; it's an athlete's malady, which only exercise can remedy. (*The Magistrate returns; he too now has an evident reason to desire peace.*)

Magistrate   Can anybody tell us where Lysistrata is? Surely she will have some compassion on our condition.

Leader of Chorus of Old Men *(pointing)* Look! now he has the very same complaint. *(To the Magistrate)* Don't you feel a strong nervous tension in the morning?

Magistrate Yes, and a dreadful, dreadful torture it is! Unless peace is made very soon, we shall find no recourse but to make love to Clisthenes.

Leader of Chorus of Old Men Take my advice, and arrange your clothes as best you can; one of the fellows who mutilated the Hermae might see you.

Magistrate Right, by Zeus.

(He endeavors, not too successfully, to conceal his condition.)

Laconian Envoy Quite right, by the Dioscuri. There, I will put on my tunic.

Magistrate Oh! what a terrible state we are in! Greeting to you, Laconian fellow-sufferers.

Laconian Envoy *(addressing one of his countrymen)* Ah! my boy, what a terrible thing it would have been if these fellows had seen us just now when we were on full stand!

Magistrate Speak out, Laconians, what is it brings you here?

Laconian Envoy We have come to treat for peace.

Magistrate Well said; we are of the same mind. Better call Lysistrata, then; she is the only person who will bring us to terms.

Laconian Envoy Yes, yes—and Lysistratus into the bargain, if you will.

Magistrate Needless to call her; she has heard your voices, and here she comes.
                    (She comes out of the Acropolis.)

Leader of Chorus of Old Men Hail, boldest and bravest of womankind! The time is come to show yourself in turn uncompromising and conciliatory, exacting and yielding, haughty and condescending. Call up all your skill and artfulness. Lo! the foremost men in Hellas, seduced by your fascinations, are agreed to entrust you with the task of ending their quarrels.

Lysistrata It will be an easy task—if only they refrain from mutual indulgence in masculine love; if they do, I shall know the fact at once. Now, where is the gentle goddess Peace? *(The goddess, in the form of a beautiful nude girl is brought in by the Machine.)* Lead hither the Laconian envoys. But, look you, no roughness or violence; our husbands always behaved so boorishly. Bring them to me with smiles, as women should. If any refuse to give you his hand, then take hold of his tool. Bring up the Athenians too; you may lead them either way. Laconians, approach; and you, Athenians, on my other side. Now hearken all! I am but a woman; but I have good common sense; Nature has endowed me with discriminating judgment, which I have yet further developed, thanks to the wise teachings of my father and the elders of the city. First I must bring a reproach against you that applies equally to both sides. At Olympia, and Thermopylae, and Delphi, and a score of other places too numerous to mention, you celebrate before the same altars ceremonies common to all Hellenes; yet you go cutting each other's throats, and sacking Hellenic cities, when all the while the barbarian yonder is threatening you! That is my first point.

Magistrate *(devouring the goddess with his eyes)* Good god, this erection is killing me!

Lysistrata Now it is to you I address myself, Laconians. Have you forgotten how Periclidas, your own countryman, sat a suppliant before our altars? How pale he was in his purple robes! He had come to crave an army of us; it was the time when Messenia was pressing you sore, and the Sea-god was shaking the earth. Cimon marched to your aid at the head of four thousand hoplites, and saved Lacedaemon. And, after such a service as that, you ravage the soil of your benefactors!

Magistrate They do wrong, very wrong, Lysistrata.

Laconian Envoy We do wrong, very wrong. *(Looking at the goddess)* Ah! great gods! what a lovely bottom Peace has!

Lysistrata And now a word to the Athenians. Have you no memory left of how, in the days when you wore the tunic of slaves, the Laconians came, spear in hand, and slew a host of Thessalians and partisans of Hippias the tyrant? They, and they only, fought on your side on that eventful day; they delivered you from despotism, and thanks to them our nation could change the short tunic of the slave for the long cloak of the free man.

Laconian Envoy *(looking at Lysistrata)* I have never seen a woman of more gracious dignity.

Magistrate *(looking at Peace)* I have never seen a woman with a finer body!

Lysistrata Bound by such ties of mutual kindness, how can you bear to be at war? Stop, stay the hateful strife, be reconciled; what hinders you?

Laconian Envoy We are quite ready, if they will give us back our rampart.

Lysistrata What rampart, my dear man?

Laconian Envoy Pylos, which we have been asking for and craving for ever so long.

Magistrate In the Sea-god's name, you shall never have it!

Lysistrata Agree, my friends, agree.

Magistrate But then what city shall we be able to stir up trouble in?

Lysistrata Ask for another place in exchange.

Magistrate Ah! that's the ticket! Well, to begin with, give us Echinus, the Maliac gulf adjoining, and the two legs of Megara.

Laconian Envoy No, by the Dioscuri, surely not all that, my dear sir.

Lysistrata Come to terms; never make a difficulty of two legs more or less!

Magistrate *(his eye on Peace)* Well, I'm ready to strip down and get to work right now.
(He takes off his mantle.)

Laconian Envoy *(following out this idea)* And I also, to dung it to start with.

Lysistrata That's just what you shall do, once peace is signed. So, if you really want to make it, go consult your allies about the matter.

Magistrate What allies, I should like to know? Why, we are *all* erected; there's no one who is not mad to be mating. What we all want is to be in bed with our wives; how should our allies fail to second our project?

Laconian Envoy And ours too, for certain sure!

Magistrate The Carystians first and foremost, by the gods!

Lysistrata Well said, indeed! Now go and purify yourselves for entering the Acropolis, where the women invite you to supper; we will empty our provision baskets to do you honor. At table, you will exchange oaths and pledges; then each man will go home with his wife.

Magistrate Come along then, and as quick as may be.

Laconian Envoy Lead on; I'm your man.

Magistrate Quick, quick's the word, say I.
(They follow Lysistrata into the Acropolis.). . . .

LYSIAS (CA. 440–380 B.C.)
The Olympiacus

$\mathcal{B}$orn in Athens, the son of Cephalus, an affluent Syracusan befriended by Pericles, Lysias was sent to southern Italy at the age of fifteen to study with the teacher of rhetoric Tisias. When he returned in 412 B.C., he settled in Piraeus, where he and his brother Polemarchus manufactured shields. In 404 B.C., during the Thirty Tyrants' reign of terror, the wealthy "alien resident" brothers were arrested essentially for being on the wrong side of the revolution. Their property was confiscated.

- Tried and condemned for having democratic leanings, Polemarchus was executed by the leaders of the oligarchy. Lysias managed to flee to the safety of Megara. When the democrats prevailed in 403 B.C., he returned to Athens where he moved in the highest circles of society. To restore his finances lost to the Thirty, he began writing legal speeches for litigants. Though his bid for citizenship failed and he therefore was not allowed to speak in assembly, his reputation as an orator was recognized with his *Against Eratosthenes,* seeking justice against the man who ordered his brother's death.

- The subjects he dealt with as a professional speechwriter are an invaluable resource for understanding the legal mechanics of Athenian society. Of his hundreds of speeches, the thirty-five that survive reflect the continuity of human vices in a cross-section of Athenian society: embezzlement, negligence in office, profiteering, assault and battery, sacrilege, draft evasion, overdue fines, and forgery of welfare benefits. Lysias had a journalist's eye for marital infidelities, murders, investment schemes, and bankruptcies.

- Lysias is the first typically classical orator of Attic Greek, renowned for his plain and simple yet graceful style based on everyday language, quite in contrast to the self-conscious elaborations of the Sophists. An oration by Lysias makes its impact through straightforward clarity instead of rhetorical pyrotechnics. His language, free of poetic contrivances, was smoothly masterful in its persuasion; his speeches are still praised for their insight and compelling characterization. The organization of a Lysian speech—introduction, narrative, evidence, and peroration—is a "classic model" of effective argument.

- In the *Olympiacus* (388 B.C.), one of the three speeches he gave in person, Lysias uses his opportunity as guest of the Olympic committee, and his perception of his audience's fear of foreign aggression (especially from Dionysius, tyrant of Syracuse, and Artaxerxes, king of Persia), to warn the Greeks against the dangers of disunity. His brief reference to the Olympic games suggests how they were perceived as a vehicle for expressing rivalries within a socially constructive framework.

Among many noble feats, gentlemen, for which it is right to remember Heracles, we ought to recall the fact that he was the first, in his affection for the Greeks, to convene this contest. For previously the cities regarded each other as strangers. But he, when he had crushed despotism and arrested outrage, founded a contest of bodily strength, a challenge of wealth, and a display of intelligence in the fairest part of Greece, that we might meet together for all these enjoyments alike of our eyes and of our ears, because he judged that our assembly here would be a beginning of mutual amity amongst the Greeks. The project of it, then, was his; and so I have not come here to talk trivialities or to wrangle over words: I take that to be the business of utterly futile professors in straits for a livelihood; but I think it behooves a man of principle and civic worth to be giving his counsel on the weightiest questions, when I see Greece in this shameful plight, with many parts of her held subject by the foreigner, and many of her cities ravaged by despots. Now if these afflictions were due to weakness, it would be necessary to acquiesce in our fate: but since they are due to faction and mutual rivalry, surely we ought to desist from the one and arrest the other, knowing that, if rivalry befits the prosperous, the most prudent views befit people in a position like ours. For we see both the gravity of our dangers and their imminence on every side: You are aware that empire is for those who command the sea, that the King has control of the money, that the Greeks are in thrall to those who are able to spend it, that our master possesses many ships, and that the despot of Sicily has many also. We ought therefore to relinquish our mutual warfare, and with a single purpose in our hearts to secure our salvation; to feel shame for past events and fear for those that lie in the future, and to compete with our ancestors, by whom the foreigner, in grasping at the land of others, was deprived of his own, and who expelled the despots and established freedom for all in common. But I wonder at the Lacedaemonians most of all: What can be their policy in tolerating the devastation of Greece, when they are leaders of the Greeks by the just claims alike of their inborn valor and their martial science, and when they alone have their dwelling-places unravaged though unwalled and, strangers to faction and defeat, observe always the same rules of life? Wherefore it may be expected that the liberty they possess will never die, and that having achieved the salvation of Greece in her past dangers they are providing against those that are to come. Now the future will bring no better opportunity than the present. We ought to view the disasters of those who have been crushed, not as the concern of others, but as our own: Let us not wait for the forces of both our foes to advance upon ourselves, but while there is yet time let us arrest their outrage. For who would not be mortified to see how they have grown strong through our mutual warfare? Those incidents, no less awful than disgraceful, have empowered our dire oppressors to do what they have done, and have hindered the Greeks from taking vengeance for their wrongs. . . .

ISOCRATES (436–399 B.C.)
Oration to Philip

*M*ost famous for his teaching of rhetoric, Isocrates was also a self-promoter, speechwriter, and orator. Born in Athens of an affluent manufacturer of musical instruments, Theodorus, Isocrates was privileged to study under the sophists Prodicos, Protagoras, Theramenes, and Gorgias; and also, perhaps, was influenced by Socrates himself. After a sojourn on Chios, the school he founded in Athens around 392 B.C., to rival Plato's Academy, focused on educating leaders through the practice of the literary and rhetorical arts. His students included the statesman Lycurgus and the historian Theopompus.

- A Hellenic nationalist and Athenian supremacist, Isocrates deplored the rivalry among the Greek city-states and argued, in his *Panegyricus,* for an enlightened monarch, similar to Plato's philosopher-king, to unite Greece around its highest cultural accomplishments and aspirations—and against Persia. At the time of his death, Philip of Macedon seemed on the brink of realizing Isocrates' lifelong dream.
- His surviving letters, essays, pamphlets, and dialogues are notable for his sophisticated representation of the highly symmetrical "periodic style" of Attic prose that would later deteriorate into preciousness and artificiality.

. . . My purpose in relating all this is that you may see that by my words I am exhorting you to a course of action which, in the light of their deeds, it is manifest that your ancestors chose as the noblest of all. Now, while all who are blessed with understanding ought to set before themselves the greatest of men as their model, and strive to become like him, it behooves you above all to do so. For since you have no need to follow alien examples but have before you one from your own house, have we not then the right to expect that you will be spurred on by this and inspired by the ambition to make yourself like the ancestor of your race? I do not mean that you will be able to imitate Heracles in all his exploits; for even among the gods there are some who could not do that; but in the qualities of the spirit, in devotion to humanity, and in the good will which he cherished toward the Hellenes, you can come close to his purposes. And it lies in your power, if you will heed my words, to attain whatever glory you

yourself desire; for it is easier for you to rise from your present station and win the noblest fame than it has been to advance from the station which you inherited to the fame which is now yours. And mark that I am summoning you to an undertaking in which you will make expeditions, not with the barbarians against men who have given you no just cause, but with the Hellenes against those upon whom it is fitting that the descendants of Heracles should wage war.

And do not be surprised if throughout my speech I am trying to incline you to a policy of kindness to the Hellenes and of gentleness and humanity. For harshness is, I observe, grievous both to those who exercise it and to those upon whom it falls, while gentleness, whether in man or in the other animals, bears a good name; nay, in the case of the gods also we invoke as the "Heavenly Ones" those who bless us with good things, while to those who are agents of calamities and punishments we apply more hateful epithets; in honor of the former, both private persons and states erect temples and altars, whereas we honor the latter neither in our prayers nor in our sacrifices, but practice rites to drive away their evil presence. Bearing ever in mind these truths, you should habitually act and strive to the end that all men shall cherish even more than they do now such an opinion of your character. Indeed, those who crave a greater fame than that of other men must map out in their thoughts a course of action which, while practicable, is at the same time close to the ideal, and seek to carry it into effect as opportunity presents a way.

From many considerations you may realize that you ought to act in this way, but especially from the experiences of Jason. For he, without having achieved anything comparable to what you have done, won the highest renown, not from what he did, but from what he said; for he kept talking as if he intended to cross over to the continent and make war upon the King. Now since Jason by use of words alone advanced himself so far, what opinion must we expect the world will have of you if you actually do this thing; above all, if you undertake to conquer the whole empire of the King, or, at any rate, to wrest from it a vast extent of territory and sever from it—to use a current phrase—"Asia from Cilicia to Sinope"; and if, furthermore, you undertake to establish cities in this region, and to settle in permanent abodes those who now, for lack of the daily necessities of life, are wandering from place to place and committing outrages upon whomsoever they encounter? If we do not stop these men from banding together, by providing suffi-

cient livelihood for them, they will grow before we know it into so great a multitude as to be a terror no less to the Hellenes than to the barbarians. But we pay no heed to them; nay, we shut our eyes to the fact that a terrible menace which threatens us all alike is waxing day by day. It is therefore the duty of a man who is high-minded, who is a lover of Hellas, who has a broader vision than the rest of the world, to employ these bands in a war against the barbarians, to strip from that empire all the territory which I defined a moment ago, to deliver these homeless wanderers from the ills by which they are afflicted and which they inflict upon others, to collect them into cities, and with these cities to fix the boundary of Hellas, making of them buffer states to shield us all. For by doing this, you will not only make them prosperous, but you will put us all on a footing of security. If, however, you do not succeed in these objects, this much you will at any rate easily accomplish—the liberation of the cities which are on the coast of Asia.

But no matter what part of this undertaking you are able to carry out, or only attempt to carry out, you cannot fail to attain distinguished glory; and it will be well deserved if only you will make this the goal of your own efforts and urge on the Hellenes in the same course. For as things now are, who would not have reason to be amazed at the turn events have taken and to feel contempt for us, when among the barbarians, whom we have come to look upon as effeminate and unversed in war and utterly degenerate from luxurious living, men have arisen who thought themselves worthy to rule over Hellas, while among the Hellenes no one has aspired so high as to attempt to make us masters of Asia? Nay, we have dropped so far behind the barbarians that, while they did not hesitate even to begin hostilities against the Hellenes, we do not even have the spirit to pay them back for the injuries we have suffered at their hands. On the contrary, although they admit that in all their wars they have no soldiers of their own nor generals nor any of the things which are serviceable in times of danger, but have to send and get all these from us, we have gone so far in our passion to injure ourselves that, whereas it lies in our power to possess the wealth of the barbarians in security and peace, we continue to wage war upon each other over trifles, and we actually help to reduce to subjection those who revolt from the authority of the King, and sometimes, unwittingly, we ally ourselves with our hereditary foes and seek to destroy those who are of our own race.

Therefore, since the others are so lacking in spirit, I think it is opportune for you to head the war against the King; and, while it is only natural for the other descendants of Heracles, and for men who are under the bonds of their polities and laws, to cleave fondly to that state in which they happen to dwell, it is your privilege, as one who has been blessed with untrammeled freedom, to consider all Hellas your fatherland, as did the founder of your race, and to be as ready to brave perils for her sake as for the things about which you are personally most concerned.

Perhaps there are those—men capable of nothing else but criticism—who will venture to rebuke me because I have chosen to challenge you to the task of leading the expedition against the barbarians and of taking Hellas under your care, while I have passed over my own city. Well, if I were trying to present this matter to any others before having broached it to my own country, which has thrice freed Hellas—twice from the barbarians and once from the Lacedaemonian yoke—I should confess my error. In truth, however, it will be found that I turned to Athens first of all and endeavored to win her over to this cause with all the earnestness of which my nature is capable, but when I perceived that she cared less for what I said than for the ravings of the platform orators, I gave her up, although I did not abandon my efforts. Wherefore I might justly be praised on every hand, because throughout my whole life I have constantly employed such powers as I possess in warring on the barbarians, in condemning those who opposed my plan, and in striving to arouse to action whoever I think will best be able to benefit the Hellenes in any way or to rob the barbarians of their present prosperity. Consequently, I am now addressing myself to you, although I am not unaware that when I am proposing this course many will look at it askance, but that when you are actually carrying it out all will rejoice in it; for no one has had any part in what I have proposed, but when the benefits from it shall have been realized in fact, everyone without fail will look to have his portion.

Consider also what a disgrace it is to sit idly by and see Asia flourishing more than Europe and the barbarians enjoying a greater prosperity than the Hellenes; and, what is more, to see those who derive their power from Cyrus, who as a child was cast out by his mother on the public highway, addressed by the title of "The Great King," while the descendants of Heracles, who because of his virtue was exalted by his father to the rank of a god, are addressed by meaner titles than they. We must not allow this state of affairs to go on; no, we must change and reverse it entirely.

Rest assured that I should never have attempted to persuade you to undertake this at all had power and wealth been the only things which I saw would come of it; for I think that you already have more than enough of such things, and that any man is beyond measure insatiable who deliberately chooses the extreme hazard of either winning these prizes or losing his life. No, it is not with a view to the acquisition of wealth and power that I urge this course, but in the belief that by means of these you will win a name of surpassing greatness and glory. Bear in mind that while we all possess bodies that are mortal, yet by virtue of good will and praise and good report and memory which keeps pace with the passage of time we partake of immortality—a boon for which we may well strive with all our might and suffer any hardship whatsoever. You may observe that even common citizens of the best sort, who would exchange their lives for nothing else, are willing for the sake of winning glory to lay them down in battle; and, in general, that those who crave always an honor greater than they already possess are praised by all men, while those who are insatiable with regard to any other thing under the sun are looked upon as intemperate and mean. But more important than all that I have said is the

truth that wealth and positions of power often fall into the hands of our foes, whereas the good will of our fellow-countrymen and the other rewards which I have mentioned are possessions to which none can fall heir but our own children, and they alone. I could not, therefore, respect myself if I failed to advance these motives in urging you to make this expedition and wage war and brave its perils.

You will best resolve upon this question if you feel that you are summoned to this task, not by my words only, but by your forefathers, by the cowardice of the Persians, and by all who have won great fame and attained the rank of demigods because of their campaigns against the barbarians, and, most of all, by the present opportunity, which finds you in the possession of greater power than has any of those who dwell in Europe, and finds him against whom you are to make war more cordially hated and despised by the world at large than was ever any king before him.

I should have given much to be able to blend into one all the speeches I have delivered on this question; for the present discourse would then appear more worthy of its theme. But, as things are, it devolves upon you to search out and consider, from all my speeches, the arguments which bear upon and urge you to this war; for so you will best resolve upon the matter.

Now I am not unaware that many of the Hellenes look upon the King's power as invincible. Yet one may well marvel at them if they really believe that the power which was subdued to the will of a mere barbarian—an ill-bred barbarian at that—and collected in the cause of slavery, could not be scattered by a man of the blood of Hellas, of ripe experience in warfare, in the cause of freedom—and that too although they know that while it is in all cases difficult to construct a thing, to destroy it is, comparatively, an easy task.

Bear in mind that the men whom the world most admires and honors are those who unite in themselves the abilities of the statesman and the general. When, therefore, you see the renown which even in a single city is bestowed on men who possess these gifts, what manner of eulogies must you expect to hear spoken of you, when among all the Hellenes you shall stand forth as a statesman who has worked for the good of Hellas, and as a general who has overthrown the barbarians? I, for my part, think that this will set a limit to human endeavor; for no other man will ever be able to do deeds greater than these, because among the Hellenes there will never be again so great an enterprise as that of leading us forward out of our innumerable wars into a spirit of concord; nor, among the barbarians, is it likely that so great a power will ever be built up again if once you shatter that which they now possess. Therefore, in generations yet to come, no one, no matter how surpassing his genius, will ever be in a position to do so great a thing. Yes, and speaking of those who lived before your time, I could show that their deeds are excelled by the things which you have even now accomplished, in no specious sense but in very truth; for since you have overthrown more nations than any of the Hellenes has ever taken cities, it would not be hard for me to prove, comparing you with each of them in

turn, that you have accomplished greater things than they. But I have deliberately abstained from this mode of comparison, and for two reasons: because some writers employ it in season and out of season, and also because I am unwilling to represent those whom the world regards as demigods as of less worth than men who are now living.

Ponder well the fact (to touch upon examples from the distant past) that while no man, whether poet or writer of prose, would applaud the wealth of Tantalus, or the rule of Pelops, or the power of Eurystheus, all the world, with one accord, would praise—next to the unrivaled excellence of Heracles and the goodness of Theseus—the men who marched against Troy and all others who have proved to be like them. And yet we know that the bravest and most famous of them held their sway in little villages and petty islands; nevertheless they left behind them a name which rivals that of the gods and is renowned throughout the world. For all the world loves, not those who have acquired the greatest power for themselves alone, but those who have shown themselves to be the greatest benefactors of Hellas.

And you will observe that this is the opinion which men hold, not of these heroes only, but of all mankind. Thus, no one would praise our city either because she was once mistress of the sea, or because she extorted such huge sums of money from her allies and carried them up into the Acropolis, nor yet, surely, because she obtained power over many cities—power to devastate them, or aggrandize them, or manage them according to her pleasure (for all these things it was possible for her to do); no, all these things have been the source of many complaints against her, while because of the battle of Marathon, the naval battle at Salamis, and most of all because her citizens abandoned their own homes to insure the deliverance of Hellas, she enjoys the encomiums of all mankind. The same opinion is held regarding the Lacedaemonians also; their defeat at Thermopylae is more admired than their many victories; the trophy which was erected by the barbarians over the Lacedaemonians is an object of affectionate regard and of pilgrimages, while the trophies erected by the Lacedaemonians over their enemies call forth, not praise, but odium; for the former is regarded as a proof of valor, the latter of selfish greed.

Now if, after examining and reviewing all these admonitions in your own mind, you feel that my discourse is in any part rather weak and inadequate, set it down to my age, which might well claim the indulgence of all; but if it is up to the standard of my former publications, I would have you believe that it was not my old age that conceived it but the divine will that prompted it, not out of solicitude for me, but because of its concern for Hellas, and because of its desire to deliver her out of her present distress and to crown you with a glory far greater than you now possess. I think that you are not unaware in what manner the gods order the affairs of mortals: for not with their own hands do they deal out the blessings and curses that befall us; rather they inspire in each of us such a state of mind that good or ill, as the case may be, is visited upon us through one another. For example, it may be that even now the gods have assigned to me the task of speech while to you they allot the task of action, considering

that you will be the best master in that province, while in the field of speech I might prove least irksome to my hearers. Indeed, I believe that even your past achievements would never have reached such magnitude had not one of the gods helped you to succeed; and I believe he did so, not that you might spend your whole life warring upon the barbarians in Europe alone, but that, having been trained and having gained experience and come to know your own powers in these campaigns, you might set your heart upon the course which I have urged upon you. It were therefore shameful, now that fortune nobly leads the way, to lag behind and refuse to follow whither she desires to lead you forward.

It is my belief that, while you ought to honor everyone who has any praise for your past accomplishments, you ought to consider that those laud you in the noblest terms who judge your nature capable of even greater triumphs, and not those whose discourse has gratified you for the moment only, but those who will cause future generations to admire your achievements beyond the deeds of any man of the generations that are past. I would like to say many things in this strain, but I am not able; the reason why, I have stated more often than I ought.

It remains, then, to summarize what I have said in this discourse, in order that you may see in the smallest compass the substance of my counsels. I assert that it is incumbent upon you to work for the good of the Hellenes, to reign as king over the Macedonians, and to extend your power over the greatest possible number of the barbarians. For if you do these things, all men will be grateful to you: the Hellenes for your kindness to them; the Macedonians if you reign over them, not like a tyrant, but like a king; and the rest of the nations, if by your hands they are delivered from barbaric despotism and are brought under the protection of Hellas.

How well this discourse has been composed with respect to appropriateness and finish of style is a question which it is fair to ask my hearers to answer; but that no one could give you better advice than this, or advice more suited to the present situation—of this I believe that I am well assured.

PLATO (CA. 429–347 B.C.)
The Republic

❦

*T*he greatest original philosopher of classical Greece and second only to Homer in his impact on its value system was born to a distinguished Athenian family, the son of Ariston and Perictione (his mother was a relative of Solon and Critias). Plato's stepfather Pyrilampes was one of Pericles' close friends and advisers. He was named Aristocles after his grandfather; but was nicknamed "Plato," "wide forehead," by his mentor Socrates because of the breadth of his speech and knowledge. He was trained in music and gymnastics, and began his literary career as a poet. But under the tutelage of Heraclitus' student Cratylus he turned to the study of philosophy, becoming an associate of Socrates when he was twenty. When Socrates was condemned to death in 399 B.C., Plato, horrified by Athenian politics, left Athens and traveled widely from Egypt to Italy.

In southern Italy and in the court of Dionysius I of Syracuse, Plato came into contact with Pythagorean thought. He returned to Athens to found the Academy, which may be called the first university in the western world; and researched and taught there for forty years, dedicating his work to preparing leaders worthy of governing. His most famous student was Aristotle. Whereas his competitor Isocrates educated leaders primarily in rhetoric, Plato's curriculum included law, political theory, and mathematics. Plato wrote thirty-six dialogues and many letters, in compelling, metaphorically rich and unequaled Attic prose. Everything he wrote has survived. Some of his most important dialogues, and their subject matter, are:

- *The Symposium,* various views of the nature of love
- *The Republic,* on the ideal commonwealth and the nature of justice
- *The Apology, Crito,* and *Phaedo,* on the trial and death of Socrates
- *The Meno,* on the nature of the "good"

- *The Sophist,* on being and not-being, and the insufficiency of dialectic
- *The Timaeus,* on the evolution of the universe and mankind

- Plato's most influential theory, the "theory of ideas," posited a distinction between the "real" world of perception and the "really real" world of ideas that lay behind this veil of illusion (no doubt influenced by eastern thought, transmitted by way of Egypt and Pythagoreanism). Because our souls lived in the ideal world before entering our bodies, our minds can "recall" true knowledge if led to the recollection by the questioning of an astute master such as Socrates. In keeping with this theory, Plato believed in the "transmigration of souls" (reincarnation).
- Although Plato attacked poetry as being inferior to philosophy because it has no loyalty to truth, he himself was a considerable poet as well as one of the most poetic of prose writers. The British poet Shelley commended Plato for the "melody of his language," for his ability to "kindle a harmony in thoughts," and for the "truth and splendour of his imagery." Despite all he did for the creation of a logical language with which to pursue metaphysics, Plato in his late dialogues, *The Sophist* and *Theatetus,* evolved to the belief that language and logic alone could never ultimately capture the "truth." The apex of his poetic penchant is his conclusion that only intuition, albeit based on reason's spadework, allows the philosopher to grasp the "really real." The dialogue, which Plato perfected, is, after all, a dramatic form.
- In his most famous dialogue, *The Republic,* Plato outlines the dimensions of a political utopia presided over by the ideal philosopher-king. In this perfectly harmonious world, all the parts of the "body politic" (a term he invented) serve the greater good; offending parts would be cut off. In the parable of the cave, which follows, he introduces the distinction between the world of the senses in which we live and the world of true reality from which we came and to which we will go after death. The excerpt which follows, from Book 8, moves, in Socrates' interrogation of Glaucon, from the metaphor of the cave to an outline of the ideal education, including Plato's own dialectical method that the dialogue itself exemplifies.

And now, I said, let me show in a figure how far our nature is enlightened or unenlightened: Behold! human beings living in an underground den, which has a mouth open toward the light and reaching all along the den; here they have been from their childhood, and have their legs and necks chained so that they cannot move, and can only see before them, being prevented by the chains from turning around their heads. Above and behind them a fire is blazing at a distance, and between the fire and the prisoners there is a raised way; and you will see, if you look, a low wall built along the way, like the screen which marionette-players have in front of them, over which they show the puppets.

I see.

And do you see, I said, men passing along the wall carrying all sorts of vessels, and statues and figures of animals made of wood and stone and various materials, which appear over the wall? Some of them are talking, others silent.

You have shown me a strange image, and they are strange prisoners.

Like ourselves, I replied; and they see only their own shadows, or the shadows of one another, which the fire throws on the opposite wall of the cave?

True, he said; how could they see anything but the shadows if they were never allowed to move their heads?

And of the objects which are being carried in like manner they would only see the shadows?

Yes, he said.

And if they were able to converse with one another, would they not suppose that they were naming what was actually before them?

Very true.

And suppose further that the prison had an echo which came from the other side, would they not be sure to fancy when one of the passersby spoke that the voice which they heard came from the passing shadow?

No question, he replied.

To them, I said, the truth would be literally nothing but the shadows of the images.

That is certain.

And now look again, and see what will naturally follow if the prisoners are released and disabused of their error. At first, when any of them is liberated and compelled suddenly to stand up and turn his neck around and walk and look toward the light, he will suffer sharp pains; the glare will distress him, and he will be unable to see the realities of which in his former state he had seen the shadows; and then conceive someone saying to him, that what he saw before was an illusion, but that now, when he is approaching nearer to being and his eye is turned toward more real existence, he has a clearer vision—what will be his reply? And you may further imagine that his instructor is pointing to the objects as they pass and requiring him to name them—will he not be perplexed? Will he not fancy that the shadows which he formerly saw are truer than the objects which are now shown to him?

Far truer.

And if he is compelled to look straight at the light, will he not have a pain in his eyes which will make him turn away to take refuge in the objects of vision which he can see, and which he will conceive to be in reality clearer than the things which are now being shown to him?

True, he said.

And suppose once more, that he is reluctantly dragged up a steep and rugged ascent, and held fast until he is forced into the presence of the sun himself, is he not likely to be pained and irritated? When he approaches the light his eyes will be dazzled, and he will not be able to see anything at all of what are now called realities.

Not all in a moment, he said.

He will require to grow accustomed to the

sight of the upper world. And first he will see the shadows best, next the reflections of men and other objects in the water, and then the objects themselves; then he will gaze upon the light of the moon and the stars and the spangled heaven; and he will see the sky and the stars by night better than the sun or the light of the sun by day?

Certainly.

Last of all he will be able to see the sun, and not mere reflections of him in the water, but he will see him in his own proper place, and not in another; and he will contemplate him as he is.

Certainly.

He will then proceed to argue that this is he who gives the season and the years, and is the guardian of all that is in the visible world, and in a certain way the cause of all things which he and his fellows have been accustomed to behold?

Clearly, he said, he would first see the sun and then reason about him.

And when he remembered his old habitation, and the wisdom of the den and his fellow prisoners, do you not suppose that he would felicitate himself on the change, and pity him?

Certainly, he would.

And if they were in the habit of conferring honors among themselves on those who were quickest to observe the passing shadows and to remark which of them went before, and which followed after, and which were together; and who were therefore best able to draw conclusions as to the future, do you think that he would care for such honors and glories, or envy the possessors of them? Would he not say with Homer,

"Agora, Athens"

"Better to be the poor servant of
a poor master,"

and to endure anything, rather than think as they do and live after their manner?

Yes, he said, I think that he would rather suffer anything than entertain these false notions and live in this miserable manner.

Imagine once more, I said, such a one coming suddenly out of the sun to be replaced in his old situation; would he not be certain to have his eyes full of darkness?

To be sure, he said.

And if there were a contest, and he had to compete in measuring the shadows with the prisoners who had never moved out of the den, while his sight was still weak, and before his eyes had become steady (and the time which would be needed to acquire this new habit of sight might be very considerable), would he not be ridiculous? Men would say of him that up he went and down he came without his eyes; and that it was better not even to think of ascending; and if anyone tried to loose another and lead him up to the light, let them only catch the offender, and they would put him to death.

No question, he said.

This entire allegory, I said, you may now append, dear Glaucon, to the previous argument; the prison-house is the world of sight, the light of the fire is the sun, and you will not misapprehend me if you interpret the journey upward to be the ascent of the soul into the intellectual world according to my poor belief, which, at your desire, I have expressed— whether rightly or wrongly, God knows. But, whether true or false, my opinion is that in the world of knowledge the idea of good appears last of all, and is seen only with an effort; and, when seen, is also inferred to be the universal author of all things beautiful and right, parent of light and of the lord of light in this visible world, and the immediate source of reason and truth in the intellectual; and that this is the power upon which he who would act rationally either in public or private life must have his eye fixed.

I agree, he said, as far as I am able to understand you.

Moreover, I said, you must not wonder that those who attain to this beatific vision are unwilling to descend to human affairs; for their souls are ever hastening into the upper world where they desire to dwell; which desire of theirs is very natural, if our allegory may be trusted.

Yes, very natural.

And is there anything surprising in one who passes from divine contemplations to the evil state of man, misbehaving himself in a ridiculous manner; if, while his eyes are blinking and

before he has become accustomed to the surrounding darkness, he is compelled to fight in courts of law, or in other places, about the images or the shadows of images of justice, and is endeavoring to meet the conceptions of those who have never yet seen absolute justice?

Anything but surprising, he replied.

Anyone who has common sense will remember that the bewilderments of the eyes are of two kinds, and arise from two causes, either from coming out of the light or from going into the light, which is true of the mind's eye, quite as much as of the bodily eye; and he who remembers this when he sees anyone whose vision is perplexed and weak, will not be too ready to laugh; he will first ask whether that soul of man has come out of the brighter life, and is unable to see because unaccustomed to the dark, or having turned from darkness to the day is dazzled by excess of light. And he will count the one happy in his condition and state of being, and he will pity the other; or, if he have a mind to laugh at the soul which comes from below into the light, there will be more reason in this than in the laugh which greets him who returns from above out of the light into the den.

That, he said, is a very just distinction.

But then, if I am right, certain professors of education must be wrong when they say that they can put a knowledge into the soul which was not there before, like sight into blind eyes.

They undoubtedly say this, he replied.

Whereas, our argument shows that the power and capacity of learning exists in the soul already; and that just as the eye was unable to turn from darkness to light without the whole body, so too the instrument of knowledge can only by the movement of the whole soul be turned from the world of becoming into that of being, and learn by degrees to endure the sight of being, and of the brightest and best of being, or, in other words, of the good.

Very true.

And must there not be some art which will effect conversion in the easiest and quickest manner; not implanting the faculty of sight, for that exists already, but has been turned in the wrong direction, and is looking away from the truth?

Yes, he said, such an art may be presumed.

And whereas the other so-called virtues of the soul seem to be akin to bodily qualities, for even when they are not originally innate they can be implanted later by habit and exercise, the virtue of wisdom more than anything else contains a divine element which always remains, and by this conversion is rendered useful and profitable; or, on the other hand, hurtful and useless. Did you never observe the narrow intelligence flashing from the keen eye of a clever rogue—how eager he is, how clearly his paltry soul sees the way to his end; he is the reverse of blind, but his keen eyesight is forced into the service of evil, and he is mischievous in proportion to his cleverness?

Very true, he said.

But what if there had been a circumcision of such natures in the days of their youth; and they had been severed from those sensual pleasures, such as eating and drinking, which, like leaden weights, were attached to them at their birth, and which drag them down and turn the vision of their souls upon the things that are below—if, I say, they had been released from these impediments and turned in the opposite direction, the very same faculty in them would have seen the truth as keenly as they see what their eyes are turned to now.

Very likely.

Yes, I said; and there is another thing which is likely, or rather a necessary inference from what has preceded, that neither the uneducated and uninformed of the truth, nor yet those who never make an end of their education, will be able ministers of the State; not the former, because they have no single aim of duty which is the rule of all their actions, private as well as public; nor the latter, because they will not act at all except upon compulsion, fancying that they are already dwelling apart in the islands of the blessed.

Very true, he replied.

Then, I said, the business of us who are the founders of the State will be to compel the best minds to attain that knowledge which we have already shown to be the greatest of all—they must continue to ascend until they arrive at the good; but when they have ascended and seen enough we must not allow them to do as they do now.

What do you mean?

I mean that they remain in the upper world: but this must not be allowed; they must be made to descend again among the prisoners in the den, and partake of their labors and honors, whether they are worth having or not.

But is not this unjust? he said; ought we to give them a worse life, when they might have a better?

You have again forgotten, my friend, I said,

the intention of the legislator, who did not aim at making any one class in the State happy above the rest; the happiness was to be in the whole State, and he held the citizens together by persuasion and necessity, making them benefactors of the State, and therefore bene-factors of one another; to this end he created them, not to please themselves, but to be his instruments in binding up the State.

True, he said, I had forgotten.

Observe, Glaucon, that there will be no in-justice in compelling our philosophers to have a care and providence of others; we shall ex-plain to them that in other States, men of their class are not obliged to share in the toils of politics: and this is reasonable, for they grow up at their own sweet will, and the govern-ment would rather not have them. Being self-taught, they cannot be expected to show any gratitude for a culture which they have never received. But we have brought you into the world to be rulers of the hive, kings of your-selves and of the other citizens, and have edu-cated you far better and more perfectly than they have been educated, and you are better able to share in the double duty. Wherefore each of you, when his turn comes, must go down to the general underground abode, and get the habit of seeing in the dark. When you have acquired the habit, you will see ten thou-sand times better than the inhabitants of the den, and you will know what the several im-ages are, and what they represent, because you have seen the beautiful and just and good in their truth. And thus our State, which is also yours, will be a reality, and not a dream only, and will be administered in a spirit unlike that of other States, in which men fight with one another about shadows only and are distracted in the struggle for power, which in their eyes is a great good. Whereas the truth is that the State in which the rulers are most reluctant to govern is always the best and most quietly gov-erned, and the State in which they are most eager, the worst.

Quite true, he replied.

And will our pupils, when they hear this, refuse to take their turn at the toils of State, when they are allowed to spend the greater part of their time with one another in the heavenly light?

Impossible, he answered; for they are just men, and the commands which we impose upon them are just; there can be no doubt that every one of them will take office as a stern ne-cessity, and not after the fashion of our present rulers of State.

Yes, my friend, I said; and there lies the point. You must contrive for your future rulers another and a better life than that of a ruler, and then you may have a well-ordered State; for only in the State which offers this, will they rule who are truly rich, not in silver and gold, but in virtue and wisdom, which are the true blessings of life. Whereas, if they go to the ad-ministration of public affairs, poor and hunger-ing after their own private advantage, thinking that hence they are to snatch the chief good, order there can never be; for they will be fight-ing about office, and the civil and domestic broils which thus arise will be the ruin of the rulers themselves and of the whole State.

Most true, he replied.

And the only life which looks down upon

the life of political ambition is that of true phi-losophy. Do you know of any other?

Indeed, I do not, he said.

And those who govern ought not to be lovers of the task? For, if they are, there will be rival lovers, and they will fight.

No question.

Who, then, are those whom we shall com-pel to be guardians? Surely they will be the men who are wisest about affairs of State, and by whom the State is best administered, and who at the same time have other honors and an-other and a better life than that of politics?

They are the men, and I will choose them, he replied.

And now shall we consider in what way such guardians will be produced, and how they are to be brought from darkness to light—as some are said to have ascended from the world below to the gods?

By all means, he replied.

The process, I said, is not the turning over of an oyster shell, but the turning around of a soul passing from a day which is little better than night to the true day of being, that is, the ascent from below, which we affirm to be true philosophy?

Quite so.

And should we not inquire what sort of knowledge has the power of effecting such a change?

Certainly.

. . . And so, Glaucon, I said, we have at last arrived at the hymn of dialectic. This is that strain which is of the intellect only, but which the faculty of sight will nevertheless be found to imitate; for sight, as you may remember, was imagined by us after a while to behold the real animals and stars, and last of all the sun him-self. And so with dialectic; when a person starts on the discovery of the absolute by the light of reason only, and without any assistance of sense, and perseveres until by pure intelligence he arrives at the perception of the absolute good, he at last finds himself at the end of the intellectual world, as in the case of sight at the end of the visible.

Exactly, he said.

Then this is the progress which you call di-alectic?

True.

But the release of the prisoners from chains, and their translation from the shadows to the images and to the light, and the ascent from the underground den to the sun, while in his presence they are vainly trying to look on animals and plants and the light of the sun, but are able to perceive even with their weak eyes the images in the water (which are di-vine), and are the shadows of true existence (not shadows of images cast by a light of fire, which compared with the sun is only an im-age)—this power of elevating the highest prin-ciple in the soul to the contemplation of that which is best in existence, with which we may compare the raising of that faculty which is the very light of the body to the sight of that which is brightest in the material and visible world—this power is given, as I was saying, by all that study and pursuit of the arts which have been described. . . .

XENOPHON (428–354 B.C.)
Anabasis

Of a wealthy Athenian family, Xenophon, son of Gryllus, served in the Persian army under Cyrus the younger, received an estate from Sparta where he spent much of his life, and died on a visit to Corinth. Along the way he became a leading associate of Socrates, as well as an adviser to Spartan king Agesilaus, whom he aided in his war against Athens and Boeotia.

- Xenophon served as a mercenary for the Persian Cyrus in his campaign to overthrow his brother, King Artaxerxes. When Xenophon and his fellow countrymen were left leaderless after Cyrus' battlefield death at Cunaxa, he (along with Chirisophus) was elected general; and successfully guided the "ten thousand" out of Persia to the safety of Greek cities on the Black Sea. This exploit is the subject of his seven-book *Anabasis*.
- Xenophon's other works included the *Oeconomicus,* on estate and household management, important for its insight into the place of women in classical Athens; the *Cyropaedia,* an idealized biography of the education of Cyrus the elder; the *Hellenica,* a sequel to Thucydides' history, describing Greek history 411–362 B.C. from a very pro-Sparta bias; and *Memorabilia,* memoirs of Socrates, in four books.

BOOK III—A COUNCIL OF GREEK GENERALS

What the Greeks did in their march up the country with Cyrus, until the time of the battle, and what occurred after Cyrus was dead, when the Greeks set out to return with Tissaphernes in reliance on a truce, has been related in the preceding part of the work.

After the generals were made prisoners, and such of the captains and soldiers as had accompanied them were put to death, the Greeks were in great perplexity, reflecting that they were not far from the king's residence; that there were around them, on all sides, many hostile nations and cities; that no one would any longer secure them opportunities of purchasing provisions; that they were distant from Greece not less than ten thousand stadia; that there was no one to guide them on the way; that impassable rivers would intercept them in the midst of their course; that the Barbarians who had gone up with Cyrus had deserted them; and that they were left utterly alone, having no cavalry to support them, so that it

"Charioteer, Delphi." Michos Tzovaras Photography. By permission of Art Resource.

was certain, even if they defeated their enemies, that they would not kill a man of them, and that, if they were defeated, none of themselves would be left alive; reflecting, I say, on these circumstances, and being disheartened at them, few of them tasted food for that evening, few kindled fires, and many did not come to the place of arms during the night, but lay down to rest where they severally happened to be, unable to sleep for sorrow and longing for their country, their parents, their wives and children, whom they never expected to see again. In this state of mind they all went to their resting places.

There was in the army a certain Xenophon, an Athenian, who accompanied it neither in the character of general, nor captain, nor common soldier, but it had happened that Proxenus, an old guest-friend of his, had sent for him from home, giving him a promise that, if he came, he would recommend him to the friendship of Cyrus, whom he considered, he said, as a greater object of regard than his own country. Xenophon, on reading the letter, consulted Socrates the Athenian, as to the propriety of making the journey; and Socrates, fearing that if he attached himself to Cyrus it might prove a ground of accusation against him with his country, because Cyrus was thought to have zealously assisted the Lacedaemonians in their war with Athens, advised Xenophon to go to Delphi, and consult the god respecting the expedition. Xenophon, having gone thither accordingly, inquired of Apollo to which of the gods he should sacrifice and pray, in order most honorably and successfully to perform the journey which he contemplated, and, after prosperously accomplishing it, to return in safety. Apollo answered him that "he should sacrifice to the gods to whom it was proper for him to sacrifice." When he returned, he repeated the oracle to Socrates, who, on hearing it, blamed him for not asking Apollo in the first place, whether it were better for him to go or stay at home; whereas, having settled with himself that he would go, he only asked how he might best go; "but since you have," said he, "put the question thus, you must do what the god has directed." Xenophon, therefore, having sacrificed to the gods as Apollo commanded, set sail, and found Proxenus and Cyrus at Sardis, just setting out on their march up the country, and was presented to Cyrus. Proxenus desiring that he should remain with them, Cyrus joined in the same desire, and said that as soon as the expedition was ended, he would send him home again. The expedition was said to be intended against the Pisidians. Xenophon accordingly joined in the enterprise, being thus deceived, but not by Proxenus; for he did not know that the movement was against the king, nor did any other of the Greeks, except Clearchus.

When they arrived in Cilicia, however, it appeared manifest to every one that it was against the king that their force was directed; but, though they were afraid of the length of the journey, and unwilling to proceed, yet the greater part of them, out of respect both for one another and for Cyrus, continued to follow him; of which number was Xenophon.

When this perplexity occurred, Xenophon was distressed as well as the other Greeks, and unable to rest, but having at length got a little sleep, he had a dream in which, in the midst of a thunderstorm, a bolt seemed to him to fall upon his father's house, and the house in consequence became all in a blaze. Being greatly frightened, he immediately awoke, and considered his dream as in one respect favorable (inasmuch as, being in troubles and dangers, he seemed to behold a great light from Jupiter), but in another respect he was alarmed (because the dream appeared to him to be from Jupiter who was a king, and the fire to blaze all around him), lest he should be unable to escape from the king's territories, but should be hemmed in on all sides by inextricable difficulties.

What it betokens, however, to see such a dream, we may conjecture from the occurrences that happened after the dream. What immediately followed was this. As soon as he awoke, the thought that first occurred to him was, "Why do I lie here? The night is passing away. With daylight it is probable that the enemy will come upon us; and if we once fall into the hands of the king, what is there to prevent us from being put to death with ignomy, after witnessing the most grievous sufferings among our comrades, and enduring every severity of torture ourselves? Yet no one concerts measures, or takes thought, for our defense, but we lie still, as if we were at liberty to enjoy repose. From what city, then, do I expect a leader to undertake our defense? What age am I waiting for to come to myself? Assuredly I shall never be older, if I give myself up to the enemy today." After these reflections he arose, and called together, in the first place, the captains that were under Proxenus.

When they were assembled, he said, "For my part, captains, I cannot sleep, nor, I should think, can you, nor can I lie still any longer, when I consider in what circumstances we are placed; for it is plain that the enemy did not openly manifest hostility toward us, until they thought that they had judiciously arranged their plans; but on our side no one takes any thought how we may best maintain a contest with them. Yet if we prove remiss, and fall into the power of the king, what may we not expect to suffer from a man who cut off the head and hand of his own brother by the same mother and father, even after he was dead, and fixed them upon a stake? What may not we, I say, expect to suffer, who have no relative to take our part, and who have marched against him to make him a subject instead of a monarch, and to put him to death if it should lie in our power? Will he not proceed to every extremity, that by reducing us to the last degree of ignominious suffering, he may inspire all men with a dread of ever taking the field against him? We must, however, try every expedient not to fall into his hands. For myself, I never ceased, while the truce lasted, to consider ourselves as objects of pity, and to regard the king and his people as objects of envy, as I contemplated how extensive and valuable a country they possessed, how great an abundance of provisions, how many slaves and cattle, and how vast a quantity of gold and raiment; while, on the other hand, when I reflected on the condition of our own soldiers, that we had no share in any of all these blessings, unless we bought it, and knew that few of us had any longer money to buy, and that our oaths restrained us from getting provisions otherwise than by buying, I sometimes, on taking all these circumstances into consideration, feared the continuance of peace more than I now fear war. But since they have put an end to peace, their own haughtiness, and our mistrust, seem likewise to be brought to an end; for the advantages which I have mentioned lie now as prizes between us, for whichsoever of us shall prove the better men; and the gods are the judges of the contest, who, as is just, will be on our side; since the enemy have offended them by perjury, while we, though seeing many good things to tempt us, have resolutely abstained from all of them through regard to our oaths; so that, as it seems to me, we may advance to the combat with much greater confidence than they can feel. We have bodies, moreover, better able than theirs to endure cold, and heat, and toil; and we have, with the help of the gods, more resolute minds; while the enemy, if the gods, as before, grant us success, will be found more obnoxious to wounds and death than we are. But possibly others of you entertain the same thoughts; let us not, then, in the name of heaven, wait for others to come and exhort us to noble deeds, but let us be ourselves the first to excite others to exert their valor. Prove yourselves the bravest of the captains, and more worthy to lead than those who are now leaders. As for me, if you wish to take the start in the course, I am willing to follow you, or, if you appoint me to be a leader, I shall not make my youth an excuse, but shall think myself sufficiently mature to defend myself against harm."

Thus spoke Xenophon; and the captains, on hearing his observations, all desired him to be their leader, except a certain Apollonides, who resembled a Boeotian in his manner of speaking; this man said that "whoever asserted they could gain safety by any other means than by obtaining, if he could, the king's consent to it, talked absurdly"; and at the same time began to enumerate the difficulties surrounding them. But Xenophon, interrupting him, said, "O most wonderful of men! you neither understand what you see, nor remember what you hear. Yet you were on the same spot with those here present, when the king, after Cyrus was dead, being in high spirits at the circumstance, sent to demand that we should deliver up our arms; and, when we, refusing to deliver them up, and appearing in full armor, went and encamped over against him, what means did he not try, sending deputies, asking for a truce, and supplying us with provisions until he obtained a truce? But when, on the other hand, our generals and captains went to confer with the Barbarians, as you now advise us to do, without their arms, and relying on the truce, were they not beaten, goaded, insulted, and are they not unable, wretched men, to die, though, I should think, greatly longing for death? And do you, knowing all these occurrences, say to those who exhort us to defend ourselves, talk absurdly, and advise us to go again to try persuasion? To me, O captains, it seems that we should no longer admit this man into the same service with ourselves, but take from him his captaincy, and laying baggage on his back, make use of him in that capacity; for he disgraces both his own country and all Greece, inasmuch as, being a Greek, he is of such a character." Here Agasias of Stymphalus, proceeding to speak, said, "But this man, assuredly, has nothing to do either with Boeotia or with Greece at all, for I have observed that he has both his ears bored, like a Lydian." Such indeed was the case; and they accordingly expelled him.

The rest, proceeding to the different divisions of the troops, called up the general wherever there was a general surviving, and the lieutenant-general where the general was dead, and the captain wherever there was a captain surviving. When they were all come together, they sat down before the place where the arms were piled; and the generals and captains assembled were about a hundred in all. The time when the meeting took place was about midnight.

Hieronymus, a native of Elis, the oldest of all the captains that had served under Proxenus, was the first to speak, as follows: "It has seemed proper to us, O generals and captains, on contemplating the present state of our affairs, to meet together ourselves, and to call upon you to join us, that we may determine, if we can, on some plan for our benefit. But do you, Xenophon, first represent to the assembly what you have already observed to us." Xenophon accordingly said, "We are all aware that the king and Tissaphernes have made prisoners of as many of us as they could; and it is evident that they are forming designs against the rest of us, that they may put us to death if they can. But on our parts I think that every means should be adopted in order that we may not fall into the Barbarians' hands, but rather that they, if we can accomplish it, may fall into ours. Be well assured then, that you, who have now met together in such numbers, have upon you a most important responsibility; for all the soldiers look to you, and, if they see you dispirited, they will themselves lose courage, but if both you yourselves appear well prepared to meet the enemy, and exhort others to be equally prepared, be certain that they will follow you, and strive to imitate you. Perhaps, too, it is right that you should show some superiority over them; for you are their generals, their officers, and their captains, and, when there was peace, you enjoyed advantages over them in fortune and honor; and now, in consequence, when war arises, you ought to prove yourselves preeminent over the multitude, and to take the lead in forming plans for them, and should it ever be necessary, in toiling for them.

And, in the first place, I think that you will greatly benefit the army, if you take care that generals and captains be chosen, as soon as possible, in the room of those whom we have lost; for without commanders nothing honorable or advantageous can be achieved, I may say in one word, anywhere, but least of all in the field of battle. Good order conduces to safety, but want of order has already proved fatal to many. Again, when you have appointed as many commanders as are requisite, I consider that if you were to assemble and encourage the rest of the soldiers, you would act very suitably to the occasion; for you perhaps observe, as well as myself, how dejectedly they have now come to the place of arms, and how dejectedly they go upon guard, so that, while they are in such a condition, I know not for what service anyone could employ them, whether required by night or by day. But if anyone could change the direction of their thoughts, so that they may not merely contemplate what they are likely to suffer, but what they may be able to do, they will become much more eager for action; for you are certain that it is neither numbers nor strength which gives the victory in war, but that whichsoever side advances on the enemy with the more resolute courage, their opponents, in general, cannot withstand their onset. I have also remarked, fellow soldiers, that such as are eager in the field to preserve their lives at any rate, for the most part perish wretchedly and igno-

miniously, while I see that such as reflect that death is to all men common and inevitable, and seek in battle only to fall with honor, more frequently, from whatever cause, arrive at old age, and live, while they live, with greater happiness. Being aware, then, of these facts, it behooves us, such are the circumstances in which we are placed, both to prove ourselves to be brave soldiers, and to exhort others to be so likewise." Having spoken thus, he stopped.

After him Cheirisophus said, "Till the present moment, O Xenophon, I knew nothing of you, except having heard that you were an Athenian, but now I have to praise you both for what you say and what you do, and could wish that there were very many like you; for it would be a general good. And now," he added, "let us not delay, my fellow soldiers, but proceed at once, you who want them, to choose commanders, and when you have elected them, come to the center of the camp, and bring those that are chosen; and we will then call the rest of the soldiers together there. And let Tolmides the herald," said he, "come with us." As he said this, he rose up, that the necessary measures might not be delayed, but carried at once into execution. There were accordingly chosen commanders, Timasion, a Dardanian in the room of Clearchus, Xanthicles an Achaean in that of Socrates, Cleanor an Arcadian in that of Agias, Philesius an Achaean in that of Menon, and Xenophon of Athens in that of Proxenus.

Aeneas the Tactician (fl. 357 b.c.)
On the Defense of Fortified Positions

*O*ne of the earliest Greek writers on the art of war, Aeneas wrote a number of treatises and military manuals. *On the Defense of Fortified Positions* is the only one that survives.

- He was probably from Stymphalos in the Peloponnesus, and fought as a general in the Arcadian Confederacy in the Aegean and Asia Minor. Many of his illustrations are drawn from firsthand experience.
- Writing his didactic handbook in the Hellenistic *Koine* dialect, Aeneas advises the defenders of a besieged city on the best tactics for strengthening and maintaining their fortifications, and for defending against internal squabbles; he uses historical examples to corroborate his points. His mention of signal fires gives evidence of how long-distance communication was accomplished in ancient Greece, explaining the opening of Aeschylus' *Agamemnon,* where the watchman stands on the roof awaiting sign of the king's return to Mycenae. The handbook is particularly valuable for the perspective it provides on fourth-century political and living conditions.

When men set out from their own country to encounter strife and perils in foreign lands and some disaster befalls them by land or sea, the survivors still have left their native soil, their city, and their fatherland, so that they are not all utterly destroyed. But for those who are to incur peril in defense of what they most prize, shrines and country, parents and children, and all else, the struggle is not the same nor even similar. For if they save themselves by a stout defense against the foe, their enemies will be intimidated and disinclined to attack them in the future, but if they make a poor showing in the face of danger, no hope of safety will be left. Those, therefore, who are to contend for all these precious stakes must fail in no preparation and no effort, but must take thought for many and varied activities, so that a failure may at least not seem due to their own fault. But if after all a reverse should befall them, yet at all events the survivors may some time restore their affairs to their former condition, like certain Greek peoples who, after being reduced to extremes, have re-established themselves.

I.

Now the disposition of the troops is to be made with reference to the size of the state and the topography of the town, its sentries and patrols, and any other service for which troops are required in the city—in view of all this the assignments are to be made. So men who are going to fight outside the walls must be drawn up in a manner suitable to the country along their line of march, according as they are to march past dangerous or fortified places, through narrow passes or across plains, past higher ground upon the right and points exposed to ambush, with reference also to the river crossings and the formation of a line of battle under such conditions. But the forces which are to defend the walls and keep watch over the citizens need not be so arranged, but rather with reference to the positions within the city and to the immediate danger. First, then, it is necessary to select the most prudent citizens and those most experienced in war for attendance upon the civil authorities. Next one must pick out men capable of the greatest physical exertion and divide them into companies, that they may be ready for sallies, for patrolling the city, for the relief of those hard pressed, or for any other similar service, these who are picked men and able to give assistance. They must be both loyal and satisfied with the existing order, since it is a great thing to have such a group acting like a fortress against the revolutionary designs of the other party, for it would be a terror to the opposition inside the city. And let the man who is to lead and have charge of them be not merely prudent and vigorous, but also one who would run

"Inside the Cyclopean walls of Mycenae"

the greatest risks from a change of government. From the rest the strongest, in the prime of manhood, should be chosen for the watches and the walls, while the remainder should be divided and apportioned according to the length of the nights and the number of the watches. Of the common soldiers some should be stationed in the marketplace, some in the theater, and the rest in the open places in the city, so that as far as the city's power permits no part may be unguarded.

II.

And that there may be no need of troops to guard them, it is best to block up the useless open places in the city by digging ditches and by making them as inaccessible as possible to any who might wish to start a revolt and begin by taking possession of them. So, when the Thebans had broken in, the Lacedaemonians, some here and others there, filled baskets with earth and stones from the nearest houses, which they tore down, and from fences and walls, making use also, it is said, of the many massive bronze tripods from the temples, and with these they managed, in advance of the Thebans, to block up the entrances and passages and open places and kept them out when they tried to break into the city proper.

On another occasion, when the Plataeans became aware during the night that the Thebans were in the city, they perceived that there were not many of them and that they were taking none of the proper precautions because they fancied that they were in possession of the town. The Plataeans concluded, therefore, that they could easily defeat them by an attack, and so promptly devised the following scheme. Some of the authorities engaged the Thebans in the marketplace in a discussion of terms, while others were secretly passing the word around to the rest of the citizens not to go out of their houses singly, but one or two at a time to break through the party-walls and assemble stealthily in one another's houses. When a sufficient fighting force was ready, they blocked up the streets and alleys, using wagons without the draft animals, and rushing together at a given signal, fell upon the Thebans. At the same time

the womenfolk and the house slaves were on the tile roofs. The result was that when the Thebans wished to act and to defend themselves in the darkness they suffered no less harm from the wagons than from their assailants, since they fled without knowing which way to turn for safety because of the barricades of wagons, while their pursuers, being acquainted with the ground, soon killed many of them.

Yet it is necessary to set forth also the reasons which make against this practice, such as the great danger to the besieged if there is only one open place and the conspirators are the first to seize it. For when there is only one such common spot, the advantage would lie with those who first take it. But if there are two or three such places, there would be these advantages: If the conspirators should seize one or two there would still be one left for their opponents; and if they should seize them all, by separation and division they would be weaker in the face of their united opponents, unless indeed each division were numerically superior to the defenders of the city. In the same way in all other decisions one should consider the inherent objections to the prescribed rules, that one may not inadvisedly adopt another course.

III. [*ANOTHER ORGANIZATION OF CITY GUARDS*]

When sudden fear falls upon a city without military organization, one could most speedily organize the citizens for its defense by allotting to each ward a section of the wall to which it is to hurry and mount guard, letting the number of the inhabitants of the ward determine the extent of that section of the wall to whose defense it is appointed. The next step is to assign the able-bodied men from each ward to duty at the marketplace, upon patrols, and wherever else such men may be needed. Similarly when a stronghold is occupied by allies, let a section of the wall be given to each contingent of the allies to defend. Should the citizens, however, suspect one another, trustworthy men should be stationed at the several places for ascending the wall, who, if anyone else attempts to mount, will prevent him from doing so. In peace, also, the citizens ought to be organized in the following manner. First of all one should appoint as captain of each precinct the most capable and prudent man, to whom the citizens are to rally if anything unexpected occurs at night. The precinct captains should muster at the marketplace the men of those precincts nearest the marketplace, at the theater the men of those precincts nearest the theater, and so for the other open places the precinct captains with the armed men who have reported to them should gather, each in the one that lies nearest to him. For this is the quickest way by which each group would both reach their stations and be near their own homes, and so, as heads of families, could communicate with their households, that is, with their children and wives, because stationed not far from them. And it should be determined beforehand by lot to which quarter each of the authorities should go and send detachments of troops to the battlements. Moreover, there will be leaders to look after everything else, provided that they thus assume immediate command. . . .

AESCHINES (CA. 397–CA. 322 B.C.)
Against Timarchus (345 B.C.)

*A*eschines, though no match for his lifelong political enemy Demosthenes, was a distinguished orator and elegant presence in the Athenian forum. He was born the son of the priestess Glaukothea (sister of general Cleobulus) and the democratic schoolmaster Atrometus in Athens, and was raised in his father's elementary school. Aeschines made ends meet by serving as a soldier at Phlius and at Mantinea in the Theban Wars and in the Euboean expedition of 348 B.C., where he won great honor for his bravery. When he returned home, he supported himself by working as a law clerk for the Athenian assembly, and by acting in company with the two greatest actors of his time, Theodorus and Aristodemus.

When an accident ended his acting career, Aeschines worked as an assistant to Athenian statesmen Aristophon and Eubulus. His acting served him in good stead when he began speaking in public, where he became distinguished for his dignity and elocution. Originally, like Demosthenes, opposed to Philip of Macedon after he had conquered Olynthus and controlled the Chalcidic peninsula, and favoring a new Panhellenic confederation, Aeschines came to regard a Macedonian takeover as inevitable and saw the wisdom of negotiating with the king and his charismatic son. Aeschines' pragmatism drew Demosthenes' wrath, and he was eventually forced into exile on Rhodes by the force of Demosthenes' *On the Crown*—which he himself had provoked with his speech *Against Ctesiphon* (330 B.C.), an attack on those who wished to honor his hated rival. He died on Samos.

- After Philip's conquest of Olynthus, in 347/6 B.C., Aeschines, along with Demosthenes and Philocrates, negotiated a peaceful alliance with the Macedonian king. But Demosthenes and Timarchus, unhappy with the results of the embassy, accused Aeschines of accepting bribes from Philip. He may not have been guilty of the bribes, but he was certainly influenced by Philip's praise, his speechmaking abilities no match for Philip's diplomatic wiles. Philip's purpose was to buy time in which to consolidate his power over Greece; Aeschines gave him the time, whether intentionally or not. Much of our knowledge about the relationship between Macedon and Athens is derived from the interchange between Aeschines and Demosthenes.
- Part of the Athenian philosophy of excellence required that only men above reproach could address the assembly. Aeschines' *Against Timarchus,* one of his three surviving speeches known as "the three Graces" to ancient historians, responds to Demosthenes' accusations of bribery by successfully impugning the profligate private life of Demosthenes' partner Timarchus. The speech shows Aeschines' careful reflection, ready use of allusion, and shapely expression, making him the greatest Attic orator after Demosthenes.

I have never, fellow citizens, brought indictment against any Athenian, nor vexed any man when he was rendering account of his office; but in all such matters I have, as I believe, shown myself a quiet and modest man. But when I saw that the city was being seriously injured by the defendant, Timarchus, who, though disqualified by law, was speaking in your assemblies, and when I myself was made a victim of his blackmailing attack—the nature of the attack I will show in the course of my speech—I decided that it would be a most shameful thing if I failed to come to the defense of the whole city and its laws, and to your defense and my own; and knowing that he was liable to the accusations that you heard read a moment ago by the clerk of the court, I instituted this suit, challenging him to official scrutiny. Thus it appears, fellow citizens, that what is so frequently said of public suits is no mistake, namely, that very often private enmities correct public abuses.

You will see, then, that Timarchus cannot blame the city for any part of this prosecution, nor can he blame the laws, nor you, nor me, but only himself. For because of his shameful private life the laws forbade him to speak before the people, laying on him an injunction not difficult, in my opinion, to obey—nay, most easy; and had he been wise, he need not have made his slanderous attack upon me. I hope, therefore, that in this introduction I have spoken as a quiet and modest citizen ought to speak.

I am aware, fellow citizens, that the statement which I am about to make first is something that you will undoubtedly have heard from other men on other occasions; but I think the same thought is especially timely on this occasion, and from me. It is acknowledged, namely, that there are in the world three forms of government, autocracy, oligarchy, and democracy: Autocracies and oligarchies are administered according to the tempers of their lords, but democratic states according to established laws. And be assured, fellow citizens, that in a democracy it is the laws that guard the person of the citizen and the constitution of the state, whereas the despot and the oligarch find their protection in suspicion and in armed guards. Men, therefore, who administer an oligarchy, or any government based upon inequality, must be on their guard against those who attempt revolution by the law of force; but you, who have a government based upon equality and law, must guard against those whose words violate the laws or whose lives have defied them; for then only will you be strong, when

you cherish the laws, and when the revolutionary attempts of lawless men shall have ceased. And it behooves us, I think, not only when we are enacting laws, to consider always how the laws that we make may be good and advantageous to the democracy, but when once we have enacted them, it equally behooves us, if all is to be well with the state, to obey the laws that we have enacted, and to punish those who do not obey them.

Consider, fellow citizens, how much attention that ancient lawgiver, Solon, gave to morality, as did Draco and the other lawgivers of those days. First, you recall, they laid down laws to protect the morals of our children, and they expressly prescribed what were to be the habits of the freeborn boy, and how he was to be brought up; then they legislated for the lads, and next for the other age groups in succession, including in their provision not only private citizens, but also the public men. And when they had inscribed these laws, they gave them to you in trust, and made you their guardians.

Now it is my desire, in addressing you on this occasion, to follow in my speech the same order which the lawgiver followed in his laws. For you shall hear first a review of the laws that have been laid down to govern the orderly conduct of your children, then the laws concerning the lads, and next those concerning the other ages in succession, including not only private citizens, but the public men as well. For so, I think, my argument will most easily be followed. And at the same time I wish, fellow citizens, first to describe to you in detail the laws of the state, and then in contrast with the laws to examine the character and habits of

Timarchus. For you will find that the life he has lived has been contrary to all the laws.

In the first place, consider the case of the teachers. Although the very livelihood of these men, to whom we necessarily entrust our own children, depends on their good character, while the opposite conduct on their part would mean poverty, yet it is plain that the lawgiver distrusts them; for he expressly prescribes, first, at what time of day the freeborn boy is to go to the schoolroom; next, how many other boys may go there with him, and when he is to go home. He forbids the teacher to open the schoolroom, or the gymnastic trainer the wrestling school, before sunrise, and he commands them to close the doors before sunset; for he is exceeding suspicious of their being alone with a boy, or in the dark with him. He prescribes what children are to be admitted as pupils, and their age at admission. He provides for a public official who shall superintend them, and for the oversight of slave attendants of schoolboys. He regulates the festivals of the Muses in the schoolrooms, and of Hermes in the wrestling schools. Finally, he regulates the companionships that the boys may form at school, and their cyclic dances. He prescribes, namely, that the choregus, a man who is going to spend his own money for your entertainment, shall be a man of more than forty years of age when he performs this service, in order that he may have reached the most temperate time of life before he comes into contact with your children.

These laws, then, shall be read to you, to prove that the lawgiver believed that it is the boy who has been well brought up that will be a useful citizen when he becomes a man. But when a boy's natural disposition is subjected at the very outset to vicious training, the product of such wrong nurture will be, as he believed, a citizen like this man Timarchus. *(To the Clerk of the Court.)* Read these laws to the jury.

LAWS

[The teachers of the boys shall open the schoolrooms not earlier than sunrise, and they shall close them before sunset. No person who is older than the boys shall be permitted to enter the room while they are there, unless he be a son of the teacher, a brother, or a daughter's husband. If any one enter in violation of this prohibition, he shall be punished with death. The superintendents of the gymnasia shall under no conditions allow any one who has reached the age of manhood to enter the contests of Hermes together with the boys. A gymnasiarch who does permit this and fails to keep such a person out of the gymnasium, shall be liable to the penalties prescribed for the seduction of freeborn youth. Every choregus who is appointed by the people shall be more than forty years of age.]

Now after this, fellow citizens, he lays down laws regarding crimes which, great as they undoubtedly are, do actually occur, I believe, in the city. For the very fact that certain unbecoming things were being done was the reason for the enactment of these laws by the men of old. At any rate the law says explicitly: If any boy is let out for hire as a prostitute, whether it be by father or brother or uncle or guardian, or by anyone else who has control of him, prosecution is not to lie against the boy himself, but against the man who let him out for hire and the man who hired him; against the one because he let him out for hire, and against the other, it says, because he hired him. And the law has made the penalties for both offenders the same. Moreover the law frees a son, when he has become a man, from all obligation to support or to furnish a home to a father by whom he has been hired out for prostitution; but when the father is dead, the son is to bury him and perform the other customary rites. See, gentlemen, how admirably this legislation fits the case: So long as the father is alive he is deprived of all the benefits of fatherhood, precisely as he deprived his son of a citizen's right to speak; but when he is dead, and unconscious of the service that is being rendered him, and when it is the law and religion that receive the honor, then at last the lawgiver commands the son to bury him and perform the other customary rites.

But what other law has been laid down for the protection of your children? The law against panders. For the lawgiver imposes the heaviest penalties if any person act as pander in the case of a freeborn child or a freeborn woman.

And what other law? The law against outrage, which includes all such conduct in one summary statement, wherein it stands expressly written: If anyone outrage a child (and surely he who hires, outrages) or a man or woman, or anyone, free or slave, or if he commit any unlawful act against any one of these.

Here the law provides prosecution for outrage, and it prescribes what bodily penalty he shall suffer, or what fine he shall pay. *(To the Clerk.)* Read the law.

LAW

[If any Athenian shall outrage a freeborn child, the parent or guardian of the child shall prosecute him before the Thesmothetae, and shall demand a specific penalty. If the court condemn the accused to death, he shall be delivered to the constables and be put to death the same day. If he be condemned to pay a fine, and be unable to pay the fine immediately, he must pay within eleven days after the trial, and he shall remain in prison until payment is made. The same action shall hold against those who abuse the persons of slaves.]

Now perhaps some one, on first hearing this law, may wonder for what possible reason this word "slaves" was added in the law against outrage. But if you reflect on the matter, fellow citizens, you will find this to be the best provision of all. For it was not for the slaves that the lawgiver was concerned, but he wished to accustom you to keep a long distance away from the crime of outraging free men, and so he added the prohibition against the outraging even of slaves. In a word, he was convinced that in a democracy that man is unfit for citizenship who outrages any person whatsoever. And I beg you, fellow citizens, to remember this also, that here the lawgiver is not yet addressing the person of the boy himself, but those who are near him, father, brother, guardian, teachers, and in general those who have control of him. But as soon as the young man has been registered in the list of citizens, and knows the laws of the state, and is now able to distinguish between right and wrong, the lawgiver no longer addresses another, Timarchus, but now the man himself. And what does he say? "If any Athenian," he says, "shall have prostituted his person, he shall not be permitted to become one of the nine archons," because, no doubt, that official wears the wreath; "nor to discharge the office of priest," as being not even clean of body; "nor shall he act as an advocate for the state," he says, "nor shall he ever hold any office whatsoever, at home or abroad, whether filled by lot or by election; nor shall he be a herald or an ambassador"—nor shall he prosecute men who have served as ambassadors, nor shall he be a hired slanderer—"nor ever address senate or assembly," not even though he be the most eloquent orator in Athens. And if anyone act contrary to these prohibitions, the lawgiver has provided for criminal process on the charge of prostitution, and has prescribed the heaviest penalties therefor. *(To the Clerk.)* Read to the jury this law also, that you may know, gentlemen, in the face of what established laws of yours, so good and so moral, Timarchus has had the effrontery to speak before the people—a man whose character is so notorious. . . .

ARISTOTLE (384–322 B.C.)

Poetics

⚬━✦━⚬

The first and greatest logical philosopher was born in Thracian Stagira, in a region known as Chalcidice, just south of Macedon, the son of Nicomachus, the court physician in Pella of Amyntas II, king of Macedon. Called by Dante "the master of those that know," he was the supreme polymath of classical Greece, his curiosity ranging over every known field of knowledge and classifying its findings into major categories still in use today. It's fair to say that Aristotle defined the principles of reasoning underlying western civilization, and pioneered the biological sciences. He countered the idealistic philosophy of his master, Plato, with a philosophy based instead on empirical realism.

At the age of seventeen Aristotle became Plato's student at the Academy and began his zoological studies and research into all areas of knowledge, staying until Plato's death twenty years later. Plato called him "the reader." When Speusippus was elected to succeed Plato, Aristotle decided it was time to travel. He settled next in Asia Minor, founding an academy of his own at Assos. There he married Pythias, daughter of the ruler Hermeias, a fellow academician. He journeyed next to Lesbos to study marine biology at Mytilene under Theophrastus, but two years later accepted the invitation of Philip of Macedon to tutor his son Alexander in Homer and politics.

Returning to Athens in 335, Aristotle established the Lyceum (in the grove of Apollo Lyceius), whose porticoed courtyard, in which master and students walked and talked together, gave his academy the name Peripatetic School (from *peripatos,* "strolling"). The school was organized around the library he founded (and to which his pupil Alexander added as he made his way through Asia), a museum, and a collection of maps. Here Aristotle supervised graduate study and lectured on his wide range of interests until the death of Alexander in 323, when he retired from Athens because the newly nationalistic Athenians accused him of impiety, as they had Socrates, and he did not want Athens, as he said, "to sin twice against philosophy." He died at Chalcis, in Euboia, the same year.

- Aristotle wrote voluminously on logic and analysis, physics, politics, ethics, zoology, dreams, biology, metaphysics, and literature. His most important surviving works, many of which appear to have been more like lecture notes than polished essays or dialogues, include:

  - *The Constitution of Athens,* the new codification of democratic law
  - *The Organon,* a collection of treatises on logic
  - *The Physics,* dealing with natural phenomena
  - *Historia animalium* and *De generatione,* dealing with zoological structures, the "progression of animals," influencing Charles Darwin
  - *De anima,* the first "definitive work on psychology"
  - *The Metaphysics,* 14 books dealing with "being"
  - *The Nicomachean Ethics,* dealing with vice and virtue and the concept of "the golden mean"
  - *The Politics,* dealing with political theory, education, and the government of the city-state *(polis)* in its relationship to the individual

In other works he systematically investigated dramatic structure and the nature of art, astronomy, memory, life and death, cosmic teleology, oratory and literature, "indivisible lines," and the evolutionary process. Where his master Plato had sought out universal *ideas,* Aristotle focused on the facts; moving toward generalizations only after classifying specific data. He developed and clarified the "dialectical process" of reasoning by which thesis generates first antithesis, then synthesis; which, in turn, becomes a new thesis. Aristotle also invented the great majority of scientific categories still in use today, such as species and genus. In his own version of the "theory of ideas," he argued that the *form* of things is inherent in each thing.

- When the great classifier and master of synthesis focused on moral behavior in the *Nicomachean Ethics,* so named because it was dedicated to his son Nicomachus, he established an approach that defined this area of human thought for nearly two thousand years. Thomas Aquinas, the great codifier of the Roman Catholic Church, incorporated Aristotelian thought into his *Summa Theologica.* Aristotle defined virtue in moderation as the "golden mean" between two vicious extremes. On one end of the spectrum, a miser; on the other, a spendthrift; in the middle, a balanced financial manager.

- Turning his analytical eye to the elements of poetry and dramatic fiction, Aristotle's *Poetics* is the first surviving work of fundamental literary criticism and theory, and is especially important for formulating:

  1. the importance of character as the source of all effective dramatic action;
  2. the emotional impact of well-wrought drama, which Aristotle called *katharsis* ("a purging"), that comes from causing the audience to experience pity and fear, and to be purged from those emotions by play's end. He would argue that drama cannot cause violence, but instead is a primary social method of diffusing it by allowing it to be experienced and dissolved in the public forum of theater;
  3. the concept of poetry and drama as *mimesis,* a Greek term that is badly translated as "imitation of action" but which more closely means "reproduction" or "re-creation";
  4. because poetic *mimesis* contains a clear-cut and involving *beginning,* a complex and rhythmically satisfying *middle,* and a powerful and conclusive *ending,* it is psychologically preferable to life itself; this led Aristotle to make the statement that poetry is more scientific and philosophical than history because it shows us things that "might be" instead of merely "things that are, or were";
  5. the dramatic "unities" of character, action, time, and place (although these unities were further defined in the Renaissance);
  6. the idea of "beginning in the middle of things," or, as screenwriter William Goldman echoes, "Start as far into a scene as possible, and get out of it as quickly as you can."

Because what is published under the title *Poetics* seem to have been lecture notes, the text is not completely "filled in." Aristotle's meaning, however, is so clear that the gaps can be filled by the reader's intuition.

. . . It is clear that the general origin of poetry was due to two causes, each of them part of human nature. Imitation is natural to man from childhood, one of his advantages over the lower animals being this, that he is the most imitative creature in the world, and learns at first by imitation. And it is also natural for all to delight in works of imitation. The truth of this second point is shown by experience: though the objects themselves may be painful to see, we delight to view the most realistic representations of them in art, the forms for example of the lowest animals and of dead bodies. The explanation is to be found in a further fact: to be learning something is the greatest of pleasures not only to the philosopher but also to the rest of mankind, however small their capacity for it; the reason of the delight in seeing the picture is that one is at the same time learning—gathering the meaning of things, e.g. that the man there is so-and-so; for if one has not seen the thing before, one's pleasure will not be in the picture as an imitation of it, but will be due to the execution or coloring or some similar cause. Imitation, then, being natural to us—as also the sense of harmony and rhythm, the meters being obviously species of rhythms—it was through their original aptitude, and by a series of improvements for the most part gradual on their first efforts, that they created poetry out of their improvisations.

Poetry, however, soon broke up into two kinds according to the differences of character in the individual poets; for the graver among them would represent noble actions, and those of noble personages; and the meaner sort the actions of the ignoble. The latter class pro-

"Alexander the Great, student of Aristotle; from Magnesia at Sipylos." Bildarchiv Foto Marburg. Istanbul Museum. By permission of Art Resource.

duced invectives at first, just as others did hymns and panegyrics. We know of no such poem by any of the pre-Homeric poets, though there were probably many such writers among them; instances, however, may be found from Homer downwards, e.g. his *Margites*, and the similar poems of others. In this poetry of invective its natural fitness brought an iambic meter into use; hence our present term "iambic," because it was the meter of their "iambs" or invectives against one another. The result was that the old poets became some of them writers of heroic and others of iambic verse. Homer's position, however, is peculiar: just as he was in the serious style the poet of poets, standing alone not only through the literary excellence, but also through the dramatic character of his imitations, so too he was the first to outline for us the general forms of Comedy by producing not a dramatic invective, but a dramatic picture of the Ridiculous; his *Margites* in fact stands in the same relation to our comedies as the *Iliad* and *Odyssey* to our tragedies. As soon, however, as Tragedy and Comedy appeared in the field, those naturally drawn to the one line of poetry became writers of comedies instead of iambs, and those naturally drawn to the other, writers of tragedies instead of epics, because these new modes of art were grander and of more esteem than the old.

If it be asked whether Tragedy is now all that it need be in its formative elements, to consider that, and decide it theoretically and in relation to the theaters, is a matter for another inquiry.

It certainly began in improvisations—as did also Comedy; the one originating with the authors of the Dithyramb, the other with those of the phallic songs, which still survive as institutions in many of our cities. And its advance after that was little by little, through their improving on whatever they had before them at each stage. It was in fact only after a long series of changes that the movement of Tragedy stopped on its attaining to its natural form. (1) The number of actors was first increased to two by Aeschylus, who curtailed the business of the Chorus, and made the dialogue, or spoken portion, take the leading part in the play. (2) A third actor and scenery were due to Sophocles. (3) Tragedy acquired also its magnitude. Discarding short stories and a ludicrous diction, through its passing out of its satyric stage, it assumed, though only at a late point in its progress, a tone of dignity; and its meter changed then from trochaic to iambic. The reason for their original use of the trochaic tetrameter was that their poetry was satyric and more connected with dancing than it now is. As soon,

however, as a spoken part came in, nature herself found the appropriate meter. The iambic, we know, is the most speakable of meters, as is shown by the fact that we very often fall into it in conversation, whereas we rarely talk hexameters, and only when we depart from the speaking tone of voice. (4) Another change was a plurality of episodes or acts. As for the remaining matters, the superadded embellishments and the account of their introduction, these must be taken as said, as it would probably be a long piece of work to go through the details.

As for Comedy, it is (as has been observed) an imitation of men worse than the average; worse, however, not as regards any and every sort of fault, but only as regards one particular kind, the Ridiculous, which is a species of the Ugly. The Ridiculous may be defined as a mistake or deformity not productive of pain or harm to others; the mask, for instance, that excites laughter, is something ugly and distorted without causing pain.

Though the successive changes in Tragedy and their authors are not unknown, we cannot say the same of Comedy; its early stages passed unnoticed, because it was not as yet taken up in a serious way. It was only at a late point in its progress that a chorus of comedians was officially granted by the archon; they used to be mere volunteers. It had also already certain definite forms at the time when the record of those termed comic poets begins. Who it was who supplied it with masks, or prologues, or a plurality of actors and the like, has remained unknown. The invented Fable, or Plot, however, originated in Sicily, with Epicharmus and Phormis; of Athenian poets Crates was the first to drop the Comedy of invective and frame sto ries of a general and non-personal nature, in other words, Fables or Plots.

Epic poetry, then, has been seen to agree with Tragedy to this extent, that of being an imitation of serious subjects in a grand kind of verse. It differs from it, however, (1) in that it is in one kind of verse and in narrative form; and (2) in its length—which is due to its action having no fixed limit of time, whereas Tragedy endeavors to keep as far as possible within a single circuit of the sun, or something near that. This, I say, is another point of difference between them, though at first the practice in this respect was just the same in tragedies as in epic poems. They differ also (3) in their constituents, some being common to both and others peculiar to Tragedy—hence a judge of good and bad in Tragedy is a judge of that in epic poetry also. All the parts of an epic are included in Tragedy; but those of Tragedy are not all of them to be found in the Epic.

Reserving hexameter poetry and Comedy for consideration hereafter, let us proceed now to the discussion of Tragedy; before doing so, however, we must gather up the definition resulting from what has been said. A tragedy, then, is the imitation of an action that is serious and also, as having magnitude, complete in itself; in language with pleasurable accessories, each kind brought in separately in the parts of the work; in a dramatic, not in a narrative form; with incidents arousing pity and fear, wherewith to accomplish its catharsis of such emotions. Here by "language with pleasurable accessories" I mean that with rhythm and harmony or song superadded; and by "the kinds separately" I mean that some portions are worked out with verse only, and others in turn with song.

I. As they act the stories, it follows that in the first place the Spectacle (or stage-appearance of the actors) must be some part of the whole; and in the second Melody and Diction, these two being the means of their imitation. Here by "Diction" I mean merely this, the composition of the verses; and by "Melody," what is too completely understood to require explanation. But further: the subject represented also is an action; and the action involves agents, who must necessarily have their distinctive qualities both of character and thought, since it is from these that we ascribe certain qualities to their actions. There are in the natural order of things, therefore, two causes, Character and Thought, of their actions, and consequently of their success or failure in their lives. Now the action (that which was done) is represented in the play by the Fable or Plot. The Fable, in our present sense of the term, is simply this, the combination of the incidents, or things done in the story; whereas Character is what makes us ascribe certain moral qualities to the agents; and Thought is shown in all they say when proving a particular point or, it may be, enunciating a general truth. There are six parts consequently of every tragedy, as a whole, that is, of such or such quality, viz, a Fable or Plot, Characters, Diction, Thought, Spectacle and Melody; two of them arising from the means, one from the manner, and three from the objects of the dramatic imitation; and there is nothing else besides these six. Of these, its formative elements, then, not a few of the dramatists have made due use, as every play, one may say, admits of Spectacle, Character, Fable, Diction, Melody, and Thought.

II. The most important of the six is the

combination of the incidents of the story. Tragedy is essentially an imitation not of persons but of action and life, of happiness and misery. All human happiness or misery takes the form of action; the end for which we live is a certain kind of activity, not a quality. Character gives us qualities, but it is in our actions—what we do—that we are happy or the reverse. In a play accordingly they do not act in order to portray the Characters; they include the Characters for the sake of the action. So that it is the action in it, i.e. its Fable or Plot, that is the end and purpose of the tragedy; and the end is everywhere the chief thing. Besides this, a tragedy is impossible without action, but there may be one without Character. The tragedies of most of the moderns are characterless—a defect common among poets of all kinds, and with its counterpart in painting in Zeuxis as compared with Polygnotus; for whereas the latter is strong in character, the work of Zeuxis is devoid of it. And again: one may string together a series of characteristic speeches of the utmost finish as regards Diction and Thought, and yet fail to produce the true tragic effect; but one will have much better success with a tragedy which, however inferior in these respects, has a Plot, a combination of incidents, in it. And again: the most powerful elements of attraction in Tragedy, the Peripeties and Discoveries, are parts of the Plot. A further proof is in the fact that beginners succeed earlier with the Diction and Characters than with the construction of a story; and the same may be said of nearly all the early dramatists. We maintain, therefore, that the first essential, the life and soul, so to speak, of Tragedy is the Plot; and that the Characters come second—compare

the parallel in painting, where the most beautiful colors laid on without order will not give one the same pleasure as a simple black-and-white sketch of a portrait. We maintain that Tragedy is primarily an imitation of action, and that it is mainly for the sake of the action that it imitates the personal agents. Third comes the element of Thought, i.e. the power of saying whatever can be said, or what is appropriate to the occasion. This is what, in the speeches in Tragedy, falls under the arts of Politics and Rhetoric; for the older poets make their personages discourse like statesmen, and the moderns like rhetoricians. One must not confuse it with Character. Character in a play is that which reveals the moral purpose of the agents, i.e. the sort of thing they seek or avoid, where that is not obvious—hence there is no room for Character in a speech on a purely indifferent subject. Thought, on the other hand, is shown in all they say when proving or disproving some particular point, or enunciating some universal proposition. Fourth among the literary elements is the Diction of the personages, i.e. as before explained, the expression of their thoughts in words, which is practically the same thing with verse as with prose. As for the two remaining parts, the Melody is the greatest of the pleasurable accessories of Tragedy. The Spectacle, though an attraction, is the least artistic of all the parts, and has least to do with the art of poetry. The tragic effect is quite possible without a public performance and actors; and besides, the getting-up of the Spectacle is more a matter for the costumier than the poet.

Having thus distinguished the parts, let us now consider the proper construction of the

Fable or Plot, as that is at once the first and the most important thing in Tragedy. We have laid it down that a tragedy is an imitation of an action that is complete in itself, as a whole of some magnitude; for a whole may be of no magnitude to speak of. Now a whole is that which has beginning, middle, and end. A beginning is that which is not itself necessarily after anything else, and which has naturally something else after it; an end is that which is naturally after something itself, either as its necessary or usual consequent, and with nothing else after it; and a middle, that which is by nature after one thing and has also another after it. A well-constructed Plot, therefore, cannot either begin or end at any point one likes; beginning and end in it must be of the forms just described. Again: to be beautiful, a living creature, and every whole made up of parts, must not only present a certain order in its arrangement of parts, but also be of a certain definite magnitude. Beauty is a matter of size and order, and therefore impossible either (1) in a very minute creature, since our perception becomes indistinct as it approaches instantaneity; or (2) in a creature of vast size—one, say, 1000 miles long—as in that case, instead of the object being seen all at once, the unity and wholeness of it is lost to the beholder. Just in the same way, then, as a beautiful whole made up of parts, or a beautiful living creature, must be of some size, a size to be taken in by the eye, so a story or Plot must be of some length, but of a length to be taken in by the memory. As for the limit of its length, so far as that is relative to public performances and spectators, it does not fall within the theory of poetry. If they had to perform a hundred tragedies, they would be timed by water-clocks, as they are said to have been at one period. The limit, however, set by the actual nature of the thing is this: the longer the story, consistently with its being comprehensible as a whole, the finer it is by reason of its magnitude. As a rough general formula, "a length which allows of the hero passing by a series of probable or necessary stages from misfortune to happiness, or from happiness to misfortune," may suffice as a limit for the magnitude of the story.

The Unity of a Plot does not consist, as some suppose, in its having one man as its subject. An infinity of things befall that one man, some of which it is impossible to reduce to unity; and in like manner there are many actions of one man which cannot be made to form one action. One sees, therefore, the mistake of all the poets who have written a *Heracleid*, a *Theseid*, or similar poems; they suppose that, because Heracles was one man, the story also of Heracles must be one story. Homer, however, evidently understood this point quite well, whether by art or instinct, just in the same way as he excels the rest in every other respect. In writing an *Odyssey*, he did not make the poem cover all that ever befell his hero—it befell him, for instance, to get wounded on Parnassus and also to feign madness at the time of the call to arms, but the two incidents had no probable or necessary connexion with one another—instead of doing that, he took an action with a Unity of the kind we are describing as the subject of the *Odyssey*, as also of the *Iliad*. The truth is that, just as in the other imitative arts one imitation is always of one thing, so in poetry the story, as an imitation of action, must represent one action, a complete whole, with its several incidents so closely connected that the transposal or withdrawal of any one of them will disjoin and dislocate the whole. For that which makes no perceptible difference by its presence or absence is no real part of the whole.

From what we have said it will be seen that the poet's function is to describe, not the thing that has happened, but a kind of thing that might happen, i.e. what is possible as being probable or necessary. The distinction between historian and poet is not in the one writing prose and the other verse—you might put the work of Herodotus into verse, and it would still be a species of history; it consists really in this, that the one describes the thing that has been, and the other a kind of thing that might be. Hence poetry is something more philosophic and of graver import than history, since its statements are of the nature rather of universals, whereas those of history are singulars. . . .

DEMOSTHENES (384–322 B.C.)
On the Crown

The most famous orator of classical Greece, Demosthenes was also the last great spokesman of a free Athens. The son of a wealthy arms manufacturer also named Demosthenes and his Scythian wife Cleobule, he learned rhetoric and law from Isaeus. He became a working attorney, assistant prosecutor in public trials, and lifelong political opponent of Philip and his son, Alexander the Great of Macedon. Demosthenes, betrayed by his own fellow citizens and best friend Demades, fled a conquered Athens to seek refuge in the temple of Poseidon in Calauria. Rather than submit to Alexander's general, Antipater, the great orator took poison by his own hand.

- Demosthenes' father died when he was seven, leaving him and his sisters at the mercy of embezzling guardians for their patrimony. A sickly child raised by his mother, he became an introvert, painfully shy and stammering, who sought solace in his studies. At the age of sixteen he was inspired by the orator Callistratus to develop his own rhetorical skills. Plutarch tells us he practiced in front of a mirror, walked along the seashore with pebbles in his mouth to develop his speaking voice, and in an underground study repeatedly recopied the speeches reported by Thucydides in his *History of the Peloponnesian War* to internalize their forcefulness. Though he won his legal case against the guardians, Demosthenes was forced to earn a living by speechwriting and by representing citizens in court.

After Philip of Macedon conquered Athens' ally Olynthus in 348 B.C., Demosthenes, Philocrates, and Aeschines were sent as ambassadors to conclude peace with the king. Philocrates and Aeschines accepted Macedonian bribes, which led the Macedonians to occupy Thermopylae, commanding the entrance to Attica. Demosthenes himself fought with Athens' allies, the Thebans, at the battle of Chaeronea (338 B.C.), from which he fled—and from which Philip emerged as conqueror of Greece. Demosthenes was first blamed for the defeat, then exonerated by his fellow citizens. Ctesiphon, in recognition of Demosthenes' long service to Athens, proposed to give him a golden crown and to honor him publicly at the Dionysian festival. Aeschines, who was now in the pay of Philip's son Alexander, conqueror of Thebes, responded by claiming this honor was illegal and undeserved.

- Demosthenes' primary political goal throughout his career was to awaken a complacent Athens to the danger of Philip of Macedon, and to inspire his beloved city to regain its former vigorous leadership. So eloquent was he in his first speeches (called *Philippics)* against Macedon that Philip himself is said to have claimed it was not Athens he fought but Demosthenes. *On the Crown,* typical of his careful thought and compelling rhetoric and regarded as one of the greatest speeches of all time, compares Athens' deteriorating political situation over the past twenty years to its golden past, recapitulates his own political service to the city, outlines Aeschines' treachery with the Macedonians, and contrasts his personal life with Aeschines'. His name-calling of his opponent to discredit him in front of the audience reminds us of the tactics of contemporary litigators like F. Lee Bailey and Melvin Belli.
- The jury of 500 responded to this speech by failing to give Aeschines the necessary one-fifth of their votes. Demosthenes' enemy was banished to Rhodes. The entire oration illustrates the controlled spontaneity and fiery spirit of Demosthenes' highly polished yet powerfully eloquent rhetoric, revealing what he himself regarded to be the most important requisite: delivery. When asked what he thought were the second and third most important requisites, he replied: "Delivery, and delivery."

I begin, men of Athens, by praying to every God and Goddess that the same goodwill, which I have ever cherished toward the commonwealth and all of you, may be requited to me on the present trial. I pray likewise—and this especially concerns yourselves, your religion, and your honor—that the Gods may put it in your minds, not to take counsel of my opponent touching the manner in which I am to be heard—that would indeed be cruel!—but of the laws and of your oath; wherein (besides the other obligations) it is prescribed that you shall hear both sides alike. This means not only that you must pass no pre-condemnation, not only that you must extend your goodwill equally to both, but also that you must allow the parties to adopt such order and course of defense as they severally choose and prefer.

Many advantages hath Aeschines over me on this trial; and two especially, men of Athens. First, my risk in the contest is not the same. It is assuredly not the same for me to forfeit your regard, as for my adversary not to succeed in his indictment. To me—but I will say nothing untoward at the outset of my address. The prosecution however is play to him. My second disadvantage is the natural disposition of mankind to take pleasure in hearing invective and accusation, and to be annoyed by those who praise themselves. To Aeschines is assigned the part which gives pleasure; that which is (I may fairly say) offensive to all, is left for me. And if, to escape from this, I make no mention of what I have done, I shall appear to be without defense against his charges, without proof of my claims to honor: whereas, if I proceed to give an account of my conduct and measures, I shall be forced to speak frequently of myself. I will endeavor then to do so with all becoming modesty: what I am driven to by the necessity of the case will be fairly chargeable to my opponent who has instituted such a prosecution.

I think, men of the jury, you will all agree that I, as well as Ctesiphon, am a party to this proceeding, and that it is a matter of no less concern to me. It is painful and grievous to be deprived of anything, especially by the act of one's enemy; but your goodwill and affection are the heaviest loss, precisely as they are the greatest prize to gain.

Such being the matters at stake in this cause, I conjure and implore you all alike to hear my defense to the charge in that fair manner which the laws prescribe—laws to which

"Temple of Athena Nike, Acropolis, Athens"

their author, Solon, a man friendly to you and to popular rights, thought that validity should be given, not only by the recording of them, but by the oath of you the jurors: not that he distrusted you, as it appears to me; but, seeing that the charges and calumnies, wherein the prosecutor is powerful by being the first speaker, cannot be got over by the defendant, unless each of you jurors, observing his religious obligation, shall with like favor receive the arguments of the last speaker, and lend an equal and impartial ear to both, before he determines upon the whole case.

As I am, it appears, on this day to render an account both of my private life and my public measures, I would fain, as in the outset, call the Gods to my aid; and in your presence I implore them, first, that the goodwill which I have ever cherished toward the commonwealth and all of you may be fully requited to me on the present trial; next, that they may direct you to such a decision upon this indictment, as will conduce to your common honor, and to the good conscience of each individual.

Had Aeschines confined his charge to the

subject of the prosecution, I too would have proceeded at once to my justification of the decree. But since he has wasted no fewer words in the discussion of other matters, in most of them calumniating me, I deem it both necessary and just, men of Athens, to begin by shortly adverting to these points, that none of you may be induced by extraneous arguments to shut your ears against my defense to the indictment.

To all his scandalous abuse of my private life, observe my plain and honest answer. If you know me to be such as he alleged—for I have lived nowhere else but among you—let not my voice be heard, however transcendent my statesmanship! Rise up this instant and condemn me! But if, in your opinion and judgment, I am far better and of better descent than my adversary; if (to speak without offense) I am not inferior, I or mine, to any respectable citizens; then give no credit to him for his other statements—it is plain they were all equally fictions—but to me let the same goodwill, which you have uniformly exhibited upon many former trials, be manifested now. With all your malice, Aeschines, it was very simple to suppose that I should turn from the discussion of measures and policy to notice your scandal. I will do no such thing: I am not so crazed. Your lies and calumnies about my political life I will examine forthwith; for that loose ribaldry I shall have a word hereafter, if the jury desire to hear it.

The crimes whereof I am accused are many and grievous: for some of them the laws enact heavy—most severe—penalties. The scheme of this present proceeding includes a combination of spiteful insolence, insult, railing, aspersion, and everything of the kind; while for the said charges and accusations, if they were true, the state has not the means of inflicting an adequate punishment, or anything like it. For it is not right to debar another of access to the people and privilege of speech; moreover, to do so by way of malice and insult—by heaven! is neither honest, nor constitutional, nor just. If the crimes which he saw me committing against the state were as heinous as he so tragically gave out, he ought to have enforced the penalties of the law against them at the time; if he saw me guilty of an impeachable offense, by impeaching and so bringing me to trial before you; if moving illegal decrees, by indicting me for them. For surely, if he can prosecute Ctesiphon on my account, he would not have forborne to indict me myself, had he thought he could convict me. In short, whatever else he saw me doing to your prejudice, whether mentioned or not mentioned in his catalog of slander, there are laws for such things, and punishments, and trials, and judgments, with sharp and severe penalties; all of which he might have enforced against me: and had he done so—had he thus pursued the proper method with me, his charges would have been consistent with his conduct. But now he has declined the straightforward and just course, avoided all proofs of guilt at the time, and after this long interval gets up, to play his part withal, a heap of accusation, ribaldry, and scandal. Then he arraigns me, but prosecutes the defendant. His hatred of me he makes the prominent part of the whole contest; yet, without having ever met me upon that ground, he openly seeks to deprive a third party of his privileges. Now, men of Athens, besides all the other arguments that may be urged in Ctesiphon's behalf, this, methinks, may very fairly be alleged—that we should try our own quarrel by ourselves; not leave our private dispute, and look what third party we can damage. That surely were the height of injustice. . . .

When the Phocian war had broken out—not through me, for I had not then commenced public life—you were in this position: You wished the Phocians to be saved, though you saw they were not acting right; and would have been glad for the Thebans to suffer anything, with whom for a just reason you were angry; for they had not borne with moderation their good fortune at Leuctra. The whole of Peloponnesus was divided: They that hated the Lacedaemonians were not powerful enough to destroy them; and they that ruled before by Spartan influence were not masters of the states; among them, as among the rest of the Greeks, there was a sort of unsettled strife and confusion. Philip, seeing this—it was not difficult to see—lavished bribes upon the traitors in every state, embroiled and stirred them all up against each other; and so, by the errors and follies of the rest, he was strengthening himself, and growing up to the ruin of all. But when every one saw that the then overbearing, but now unfortunate, Thebans, harassed by so long a war, must of necessity have recourse to you; Philip, to prevent this, and obstruct the union of the states, offered to you peace, to them succor. What helped him then almost to surprise you in a voluntary snare? The cowardice, shall I call it? or ignorance—or both—of the other Greeks; who, while you were waging a long and incessant war—and that too for their common benefit, as the event has shown—assisted you

neither with money nor men, nor anything else whatsoever. You, being justly and naturally offended with them, lent a willing ear to Philip.

The peace then granted was through such means brought about, not through me, as Aeschines calumniously charged. The criminal and corrupt practices of these men during the treaty will be found, on fair examination, to be the cause of our present condition. The whole matter am I for truth's sake discussing and going through; for let there appear to be ever so much criminality in these transactions, it is surely nothing to me. The first who spoke and mentioned the subject of peace was Aristodemus the actor: the seconder and mover, fellow-hireling for that purpose with the prosecutor, was Philocrates the Agnusian—your associate, Aeschines, not mine, though you should burst with lying. Their supporters, from whatever motives—I pass that by for the present—were Eubulus and Cephisophon. I had nothing to do with it.

Notwithstanding these facts, which I have stated exactly according to the truth, he ventured to assert—to such a pitch of impudence had he come—that I, besides being author of the peace, had prevented the country making it in a general council with the Greeks. Why, you—I know not what name you deserve!—when you saw me robbing the state of an advantage and connection so important as you described just now, did you ever express indignation? did you come forward to publish and proclaim what you now charge me with? If indeed I had been bribed by Philip to prevent the conjunction of the Greeks, it was your business not to be silent, but to cry out, to protest, and inform the people. But you never did so—your voice was never heard to such a purpose, and no wonder; for at that time no embassy had been sent to any of the Greeks—they had all been tested long before; and not a word of truth upon the subject has Aeschines spoken.

Besides, it is the country that he most traduces by his falsehoods. For if you were at the same time calling on the Greeks to take arms, and sending your own ambassadors to treat with Philip for peace, you were performing the part of an Eurybatus, not the act of a commonwealth, or of honest men. But it is false, it is false. For what purpose could ye have sent for them at that period? For peace? They all had it. For war? You were yourselves deliberating about peace. It appears, therefore, I was not the adviser or the author of the original peace; and none of his other calumnies against me are shown to be true.

Observe again, after the state had concluded the peace, what line of conduct each of us adopted. Hence you will understand who it was that cooperated in everything with Philip; who that acted in your behalf, and sought the advantage of the commonwealth.

I moved in the council that our ambassadors should sail instantly for whatever place they heard Philip was in, and receive his oath; they would not, however, notwithstanding my resolution. What was the effect of this, men of Athens? I will explain. It was Philip's interest that the interval before the oaths should be as long as possible; yours, that it should be as short. Why? Because you discontinued all your warlike preparations, not only from the day of swearing peace, but from the day that you conceived hopes of it; a thing which Philip was from the beginning studious to contrive, believ-ing—rightly enough—that whatever of our possessions he might take before the oath of ratification he should hold securely; as none would break the peace on such account. I, men of Athens, foreseeing and weighing these consequences, moved the decree, to sail for whatever place Philip was in, and receive his oath without delay; so that your allies, the Thracians, might be in possession of the places which Aeschines ridiculed just now (Serrium, Myrtium, and Ergisce) at the time of swearing the oaths; and that Philip might not become master of Thrace by securing the posts of vantage, nor provide himself with plenty of money and troops to facilitate his further designs. Yet this decree he neither mentions nor reads; but reproaches me, because, as Councillor, I thought proper to introduce the ambassadors. Why, what should I have done? Moved not to introduce men who were come for the purpose of conferring with you? or ordered the Manager not to assign them places at the theater? They might have had places for their two obols, if the resolution had not been moved. Was it my duty to guard the petty interests of the state, and have sold our main interests like these men? Surely not. . . .

I conjure and beseech you, men of Athens, throughout the trial to remember this; that, if Aeschines in his charge had not traveled out of the indictment, neither would I have spoken a word irrelevant; but since he has resorted to every species both of accusation and calumny, it is necessary for me to reply briefly to each of his charges.

What then were the statements made by Aeschines, through which everything was lost? That you should not be alarmed by Philip's having passed Thermopylae—that all would be as you desired, if you kept quiet; and in two or three days you would hear he was their friend to whom he had come as an enemy, and their enemy to whom he had come as a friend—it was not words that cemented attachments (such was his solemn phrase), but identity of interest; and it was the interest of all alike, Philip, the Phocians, and you, to be relieved from the harshness and insolence of the Thebans. His assertions were heard by some with pleasure, on account of the hatred which then subsisted against the Thebans.

But what happened directly, almost immediately, afterwards? The wretched Phocians were destroyed, their cities demolished; you that kept quiet, and trusted to Aeschines, were shortly bringing in your effects out of the country, while Aeschines received gold; and yet more—while you got nothing but your enmity with the Thebans and Thessalians, Philip won their gratitude for what he had done. . . .

When you had been deceived by Philip through the agency of these men, who sold themselves in the embassies, and reported not a word of truth to you—when the unhappy Phocians had been deceived and their cities destroyed—what followed? The despicable Thessalians and stupid Thebans looked on Philip as a friend, a benefactor, a savior: He was everything with them—not a syllable would they hear from anyone to the contrary. You, though regarding his acts with suspicion and anger, still observed the peace; for you could have done nothing alone. The rest of the Greeks, cheated and disappointed like yourselves, gladly observed the peace, though they also had in a manner been attacked for a long time. For when Philip was marching about, subduing Il-

lyrians and Triballians and some also of the Greeks, and gaining many considerable accessions of power, and certain citizens of the states (Aeschines among them) took advantage of the peace to go there and be corrupted; all people then, against whom he was making such preparations, were attacked. If they perceived it not, that is another question, no concern of mine. I was forever warning and protesting, both at Athens and wheresoever I was sent. But the states were diseased; one class in their politics and measures being venal and corrupt, while the multitude of private men either had no foresight, or were caught with the bait of present ease and idleness; and all were under some such influence, only they imagined each that the mischief would not approach themselves, but that by the peril of others they might secure their own safety when they chose. The result, I fancy, has been that the people, in return for their gross and unseasonable indolence, have lost their liberty: the statesmen, who imagined they were selling everything but themselves, discovered they had sold themselves first; for, instead of friends, as they were named during the period of bribery, they are now called parasites, and miscreants, and the like befitting names. Justly. For no man, O Athenians, spends money for the traitor's benefit, or, when he has got possession of his purchase, employs the traitor to advise him in future proceedings: else nothing could have been more fortunate than a traitor. But it is not so—it never could be—it is far otherwise! When the aspirant for power has gained his object, he is master also of those that sold it; and then—then, I say, knowing their baseness, he loathes and mistrusts and spurns them.

Consider only—for, though the time of the events is past, the time for understanding them is ever present to the wise: Lasthenes was called the friend of Philip for a while, until he betrayed Olynthus—Timolaus for a while, until he destroyed Thebes—Eudicus and Simus of Larissa for a while, until they brought Thessaly under Philip's power. Since then the world has become full of traitors, expelled, and insulted, and suffering every possible calamity. How fared Aristratus in Sicyon? how Perilaus in Megara? Are they not outcasts? Hence, one may evidently see, it is the vigilant defender of his country, the strenuous opponent of such men, who secures to you traitors and hirelings, Aeschines, the opportunity of getting bribes: Through the number of those that oppose your wishes, you are in safety and in pay; for had it depended on yourselves, you would have perished long ago.

Much more could I say about those transactions, yet methinks too much has been said already. The fault is my adversary's, for having spirted over me the dregs, I may say, of his own wickedness and iniquities, of which I was obliged to clear myself to those who are younger than the events. You too have probably been disgusted, who knew this man's venality before I spoke a word. He calls it friendship indeed; and said somewhere in his speech—"the man who reproaches me with the friendship of Alexander." I reproach you with friendship of Alexander! Whence gotten, or how merited? Neither Philip's friend nor Alexander's should I ever call you; I am not so mad; unless we are to call reapers and other hired laborers the friends of those that hire them. That however is not so—how could it be? It is nothing of the kind. Philip's hireling I called you once, and Alexander's I call you now. So do all these men. If you disbelieve me, ask them; or rather I will do it for you. Athenians! is Aeschines, think ye, the hireling, or the friend of Alexander? You hear what they say. . . .

"THEOPHRASTUS" TYRTAMOS (371–287 B.C.)
The Characters (319 B.C.)

❦

*T*yrtamos was born in Eresos, in Lesbos. A student of Plato and Aristotle, he inherited the guardianship of Aristotle's son, the philosopher's manuscripts, and the presidency of his Lyceum in Athens, in 322 B.C. Reportedly it was also Aristotle who dubbed him "Theophrastus," "marked by the gods," for his oratorical mastery. Theophrastus remained the head of the Peripatetic school until he died in his eighty-fifth year, supervising the instruction of thousands of students from all over Greece. He personally lectured in philosophy, history of philosophy, politics, law, cultural history, mineralogy, zoology, ethics, religion, sense perception, physics, metaphysics, education, rhetoric, mathematics, botany, astronomy, logic, and meteorology—and wrote hundreds of treatises. His fifteen books of lecture notes on the habitat, physiology, classification, and etiology of plants were perhaps his most important scientific work.

- Aristotle's *Nicomachean Ethics* classifies virtues by reference to their extreme vices. Theophrastus' *Characters* may have been conceived to illustrate the vices; the collection falls short of fulfilling such a mission, but is an enjoyable read in its own right. Although Theophrastus wrote a description of virtuous characters, only his character sketches of "vicious" men survive. By 338 B.C., Athens was no longer a free democracy but had been subdued by Philip of Macedon, and the city was ruled in absentia by Antipater, one of Alexander's generals. The atmosphere of Athens, as a result, had deteriorated from one of philosophically driven magnanimity to preoccupation with the daily routine and obsession with the latest gossip or scandal.
- The *Characters* applies Theophrastus' system of classification to human beings. As snapshots of contemporary Athenian society, and also as a study of types of people ("characters" means "distinguishing marks"), the book became an indispensable reference tool for dramatists and actors. The playwright Menander may have been one of his students. Its curmudgeonly humor and avuncular perspective, similar to that of Art Buchwald in our own time, makes the *Characters* one of the most accessible documents of the late classical period.

---

1. THE IRONICAL MAN

Irony, if summarily defined, would appear to be an affectation of the worse in word and deed.

The ironical man is one who goes up to people he detests and is ready to chat with them without any sign of dislike. He praises to their face men whom he has attacked behind their backs, and sympathizes with them when they are meeting ill success. He is indulgent towards those who slander him, and unconcerned about what is being said. He talks blandly with people who are being ill-treated and who resent it. When people want to see him urgently, he tells them to come back another time. He never admits to anything he is doing, but says he is thinking of it. He pretends that he "has only just arrived," that he "was too late," or "was not well." To those who ask for a loan or a subscription he replies that he is not a rich man. When he has something to sell, he "is not selling," and if in fact he is not selling he says he is. He pretends he didn't hear, when he did; that he hasn't seen, when he has; when he has made an admission, that he doesn't remember making it. "I thought about that," he says; or, "I've no idea"; or, "That surprises me"; or, "I once reached a similar conclusion myself." In short, he is always using phrases of this kind: "I don't believe it," "I don't understand," "You astonish me"; or, "You give a different account of it; that wasn't the story he told *me*"; or, "I think the whole thing's absurd"; or, "Tell that to someone else"; or, "I don't see how I can either disbelieve you, or condemn him"; or, "All the same, don't be in a hurry to believe it."

2. THE TOADY, OR FLATTERER

Flattery may be thought of as an attitude or relationship which is degrading in itself, but profitable to the one who flatters.

The toady is the sort of person who will say to the man he is walking with, "Do you notice how people look at you? You're the only man in Athens they study in that way." Or perhaps, "You were being complimented yesterday in the Arcade. There was a group of thirty or more sitting talking; and the question cropped up, Who was our best citizen? Starting from that, we all came back finally to your name." While he is going on like this, he picks a stray thread off the other's cloak; or if a bit of chaff has blown into his hair, he takes it out, and says with a laugh, "Look at that! Because I haven't seen you for two days, you've got a beard full of gray hairs; though if anyone's hair keeps its color in spite of years, yours does." Then he will tell the company to keep silent while the great man is speaking; he will praise him when he is listening; and when he pauses in his talk he will back him up with "Hear, hear!" When his patron makes a feeble joke he laughs, stuffing his cloak into his mouth as if he couldn't contain his merriment. He asks people they meet in the street to wait until "He" has passed. He buys apples and pears, brings them in and gives them to the children when their father is watching, kisses them and says, "Well, youngsters, you've got a splendid father." If he goes with his patron to help him buy some shoes, he remarks that the foot is more shapely than the shoe. If the other is on his way to visit some friend, the toady will run ahead and tell the friend, "He's coming to see you," and then turn back and say, "I have announced you." He is even capable of running errands, at a moment's notice, to the women's market. At a dinner party he is the first to praise the wine, and he may be relied on to exclaim, "How delicate your food is!" Then he picks up something from the table, and says, "Now, isn't that choice?" He will ask his friend if he is cold and if he would like to put something more on; and while still asking he puts a wrap around him. What's more, he leans over to whisper in his ear; or, when talking to other guests, keeps glancing at their host. Then in the theater, he will take the cushions from the slave, and himself arrange them on his patron's seat. His patron's house, he will say, is beautifully built; his land has been nicely planted; and his portrait is an excellent likeness.

3. THE CHATTERER

Chatter is the churning-out of long-winded, unconsidered talk.

The chatterer is the sort of man who sits down beside someone he doesn't know and begins by delivering a panegyric on his own wife; continues with an account of his dream of the night before; then describes in detail what he had for supper. Next, getting into his stride, he remarks how far inferior men of the present day are to the ancients; how reasonable wheat is now in the shops; how full of foreigners Athens is getting. He observes that since the Dionysia it has been good sailing weather; and that if only Zeus would send more rain it would be better for the farmers. Then he tells you what part of his land he will put down to crops next year; and how difficult it is to live; and that Damippus has set up an enormous torch at the Mysteries; and "How many columns has the Odeion?" and "I was violently sick yesterday"; and "What day of the month is it today?" Then he tells you that the Mysteries are in September, the Apaturia in October, and the Rural Dionysia in December. In fact, if you put up with him, he will never stop.

4. THE BOOR

Boorishness I would define as uncivilized ignorance.

The boor is the sort of man who drinks barley-brew before going into the Assembly; who asserts that garlic smells as sweet as any perfume; wears shoes too big for his feet; and can't talk without bellowing. He won't trust his friends and relations, but he'll consult his slaves about his most important business; and he'll retail all the affairs of the Assembly to the laborers he employs on his farm. He sits down with his clothes hitched above the knee, exposing his nakedness. In the streets, other sights arouse in him no interest or surprise whatever, but if he sees a cow or a donkey or a goat he stops and inspects it. He can't fetch a bit of food from the cupboard without nibbling at it on the way; he drinks his wine neat. He quietly tries to rumple the bakery-maid, after he's helped her to do the grinding for the whole household, himself included. He feeds his horses while still eating his own breakfast. He

answers the front door himself; and calls his dog and takes hold of it by the nose, and says, "This fellow guards the house and the whole place." When he has been paid by someone with a silver coin, he rejects it, saying it is worn too smooth, and takes another instead. If he has lent his plow, or a basket, or a sickle, or a bag, he remembers it as he lies awake and goes to ask for it in the middle of the night. On his way down to town he asks anyone he meets what price hides or bloaters were fetching, or whether the new-moon festival is being held today. And in the same breath he tells you he's going down to get his hair cut; and while he's passing that way he means to call at Archias' for some fish. He sings in the public bath; and he drives hobnails into his shoes.

5. ANXIETY TO PLEASE

Anxiety to please (to compass it in a definition) is a quality designed to give pleasure, but whose impact does not make the best impression.

The ingratiating man is, shall we say, the sort who greets you from fifty yards off with "My dear man," gazes at you full of admiration, holds you by both hands and won't let go, and then after accompanying you a little way and asking when he is to see you next, finally departs on a note of eulogy. When he is called in to an arbitration he is anxious to please not only the man he is supporting but also his opponent, so as to appear impartial. In a dispute between foreigners and Athenians he will say the foreigners are in the right. When invited out to dinner he will ask his host to call the children; and when they come in he will say they are as like their father as so many peas in a pod. Then he pulls them towards him, kisses them and makes them stand by him. Then he romps with them, and sings the words of the game himself—

> Atishoo, atishoo,
> We all fall down!

—and he lets some of them fall asleep on his stomach, in spite of the cramp it gives him.

9. THE SHAMELESS MAN

Shamelessness may be defined as indifference to ill repute for the sake of gain.

The shameless man is one who will go to borrow money from the very person he is defrauding; one who after sacrificing to the gods will himself go out to dinner with someone else, and then salt down the meat and store it. At his host's table he calls his slave, then picks up meat and bread from the table and gives it to him, saying so that everyone can hear, "Make a good meal, Tibeios!" When he goes shopping he reminds the butcher of any little service he may have done him; and he stands near the scale and slips on to it some meat if possible, otherwise a bone to make soup; and if he gets away with it he's happy, and if not, he whips a bit of tripe off the table and chuckles as he hurries away with it. When he has guests from another city he buys (with their money) seats for a theater performance, and thus sees the play without paying his share; and the next day he even brings his sons, and their tutor. If you are carrying something you've bought at a bargain price, he will always ask you to share it with him. He will go to a neighbor's door and borrow barley, or perhaps bran, and then get the person who has lent it to carry it over to his house. In the public baths,

what he likes to do is to go over to where the jugs are kept, fill one (while the bath-man bawls at him), throw water over his own head, and then announce that he has had his bath, adding as he goes out, "And no thanks to you!"

10. THE SKINFLINT, OR STINGY MAN

Stinginess is a disproportionate avoidance of expense.

The stingy man is the sort who will come to your house in the middle of the month and ask you for half a month's interest on his loan. When he is at table with others, he will count how many cups each person has drunk; and of the whole company at dinner, he will pour the smallest libation to Artemis. If you buy anything for him, however cheaply, he will say, when you send in your account, that it has taken his last penny. If a servant breaks a jug or a dish, he takes the price of it out of his allowance. If his wife has dropped a threepenny-bit, he is the sort of person to start moving the furniture, shifting couches and cupboards, rummaging among rugs. If he has anything to sell, he will only let it go at a price which means a bad bargain for the buyer. He would never let you eat a fig out of his garden, or walk through his land, or pick up one of his windfall olives or dates. Every single day he inspects his boundaries to see if they have been tampered with. He is a terror, too, for enforcing the right of distraint, and for charging compound interest. When it is his turn to give the parish dinner, he cuts the meat into tiny slices to serve out. He goes off to market, and comes home again without buying anything. He forbids his wife to lend salt, or lamp-wick, or herbs, or barley-grains, or garlands, or holy-cakes. "These things all mount up, you know," he says, "in a twelvemonth."...

MENANDER (341–290 B.C.)
The Dyskolos (316 B.C.)

The single surviving play of the master of New Comedy won the annual prize in the year 316 B.C. Yet its author, Menander, produced over one hundred plays after writing his first, *Anger,* when he was twenty. Nearly a thousand fragments of his work remain to represent the last flowering of Athenian drama. The Romans Plautus and Terence, though lacking Menander's subtlety and nuance, "translated" his plays into Latin, thereby ensuring that Menander's plots would be available to be plundered by playwrights to this day. But Menander would not have minded; he stole his own plots, most of which can be summarized in one sentence: "A young man in love needs money." Shakespeare's *Much Ado about Nothing, All's Well That Ends Well,* and *Love's Labour's Lost* are influenced by Menander via these Roman imitators.

- The nephew of the playwright Alexis, who may have been his dramatic mentor, Menander belonged to a wealthy aristocratic Athenian family. Friends he entertained at his estate in Piraeus included the philosophers Theophrastus, Demetrius, and Epicurus. When Ptolemy I invited him to Egypt, Menander declined, preferring to enjoy the affluent comforts of home. He died while bathing in Piraeus, at the age of fifty-two. Despite his enormous popularity he won only eight prizes, losing regularly to his rival Philemon. Major fragments of *The Arbitrants, The Hero, Shorn, The Woman from Samos,* and *The Man from Sicyon* survive.

- In Menander's plays the chorus is shifted from a central role to that of providing interludes, and masks are customized to express character. Menander was said to have held "a mirror up to life" with his ironical and accurate depiction of contemporary foibles. He was applauded for his originality, clever plots, sophisticated wit, rapid-fire dialogue, elegant trimeter, and proverbial style. The dramatic elements of mistaken identity, orphaned children, unreasonable parents, strutting soldiers, separated twins, kidnapped daughters, thwarted lovers, scheming slaves, blustering rich men, jealous brothers, jilted suitors, and monologues involving the audience and showing off the actor's skill are grist for New Comedy's mill. These plays read like parodies of soap operas. *A Funny Thing Happened on the Way to the Forum* provides a taste for the fun and bawdy wit (with, of course, a Roman accent).

- Recovered from an Egyptian papyrus in 1958, *The Dyskolos* ("Misanthrope"), which won Menander first prize at the age of twenty-five, describes the contrary life of a man who "didn't like people," and who especially cannot stand his daughter's lover. Like most of Menander's plays, this one is preoccupied not with Hellenic political issues and events, but with domestic affairs. When the grumbling Knemon falls into a well, his would-be son-in-law rescues him; reluctantly, he takes part in the wedding. Like the Old Comedy of Aristophanes, Menander's plays end with a *gamos,* a celebration of life. But where Aristophanes bases his drama on the exploration of an idea, Menander's art, like the film *Four Weddings and a Funeral,* centers on manners and the subtleties of character, taking its lead from the tragic playwrights. As in his best plays, the characters here develop as the story unfolds, speaking in a characteristic manner that became a standard for good theatrical dialogue. That Menander was the darling of his fellow citizens indicates the self-consciousness into which Alexandrian Athens had fallen—far afield from the vigorous and thought-challenging culture of the golden fifth century B.C. Instead of the arrogance of excellence, the message of Menander's entertainment is understanding and good-humored acceptance.

THE MAN WHO DIDN'T LIKE PEOPLE

PROLOGUE
(Enter Pan, from his shrine. He addresses the audience.)

Pan   I would like you to imagine that this scene here represents Phyle, a village in Attica. This shrine I've emerged from belongs to the people of the place—and to anybody who's got the ability to farm these rocks. It's quite a celebrated shrine. Now this farm here on the right—it belongs to Knemon. He's an inhuman human—very inhuman: a fellow who's bad-tempered with everybody. And he doesn't like crowds. Crowds, eh? Why, he's never said a kind word to any individual in all his life, and he's lived a pretty long time. He's never gone up to anybody to greet him with a polite "Good morning," apart from me. And he only does it to me because he has to, out of religious form, through living next door to me and always going past my shrine. Oh, by the way, I'm the god

Pan. Anyway, I'm quite sure he changes his mind about being polite to me the minute he's gone past my shrine!

Well, for all his solitary ways, he actually got married—to a widow, whose first husband had died and left her with a little baby boy. He was at loggerheads with his wife from the start, and he spent all the daytime and a large part of the night, too, having a miserable time. Then they had a little daughter born to them. That made it worse, and when the trouble reached a point where you couldn't ever expect any change, and life was all hardship and misery, his wife left him. She went back to her son, the boy who was born before her second marriage. He owned a little farm here, nearly next door to the old man. That's the place where he's now looking after his mother and a loyal family servant, as well as himself. But they don't do so well. He's quite a young man now, with a head on him that's older than his years. It's Experience of Life—that's what has schooled him. And all this time the old man's been living all by himself, except for his daughter and an old woman who looks after them. Old Knemon's always working, collecting firewood or digging on his land, and detesting every human being, beginning with his neighbors here, and going on right down to the plain of Attica over there. But as for the old man's daughter, well, she's grown up like her environment—quite unsophisticated: not a wicked notion in her head. She looks after the shrine and the nymphs who share it with me, yes, she's so devoted and respectful to us that we've been persuaded to look after her in return. There's a fellow who farms a lot of land near here, worth thousands of pounds, and he has a son. Just about eighteen, and rather a man about town. Now this young man has been out hunting with a servant of his, and the chase has brought them to these parts, as it happens, and I've put him under a spell. That's the top and bottom of the situation. As for the details, you are going to see them, if you like—and you'd better like! As a matter of fact, I think I can see the young man coming this way now, and his parasite with him. They're having a private discussion about the recent events.

(Pan retires into his shrine.)

ACT ONE
(Pan having retired into his shrine to avoid being seen by them, Sostratos and his parasite Chaireas now enter. Sostratos is wearing a fine woolen cloak, and Chaireas is clothed in the traditional black of his profession; the two are in the middle of a conversation.)

Chaireas   What's that? You saw a free girl here putting garlands on the heads of the nymphs next door, and you'd fallen in love with her before you could get away? At first sight, Sostratos?

Sostratos   Yes, at first sight.

Chaireas   Quick work! Now you're sure you hadn't made up your mind to fall in love before you came out?

Sostratos   You're laughing at me, but really, Chaireas, I feel terrible.

Chaireas   I'm willing to believe you.

Sostratos   That's why I've brought you in on this affair. I thought you were a good friend—and practical, too.

Chaireas   Sostratos, that's just what I am in things like this. Now suppose friend number one's in love with a you-know-what. Well, he calls me in to help. Not a minute's delay. I grab her, carry her off, get drunk, burn her door down if she's awkward. In short, I've no time for the rationalistic approach. You've got to get her even before you've asked her name. If you take too long, the fellow's infatuation gets out of control. Be quick about it, and you can stop quickly. Now suppose friend number two is burbling about "settling down" and "a nice goodclass girl." I'm quite a different person then. I make inquiries: you know, about her family, how much money they've got, and about what the girl's really like. That way I leave a sort of permanent reminder to my friend: It doesn't matter how I arrange the courting, the results are permanent.

Sostratos   Yes, yes, and you do it very well. But not in the way that I want it (*this last remark probably aside*).

Chaireas   And now we must hear all about it.

Sostratos   Well, just after daybreak I sent Pyrrhias, the fellow who was out hunting with me, on an errand.

Chaireas   Where to?

Sostratos   I sent him to see the girl's father, or whoever's the legal guardian of the house where she lives.

Chaireas   Herakles! What a thing to do!

Sostratos   It was all wrong, I admit it. It's not done to give that kind of job to a servant. But you know, when you're in love, it's not so easy to know the right thing to do. Anyhow, he's been away a long time now, I wonder what's causing the delay; I told him to report back home to me as soon as he had discovered how things were.

   (*At this moment the servant Pyrrhias rushes blindly onto the stage.*)

Pyrrhias   Let me get past, look out, get out of the way, everybody—he's insane, the chap who's chasing me, he's off his rocker.

Sostratos   What's the matter, boy?

Pyrrhias   He's throwing lumps of earth at me, and stones. I'm all in.

Sostratos   Throwing? Where, you fool?

Pyrrhias   Perhaps . . . he's not . . . chasing me any longer?

Sostratos   No, he isn't.

Pyrrhias   I thought he was.

Sostratos   What are you talking about?

Pyrrhias   Please, let's get away from here.

Sostratos   Where to?

Pyrrhias   As far away from that door there (*he points to Knemon's door*) as we possibly can. He's a son of grief, a madman, a raving lunatic, that fellow you sent me to see, who lives there. Herakles! It's awful. I've broken practically all my toes with tripping over these rocks.

Sostratos   (*to Chaireas*) This fellow's acting as if he's drunk, it's plain to see.

Pyrrhias   (*thinking that the last remark was a reference to Knemon, not to himself*) Yes, he's quite out of his mind. But Sostratos, I'll be murdered. We've got to be careful. But I can't get my breath to speak. It's sticking in my throat . . . Well, I knocked at the door of that house. A miserable old hag came out. I said I was looking for the owner. She pointed him out to me from here, where I'm standing now as I tell you this. He was mucking about, gathering pears on the hilltop, or collecting faggots.

Sostratos   Temper, temper!

Pyrrhias   What's that, sir? Well, I climbed onto his land and started walking up to him. Now I wanted to make the right impression on him from a long way off, you know, I wanted to look like a friendly sort of chap. So I gave him a shout and said, "I've come to see you, sir," I said, "there's a matter I want to see you about, it concerns you." But he came back at me right away, with "You damnable blackguard you, why the hell are you trespassing on my land?", and he picked up a lump of earth and threw it right into my face.

Chaireas   Good heavens!

Pyrrhias   Well, while I had my eyes closed and my mouth open—I was going to tell him where to go—well, he picked up a stick again, and he began to clean the bark off it, and he shouted "What business have you got with me, eh? Don't you know the public way?" He was screaming away at the top of his voice.

Chaireas   This farmer sounds absolutely insane.

Pyrrhias   Well, in the end I ran for it, and he's chased me nearly a couple of miles, first around the hill, and then down here into the wood, slinging sods and rocks at me, and his pears too, he hadn't anything else. It's a barbarous sort of business, he's a perfectly murderous old man. I do beg you, get out of here.

Sostratos   That's cowardice.

Pyrrhias   But you don't realize what sort of trouble this is. He'll eat us alive!

Chaireas   Perhaps he's a bit upset now. I really think we ought to put our visit off for the present. You know, Sostratos, there's nothing so effective, whatever you're doing, as tact.

Pyrrhias   That's sensible, now.

Chaireas   A poor farmer's inclined to be rather touchy. It's not just him alone, they're practically all like that. Now tomorrow, I'll go and see him myself, first thing, I know where he lives. And you go home and wait (*he is addressing Sostratos*). This'll turn out just as we want it.

Pyrrhias   Yes, let's do that (*exit Chaireas*).

Sostratos   He was glad enough to have an excuse for leaving as soon as he could. Obviously he didn't like the idea of walking here with me, he didn't think much of my keenness in wanting to get married. But as for you, my boy, damn you for your stupidity!

Pyrrhias   But what have I done wrong, Sostratos?

Sostratos   You trespassed on his property, that's clear enough.

Pyrrhias   But I wasn't stealing anything.

Sostratos   Now would anyone be after your hide if you weren't doing anything wrong?

Pyrrhias   Oh, look, he's coming now.

Sostratos Now, my dear boy, you can go up to him first.

Pyrrhias No, you talk to him.

Sostratos I couldn't. I'm not very good at conversation. I couldn't convince anybody. *(Knemon now enters, with purposeful gait, ignoring all in his path and muttering to himself.)*

Pyrrhias Well, what's your opinion of him now? *(Pyrrhias here backs into the temple, remaining visible to the audience, but hiding himself from Knemon.)*

Sostratos No, he doesn't seem to have a very friendly look on his face. Heavens, he is in a hurry! I think I'll stand a little way out of his path, away from his door. That's better. Why, he's yelling at the top of his voice, and he's all by himself. I don't think he can be in his right mind.

Knemon That fellow Perseus was a lucky chap, in two ways. He had a pair of wings, so he didn't have to meet any pedestrians walking about on the ground. And second, he had a contraption that turned everybody who irritated him into stone. I wish I had something like that now. There'd be no shortage of stone statues around here then. *(He gazes intently at the audience.)* But as it is, life's just not worth living. People come chattering and trespassing on your property nowadays. Yes, you know, I once used to spend my time working by the side of the road. But I don't do that any longer; I've given up cultivating all that part of my land that touches the road. I've left it because of the

people who are always passing. But now they chase me right up to the hilltops. Oh, there's far too many people in this world, far too many people. Oh no! Who's that standing by my door?

Sostratos Is he going to give *me* a hiding?

Knemon *(He ignores the words of Sostratos)* A man can't find a quiet place anywhere, no, not even if he wants to hang himself.

Sostratos He's vexed with me. *(To Knemon)* Oh, sir, I'm waiting for somebody here, I arranged to meet him.

Knemon Didn't I just say so? You all think this is a park or a public place. Well then, if you want to meet anybody near my door, why don't you get it all organized just as you like? Go on, put up a bench to sit on, if you want. No, build a whole stadium! It's an absolute scandal, this disgusting behavior, as if I haven't got enough to be worried about! *(Exit into his house, slamming the door.)*

Sostratos This affair is going to require some extra-special hard work, I think; obviously it needs a bit more initiative. Now I wonder, shall I go and see father's servant? Yes, I will: Getas is just the man. He's got a lively brain, and he's well up in all sorts of things. He'll get rid of that fellow's crabby temper, I know. I'm all against delay in this affair; a lot could happen in one day. But someone's unlatched the door.

(Knemon's daughter enters from her father's house, carrying a pitcher.)

Daughter   Oh dear, dear me, how awful things are! What am I going to do now? Nurse has dropped the big water jar into the well as she was drawing it up. . . .

Sostratos   (aside) O father Zeus, O healer Apollo, O dear Castor and Pollux, what irresistible beauty!

Daughter   . . . and when Daddy went out, he told us to get some hot water ready for him . . .

Sostratos   (aside) My dear fellows, she's beautiful!

Daughter   . . . and if he finds out he'll beat the life out of her. Oh dear, I haven't much time. I know, my darling nymphs: I think I'll get the water from your shrine. But still, I'm rather frightened of disturbing anybody inside; there may be some people sacrificing.

Sostratos   Er, if you're willing to let me have the jar, I'll dip it in and bring it back to you.

Daughter   (making up her mind suddenly, after a doubtful pause.) Yes, certainly you may, but you'd better hurry. (She hands him the jar.)

Sostratos   (entering the shrine, and in an aside) She may have been brought up on a farm, but she certainly knows how to behave!

Daughter   Oh, I wish I knew how we could get out of this mess. Oh dear, the door. Surely it's not Daddy coming out? He'll give me a good spanking if he finds me outside.

(Daos enters from Gorgias' house, and addresses his first words to someone in the house.)

Daos   I've spent a long time here, madam, looking after your needs, and master's been all by himself working on the farm. It's time I went and joined him. Oh, damn this poverty of ours. Poverty. Why did we have to be so poor? Why did Lady Have-Nowt have to choose our house for her permanent residence, year in, year out?

Sostratos   (bringing back the full jar, and now accompanied by Pyrrhias) Here you are.

Daughter   Let me have it here.

Daos   (aside, and suspicious) Whatever does this fellow want?

Sostratos   Good-bye, and look after your father. (Exit daughter into her father's house.) Oh, I do feel terrible.

Pyrrhias   Stop moaning, Sostratos, it'll be all right.

Sostratos   What'll be all right?

Pyrrhias   Cheer up, do what you were going to do just now, find Getas and tell him all about it properly, and then you can come back here.

(Exeunt Sostratos and Pyrrhias, left.)

Daos   What's going on here? I don't like it one little bit, a young man fetching and carrying for a girl, it's wrong. Damn you, Knemon, damn you for the villain you are, leaving a poor girl that wouldn't harm a fly all alone here in a wilderness, and not a single person to look after her if anything happened. You might as well leave her out on a mountaintop. I bet that young toff found out about it and was here in a flash. Thought it was a lucky strike, I'll warrant. Still, I'd better be quick and tell her step-brother about this, and then we might be able to see that the girl's properly looked after. I think I'll go and do that now. Why, here's the local choir on its rounds. They look a bit drunk; I think it'd be as well to keep out of their way *(Exit right.)*

(The local choir [in the original Greek, a reveling chorus of votaries of Pan or Apollo, young men garlanded and carrying lit torches, and rather tipsy] enter, and entertain the audience with an entr'acte.)

EPICURUS (341–270 B.C.)
Letter to Herodotus

*E*picureanism, the hedonistic philosophy based on seeking maximum sensual pleasure and minimum pain as the highest good in a turbulent world of mortal life among fortuitous circumstances and random happenings, was so hated by virtuous Romans and the early Christians that few of its founder's writings survive. The moral and natural philosopher Epicurus was born on the island of Samos and died in Athens, the home of his father Neocles, who was a schoolmaster. His mother was Chaerestrate.

As a youth, he studied at Plato's Academy under Xenocrates, with Menander as a classmate. From Nausiphanes in Teos he learned about the atomists, especially Democritus and Leucippus, who deeply influenced his thinking about the natural world. At his "Garden" in Athens, as well as in Mytilene on Lesbos and at Lampsacus, Epicurus set up his own residential schools around discussion groups. Women and slaves were allowed to participate.

- Its reputation to the contrary, the followers of Epicurus, who lived together in commune style, practiced an austere asceticism reminiscent of Pythagoreanism and later influential on the meditations of Emperor Marcus Aurelius.
- Epicurus' most important historian, Diogenes Laertius, records that Epicurus wrote prodigiously—more than 300 documents. Only these remain:

- The Letter to Pythocles, about the heavens.
- The Letter to Menoeceus, summarizing his views on ethics, the gods, and morality.
- And two collections of maxims and sayings, samples given below.

- We know as much as we do about Epicurus' worldview from a Roman poem by Lucretius, *On the Nature of Things,* which borrowed heavily from him. Epicurus believed that:

  - The purpose of philosophy is to help man achieve happiness in this life; "pleasure is the beginning and end of living happily."
  - Positive pleasure comes from enjoyable physical sensations; "negative" pleasure comes from the absence of pain.
  - Nothing immaterial exists. Everything is material except empty space, and matter is composed of invisible, indivisible *atomoi,* atoms.
  - The soul, like the body, is mortal. Knowing this, man is freed from his fear of death.
  - The gods, themselves material, exist on an entirely separate plane where there is no pain. Prayers to them are useless, for they have no interest in or impact on human affairs.
  - The ideal in life is freedom from disturbance. Renouncing worldly ambitions, Epicureans rise above the ups and downs of political engagement as well as of emotional commitments.

Yet Epicurean communities were known for loyalty among members as well as for their moderation.

The physics of Epicurus, especially in its description of the "rain of atoms" that ceaselessly causes change in the universe, looks forward to the great discoveries of the twentieth century in atomic physics. We learn directly about Epicurus' philosophy of nature in his "Letter to Herodotus," written as a summary of his scientific thought to the famous historian. We owe the existence of this letter to its preservation by Diogenes Laertius.

The first thing we must fix in our minds in the study of physics, Herodotus, is the reference of the terms used, so that we may have a sure standard of judgment in our investigations, and so that an unproved assumption may not spawn meaningless phrases forever. For every word we utter we must be able to call up a clear mental picture, which needs no further definition, to which we can refer our problems. In the second place, it is axiomatic that we must refer constantly to our sensations, to the judgments of our mind or any other standard we accept, as well as the reports of our senses. Thus only can we confirm the obscure and uncertain.

When these two points are well understood, we can begin to study things which are not obvious. First of all, nothing can come into being where nothing was before, for if it could, anything could arise from any origin, since it would have no need of its own proper source. And nothing can disappear into nothingness; if a thing which disappears to the sight were really annihilated, everything in the world would long since have perished without a trace. The sum of the matter in the world has always been just what it now is and what it always will be. There is nothing outside matter into which matter can change, nor is there anything nonmaterial which could enter in and cause such a transformation.

The whole universe is made up only of matter and empty space. Our own senses bear witness that matter exists, and it is on our senses that the reason must base its advances into the unknown.

Now if there were no empty space—call it "void" or "room to move in" or "the intangible" or what you will—there would be no place in which bodies could exist or move about, as we see them doing. Aside from these two, matter and void, there is nothing of which we can form a mental picture, nothing of which we can conceive on the analogy of anything else. . . .

There is an unlimited number of worlds, some like this one, some not. For the atoms, which are infinite in number, are always spreading out further and further; and the particles from which a world could be formed could not all have been used up in making this one

. . . We should realize that we see things and think about them when something material passes into us from them. For it is unlikely that external objects should register their shape and color on our minds by pressing the air between them and us, or by rays or currents passing from us to them; it is more reasonable that films of atoms enter us, of the same shape and color as the objects from which they arise. Once in, these films stimulate the sense organs or the mind, depending on the size of their atoms. These films move at enormous speed, which is why they present us with a single continuous image. Their atoms keep the same relative position that was impressed on them by the atoms in the depths of the object. Whenever we have an image of something's shape or other property, in our eyes or in our minds, it is that of the object and not of something else; it is produced because the atoms of the film cling together, or, at least, part of them do. Falsehood and error arise, not from our perceptions, but from the conclusions to which we jump about things which have not yet been established as true; in such cases further investigation may not confirm our first opinions, and may even disprove them. . . .

Most of our capacity to perceive resides in the soul, but this could not be so unless the soul were contained in the body and permeated its every part. The body, by providing the necessary framework, shares with the soul the responsibility for perception, but does not possess all the soul's powers. When the atoms of the soul are scattered in death the body loses its ability to perceive. This power it does not possess of itself, but only as a loan from the soul, which is born with the body. The soul is potentially able to feel; when its atoms are set in motion the potentiality becomes real. It then imparts this power it has gained to the body by its penetration and intimate connection. . . .

The greatest anxiety suffered by the human mind arises from the belief that the heavenly bodies are divine and imperishable, but still are able to desire and act and cause things. Moreover, men cringe in dread as if they were doomed to some unending evil, probably because of the fairy stories they have heard, and await in terror the unfeeling nothingness of death—as if, forsooth, that affected us at all! They do not suffer thus because they have thought things out, but through a quite unreasoning panic. Indeed, those who set no limit to their frightened pondering are perturbed as much as or more than men who make only random and careless conjectures on these matters. Real peace of mind means freeing one's self from all these bugbears and constantly remembering the real and supreme truths.

Let us, then, confine ourselves to the evidence of sense and feeling, our own and that common to all men, and pay attention only to what can be clearly judged by reliable standards. If we study this evidence, we will understand and eliminate the causes of our fears and anxieties, and will be able to observe with tranquility the happenings in the sky, and other portents which cause the most extreme terror in the rest of mankind. . . .

First believe that God is alive, immortal, and blessed, as the consensus of mankind indicates, but do not attach to him anything inconsistent with his immortality and blessed state; rather believe what supports them. For assuredly the gods exist, and knowledge of them is certain; but they are not like those in whom most men believe, for the multitude is not consistent in the conception it forms of the gods. . . .

Accustom yourself to the realization that death concerns us not at all. For good and bad exist only by being perceived, and death deprives us of perception. Once we understand this truth, that death does not concern us, even our mortality becomes a source of pleasure: We give up our attempts to add eternity to our span of life here, and can abandon our vain longing for immortality. Life holds no terrors for him who realizes that there are none in death. This worst of horrors, the fear of death, affects us not at all; for while we are, death is not, and when death is, we are not.

We must remember that of our desires some are natural, others purposeless; of the natural ones, some are necessary, others not. Of the necessary desires, some are essential to life, others to bodily comfort, others to happiness.

The man who understands this will govern his choices and his rejections by considering the health of his body and the tranquility of his soul; this is the purpose of a happy life. To this end of feeling no pain or insecurity we direct all our actions; when once we have gained this, the storms that trouble the soul are calmed, and we no longer need to go in search of what we lack or hunt for anything good to fulfill the needs of body or soul. When we suffer from a lack of pleasure, then only do we feel its need; when we are not in pain, we need no more. Pleasure, then, we call the beginning and end of a happy life. We know that it is our first and inborn good; for its sake we choose or avoid things; we use our feelings as the standard for measuring every good.

Pleasure is our greatest good, and desire for it

is born in us; yet we do not clutch at every pleasure that offers itself but sometimes pass over delights from which a greater pain may result. Pain itself, indeed, often seems preferable to pleasure, if greater pleasure will follow our enduring it. Everything pleasant is good, for it is naturally fitted to us, but it does not follow that we should choose it. In like manner every pain is an evil, but not all painful things must be avoided.

By a sort of calculus, by examining and comparing the good or evil in things, we must decide our course. Sometimes we will regard pleasure as an evil and pain as a good.

Independence of external things, too, we regard as a great good, not in order that we may always want to live frugally, but that we may be content to do so if we should have to. For we are convinced that those who need luxury least enjoy it most. Natural pleasures are easily gained; it is the useless ones which are costly. Simple food brings as much delight as rare and choice dishes, even when the edge of appetite is dulled, and bread and water bring the highest pleasure to one in real need of food. . . .

When we assert that pleasure is the chief motive of life, we are not speaking of dissipation and intemperance, as some ignorant, prejudiced, or malicious people think. No; we mean the absence of discomfort in the body and disturbance in the soul. Wild revels and orgies, gorges of rich food, cannot produce a happy life; the soul can best free itself from anxiety and tumult which haunt it by sober thought and searching out the reasons for its choices and rejections. Common sense is the beginning of this, and is the most valuable thing a man can have. It is more precious even than philosophy, for all the other virtues arise

from it. It shows that we cannot live happily unless we live with intelligence, honor, and justice, and that we cannot live intelligently, honorably, and justly without being happy. All the virtues merge in the happy life, which cannot be separated from them.

Can you think of anyone who is better off than a man who leads this life? His ideas about the gods are reverent. He has no terror at the thought of death, which he views as the end established for us by nature. He knows how easily his natural desires can be fulfilled, and that any evils which he suffers are either short-lived or not severe. Destiny, which some [the Stoics] bring in as the ruler of all things, he laughs at: Some things, he says are predestined, some happen by chance, and some come about through our own activity; if destiny ruled, man would have no responsibility, and if chance, she is a fickle tyrant. No; our choice is free, and on the choices we make depends the praise or blame we deserve. . . .

THE GOLDEN MAXIMS

1. A blessed and immortal being feels no trouble in himself and makes none for others. He is, therefore, subject neither to anger nor to affection, things which only accompany weakness.

2. Death is nothing to us; for when the body has been destroyed it feels nothing, and a state of feeling nothing is no concern to us.

3. The limit of the intensity of pleasure is the removal of all pain. As long as we feel pleasure, there can be no pain or sorrow in the body or the mind.

4. Severe pain of the flesh does not last long. Extreme anguish is very short-lived, and even pain which barely outweighs pleasure re-

mains only for a few days. Diseases which do last a long time may even allow the sufferer to feel more pleasure than pain. . . .

11. If the phenomena of the heavens had never terrified us, if we had never felt ourselves somehow concerned with death, and if we had never failed to recognize the limits of pain and desire, we would never have had any need to study the workings of nature. . . .

14. First of all we seek a reasonable degree of security from other men. After that our desire seeks something else, the security of a quiet life, withdrawn from the crowd. This depends on our having a comfortable prosperity and wealth enough to support us. . . .

18. Pleasure cannot be increased in the flesh once the pain caused by want has been removed; from then on it can only be varied. . . .

31. Natural justice is a short term for the expediency found in not harming others on condition that they shall not harm us. . . .

33. There never was such a thing as abstract or absolute justice, but men made contracts in various times and places not to harm others or be harmed themselves. . . .

37. If the letter of any law is admitted to be appropriate to the conditions of men's relations that exist, by that very fact the law acquires the character of justice, whether or not it be the same for all. But if someone writes a law which turns out not to be useful in men's relations, it no longer shares the spirit of justice. If conditions of usefulness change, so that they fit the terms expressed in the law only for a little while, the law is just for that little while and no more—if, that is, we look at the facts and do not bother our heads with mere empty verbiage.

EUCLID (FL. 300 B.C.)
The Elements of Geometry

𝒯he writer of the standard handbook of arithmetic and geometry still in use today taught mathematics in Alexandria, Egypt, at a school he founded during the reign of Ptolemy I. Ptolemy himself was among his many distinguished students. Almost nothing is known about Euclid's personal life. In addition to mathematics, he wrote about astronomy, optics, and music. When asked for a shortcut by Ptolemy, he is said to have replied: "There is no royal road to mathematics."

- Compiling, reorganizing, clarifying, and correcting previous works on mathematics and geometry by Theudius (whose text was used by Aristotle), Hippocrates of Chios, Theaetetus, Leon, and Eudoxus, Euclid's work immediately replaced them all and was translated into many languages within the author's lifetime. In the next 2,300 years his little book would sell nearly as many copies as the Bible.

- Though Thales and Pythagoras may have laid the foundations, Euclid's systematic presentation makes him the father of mathematics. The *Elements,* concise and clearly written, is divided into thirteen books, dealing with plane and solid geometry, arithmetic, and the theory of numbers.

BOOK I.
DEFINITIONS.

I. A *point* is that which has not parts.

II. A *line* is length without breadth.

III. The extremities of a line are points.

IV. A *right line* is that which lies evenly between its extremities.

V. A *surface* is that which has length and breadth only.

VI. The extremities of a surface are lines.

VII. A *plane surface* is that which lies evenly between its extremities.

VIII. A *plane angle* is the inclination of two lines to one another, in a plane, which meet together, but are not in the same direction.

IX. A *plane rectilinear angle* is the inclination of two right lines to one another, which meet together, but are not in the same right line.

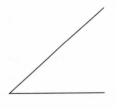

X. When a right line standing on another right line makes the adjacent angles equal, each of these angles is called a *right angle,* and each of these lines is said to be *perpendicular* to the other.

XI. An *obtuse* angle is an angle greater than a right angle.

XII. An *acute* angle is an angle less than a right angle.

XIII. A term or boundary is the extremity of any thing.

XIV. A figure is a surface, enclosed on all sides by a line or lines.

XV. A *circle* is a plane figure, bounded by one continued line, called its *circumference* or *periphery;* and having a certain point within it, from which all right lines drawn to its circumference are equal.

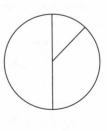

XVI. This point (from which the equal lines are drawn) is called the center of the circle.

XVII. A *diameter* of a circle is a right line drawn through the center, terminated both ways in the circumference.

XVIII. A semicircle is the figure contained by the diameter, and the part of the circle cut off by the diameter.

XIX. A segment of a circle is a figure contained by a right line, and the part of the circumference which it cuts off.

XX. A figure contained by right lines only is called a *rectilinear figure*.

XXI. A triangle is a rectilinear figure included by three sides.

XXII. A quadrilateral figure is one which is bounded by four sides. The right lines, AC, BD, connecting the vertices of the opposite angles of a quadrilateral figure, are called its *diagonals*.

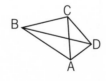

XXIII. A polygon is a rectilinear figure, bounded by more than four sides.

XXIV. A triangle whose three sides are equal is said to be equilateral.

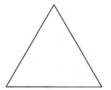

XXV. A triangle which has only two sides equal is called an isosceles triangle.

XXVI. A *scalene triangle* is one which has no two sides equal.

XXVII. A right-angled triangle is that which has a right angle.

XXVIII. An obtuse-angled triangle is that which has an obtuse angle.

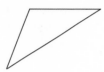

XXIX. An acute-angled triangle is that which has three acute angles.

XXX. An equilateral quadrilateral figure is called a *lozenge*.

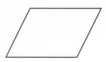

XXXI. An equiangular lozenge is called a *square*.

XXXII. An *oblong* is a quadrilateral, whose angles are all right, but whose sides are not equal.

XXXIII. A *rhomboid* is a quadrilateral whose opposite sides are equal.

XXXIV. All other quadrilateral figures are called *trapeziums*.

XXXV. Parallel right lines ——————— are such as are in the ——————— same plane, and which, being produced continually in both directions, would never meet.

POSTULATES.

I. Let it be granted that a right line may be drawn from any one point to any other point.

II. Let it be granted that a finite right line may be produced to any length in a right line.

III. Let it be granted that a circle may be described with any center at any distance from that center.

AXIOMS.

I. Magnitudes which are equal to the same are equal to each other.

II. If equals be added to equals the sums will be equal.

III. If equals be taken away from equals the remainders will be equal.

IV. If equals be added to unequals the sums will be unequal.

V. If equals be taken away from unequals the remainders will be unequal.

"Lion's Gate, Mycenae" Bildarchiv Foto Marburg. Istanbul Museum. By permission of Art Resource.

VI. The doubles of the same or equal magnitudes are equal.

VII. The halves of the same or equal magnitudes are equal.

VIII. Magnitudes which coincide with one another, or exactly fill the same space, are equal.

IX. The whole is greater than its part.

X. Two right lines cannot include a space.

XI. All right angles are equal.

XII. If two right lines (AB, CD) meet a third right line (AC) so as to make the two interior angles (BAC and DCA)

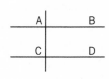

on the same side less than two right angles, these two right lines will meet if they be produced on that side on which the angles are less than two right angles . . .

LEONIDAS OF TARENTUM (FL. CA. 280 B.C.)
Lyrics

*S*urviving only in the Greek Anthology, the poems of Leonidas of Tarentum, one of the earliest Hellenistic epigrammatists, are various in subject matter and graceful, if not brilliant, in style.

- Though his patrons included King Pyrrhus of Epirus, Leonidas' poems often dealt with everyday events in the lives of sailors, shepherds, fishermen, and farmers.
- He may be more important for those he inspired, including the Roman Propertius, than for the artistic merits of his own work.

'Tis time to sail—the swallow's note is heard,
Who chattering down the soft west wind is
    come,
The fields are all aflower, the waves are dumb
Which erst the winnowing blast of winter
    stirred.

Loose cable, friend, and bid your anchor rise,
Crowd all your canvas at Priapus' hest,
Who tells you from your harbors—"Now
    'twere best,

Sailor, to sail upon your merchandise."

Fair Kypris, rising from her mother's breast,
    Her beauty with the salt sea foam aglow,
Apelles saw and bade the loveliest
    Vision of joy upon his canvas grow.
A living form, which seems to breathe and
    move!
    She draws her taper fingers through her
    hair;
In her calm eye shines soft the light of love;

Her quince-shaped breasts her wondrous
    charms declare.
Then, then Athena and great Hera yield
Confessing, "Zeus, for her we quit the field."

A FIG-TREE

Democritus fig-loving shouldst thou see,
Bear him this message, traveler, from me:
The luscious fruit, maturely beautiful,
Weighs upon me, and waits for him to cull;
But fence is none; so, if he wish to taste,
'Tis fit that thou and he should both make
    haste.

Not solely from the summer's sultry heat
Seek I in shady glades a cool retreat,
And sip up dew, and utter from the pine
Music unbought, the traveler's joy and mine;
But on the shining point of Pallas' spear
I perch a warlike grasshopper; for dear
As I to Muses, is to me the maid
Whose skill inventive first the flute essayed.

They say that I am small and frail,
    And cannot live in stormy seas;
It may be so; yet every sail
    Makes shipwreck in the swelling breeze.
Not strength nor size can then hold fast;
    But Fortune's favor, Heaven's decree:
Let others trust in oar and mast;
    But may the gods take care of me.

Venus, at Rhodo's prayer this stick, and these
Sandals, the spoil of sage Posochares;
This dirty leather flask, this wallet torn,
Suffer thy sanctuary to adorn:
Trophies not rich but glorious, for they prove
Philosophy's subjection unto Love.

With courage seek the kingdom of the dead;

The path before you lies,
It is not hard to find, nor tread;
No rocks to climb, no lanes to thread;
But broad, and straight, and even still,
And ever gently slopes downhill;
You cannot miss it, though you shut your eyes.

THE TOMB OF CRETHON

I am the tomb of Crethon; here you read
His name; himself is number'd with the dead;
Who once had wealth not less than Gyges'
    gold:
Who once was rich in stable, stall, and fold;
Who once was blest above all living men—
With lands, how narrow now, how ample then:

Shepherds that on this mountain ridge abide,
Tending your goats and fleecy flocks alway,
A little favor, but most grateful, pay
Cleitagoras, nor be the boon denied!
For sake of mother earth, and by the bride
Of Hades under earth, let sheep, I pray,
Bleat near me, and the shepherd softly play
From the scarred rock across the pasture wide.

Ah! but, in early spring, cull meadowsweet,
Neighbor, and weave a garland for my tomb;
And with ewe's milk be the stone edge
    bedewed
When the lambs play about their mother's
    feet.
So shall you honor well the shades, from
    whom
Are thanks—and from the dead is gratitude.

THE FISHERMAN

Theris the old, the waves that harvestèd,
    More keen than birds that labor in the sea,
With spear and net, by shore and rocky bed

Not with the well-manned galley, labored
   he;
Him not the Star of Storms, nor sudden
   sweep
   Of wind with all his years hath smitten and
   bent.
But in his hut of reeds he fell asleep,
   As fades a lamp when all the oil is spent:
This tomb nor wife nor children raised, but we
   His fellow-toilers, fishers of the sea.

THE SPINNING WOMAN

Morning and evening, sleep she drove away,
   Old Platthis, warding hunger from the door,
And still to wheel and distaff hummed her lay
   Hard by the gates of Eld, and bent and
   hoar:
Plying her loom until the dawn was gray,
   The long course of Athene did she tread:
With withered hand by withered knee she
   spun

Sufficient for the loom of goodly thread,
Till all her work and all her days were done.
   And in her eightieth year she saw the wave
   Of Acheron—old Platthis—kind and brave.

Unnumbered were the ages past, O man,
   Before thy day began.
Unnumbered, too, the ages yet shall be,
   That Hades hath for thee.

What store of life, then, doth to thee remain?
   Scarce as it were a grain!
Scanty thy life and short—nor mayest thou
   Even enjoy it now;
For it is hateful, and its poisoned breath
   More dire than loathèd death.

Then scorn this stormy life of thine and
   shun—
   As I indeed have done,
I, Pheido, son of Krita—and like me,
Seek the still haven of tranquility,
The haven of dark Hades' silent sea.

THEOCRITOS (CA. 310–250 B.C.)
Thyrsis: The Death of Daphnis

*T*he master of Greek pastoral poetry and the finest poet of the Hellenistic period traveled from his native Syracuse to the island of Cos, off Asia Minor, to study with Philetas' "School of Poets." After a brief sojourn in Ptolemy II's Alexandria, where he also studied with the poets Asclepiades and Aratus, Theocritos returned either to Cos or to Hieron II's Sicily, where he spent the remainder of his life.

- Alexandrian literature was typically highly polished, erudite, and stylistically affected, enamored of the exotic and of novel variations on traditional themes. Pastoral poetry after Theocritos shares many of these self-consciously artificial qualities, rarely suggesting a real connection between subject matter and author. But Theocritos himself may have left Alexandria precisely because his muse did not respond to its precious literary atmosphere, and his descriptions of nature's charms are heartfelt and generally free of "Alexandrian" influence. Some say he wrote so vividly and persuasively about rural life because he was also disappointed with his lack of patronage from Sicily's Hieron II. In Homer's *Iliad* the peacefulness of the shepherds' life was presented in contrast with the senseless violence of war. Theocritos, from personal experience, expanded Homer's metaphor into a new kind of poetry.

- Theocritos' Idylls (from the Greek word for "pictures"), all but three written in the Doric dialect spoken in Sicily, are the first great "pastoral" or "bucolic" poems in western literature. In an age of sophisticated decadence and decline of moral values in favor of experimentalism, they celebrate compellingly the innocence and moral purity of the countryside and of everyday joys and woes of common people. Their dramatic power may rise from their being as much romanticization as remembrance, their realistic vitality based on Theocritos' own positive experience of the pastoral hillsides and bustling harbors of his Syracusan origins.

- His poetry, in contrast with the puritanical cynicism of Hesiod's, created a philosophically reflective and romantically evocative genre that would be developed by the Romans Horace and Virgil, Renaissance writers from Jacopo Sannazaro to John Milton, and Romantics William Wordsworth and John Keats.

- The first Idyll evokes Pan the protector of shepherds, who entertain themselves and their animals by playing his reed pipe (the *syrinx*). The poem describes the young man Daphnis, the mythical inventor of pastoral song, who wastes away and dies from struggling against a love to which he refuses to yield. Theocritos compares Daphnis' love problems with those of Aphrodite (Cypris), the goddess whom Daphnis defies.

IDYLL I

Thyrsis: Sweet is the whisper of wind as it plays in that pine
Near the spring, O goatherd, and sweet, too, is your piping;
In a contest with Pan you would win second prize.
If he took the horned he-goat, you'd win the dam,

But should his prize be the dam, the kid would be yours,
And a kid before it gives milk is delectable eating.

Goatherd: Sweeter, O shepherd, pours forth the song from your lips
Than the water tumbling down from those rocks overhead.
Should the Muses bear away a ewe as their gift,

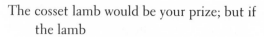

The cosset lamb would be your prize; but if
the lamb
Should content them, you next would be
awarded the ewe.

Thyrsis: By the nymphs, goatherd, would it
please you to sit down
On this sloping hillock here where the
tamarisks grow
And play your syrinx, while I meanwhile look
after your goats?

Goatherd: Custom forbids, O shepherd, that
at noontime we play
  on the syrinx,
For we go in fear of great Pan. At this time of
day,
Weary, he rests from the chase. He has an
irascible temper,
And bitter gall perches forever over his
nostrils.
But you, Thyrsis, sing of the sorrows of
Daphnis
And are skilled in the pastoral song of the
Muses.
Let us sit down here under the elm tree facing
Priapos
And the nymphs of the spring, where stand
the oaks
And the bench of the shepherds, and if you
sing as you did
When vying in song once with Chromis of
Libya,
I will let you have a twin-bearing goat for
three milkings,
Who, besides feeding two kids, yields up two
milk pails,

And a deep ivywood drinking cup coated with
sweet-scented wax,
Two-handled and newly wrought, and from
the chisel still fragrant.
Ivy twines high along the lip of the cup,
And scattered among the ivy leaves are
helichryse blossoms,
And the spiraling tendrils below are glorious
with golden fruit.
Inside the cup a woman, carved as by one of
the gods,
Wearing a peplos and headband; two men
stand beside her
With fine long hair, contending with
speeches, first one,
Then the other in turn, but they cannot
kindle her heart.
At one moment, laughing, she looks on this
man,
The next moment turns her mind to the
other, while they,
Long heavy-eyed from love's suffering, labor
in vain.
Near them is engraved a fisherman on a rough
rock,
An old man who visibly strains as he gathers
up
His great net for a cast, like a man worn out
with hard work.
You might say he was fishing with all the
strength of his limbs
From the swollen sinews that stand out all
over his neck,
But gray-haired though he is, his strength is
that of a youth.
And not far away from this seaworn old man is
a vineyard
Heavily laden with ripening clusters of grapes,

Where on a dry-stone wall a small boy sits on
  guard.
Two foxes flank him: One prowls up and down
  the vine rows,
Pilfering the already ripe fruit, while the other
Directs all her cunning toward the boy's
  wallet, and vows not to rest
Until she has left him lean fare for his
  breakfast.
But he, plaiting with asphodel stalks a fine
  cage for locusts,
Fits in a reed and thinks not at all of his
  wallet
Or of the vines, so great is his joy in his
  weaving.
And all over the cup is spread the wavy
  acanthus—
A sight for goatherds! The marvelous thing
  will amaze you!
I gave the Calydnian boatman a she-goat in
  payment
And a great wheel of white cheese. Never so
  far
Has it been touched by my lips, but still lies
  unsullied.
It would be a pleasure indeed, my friend, to
  give it to you
If you would sing for me that beautiful song.
I do not mock you. Come, sir, for to hoard it
Will not serve you at all in Hades' realm
  where all is forgotten.

Thyrsis: *Begin the pastoral song, dear Muses,*
  begin the song.
Thyrsis of Etna am I, and this is the sweet
  voice of Thyrsis.
Where were you, nymphs, where were you
  when Daphnis was wasting?

In Tempe, the lovely vale of Peneios, or off on
  the slopes of the Pindos?
For not then did you haunt the great stream
  of the river Anapos
Or Etna's high peak or the holy waters of Acis.

  Begin the pastoral song, dear Muses, begin
the song.

For him the jackals lamented, for him the
  wolves howled,
For him, dead, the lion mourned in the oak
  wood.

  Begin the pastoral song, dear Muses, begin
the song.

Around him cows without number and bulls
  made lament,
Many a heifer and many a calf too bewailed
  him.

  Begin the pastoral song, dear Muses, begin
the song.

Hermes came from the hill first of all and
  said, "Daphnis,
Who wastes away your life thus? For whom,
  good man, such desire?"

  Begin the pastoral song, dear Muses, begin
the song.

The cowherds came, the shepherds came, and
  the goatherds,
And all of them asked why he suffered.
    Priapos came too

And said, "Daphnis, poor wretch, why are you
    pining? The girl
On hastening feet goes to every spring, every
    grove searching.

   *Begin the pastoral song, dear Muses, begin
the song.*

"A laggard in love are you and helpless indeed!
Cowherd you were called, but now you
    resemble a goatherd—
A goatherd, forsooth, who when he sees
    nannies mounted
Pines, teary-eyed, because he was not born a
    he-goat.

   *Begin the pastoral song, dear Muses,
begin the song.*

"And you, whenever you chance to see
    maidens laughing,
Pine, teary-eyed, because you cannot dance
    among them."
To all of this the herdsman made no reply,
But endured his bitter love, bore it out to the
    end preordained.

   *Begin the song, Muses, begin again the pas-
toral song.*

Cypris came too, sweetly laughing but
    laughing falsely,
Holding back the wrath deep in her heart,
And said, "Daphnis, you vowed to wrestle
    Love to a fall,
But have not you yourself been thrown by
    mischievous Eros?"

   *Begin the song, Muses, begin again the pas-
toral song.*

And to her then Daphnis replied,
    "Hardhearted Cypris,
Cypris the terrible, Cypris hateful to mortals,
Are you so sure that all my suns have already
    set?
Even in Hades will Daphnis be bitter trouble
    for Eros.

   *Begin the song, Muses, begin again the pas-
toral song.*

"Is it not said that with Cypris a cowherd
    once—? Creep off to Ida,
Crawl to Anchises; oak trees grow there and
    galingale,
And bees murmurously hum in swarms round
    the hives.

   *Begin the song, Muses, begin again the pas-
toral song.*

"Adonis, too, in the prime of his youth
    pastures his flocks,
And shoots hares and hunts every wild beast
    in the chase.

   *Begin the song, Muses, begin again the pas-
toral song.*

"Or go take up your stand again before
    Diomedes
And say, 'I overcame Daphnis the herdsman,
    but come on and fight
    me.'

Begin the song, Muses, begin again the pastoral song.

"O wolves, O jackals, O bears lurking in dens
     in the mountains,
Farewell. No more will I, Daphnis the
     herdsman, pass through your forest,
No more through your oak woods or groves.
     Farewell, Arethusa,
And rivers whose rushing water pours down
     from Thybris.

Begin the song, Muses, begin again the pastoral song.

"I, that Daphnis who here pastured his cattle,
The Daphnis who here watered his bulls and
     his calves.

Begin the song, Muses, begin again the pastoral song.

"O Pan, Pan, whether you range the lofty
     peaks of Lycaios
Or busy yourself on high Mainalos, come to
     the island
Of Sicily, leaving Helike's mound and the tall
     tomb
Of the son of Lycaon's daughter, at which
     even the blessed ones marvel.

Cease the song, Muses, cease now the pastoral song.

"Come, lord, and take this sweet-breathing
     syrinx smelling of honey

And beeswax, and bound securely around the
     fine lip,
For now, defeated by Eros, I go down to
     Hades.

Cease the song, Muses, cease now the pastoral song.

"Now you brambles, you thornbushes, may
     you bear violets,
May the lovely narcissus on junipers bloom,
Let all be confounded, and pears grow on pine
     trees,
Since Daphnis is dying; may deer drag down
     dogs,
And may owls from the mountains to
     nightingales sing."

Cease the song, Muses, cease now the pastoral song.

So much he said, then was silent. Willingly
     would Aphrodite
Have spared him but the whole thread of his
     fate had run out,
And Daphnis went to the stream. The swirling
     waters washed over
The man dear to the Muses, the man not
     abhorred by the nymphs.

Cease the song, Muses, cease now the pastoral song.

Now give me the goat and the cup, so I may
     milk her
And pour out to the Muses an offering.
     Muses, farewell,

Many times farewell, but I will sing you a
sweeter song later.

Goatherd: May your lovely mouth be filled
with honey, Thyrsis,
Filled too with honeycomb, and may you
munch the sweet figs
Of Aigilia, for you sing to surpass the cicada.

See, here is the cup; notice, my friend, its fine
fragrance.
It would make you think it was dipped in the
spring of the Hours.
Come here, Cissaitha!—you milk her. Don't
frisk around,
You other nannies! Calm down lest the billy
goat mount you.

APOLLONIUS OF RHODES (295–247 B.C.)
The Voyage of Argo (Argonautica)

The last great epic poet of Greek antiquity, Apollonius was born in Alexandria, Egypt, where he served as scholar at the great Library. When his mentor and rival Callimachus led the attack on his *Argonautica,* Apollonius retired to the island of Rhodes, where he was honored for the epic Alexandria rejected. When, after years of teaching rhetoric on Rhodes, he returned to Alexandria, he was given a hero's welcome, and his epic was applauded by the literary circle. Ptolemy I appointed him curator of the Library. Callimachus now reported to him.

- Apollonius' ongoing literary feud with Callimachus was based on the latter's belief that epic poetry was obsolete. Apollonius, it is said, wrote the *Argonautica* to prove his fellow scholar wrong. Callimachus, whose preference was for elaborate and artificial Hellenistic style and for short, highly polished poems, was not convinced by Apollonius' effort.
- Though it is filled with allusions to the Homeric cycle, Apollonius' poem achieves its own distinction in the history of epic poetry. Though it is largely flawed—incomplete, rambling, faltering in action—even its flaws are noteworthy. Most remarkably its main character, Jason, unlike Homer's wrathful Achilles or many-minded Odysseus, is the first example in western literature of the reluctant hero. When he is called to undertake the epic quest, for the legendary golden fleece, Jason is filled with trepidation and anxiety, reminding us of no one as much as Shakespeare's Hamlet.

- Apollonius may be tedious at times, but he is a master of empathy, showing a talent for getting inside his characters to discover and to express their precise feelings in a moment of crisis. The *Argonautica* is, as this excerpt shows, romantic, delicately portraying nuances of mood and emotions as only an inward-turning, self-reflexive culture is capable of appreciating. Apollonius' portrait of Medea, so much more convincing psychologically than his Jason, betrays a fascination with female psychology in a manner that both recalls the women of Sappho and Euripides and anticipates the Dido of Virgil's *Aeneid*. The epic, which tells the story of Jason's quest for the golden fleece and his encounter with a king's daughter, Medea, who helps him succeed in obtaining it, was divided, by Apollonius himself, into four books, and was written in an enhanced Homeric language that mirrors the sentimental culture of third-century B.C. Alexandria. The "golden fleece" is a metaphor for the sheep-stock and gold brought back to Greece from the Black Sea. Jason's quest, accordingly, is a mythic parallel to the story of the Trojan War.

BOOK THREE, *JASON AND MEDEA*

Come, Erato, come lovely Muse, stand by me and take up the tale. How did Medea's passion help Jason to bring back the fleece to Iolcus? You that share Aphrodite's powers must surely know; you that fill virgin hearts with love's inquietude and bear a name that speaks of love's delights.

We left the young lords lying there concealed among the rushes. But ambushed though they were, Here and Athene saw them and at once withdrew from Zeus and the rest of the immortal gods into a private room to talk the matter over.

Here began by sounding Athene. "Daughter of Zeus," she said, "let me hear you first. What are we to do? Will you think of some ruse that might enable them to carry off Aeetes' golden fleece to Hellas? Or should they speak him fair in the hope of winning his consent? I know the man is thoroughly intractable. But all the same, no method of approach should be neglected."

"Here," said Athene quickly, "you have put to me the very questions I have been turning over in my mind. But I must admit that, though I have racked my brains, I have failed so far to think of any scheme that might commend itself to the noble lords."

For a while the two goddesses sat staring at the floor, each lost in her own perplexities. Here was the first to break the silence; an idea had struck her. "Listen," she said. "We must have a word with Aphrodite. Let us go together and ask her to persuade her boy, if that is possible, to loose an arrow at Aeetes' daughter, Medea of the many spells, and make her fall in love with Jason. I am sure that with her help he will succeed in bearing off the fleece to Hellas.". . .

Meanwhile Eros, passing through the clear

"Vase with tomb of Patroklos." Copyright Archivi Alinari, 1989. By permission of Art Resource.

air, had arrived unseen and bent on mischief, like a gadfly setting out to plague the grazing heifers, the fly that cowherds call the breese. In the porch, under the lintel of the door, he quickly strung his bow and from his quiver took a new arrow, fraught with pain. Still unobserved, he ran across the threshold glancing around him sharply. Then he crouched low at Jason's feet, fitted the notch to the middle of the string, and drawing the bow as far as his hands would stretch, shot at Medea. And her heart stood still.

With a happy laugh Eros sped out of the high-roofed hall on his way back, leaving his shaft deep in the girl's breast, hot as fire. Time and again she darted a bright glance at Jason.

All else was forgotten. Her heart, brimful of this new agony, throbbed within her and overflowed with the sweetness of the pain.

A working woman, rising before dawn to spin and needing light in her cottage room, piles brushwood on a smoldering log, and the whole heap kindled by the little brand goes up in a mighty blaze. Such was the fire of Love, stealthy but all-consuming, that swept through Medea's heart. In the turmoil of her soul, her soft cheeks turned from rose to white and white to rose.

By now the servants had prepared a banquet for the newcomers, who gladly sat down to it after refreshing themselves in warm baths. When they had enjoyed the food and drink, Aeetes put some questions to his grandsons:

"Sons of my daughter and of Phrixus, the most deserving guest I have ever entertained, how is it that you are back in Aea? Did some misadventure cut your journey short? You refused to listen when I told you what a long way you had to go. But I knew; for I myself was whirled along it in the chariot of my father Helios, when he took my sister Circe to the Western Land and we reached the coast of Tyrrhenia, where she still lives, far, far indeed from Colchis. But enough of that. Tell me plainly what befell you, who your companions are, and where you disembarked."

To answer these questions, Argus stepped out in front of his brothers, being the eldest of the four. His heart misgave him for Jason and his mission; but he did his best to conciliate the king. "My lord," he said, "that ship of ours soon fell to pieces in a storm. We hung on to one of her planks and were cast ashore on the Island of Ares in the pitch-dark night. But Providence looked after us: There was not a sign of the War-god's birds, who used to haunt the desert isle. They were driven off by these men, who had landed on the previous day and been detained there by the will of Zeus in pity for ourselves—or was it only chance? In any case, they gave us plenty of food and clothing directly they heard the illustrious name of Phrixus, and your own, my lord, since it was your city they were bound for. As to their purpose, I will be frank with you. A certain king, wishing to banish and dispossess this man because he is the most powerful of the Aeolids, has sent him here on a desperate venture, maintaining that the House of Aeolus will not escape the inexorable wrath of Zeus, the heavy burden of their guilt, and vengeance for the sufferings of Phrixus, till the fleece returns to Hellas. The ship that brought him was built by Pallas Athene on altogether different lines from the Colchian craft, the rottenest of which, as luck would have it, fell to us. For *she* was smashed to pieces by the wind and waves, whereas the bolts of *Argo* hold her together in any gale that blows, and she runs as sweetly when the crew are tugging at the oars as she does before the wind. This ship he manned with the pick of all Achaea, and in her he has come to your city, touching at many ports and crossing formidable seas, in the hope that you will let him have the fleece. But it must be as you wish. He has not come here to force your hand. On the contrary, he is willing to repay you amply for the gift by reducing for you your bitter enemies, the Sauromatae, of whom I told him. But now you may wish to know the names and lineage of your visitors. Let me tell you. Here is the man to whom the others rallied

from all parts of Hellas, Jason son of Aeson, Cretheus' son. He must be a kinsman of our own on the father's side, if he is a grandson of Cretheus, for Cretheus and Athamas were both sons of Aeolus, and our father Phrixus was a son of Athamas. Next, and in case you have heard that we have a son of Helios with us, behold the man, Augeias. And this is Telamon, son of the illustrious Aeacus, a son of Zeus himself. Much the same is true of all the rest of Jason's followers. They are all sons or grandsons of immortal gods."

The king was filled with rage as he listened to Argus. And now, in a towering passion, he gave vent to his displeasure, the brunt of which fell on the sons of Chalciope, whom he held responsible for the presence of the rest. His eyes blazed with fury as he burst into speech:

"You scoundrels! Get out of my sight at once. Get out of my country, you and your knavish tricks, before you meet a Phrixus and a fleece you will not relish. It was no fleece that brought you and your confederates from Hellas, but a plot to seize my scepter and my royal power. If you had not eaten at my table first, I would tear your tongues out and chop off your hands, both of them, and send you back with nothing but your feet, to teach you to think twice before starting on another expedition. As for all that about the blessed gods, it is nothing but a pack of lies." . . .

Jason's obsequious address had no effect. The king was plunged in sullen cogitation, wondering whether to leap up and kill them on the spot or to put their powers to the proof. He ended by deciding for a test and said to Jason:

"Sir, there is no need for me to hear you out. If you are really children of the gods or have other grounds for approaching me as equals in the course of your piratical adventure, I will let you have the golden fleece—that is, if you still want it when I have put you to the proof. For I am not like your overlord in Hellas, as you describe him; I am not inclined to be ungenerous to men of rank.

"I propose to test your courage and abilities by setting you a task which, though formidable, is not beyond the strength of my two hands. Grazing on the plain of Ares, I have a pair of bronze-footed and fire-breathing bulls. These I yoke and drive over the hard fallow of the plain, quickly plowing a four-acre field up to the ridge at either end. Then I sow the furrows, not with corn, but with the teeth of a monstrous serpent, which presently come up in the form of armed men, whom I cut down and kill with my spear as they rise up against me on all sides. It is morning when I yoke my team and by evening I have done my harvesting. That is what I do. If you, sir, can do as well, you may carry off the fleece to your king's palace on the very same day. If not, you shall not have it—do not deceive yourself. It would be wrong for a brave man to truckle to a coward." . . .

They left the palace with heavy hearts. Meanwhile Chalciope, to save herself from Aeetes' wrath, had hastily withdrawn to her own room together with her sons. Medea too retired, a prey to all the inquietude that Love awakens. The whole scene was still before her eyes—how Jason looked, the clothes he wore, the things he said, the way he sat, and how he walked to the door. It seemed to her, as she reviewed these images, that there was nobody like Jason. His voice and the honey-sweet words that he had used still rang in her ears. But she

feared for him. She was afraid that the bulls or Aeetes with his own hands might kill him; and she mourned him as one already dead. The pity of it overwhelmed her; a round tear ran down her cheek; and weeping quietly she voiced her woes:

"What is the meaning of this grief? Hero or villain (and why should I care which?) the man is going to his death. Well, let him go! And yet I wish he had been spared. Yes, sovereign Lady Hecate, this is my prayer. Let him live to reach his home. But if he must be conquered by the bulls, may he first learn that I for one do not rejoice in his cruel fate." . . .

Medea was the first to speak. "Sister," she said, "you left me speechless when you talked of curses and avenging Furies. How can I set your mind at rest? I only wish we could be sure of rescuing your sons. However, I will do as you ask and take the solemn oath of the Colchians, swearing by mighty Heaven and by Earth below, the Mother of the Gods, that provided your demands are not impossible I will help you as you wish, with all the power that in me lies."

When Medea had taken the oath, Chalciope said: "Well now, for the sake of my sons, could you not devise some stratagem, some cunning ruse that the stranger could rely on in his trial? He needs you just as much as they do. In fact he has sent Argus here to urge me to enlist your help. I left him in the palace when I came to you just now."

At this, Medea's heart leaped up. Her lovely cheeks were crimsoned and her eyes grew dim with tears of joy. "Chalciope," she cried, "I will do anything to please you and your sons, anything to make you happy. May I never see the light of dawn again and may you see me in the world no more, if I put anything before your safety and the lives of your sons, who are my brothers, my dear kinsmen, with whom I was brought up. And you, am I not as much your daughter as your sister, you that took me to your breast as you did them, when I was a baby, as I often heard my mother say? But go now and tell no one of my promise, so that my parents may not know how I propose to keep it. And at dawn I will go to Hecate's temple with magic medicine for the bulls."

Thus assured, Chalciope withdrew from her sister's room and brought her sons the news of her success. But Medea, left alone, fell a prey once more to shame and horror at the way in which she planned to help a man in defiance of her father's wishes. . . .

With that she went and fetched the box in which she kept her many drugs, healing or deadly, and putting it on her knees she wept. Tears ran unchecked in torrents down her cheeks and drenched her lap as she bemoaned her own sad destiny. She was determined now to take a poison from the box and swallow it; and in a moment she was fumbling with the fastening of the lid in her unhappy eagerness to reach the fatal drug. But suddenly she was overcome by the hateful thought of death, and for a long time she stayed her hand in silent horror. Visions of life and all its fascinating cares rose up before her. She thought of the pleasures that the living can enjoy. She thought of her happy playmates, as a young girl will. And now, setting its true value on all this, it seemed to her a sweeter thing to see the sun than it had ever been before. So, prompted by Here, she changed her mind and put the box away. Irresolute no longer, she waited eagerly for Dawn to come, so that she could meet the stranger face to face and give him the magic drug as she had promised. Time after time she opened her door to catch the first glimmer of day; and she rejoiced when early Dawn lit up the sky and people in the town began to stir.

Argus left the palace and returned to the ship. But he told his brothers to wait before following him, in order to find out what Medea meant to do. She herself, as soon she saw the first light of day, gathered up the golden locks that were floating around her shoulders in disorder, washed the stains from her cheeks and cleansed her skin with an ointment clear as nectar; then she put on a beautiful robe equipped with cunning brooches, and threw a silvery veil over her lovely head. And as she moved about, there in her own home, she walked oblivious of all evils imminent, and worse to come.

She had twelve maids, young as herself and all unmarried, who slept in the antechamber of her own sweet-scented room. She called them now and told them to yoke the mules to her carriage at once, as she wished to drive to the splendid Temple of Hecate; and while they were getting the carriage ready she took a magic ointment from her box. This salve was named after Prometheus. A man had only to smear it on his body, after propitiating the only-begotten Maiden with a midnight offering, to become invulnerable by sword or fire and for that day to surpass himself in strength and daring. It first appeared in a plant that sprang from the blood-like ichor of Prometheus in his torment, which the flesh-eating eagle had dropped on the spurs of Caucasus. The flowers, which grew on twin stalks a cubit high, were of the color of Corycian saffron, while the root looked like flesh that has just been cut, and the juice like the dark sap of a mountain oak. To make the ointment, Medea, clothed in black, in the gloom of night, had drawn off this juice in a Caspian shell after bathing in seven perennial streams and calling seven times on Brimo, nurse of youth, Brimo, night-wanderer of the underworld, Queen of the dead. The dark earth shook and rumbled underneath the Titan root when it was cut, and Prometheus himself groaned in the anguish of his soul.

Such was the salve that Medea chose. Placing it in the fragrant girdle that she wore beneath her bosom, she left the house and got into her carriage, with two maids on either side. They gave her the reins, and taking the well-made whip in her right hand, she drove off through the town, while the rest of the maids tucked up their skirts above their white knees and ran behind along the broad highway, holding on to the wicker body of the carriage. . . .

But it was not so very long before the sight of Jason rewarded her impatient watch. Like Sirius rising from Ocean, brilliant and beautiful but full of menace for the flocks, he sprang into view, splendid to look at but fraught with trouble for the lovesick girl. Her heart stood still, a mist descended on her eyes, and a warm flush spread across her cheeks. She could neither move toward him nor retreat; her feet were rooted to the ground. And now her servants disappeared, and the pair of them stood face to face without a word or sound, like oaks or tall pines that stand in the mountains side by side in silence when the air is still, but when the wind has stirred them chatter without end. So these two, stirred by the breath of Love, were soon to pour out all their tale.

Jason, seeing how distraught Medea was, tried to put her at her ease. "Lady," he said, "I am alone. Why are you so fearful of me? I am not a profligate as some men are, and never was, even in my own country. So you have no need to be on your guard, but may ask or tell me anything you wish. We have come together here as friends, in a consecrated spot which must not be profaned. Speak to me, question me, without reserve; and since you have already promised your sister to give me the talisman I need so much, pray do not put me off with pleasant speeches. I plead to you by Hecate herself, by your parents, and by Zeus. His hand protects all suppliants and strangers, and I that now address my prayers to you in my necessity am both a stranger and a suppliant. Without you and your sister I shall never succeed in my appalling task. Grant me your aid and in the days to come I will reward you duly, repaying you as best I can from the distant land where I shall sing your praises. My comrades too when they are back in Hellas will immortalize your name. So will their wives and mothers, whom I think of now as sitting by the sea, shedding tears in their anxiety for us—bitter tears, which you could wipe away. Remember Ariadne, young Ariadne, daughter of Minos and Pasiphae, who was a daughter of the Sun. She did not scruple to befriend Theseus and save him in his hour of trial; and then, when Minos had relented, she left her home and sailed away with him. She was the darling of the gods and she has her emblem in the sky: All night a ring of stars called Ariadne's Crown rolls on its way among the heavenly constellations. You too will be thanked by the gods if you save me and all my noble friends. Indeed your loveliness assures me of a kind and tender heart within."

Jason's homage melted Medea. Turning her eyes aside she smiled divinely and then, uplifted by his praise, she looked him in the face. How to begin, she did not know; she longed so much to tell him everything at once. But with the charm, she did not hesitate; she drew it out from her sweet-scented girdle and he took it in his hands with joy. She reveled in his need of her and would have poured out all her soul to him as well, so captivating was the light of love that streamed from Jason's golden head and held her gleaming eyes. Her heart was warmed and melted like the dew on roses under the morning sun.

At one moment both of them were staring at the ground in deep embarrassment; at the next they were smiling and glancing at each other with the lovelight in their eyes. But at last Medea forced herself to speak to him. "Hear me now," she said. "These are my plans for you. When you have met my father and he has given you the deadly teeth from the serpent's jaws, wait for the moment of midnight and after bathing in an ever-running river, go out alone in somber clothes and dig a round pit in the earth. There, kill a ewe and after heaping up a pyre over the pit, sacrifice it whole, with a libation of honey from the hive and prayers to Hecate, Perses' only daughter. Then, when you have invoked the goddess duly, withdraw from

the pyre. And do not be tempted to look behind you as you go, either by footfalls or the baying of hounds, or you may ruin everything and never reach your friends alive.

"In the morning, melt this charm, strip, and using it like oil, anoint your body. It will endow you with tremendous strength and boundless confidence. You will feel yourself a match, not for mere men, but for the gods themselves. Sprinkle your spear and shield and sword with it as well; and neither the spear-points of the earthborn men nor the consuming flames that the savage bulls spew out will find you vulnerable. But you will not be immune for long—only for the day. Nevertheless, do not at any moment flinch from the encounter.

"And here is something else that will stand you in good stead. You have yoked the mighty bulls; you have plowed the stubborn fallow (with those great hands and all that strength it will not take you long); you have sown the serpent's teeth in the dark earth; and now the giants are springing up along the furrows. Watch till you see a number of them rise from the soil, then, before they see you, throw a great boulder in among them; and they will fall on it like famished dogs and kill one another. That is your moment; plunge into the fray yourself.

"And so the task is done and you can carry off the fleece to Hellas—a long, long way from Aea, I believe. Go none the less, go where you will; go where the fancy takes you when you part from us. . . ."

ARCHIMEDES (287–212 B.C.)
The Sand-reckoner

The greatest Greek mathematician, geometrician, and physicist was son of the astronomer Phidias, and born in Syracuse, where he was adviser and military engineer to his relative Hieron II and Hieron's son Gelon. We know little of Archimedes' life except that he was educated at Alexandria with the philosopher Conon of Samos and the followers of Euclid; calculated the value of π; and built a planetarium. His earliest known work, *On Mechanical Theorems,* was dedicated to Eratosthenes the philologist. Legend has it that Archimedes was so preoccupied among his catapults and burning-glasses at the siege of Syracuse by the Romans under Marcus Claudius Marcellus that he was unaware the city had fallen, and was killed by a Roman soldier who mistook his gleaming instruments for gold. In 75 B.C. Cicero discovered his tomb, which displayed one of his most famous formulas.

- Archimedes' writings, in the Doric dialect, are voluminous. They include theoretical works on elementary mechanics, hydrostatics, spheres and cylinders, measurement of the circle, spirals, parabolas, the equilibrium and centers of gravity of planes, astronomy, statics, and levers. Roman historian Livy called him "a singular observer of the heavens and the stars." He apparently had little use for his many inventions, and *On Sphere-making* was his only writing of a purely practical bent. Plutarch, in his *Marcellus,* states that Archimedes

> possessed so high a spirit, so profound a soul, and such treasures of scientific knowledge that, though these inventions had obtained for him the renown of more than human sagacity, he yet would not deign to leave behind him any written work on such subjects but, regarding as ignoble and sordid the business of mechanics, and every sort of art which is directed to use and profit, he placed his whole ambition in those speculations in whose beauty and subtlety there is no admixture of the common needs of life.

His fabled "Eureka!" (meaning "I found it!"), the phrase used when he accidentally discovered that a body displaces its own weight in water, gave a name to the "revelation" stage of the creative process. All his works were published in the form of correspondence with other mathematicians of his time.

- Archimedes is credited with saying, "Give me somewhere to stand and I will move the earth." He constructed long, movable poles for dropping heavy weights on enemy ships; and a "triple pulley" that allowed him to move an enormous ship using only his left hand. Lucian reports that Archimedes' multiple hexagonal mirrors, focusing the noonday sun, set fire to Marcellus' ships. He figured out the ratio of the radius to the circumference, that of the cylinder to the sphere, and the law that a body displaces its own volume of water; and invented the pulley, the endless screw used to launch ships, and the water screw used to pump water from flooded fields. His breadth and freedom of vision and unconventional boldness of thought make him one of the most remarkable scientific thinkers of all time.

- Like many of the great Nobel Prize–winning mathematicians and physicists of the twentieth century, Archimedes had a great sense of humor. In *The Sand-reckoner,* addressed to Hieron's son Gelon, Archimedes argues that hypothetically the number of grains of sand in the universe is countable, and gives it as 10^{63}; invents a place-value system of notation that remedied shortcomings of the Greek notational system; and also describes his method for using an instrument to determine the sun's diameter and radius.

- His description of the heliocentric system of Aristarchus of Samos, which theorized that the earth moves around the fixed sun on the orbit of a circle, is the best account we have of the Greek heliocentric theory. While others of his time satisfied themselves with revisions and compilations of preceding thought, Archimedes was satisfied only with something new that added to the sum of human knowledge.

"There are some, king Gelon, who think that the number of the sand is infinite in multitude; and I mean by the sand not only that which exists about Syracuse and the rest of Sicily but also that which is found in every region whether inhabited or uninhabited. Again there are some who, without regarding it as infinite, yet think that no number has been named which is great enough to exceed its multitude. And it is clear that they who hold this view, if they imagined a mass made up of sand in other respects as large as the mass of the earth, including in it all the seas and the hollows of the earth filled up to a height equal to that of the highest of the mountains, would be many times further still from recognizing that any number could be expressed which exceeded the multitude of the sand so taken. But I will try to show you by means of geometrical proofs, which you will be able to follow, that, of the numbers named by me and given in the work which I sent to Zeuxippus, some exceed not only the number of the mass of sand equal in magnitude to the earth filled up in the way described, but also that of a mass equal in magnitude to the universe. Now you are aware that 'universe' is the name given by most astronomers to the sphere whose center is the

"Clepsydra (water clock) in the agora, at Athens."
Alinari Scala. By permission of Art Resource.

center of the earth and whose radius is equal to the straight line between the center of the sun and the center of the earth. This is the common account... as you have heard from astronomers. But Aristarchus of Samos brought out a book consisting of some hypotheses, in which the premises lead to the result that the universe is many times greater than that now so called. His hypotheses are that the fixed stars and the sun remain unmoved, that the earth revolves about the sun in the circumference of a circle, the sun lying in the middle of the orbit, and that the sphere of the fixed stars, situated about the same center as the sun, is so great that the circle in which he supposes the earth to revolve bears such a proportion to the

distance of the fixed stars as the center of the sphere bears to its surface. Now it is easy to see that this is impossible; for, since the center of the sphere has no magnitude, we cannot conceive it to bear any ratio whatever to the surface of the sphere. We must however take Aristarchus to mean this: Since we conceive the earth to be, as it were, the center of the universe, the ratio which the earth bears to what we describe as the 'universe' is the same as the ratio which the sphere containing the circle in which he supposes the earth to revolve bears to the sphere of the fixed stars. For he adapts the proofs of his results to a hypothesis of this kind, and in particular he appears to suppose the magnitude of the sphere in which he represents the earth as moving to be equal to what we call the 'universe.'

I say then that, even if a sphere were made up of the sand, as great as Aristarchus supposes the sphere of the fixed stars to be, I shall still prove that, of the numbers named in the *Principles*, some exceed in multitude the number of the sand which is equal in magnitude to the sphere referred to, provided that the following assumptions be made.

1. *The perimeter of the earth is about* 3,000,000 *stadia and not greater.*

It is true that some have tried, as you are of course aware, to prove that the said perimeter is about 300,000 stadia. But I go further and, putting the magnitude of the earth at ten times the size that my predecessors thought it, I suppose its perimeter to be about 3,000,000 stadia and not greater.

2. *The diameter of the earth is greater than the diameter of the moon, and the diameter of the sun is greater than the diameter of the earth.*

In this assumption I follow most of the earlier astronomers.

3. *The diameter of the sun is about* 30 *times the diameter of the moon and not greater.*

It is true that, of the earlier astronomers, Eudoxus declared it to be about 9 times as great, and Pheidias my father 12 times, while Aristarchus tried to prove that the diameter of the sun is greater than 18 times but less than 20 times the diameter of the moon. But I go even further than Aristarchus, in order that the truth of my proposition may be established beyond dispute, and I suppose the diameter of the sun to be about 30 times that of the moon and not greater.

4. *The diameter of the sun is greater than the side of the chiliagon inscribed in the greatest circle in the (sphere of the) universe.*

I make this assumption because Aristarchus discovered that the sun appeared to be about $\frac{1}{720}$th part of the circle of the zodiac, and I myself tried, by a method which I will now describe, to find experimentally (ὀργανικῶς) the angle subtended by the sun and having its vertex at the eye (τὰν γωνίαν, εἰς ἂν ὁ ἅλιος ἐναρμόζει τὰν κορυφὰν ἔχουσαν ποτὶ τᾷ ὄψει)."

The result of the experiment was to show that the angle subtended by the diameter of the sun was less than $\frac{1}{164}$th part, and greater than $\frac{1}{200}$th part, of a right angle.

To prove that (on this assumption) the diameter of the sun is greater than the side of a chiliagon, or figure with 1,000 *equal sides, inscribed in a great circle of the "universe."*

Suppose the plane of the paper to be the plane passing through the center of the sun, the center of the earth and the eye, at the time when the sun has just risen above the horizon. Let the plane cut the earth in the circle *EHL* and the sun in the circle *FKG*, the centers of the earth and sun being *C, O* respectively, and *E* being the position of the eye.

Further, let the plane cut the sphere of the "universe" (i.e. the sphere whose center is *C* and radius *CO*) in the great circle *AOB.* . . .

Application to the number of the sand.

By Assumption 5

(diam. of poppy-seed) $\not> \frac{1}{40}$ (finger-breadth); and, since spheres are to one another in the triplicate ratio of their diameters, it follows that

$$
\left.
\begin{array}{l}
\text{(sphere of diam.} \\
\text{1 finger-breadth)} \not> 64{,}000 \text{ poppy-seeds} \\
\qquad\qquad \not> 64{,}000 \times 10{,}000 \\
\qquad\qquad \not> 640{,}000{,}000 \\
\qquad\qquad \not> 6 \text{ units of } second \\
\qquad\qquad\quad order +40{,}000{,}000 \\
\qquad\qquad\quad \text{units of first order} \\
(a\ fortiori) < 10 \text{ units of} \\
\qquad\qquad second\ order \text{ of} \\
\qquad\qquad \text{numbers.}
\end{array}
\right\} \text{grains of sand}
$$

We now gradually increase the diameter of the supposed sphere, multiplying it by 100 each time. Thus, remembering that the sphere is thereby multiplied by 100^3 or 1,000,000, the number of grains of sand which would be contained in a sphere with each successive diameter may be arrived at as follows.

Diameter of sphere.	Corresponding number of grains of sand.
(1) 100 finger-breadths	<1,000,000 × 10 units of *second order* <(7th term of series)

× (10th term of
series)
<16th term of series
[i.e. 10^{15}]
<[10^7 or] 10,000,000
units of the *second*
order.

(2) 10,000 finger-
breadths

<1,000,000 × (last
number)
<(7th term of series)
× (16th term)
<22nd term of series
[i.e. 10^{21}]
<[10^5 or] 100,000
units of *third order.*

(3) 1 stadium
(<10,000 finger-
breadths)

(4) 100 stadia

<100,000 units of
third order.

<1,000,000 × (last
number)
<(7th term of series)
× (22nd term)
<28th term of series
[10^{27}]
<[10^3 or] 1,000 units
of *fourth order.*

(5) 10,000 stadia

<1,000,000 × (last
number)
<(7th term of series)
× (28th term)
<34th term of series
[10^{33}]
<10 units of *fifth*
order.

(6) 1,000,000 stadia

<(7th term of series)
x (34th term)
<40th term
[10^{39}]

<[10^7 or] 10,000,000
units of *fifth*
order.

(7) 100,000,000 stadia

<(7th term of series)
× (40th term)
<46th term
[10^{45}]
<[10^5 or] 100,000
units of *sixth order.*

(8) 10,000,000,000
stadia

<(7th term of series)
× (46th term)
<52nd term of series
[10^{51}]
<[10^3 or] 1,000 units
of *seventh order.*

But, by the proposition above,
(diameter of "universe")<10,000,000,000
stadia.

Hence *the number of grains of sand which coud be contained in a sphere of the size of our "universe" is less than* 1,000 *units of the seventh order of numbers* [or 10^{51}].

From this we can prove further that *a sphere of the size attributed by Aristarchus to the sphere of the fixed stars would contain a number of grains of sand less than* 10,000,000 *units of the eight order of numbers* [or $10^{56+7}=10^{63}$].

For, by the hypothesis,
(earth) : ("universe") = ("universe") :
(sphere of fixed stars).
And
(diameter of "universe")<
10,000 (diam. of earth);
whence
(diam. of sphere of fixed stars)<
10,000 (diam. of "universe").
Therefore
(sphere of fixed stars)<$(10,000)^3$.("universe").

It follows that the number of grains of sand which would be contained in a sphere equal to the sphere of the fixed stars

$< (10,000)^3 \times 1,000$ units of *seventh order*

$<$ (13th term of series) $\times$ (52nd term of series)

$<$64th term of series   [i.e. 10^{63}]

$< [10^7$ or] 10,000,000 units of *eighth order* of numbers.

Conclusion

"I conceive that these things, king Gelon, will appear incredible to the great majority of people who have not studied mathematics, but that to those who are conversant therewith and have given thought to the question of the distances and sizes of the earth, the sun and the moon, and the whole universe the proof will carry conviction. And it was for this reason that I thought the subject would not be inappropriate for your consideration.

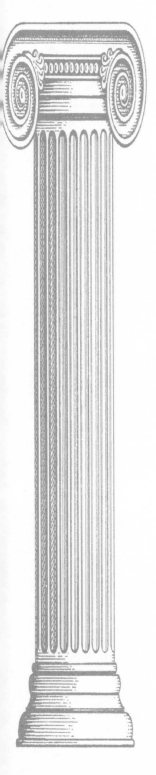

PART THREE

Postclassical

Polybius (ca. 203–122 b.c.)

The General History of the Wars of the Romans

The son of a leading statesman and general of the Achaean League, Lycortas of Megalopolis (in Arcadia), Polybius was raised around politics and the military. For his opposition to all things Roman and service as a commander in the League's cavalry, he was transported, after the Roman victory at Perseus, with 1,000 other Achaean nobles as hostages to Rome. In the household of statesman Aemilius Paulus, Polybius became the tutor of Scipio Aemilianus, his lifelong friend and patron. His position in Scipio's circle gave him freedom of speech and freedom of travel, and he accompanied Scipio to Africa and witnessed his triumph over Carthage.

- Polybius used his skills to write a *Treatise on Tactics* and the *Life of Philopoemen* (his father's associate). After his *History of the Numantine War,* Polybius went on to write forty volumes about the Roman rise to power throughout the Mediterranean, from 220 b.c. through the destruction of Carthage and the conquest of Corinth in 145 b.c..

- Although its style is sometimes redundant, often coarse, and generally undistinguished, the intelligence and clarity of Polybius' observations based on his widespread experience makes *The General History,* of which five of its forty books survive, an invaluable sourcebook and study in military cause and effect—fulfilling his aim to write a history that would benefit future leaders and prepare the general reader to face military disaster. In addition to his own observations, Polybius used eyewitnesses and documentary sources to detail the history of the years 220–168 during which Rome moved from the wars against Hannibal, the Macedonians, the Syrians, and the Spanish—to total domination of the Mediterranean. He saw Rome's rise as the inevitable outcome of its excellence in both strategy and tactics. According to Polybius, "truth is to history what eyesight is to the living creature."

In the year, then, which was the nineteenth after the engagement near Aegospotamus, and the sixteenth before the battle of Leuctra; the year when the Lacedaemonians confirmed the treaty which Antalcidas had made with the Persians; and the elder Dionysius, having some time before defeated the Greeks of Italy near the river Helleporus, laid siege to Rhegium: In this same year the Gauls took Rome by storm, and remained masters of all the city, the capital only excepted. But the Romans, having yielded to such conditions as the conquerors thought proper to impose, were once more restored, beyond all hope, to the possession of their country. From this time, being as it were again renewed in strength and vigor, they made war upon the states that were contiguous to their own; and having, partly by their bravery, and partly by the aid of fortune, reduced all the Latins to their yoke, they next attacked the Tyrrhenians; after these the Gauls, and then the Samnites, whose country lay contiguous to the territory of the Latins, and bounded it towards the north and east. Some time afterwards, the people of Tarentum, having treated an embassy from Rome with great indignity and insult, and being apprehensive that the Romans were preparing vengeance for the affront, invited Pyrrhus into Italy. This happened the year before the Gauls invaded Greece, and received that signal overthrow at Delphi, which drove them, with the remains of their army, into Asia. But the Romans, who had already reduced the Tyrrhenians and the Samnites to their yoke, and had returned with conquest from many engagements also with the Gauls, were now beginning to enlarge their views, and

resolved to seize upon the rest of Italy, as if the whole country had belonged to them by a natural and proper right. Their former combats had completely trained and exercised them in the use of arms. They attacked the Tarentines with vigor, and persisted in the war with so much firmness, that they at last drove Pyrrhus out of Italy, and then turned their arms against the cities which had been confederated with that prince against them: and having, by a course of wonderful success, forced all the inhabitants of Italy, except the Gauls, to receive their laws, they were now at leisure to march against a body of Roman soldiers, who had possessed themselves of Rhegium.

The two cities, Messana and Rhegium, both situated upon the same straits, had both experienced the same misfortune. Not long before this time, a body of Campanian mercenaries, who had served in the armies of Agothocles, invited by the beauty and rich condition of Messana, watched their time for gaining possession of the place by treachery. They soon found means to be received as friends within the city, where they killed one part of the inhabitants, and drove the rest without the walls. And, having taken to themselves the wives and children of those unhappy men, as they fell into the hands of everyone at the very time of the disorder, they made afterward a division of their lands and riches; and thus, with little difficulty, gained a full possession of a very splendid city, and fertile territory. This success soon excited others to follow the example. The inhabitants of Rhegium, alarmed by the entrance of Pyrrhus into Italy, and being also under no small apprehensions of some danger from the

Carthaginians, who were at that time the sole masters of the sea, implored the assistance of the Romans, who sent them a garrison of four thousand men, under the command of Decius Companus. These, for some time, remained firm in their duty, and guarded the liberties of the city; but, being at last seduced by the commodious situation of the place, and by the wealth and flourishing condition of the citizens, they resolved to imitate the example which the Campanians had so lately set before them; and, being assisted also by them in the execution of their design, they drove out or killed the inhabitants, and obtained entire possession of the city.

This horrid act of treachery raised great indignation in the Romans, but the wars in which they were then involved restrained their vengeance. As soon as these were ended, they marched and laid siege to Rhegium. The place soon fell into their hands; but the greatest part of the garrison was destroyed in the assault: for they fought like men who well foresaw the consequences of their crime. About three hundred only that were taken alive were sent to Rome; and, being conducted by the praetors into the forum, were first scourged, and then beheaded. By this just severity the Romans hoped that they should again recover their character of good faith among their allies: They restored the city also, with all the lands, to the former inhabitants.

The Mamertines of Messana, for this was the name which the Campanian mercenaries had assumed, as long as they were supported by the Romans who had possessed themselves of Rhegium not only remained in quiet and secure enjoyment of their own city and proper territory, but made frequent incursions also into the adjacent countries; creating no small terror and disturbance, both to the Carthaginians and the Syracusans, and exacting contributions from many parts of Sicily.

But no sooner had the siege of Rhegium deprived them of the assistance of those allies than they were themselves so vigorously pressed by the Syracusan forces that they were constrained to abandon all the open country, and to keep close behind their walls. The occasion was as follows:

A little before this time, when some dissension had been raised between the citizens of Syracuse and the army, the troops, while they lay encamped in the neighborhood of Mergana, elected two magistrates out of their own body, Artemidorus, and Hiero, who was afterward king. Hiero was then extremely young, but he seemed to have been singularly formed by nature to sustain the regal dignity. As soon as he was invested with this new authority he found some means, by the assistance of his friends, to gain admission into the city: and, having there drawn all the chiefs of the opposite faction into his power, he showed, in his whole deportment, such proofs of clemency and true greatness that the people, though they were by no means satisfied with the liberty which the army had assumed, with one voice declared him praetor. But it was easy to discern, from his first behavior in this office, that he had some more exalted post in view: for, having remarked that as often as the forces, with the magistrates at their head, were obliged to take the field, some new commotions and disorders were always raised among the citizens; and observing also that a certain Syracusan, named Leptines, was the first in favor with the people, and far superior in his influence and credit to all the rest of the inhabitants, he resolved to contract a close alliance with him, and to marry his daughter, being persuaded that, by the help of his authority, he would be able to keep all things quiet and secure at home, whenever himself should be engaged in the command of the army abroad. Some time afterward, observing that the mercenaries, who had been long employed in the Syracusan armies, had become untractable and mutinous, he ordered all the forces to take the field, and to march against the barbarians of Messana. Being encamped within sight of the enemy near Centuripe, he drew up his army in order of battle, along the side of the Cyamosorus. But, having stationed the Syracusan troops, both infantry and cavalry, at a distance from the rest, as if he had intended an attack from a different quarter, he opposed the mercenaries only to the enemy, by whom they were entirely defeated and destroyed, but as soon as the slaughter had begun, himself, with all the forces of the city, returned back again to Syracuse. Having thus happily accomplished his design, and cleared the army of its seditious members, and having filled their place with a sufficient number of new mercenaries levied by himself, from that time he continued to discharge the duties of his post, without any tumult or disorder. And when the Mamertines, elated by their past success, had spread themselves over all the country, without any fear or caution, he led against them the forces of the city, which were now completely armed and disciplined, and came to an engagement with them upon the banks of the river Longanus, in the plain of Mylae; and,

having obtained an entire victory, in which their generals also were taken prisoners, he gave an effectual check to the insolence of those barbarians, and, on his return to Syracuse, was saluted king by the army.

The Mamertines, who had been before deprived of the assistance which they had been accustomed to receive from Rhegium, were now so broken and disheartened by this last defeat that they considered their affairs as almost desperate. In this state some among them had recourse to the Carthaginians, and delivered the citadel into their hands; while the rest sent ambassadors to Rome, to make an offer of their city, and to implore the protection of the Romans for a people sprung, as they pretended, from one common stock with themselves. The Romans were, for some time, under great perplexity and doubt. To comply with this demand appeared to be in a high degree improper and absurd. They had lately punished, with the last severity, a body of their own citizens, for having betrayed the public faith in seizing Rhegium; and, if they now should support the Mamertines, who not only had surprised Messana by the very same kind of perfidy, but had assisted in taking Rhegium also, it would be difficult to find any fair apology for such conduct. On the other hand, as the Carthaginians, besides the dominions which they possessed in Afric, were masters also of many parts of Spain, and of all the islands in the Sardinian and Tyrrhenian seas, it was greatly to be feared that, if Sicily should now fall into their hands, they would soon become too formidable neighbors, since they would then lie close to every part of Italy, and encircle them on every side. It was easy also to discern that they must very soon be able to reduce the island, if the Mamertines were not now supported: for, if once they were permitted to possess Messana, they would find it no hard task to conquer Syracuse, since they were already masters of all the other parts of Sicily. The Romans saw the danger, and considered it as a matter of the last necessity to obviate and prevent these consequences, and not suffer Messana to fall into the hands of those who might, from thence, be able to lay, as it were, a bridge for passing into Italy. Yet, after many long debates upon the subject, the senate even at last refused to pass any decree concerning it; because the manifest absurdity on one side seemed still to draw with equal weight against the advantage on the other. But the people, who had been much exhausted by their former wars, and wished for some occasion to repair their shattered fortunes, being incited partly by the great utility which would confessedly accrue to the republic from the war, and animated also by the show of those advantages with which the praetors, in their speeches, flattered every private man, resolved that the desired assistance should be sent, and made a law for that purpose, commanding Appius Claudius, one of the consuls, to pass over to Messana. The Mamertines, partly by the means of fraud, and partly by open force, drove out the Carthaginian commander from the citadel, and delivered the city to the Romans.

The Carthaginians, when they had first crucified their general for his cowardice and ill conduct in relinquishing the citadel, made haste to draw together all their forces to retake Messana: and, having stationed their fleet near Pelorus, and posted their land army on the side of Senae, they began to press the siege with

vigor. At the same time Hiero, imagining that this occasion might be favorable for driving the Mamertines entirely out of Sicily, entered into treaty with the Carthaginians; and, beginning his march from Syracuse, he came and invested the city on the other side, having encamped near the mountain called Chaleidicus.

The consul Appius passed the Straits in an adventurous manner by night, and was received into Messana; but finding that the place was closely pressed on every side, and reflecting with himself that the affair was full of hazard, and that little reputation was likely to be gained from a war in which the enemy were so much superior both by land and sea, he sent offers of accommodation to both camps, desiring only that the Mamertines might remain unmolested. But, as this proposal was rejected, he was forced to venture on a battle, and resolved to make his first attack upon the Syracusans. He accordingly drew his forces out of the city, and offered battle to Hiero, who readily accepted it. The fight was long and obstinate; but at last the Romans obtained the victory, and drove back the enemy to their camp; and, having spoiled the dead, they returned again to Messana.

But Hiero, beginning now to apprehend some worse event, as soon as night came on, returned back again with his army, in all haste, to Syracuse. When Appius, on the following day, was informed of this retreat, he immediately conceived new hopes, and resolved to attack the Carthaginians without delay. He gave orders, therefore, to the troops, to take their repast betimes; and, marching out of the city at break of day, he charged the enemy, killed great numbers of them, and forced the rest to fly to the neighboring cities. After these signal victories, the siege being raised, and no forces appearing in the field, the Romans wasted, at their leisure, the country of the Syracusans and their allies, and at last advanced to Syracuse itself, in order to besiege it.

Such were the causes, and such the time and manner, of the first expedition of the Romans out of Italy, and here I fix the beginning of my work; having first run through the times which just before preceded it, in order more clearly to explain the genuine and real grounds of this transaction: for, that the reader might be able to obtain a just and perfect knowledge of the causes of the present power and greatness of the Romans, it was proper previously to acquaint him both with the time and manner in which this people first recovered into better hopes, after they had beheld their country lost; and by what means afterward, when they had vanquished all the neighboring states, they found occasion to extend their conquests beyond the bounds of Italy. Nor let it be thought in any manner strange, if, in the subsequent parts of this history, when I was speaking of the states that are chiefly celebrated in the world, I should look back to ages that are more remote: for this I shall do, merely for the sake of beginning from such facts as will best enable me to discern from what causes, and in what time and manner, they severally grew to that condition in which they are seen to flourish in the

present times. But I now must hasten to the task that is before me; mentioning first, in few words, the events which are designed to be the subject of these preliminary books.

The first then is the war in Sicily between the Carthaginians and the Romans; and, after it, the African war. Next will follow a recital of the actions of Amilcar and of Asdrubal in Spain, with the invasion also of Illyria by the Romans, who then, for the first time, sent their armies into those parts of Europe. After these transactions come the battles which the Romans were forced to sustain in Italy against the Gauls: about which time it was that the war of Cleomenes broke out in Greece; with an account of which I shall conclude the second book, and close the introduction to my history.

To enter into a minute detail of all the parts and circumstances of these wars, would be labor quite unnecessary to myself, and attended with no great advantage to the reader: for it is not my design to write the history, but rather to give a general and summary account of these transactions, such as may serve for an introduction to my history; and by making a short recital of the chief events in the order in which they were transacted, and carrying on the narration, in one regular and connected series, to the time from whence my own work commences, to prepare the reader for the accounts that follow, and make the whole both easy and intelligible. . . .

NICANDER (FL. CA. 170 B.C.)
Theriaca

The son of Damaeus, as he tells us, Nicander wrote didactic poems on scientific subjects dealing primarily with animals and plants. He was born in Clarus, near Colophon in Asia Minor. Nicander may have inherited a priestly position at the shrine of Apollo from his father.

Nicander's style, an awkward, overblown imitation of Homeric hexameters, is generally atrocious. But his compilation of accepted wisdom on folk cures provides unique insight into the herbal industry of both his own time and of earlier antiquity. His most important works were the *Theriaca* ("On Poisonous Animals"), the *Alexipharmaca* ("Antidotes"), and the *Georgica,* which dealt with agriculture and beekeeping and influenced Virgil. His writings on mythology were one of the Roman Ovid's primary sources for his *Metamorphoses.*

Readily, dear Hermesianax, most honored of my many kinsmen, and in due order will I expound the forms of savage creatures and their deadly injuries which smite one unforeseen, and the countering remedy for the harm. And the toiling plowman, the herdsman, and the woodcutter, whenever in forest or at the plow one of them fastens its deadly fang upon him, shall respect you for your learning in such means for averting sickness.

Now I would have you know, men say that noxious SPIDERS, together with the grievous reptiles, and vipers and the earth's countless burdens, are of the Titans' blood—if indeed he spoke the truth, Ascraean Hesiod on the steeps of secluded Melisseeis by the waters of Permessus. And it was the Titan's daughter who sent forth the blighting Scorpion with sharpened sting, when she compassed an evil end for Boeotian Orion, and attacked him after he had laid violent hands upon the immaculate raiment of the goddess. Thereupon the Scorpion, which had lurked unobserved beneath a small stone, struck him in the ankle of his strong foot. But Orion's wondrous sign is set conspicuous, fixed there amid the constellations, as of one hunting, dazzling to behold.

You for your part will easily chase and dispel all creeping things from farmstead and cottage, or from steep bank, or from couch of natural herbage, in the hour when, to shun parching summer's fiery breath, beneath the sky you make your bed on straw at nightfall in the fields and sleep, or else beside some unwooded hill or on the edge of a glen, where poisonous creatures feed in multitudes upon the forest, or be-

"Minoan serpent goddess." Photographie Giraudon. National Museum of Heraklion, Crete. By permission of Art Resource.

side the leveled perimeter of the threshing-floor, and where the grass at its first burgeoning brings bloom to the shady water-meadows, at the time when the snake sloughs the withered scales of age, moving feebly forward, when in spring he leaves his den, and his sight is dim; but a meal of the fennel's sappy shoots makes him swift and bright of eye.

You may expel the hot and harmful doom that snakes bring, if you char the tined horn of a STAG, or else set fire to dry LIGNITE, which not even the violence of a fierce flame consumes. Cast also upon the fire the foliage of the MALE FERN with its cloven fronds, or take the heated root of the FRANKINCENSE-TREE mixed with an equal measure of GARDEN-CRESS; and mingle the fresh, pungent horn of a ROE, putting an equal weight of it in the balance. Burn also a portion no less heavy of the strong-smelling BLACK CUMIN, or else of SULPHUR, or again of BITUMEN. Or you may ignite in the fire the THRACIAN STONE, which when soaked in water glows, yet quenches its brightness at the least smell of a drop of oil. Herdsmen gather it for themselves from the river of Thrace which they call *Pontus*, where the Thracian shepherds who eat ram's flesh follow after their leisurely flocks. Again, the heavy-scented JUICE OF ALL-HEAL stimulated over a fire, and the STINGING NETTLE, and CEDAR cut with saws and ground to dust by their many-toothed jaws produce in burning a smoky and repellent stench. With these means you may clear hollow clefts and couches in the woods, and may sink upon the ground and take your fill of sleep.

But if these things involve trouble, and night brings bedtime near, and you are longing for rest when your work is done, then gather to yourself among the eddies of some rushing river the water-loving, leafy MINT, for it grows in plenty by streams and is fed with the moisture about their edges, as it delights in gleaming rivers. Or you should cut and strew beneath you the flowering WILLOW, or the strong-smelling HULWORT, which has a most offensive odor; so too have VIPER'S BUGLOSS and the leaves of MARJORAM, aye, or of WORMWOOD, which grows wild upon the hills in some chalky glen, or of TUFTED THYME from pasture-lands: Tenacious of life it draws sustenance from a damp soil, deep-rooted, ever furnished with hairy leaves. And you should mark the pale spikes of the low-growing FLEABANE and of the AGNUS CASTUS, and the pungent STINKING BEAN-TREFOIL. Likewise cut the rough twigs of the POMEGRANATE, or else young and flourishing shoots of the ASPHODEL, and DEADLY NIGHTSHADE, and the horrid HYPER-ICUM which injures the herdsman in the springtime when his cows are poisoned by eating the stalks; and further stems of the heavy-scented SULPHURWORT whose very odor scares snakes and chases them away should they approach you. So place some of these by you wherever you make a casual couch in the fields; others where snakes lurk, and a double quantity at their holes.

Now make in an earthen vessel or an oil-flask a paste of JUNIPER BERRIES and anoint your supple limbs—or of the heavy-scented SULPHURWORT; or else pound thoroughly in oil the dried leaves of FLEABANE from the hills, and likewise the healing SALVIA, adding the root of SILPHIUM, which the grater's teeth should grind small—many a time too have noxious creatures fled in terror from the scent of a man's spittle. But if you rub a CATERPILLAR from the garden in a little vinegar, the dewy caterpillar with a green back, or if you anoint your limbs all about with the teeming fruit of the MARSH MALLOW, then you will pass the night unscathed. Also cast in and rub down in the stony heart of a mortar two leafy sprays of WORMWOOD mixed with GARDEN-CRESS—an

obol's weight is suitable—and with a pestle pound therein to smoothness a handful of fresh berries from the BAY; then mold into rounds and put to dry in a shady, windswept spot; when dry break them in pieces in an oil-flask, and you can anoint your limbs with it at once.

If however you can cast SNAKES coupled at a crossroads, alive and just mating, into a pot, and the following medicaments besides, you have a preventive against deadly disasters. Throw in thirty drachms' weight of the marrow of a freshly killed STAG and one-third of a *chous* of ROSE-OIL—essence which perfumers style "prime" and "medium" and "well-ground"— and pour on an equal measure of raw, gleaming OIL and one-quarter of WAX. These you must quickly heat in a round, bellying pot until the fleshy portions are softened and come in pieces about the spine. Next take a shaped, well-made pestle and pound up these many ingredients in a mixture with the snakes; but cast aside the vertebrae, for in them a venom no less deadly is engendered. Then anoint all your limbs, be it for a journey or for a sleep or when you gird yourself after work at the threshing-floor in summer's drought and with pronged forks winnow the high pile of grain.

BION (FL. 100 B.C.)
Lament for Adonis

Though he spent most of his life in Sicily, the poet Bion was born in Smyrna, in Asia Minor. He wrote in the pastoral tradition, though his work was more erotic and lyric than that of Theocritos or Moschus.

- Six of his *Idylls* survive. The style of his *Bucolica* is praised for its grace, playfulness, and sensual, if sometimes excessive, emotionalism.
- The translation of his most famous poem which follows is by Elizabeth Barrett Browning. The subject matter of the "Lament" may reflect the power of his homeland's cult of Adonis.

I mourn for Adonis—Adonis is dead,
  Fair Adonis is dead and the Loves are
    lamenting.
Sleep, Cypris, no more on thy purple-strewed
  bed:
  Arise, wretch stoled in black; beat thy breast
    unrelenting,
And shriek to the worlds, "Fair Adonis is
    dead!"

I mourn for Adonis—the Loves are
    lamenting.
  He lies on the hills in his beauty and death;
The white tusk of a boar has transpierced his
    white thigh.
  Cytherea grows mad at his thin gasping
    breath,
While the black blood drips down on the pale
    ivory,

And his eyeballs lie quenched with the
    weight of his brows;
The rose fades from his lips, and upon them
  just parted
The kiss dies the goddess consents not to lose,
Though the kiss of the Dead cannot make her
    glad hearted:
He knows not who kisses him dead in the
    dews.

I mourn for Adonis—the Loves are lamenting.
  Deep, deep in the thigh is Adonis's wound,
But a deeper is Cypris's bosom presenting.
  The youth lieth dead while his dogs howl
    around,
And the nymphs weep aloud from the mists of
    the hills,
And the poor Aphrodite, with tresses
    unbound,

All disheveled, unsandaled, shrieks mournful
and shrill
Through the dusk of the groves. The thorns
tearing his feet,
Gather up the red flower of her blood which is
holy,
Each footstep she takes; and the valleys
repeat
The sharp cry she utters and draw it out
slowly.
She calls on her spouse, her Assyrian, on
him
Her own youth, while the dark blood spreads
over his body,
The chest taking hue from the gash in the
limb,
And the bosom, once ivory, turning to ruddy.

Ah, ah, Cytherea! the Loves are lamenting.
She lost her fair spouse and so lost her fair
smile:
When he lived she was fair, by the whole
world's consenting,
Whose fairness is dead with him: woe worth
the while!
All the mountains above and the oaklands
below
Murmur, ah, ah, Adonis! the streams
overflow
Aphrodite's deep wail; river-fountains in pity
Weep soft in the hills, and the flowers as
they blow
Redden outward with sorrow, while all hear
her go
With the song of her sadness through
mountain and city.

Ah, ah, Cytherea! Adonis is dead.
Fair Adonis is dead—Echo answers, Adonis!

Who weeps not for Cypris, when bowing her
head
She stares at the wound where it gapes and
astonies?
—When, ah, ah!—she saw how the blood ran
away
And empurpled the thigh, and, with wild
hands flung out,
Said with sobs: "Stay, Adonis! unhappy one,
stay,
Let me feel thee once more, let me ring
thee about
With the clasp of my arms, and press kiss into
kiss!
Wait a little, Adonis, and kiss me again,
For the last time, beloved—and but so much
of this
That the kiss may learn life from the
warmth of the strain!
—Till thy breath shall exude from the soul to
my mouth,
To my heart, and, the love-charm I once
more receiving,
May drink thy love in it and keep of a truth
That one kiss in the place of Adonis the
living.

Thou fliest me, mournful one, fliest me far,
My Adonis, and seekest the Acheron
portal—
To Hell's cruel King goest down with a scar,
While I weep and live on like a wretched
immortal,
And follow no step! O Persephone, take him,
My husband—thou'rt better and brighter
than I,
So all beauty flows down to thee: I cannot
make him

Look up at my grief; there's despair in my
   cry.
Since I wail for Adonis who died to me—died
   to me—
   Then, I fear *thee!*—Art thou dead, my
    Adored?
Passion ends like a dream in the sleep that's
   denied to me.
   Cypris is widowed, the Loves seek their lord
All the house through in vain. Charm of
   cestus has ceased
   With thy clasp! O too bold in the hunt past
   preventing,
Ay, mad, thou so fair, to have strife with a
   beast!"
   Thus the goddess wailed on—and the Loves
   are lamenting.

Ah, ah, Cytherea! Adonis is dead.
She wept tear after tear with the blood which
   was shed,
And both turned into flowers for earth's
   garden-close,
Her tear to the wind-flower; his blood to the
   rose.

I mourn for Adonis—Adonis is dead.
   Weep no more in the woods, Cytherea, thy
   lover!
So, well: make a place for his corse in thy bed,
   With the purples thou sleepest in, under
   and over.
He's fair though a corse—a fair corse, like a
   sleeper.
   Lay him soft in the silks he had pleasure to
   fold
When, beside thee at night, holy dreams deep
   and deeper

Enclosed his young life on the couch made
   of gold.
Love him still, poor Adonis; cast on him
   together
   The crowns and the flowers: since he died
   from the place,
Why, let all die with him; let blossoms go
   wither,
   Rain myrtles and olive-buds down on his
   face.
Rain the myrrh down, let all that is best fall
   a-pining,
   Since the myrrh of his life from thy keeping
   is swept.
Pale he lay, thine Adonis, in purples reclining;
   The Loves raised their voices around him
   and wept.
They have shorn their bright curls off to cast
   on Adonis;
One treads on his bow—on his arrows,
   another—
One breaks up a well-feathered quiver, and
   one is
   Bent low at a sandal, untying the strings,
   And one carries the vases of gold from the
   springs,
While one washes the wound—and behind
   them a brother
Fans down on the body sweet air with his
   wings.
Cytherea herself now the Loves are lamenting.
   Each torch at the door Hymenaeus blew
   out;
And, the marriage-wreath dropping its leaves
   as repenting,
   No more "Hymen, Hymen," is chanted
   about,
But the *ai ai* instead—"ai alas!" is begun

For Adonis, and then follows "Ai
 Hymenaeus!"
The Graces are weeping for Cinyris' son,
 Sobbing low each to each, "His fair eyes
 cannot see us!"
Their wail strikes more shrill than the sadder
 Dione's.
The Fates mourn aloud for Adonis, Adonis,

Deep chanting; he hears not a word that they
 say:
 He *would* hear, but Persephone has him in
 keeping.
—Cease moan, Cytherea! leave pomps for today,
And weep new when a new year refits thee for
 weeping.

STRABO (CA. 63 B.C.–CA. A.D. 24)
The Geography

*S*trabo (Greek: *Strabon)* was born in Amaseia, in Pontus, of an aristocratic family. He traveled widely in Greece, Italy, Egypt, Ethiopia, and Asia Minor and was educated in philosophy, history, and geography. In 44 B.C. he continued his studies in Augustan Rome under the finest Greek teachers, including the Aristotelians Tyrannion and Xenarchus. He studied Stoicism under Octavius' tutor Athenodorus.

- His *Geographica,* in seventeen volumes, and completed around A.D. 20, is the most important surviving work of ancient geography. Its description of regions, cities, and their inhabitants is based on both personal observation and on previous authoritative works such as that by Eratosthenes. The *Geography* remained a standard text in Europe well into the Renaissance. Strabo viewed the world as spherical, with inhabited lands forming a central island surrounded by ocean.
- Strabo's simple, straightforward, and compelling style is aimed at educating influential public figures and rulers by providing them with information they should have to better understand the world. He was an unabashed admirer of Roman culture and of the Roman Empire.

CHAPTER II

1. Sicily is triangular in form, and on this account was at first called Trinaeria, but afterward the name was softened and it was changed into Thrinacia. Three low headlands bound the figure: Pelorias is the name of that toward Caenys and the Columna Rheginorum which forms the strait; Pachynus is that which stretches towards the east, and is washed by the Sea of Sicily, looking toward the Peloponnesus and in the direction of the passage to Crete; the third is Lilybaeum, and is next to Africa, looking toward that region and the setting of the sun in winter. Of the sides which these three headlands bound, two are somewhat concave, while the third is slightly convex; it runs from Lilybaeum to Pelorias, and is the longest, being, as Posidonius has said, 1,700 stadia, adding further twenty. Of the others, that extending to Pachynus from Lilybaeum is the longer, while the shortest faces the Strait and Italy, extending from Pelorias to Pachynus, being about 1,120 or 1,130 stadia. Posidonius shows that the circumference is 4,400 stadia, but in the Chorography the distances are declared to exceed the above numbers, being severally reckoned in miles. Thus from Cape Pelorias to Mylae, 25 miles; from Mylae to Tyndaris, 25; thence to Agathyrnum, 30; from Agathyrnum to Alaesa, 30; from Alaesa to Cephaloedium, 30; these are but insignificant places; from Cephaloedium to the river Himera, which runs through the midst of Sicily, 18; from thence to Panormus, 35; [thence] to the Emporium of the Aegestani, 32; leaving to Lilybaeum a distance of 38; thence having doubled the Cape and coasting

the adjacent side to Heracleum, 75; and to the Emporium of the Agrigentini, 20; and to Camarina, another 20; then to Pachynus, 50; thence again along the third side to Syracuse, 36; from Syracuse to Catana, 60; then to Tauromenium, 33; thence to Messana, 30. Thus on foot from Pachynus to Pelorias we have 168 [miles], and from Messana to [Cape] Lilybaeum, on the Via Valeria, we have 235 [miles]. Some have estimated the circuit in a more simple way, as Ephorus, who says that the compass of the island by sea takes five days and nights. Posidonius attempts to determine the situation of the island by climata, and places Pelorias to the north, Lilybaeum to the south, and Pachynus to the east. We however consider that of necessity all climata are set out in the manner of a parallelogram, but that districts portrayed as triangles, and especially such triangles as are scalene, and whereof no one side lies parallel to a side of the parallelogram, cannot in any way be assimilated to climata on account of their obliquity. However, we must allow that in treating of Sicily, Pelorias, which lies to the south of Italy, may well be called the most northern of the three angles, so that we say that the line which joins it to Pachynus faces the east but looks towards the north. Now this line [of coast] will make the side next the Strait [of Messina], and it must have a slight inclination toward the winter sunrise; for thus the shore slightly changes its direction as you travel from Catana toward Syracuse and Pachynus. Now the transit from Pachynus to the mouth of the Alpheus is 4,000 stadia. But when Artemidorus says that from Pachynus to Taenarum it is 4,600, and from the Alpheus to the Pamisus is 1,130 stadia, he appears to me to lie open to the objection of having given distances which do not accord with the 4,000 stadia from Pachynus to the Alpheus. The line run from Pachynus to Lilybaeum (which is much to the west of Pelorias) is considerably diverged from the south toward the west, having at the same time an aspect looking toward the east and toward the south. On one side it is washed by the sea of Sicily, and on the other by the Libyan Sea, extending from Carthage to the Syrtes. The shortest run is 1,500 stadia from Lilybaeum to the coast of Africa about Carthage; and, according to report, a certain very sharp-sighted person, placed on a watchtower, announced to the Carthaginians besieged in Lilybaeum the number of the ships which were leaving Carthage. And from Lilybaeum to Pelorias the side must necessarily incline toward the east, and look in a direction towards the west and north, having Italy to the north, and the Tyrrhenian Sea with the islands of Aeolus to the west.

2. The cities situated on the side which forms the Strait are, first Messana, then Tauromenium, Catana, and Syracuse; between Catana and Syracuse were the ruined cities Naxos and Megara, situated where the rivers descending from Aetna fall into the sea, and afford good accommodation for shipping. Here is also the promontory of Xiphonia. They say that Ephorus founded these first cities of the Greeks in Sicily in the tenth generation from the Trojan war. For those who preceded him were so terrified by the piratical customs of the Tyrrheni, and the ferocity of the savages of the neighborhood, that they did not even venture

to resort thither for the purposes of commerce. Theocles the Athenian, however, having been driven to Sicily by storms, observed both the weakness of the inhabitants and the excellence of the soil. On his return home, he was unable to persuade the Athenians to make any attempt, but he collected a numerous band of Chalcidians in Euboea, with some Ionians and Dorians, whereof the most part were Megarenses, and sailed. The Chaleidians founded Naxos, and the Dorians Megara, which was at first called Hybla. These cities no longer exist, but the name of Hybla survives on account of the Hyblaean honey.

3. The first of the cities which at present remain on the aforesaid side is Messana, built at the head of the gulf of Pelorias, which is curved very considerably towards the east, and forms a bay. The passage across to Rhegium is 60 stadia, but the distance to the Columna Rheginorum is much less. It was from a colony of the Messenians of the Peloponnesus that it was named Messana, having been originally called Zanele, on account of the great inequality of the coast (for anything irregular was termed ζάγκλιογ). It was originally founded by the people of Naxos near Catana. Afterwards the Mamertini, a tribe of Campanians, took possession of it. The Romans, in the war in Sicily against the Carthaginians, used it as an arsenal. Still more recently, Sextus Pompeius assembled his fleet in it, to contend against Augustus Caesar; and when he relinquished the island, he took ship from thence. Charybdis is pointed out at a short distance from the city in the Strait, an immense gulf, into which the back currents of the Strait frequently impel ships, carrying them down with a whirl and the vio-

lence of the eddy. When they are swallowed down and shattered, the wrecks are cast by the stream on the shore of Tauromenia, which they call, on account of this kind of accumulation, the dunghill. So greatly have the Mamertini prevailed over the Messenians, that they have by degrees wrested the city from them. The inhabitants generally are rather called Mamertini than Messenians. The district abounds in wine, which we do not call Messenian, but Mamertinian: it vies with the best produced in Italy. The city is well peopled, but Catana is more populous, which has been colonized by the Romans. Tauromenium is less populous than either. Catana was founded by people from Naxos, and Tauromenium by the Zanclaeans of Hybla, but Catana was deprived of its original inhabitants when Hiero, the tyrant of Syracuse, introduced others, and called it by the name of Aetna instead of Catana. It is of this that Pindar says he was the founder, when he sings,

> "Thou understandest what I say, O father, that bearest the same name with the splendid holy sacrifices, thou founder of Aetna."

But on the death of Hiero, the Catanaeans returned and expelled the new inhabitants, and demolished the mausoleum of the tyrant. The Aetnaeans, compelled to retire, established themselves on a hilly district of Aetna, called Innesa, and called the place Aetna. It is distant from Catana about 80 stadia. They still acknowledged Hiero as their founder.

Aetna lies the highest of any part of Catana, and participates the most in the inconve-niences occasioned by the mouths of the volcano, for the streams of lava flowing down in Catanaea pass through it first. It was here that Amphinomus and Anapias set the example of filial piety so greatly celebrated, for they, seizing their parents, carried them on their shoulders to a place of safety from the impending ruin; for whenever, as Posidonius relates, there is an eruption of the mountain the fields of the Catanaeans are buried to a great depth. However, after the burning ashes have occasioned a temporary damage, they fertilize the country for future seasons, and render the soil good for the vine and very strong for other produce, the neighboring districts not being equally adapted to the produce of wine. They say that the roots which the districts covered with these ashes produce are so good for fattening sheep that they are sometimes suffocated, wherefore they bleed them in the ear every four or five days, in the same way as we have related a like practice at Erythia. When the stream of lava cools it covers the surface of the earth with stone to a considerable depth, so that those who wish to uncover the original surface are obliged to hew away the stone as in a quarry. For the stone is liquefied in the craters and then thrown up. That which is cast forth from the top is like a black moist clay and flows down the hillsides, then congealing it becomes millstone, preserving the same color it had while fluid. The ashes of the stones which are burnt are like what would be produced by wood, and, as rue thrives on wood ashes, so there is probably some quality in the ashes of Aetna which is appropriate to the vine.

4. Archias, sailing from Corinth, founded Syracuse about the same period that Naxos and

Megara were built. They say that Myscellus and Archias having repaired to Delphi at the same time to consult the oracle, the god demanded whether they would choose wealth or health, when Archias preferred wealth and Myscellus health, upon which the oracle assigned Syracuse to the former to found, and Crotona to the latter. And certainly, in like manner as it fell out that the Crotoniatae should inhabit a state so notable for salubrity as we have described, so such great riches have accrued to the Syracusans that their name has been embodied in the proverb applied to those who have too great wealth, viz. that they have not yet attained to a tithe of the riches of the Syracusans. While Archias was on his voyage to Sicily, he left Chersicrates, a chief of the race of the Heracleidae, with a part of the expedition to settle the island now called Corcyra, but anciently called Scheria, and he, having expelled the Liburni who possessed it, established his colony in the island. Archias, pursuing his route, met with certain Dorians at Zephyrium, come from Sicily, and who had quitted the company of those who had founded Megara; these he took with him, and in conjunction with them founded Syracuse. The city flourished on account of the fertility of the country and the convenience of the harbors, the citizens became great rulers; while under tyrants themselves, they domineered over the other states [of Sicily], and when freed from despotism, they set at liberty such as had been enslaved by the barbarians: Of these barbarians some were the aboriginal inhabitants of the island, while others had come across from the continent. The Greeks suffered none of the barbarians to approach the shore, although they were not able to expel them entirely from the interior, for the Siculi, Sicani, Morgetes, and some others, still inhabit the island to the present day, among whom also were the Iberians, who, as Ephorus relates, were the first of the barbarians that are considered to have been settlers in Sicily. It seems probable that Morgantium was founded by the Morgetes. Formerly it was a city, but now it is not. When the Carthaginians endeavored to gain possession of the island they continually harassed both the Greeks and the barbarians, but the Syracusans withstood them; at a later period the Romans expelled the Carthaginians and took Syracuse after a long siege. And [Sextus] Pompeius, having destroyed Syracuse in the same way as he had done by the other cities, Augustus Caesar in our own times sent thither a colony, and to a great extent restored it to its former importance, for anciently it consisted of five towns enclosed by a wall of 180 stadia, but there being no great need that it should fill this extensive circle, he thought it expedient to fortify in a better way the thickly inhabited portion lying next the island of Ortygia, the circumference of which by itself equals that of an important city. Ortygia is connected to the mainland by a bridge, and [boasts of] the fountain Arethusa, which springs in such abundance as to form a river at once, and flows into the sea. They say that it is the river Alpheus which rises in the Peloponnesus, and that it flows through the land beneath the sea to the place where the Arethusa rises and flows into the sea. Some such proofs as these are given in support of the fact. A certain chalice having fallen into the river at Olympia was cast up by the springs of Arethusa; the fountain too is troubled by the sacrifices of oxen at Olympia. And Pindar, following such reports, thus sings,

> "Ortygia, revered place of reappearing of
>   the Alpheus,
> The offset of renowned Syracuse."

Timaeus the historian advances these accounts in like manner with Pindar. Undoubtedly if before reaching the sea the Alpheus were to fall into some chasm, there would be a probability that it continued its course from thence to Sicily, preserving its potable water unmixed with the sea; but since the mouth of the river manifestly falls into the sea, and there does not appear any opening in the bed of the sea there, which would be capable of imbibing the waters of the river (although even if there were they could not remain perfectly fresh, still it might be possible to retain much of the character of fresh water, if they were presently to be swallowed down into a passage running below the earth which forms the bed of the sea), it is altogether impossible; and this the water of Arethusa clearly proves, being perfectly fit for beverage; but that the flow of the river should remain compact through so long a course, not mixing with the sea until it should fall into the fancied channel, is entirely visionary; for we can scarcely credit it of the Rhone, the body of the waters of which remains compact during its passage through the lake, and preserves a visible course, but in that instance both the distance is short and the lake is not agitated by waves like the sea, but in this case of the Alpheus, where there are great storms and the waters are tossed with violence, the supposition is by no means worthy of attention. The fable

of the chalice being carried over is likewise a mere fabrication, for it is not calculated for transfer, nor is it by any means probable it should be washed away so far, nor yet by such difficult passages. Many rivers, however, and in many parts of the world, flow beneath the earth, but none for so great a distance. Still, although there may be no impossibility in this circumstance, yet the above-mentioned accounts are altogether impossible, and almost as absurd as the fable related of the Inachus: this river, as Sophocles feigns,

> "Flowing from the heights of Pindus and
> Lacmus, passes from the country of the
> Perrhoebi to that of the Amphilochi and
> the Acarnanians, and mingles its waters
> with the Achelous":

and further on [he says],

> "Thence to Argos, cutting through the
> waves, it comes to the territory of Lyr-
> ceius."

Those who would have the river Inopus to be a branch of the Nile flowing to Delos exaggerate this kind of marvel to the utmost. Zoïlus the rhetorician, in his Eulogium of the people of Tenedos, says that the river Alpheus flows from Tenedos: yet this is the man who blames Homer for fabulous writing. Ibycus also says that the Asopus, a river of Sicyon, flows from Phrygia. Hecataeus is more rational, who says that the Inachus of the Amphilochi, which flows from Mount Laemus, from whence also the Aeas descends, was distinct from the river of like name in Argolis, and was so named after

Amphilochus, from whom likewise the city of Argos was denominated Amphilochian. He says further that this river falls into the Achelous, and that the Aeas flows to Apollonia toward the west. On each side of the island there is an extensive harbor; the extent of the larger one is 80 stadia. [Augustus] Caesar has not only restored this city, but Catana, and likewise Centoripa, which had contributed much toward the overthrow of [Sextus] Pompey. Centoripa is situated above Catana and confines with the mountains of Aetna and the river Giaretta, which flows into Catanaea.

5. One of the remaining sides, that stretching from Pachynus to Lilybaeum, is entirely deserted; still it preserves a few traces of the ancient inhabitants, one of whose cities was Camarina. Acragas, which was a colony of the Geloi, together with its port and Lilybaeum, still exist. In fact, these regions, lying opposite to Carthage, have been wasted by the great and protracted wars which have been waged. The remaining and greatest side, although it is by no means densely peopled, is well occupied, for Alaesa, Tyndaris, the emporium of the Aegestani and Cephaloedium, are respectable towns. Panormus has received a Roman colony: they say that Aegesta was founded by the Greeks who passed over, as we have related when speaking of Italy, with Philoctetes to the Crotoniatis, and were by him sent to Sicily with Aegestus the Trojan.

MELEAGER (FL. 100–60 B.C.)

Lyrics

From Gadara, in Syria, philosopher-poet Meleager was, as he tells us in his lyric "On Himself," the son of Eucrates. Although his satires do not survive, over one hundred of Meleager's love poems, epigrams written in the florid style called "Asian," survive in the Greek Anthology; Meleager's *Stephanos ("Garland")*, which was the first such collection, formed that anthology's nucleus. Meleager, who spoke Greek, Syrian, and Phoenician, also lived in Tyre and Cos. His work, characterized by precise metrics and excessively ornate metaphor and philosophical conceit, is largely adapted from poems by earlier epigrammists. Nonetheless the sensitive emotions and erotic fervor his poetry expresses appear to be genuine.

SHINING FOE

O morning star, bright enemy of love,
how slowly you turn around the world
while Demos lies warm with another
    under her cloak.
But when my slender love lay on my chest,
how swiftly you came to stand above us,
drenching us with light that seemed to laugh
    at our loss.

MYISKOS

By Love, I swear it!
Tender are the boys whom Tyros nurtures.
Yet Myiskos is the sun,
and when he illuminates the world
bright stars fade under his light.

AFTER CHARYBDIS

Where are you driving me,
foul waves of love,
huge sleepless winds of jealousy,
turbulent sea of orgy?

The rudder of my heart is broken:
I drift.
Will I ever again see
the voluptuous Skylla?

THE WINE CUP

The wine cup is happy. It rubbed against
warm Zenophila's erotic mouth. O bliss!
I wish she would press her lips under my lips

and in one breathless gulp drain down my
    soul.

LOVE ON THE BLUE WATER

Asklepias adores making love. She gazes at a
    man,
her aquamarine eyes calm like the summer
    seas,
and persuades him to go boating on the lake
    of love.

HELIODORA'S FINGERNAIL

Your fingernail, Heliodora, was grown by Eros
and sharpened by him. How else could
your mere scratching be a claw against my
    heart?

THE KISS

Your eyes are fire, Timarian, your kiss
    birdlime.
You look at me and I burn. You touch me and
    I stick!

HOUR OF THE SPRING

Winter squalls are drained out of the sky,
the violet season of flowering spring smiles,
the black earth glitters under a green lawn,
swelling plants pop open with tiny petals,
meadows laugh and suck the dew of morning
while the rose unfolds.

DIONYSIUS OF HALICARNASSUS (FL. CA. 30 B.C.)
The Roman Antiquities

*D*ionysius of Halicarnassus moved to Rome around 30 B.C., when the civil war between Augustus and Antony came to an end. He was so grateful for the welcome he received from the Romans as a rhetoric teacher that he wrote a social history of Rome from earliest times through the First Punic War.

- Rome was so busy with political affairs that its leaders eagerly welcomed those who could help it establish glorious mythological and literary roots. For this reason, Dionysius spends many words trying to prove that the Romans are descended from the Greeks, following Virgil's *Aeneid,* where the Homeric hero Aeneas was considered to have fled from defeated Troy to "found a new race" that would become the mighty Roman Empire. At the same time, Dionysius served as a propagandist, providing his fellow Greeks with an image of Rome that might allow them to revise their view of their conquerors as barbarians and hopefully make their conquest more palatable. He also wrote on literary theory, literary criticism, rhetoric, history of oratory, and style.
- The importance of *Roman Antiquities* is twofold:

  - It preserved, in a quite laborious fashion, the arguments among previous historians, providing invaluable insight into otherwise lost accounts of Roman prehistory;
  - Dionysius, who insisted on exploring the causality behind events, is a master of thorough and systematic analysis, showing scholars, researchers, and attorneys after him how to create the maximum brief on any particular topic.

He argues that the two fundamental historical principles are choosing subjects of serious importance to readers and using the greatest precision and judgment in collecting information in the pursuit of truth. He is ever conscious of the role of history as a cautionary tale for politicians who should learn from it not to repeat its disastrous mistakes. As Dionysius praises the past he is also gently upbraiding his Roman audience for not living up to its own magnificent origins.

BOOK I

I. Although it is much against my will to indulge in the explanatory statements usually given in the prefaces to histories, yet I am obliged to prefix to this work some remarks concerning myself. In doing this it is neither my intention to dwell too long on my own praise, which I know would be distasteful to the reader, nor have I the purpose of censuring other historians, as Anaximenes and Theopompus did in the prefaces to their histories; but I shall only show the reasons that induced me to undertake this work and give an accounting of the sources from which I gained the knowledge of the things I am going to relate. For I am convinced that all who propose to leave such monuments of their minds to posterity as time shall not involve in one common ruin with their bodies, and particularly those who write histories, in which we have the right to assume that Truth, the source of both prudence and wisdom, is enshrined, ought, first of all, to make choice of noble and lofty subjects and such as will be of great utility to their readers, and then, with great care and pains, to provide themselves with the proper equipment for the treatment of their subject. For those who base historical works upon deeds inglorious or evil or unworthy of serious study, either because they crave to come to the knowledge of men and to get a name of some sort or other, or because they desire to display the wealth of their rhetoric, are neither admired by posterity for their fame nor praised for their eloquence; rather, they leave this opinion in the minds of all who take up their histories, that they themselves admired lives which were of a piece with

the writings they published, since it is a just and a general opinion that a man's words are the images of his mind. Those, on the other hand, who, while making choice of the best subjects, are careless and indolent in compiling their narratives out of such reports as chance to come to their ears gain no praise by reason of that choice; for we do not deem it fitting that the histories of renowned cities and of men who have held supreme power should be written in an offhand or negligent manner. As I believe these considerations to be necessary and of the first importance to historians and as I have taken great care to observe them both, I have felt unwilling either to omit mention of them or to give it any other place than in the preface to my work.

II. That I have indeed made choice of a subject noble, lofty, and useful to many will not, I think, require any lengthy argument, at least for those who are not utterly unacquainted with universal history. For if anyone turns his attention to the successive supremacies both of cities and of nations, as accounts of them have been handed down from times past, and then, surveying them severally and comparing them together, wishes to determine which of them obtained the widest dominion and both in peace and war performed the most brilliant achievements, he will find that the supremacy of the Romans has far surpassed all those that are recorded from earlier times, not only in the extent of its dominion and in the splendor of its achievements—which no account has as yet worthily celebrated—but also in the length of time during which it has endured down to our day. For the empire of the Assyrians, ancient as it was and running back to legendary times, held sway over only a small part of Asia. That of the Medes, after overthrowing the Assyrian empire and obtaining a still wider dominion, did not hold it long, but was overthrown in the fourth generation. The Persians, who conquered the Medes, did, indeed, finally become masters of almost all Asia; but when they attacked the nations of Europe also, they did not reduce many of them to submission, and they continued in power not much above two hundred years. The Macedonian dominion, which overthrew the might of the Persians, did, in the extent of its sway, exceed all its predecessors, yet even it did not flourish long, but after Alexander's death began to decline; for it was immediately partitioned among many commanders from the time of the Diadochi, and although after their time it was able to go on to the second or third generation, yet it was weakened by its own dissensions and at the last destroyed by the Romans. But even the Macedonian power did not subjugate every country and every sea; for it neither conquered Libya, with the exception of the small portion bordering on Egypt, nor subdued all Europe, but in the North advanced only as far as Thrace and in the West down to the Adriatic Sea.

III. Thus we see that the most famous of the earlier supremacies of which history has given us any account, after attaining to so great vigor and might, were overthrown. As for the Greek powers, it is not fitting to compare them to those just mentioned, since they gained neither magnitude of empire nor duration of eminence equal to theirs. For the Athenians ruled only the seacoast, during the space of sixty-eight years, nor did their sway extend even over all that, but only to the part between the Euxine and the Pamphylian seas, when their naval supremacy was at its height. The Lacedaemonians, when masters of the Peloponnesus and the rest of Greece, advanced their rule as far as Macedonia, but were checked by the Thebans before they had held it quite thirty years. But Rome rules every country that is not inaccessible or uninhabited, and she is mistress of every sea, not only of that which lies inside the Pillars of Hercules but also of the Ocean, except that part of it which is not navigable; she is the first and the only State recorded in all time that ever made the risings and the settings of the sun the boundaries of her dominion. Nor has her supremacy been of short duration, but more lasting than that of any other commonwealth or kingdom. For from the very beginning, immediately after her founding, she began to draw to herself the neighboring nations, which were both numerous and warlike, and continually advanced, subjugating every rival. And it is now 745 years from her foundation down to the consulship of Claudius Nero, consul for the second time, and of Calpurnius Piso, who were chosen in the 193rd Olympiad. From the time that she mastered the whole of Italy she was emboldened to aspire to govern all mankind, and after driving from off the sea the Carthaginians, whose maritime strength was superior to that of all others, and subduing Macedonia, which until then was reputed to be the most powerful nation on land, she no longer had as rival any nation either barbarian or Greek; and it is now in my day already the seventh generation that she has continued to hold sway over every region of the world, and there is no nation, as I may say, that disputes her universal dominion or protests against being ruled by her. However, to prove my statement that I have neither made choice of the most trivial of subjects nor proposed to treat of mean and insignificant deeds, but am undertaking to write not only about the most illustrious city but also about brilliant achievements to whose like no man could point, I know not what more I need say.

IV. But before I proceed, I desire to show in a few words that it is not without design and mature premeditation that I have turned to the early part of Rome's history, but that I have well-considered reasons to give for my choice, to forestall the censure of those who, fond of finding fault with everything and not as yet having heard of any of the matters which I am about to make known, may blame me because, in spite of the fact that this city, grown so famous in our days, had very humble and inglorious beginnings, unworthy of historical record, and that it was but a few generations ago, that is, since her overthrow of the Macedonian powers and her success in the Punic wars, that she arrived at distinction and glory, nevertheless, when I was at liberty to choose one of the famous periods in her history for my theme, I turned aside to one so barren of distinction as her antiquarian lore. For to this day almost all the Greeks are ignorant of the early history of Rome and the great majority of them have been imposed upon by sundry false opinions grounded upon stories which chance has brought to their ears and led to believe that, having come upon various vagabonds without house or home and barbarians, and even those not free men, as her founders, she in the course of time arrived at world domination, and this

not through reverence for the gods and justice and every other virtue, but through some chance and the injustice of Fortune, which inconsiderately showers her greatest favors upon the most undeserving. And indeed the more malicious are wont to rail openly at Fortune for freely bestowing on the basest of barbarians the blessings of the Greeks. And yet why should I mention men at large, when even some historians have dared to express such views in the writings they have left, taking this method of humoring barbarian kings who detested Rome's supremacy—princes to whom they were ever servilely devoted and with whom they associated as flatterers—by presenting them with "histories" which were neither just nor true?

V. In order, therefore, to remove these erroneous impressions, as I have called them, from the minds of the many and to substitute true ones in their room, I shall in this Book show who the founders of the city were, at what periods the various groups came together, and through what turns of fortune they left their native countries. By this means I engage to prove that they were Greeks and came together from nations not the smallest nor the least considerable. And beginning with the next Book I shall tell of the deeds they performed immediately after their founding of the city and of the customs and institutions by virtue of which their descendants advanced to so great dominion; and, so far as I am able, I shall omit nothing worthy of being recorded in history, to the end that I may instill in the minds of those who shall then be informed of the truth the fitting conception of this city—unless they have already assumed an utterly violent and hostile attitude toward it—and also that they may neither feel indignation at their present subjection, which is grounded on reason (for by an universal law of Nature, which time cannot destroy, it is ordained that superiors shall ever govern their inferiors), nor rail at Fortune for having wantonly bestowed upon an undeserving city a supremacy so great and already of so long continuance, particularly when they shall have learned from my history that Rome from the very beginning, immediately after its founding, produced infinite examples of virtue in men whose superiors, whether for piety or for justice or for lifelong self-control or for warlike valor, no city, either Greek or barbarian, has ever produced. This, I say, is what I hope to accomplish, if my readers will but lay aside all resentment; for some such feeling is aroused by a promise of things which run counter to received opinion or excite wonder. And it is a fact that all those Romans who bestowed upon their country so great a dominion are unknown to the Greeks for want of a competent historian. For no accurate history of the Romans written in the Greek language has hitherto appeared, but only very brief and summary epitomes.

VI. The first historian, so far as I am aware, to touch upon the early period of the Romans was Hieronymus of Cardia, in his work on the Epigoni. After him Timaeus of Sicily related the beginnings of their history in his general history and treated in a separate work the wars with Pyrrhus of Epirus. Besides these, Antigonus, Polybius, Silenus, and innumerable other authors devoted themselves to the same themes, though in different ways, each of them recording some few things compiled without accurate investigation on his own part but from reports which chance had brought to his ears. Like to these in all respects are the histories of those Romans, also, who related in Greek the early achievements of the city; the oldest of these writers are Quintus Fabius and Lucius Cincius, who both flourished during the Punic wars. Each of these men related the events at which he himself had been present with great exactness, as being well acquainted with them, but touched only in a summary way upon the early events that followed the founding of the city. For these reasons, therefore, I have determined not to pass over a noble period of history which the older writers left untouched, a period, moreover, the accurate portrayal of which will lead to the following most excellent and just results: In the first place, the brave men who have fulfilled their destiny will gain immortal glory and be extolled by posterity, which things render human nature like unto the divine and prevent men's deeds from perishing together with their bodies. And again, both the present and future descendants of those godlike men will choose, not the pleasantest and easiest of lives, but rather the noblest and most honorable, when they consider that all who are sprung from an illustrious origin ought to set a high value on themselves and indulge in no pursuit unworthy of their ancestors. And I, who have not turned aside to this work for the sake of flattery, but out of a regard for truth and justice, which ought to be the aim of every history, shall have an opportunity, in the first place, of expressing my attitude of goodwill toward all good men and toward all who take pleasure in the contemplation of great and noble deeds; and, in the second place, of making the most grateful return that I may to the city in re membrance of the education and other blessings I have enjoyed during my residence in it.

VII. Having thus given the reason for my choice of subject, I wish now to say something concerning the sources I used while preparing for my task. For it is possible that those who have already read Hieronymus, Timaeus, Polybius, or any of the other historians whom I just now mentioned as having slurred over their work, since they will not have found in those authors many things mentioned by me, will suspect me of inventing them and will demand to know how I came by the knowledge of these particulars. Lest anyone, therefore, entertain such an opinion of me, it is best that I should state in advance what narratives and records I have used as sources. I arrived in Italy at the very time that Augustus Caesar put an end to the civil war, in the middle of the 187th Olympiad; and having from that time to this present day, a period of twenty-two years, lived at Rome, learned the language of the Romans, and acquainted myself with their writings, I have devoted myself during all that time to matters bearing upon my subject. Some information I received orally from men of the greatest learning, with whom I associated; and other data I gathered from histories written by the approved Roman authors—Porcius Cato, Fabius Maximus, Valerius Antias, Licinius Macer, the Aelii, Gellii and Calpurnii, and many others of note; with these works, which are like the Greek annalistic accounts, as a basis, I set about the writing of my history. So much, then, concerning myself. But it yet remains for me to say something also concerning the history itself—to what periods I limit it, what subjects I describe, and what form I give to the work.

VIII. I begin my history, then, with the most ancient legends, which the historians before me have omitted as a subject difficult to be cleared up without diligent study; and I bring the narrative down to the beginning of the First Punic War, which fell in the third year of the 128th Olympiad. I relate all the foreign wars that the city waged during that period and all the internal seditions with which she was agitated, showing from what causes they sprang and by what methods and by what arguments they were brought to an end. I give an account also of all the forms of government Rome used, both during the monarchy and after its overthrow, and show what was the character of each. I describe the best customs and the most remarkable laws; and, in short, I show the whole life of the ancient Romans. As to the form I give this work, it does not resemble that which the authors who make wars alone their subject have given to their histories, nor that which others who treat of the several forms of government by themselves have adopted, nor is it like the annalistic accounts which the authors of the *Atthides* have published (for these are monotonous and soon grow tedious to the reader), but it is a combination of every kind, forensic, speculative and narrative, to the intent that it may afford satisfaction both to those who occupy themselves with political debates and to those who are devoted to philosophical speculations, as well as to any who may desire mere undisturbed entertainment in their reading of history. Such things, therefore, will be the subjects of my history and such will be its form. I, the author, am Dionysius of Halicarnassus, the son of Alexander. And at this point I begin. . . .

DIOSCORIDES (CA. A.D. 40–90)
Materia medica

$\mathcal{P}$edanios Dioscorides, from Anabarzus in Cilicia, was primarily a botanist and herbalist who collected in his five-book *Materia medica* (published around the year 70) his observations on 600 plants—including cannabis, hemlock, and opium (the last for "sleeping potions" useful for surgery)—and a thousand animal and mineral remedies encountered during his wide-flung travels. We know little about him except that he was a surgeon in the Roman armies of Claudius and Nero, familiar with the anesthetic use of opium and mandragora. His *Herbal,* as the *Materia medica* became known, was widely popular as a sober-minded and superstition-free botanical, zoological, and pharmacological reference both in his own time, and, translated into seven European languages including Arabic, well into the Renaissance.

FROM MATERIA MEDICA

BOOK II

In the first booke, most louing Areius, that we made of Medicinall matters, we haue discourst of Aromata, of Oyles, of Ointments, of Trees, & of ye Liquors and Teares and Fruits that come of them. But in this being ye second book, we shall comme to discourse both of Liuing creatures, and of Hony, and of Milke, and of Adeps, and of those thinges which they call Frumentacea, as also of Pot-hearbs, annexing vnto those such Herbes as are endued with a sharpe qualitie, because such are neare of kinne, as are garlick & onions, & mustard seed, that the qualities of those thinges soe like of nature should not be severed.

LIVING CREATURES. I-74

11. KOCHLIAS. HELIX POMATIA AND OTHER SNAILS

The earth Snaile is good for the stomach, hardly corrupted. That is the best which is in Sardinia, & Africa, & Astyypalia, & in Sicilia, & Chios, as also that which is in the Alpes by Liguria, surnamed Pomatias (because of its covering). And ye Sea Snaile also is good for the stomach, & is easily transient, but ye River Snaile is poysonous. The Field snaile which hangeth upon bushes & shrubs, which somme call Sesilon or Seselita is a troubler or disturber of ye belly & stomach, causing vomiting. But the shells of all of them being burnt, haue the power to heate & burne, to cleanse Leprosies, the Vitiligines &

the teeth. Being burnt whole with their flesh & beaten small, & anointed on with hony, they take away the Cicatrices in the eyes, & the Albugines, and ye sunspots, & ye dullnesse of ye sight. But being applyed raw with their shells, they dry up hydropicall tumors, & doe not fall off till all the moisture be exhausted. They doe also lenifie podagricall inflammations & draw out thornes, being applyed after the like manner. Being beaten small, & soe applyed, they expell the Menstrua. But the flesh of them being beaten small, & layd on as a Cataplasme with Myrrhe & Franckincense, doth conglutinate wounds, & especially those about the Sinewes; & they stay the bleeding out of the Nosthrills, being beaten small with vinegar. But the live flesh, especially of ye African, being devoured, doth pacifie the paines of the stomach. But being whole with ye shell & a little of it dranck with wine & Myrrhe it doth cure such as are troubled with the colick & the paines of the bladder. The earth snaile doth conglutinate the falling haire if one, thrusting a needle through ye flesh of ye snaile, doe touch the haire with the slymie matter that ariseth thence.

12. KARKINOI. THELPHUSA SP.

The ashes of burnt Crevises or River Crabs, to ye quantitie of twoe spoonefulls, with one spoonefull of ye roote of Gentian, & being dranck in wine for three dayes together, doth manifestly help such as are bitten of a mad dogge. And with sod Hony they doe lenifie the chaps which are in ye feet, and those which are in the seate, and ye Perniones, & ye Carcinomata. Being beaten when they are raw & dranck with Asses milk they help the bitings of Serpents & the stroakes of the Phalangii &

Scorpions. But being sod, and eaten with their broth, they are good for such as are in a consumption, & such as haue swallowed a Sea Hare. But being beaten together with Ocimum, & layd vnto them, they kill Scorpions.

The Sea Crabs can doe ye same things, but they worke somewhat lesse effectually than these.

13. SKORPIOS CHERSAIOS

The earthly Scorpion, being taken raw, beaten small and soe layd on, is a remedie for ye hurt donne by it: it is found also rosted for ye same purpose.

19. OPHEOS GERAS. THE SLOUGH OF SNAKES

The Senecta anguium (which is the skinne that ye snake casts in ye spring tyme) being sod in wine, is a remedie for ye paine in the eares if it be poured into them, & for ye paine of the teeth when taken by way of collution. They mix it, especially that of the sea viper, with eye medicines.

21. LAGOOS CHERSAIOS. LEPUS TIMIDUS. HARE

The braine of a Land Hare, being eaten roasted, is good for ye trembling that commes of a feare, as also for ye toothing in children, being rubbed on, or eaten. The head thereof being burnt, and anointed on with Beares grease, or vinegar, doth cure the Alopeciae. The Coagulum thereof being dranck after three dayes after ye menstrual courses, is reported to cause sterilitie. Likewise it stops the flux of ye wombe & of the belly. It helps them also which haue ye falling sicknesse; and dranck with vinegar it is good against poisons, especially for ye curdling of ye milke, and the bitings of vipers. But ye blood thereof being anointed on while it is warme, doth cure ye sun-spotts, & ye vitiligines, & ye Lentigines.

25. ORCHIS HIPPOPOTAMOU. HIPPOPOTAMUS

The stones of the Hippopotamus, being dryed, & beaten small, is dranck in wine against the bitings of Serpents.

26. KASTOROS ORCHIS. CASTOREUM OF BEAVER

The Castor is a living creature of a double nature, being nourisht for ye most part in ye waters with ye fishes & Crabs. The stones thereof are good against ye poysons of serpents. It is good also to cause sneesing, & generally, it is vsefull for many purposes. For two dragms thereof being dranck with Pulegium, doe provoke the menstrua, & doe cast out ye Embryons and the secondines. It is also dranck with vinegar against the Inflationes, the tormina, the singultas, deadly poysons, the

Ixia. Being moystened with vinegar & Rosaceum, it doth fetch againe the lethargicall, or those which are borne downe by any manner. And it doth doe ye like being smelt to, or being suffumigated. It is good also for tremblings & convulsions, & for all ye diseases of the Nerves, being either dranck or anointed on, and generally it hath a warming facultie. But ever choose those stones, which are connexed together from one beginning (for it is impossible to finde two folliculi knit together in one Membrane); & hauing that within it waxie, of a strong smell, & poysonnous, sharp, biting taste, easily crumbled, ever distinguished by their naturall tunicles. Somme doe adulterate it by pouring in Ammoniacum, or gumme tempered with blood & Castoreum into the folliculus, and drying it. But it is a vaine report, that this beast when it is pursued, doth bite off his stones & cast them away, for it is impossible that hee should touch them, being knit under, as those of a Boare. But they who take off the skinne, must take the liquor therein looking like hony, together with ye tunicle that containes it, & soe hauing dryed it, lay it vp in store.

28. BATRACHOI. FROGS

Frogs are an Antidot against the (poyson) of all serpents, they being sod into a broth in salt & oyle, the broth being likewise taken, & for ye diuturnos abscessus tendinum. But being burnt, & soe cast upon, they stanch bleeding, & they cure ye Alopecias, being anointed on with liquid pitch. But the blood of Green Frogs being dropt on, doth forbid the haire euer to comme up againe, where it hath once been pulled off from the eye lidds. They are good also for the toothache, being sod together with water & vinegar, & ye teeth being washt therewith.

36. KOREIS. BED BUGS

Cimices of ye bed, (being taken) to the number of seven of them & put in meate with beanes, and swallowed downe before the fitt, doe help such as haue ye quartaine ague. And being swallowed downe without beanes, (they help such as are) bitten by an Aspick. Being smellt vnto, they call back such againe as are fallen into a swoune by the strangulation of the Vulua. Being dranck with wine or vinegar, they expell horse leaches. Being beaten small & put into the Urinaria Fistula they cure the Dysuria.

38. SILPHE. BLATTA ORIENTALIS. COCKROACH

The inward parts of that kind of Blatta which is found in Bakehowses, & millhowses, being beaten with oyle, or sodd & dropt into the eares doth assuage their paine.

41. PNEUMON ALOPEKOS. LUNGS OF FOX

And the Lunges of a Fox, being dryed, & dranck, doth help the Asthmaticall; & the grease of the same, being melted, & poured in, doth assuage the paine of ye eare.

42. HEPAR ONEIRON. ASS'S LIVER

An Ass's Liuer being eaten roasted, is good for the Epilepticall, but let them take it fasting.

43. AIDOION ARRENOS ELAPHOU. TESTES OF DEER

The genitall of a male Hart, being beaten small, & dranck with wine, doth help those who haue been bitten of Vipers.

44. ONUCHES ONON. ASS'S HOOFS

An Ass's hoofes being burnt, & the quantitie of twoe spoonefulls thereof being dranck for many daies together, are sayd to cure the Epilepticall; but being macerated in oyle, they dissolve ye strumae, being sprinckled on also they heale ye Perniones.

45. LEICHENES HIPPON. SPAVINS OF HORSES

The Lichenes of Horses, are (according to description) that obdurate substance, which growes hardened at their knees, & at their hoofs, which being beaten small, & dranck with vinegar, are sayd to cure Epilepses.

51. KATTUMATA. OLD LEATHER

The old leather of old soles of shooes, beeing burnt, beaten to powder, & soe layed on, do help burnings, intertrigines, gallings occasioned by wearing of shooes.

56. TETTIGES. GRASSHOPPERS

Grasshoppers if they be eaten roasted, doe help the griefs about the bladder.

57. AKRIDES. LOCUSTS

Locusts being suffumigated, doe help the difficulties of pissing, especially in women folke, but they haue a flesh that is vnprofitable.

But that kinde of Locust, which is called Asiracos, or Onos, is without wings, hauing great members when it is young. This being dryed, & dranck with wine doth greatly help such as are bitten of Scorpions, but the Africans which inhabit Leptis feed on these abundantly.

72. ENTERA GES. EARTH-WORMS

The Wormes of the earth, being beaten small, & soe layd on, doth glue together Sinews cut asunder. And they doe also dissolue tertians. But being sod with Goose-grease, they doe cure ye diseases of the eares being dropt therein. And being sod together with oyle, & poured into ye contrary eare, they help tooth-aches. They being beaten small, & dranck with Passum doe expell the urine.

78. GALA GUNAIKOS. WOMAN'S MILK

But woman's milke is ye sweetest and most nourishing. Being sucked it is good for the gnawing of ye stomach & the Consumption. It is good also for one that hath dranck downe a Sea-Hare. Being mixed with Franckincense beaten small, it is dropt into eyes that are bloudshot by a blow. And it is good for the goutie being anointed on with Meconium & Ceratium. But all milke is naught for ye spleneticall, the Hepaticall, for ye Vertiginous, Epileptical, & such as are troubled in their sinewes, for such as haue feauers, or whose heads doe ake, unless at any tyme one give them whey for purgation sake, as hath been formerly showed.

Some say that the milke of a bitch when shee doth first whelp, doth do away haire being anointed on, & that being dranck, it is an Antidot against Poysonous medicines, & that it is a caster out of dead Embryos.

79. TUROS NEAROS. NEW CHEESE

New cheese being eaten without salt, is nourishing, good for ye stomach, easy of digestion, encreasing the flesh, & indifferently mollifying ye belly. Yet somme is better than other according to ye nature of the milke of which it is made. But being sod, & strained out, afterward roasted, it doth binde the belly, and being layed on it is good for the inflammations, & sugillations of ye eyes.

"LONGINUS" (FIRST CENTURY A.D.)

On the Sublime

Although this philosophical treatise on great writing, the psychology of writing, genius, and aesthetics was attributed mistakenly to Cassius Longinus (a teacher of rhetoric in Palmyra in the third century B.C.), its true author is unknown. Scholars, in their inimitably witty way, have decided to call him Pseudo-Longinus.

- We know from internal evidence that the treatise was written to correct the inadequacy of a previous work on the same topic by Caecilius of Calacte, whom this author attacks for having failed to give sufficient importance to the emotional content of elevated writing. The author, whose aim is to "clarify and instruct," laments that his is an age of decadence, when most men pursue material rather than spiritual goals. Neither political circumstances nor loss of democracy account for the dearth of great writing as much as a society's distorted value system. No wonder writers of the present are inferior to the great noble writers of the past.
- The author of *On the Sublime* argues, in a vigorous and sophisticated style worthy of his subject, that the highest form of literature, "the sublime," bears five characteristics, all of them reflecting "greatness of spirit":

  1. the natural and/or innate ability to choose thought and expression that serve a distinguished, grand conception—as when Herman Melville writes, in *Moby Dick,* "to write a mighty book you must have a mighty theme."
  2. intense emotion and passion (the Greek word is *páthos).*
  3. effective figures of speech.
  4. noble diction.
  5. harmonious structure, including rhythmic word- and thought-order.

The last three characteristics are *technical,* the first two *innate.* A great writer is a natural storyteller, who then perfects his craft. Longinus is a stickler for quality and a closely focused textual critic, analyzing passages from Homer, Sappho, Demosthenes, Thucydides, and Plato. Writing fails to attain the sublime generally for four reasons:

  1. it may be *turgid,* displaying impropriety in the relationship between thought and expression, and a worthy subject matter;
  2. it may be *puerile,* showing impropriety of expression and thought on an unworthy subject;
  3. it may be *histrionic,* showing excessive emotion and passion;
  4. it may be *frigid,* imprecisely using figures of speech.

The author examines the relationship between genius and discipline, between nature and art. By arguing that the greatness of a work is directly linked to the writer's magnanimity, which if not inborn can be achieved through modeling great authors, Longinus breaks with tradition that credits great writing to divine inspiration. *On the Sublime* is required reading for every aspiring writer.

1. You know, my dear Postumius Terentianus, that when we were studying together Cecilius's little treatise on the Sublime we found it was too trivial to satisfy the full demands of the subject and omitted altogether to touch upon the main points, and that consequently it does not render to its readers very much of that assistance which should be an author's chief aim. Moreover, in every systematic treatise there are two requisites: The author must first define his subject, and secondly, though this is really more important, he must show us how and by what means of study we may reach the goal ourselves. Cecilius, however, while assuming our ignorance and endeavoring by a thousand instances to demonstrate the nature of the sublime, apparently thought it unnecessary to deal with the means by which we may be enabled to educate our natures to the proper pitch of elevation. Still, so far as Cecilius is concerned, we ought perhaps rather to praise him for the mere conception of such a treatise and the trouble spent upon it than to blame him for his omissions. But since you have now required me in my turn to prepare some notes on the sublime purely for your own sake, let us then see whether our views have any real value for public speakers; and in the details of our inquiry you yourself, my friend, will, I am sure, do what duty and your heart alike dictate and give me the benefit of your unbiased judgment. For he spoke well who, in answer to the question, "What have we in common with the gods?" said "Kindness and Truth." Further, writing for a man of such learning and culture as yourself,

dear friend, I almost feel freed from the need of a lengthy preface showing how the Sublime consists in a consummate excellence and distinction of language, and that this alone gave to the greatest poets and historians their preeminence and clothed them with immortal fame. For the effect of genius is not to persuade the audience but rather to transport them out of themselves. Invariably what inspires wonder casts a spell upon us and is always superior to what is merely convincing and pleasing. For our convictions are usually under our own control, while such passages exercise an irresistible power of mastery and get the upper hand with every member of the audience.

Again inventive skill and the due disposal and marshaling of facts do not show themselves in one or two touches: They gradually emerge from the whole tissue of the composition, while, on the other hand, a well-timed flash of sublimity scatters everything before it like a bolt of lightning and reveals the full power of the speaker at a single stroke. But, as I say, my dear Terentianus, these and other such hints you with your experience could supply yourself.

2. We must begin now by raising the question whether there is an art of sublimity or profundity, for some think those are wholly at fault who try to bring such matters under systematic rules. Genius, it is said, is born and does not come of teaching, and the only art for producing it is nature. Works of natural genius, so people think, are spoiled and utterly demeaned by being reduced to the dry bones of rule and precept. For my part I hold that the

opposite may be proved, if we consider that while in lofty emotion Nature for the most part knows no law, yet it is not the way of Nature to work at random and wholly without system. In all production Nature is the prime cause, the great exemplar; but as to all questions of degree, of the happy moment in each case, and again of the safest rules of practice and use, such prescriptions are the proper contribution of an art or system. We must remember also that mere grandeur runs the greater risk, if left to itself without the stay and ballast of scientific method, and abandoned to the impetus of uninstructed enterprise. For genius needs the curb as often as the spur. Speaking of the common life of men Demosthenes declares that the greatest of all blessings is good fortune, and that next comes good judgment, which is indeed quite as important, since the lack of it often completely cancels the advantage of the former. We may apply this to literature and say that Nature fills the place of good fortune, Art that of good judgment. And above all we must remember this: The very fact that in literature some effects come of natural genius alone can only be learned from art. If then, I say, those who censure the students of this art would lay these considerations to heart, they would not, I fancy, be any longer inclined to consider the study of these subjects superfluous and useless.

[*Two pages of the* MS. *are missing here.*]

3. . . .
Yea, though they check the chimney's
    towering flame.

For, if I spy one hearthholder alone,
I'll weave one torrent coronal of flame
And fire the steading to a heap of ash.
But not yet have I blown the noble
    strain.

All this has lost the tone of tragedy: It is pseudo-tragic—the "coronals" and "spewing to heaven" and making Boreas a flute-player and all the rest of it. The phrasing is turbid, while the images make for confusion rather than intensity. Examine each in the light of day and it gradually declines from the terrible to the ridiculous. Now seeing that in tragedy, which is essentially a majestic matter and admits of bombast, misplaced tumidity is none the less unpardonable, surely it is not likely to suit real speeches. Thus it is that people laugh at Gorgias of Leontini for calling Xerxes "the Persian Zeus," and vultures "living sepulchers"; also at certain phrases of Callisthenes which are not sublime but highfalutin, and still more at some of Cleitarchus's efforts, an affected creature, blowing, as Sophocles says, "on scrannel pipes, yet wasting all his wind." You find the same sort of thing in Amphicrates too, and in Hegesias and Matris. For often when they think themselves inspired, their supposed ecstasy is merely childish folly. Speaking generally, tumidity seems one of the hardest faults to guard against. For all who aim at grandeur, in trying to avoid the charge of being feeble and arid, fall somehow into this fault, pinning their faith to the maxim that "to miss a high aim is to fail without shame." Tumors are bad things whether in books or bodies, those empty inflations, void of sincerity, as likely as not producing the opposite to the effect intended. For, as they say, "there's naught so dry as dropsy."

Tumidity then comes of trying to outdo the sublime. Puerility, on the other hand, is the exact opposite of grandeur; utterly abject, mean-spirited, and in fact the most ignoble of faults. What then is puerility? Is it not obviously the academic attitude, where overelaboration ends in frigid failure? Writers fall into this fault through trying to be uncommon and exquisite, and above all to please, and founder instead upon the tinsel reefs of affectation. Closely allied to this is a third kind of fault peculiar to emotional passages, what Theodorus used to call "Parenthyrson." This is emotion misplaced and pointless where none is needed, or unrestrained where restraint is required. For writers often behave as if they were drunk and give way to outbursts of emotion which the subject no longer warrants. Such emotion is purely subjective and consequently tedious, so that to an audience which feels none of it their behavior looks unseemly. And naturally so, for while they are in ecstasy, the audience are not. However we have reserved another place in which to treat of emotional passages.

EPICTETUS (CA. A.D. 55–135)
The Encheiridion (Handbook) recorded by Arrian

Born in Hierapolis, in Phyrgia, the philosopher Epictetus lived in Rome as the slave of the freedman Epaphroditos, who was at the time an administrative assistant to the Emperor Nero. He studied Stoicism under Musonius Rufus and, when Epaphroditos freed him, became himself a teacher of Stoicism until Domitian expelled the philosophers from Rome. Then he went to Nikopolis, in Epirus, and lived out his life there as a schoolmaster, passionately defending freedom in everything he said and wrote.

- Like Socrates, Epictetus taught through dialectic and conversations. He left no writing of his own, but his teachings were recorded by his students. One of them, the historian Arrian, is probably responsible for transcribing the text we have today. The Emperor Marcus Aurelius was influenced by Epictetus more than by any other philosopher.
- The *Handbook* is probably the most important statement of the Stoic philosophy that has come down to us, espousing unequivocal acceptance of Providence as the ultimate buttress against every misfortune: "To endure and to renounce." Epictetus' doctrine of self-sufficiency, and the mind's power over matter, is strikingly modern, echoed in Norman Cousins' *Anatomy*

of an Illness and *Head First,* Scott Peck's *The Road Less Traveled,* and Anthony Robbins' *Unlimited Power.* He believed that self-mastery was the highest aim in life. If Epictetus had lived in the twentieth century, he would have "done the circuit" of the self-help industry.

1.

Of things some are in our power, and others are not. In our power are opinion, movement towards a thing, desire, aversion, turning from a thing; and in a word, whatever are our acts. Not in our power are the body, property, reputation, offices, and in a word, whatever are not our own acts. And the things in our power are by nature free, not subject to restraint or hindrance; but the things not in our power are weak, slavish, subject to restraint, in the power of others. Remember then, that if you think the things which are by nature slavish to be free, and the things which are in the power of others to be your own, you will be hindered, you will lament, you will be disturbed, you will blame both gods and men; but if you think that only which is your own to be your own, and if you think that what is another's, as it really is, belongs to another, no man will ever compel you, no man will hinder you, you will never blame any man, you will accuse no man, you will do nothing involuntarily, no man will harm you, you will have no enemy for you will not suffer any harm.

If then you desire such great things remember that you must not lay hold of them with a small effort; but you must leave alone some things entirely, and postpone others for the present. But if you wish for these things also, and power and wealth, perhaps you will not gain

even these very things because you aim also at those former things; certainly you will fail in those things through which alone happiness and freedom are secured. Straightway then practice saying to every harsh appearance: You are an appearance, and in no manner what you appear to be. Then examine it by the rules which you possess, and by this first and chiefly, whether it relates to the things which are in our power or to things which are not in our power; and if it relates to anything which is not in our power, be ready to say that it does not concern you.

2.

Remember that desire contains in it the profession of obtaining that which you desire; and the profession in aversion is that you will not fall into that which you attempt to avoid; and he who fails in his desire is unfortunate; and he who falls into that which he would avoid is unhappy. If then you attempt to avoid only the things contrary to nature which are within your power you will not be involved in any of the things which you would avoid. But if you attempt to avoid disease, or death, or poverty, you will be unhappy. Take away then aversion from all things which are not in our power, and transfer it to the things contrary to nature which are in our power. But destroy desire completely for the present. For if you desire anything which is not in our power, you must be unfortunate; but of the things in our power, and which it would be good to desire, nothing yet is before you. But employ only the power of moving towards an object and retiring from it; and these powers indeed only slightly and with exceptions and with remission.

3.

In everything which pleases the soul, or supplies a want, or is loved, remember to add this to the notion: What is the nature of each thing, beginning from the smallest? If you love an earthen vessel, say it is an earthen vessel which you love; for when it has been broken you will not be disturbed. If you are kissing your child or wife, say that it is a human being whom you are kissing, for when the wife or child dies you will not be disturbed.

4.

When you are going to take in hand any act remind yourself what kind of an act it is. If you are going to bathe, place before yourself what happens in the bath; some splashing the water, others pushing against one other, others abusing one another, and some stealing; and thus with more safety you will undertake the matter, if you say to yourself, I now intend to bathe, and to maintain my will in a manner conformable to nature. And so you will do in every act; for thus if any hindrance to bathing shall happen let this thought be ready. It was not this only that I intended, but I intended also to maintain my will in a way conformable to nature; but I shall not maintain it so if I am vexed at what happens.

5.

Men are disturbed not by the things which happen, but by the opinions about the things; for example, death is nothing terrible, for if it were it would have seemed so to Socrates; for the opinion about death that it is terrible, is the terrible thing. When then we are impeded, or disturbed, or grieved, let us never blame others, but ourselves—that is, our opinions. It is the act of an ill-instructed man to blame others for his own bad condition; it is the act of one who has begun to be instructed, to lay the blame on himself; and of one whose instruction is completed, neither to blame another, nor himself.

6.

Be not elated at any advantage which belongs to another. If a horse when he is elated should say, I am beautiful, one might endure it. But when you are elated, and say, I have a beautiful horse, you must know that you are elated at having a good horse. What then is your own? The use of appearances. Consequently when in the use of appearances you are conformable to nature, then be elated, for then you will be elated at something good which is your own.

7.

As on a voyage when the vessel has reached a port, if you go out to get water it is an amusement by the way to pick up a shellfish or some bulb, but your thoughts ought to be directed to the ship, and you ought to be constantly watching if the captain should call, and then you must throw away all those things, that you may not be bound and pitched into the ship like sheep. So in life also, if there be given to you instead of a little bulb and a shell a wife and child, there will be nothing to prevent you from taking them. But if the captain should call, run to the ship and leave all those things without regard to them. But if you are old, do not even go far from the ship, lest when you are called you make default.

8.

Seek not that the things which happen should happen as you wish; but wish the things which happen to be as they are, and you will have a tranquil flow of life.

PLUTARCH (MESTRIUS PLUTARCHUS) (CA. A.D. 45–CA. 127)
The Life of Alexander the Great

*P*lutarch was one of the most remarkable and prolific men of Greek antiquity, a "Renaissance man" long before the Renaissance gave such a being a name. Known today primarily for his biographies of the great Greeks and Romans (*Parallel Lives*), he was also an essayist, researcher, literary historian, literary comparatist, historian of religion, mythographer, Platonic philosopher (who attacked the Epicureans and Stoics), active politician (granted an office in Achaea by the Emperor Hadrian), educator, writer of handbooks for the average person, and even a priest and reformer at Apollo's shrine at Delphi. His *Parallel Lives,* as translated by Sir Thomas North, was a tremendous influence on the Elizabethan Renaissance in general and Shakespeare's Roman plays in particular.

- Plutarch was born the son of the biographer Aristobulus, of an affluent family in Chaeronea, Boeotia, and educated in Athens under Ammonius. He married a woman named Timoxena. Though he lived much of his life as a magistrate, and died in his hometown, Plutarch also traveled extensively—especially to Rome where his lectures on philosophy introduced him to the highest circles of imperial society, including the emperors Trajan and Hadrian. Plutarch was also a citizen of Athens, and remained in close touch with the Academy throughout his life. His essays and dialogues, in powerful Attic, display his interest in the full human spectrum, including science as well as literature, philosophy, political science, archaeology, and history.
- *The Life of Alexander the Great,* which was set opposite the *Life of Caesar,* is typical of Plutarch's *Parallel Lives;* character sketches designed to harmonize Romans and Greeks by

displaying their common heroic propensities, in its anecdotal and philosophical idealization of a man whom antiquity had long since enshrined as a demi-god for his military prowess and imperial expansionism. As in all the *Lives,* which emphasize the balance or imbalance of vice and virtue, Plutarch follows the pattern of *family and upbringing, education, first public actions, climactic turning points,* and *changes in the hero's fortunes.* The author's purpose is to provide in an entertaining way cautionary tales and models for optimal behavior—political, social, intellectual, and moral. Especially interesting in this regard is Plutarch's account, combining his own intuitive acumen with both the oral tradition and previous historians, of Alexander's relationship with his tutor Aristotle.

. . . Now Philip putting no great affiance in his schoolmasters of music and humanity, for the instruction and education of his son, whom he had appointed to teach him, but thinking rather that he needed men of greater learning than their capacities would reach unto: and that as Sophocles saith,

He needed many reins, and many bits at once:

he sent for Aristotle (the greatest philosopher in his time, and best learned) to teach his son, unto whom he gave honourable stipend. For Philip having won and taken before, the city of Stagira, where Aristotle was born: for his sake he built it again, and replenished it with inhabitants which fled away, or otherwise were in bondage. He appointed them for a school-house and dwelling-place, the pleasant house that is by the city of Mieza. In that place are yet seen seats of stone which Aristotle caused to be made, and close walks to walk in the shadow. It is thought also, that Alexander did not only learn of Aristotle, moral philosophy and humanity, but also he heard of him other more secret, hard, and grave doctrine, which Aristotle's scholars do properly call Acroamata, or Epoptica, meaning things speculative, which requireth the master's teaching to understand them, or else are kept from common knowledge: which sciences, they did not commonly teach. Alexander being passed into Asia, and hearing that Aristotle had put out certain books of that matter: for the honor's sake of philosophy, he wrote a letter unto him, somewhat too plain, and of this effect. Alexander unto Aristotle greeting. Thou has not done well to put forth the Acroamatical sciences. For wherein shall we excel other, if those things which thou hast secretly taught us, be made common to all? I do thee to understand, that I had rather excel others in excellency of knowledge, than in greatness of power. Farewell. Whereunto Aristotle to pacify this his ambitious humor, wrote unto him again, that these books were published, and not published. For to say truly, in all his treatises which he called μετὰ τὰ φυσικὰ: there is no plain instruction profitable for any man, neither to pick out by himself, nor yet to be taught by any other, than Aristotle himself, or his scholars. So that it is written as a memorial for them that have been entered and brought up in the Peripatetic sect and doctrine. It seemeth also, that it was Aristotle above all other, that made Alexander take delight to study physick. For Alexander did not only like the knowledge of speculation, but would exercise practice also, and help his friends when they were sick: and made besides certain remedies, and rules to live by: as appeareth by his letters he wrote, that of his own nature he was much given to his book, and desired to read much. He learned also the Iliads of Homer, of Aristotle's correction, which they call τὴν ἐκ τοῦ νάρθηκος the corrected, as having passed under the rule: and laid it every night under his bed's-head with his dagger, calling it (as Onesicrates writeth) the institution of martial discipline. And when he was in the high countries of Asia, where he could not readily come by other books, he wrote unto Harpalus to send them to him. Harpalus sent him the histories of Philistas, with divers tragedies of Euripides, Sophocles, and Aeschylus: and certain hymns of Telestas and Philoxenus. Alexander did reverence Aristotle at the first, as his father, and so he termed him: because from his natural father he had life, but from him, the knowledge to live. But afterwards he suspected him somewhat, yet he did him no hurt, neither was he so friendly to him as he had been: whereby men perceived that he did not bear him the good-will he was wont to do. This notwithstanding, he left not that zeal and desire he had to the study of philosophy, which he had learned from his youth, and still continued with him. For he shewed divers testimonies thereof. As, the honor he did unto Anaxarchus the Philosopher. The fifty talents which he sent unto Xenocrates, Dandamis, and Calanus: of whom he made great account. When King Philip made war with the Byzantines, Alexander being but sixteen years old, was left his lieutenant in Macedon, with the custody and charge of his great seal: at what time he also subdued the Medarians which had rebelled against him, and having won their city by assault, he drave out the barbarous people, and made a colony of it of sundry nations, and called it Alexandropolis, to say, the city of Alexander. He was with his father at the battell of Chaeronea against the Grecians, where it was reported, that it was he that gave charge first of all upon the holy band of the Thebans. Furthermore, there was an old oak seen in my time, which the countrymen commonly call Alexander's oak, because his tent or pavilion was fastened to it: and not far from thence is the charnel house, where those Macedonians were buried that were slain at the battell. For these causes, his father Philip loved him very dearly, and was glad to hear the Macedonians call Alexander king, and himself their captain. Howbeit the troubles that fell out in his court afterwards, by reason of Philip's new marriages and loves, bred great quarrel and strife amongst the women: for the mischief of dissension and jealousy of women, doth separate the hearts of kings one from another, whereof was chiefest cause, the sharpness of Olympias, who being a jealous woman, fretting, and of a revenging mind, did incense Alexander against his father. But the chiefest cause that provoked Alexander, was Attalus at the marriage of Cleopatra, whom Philip married a maiden, falling in fancy with her when himself was past marriage. This was the matter: Attalus being uncle unto this Cleopatra, fell drunk at the marriage, and having in his cups, he persuaded the Macedonians that were at the feast, to pray to the gods, that they might have a lawful heir of Philip and Cleopatra, to succeed him in the kingdom of Macedon. Alexander being in a rage therewith threw a cup at his head, and said unto him: Why, traitor, what am I: dost thou take me for a bastard? Philip seeing that, rose from the board, and drew out his sword, but by good fortune for them both, being troubled with choler and wine, he fell down on the ground. Then Alexander mocking him, Lo, said he, to the Macedonians, here is the man that prepared to go out of Europe into Asia, and stepping only from one bed to another, ye see him laid along on the ground. After this great insolency, he took his mother Olympias away with him, and carrying her into his country of Epirus, he left her there, and himself afterwards went into Illyria. In the meantime, Demaratus Corinthian, a friend of King Philip's, and very familiar with him, came to see him. Philip when he had courteously welcomed him, asked him how the Grecians did agree together. Truly, O king, quoth he, it imports you much to inquire of the agreement of the Grecians, when your own court is so full of quarrel and contention. These words nipped Philip in such sort, and caused him to know his fault, that through Demaratus' means, whom he sent to persuade Alexander to return, Alexander was made to come back again. Now

when Pexodorus, a prince of Caria (desiring for necessity's sake, to enter in league and friendship with Philip) offered his eldest daughter in marriage unto Arrhidaeus King Philip's son, and had sent Aristocritus ambassador into Macedon for that purpose: the friends of Alexander and his mother, began again to inveigle him with new reports and suspicions, how Philip by this great marriage would advance Arrhidaeus to his utter undoing, and leave him his heir in the kingdom. Alexander being nettled therewith, sent one Thessalus a player of tragedies into Caria to Pexodorus: to persuade him to leave Arrhidaeus, that was a bastard and a fool, and rather to make alliance with Alexander. This offer pleased Pexodorus far better, to have Alexander his son-in-law, than Arrhidaeus. Philip understanding this, went himself into Alexander's chamber, taking Philotas with him (the son of Parmenio) one of his familiars, and bitterly took up Alexander, telling him that he had a base mind, and was unworthy to be left his heir after his death, if he would cast himself away, marrying the daughter of a Carian, that was a slave and subject of a barbarous king. Thereupon he wrote letters unto Corinth, that they should send Thessalus bound unto him. And furthermore, he banished out of Macedon, Harpalus, Nearchus, Phrygius, and Ptolemy, his son's companions: whom Alexander afterwards called home again and placed them in great authority about him. Shortly after, Pausanias sustaining villainy by the counsel and commandment of Attalus and Cleopatra, craving justice of Philip, and finding no amends: he converted all his anger against him, and for spite slew him himself. Of this murder, most men accused Queen Olympias, who (as it is reported) allured this young man, having just cause of anger, to kill him. And Alexander also went not clear from suspicion of this murder. For some say, that Pausanias after this villainy was done him, complained unto Alexander, and told him how he had been abused: who recited these verses to him of Euripides, in the tragedy of *Medea*, where she said in anger, that she would be revenged:

Both of the bridegroom and the bride,
And of the father-in-law.

Notwithstanding, afterwards he caused diligent search to be made, and all them to be severely punished that were of the conspiracy: and was angry also that his mother Olympias had cruelly slain Cleopatra. So he came to be king of Macedon at twenty years of age, and found his realm greatly envied and hated of dangerous enemies, and every way full of danger. . . .

Against Going into Debt

$\mathcal{P}$lutarch's lifelong fascination with character analysis, his concern with ethics, and his love for contemporary and literary anecdote are evident in his wide-ranging essay *Against Going into Debt* (from the category of his works known as *Moralia*). As he does in the *Lives,* Plutarch here studies the interplay of vice and virtue and how each quality in the individual affects the body politic. Discussing debtors and creditors, the evils of usury, the power of positive thinking and self-determination, the virtues of self-control, the dangers of addiction to "keeping up with the Joneses," Plutarch could be describing our own times—though living in the century of credit cards and "Other People's Money" would make him a frequent guest on *Larry King Live.* His view on the subject of indebtedness makes Shakespeare's Polonius, in his advice to Hamlet ("Neither a borrower nor a lender be"), seem a libertine by comparison. That Plutarch and his affluent contemporaries regarded "debt" with such fear and loathing is indeed a cautionary tale for our world, in which borrowing has become a way of life.

"Greek coins." Photographie Giraudon. The Louvre, Paris. By permission of Art Resource.

Plato in his Laws permits not anyone to go and draw water from his neighbor's well, who has not first dug and sunk a pit in his own ground till he is come to a vein of clay, and has by his sounding experimented that the place will not yield a spring. For the clay or potter's earth, being of its own nature fatty, solid, and strong, retains the moisture it receives, and will not let it soak or pierce through. But it must be lawful for them to take water from another's ground, when there is no way or means for them to find any in their own; for the law ought to provide for men's necessity, but not for their laziness. Should there not be the like ordinance also concerning money; that none should be allowed to borrow money upon usury, nor to go and dive into other men's purses—as it were into their wells and fountains—before they have first searched at home and sounded every means for obtaining it; having collected (as it were) and gathered together all the gutters and springs, to try if they can draw from them what may suffice to supply their most necessary occasions? But on the contrary, many there are who,

to defray their idle expenses and to satisfy their extravagant and superfluous delights, make not use of their own, but have recourse to others, running themselves deeply into debt without any necessity. Now this may be easily judged, if one does but consider that usurers do not ordinarily lend to those which are in distress, but only to such as desire to obtain somewhat that is superfluous and of which they stand not in need. So that the credit given by the lender is a testimony sufficiently proving that the borrower has of his own; whereas on the contrary, since he has of his own, he ought to keep himself from borrowing.

Why shouldst thou go and make thy court to a banker or a merchant? Borrow from thine own table. Thou hast tankards, dishes, and basins of silver. Make use of them for thy necessity, and when they are gone to supply thy wants, the pleasant town of Aulis or isle of Tenedos will again refurnish thy board with fair vessels of earth, far more cleanly and neat than those of silver. For they are not scented with strong and unpleasant smell of usury, which, like rust, daily more and more sullies and tarnishes the luster of thy sumptuous magnificence. They will not be every day putting thee in mind of the Kalends and new moons, which, being of themselves the most holy and sacred days of the months, are by reason of usuries rendered the most odious and accursed. For as to those who choose rather to carry their goods to the brokers and there lay them in pawn for money taken upon usury than to sell them outright, I do not believe that Jupiter Ctesius himself can preserve them from beggary. They are ashamed forsooth to receive the full price and value of their goods; but they are not ashamed to pay use for the money they have borrowed on them. And yet the great and wise Pericles caused that costly ornament of fine gold, weighing about forty talents, with which Minerva's statue was adorned, to be made in such a manner that he could take it off and on at his pleasure; to the end (said he) that when we shall stand in need of money to support the charges of war, we may take it and make use of it, putting afterwards in its place another of no less value. Thus we ought in our affairs, as in a besieged town, never to admit or receive the hostile garrison of a usurer, nor to endure before our eyes the delivering up of our goods into perpetual servitude; but rather to cut off from our table what is neither necessary nor profitable, and in like manner from our beds, our couches, and our ordinary expenses, and so to keep ourselves free and at liberty, in hopes to restore again what we shall have retrenched, if Fortune shall hereafter smile upon us.

The Roman ladies heretofore willingly parted with their jewels and ornaments of gold, for the making a cup to be sent as an offering to the temple of Apollo Pythius in the city of Delphi. And the Carthaginian matrons did with their own hands cut the hair from their heads, to make cords for the managing of their warlike engines and instruments, in the defense of their besieged city. But we, as if we were ashamed of being able to stand on our own legs without being supported by the assistance of others, go and enslave ourselves by engagements and obligations; whereas it were much better that, restraining our ambition and confining it to what is profitable for us, we should of our useless and superfluous plate, which we should either melt or sell, build a temple of Liberty for ourselves, our wives, and our children. The Goddess Diana in the city of Ephesus gives to such debtors as can fly into her temple freedom and protection against their creditors; but the sanctuary of parsimony and moderation in expenses, into which no usurer can enter to pluck thence and carry away any debtor prisoner, is always open for the prudent, and affords them a long and large space of joyful and honorable repose. For as the prophetess which gave oracles in the temple of the Pythian Apollo, about the time of the Persian wars, answered the Athenians, that God had for their safety given them a wall of wood, upon which, forsaking their lands, their city, their houses, and all their goods, they had recourse to their ships for the preservation of their liberty; so God gives us a table of wood, vessels of earth, and garments of coarse cloth, if we desire to live and continue in freedom.

"Aim not at gilded coaches, steeds of price,
And harness, richly wrought with quaint
    device";

for how swiftly soever they may run, yet will usuries overtake them and outrun them.

Take rather the first ass thou shalt meet or the first pack-horse that shall come in thy way, and fly from that cruel and tyrannical enemy the usurer, who asks thee not earth and water, as heretofore did the barbarous king of Persia, but—which is worse—touches thy liberty, and wounds thy honor by proscriptions. If thou payest him not, he troubles thee; if thou hast wherewithal to satisfy him, he will not receive it, unless it be his pleasure. If thou sellest, he will have thy goods for nothing, or at a very moderate rate; and if thou wilt not sell, he will force thee to it; if thou suest him, he speaks to thee of an accommodation; if thou swearest to give him content, he will domineer over thee; if thou goest to his house to discourse with him, he shuts his door against thee; if thou stayest at home, he is always knocking at thy door and will never stir from thee.

Of what use to the Athenians was the decree of Solon, by which he ordained that the body should not be obliged for any public debt? For they who owe are in bondage to all bankers, and not to them alone (for then there would be no great hurt), but to their very slaves, who are proud, insolent, barbarous, and outrageous, and in a word exactly such as Plato describes the devils and fiery executioners to be, who in hell torment the souls of the wicked. For thus do these wretched usurers make the court where justice is administered a hell to the poor debtors, preying on some and gnawing them, vulture-like, to the very bones, and

"Piercing into their entrails with sharp beaks";

standing over others, who are, like so many Tantaluses, prohibited by them from tasting the corn and fruits of their own ground and drinking the wine of their own vintage. And as King Darius sent to the city of Athens his lieutenants Datis and Artaphernes with chains and cords, to bind the prisoners they should take; so these usurers, bringing into Greece boxes full of schedules, bills, and obligatory contracts, as so many irons and fetters for the shackling of poor criminals, go through the cities, sowing in them, as they pass, not good and profitable seed—as did heretofore Triptolemus, when he went through all places teaching the people to sow corn—but roots and grains of debts, that produce infinite labors and intolerable usuries, of which the end can never be found, and which, eating their way and spreading their sprouts round about, do in fine make cities bend under the burden, till they come to be suffocated. They say that hares at the same time suckle one young leveret, are ready to kindle and bring forth another, and conceive a third; but the usuries of these barbarous and wicked usurers bring forth before they conceive. For at the very delivery of their money, they immediately ask it back, taking it up at the same moment they lay it down; and they let out that again to interest which they take for the use of what they have lent before. . . .

DIO(N) CHRYSOSTOMOS (DIO COCCEIANUS)
(CA. A.D. 40–CA. 115)

The Hunters of Euboea

From Prusa, in Bithynia, Dio Chrysostomos was an aristocratic Hellenistic philosopher and teacher of rhetoric who came into favor with the Emperor Vespasian in Egypt, and subsequently moved to Rome under Domitian. Exiled from Rome in A.D. 82 for his association with Titus and Flavius Sabinus, who conspired against the emperor, the orator traveled in virtuous poverty for fourteen years in the farthest northern points of the Empire.

- He was called "Chrysostomos" ("golden-mouthed") because of his eloquent oratory. Eighty of his essay-like orations and public speeches survive, on topics as diverse as ethics, philosophy, and politics. His style is classical, modeled upon that of Plato and Demosthenes.
- When Domitian died, Dio Chrysostomos returned to Rome and eventually returned to imperial favor under Trajan. "The Hunters of Euboea" is taken from his "Euboean Speech" *(Euboicus),* dealing metaphorically and sociologically with virtue and poverty in the peninsular island of Euboea.

The story I shall tell is not a thing I heard from others, but what I myself saw. Wordiness is an old man's way: It is not easy to put a graybeard off once he has begun to talk. But maybe it is a vagabond's way too. The reason is old men and vagabonds alike have lived through much and like to recall their experiences. What I shall tell about are some men I met practically in the heart of Greece, and the kind of life they lived.

I happened to be sailing across from Chios with some fishermen. Summer voyaging was over and our craft was tiny, so when a storm blew up we barely got safe to the Hollows of Euboea. The fishermen ran their boat up on a rough shingle under the cliffs and smashed it, then went off to join some purple fishers who were moored at a nearby spur. Their thought was to stay there and work with the purple fishers. I was left all alone. I knew no city where I might find shelter, and so roamed down by the sea in the hope of spying some boat sailing by or riding at anchor. For a considerable piece I rambled on without seeing a living creature, but then did I spy a deer which had tumbled down the cliff and was gasping its life away on the shingle, where the waves were sweeping over it. After a bit I thought I heard dogs barking above me, but it was hard to be sure on account of the noise from the sea. I went forward and with great exertion climbed the height, from which I saw the actual dogs, baffled and running in circles; it was they, I conjectured, who had forced the creature to jump down the cliff. Presently I saw a man. By his looks and dress I judged he was a hunter. He had a healthy beard to his face, not just the ordinary shabby shag behind that Homer says the Euboeans who went to Troy had. Homer was having his joke at the expense of the Euboeans, I am sure: While the other Achaeans made a fine show the Euboeans were half tonsured.

The man accosted me: "Stranger, have you seen a startled deer hereabouts?" "Yonder he is now in the surf," said I to him, and then took him and pointed it out to him. He dragged it out of the surf and flayed its skin off with his knife, with me trying to help as best I could. Then he lopped off the hindquarters to take home with the hide. He invited me to come along too, and share his venison feast. His house, he said, was no great distance off. . . .

We had about five miles to go, and as we walked he told me all about himself and the kind of life he led with his wife and children. "There are two of us, stranger," said he, "who live in the same place. Each is married to the sister of the other, and we have children, both boys and girls. We live by hunting for the most part, but we work a bit of land, too. The place is not really ours; we neither inherited nor bought it. Our fathers were free men, indeed, but just as poor as we. They were herdsmen, and kept cattle for a rich man who lived on this island. This man owned many herds of horses and cows, many sheep, many fine fields, many other valuables, and all these hills. When he died his property was confiscated—people say the emperor did him in for his property. His herds were immediately driven off to be butchered, and with them our own few head of cattle. Nobody paid our wages. For the time we could only stay where we had been keeping the cattle. We had built huts and a wooden corral for the calves. It was not very big or very sturdy, but a makeshift for the summer. In the winter we used to graze in the plain, where we had plenty of pasturage and a good store of fodder, but in the summer we would drive the cattle to the hills. It was this place our fathers chose for their steading. . . .

"There, then, our fathers stayed on in their huts, waiting to find some employer or work. They supported themselves by a tiny plot they cultivated near the byre; being well manured, it satisfied their needs. With no cows to keep them busy they turned to hunting; sometimes by themselves, sometimes with dogs. Two shepherd dogs had followed the cattle for quite a distance, but when they could not find their masters they left the herd and returned to the huts. At first these dogs would merely follow along, as if they had some different business. If they sighted wolves they would chase them a piece, but they were not interested in boars or deer. But if ever they sighted a bear, early or late, they would make a stand yelping and fending him off as if it were a man they were fighting. When they had got the taste of blood and had got used to pork and venison, they learned new tricks late in life and got a liking for meat instead of bread. If any game was taken they gorged; if not they starved, and so they paid more attention to hunting and chased everything they sighted. Somehow or other they managed to pick up scents and trails, and from shepherd dogs they turned into hunting hounds, late learners, to be sure, and a little slow.

"When winter came on there was no work in sight; they could find none in town or in any village. So they boarded up the walls of their huts and made their yard stouter and so got through the winter. Now they worked the whole of their plot, and winter made hunting easier. Tracks marked on damp ground are clearer, and the snow makes them visible at a distance. This made a kind of highway to the game, and there was no need to bother with searching it out. The animals, too, were sluggish, and waited to be caught; rabbits and deer could actually be taken in their lairs. From that time on our fathers continued that kind of life and wanted no other. And they got us married, each giving his daughter to the other's son. Both died about a year ago; the years of their lives were many, but their bodies were still rugged and youthful and vigorous. Of our mothers only mine is still living.

"My comrade has never been down to town at all, though he is fifty years old. I have been down twice, once as a boy with my father, when we still had the cows, and later when a man came to ask for money. He imagined we had some, and ordered us to come to the city with him. We hadn't any money, and swore we hadn't: we'd have given it to him if we had had any. We gave him the best hospitality we could, and made him a present of two deerskins. It was I that went to the city with him, for he said

that one of us must by all means go and explain how things were.

"The sights were like those I had seen on my other trip. There were many large houses and a strong wall outside, and high, square rooms on the wall. There were many boats riding at anchor, completely motionless, as if it were a lake. There is nothing like that here where you landed, and that is why ships are wrecked. That is what I saw. It is a great crowd of people shut into the same place and a frightening roar and shouting; I thought they were all fighting with one another. Well, the man brought me before certain magistrates and said with a laugh, 'This is the fellow you sent me for. He has nothing but his long hair and a hut of very strong timbers.' The magistrates strode to the theater, and I with them. The theater is a sort of hollow valley, not, however, straight up and down, but half round. It is not a natural formation, but built of stones. You are probably laughing at me for explaining what you know perfectly well.

"At first the crowd spent a long time attending to other business. They kept shouting, sometimes amiably and with good temper, when they wished to applaud, but sometimes angrily and in bad temper. . . .

"At last they settled down, and in an interval of quiet they brought me forward. One man spoke out: 'This man, gentlemen, is one of those who have been exploiting our public domain for many years, and not he alone, but his father before him. They graze our hills, they farm, they hunt, they build many houses, they set out vines, and they have many other good things, but they pay no one any rent for the land, nor have they received it from the state as a gift. For what services could they ever have received it? They hold in possession what is ours, and though they wax rich on it they never perform any public service whatever nor pay any share of their income in tax. Without paying taxes or contributing the required services they go blithely on as if they were exempted for benefactions to the city. I verily believe,' he continued, 'that they have never even come here before.' I shook my head, and the crowd laughed when they saw. The laughter infuriated the speaker, and he abused me for it. Then he turned back to the crowd and said, 'If you approve of these things so heartily, we had all better lose no time in looting the public property. Some can take the city's money, as certain persons are surely doing this moment, and some can squat upon the land without your consent, if you are going to let these beasts hold as dowry more than two hundred and fifty acres of fine land, from which you could collect three Attic quarts of grain for each citizen.'

"When I heard this I laughed as hard as I could. But the crowd did not laugh as before: Now they raised a tumult. The man grew angry and gave me a terrible stare. 'Do you notice the sarcasm and impudence of that scum?' he said. 'Do you mark how brazenly he laughs? I am minded to jail him, and his partner too. The two, I understand, are ringleaders of the gang that has grabbed virtually all the land in our hills. Nor do these same fellows, I am sure, keep their hands from the wrecks that are from time to time cast up on rocks of Caphereus; they live just above the place. How else would they acquire such valuable fields—whole villages, I had better say—and such quantities of cattle, work animals, and slaves? Perhaps you have no-

ticed how shabby his smock is and the skin he has put on to come here, on purpose to deceive you into thinking he is a pauper and has nothing. For my part,' said he, 'when I look at him I am almost frightened, as I imagine I should be if I saw Nauplius himself coming from Caphereus. I verily believe he lights beacons on the heights to lure mariners onto the rocks.' As he was saying these things and much more besides, the crowd growled savagely. I was at a loss, and feared they might do me some mischief.

"There came forward then another speaker, a kindly man, to judge from the words he spoke and from his appearance. First he asked the people to be quiet, and they did fall silent.

And then in a gentle voice he told them that people who worked idle land and put it into condition committed no wrong, but on the contrary might justly receive commendation. Not those who cultivated public land and planted it should be penalized, but those who ruined it. 'Even now, gentlemen,' he said, 'almost two thirds of our country is desolate because of neglect and depopulation. I, too, own many acres, as I imagine others here do, not only in the hills but also in the plains, and if anyone were willing to farm them I should not only let him do so gratis, but gladly pay him money besides. Obviously their value is increased, and besides land that is lived on and worked makes an agreeable sight. Wasteland is not only a useless encumbrance to its owner but a pitiful advertisement of the master's misfortune.

"'In my judgment, therefore, you should rather encourage as many other citizens as you can to take some of the public land and work it.

Those who have some capital should take more, and the poor as much as each can manage. Thus your land would be worked, and the citizens who volunteer relieved of two great evils, idleness and poverty. For ten years let them hold the land without charges, and after that period let them pay a small assessment on their tilth, but none on livestock. If a non-citizen works the land he too should pay nothing for five years, and thereafter twice the sum citizens pay. And any non-citizen who works as many as fifty acres ought to be given citizenship, in order to encourage the greatest possible number. As things are now the land outside our very gates has run wild and is extremely ugly, as if it were some deep wilderness and not the approach of a city. Inside the walls, furthermore, most of the land is sown or grazed. In view of this,' said he, 'the conduct of our orators is very strange. Against the hard-working people of Caphereus, in a remote corner of Euboea, they trump up charges, but they see no harm in men plowing up the gymnasium and grazing cattle in the market square. See for yourselves: Your gymnasium they have made into a grainfield, and the stalks have completely hidden the Heracles and many other statues; heroes and gods are covered. Every day sheep belonging to the previous speaker take over the market square at dawn and graze around the senate house and administration buildings. When strangers first come to our city some of them laugh at it and others pity it.' When the crowd heard this they directed their fury against the first speaker and raised a clamor.

" 'That sort of thing the man does himself,' he continued, 'but he holds that ordinary folk who struggle for livelihood ought to be jailed. Obviously he intends that no one shall work in future; those outside the city must turn highwaymen and those inside footpads. I propose that we remit to these men what they themselves have created. For the future let them pay a moderate tax, but they must not be obligated for arrears. They have earned remission by putting under cultivation land that was deserted and useless. If they wish to put down a price for the land, we must sell it to them for less than to others.' After this speech the first man spoke in rebuttal, and there were harsh words on both sides. At length I too was bidden to say whatever I liked.

" 'What kind of thing must I say?' said I. 'Speak to what has been said,' said a man in the audience. 'Then I say,' said I, 'that there is no truth at all in what he said. When he babbled on about fields and villages and the like I thought, sirs, that I must be dreaming. We have no villages or horses or asses or cattle. I wish we did have all the fine things he mentions: We could give some to you and be rich ourselves. But what we do have is enough for us, and if you want any of it, take it. Take it all, if you like; we shall get another supply.' They applauded what I said, and the magistrate then asked me what we could give the people. 'Four very fine deerskins,' said I. Most of the people laughed, and the magistrate was vexed at me. 'I offer the deer because the bearskins are tough,' said I, 'and the goatskins are not their equal; some are old and some are small. But if you like take them too.' Again the man was vexed, and called me a stupid field hand. 'There you go talking about fields again,' said I. 'Didn't you hear me say that we have no fields?'

"The magistrate now asked whether we

would be willing to contribute one hundred pounds each. 'We do not weigh our meat,' I said, 'but whatever it amounts to we will give it to you. A little of it is salted down, and the rest is smoked, but nearly as good. There are sides of bacon and venison and other fine meat.' There was an uproar indeed at this point, and they said I was lying. But the man went on to ask me whether we had any grain, and how much. I told him the whole truth. 'Three bushels of wheat,' I said, 'six of barley, the same of millet, but only four quarts of beans: they did not thrive this year. You take the wheat and barley,' said I, 'and leave us the millet. But if you need millet take that too.' 'Don't you make any wine?' another man asked. 'We do,' I said; 'if any of you comes we shall let him have it. But be sure to bring a wineskin, for we haven't any.' 'How many vines have you?' 'Two,' said I, 'at the house door, twenty inside the yard, and the same number on the other side of the creek, which we lately set out. They are very fine and produce big clusters, when passersby let them be. But to save you the trouble of asking item by item I shall tell you what else we have: eight she-goats, a mulley cow, her pretty calf, four sickles, four hoes, three spears, and each of us has a knife for hunting. For crockery . . . But why speak of that? We have wives and children. We live in two fine huts, and there is a third for storing the grain and the skins.' 'Yes, by Zeus,' the speaker said, 'and for burying your money, too, belike.' 'Then go and dig it up, fool. Who buries money? It doesn't grow, you know.' Here everybody laughed, and I thought it was him they were laughing at.

" 'That is what we have. If you want all of it we will give it you for the asking: You don't have to seize it from us as if we were foreigners or wicked folk unwilling to give it up. We, too, mark you, are citizens of this city, as my father used to say. Once when he came here there was a distribution of cash bonuses to citizens, and he got his with the rest. Our children, too, we are raising to be your fellow citizens, and if you are ever in need they will help you, against robbers or enemies. Now, of course, there is peace; but if such an emergency should arise you will pray for more like us to show up. Don't imagine that this speaker here will ever fight for you; he can scold, of course, like a woman. We will give you a share of meat and hides when we catch any game; just send someone to fetch them. If you bid us pull our huts down we shall pull them down if they harm you. But then give us housing here, else how can we endure this winter? There are plenty of houses inside your walls which no one lives in; one of them will be enough for us. But if we do not live here, if we do not add to the congestion of so many people living in the same spot, does that make us candidates for resettlement?' . . .

"While I was making my speech a man in the audience arose, and I thought to myself, 'There was another of the same ilk, doubtless ready to lie about me.' But this is what he said: 'Gentlemen, I have long been in two minds about this man. I could not believe he was the man I thought, but now I am positive that he is. It would be criminal, or worse, sinful, not to declare what I know and render payment in mere words for the substantial acts of kindness I experienced. I am, as you are aware, a citizen,' he continued, and, pointing to his neighbor who then also rose from his seat, said, 'and so is this man. Two years ago it happened that we were sailing in Socles' boat. The boat was wrecked off Caphereus, with the loss of all but very few of its passengers. Of these some were taken in by purple fishers, for they had money in their purses. But we were stripped bare when we were cast up, and so walked along a track hoping to find some shepherds' or cowherds' shelter. We might have died of hunger and thirst, but after a struggle got to some huts, where we stopped and called for help. This man came up and brought us in and kindled a slow fire, which he increased by degrees. He himself rubbed one of us down and his wife the other—with lard, for they had no oil. Finally they poured warm water over us until they brought us round; we had been numb with cold. Then they made us lie down, covered us with what they had, and put wheat loaves before us to eat. They themselves ate parched millet, and they gave us wine to drink while they themselves drank water. Venison was plentiful, both roasted and boiled. The next day we wanted to leave, but they kept us for three days. Then they saw us down to the plain, and when we left gave us meat and a very fine skin for each of us. When he noticed that my health was still delicate from my recent exposure, he put a little tunic on me which he took off his daughter; she wrapped another rag round herself. When we got to a village I gave the tunic back. Next after the gods, then, it is due to this man that we have survived.'

"The people had listened to the man's speech with pleasure and they applauded me. Now I recollected the incident. I called out, 'Hello, Sotades!' I went up and kissed him and the other man. When I did so the people

laughed heartily, and then I realized that in the cities people do not kiss one another. Then that kindly man who had spoken for me in the beginning came forward and said, 'I propose, gentlemen, that we invite this man to dine in the town hall. If he had saved one of our citizens by shielding him in war he would have obtained many fine gifts. Now he has saved two citizens, and perhaps others who are not here: Does he deserve no reward at all? In return for the tunic which he stripped from his daughter to give to our citizen in distress, the city ought to give him a cloak as well as a tunic. This would serve as an encouragement to others to be righteous and help one another. The free use of the farm should be voted to these men and their children, and no one must trouble them. Furthermore the man should be given a hundred drachmas for tools: This sum I offer from my own funds on behalf of the city.' For this offer he was applauded, and his other proposals were carried out. The clothes and the money were brought to the theater at once. I didn't wish to accept them, but they said, 'You can't dine in the skin!' 'Well, then,' said I, 'I shall go dinnerless today.' They put the tunic on notwithstanding, and threw the cloak over my shoulders. I wanted to throw my skin on top, but they wouldn't let me. The money they could not force upon me; I swore I would not take it. 'If you are looking for someone who will take it,' said I, 'give it to that orator and let him bury it; he is obviously expert in the business.' From that time on no one has molested us."

He had hardly finished his tale when we arrived at the huts. I said with a smile, "One thing you kept hidden from your fellow citizens, and it is the finest possession of all."

"What is that?" said he. "This garden," I said; "it is very pretty and has many vegetables and trees." "It wasn't here then," he said; "we made it later." Then we went in and spent the rest of the day feasting. We reclined on a mattress of leaves and skins piled high, and the wife sat near her husband. A daughter of marriageable age waited on us and poured us a sweet dark wine to drink. The boys prepared the meat, and they themselves dined as they served. I felici-tated those people and thought their life blessed beyond any I knew. And yet I knew the houses and tables of the rich, and not of private individuals only, but of vice-regents and kings. Those latter I had always thought wretched, but particularly so when I saw liberty combined with poverty in that hut. Not even in the plea-sures of food and drink did they fall short; even here they had something of an advantage. . . .

LUCIAN (CA. A.D. 115–CA. 180)
Lyrics and Dialogues

$\mathcal{L}$ucian, from the banks of the Euphrates in Syrian Samosata, was trained as a stonemason but soon tired of blue-collar work and learned enough law to work as an itinerant advocate. Beginning his literary career as a sophist who earned his living from his public lectures, he turned to writing, in model Attic, philosophical satires and satirical lyrics and became known far and wide for his trenchant wit and personal insight.

- A frequent traveler, he was at home as much in Asia and Gaul (France) as in Greece and Italy. By the age of forty, he had settled in Athens, where he came under the influence of the Stoic Demonax as well as the Old Comedy of Aristophanes.
- Even his shortest lyrics are zingers, castigating, like his successor the French Villon, the fol-lies of the human comedy he saw around him everywhere he looked. His longer works in-clude *The Dialogues of the Gods, Peregrinus Proteus, The Dialogues of Courtesans, The Cock, How to Write History, The True History, Charon, Descent into Hades, Menippus, The Dialogues of the Dead, The Sale of Lives, Peregrinus,* and *Alexander.*

"PLAIN LIVING AND HIGH THINKING"

Stern Cynicus doth war austerely wage
With endive, lentils, chicory, and sage;
Which shouldst thou thoughtless proffer,
    "Wretch," saith he,
"Wouldst thou corrupt my life's simplicity?"
Yet is not his simplicity so great
But that he can digest a pomegranate;
And peaches, he esteems, right well agree
With Spartan fare and sound philosophy.

A FIELD

Cleon's I was, to Cleitophon was sold;
Another's soon; soon will another hold
What each calls his; but the pure truth to say,
Fortune's I am and I shall be alway.

Priapus, by devout Actemon placed
Protector of his garden's weedy waste,
Warns all disposed to search its bounds for
    pelf
That there is nought to steal except himself.

Poseidon, and all Ocean-deities,
Lucillius, 'scaped from shipwreck on the seas,
Doth dedicate to ye who bade him live
His hair, for nothing else is left to give.

A child of five short years, unknown to woe,
Callimachus my name, I rest below.
Mourn not my fate. If few the joys of life,
Few were its ills, its conflicts; brief its strife.

All mortal things from mortals glide,
And they from all that doth abide.

DIALOGUES OF THE GODS—I

PROMETHEUS OBTAINS HIS RELEASE FROM ZEUS BY A PROPHECY

Prometheus: Set me free, O Zeus, for I have already endured dreadful sufferings.

Zeus: Set you free, say you? you who ought to have heavier fetters, and all Caucasus heaped on your head; and not only your liver gnawed by sixteen vultures, but also your eyes scooped out, in return for your fashioning such animals as men, and for stealing my fire, and fabricating women. As for the tricks you put upon me in your distribution of the flesh meats, in offering me bones wrapped up in fat, and reserving the better portion of the pieces for yourself, why need I speak?

Prometheus: Have I then not paid enough penalty, nailed for such a long period of time to Caucasus, supporting that most cursed of winged creatures, the vulture, with my liver?

Zeus: Not an infinitesimal part that of what you ought to suffer.

Prometheus: Yet you shall not release me without recompense. But I will impart something to you, Zeus, exceedingly important.

Zeus: You are for outwitting me, Prometheus.

Prometheus: And what advantage should I gain? For you will not be ignorant hereafter of the whereabouts of Caucasus; neither will you be in want of chains, should I be caught playing you any trick.

Zeus: Say, first, what sort of equivalent you will pay, of so much importance to us.

Prometheus: If I tell you for what purpose you are now on your travels, shall I have credit with you, when I prophesy about the rest?

Zeus: Of course.

Prometheus: You are off to Thetis, to an intrigue with her.

Zeus: That indeed you have correct knowledge of. But what then, after that? For you seem to have some inkling of the truth.

Prometheus: Don't have anything to do with the Nereid, Zeus: for, if she should be pregnant by you, her progeny will treat you exactly as you, too, treated—

Zeus: This do you assert—that I shall be expelled from my kingdom?

Prometheus: Heaven forbid, Zeus! Intercourse with her, however, threatens something of the kind.

Zeus: Good-bye to Thetis, then. And as for you, for these timely warnings Hephaestus shall set you free.

2: ZEUS THREATENS TO PUT EROS IN FETTERS

Eros: Well, if I have really done wrong at all, Zeus, pardon me; for I am but an infant, and still without sense.

Zeus: You an infant—you the Eros, who are far older than Iapetus? Because you have not grown a beard, and don't show gray hairs, do you really claim on that account to be considered an infant, when, in fact, you are an old scamp?

Eros: But what great injury have I—the old scamp, as you call me—done you, that you intend putting me in irons?

Zeus: Consider, accursed rascal, whether they are trifling injuries you have done me, you, who make such sport of me, that there is nothing which you have not turned me into—satyr, bull, gold, swan, eagle—but not any one of them have you made to be in love with me at all; nor have I perceived that, for anything that depends upon you, I have been agreeable to any woman; but I am obliged to have recourse to juggling tricks against them, and to conceal my proper self, while they are really in love with the bull or swan, and, if they have but a glimpse of me, they die of fear.

Eros: Naturally enough, Zeus, for, being mortal women, they can't endure the sight of your person.

Zeus: How is it, then, that Branchus and Hyacinthus love Apollo?

Eros: But even from him the beauty, Daphne, fled away, for all his flowing locks and beardless chin. If you wish to be loved, don't shake your aegis, and don't take your thunderbolt with you; but make yourself as agreeable as you can, letting down your locks on both sides of your face, and tying them up again under your coronet; wear a fine purple dress, put on golden sandals, step along keeping time to the sounds of the pipe and cymbals, and you will see that more women will follow you than all the Maenads of Bacchus.

Zeus: Get away with you. I would not take the offer of being loved, on condition of becoming such a figure.

Eros: Then, Zeus, don't wish to love, either: That, at all events, is an easy matter.

Zeus: Not so; but I do wish to love, and to enjoy their society in a less vexatious fashion. Upon this, and this condition alone, I let you go.

DIALOGUES OF THE SEA-GODS—II

POLYPHEMUS COMPLAINS TO POSEIDON, HIS FATHER, OF HIS TREATMENT AT THE HANDS OF ODYSSEUS

Cyclops (blubbering):   O father, what have I endured at the hands of the accursed stranger, who made me drunk and put out my eye, assaulting me when I was lulled to sleep.

Poseidon: Who dared to do this, my poor Polyphemus?

Cyclops: In the first instance, he called himself Outis; but, when he had got clear away, and was out of reach of my arrow, he said that his name was Odysseus.

Poseidon: I know whom you speak of—him of Ithaka, and he was on his return-voyage from Ilium. But how did he do it, for he is, by no means, a man of too much courage?

Cyclops: Returning from my accustomed tending of my flocks, I caught a number of fellows in my cave, evidently having designs on my herds: for, when I placed the stone block against the door—the rock is of huge size—and had lighted the fire by igniting the tree which I brought from the mountain, evidently they appeared to be trying to conceal themselves. Well, when I had got hold of some of them, I devoured them for a pack of thieves, as was reasonable. Hereupon that most villainous rascal, whether he was Outis or Odysseus, pours out a sort of drug and gives me to drink—sweet, indeed, and of delicious smell, but most insidious, and which caused great disorder in my head: for immediately upon my drinking everything seemed to me to be in a whirl, and the cave itself was turned upside down, and I was no longer at all in my senses; and, at last, I was dragged down into sleep. Then sharpening the bar, and igniting it besides, he blinded me as I slept, and from that time, I am a blind man, at your service, Poseidon.

Poseidon: How soundly you slept, my son, that you did not jump up while you were being blinded! But as for this Odysseus, then, how did he escape? For he could not—I am well assured that he could not—move away the rock from the door.

Cyclops: Yes, but it was I who removed it, that I might the better catch him as he was going out; and, sitting down close to the door, I groped for him with extended hands, letting only my sheep pass out to pasture, after having given instructions to the ram what he was to do in my place.

Poseidon: I understand, they slipped away under them unnoticed. But you ought to have shouted, and called the rest of the Cyclopes to your aid against him.

Cyclops: I did summon them, father, and they came. But when they asked the sneaking rascal's name, and I said it was Outis, thinking I was in a mad fit, they took themselves off at once. Thus the cursed fellow tricked me with his name; and what especially vexes me is, that actually throwing my misfortune in my teeth, "Not even," says he, "will your father Poseidon cure you."

Poseidon: Never mind, my child, for I will revenge myself upon him, that he may learn that, even if it is not possible for me to heal the mutilation of people's eyes, at all events the fate of voyagers is in my hands. And he is still at sea.

PTOLEMY (FL. A.D. 121–151)
The Almagest

❦

*C*laudius Ptolemaeus began his life in Ptolemais Hermiou, Egypt, and spent most of his productive career in Alexandria. Though primarily an astronomer, he also taught and wrote on mathematics, music, optics, mechanics, the history of Egypt, and geography.

- In his eight-book *Geography,* Ptolemy outlined the rules and calculations, including tables listing latitude and longitude and climate in Africa, Asia, and Europe, to be used in mapping the world. Though considered to be authoritative until after the Renaissance, Ptolemy's geography was flawed by his basing data more on travelers' tales than on astronomical observations. He underestimated the circumference of the earth by a third, and his overestimate of the eastern extension of Asia led Christopher Columbus to believe he could reach the east by sailing west.

- His most important astronomical work, the thirteen-book *Almagest,* written with passion and clarity, used spherical trigonometry as the basis for improving the calculations of his predecessor Hipparchus. In the Ptolemaic system, in general favor until the time of Nicolaus Copernicus, the earth is considered the fixed center of the universe, around which the sun, moon, and planets revolve. His star catalog contained 1,022 stars.

. . . 4. (THAT THE EARTH TOO, TAKEN AS A WHOLE, IS SENSIBLY SPHERICAL)

That the earth, too, taken as a whole, is sensibly spherical can best be grasped from the following considerations. We can see, again, that the sun, moon, and other stars do not rise and set simultaneously for everyone on earth, but do so earlier for those more toward the east, later for those toward the west. For we find that the phenomena at eclipses, especially lunar eclipses, which take place at the same time [for all observers], are nevertheless not recorded as occurring at the same hour (that is at an equal distance from noon) by all observers. Rather, the hour recorded by the more easterly observers is always later than that recorded by the more westerly. We find that the differences in the hour are proportional to the distances between the places [of observation]. Hence one can reasonably conclude that the earth's surface is spherical, because its evenly curving surface (for so it is when considered as a whole) cuts off [the heavenly bodies] for each set of observers in turn in a regular fashion.

If the earth's shape were any other, this would not happen, as one can see from the following arguments. If it were concave, the stars would be seen rising first by those more toward the west; if it were plane, they would rise and set simultaneously for everyone on earth; if it were triangular or square or any other polygonal shape, by a similar argument, they would rise and set simultaneously for all those living on the same plane surface. Yet it is apparent that nothing like this takes place. Nor could it be cylindrical, with the curved surface in the east-west direction, and the flat sides towards the poles of the universe, which some might suppose more plausible. This is clear from the following: For those living on the curved surface none of the stars would be ever-visible, but either all stars would rise and set for all observers, or the same stars, for an equal [celestial] distance from each of the poles, would always be invisible for all observers. In fact, the farther we travel toward the north, the more of the southern stars disappear and the more of the northern stars appear. Hence it is clear that here too the curvature of the earth cuts off [the heavenly bodies] in a regular fashion in a north-south direction, and proves the sphericity [of the earth] in all directions.

There is the further consideration that if we sail toward mountains or elevated places from and to any direction whatever, they are observed to increase gradually in size as if rising up from the sea itself in which they had previously been submerged: this is due to the curvature of the surface of the water.

5. (THAT THE EARTH IS IN THE MIDDLE OF THE HEAVENS)

Once one has grasped this, if one next considers the position of the earth, one will find that the phenomena associated with it could take place only if we assume that it is in the middle of the heavens, like the center of a sphere. For if this were not the case, the earth would have to be either

(a) not on the axis [of the universe] but equidistant from both poles, or
(b) on the axis but removed toward one of the poles, or
(c) neither on the axis nor equidistant from both poles.

Against the first of these three positions militate the following arguments. If we imagined [the earth] removed towards the zenith or the nadir of some observer, then, if he were at *sphaera recta*, he would never experience equinox, since the horizon would always divide the heavens into two unequal parts, one above and one below the earth; if he were at *sphaera obliqua*, either, again, equinox would never occur at all, or, [if it did occur] it would not be at a position halfway between summer and winter solstices, since these intervals would necessarily be unequal, because the equator, which is the greatest of all parallel circles drawn about the poles of the [daily] motion, would no longer be

bisected by the horizon; instead [the horizon would bisect] one of the circles parallel to the equator, either to the north or to the south of it. Yet absolutely everyone agrees that these intervals are equal everywhere on earth, since [everywhere] the increment of the longest day over the equinoctial day at the summer solstice is equal to the decrement of the shortest day from the equinoctial day at the winter solstice. But if, on the other hand, we imagined the displacement to be toward the east or west of some observer, he would find that the sizes and distances of the stars would not remain constant and unchanged at eastern and western horizons, and that the time-interval from rising to culmination would not be equal to the interval from culmination to setting. This is obviously completely in disaccord with the phenomena.

Against the second position, in which the earth is imagined to lie on the axis removed toward one of the poles, one can make the following objections. If this were so, the plane of the horizon would divide the heavens into a part above the earth and a part below the earth which are unequal and always different for different latitudes, whether one considers the relationship of the same part at two different latitudes or the two parts at the same latitude. Only at *sphaera recta* could the horizon bisect the sphere; at a *sphaera obliqua* situation such that the nearer pole were the ever-visible one, the horizon would always make the part above the earth lesser and the part below the earth greater; hence another phenomenon would be that the great circle of the ecliptic would be divided into unequal parts by the plane of the horizon. Yet it is apparent that this is by no means so. Instead, six zodiacal signs are visible above the earth at all times and places, while the remaining six are invisible; then again [at a later time] the latter are visible in their entirety above the earth, while at the same time the others are not visible. Hence it is obvious that the horizon bisects the zodiac, since the same semicircles are cut off by it, so as to appear at one time completely above the earth, and at another [completely] below it.

And in general, if the earth were not situated exactly below the [celestial] equator, but were removed toward the north or south in the direction of one of the poles, the result would be that at the equinoxes the shadow of the gnomon at sunrise would no longer form a straight line with its shadow at sunset in a plane parallel to the horizon, not even sensibly. Yet this is a phenomenon which is plainly observed everywhere.

It is immediately clear that the third position enumerated is likewise impossible, since the sorts of objection which we made to the first [two] will both arise in that case.

To sum up, if the earth did not lie in the middle [of the universe], the whole order of things which we observe in the increase and decrease of the length of daylight would be fundamentally upset. Furthermore, eclipses of the moon would not be restricted to situations where the moon is diametrically opposite the sun (whatever part of the heaven [the luminaries are in]), since the earth would often come between them when they were not diametrically opposite, but at intervals of less than a semicircle.

6. (THAT THE EARTH HAS THE RATIO OF A POINT TO THE HEAVENS)

Moreover, the earth has, to the senses, the ratio of a point to the distance of the sphere of the so-called fixed stars. A strong indication of this is the fact that the sizes and distances of the stars, at any given time, appear equal and the same from all parts of the earth everywhere, as observations of the same [celestial] objects from different latitudes are found to have not the least discrepancy from each other. One must also consider the fact that gnomons set up in any part of the earth whatever, and likewise the centers of armillary spheres, operate like the real center of the earth; that is, the lines of sight [to heavenly bodies] and the paths of shadows caused by them agree as closely with the [mathematical] hypotheses explaining the phenomena as if they actually passed through the real center-point of the earth.

Another clear indication that this is so is that the planes drawn through the observer's lines of sight at any point [on earth], which we call "horizons," always bisect the whole heavenly sphere. This would not happen if the earth were of perceptible size in relation to the distance of the heavenly bodies; in that case only the plane drawn through the center of the earth could bisect the sphere, while a plane through any point on the surface of the earth would always make the section [of the heavens] below the earth greater than the section above it.

7. (THAT THE EARTH DOES NOT HAVE ANY MOTION FROM PLACE TO PLACE, EITHER)

One can show by the same arguments as the preceding that the earth cannot have any motion in the aforementioned directions, or indeed ever move at all from its position at the center. For the same phenomena would result as would if it had any position other than the central one. Hence I think it is idle to seek for causes for the motion of objects towards the center, once it has been so clearly established from the actual phenomena that the earth occupies the middle place in the universe, and that all heavy objects are carried toward the earth. The following fact alone would most readily lead one to this notion [that all objects fall towards the center]. In absolutely all parts of the earth, which, as we said, has been shown to be spherical and in the middle of the universe, the direction and path of the motion (I mean the proper, [natural] motion) of all bodies possessing weight is always and everywhere at right angles to the rigid plane drawn tangent to the point of impact. It is clear from this fact that, if [these falling objects] were not arrested by the surface of the earth, they would certainly reach the center of the earth itself, since the straight line to the center is also always at right angles to the plane tangent to the sphere at the point of intersection [of that radius] and the tangent.

Those who think it paradoxical that the earth, having such a great weight, is not supported by anything and yet does not move, seem to me to be making the mistake of judging on the basis of their own experience instead of taking into account the peculiar nature of the universe. They would not, I think, consider such a thing strange once they realized that this great bulk of the earth, when compared with the whole surrounding mass [of the universe], has the ratio of a point to it. For when one looks at it in that way, it will seem quite possible that that which is relatively smallest should be overpowered and pressed in equally from all directions to a position of equilibrium by that which is the greatest of all and of uniform nature. For there is no up and down in the universe with respect to itself, any more than one could imagine such a thing in a sphere; instead the proper and natural motion of the compound bodies in it is as follows: Light and rarefied bodies drift outward towards the circumference, but seem to move in the direction which is "up" for each observer, since the overhead direction for all of us, which is also called "up," points toward the surrounding surface; heavy and dense bodies, on the other hand, are carried toward the middle and the center, but seem to fall downward, because, again, the direction which is for all of us toward our feet, called "down," also points towards the center of the earth. These heavy bodies, as one would expect, settle about the center because of their mutual pressure and resistance, which is equal and uniform from all directions. Hence, too, one can see that it is plausible that the earth, since its total mass is so great compared with the bodies which fall toward it, can remain motionless under the impact of these very small weights (for they strike it from all sides), and receive, as it were, the objects falling on it. If the earth had a single motion in common with other heavy objects, it is obvious that it would be carried down faster than all of them because of its much greater size: Living things and individual heavy objects would be left behind, riding on the air, and the earth itself would very soon have fallen completely out of the heavens. But such things are utterly ridiculous merely to think of.

But certain people, [propounding] what they consider a more persuasive view, agree with the above, since they have no argument to bring against it, but think that there could be no evidence to oppose their view if, for instance, they supposed the heavens to remain motionless, and the earth to revolve from west to east about the same axis [as the heavens], making approximately one revolution each day; or if they made both heaven and earth move by any amount whatever, provided, as we said, it is about the same axis, and in such a way as to preserve the overtaking of one by the other. However, they do not realize that, although there is perhaps nothing in the celestial phenomena which would count against that hypothesis, at least from simpler considerations, nevertheless from what would occur here on earth and in the air, one can see that such a notion is quite ridiculous. Let us concede to them [for the sake of argument] that such an unnatural thing could happen as that the most rare and light of matter should either not move at all or should move in a way no different from that of matter with the opposite nature (although things in the air, which are less rare [than the heavens] so obviously move with a

more rapid motion than any earthy object); [let us concede that] the densest and heaviest objects have a proper motion of the quick and uniform kind which they suppose (although, again, as all agree, earthy objects are sometimes not readily moved even by an external force). Nevertheless, they would have to admit that the revolving motion of the earth must be the most violent of all motions associated with it, seeing that it makes one revolution in such a short time; the result would be that all objects not actually standing on the earth would appear to have the same motion, opposite to that of the earth: Neither clouds nor other flying or thrown objects would ever be seen moving toward the east, since the earth's motion toward the east would always outrun and overtake them, so that all other objects would seem to move in the direction of the west and the rear. But if they said that the air is carried around in the same direction and with the same speed as the earth, the compound objects in the air would nonetheless always seem to be left behind by the motion of both [earth and air]; or if those objects too were carried around, fused, as it were, to the air, then they would never appear to have any motion either in advance or rearwards: they would always appear still, neither wandering about nor changing position, whether they were flying or thrown objects. Yet we quite plainly see that they do undergo all these kinds of motion, in such a way that they are not even slowed down or speeded up at all by any motion of the earth. . . .

Apollodorus (FL. A.D. 140)
The Library

The Library, an invaluable systematization of the Greek gods, was attributed in ancient times to an Athenian grammarian and scholar of great learning and wide interests: Apollodorus of Athens. He was a prolific writer of grammar, mythology, geography, and history. Strabo was influenced by Apollodorus' works on geography. Apollodorus' *Chronicle* was a compendium of history from the Fall of Troy, which he dates at 1183 B.C., to his own time. He based his work primarily on the research of Eratosthenes, and composed in comic iambic trimeter. *The Library* deals with critical historical incidents, philosophical schools, and important individuals. Internal evidence shows that *The Library* could not have been composed earlier than 50 B.C. and probably not later than A.D. 150, though its omission of any reference to Rome still puzzles modern scholars. Apollodorus studied in Alexandria under Aristarchus and Panaetius the Stoic before returning to his native Athens, by way of Pergamum, where he remained until his death.

- *The Library* may well be related to a larger work, *On the Gods,* that was certainly by Apollodorus of Athens. Yet its uncritical nature, in some ways resembling the Hebrew Bible, is quite different from what we know of Apollodorus' rational approach to mythology in the earlier work, only fragments of which survive.
- Probably modeled on the lost mythography of the fifth-century B.C. Athenian Pherecydes of Leros, the surviving mythographic treatise on the gods and the heroic age traces traditional mythology from the most obscure ancient times to the historical era of Theseus. The treatise records, without philosophical or psychological distortion, what the Greeks once believed about their origins.

BOOK I

I. Sky was the first who ruled over the whole world. And having wedded Earth, he begat first the Hundred-handed, as they are named: Briareus, Gyes, Cottus, who were unsurpassed in size and might, each of them having a hundred hands and fifty heads. After these, Earth bore him the Cyclopes, to wit, Arges, Steropes, Brontes, of whom each had one eye on his forehead. But them Sky bound and cast into Tartarus, a gloomy place in Hades as far distant from earth as earth is distant from the sky. And again he begat children by Earth, to wit, the Titans as they are named: Ocean, Coeus, Hyperion, Crius, Iapetus, and youngest of all, Cronus; also daughters, the Titanides as they are called: Tethys, Rhea, Themis, Mnemosyne, Phoebe, Dione, Thia.

But Earth, grieved at the destruction of her children, who had been cast into Tartarus, persuaded the Titans to attack their father and gave Cronus an adamantine sickle. And they, all but Ocean, attacked him, and Cronus cut off his father's genitals and threw them into the sea; and from the drops of the flowing blood were born Furies, to wit, Alecto, Tisiphone, and Megaera. And, having dethroned their father, they brought up their brethren who had been hurled down to Tartarus, and committed the sovereignty to Cronus.

But he again bound and shut them up in Tartarus, and wedded his sister Rhea; and since both Earth and Sky foretold him that he would be dethroned by his own son, he used to swallow his offspring at birth. His first-born Hestia he swallowed, then Demeter and Hera, and after them Pluto and Poseidon. Enraged at this, Rhea repaired to Crete, when she was big with Zeus, and brought him forth in a cave of Dicte. She gave him to the Curetes and to the nymphs Adrastia and Ida, daughters of Melisseus, to nurse. So these nymphs fed the child on the milk of Amalthea; and the Curetes in arms guarded the babe in the cave, clashing their spears on their shields in order that Cronus might not hear the child's voice. But Rhea wrapped a stone in swaddling clothes and gave it to Cronus to swallow, as if it were the newborn child.

II. But when Zeus was full grown, he took Metis, daughter of Ocean, to help him, and she gave Cronus a drug to swallow, which forced him to disgorge first the stone and then the children whom he had swallowed, and with their aid Zeus waged the war against Cronus and the Titans. They fought for ten years, and Earth prophesied victory to Zeus if he should have as allies those who had been hurled down to Tartarus. So he slew their jaileress Campe, and loosed their bonds. And the Cyclopes then gave Zeus thunder and lightning and a thunderbolt, and on Pluto they bestowed a helmet and on Poseidon a trident. Armed with these weapons the gods overcame the Titans, shut them up in Tartarus, and appointed the Hundred-handers their guards; but they themselves cast lots for the sovereignty, and to Zeus was allotted the dominion of the sky, to Poseidon the dominion of the sea, and to Pluto the dominion in Hades.

Now to the Titans were born offspring: to Ocean and Tethys were born Oceanids, to wit, Asia, Styx, Electra, Doris, Eurynome, Amphitrite, and Metis; to Coeus and Phoebe were born Asteria and Latona; to Hyperion and Thia were born Dawn, Sun, and Moon; to Crius and Eurybia, daughter of Sea (Pontus), were born Astraeus, Pallas, and Perses; to Iapetus and Asia was born Atlas, who has the sky on his shoulders, and Prometheus, and Epimetheus, and Menoetius, he whom Zeus in battle with the Titans smote with a thunderbolt and hurled down to Tartarus. And to Cronus and Philyra was born Chiron, a centaur of double form; and to Dawn and Astraeus were born winds and stars; to Perses and Asteria was born Hecate; and to Pallas and Styx were born Victory, Dominion, Emulation, and Violence. But Zeus caused oaths to be sworn by the water of Styx, which flows from a rock in Hades, bestowing this honor on her because she and her children had fought on his side against the Titans.

And to Sea (Pontus) and Earth were born Phorcus, Thaumas, Nereus, Eurybia, and Ceto. Now to Thaumas and Electra were born Iris and the Harpies, Aello and Ocypete; and to Phorcus and Ceto were born the Phorcids and Gorgons, of whom we shall speak when we treat of Perseus. To Nereus and Doris were born the Nereids, whose names are Cymothoe, Spio, Glauconome, Nausithoe, Halie, Erato, Sao, Amphitrite, Eunice, Thetis, Eulimene, Agave, Eudore, Doto, Pherusa, Galatea, Actaea, Pontomedusa, Hippothoe, Lysianassa, Cymo, Eione, Halimede, Plexaure, Eucrante, Proto, Calypso, Panope, Cranto, Neomeris, Hipponoe, Ianira, Polynome, Autonoe, Melite, Dione, Nesaea, Dero, Evagore, Psamathe, Eumolpe, Ione, Dynamene, Ceto, and Limnoria.

III. Now Zeus wedded Hera and begat Hebe, Ilithyia, and Ares, but he had intercourse with many women, both mortals and immortals. By Themis, daughter of Sky, he had daughters, the Seasons, to wit, Peace, Order, and Justice; also the Fates, to wit, Clotho, Lachesis, and Atropus; by Dione he had Aphrodite; by Eurynome, daughter of Ocean, he had the Graces, to wit, Aglaia, Euphrosyne, and Thalia; by Styx he had Persephone; and by Memory (Mnemosyne) he had the Muses, first Calliope, then Clio, Melpomene, Euterpe, Erato, Terpsichore, Urania, Thalia, and Polymnia.

Now Calliope bore to Oeagrus or, nominally to Apollo, a son Linus, whom Hercules slew; and another son Orpheus, who practiced minstrelsy and by his songs moved stones and trees. And when his wife Eurydice died, bitten by a snake, he went down to Hades, being fain to bring her up, and he persuaded Pluto to send her up. The god promised to do so, if on the way Orpheus would not turn round until he should be come to his own house. But he disobeyed and turning round beheld his wife; so she turned back. Orpheus also invented the mysteries of Dionysus, and having been torn in pieces by the Maenads he is buried in Pieria. Clio fell in love with Pierus, son of Magnes, in consequence of the wrath of Aphrodite, whom she had twitted with her love of Adonis; and having met him she bore him a son Hyacinth, for whom Thamyris, the son of Philammon and a nymph Argiope, conceived a passion, he being the first to become enamored of males. But afterwards Apollo loved Hyacinth and killed him involuntarily by the cast of a quoit. And Thamyris, who excelled in beauty and in minstrelsy, engaged in a musical contest with the Muses, the agreement being that, if he won, he should enjoy them all, but that if he should be vanquished he should be bereft of what they would. So the Muses got the better of him and bereft him both of his eyes and his minstrelsy. Euterpe had by the river Strymon a son Rhesus, whom Diomedes slew at Troy; but some say his mother was Calliope. Thalia had by Apollo the Corybantes; and Melpomene had by Achelous the Sirens, of whom we shall speak in treating of Ulysses.

Hera gave birth to Hephaestus without intercourse with the other sex, but according to Homer he was one of her children by Zeus.

Him Zeus cast out of heaven, because he came to the rescue of Hera in her bonds. For when Hercules had taken Troy and was at sea, Hera sent a storm after him; so Zeus hung her from Olympus. Hephaestus fell on Lemnos and was lamed of his legs, but Thetis saved him.

Zeus had intercourse with Metis, who turned into many shapes in order to avoid his embraces. When she was with child, Zeus, taking time by the forelock, swallowed her, because Earth said that, after giving birth to the maiden who was then in her womb, Metis would bear a son who should be the lord of heaven. From fear of that Zeus swallowed her. And when the time came for the birth to take place, Prometheus or, as others say, Hephaestus, smote the head of Zeus with an axe, and Athena, fully armed, leaped up from the top of his head at the river Triton.

IV. Of the daughters of Coeus, Asteria in the likeness of a quail flung herself into the sea in order to escape the amorous advances of Zeus, and a city was formerly called after her Asteria, but afterward it was named Delos. But Latona for her intrigue with Zeus was hunted by Hera over the whole earth, till she came to Delos and brought forth first Artemis, by the help of whose midwifery she afterward gave birth to Apollo.

Now Artemis devoted herself to the chase and remained a maid; but Apollo learned the art of prophecy from Pan, the son of Zeus and Hybris, and came to Delphi, where Themis at that time used to deliver oracles; and when the snake Python, which guarded the oracle, would have hindered him from approaching the chasm, he killed it and took over the oracle.

Not long afterward he slew also Tityus, who was a son of Zeus and Elare, daughter of Orchomenus; for her, after he had debauched her, Zeus hid under the earth for fear of Hera, and brought forth to the light the son of Tityus, of monstrous size, whom she had borne in her womb. When Latona came to Delphi, Tityus beheld her, and overpowered by lust drew her to him. But she called her children to her aid, and they shot him down with their arrows. And he is punished even after death; for vultures eat his heart in Hades.

Apollo also slew Marsyas, the son of Olympus. For Marsyas, having found the pipes which Athena had thrown away because they disfigured her face, engaged in a musical contest with Apollo. They agreed that the victor should work his will on the vanquished, and when the trial took place Apollo turned his lyre upside down in the competition and bade Marsyas do the same. But Marsyas could not, so Apollo was judged the victor and dispatched Marsyas by hanging him on a tall pine tree and stripping off his skin.

And Artemis slew Orion in Delos. They say that he was of gigantic stature and born of the earth; but Pherecydes says that he was a son of Poseidon and Euryale. Poseidon bestowed on him the power of striding across the sea. He first married Side, whom Hera cast into Hades because she rivaled herself in beauty. Afterward he went to Chios and wooed Merope, daughter of Oenopion. But Oenopion made him drunk, put out his eyes as he slept, and cast him on the beach. But he went to the smithy of Hephaestus, and snatching up a lad set him on his shoulders and bade him lead him to the sunrise. Being come thither he was healed by the sun's rays, and having recovered his sight he hastened with all speed against Oenopion. But for him Poseidon had made ready a house under the earth constructed by Hephaestus. And Dawn fell in love with Orion and carried him off and brought him to Delos; for Aphrodite caused dawn to be perpetually in love, because she had bedded with Ares. But

Orion was killed as some say for challenging Artemis to a match at quoits, but some say he was shot by Artemis for offering violence to Opis, one of the maidens who had come from the Hyperboreans.

Poseidon wedded Amphitrite, daughter of Ocean, and there were born to him Triton and Rhode, who was married to the Sun. . . .

PAUSANIAS (FL. A.D. 175)
The Acropolis of Athens

*L*ittle is known about the geographer, art historian, and tour guide Pausanias except what can be gleaned from his terse and straightforward *Description of Greece.* A native of Lydia, during the reign of Antonines he traveled the length and breadth of Greece—as well as to Asia Minor, Egypt, and Rome—and gave us his laconic but fascinating impressions of its major cities and provinces, beginning with Attica.

- Pausanias was not among the most insightful of Greek writers. Unlike the garrulous Herodotus or the precise Thucydides, Pausanias provides only a scattering of often apparently arbitrary information about the places he visited, the sights he enjoyed, and the works of art and architecture he observed with his own eyes. Yet even his omissions tell us much about the classical Greek traveler, who is more interested in how the city he visits functions economically, and what its mythic origins are, than what to eat and where to pass the night. So rich in history is the land known as Greece that tour guides today, even the famous *Blue Guide,* have the same limitation. You'll read where Telemachos slept in the palace of Nestor, but not where you can get a night's rest; where Odysseus banqueted with Nausikaa and her mother and father, but not where a good meal can be found.
- Pausanias' eye is not that of the gourmand, nor the art critic, but of the man whose curiosity about the events of history led him to explore the places where they occurred. Yet his

faults by any standards but Greek are conscious: "From the beginning my narrative has picked out of much material the things that deserve to be recorded."

There is but one entry to the Acropolis. It affords no other, being precipitous throughout and having a strong wall. The gateway has a roof of white marble, and down to the present day it is unrivaled for the beauty and size of its stones. Now as to the statues of the horsemen, I cannot tell for certain whether they are the sons of Xenophon or whether they are made merely to beautify the place. On the right of the gateway is a temple of Wingless Victory. From this point the sea is visible, and here it was that, according to legend, Aegeus threw himself down to his death. For the ship that carried the young people to Crete began her voyage with black sails; but Theseus, who was sailing on an adventure against the bull of Minos, as it is called, had told his father beforehand that he would use white sails if he should sail back victorious over the bull. But the loss of Ariadne made him forget the signal. Then Aegeus, when from this eminence he saw the vessels borne by black sails, thinking that his son was dead, threw himself down to destruction. There is at Athens a sanctuary dedicated to him, and called the hero-shrine of Aegeus. On the left of the gateway is a building with pictures. Among those not effaced by time I found Diomedes taking the Athena from Troy, and Odysseus in Lemnos taking away the bow of Philoctetes. There in the pictures is Orestes killing Aegisthus, and Pylades killing the sons of Nauplius who had come to bring Aegisthus

succor. And there is Polyxena about to be sacrificed near the grave of Achilles. Homer did well in passing by this barbarous act. I think too that he showed poetic insight in making Achilles capture Scyros, differing entirely from those who say that Achilles lived in Scyros with the maidens, as Polygnotus has represented in his picture. He also painted Odysseus coming upon the women washing clothes with Nausicaa at the river, just like the description in Homer. There are other pictures, including a portrait of Alcibiades, and in the picture are emblems of the victory his horses won at Nemea. There is also Perseus journeying to Seriphos, and carrying to Polydectes the head of Medusa, the legend about whom I am unwilling to relate in my description of Attica. Included among the paintings—I omit the boy carrying the water-jars and the wrestler of Timaenetus—is Musaeus. I have read verse in which Musaeus receives from the North Wind the gift of flight, but in my opinion, Onomacritus wrote them, and there are no certainly genuine works of Musaeus except a hymn to Demeter written for the Lycomidae.

Right at the very entrance to the Acropolis are Hermes (called Hermes of the Gateway) and figures of Graces, which tradition says were sculptured by Socrates, the son of Sophroniscus, who the Pythia testified was the wisest of men, a title she refused to Anacharsis, although he desired it and came to Delphi to win it.

"Acropolis of Athens"

Among the sayings of the Greeks is one that there were seven wise men. Two of them were the despot of Lesbos and Periander the son of Cypselus. And yet Peisistratus and his son Hippias were more humane than Periander, wiser too in warfare and in statecraft, until, on account of the murder of Hipparchus, Hippias vented his passion against all and sundry, including a woman named Leaena (Lioness). What I am about to say has never before been committed to writing, but is generally credited among the Athenians. When Hipparchus died, Hippias tortured Leaena to death, because he knew she was the mistress of Aristogeiton, and therefore could not possibly, he held, be in ig-

norance of the plot. As a recompense, when the tyranny of the Peisistratidae was at an end, the Athenians put up a bronze lioness in memory of the woman, which they say Callias dedicated and Calamis made.

Hard by is a bronze statue of Diitrephes shot through by arrows. Among the acts reported of this Diitrephes by the Athenians is his leading back home the Thracian mercenaries who arrived too late to take part in the expedition of Demosthenes against Syracuse. He also put into the Chalcidic Euripus, where the Boeotians had an inland town Mycalessus, marched up to this town from the coast and took it. Of the inhabitants the Thracians put to the sword not only the combatants but also the women and children. I have evidence to bring. All the Boeotian towns which the Thebans sacked were inhabited in my time, as the people escaped just before the capture; so if the foreigners had not exterminated the Mycalessians the survivors would have afterward reoccupied the town. I was greatly surprised to see the statue of Diitrephes pierced with arrows, because the only Greeks whose custom it is to use that weapon are the Cretans. For the Opuntian Locrians, whom Homer represents as coming to Troy with bows and slings, we know were armed as heavy infantry by the time of the Persian wars. Neither indeed did the Malians continue the practice of the bow; in fact, I believe that they did not know it before the time of Philoctetes, and gave it up soon after. Near the statue of Diitrephes—I do not wish to write of the less distinguished portraits—are figures of gods; of Health, whom legend calls daughter of Asclepius, and of Athena, also surnamed Health. There is also a smallish stone, just large enough to serve as a seat to a little man. On it legend says Silenus rested when Dionysus came to the land. The oldest of the Satyrs they call Sileni. Wishing to know better than most people who the Satyrs are I have inquired from many about this very point. Euphemus the Carian said that on a voyage to Italy he was driven out of his course by winds and was carried into the outer sea, beyond the course of seamen. He affirmed that there were many uninhabited islands, while in others lived wild men. The sailors did not wish to put in at the latter, because, having put in before, they had some experience of the inhabitants, but on this occasion they had no choice in the matter.

The islands were called Satyrides by the sailors, and the inhabitants were redhaired, and had upon their flanks tails not much smaller than those of horses. As soon as they caught sight of their visitors, they ran down to the ship without uttering a cry and assaulted the women in the ship. At last the sailors in fear cast a foreign woman on to the island. Her the Satyrs outraged not only in the usual way, but also in a most shocking manner.

I remember looking at other things also on the Athenian Acropolis, a bronze boy holding the sprinkler, by Lycius son of Myron, and Myron's Perseus after beheading Medusa. There is also a sanctuary of Brauronian Artemis; the image is the work of Praxiteles, but the goddess derives her name from the parish of Brauron. The old wooden image is in Brauron, the Tauric Artemis as she is called. There is the horse called Wooden set up in bronze. That the work of Epeius was a contrivance to make a breach in the Trojan wall is known to everybody who does not attribute utter silliness to the Phrygians. But legend says of that horse that it contained the most valiant of the Greeks, and the design of the bronze figure fits in well with this story. Menestheus and Teucer are peeping out of it, and so are the sons of Theseus. Of the statues that stand after the horse, the likeness of Epicharinus who practiced the race in armor was made by Critias, while Oenobius performed a kind service for Thucydides the son of Olorus. He succeeded in getting a decree passed for the return of Thucydides to Athens, who was treacherously murdered as he was returning, and there is a monument to him not far from the Melitid gate. The stories of Hermolycus the pancratiast and Phormio the son of Asopichus I omit, as others have told them. About Phormio, however, I have a detail to add. Quite one of the best men at Athens and distinguished for the fame of his ancestors he chanced to be heavily in debt. So he withdrew to the parish Paeania and lived there until the Athenians elected him to command a naval expedition. But he refused the office on the ground that before his debts were discharged he lacked the spirit to face his troops. So the Athenians, who were absolutely determined to have Phormio as their commander, paid all his creditors.

In this place is a statue of Athena striking Marsyas the Silenus for taking up the flutes that the goddess wished to be cast away for good.

Opposite these I have mentioned is represented the fight which legend says Theseus fought with the so-called Bull of Minos, whether this was a man or a beast of the nature he is said to have been in the accepted story. For even in our time women have given birth to far more extraordinary monsters than this. There is also a statue of Phrixus the son of Athamas carried ashore to the Colchians by the ram. Having sacrificed the animal to some god or other, presumably to the one called by the Orchomenians Laphystius, he has cut out the thighs in accordance with Greek custom and is watching them as they burn. Next come other statues, including one of Heracles strangling the serpents as the legend describes. There is Athena too coming up out of the head of Zeus, and also a bull dedicated by the Council of the Areopagus on some occasion or other, about which, if one cared, one could make many conjectures. I have already stated that the Atheni-

ans are far more devoted to religion than other men. They were the first to surname Athena Ergane (Worker); they were the first to set up limbless Hermae, and the temple of their goddess is shared by the Spirit of Good Men. Those who prefer artistic workmanship to mere antiquity may look at the following: a man wearing a helmet, by Cleoetas, whose nails the artist has made of silver, and an image of Earth beseeching Zeus to rain upon her; perhaps the Athenians themselves needed showers, or maybe all the Greeks had been plagued with a drought. There also are set up Timotheus the son of Conon and Conon himself; Procne too, who has already made up her mind about the boy, and Itys as well—a group dedicated by Alcamenes. Athena is represented displaying the olive plant, and Poseidon the wave, and there are statues of Zeus, one made by Leochares and one called Polieus (Urban), the customary mode of sacrificing to whom I will give without adding the traditional reason thereof. Upon the altar of Zeus Polieus they place barley mixed with wheat and leave it unguarded. The ox, which they keep ready prepared for sacrifice, goes to the altar and partakes of the grain. One of the priests they call the ox-slayer, who kills the ox and then, casting aside the axe here according to the ritual, runs away. The others bring the axe to trial, as though they know not the man who did the deed.

Their ritual, then, is such as I have described. As you enter the temple that they name the Parthenon, all the sculptures you see on what is called the pediment refer to the birth of Athena, those on the rear pediment represent the contest for the land between Athena and Poseidon. The statue itself is made of ivory and gold. On the middle of her helmet is placed a likeness of the Sphinx—the tale of the Sphinx I will give when I come to my description of Boeotia—and on either side of the helmet are griffins in relief. These griffins, Aristeas of Proconnesus says in his poem, fight for the gold with the Arimaspi beyond the Issedones. The gold which the griffins guard, he says, comes out of the earth; the Arimaspi are men all born with one eye; griffins are beasts like lions, but with the beak and wings of an eagle. I will say no more about the griffins. The statue of Athena is upright, with a tunic reaching to the feet, and on her breast the head of Medusa is worked in ivory. She holds a statue of Victory about four cubits high, and in the other hand a spear; at her feet lies a shield and near the spear is a serpent. This serpent would be Erichthonius. On the pedestal is the birth of Pandora in relief. Hesiod and others have sung how this Pandora was the first woman; before Pandora was born there was as yet no womankind. The only portrait statue I remember seeing here is one of the emperor Hadrian, and at the entrance one of Iphicrates, who accomplished many remarkable achievements.

Opposite the temple is a bronze Apollo, said to be the work of Pheidias. They call it the Locust God, because once when locusts were devastating the land the god said that he would drive them from Attica. That he did drive them away they know, but they do not say how. I myself know that locusts have been destroyed three times in the past on Mount Sipylus, and not in the same way. Once a gale arose and swept them away; on another occasion violent

heat came on after rain and destroyed them; the third time sudden cold caught them and they died.

Such were the fates I saw befall the locusts. On the Athenian Acropolis is a statue of Pericles, the son of Xanthippus, and one of Xanthippus himself, who fought against the Persians at the naval battle of Mycale. But that of Pericles stands apart, while near Xanthippus stands Anacreon of Teos, the first poet after Sappho of Lesbos to devote himself to love songs, and his posture is as it were that of a man singing when he is drunk. Deinomenes made the two female figures which stand near, Io, the daughter of Inachus, and Callisto, the daughter of Lycaon, of both of whom exactly the same story is told, to wit, love of Zeus, wrath of Hera, and metamorphosis, Io becoming a cow and Callisto a bear.

By the south wall are represented the legendary war with the giants, who once dwelt about Thrace and on the isthmus of Pallene, the battle between the Athenians and the Amazons, the engagement with the Persians at Marathon and the destruction of the Gauls in Mysia. Each is about two cubits, and all were dedicated by Attalus. There stands too Olympiodorus, who won fame for the greatness of his achievements, especially in the crisis when he displayed a brave confidence among men who had met with continuous reverses, and were therefore in despair of winning a single success in the days to come. . . .

Near the statue of Olympiodorus stands a bronze image of Artemis surnamed Leucophryne, dedicated by the sons of Themistocles; for the Magnesians, whose city the King had given him to rule, hold Artemis Leucophryne in honor.

But my narrative must not loiter, as my task is a general description of all Greece. Endoeus was an Athenian by birth and a pupil of Daedalus, who also, when Daedalus was in exile because of the death of Calos, followed him to Crete. Made by him is a statue of Athena seated, with an inscription that Callias dedicated the image, but Endoeus made it. There is also a building called the Erechtheum. Before the entrance is an altar of Zeus the Most High, on which they never sacrifice a living creature, but offer cakes, not being wont to use any wine either. Inside the entrance are altars, one to Poseidon, on which in obedience to an oracle they sacrifice also to Erechtheus, the second to the hero Butes, and the third to Hephaestus. On the walls are paintings representing members of the clan Butadae; there is also inside—the building is double—seawater in a cistern. This is no great marvel, for other inland regions have similar wells, in particular Aphrodisias in Caria. But this cistern is remarkable for the noise of waves it sends forth when a south wind blows. On the rock is the outline of a trident. Legend says that these appeared as evidence in support of Poseidon's claim to the land.

Both the city and the whole of the land are alike sacred to Athena; for even those who in their parishes have an established worship of other gods nevertheless hold Athena in honor. But the most holy symbol, that was so considered by all many years before the unification of the parishes, is the image of Athena which is on what is now called the Acropolis but in early days the Polis (City). A legend concerning it says that it fell from heaven; whether this is true or not I shall not discuss. A golden lamp for the goddess was made by Callimachus. Having filled the lamp with oil, they wait until the same day next year, and the oil is sufficient for the lamp during the interval, although it is alight both day and night. The wick in it is of Carpasian flax, the only kind of flax which is fireproof, and a bronze palm above the lamp reaches to the roof and draws off the smoke. The Callimachus who made the lamp, although not of the first rank of artists, was yet of unparalleled cleverness, so that he was the first to drill holes through stones, and gave himself the title of Refiner of Art, or perhaps others gave the title and he adopted it as his . . .

GALEN (A.D. 129–199)
On the Natural Faculties

*T*he prolific philosopher-physician Galen is the second great name in Greek medicine after Hippocrates. Born in Asia Minor, he tells us that he learned as much from his mother's shrewishness as from his father's uprightness. He studied medicine in Corinth, Smyrna, and Alexandria. In A.D. 157, he returned to his native Pergamum, sacred to Asclepios, the god of healing, to attend gladiators at the god's shrine and to continue, as surgeon, his studies of anatomy and physiology.

A visit to Rome, where his skills were immediately employed by the imperial capital's intelligentsia, caught the attention of the Emperors Marcus Aurelius and Lucius Verus, who encouraged him to continue his philosophical writing and teaching. Some say he was driven from Rome by jealous rivals, who claimed he left because of a plague brought home by the returning military. Despite his refusal to join the imperial German campaign, Galen was called back in A.D. 169–170 by the emperors and granted an official position in the Roman court. Galen's experiments, operations, and demonstrations in comparative anatomy, especially on the spinal column, circulation of the blood, the valves of the heart, the structural difference between veins and arteries, the function of the liver, the seven pairs of cranial nerves, and the muscular system, were based on dissection—primarily of animals—as well as vivisection (including that of the Barbary ape). He describes an "open heart" operation he performed on a young boy. He wrote extensively on the history, philosophy, practice, and theory of medicine, covering the history of philosophy; the history and lexicography of medicine; pharmacology; diagnosis, prognosis, and treatment; anatomy and physiology; psychology; and pathology and disease.

- As a follower of Plato and Aristotle, as well as Hippocrates, Galen was an optimistic monist, though not a monotheist. He believed in the "one," a unifying principle of nature toward which all matter ascended from basest to most sublime, and which governed the relationships among parts and the whole. He accepted the "doctrine of the four humors" as a guideline for pathology. Yet he insisted on forming his own judgments through personal diagnosis and thorough dissection. Despite his theoretical bent, and his determination to provide a unified theory of medicine that covered all previous theory as well as his own findings, he understood that no theory can replace the uniqueness of the individual patient.

- Because he insisted on basing his results on direct observation, Galen corrected mistakes of previous theorists about the workings of the human body. He proved, as he demonstrates in the selection that follows, that the arteries, as well as the veins, carry blood (not air, as had been previously thought). His refusal to abandon private practice in favor of "theoretical medicine," and his refusal of specialization in favor of general practice, succeeded in elevating his profession to the highest ranks of society. At the same time his hybrid of philosophical mysticism, practical bedside experience, Hippocratic belief in the unity of the organism, and unabashed delight at appearing on the imperial lecture circuit made him the Deepak Chopra or Dr. Bernie Siegel of his day. He is considered the founder of experimental physiology, his work in dissection influencing the European Renaissance; and, by extension, giving him claim to the title "grandfather of modern medicine."

. . . Now Nature foresaw this necessity, and provided the cardiac openings of the vessels with membranous attachments, to prevent their contents from being carried backward. How and in what manner this takes place will be stated in my work "On the Use of Parts," where among other things I show that it is impossible for the openings of the vessels to be closed so accurately that nothing at all can run back. Thus it is inevitable that the reflux into the *venous artery* (as will also be made clear in the work mentioned) should be much greater than through the other openings. But what it is important for our present purpose to recognize is that everything possessing a large and appreciable cavity must, when it dilates, abstract matter from all its neighbors, and, when it contracts, must squeeze matter back into them. This should all be clear from what has already been said in this treatise and from what Erasistratus and I myself have demonstrated elsewhere respecting the tendency of a vacuum to become refilled.

XIV

And further, it has been shown in other treatises that all the arteries possess a power which derives from the heart, and by virtue of which they dilate and contract.

Put together, therefore, the two facts—that the arteries have this motion, and that everything, when it dilates, draws neighboring matter into itself—and you will find nothing strange in the fact that those arteries which reach the skin draw in the outer air when they dilate, while those which anastomose at any point with the veins attract the thinnest and most vaporous part of the blood which these contain, and as for those arteries which are near the heart, it is on the heart itself that they exert their traction. For, by virtue of the tendency by which a vacuum becomes refilled, the lightest and thinnest part obeys the tendency before that which is heavier and thicker. Now the lightest and thinnest of anything in the body is firstly pneuma, secondly vapor, and in the third place that part of the blood which has been accurately elaborated and refined.

These, then, are what the arteries draw into themselves on every side; those arteries which reach the skin draw in the outer air (this being near them and one of the lightest of things); as to the other arteries, those which pass up from the heart into the neck, and that which lies along the spine, as also such arteries as are near these—draw mostly from the heart itself; and those which are farther from the heart and skin necessarily draw the lightest part of the blood out of the veins. So also the traction exercised by the diastole of the arteries which go to the stomach and intestines takes place at the expense of the heart itself and the numerous veins in its neighborhood; for these arteries cannot get anything worth speaking of from the thick heavy nutriment contained in the intestines and stomach, since they first become filled with lighter elements. For if you let down a tube into a vessel full of water and sand, and suck the air out of the tube with your mouth, the sand cannot come up to you before the water, for in accordance with the principle of the refilling of a vacuum the lighter matter is always the first to succeed to the evacuation.

XV

It is not to be wondered at, therefore, that only a very little [nutrient matter] such, namely, as has been accurately elaborated—gets from the stomach into the arteries, since these first become filled with lighter matter. We must understand that *there are two kinds of attraction*, that by which a vacuum becomes refilled and that caused by appropriateness of quality; air is drawn into bellows in one way, and iron by the lodestone in another. And we must also understand that the traction which results from evacuation acts primarily on what is light, while that from appropriateness of quality acts frequently, it may be, on what is heavier (if this should be naturally more nearly related). Therefore, in the case of the heart and the arteries, it is in so far as they are hollow organs, capable of diastole, that they always attract the lighter matter first, while, in so far as

they require nourishment, it is actually into their *coats* (which are the real *bodies* of these organs) that the appropriate matter is drawn. Of the blood, then, which is taken into their cavities when they dilate, that part which is most proper to them and most able to afford nourishment is attracted by their actual coats.

Now, apart from what has been said, the following is sufficient proof that something is taken over from the veins into the arteries. If you will kill an animal by cutting through a number of its large arteries, you will find the veins becoming empty along with the arteries: Now, this could never occur if there were not anastomoses between them. Similarly, also, in the heart itself, the thinnest portion of the blood is drawn from the right ventricle into the left, owing to there being perforations in the septum between them: These can be seen for a great part [of their length]; they are like a kind of fossae [pits] with wide mouths, and they get constantly narrower; it is not possible, however, actually to observe their extreme terminations, owing both to the smallness of these and to the fact that when the animal is dead all the parts are chilled and shrunken. Here, too, however, our argument, starting from the principle that nothing is done by Nature in vain, discovers these anastomoses between the ventricles of the heart; for it could not be at random and by chance that there occurred fossae ending thus in narrow terminations.

And secondly [the presence of these anastomoses has been assumed] from the fact that, of the two orifices in the right ventricle, the one conducting blood in and the other out, the former is much the larger. For the fact that the insertion of the vena cava into the heart is larger than the vein which is inserted into the lungs suggests that not all the blood which the vena cava gives to the heart is driven away again from the heart to the lungs. Nor can it be said that any of the blood is expended in the nourishment of the actual body of the heart, since there is another vein which breaks up in it and which does not take its origin nor get its share of blood from the heart itself. And even if a certain amount is so expended, still the vein leading to the lungs is not to such a slight extent smaller than that inserted into the heart as to make it likely that the blood is used as nutriment for the heart: The disparity is much too great for such an explanation. It is, therefore, clear that something *is* taken over into the left ventricle.

Moreover, of the two vessels connected with it, that which brings pneuma into it from the lungs is much smaller than the great outgrowing artery from which the arteries all over the body originate; this would suggest that it not merely gets pneuma from the lungs, but that it also gets blood from the right ventricle through the anastomoses mentioned.

Now it belongs to the treatise "On the Use of Parts" to show that it was best that some parts of the body should be nourished by pure, thin, and vaporous blood, and others by thick, turbid blood, and that in this matter also Nature has overlooked nothing. Thus it is not desirable that these matters should be further discussed. Having mentioned, however, that there are two kinds of attraction, certain bodies exerting attraction along wide channels during diastole (by virtue of the principle by which a vacuum becomes refilled) and others exerting it by virtue of their appropriateness of quality, we must next remark that the former bodies can attract even from a distance, while the latter can only do so from among things which are quite close to them; the very longest tube let down into water can easily draw up the liquid into the mouth, but if you withdraw iron to a distance from the lodestone or corn from the jar (an instance of this kind has in fact been already given) no further attraction can take place.

This you can observe most clearly in connection with *garden conduits*. For a certain amount of moisture is distributed from these into every part lying close at hand but it cannot reach those lying further off: Therefore one has to arrange the flow of water into all parts of the garden by cutting a number of small channels leading from the large one. The intervening spaces between these small channels are made of such a size as will, presumably, best allow them [the spaces] to satisfy their needs by drawing from the liquid which flows to them from every side. So also is it in the bodies of animals. Numerous conduits distributed through the various limbs bring them pure blood, much like the garden water-supply, and, further, the intervals between these conduits have been wonderfully arranged by Nature from the outset so that the intervening parts should be plentifully provided for when absorbing blood, and that they should never be deluged by a quantity of superfluous fluid running in at unsuitable times.

For the way in which they obtain nourishment is somewhat as follows. In the body which is continuous throughout, such as Erasistratus supposes his *simple vessel* to be, it is the superficial parts which are the first to make use of the nutriment with which they are brought into contact; then the parts coming next draw their share from these by virtue of their contiguity; and again others from these; and this does not stop until the quality of the nutrient substance has been distributed among all parts of the corpuscle in question. And for such parts as need the humor which is destined to nourish them to be altered still further, Nature has provided a kind of storehouse, either in the form of a central cavity or else as separate caverns, or something analogous to caverns. Thus the flesh of the viscera and of the muscles is nourished from the blood directly, this having undergone merely a slight alteration; the bones, however, in order to be nourished, require very great change, and what blood is to flesh marrow is to bone; in the case of the small bones, which do not possess central cavities, this marrow is distributed in their caverns, whereas in the larger bones which do contain central cavities the marrow is all concentrated in these.

For, as was pointed out in the first book, things having a similar substance can easily change into one another, whereas it is impossible for those which are very different to be assimilated to one another without intermediate stages. Such a one in respect to cartilage is the myxoid substance which surrounds it, and in respect to ligaments, membranes, and nerves the viscous liquid dispersed inside them; for each of these consists of numerous fibers, which are homogeneous—in fact, actual *sensible elements*; and in the intervals between these fibers is dispersed the humor most suited for nutrition; this they have drawn from the blood in the veins, choosing the most appropriate possible, and now they are assimilating it step by step and changing it into their own substance.

All these considerations, then, agree with one another, and bear sufficient witness to the truth of what has been already demonstrated; there is thus no need to prolong the discussion further. For, from what has been said, anyone can readily discover in what way all the particular [vital activities] come about. For instance, we could in this way ascertain why it is that in the case of many people who are partaking freely of wine, the fluid which they have drunk is rapidly absorbed through the body and almost the whole of it is passed by the kidneys within a very short time. For here, too, the rapidity with which the fluid is absorbed depends on appropriateness of quality, on the thinness of the fluid, on the width of the vessels and their mouths, and on the efficiency of the attractive faculty. The parts situated near the alimentary canal, by virtue of their appropriateness of quality, draw in the imbibed food for their own purposes, then the parts next to them in their turn snatch it away, then those next again take it from these, until it reaches the vena cava, whence finally the kidneys attract that part of it which is proper to them. Thus it is in no way surprising that wine is taken up more rapidly than water, owing to its appropriateness of quality, and, further, that the white clear kind of wine is absorbed more rapidly owing to its thinness, while black turbid wine is checked on the way and retarded because of its thickness.

These facts, also, will afford abundant proof of what has already been said about the arteries; everywhere, in fact, such blood as is both specifically appropriate and at the same time thin in consistency answers more readily to their traction than does blood which is not so; this is why the arteries which, in their diastole, absorb vapor, pneuma, and thin blood attract either none at all or very little of the juices contained in the stomach and intestines.

PLOTINUS (A.D. 205–270)
True Happiness

*N*eo-Platonism, the last great philosophical movement in Greek antiquity, was begun in Alexandria by Ammonius Saccas but brought to focus in Rome by his student Plotinus, who was born in Lycopolis, in Egypt, but began teaching in Rome in A.D. 244. Plotinus was the center of an intellectual circle sponsored by the Emperor Gallienus, which drew from not only Plato but also Aristotle and the preSocratic philosophers. The emperor and his wife Salonina both converted to Plotinus' brand of Neo-Platonic logical mysticism. Neo-Platonists sought to continue the tradition of Greek philosophy in opposition to the growing strength of Christianity and to the influence of eastern Gnosticism, the latter believing that the universe was not monistic, but dualistic—an eternal war between spirit and matter. Neo-Platonism, like Plato's own philosophy, believed in the clear priority of spirit as the source of all in the universe, including material reality. Plotinus' lifelong ambition, to found a utopian city that would be named Platonopolis and would be governed by the rules of Plato's *Republic,* was never realized.

- The teachings of Plotinus were collected, in turn, by his student Porphyry in a work known as the *Enneads,* from which the present selection is taken. Plotinus' brand of Neo-Platonism stresses union with the "one," the principle governing the universe. His *Enneads* clearly enunciate the principles of the "world soul," the "world-mind," and the philosopher's mission to unite his mind with the higher consciousness that gives form to the universe. Awkward and absent-minded in his style, Plotinus nonetheless clearly communicates the almost religious fervor of his philosophical viewpoint.

What is happiness?

If we base happiness upon life, drawing no distinction as to kinds of life, everything that lives will be capable of happiness. We could not deny it to the irrational while allowing it to the rational. But this word *life* embraces many forms which shade down from primal to secondary, and so on—life of animal and life of plant, each phase brighter or dimmer than the next; and so it evidently must be with the good of life.

Happiness demands fullness of life and exists, therefore, where nothing is lacking of all that belongs to the idea of life. Only one that lives fully will possess happiness, for he possesses the Supreme Good if, indeed, the Supreme Good is the authentically living, life in its greatest plenitude, life in which the good is present as something essential, not as something brought in from without. The perfect life, the true and essential life, is in the Intellectual Nature beyond this sphere—all other kinds are incomplete, are phantoms of life, imperfect, not pure, not more truly life than they are its contrary. Since all living things proceed from the one Principle but possess life in different degrees, this Principle must be the first life and the most complete.

If, then, the perfect life is within human reach, the man attaining it attains happiness; if not, happiness must be made over to the gods. But since we hold that happiness is for human beings too, we must consider how this is possible. The matter may be stated thus: Man, when he commands not merely the life of sensation but also Reason and Authentic Intellection, has realized the perfect life.

But are we to picture it as something foreign imported into his nature?

No: There exists no single human being that does not either potentially or effectively possess this thing which we hold to constitute happiness. While in some men it is present as a mere portion of their total being, there is, too, the man already in possession of true felicity, who is this perfection realized, who has passed over into actual identification with it. All else is now mere clothing about the man, not to be called part of him since it lies about him unsought, not his because not appropriated to himself by any act of the will. To the man in this state, he himself is the Good by what he has and is, and the Author and Principle of what he is and holds is the Supreme. The sign that this state has been achieved is that the man seeks nothing else. What could he be seeking? Certainly none of the less worthy things, and with the Best he is already one.

Once the man is adept, the means of happiness, the way to good, are within, for nothing is good that lies outside him. Anything he desires further than this he seeks as a necessity, and not for himself but for a subordinate, for the body bound to him, to which since it has life he must minister the needs of life, not needs, however, to the true man. He knows these (to be of the lower order), and what he gives he so gives as to leave his true life undiminished.

Adverse fortune does not shake his felicity; the life so founded is stable ever. Suppose death strikes at his household or friends; he knows what death is, as the victims, if they are among the wise, know too. And if death does bring him grief, it is not to him, the true man, but to that in him which stands apart from the Supreme, that lower man in whose distress he takes no part.

If happiness did indeed require freedom from pain, sickness, misfortune, disaster, it would be utterly denied to anyone confronted by such trials; but if it lies in the acquiring of the Authentic Good, why turn away from this Term and look to means, imagining that to be happy a man must need a variety of things none of which enter into happiness? If our quest is of one term alone, that only can be elected which is ultimate and noblest, that which calls to the tenderest longings of the soul.

The quest and will of the soul are not pointed directly towards freedom from this sphere; the reason which disciplines away our concern about this life has no fundamental quarrel with things of this order; it merely resents their interference; essentially all the aspiration is not so much away from evil as toward the soul's highest and noblest: This attained, all is won and there is rest—and this is the veritably willed state of life. There can be no such thing as "willing" the acquirement of necessaries, if *will* is to be taken in its strict sense, and not misapplied to the mere recognition of need. Such things can never make part of our final object; our Term must be such that though these pleasanter conditions be absent and their contraries present, it shall remain intact.

In any case if the man that has attained felicity meets some turn of fortune that he would not have chosen, there is not the slightest lessening of his happiness for that. If there were, he would be veering and falling from felicity from day to day. What human thing is so great as not to be despised by one who has mounted above all we know here, and is bound no longer to anything below?

As for violent personal sufferings, he will carry them off as well as he can; if they overpass his endurance they will carry him off.

And so in all his pain he asks no pity; there is always the radiance in the inner soul of the man, untroubled like the light in a lantern when fierce gusts beat about it in a wild turmoil of wind and tempest. Neither ordinary experiences nor pains and sorrows, whether touching himself or others, pierce to the inner hold.

It is virtue's use to raise the general level of nature toward the better and finer, above the mass of men. And the finer is to set at nought what terrifies the common mind.

We cannot be indolent; this is an arena for the powerful combatant holding his ground against the blows of fortune and knowing that, sore though they be, they are little to him, nothing dreadful, nursery terrors. It is precisely to meet the undesired when it appears that he has the virtue which gives him, to confront it, his passionless and unshakable soul.

Thus he is ever cheerful, and the order of his life untroubled; his state is fixedly happy and nothing whatever of all that is known as evil can set it awry. If anyone seeks for some other pleasure in the life of the adept, it is not the life of the adept that he is looking for. In him is the self-gathered which can never be robbed of the vision of the All-Good.

It would be absurd to think that happiness begins and ends with the living body; happiness is the possession of the good of life; it is centered therefore in Soul, is an act of Soul. The body must be lessened, reduced, that the veritable man may show forth, the man behind the appearances; while he will safeguard his bodily health, the tyranny of the body he will work down or wear away by inattention to its claims. He would be neither wise nor in the state of happiness if he had not quitted trifling with such things and become as it were another being, having confidence in his own nature, faith that evil can never touch him. In such a spirit he can be fearless through and through; where there is dread, there is not perfect virtue; the man is some sort of a half-thing.

As for any involuntary fear rising in him and taking the judgment by surprise, the wise man will attack it and drive it out; he will, so to speak, calm the hurt and frightened child within him by reason or menace, as an infant might feel itself rebuked by a glance of severity.

This does not make the man unfriendly or harsh; giving freely to his intimates of all he has to give, he will be the best of friends by his very union with Divine Mind.

Plato rightly taught that he who is to be wise and possess happiness should draw his good from the Supreme, fixing his gaze on That, becoming like to That, living by That. He must care for no other Term than That; all else he will attend to only as he might change his residence, not in expectation of any increase to his settled felicity, but simply in a reasonable attention to the differing conditions surrounding him as he lives here or there.

He will give to the body all that he sees to be useful or possible, but he himself is of another order, and leaves it at nature's hour, although he himself is always the master to decide in its regard—the thing he tends and bears with as the musician cares for his lyre as long as it can serve him: When the lyre fails him, he will change it or give it up, as having now another craft, one that needs no lyre; and then he will let it rest unregarded at his side while he sings on without accompaniment. But it was not idly that the instrument was given him in the beginning; he has found it useful until now, many a time.

TIME AND HAPPINESS

Is it possible to think that happiness increases with time?

(No; for) if it were, then every tomorrow's well-being would be greater than today's, every later installment larger than an earlier; at once time would supplant moral excellence as the measure of felicity. If in the greater length of time the man has seen more deeply, time has certainly done something for him, but if all the process has brought him no further vision, he has only what one glance would show.

Still the one life has known pleasure longer than the other!

But pleasure cannot be fairly reckoned in with happiness, unless indeed by pleasure is meant the unhindered Act (of the true man). Even though it endure longer, it has never anything but the present; its past is over and done with.

True happiness is an unchanging state, an achieved and existing state. If there is any increase here along with that of mere time, it is in the sense that a greater happiness is the reward of a higher virtue.

If happiness lies in the living of the good

life, it clearly has to do with the life of Authentic Existence, for that life is the best. Now the life of Authentic Existence is measurable not by time but by eternity; and eternity is not a more or a less or a thing of any magnitude, but is without interval or dimension; is timeless Being.

We must not muddle together Being and non-being, time and eternity, not even everlasting time with the eternal; we cannot make laps and stages of an absolute unity; all must be taken together, wheresoever and howsoever we handle it; and it must be taken not even as an undivided block of time, but as the Life of Eternity, not made up of periods, but completely rounded, outside of all notion of time.

And what is there in the memory of past pleasures, that the man who has arrived at felicity must roam far and wide in search of gratifications and is not contented by the bliss actually within him? Men quite outside the active life may attain the state of felicity, and not in a less but in a greater degree than men of affairs. The good does not derive from the acts themselves but from the inner disposition which prompts us to noble conduct; the wise and good man harvests the good not by what he does or by what happens to him but by what he is. His contentment does not hang upon actions and events; it is his own inner habit that creates at once his felicity and whatever pleasure may accompany it.

To place happiness in actions is to put it in things that are outside virtue and outside the Soul; for the Soul's expression is not in action but in wisdom, in a contemplative operation within itself; and this, this alone, is happiness.

LONGUS (THIRD CENTURY A.D.?)
Daphnis and Chloë

*T*he history of romantic literature finds a fully developed source in the four books of *Daphnis and Chloë,* attributed to Longus. Nothing is known about the author; even his name is doubtful. Yet his pastoral romance, inspired by Eros, the god of irresistible passion, remains a compelling portrait of the beautiful simplicity of young love.

- As the power of Rome spread throughout the entire Mediterranean (which the Romans mapped as *mare nostrum,* "our lake"), the Empire turned inward to wit, manners (and the lack thereof), and circuses. At the same time that sophisticated urbanites became addicted to violence, Greek literature had entered its decadence. Against this background of elaborate ornamentation and precious conceptualizing, the story of two orphaned shepherds, possibly on the island of Lesbos, finding each other and feeling the increasingly powerful attraction of love stands like an island oasis of clarity and purity.

- Although the prose romance was an anomaly in the history of Greek literature, which preferred poetry above all other forms of expression, it finds its emotional roots in the idylls of Theocritos, and in Apollonius of Rhodes' story of Jason and Medea in the *Argonautica*. Longus' limpid prose portrays the psychology of erotic longing so authoritatively that his work becomes a primer for the modern romance writer. The purity of his romantic vision, expressed in language as elegant as it is simple, and favoring emotional nuances of character development over the contrived twists and turns of plot, transcends the commonplace and becomes truly universal.

- This early novel enshrines romance, with its fear of loss and sensation of unique vivacity, as a subject worthy of the most serious contemplation. But *Daphnis and Chloë* is more than a romance. It is an important document in the history of pastoral literature, a bucolic idyll in prose, which expresses the urban dweller's longing for an idealized, deeply sensed and appreciated countryside where humans are innocent children of nature, and where humanity can rediscover its roots. The four books of *Daphnis and Chloë* trace:

  - their growing up in the countryside raised by foster parents,
  - their falling in love,
  - their adventures,
  - their recognition of the nature of love,
  - the discovery of their real parents,
  - their marriage.

The action of the story, like comedy ending with a *gamos,* follows the cycle of the seasons, which test the lovers' passion and commitment.

PROLOGUE

When I was hunting in Lesbos, I saw, in a wood sacred to the Nymphs, the most beautiful thing that I have ever seen—a painting that told a love story. The wood itself was beautiful enough, full of trees and flowers, and watered by a single spring which nourished both the flowers and the trees; but the picture was even more delightful, combining excellent tech-nique with a romantic subject. It had become so famous that crowds of people used to go there even from abroad, partly to pray to the Nymphs, but mainly to see the picture. In it there were women having babies and other women wrapping them in swaddling clothes, babies being exposed, sheep and goats suckling them, shepherds picking them up, young people plighting their troth, pirates making a raid, enemies starting an invasion.

After gazing admiringly at many other scenes, all of a romantic nature, I was seized by a longing to write a verbal equivalent to the painting. So I found someone to explain the picture to me, and composed a work in four volumes as an offering to Love and the Nymphs and Pan, and as a source of pleasure for the human race—something to heal the sick and comfort the afflicted, to refresh the memory of those who have been in love and educate those who have not. For no one has ever escaped Love altogether, and no one ever will, so long as beauty exists and eyes can see. But as for me, I hope that the god will allow me to write of other people's experiences, while retaining my own sanity.

BOOK ONE

There is in Lesbos a large and beautiful city called Mytilene. It is intersected by canals, where the sea flows inland, and decorated with bridges of polished white stone. You will think, when you see it, that it is not so much a city as an island. Well, about twenty-two miles from this city of Mytilene was an estate belonging to a certain rich man. It was a very fine property, including mountains that supplied game, plains that produced wheat, hillsides covered with vines, and pastures full of flocks. There was also a long beach, against which the waves used to break with a soft bewitching sound.

While grazing his flock on this estate a goatherd called Lamon found a baby being suckled by one of his she-goats. There was a small wood containing a bramble-thicket, some wandering ivy, and some soft grass on which the baby was lying. The goat kept running out of sight in this direction and deserting her kid in order to stay beside the baby. Lamon noticed her running to and fro, and felt sorry for the neglected kid, so although it was the hottest time of day he went off after her and this is what he saw: The goat was standing cautiously astride the baby, so as not to hurt it by treading on it with her hooves, and the baby was sucking away at her milk just as if it came from its mother's breast. Naturally he was astonished; so he went up close and found that it was a boy—a fine big one, and better dressed than foundlings usually are, for it had a little cloak dyed with genuine purple, a golden brooch, and a dagger with an ivory hilt.

His first plan was to ignore the baby and merely go off with the tokens of its identity. But then he felt ashamed to show less humanity than a goat, so he waited until it was dark and took the whole lot home to Myrtale, his wife—tokens, baby, goat and all. Myrtale was astonished at the idea of goats having babies—until he told her the whole story, how he had found the child exposed, how he had seen it being suckled, and how he had been ashamed to leave it to die. She felt the same as he did, so they hid the things that had been left with the baby, called it their own child, and gave the job of nursing it to the goat. And to ensure that the child's name should sound adequately pastoral, they decided to call him Daphnis.

Two years went by and a shepherd in the neighboring fields whose name was Dryas found and saw something very similar. There was a cave sacred to the Nymphs which consisted of a great rock, hollow inside and rounded outside.

The images of the Nymphs themselves were made of stone. Their feet were bare, their arms were naked to the shoulder, and their hair hung down loose over their necks. They had girdles around their waists and smiles on their faces; and their whole attitude was suggestive of dancing. The mouth of the cave was in the very middle of the rock, and from it water came gushing out and flowed away in a stream; so there was an expanse of very lush meadow in front of the cave, as the moisture made the grass grow thick and soft. Hanging up in the cave were milk-pails and transverse flutes and Pan-pipes and reed-pipes, the offerings of shepherds in bygone days.

A ewe which had recently lambed kept going into this sanctuary of the Nymphs and several times made Dryas think she was lost. So wishing to punish her and get her back into good habits, he twisted a green switch into a halter like a snare and went off to the rock in the hope of catching her there. But when he arrived he did not see at all what he expected. He saw the ewe behaving just like a human being—offering her teats to the baby so that it could drink all the milk it wanted, while the baby, which was not even crying, greedily applied first to one teat and then to another a mouth shining with cleanliness, for the ewe was in the habit of licking its face with her tongue when it had had enough. This child was a girl; and like the other it had tokens lying beside it—a girdle woven with gold thread, a pair of gilded sandals, and some anklets of solid gold.

Thinking that the gods must have had a hand in this discovery and taught by the ewe's example to pity the child and love it, he took the baby up in his arms, stowed away the tokens in his knapsack, and prayed to the Nymphs to give him good luck in return for bringing up their protégée. When it was time to drive the flock back, he went home to his cottage, described to his wife what he had seen, showed her what he had found, and told her to treat the baby as her daughter and bring it up as if it were her own, without letting anyone know the truth. So Nape (for that is what she was called) immediately began to mother the child and love it, for fear of being outdone by the ewe. And to make the thing convincing, she too gave the child a pastoral name, Chloë.

These children grew up very quickly and were noticeably better-looking than ordinary country people. And now Daphnis was fifteen years old, and Chloë two years younger, when

"Kouros *(young man)*"

in the course of a single night both Dryas and Lamon had dreams that went something like this. They dreamed that the Nymphs—the ones in the cave with the spring in it, where Dryas had found the baby—were handing Daphnis and Chloë over to a very autocratic and very beautiful small boy who had wings growing out of his shoulders and carried tiny arrows and a tiny bow. This boy hit both of them with a single arrow, and gave orders that Daphnis should in future be a goatherd, and Chloë a shepherdess.

Their first reaction to this dream was disappointment, to think that the children were to be ordinary shepherds and goatherds after all, when the tokens had seemed to promise better things—for which reason they had been given especially good food, and taught to read and write and do all the things that were regarded as great accomplishments in the country. But then it seemed best to accept divine guidance in the case of children whose very survival had been due to divine providence.

So when Dryas and Lamon had told each other their dreams, and made a sacrifice in the presence of the Nymphs to "the winged boy" (for they did not know his name), they sent Daphnis and Chloë out as shepherds with their flocks, after giving them minute instructions about how to graze the animals before noon, and how to graze them when the heat of the day was over; when to drive them to water, and when to drive them back to the fold; which of them they would have to use a stick on, and which of them they could control by the voice alone. So Daphnis and Chloë took over their new job with as much satisfaction as if it had been a great command, and grew fonder of the goats and the sheep than herdsmen usually are, since Chloë was aware that she owed her life to a sheep, and Daphnis remembered that when he was exposed a goat had suckled him.

It was the beginning of spring and all the flowers were in bloom, in the woods, in the meadows, and on the mountains. Already there was a buzzing of bees, there was a sound of singing-birds, there were gambolings of new-born lambs. The lambs were gamboling on the mountains, the bees were buzzing in the meadows, and the birds were filling the thickets with enchanting song. So now that all things were possessed by the beauty of the season, these two tender young creatures began to imitate the sights and sounds around them. Hearing the birds singing they burst into song, seeing the lambs gamboling they danced nimbly about, and taking their cue from the bees they started gathering flowers, some of which they dropped into their bosoms, and the rest they wove into garlands to hang on the images of the Nymphs.

They did everything together, for they grazed their flocks side by side; and often it would be Daphnis who rounded up the sheep that had strayed, and Chloë who drove down the more adventurous goats from the high rocks. In fact it sometimes happened that one of them would look after both the flocks, because the other was busy playing with some toy.

Their toys were of a pastoral and childish nature. Chloë would go off somewhere and pick up some stalks of corn which she would weave into a cage for a locust; and while she was working on it she would forget about the sheep. And Daphnis, after cutting some slender reeds, piercing them at the joints, and fastening them together with soft wax, would practice playing the Pan-pipe until it was dark. Sometimes too they would share the same drink of milk and wine, and divide between them all the food that they brought from home. Altogether, you would have been more likely to see the sheep or the goats separated from one another, than Chloë separated from Daphnis.

While they were playing like this, Love made something serious flare up. A she-wolf with young cubs to feed had been carrying off a great many animals from other flocks in the neighboring fields, as she needed a great deal of food to rear her cubs. So one night the villagers got together and dug some pits about six feet wide and twenty-four feet deep. Most of the soil that had been dug up was carted away and scattered a long way off; but over the mouth of each pit they placed long pieces of dry wood and sprinkled the rest of the soil on top, to make the ground look the same as before. So even a hare running across it would have broken the pieces of wood, which were no stronger than twigs, and would then have realized that it was not solid earth after all, but a mere imitation of it. They dug several pits like this both on the mountains and in the plains, and never succeeded in catching the wolf, for she realized that the ground had been tampered with; but they managed to kill a great many goats and sheep, and they came very near to killing Daphnis.

It happened like this. Some he-goats got angry and started to fight. They came together rather violently, with the result that one of them had one of his horns broken and ran away snorting with pain. But the victor followed him

closely and kept him on the run. Feeling upset about the broken horn and annoyed at such unruly behavior, Daphnis began pursuing the pursuer with a stick. Since the goat was intent on getting away, and the boy was angrily intent on catching him, neither was very careful to look where he was going and they both fell into a pit—first the goat, and then Daphnis. In fact the only thing that saved Daphnis's life was using the goat to break his fall.

So Daphnis waited in tears for someone to pull him out—if anyone was ever going to. But Chloë, who had seen the whole thing, came running to the pit and finding that Daphnis was alive called a cowherd in a neighboring field to come and help. When he arrived he started looking for a long rope for Daphnis to hold on to, so as to be pulled out; and there was no rope to be found. But Chloë untied her breastband and gave the cowherd that to let down. So they stood on the edge of the pit and pulled, while Daphnis clung to the breastband with both hands and came up with it. They also pulled up the wretched goat, with both his horns broken—so quickly had the vengeance of the conquered he-goat overtaken him. He was only fit for slaughter, so they gave him to the cowherd as a reward for lifesaving, and prepared to make up a story about an attack by wolves, in case anyone at home noticed that the goat was missing. Then they went back to find out how the rest of the goats and sheep were getting on.

Having made sure that both the sheep and the goats were grazing properly, they sat down against the trunk of an oak and looked to see if Daphnis had got blood on any part of his body as a result of his fall. There was no sign of a wound and no trace of blood, but his hair and the rest of his body were plastered with loose earth and mud; and it seemed best for him to wash before Lamon and Myrtale found out what had happened.

So he went off with Chloë to the sanctuary of the Nymphs, where he gave her his shirt and knapsack to look after, while he stood in front of the spring and started washing his hair and his whole body. His hair was black and thick, and his body was slightly sunburned—it looked as though it was darkened by the shadow of his hair. It seemed to Chloë, as she watched him, that Daphnis was beautiful; and as he had never seemed beautiful to her before, she thought that this beauty must be the result of washing. Moreover, when she washed his back, she found that the flesh was soft and yielding; so she secretly touched her own body several times to see if it was any softer. Then, as the sun was setting, they drove their flocks home, and nothing out of the ordinary had happened to Chloë except that she had set her heart on seeing Daphnis washing again.

When they got to the pasture next day, Daphnis sat down under the usual oak and began to play his pipe. At the same time he kept an eye on the goats, which were lying down and apparently listening to the music. Chloë sat beside him and kept watch over her flock of sheep; but most of the time she was looking at Daphnis. While he was piping he again seemed to her beautiful, and this time she thought that the beauty was caused by the music; so when he had finished she picked up the pipe herself, in the hope that she too might become beautiful. She also persuaded him to have another wash; and while he was

washing she looked at him, and after looking at him she touched him. And again she went away full of admiration, and this admiration was the beginning of love.

She did not know what was wrong with her, for she was only a young girl who had been brought up in the country and had never even heard the word "love" used by anyone else. But she felt sick at heart, and she could not control her eyes, and she was always talking about Daphnis. She took no interest in food, she could not sleep at night, she paid no attention to her flock. One moment she would be laughing, the next she would be crying. Now she would be lying down, now she would be jumping up again. Her face would grow pale, and then grow fiery red. In fact cows that have been stung by gadflies behave less oddly than she did.

One day when she was alone she found herself talking like this:

"There's something wrong with me these days, but I don't know what it is. I'm in pain, and yet I've not been injured. I feel sad, and yet none of my sheep have got lost. I'm burning hot, and yet here I am sitting in the shade. How often I've been scratched by brambles and not cried! How often I've been stung by bees and not screamed! But this thing that's pricking my heart hurts more than anything like that. Daphnis *is* beautiful, but so are the flowers. His pipe does sound beautiful, but so do the nightingales—and I don't worry about them. If only I *were* his pipe, so that he'd breathe into me! If only I were a goat, so that I could have him looking after me! You wicked water, you made Daphnis beautiful, but when I tried washing it made no difference. Oh, Nymphs,

I'm dying—and even you do nothing to save the girl who was nursed in your cave. Who will put garlands on you when I'm gone? Who will rear the poor lambs? Who will look after my chattering locust? I had a lot of trouble catching her, so that she could talk me to sleep in front of the cave—and now I can't sleep because of Daphnis, and she chatters away for nothing."

That was how she suffered and that was how she talked, as she tried to find a name for love. But Dorcon, the cowherd who had pulled Daphnis and the he-goat out of the pit, was a youth whose beard had already begun to grow, and he knew what love was called and also what it meant. He had fallen in love with Chloë on that very day, and as other days went by his feelings had become more and more inflamed. So regarding Daphnis as too young to be taken seriously, he decided to achieve his object either by bribery or by force.

He began by bringing them presents—for Daphnis a cowherd's Pan-pipe consisting of nine reeds fastened together with bronze instead of wax, and for Chloë a Bacchic fawnskin that looked as if the colors had been put on with paint. Then, having come to be regarded as a friend, he gradually took less and less notice of Daphnis but kept bringing Chloë presents every day—either a delicious cheese, or a garland of flowers, or some summer apples. And once he actually brought her a newborn calf, and a wooden bowl decorated with gold, and some young mountain-birds. Having had no experience of the methods employed by lovers, Chloë was only too glad to accept the presents, because she thus had something to give Daphnis.

One day—for it was now Daphnis's turn to realize what love meant—he and Dorcon engaged in a beauty contest. Chloë was the judge, and the prize for victory was the privilege of kissing Chloë.

Dorcon spoke first, to this effect:

"Well, my girl, I'm bigger than Daphnis. And I'm a cowherd and he's a goatherd, so I'm as much superior to him as cows are to goats. Also my skin's as white as milk, and my hair's as red as corn that's just going to be reaped. And I was nursed by my mother, not by an animal. But this fellow's quite short, and he's as beardless as a woman and as dark as a wolf. And he grazes he-goats and smells awful as a result. And he's too poor even to keep a dog. And if it's true that he was suckled by a goat, as people say, he's really no better than a kid."

When Dorcon had said something like this, Daphnis replied:

"Certainly I was suckled by a goat—so was Zeus. And the he-goats that I graze are bigger than his cows. And they don't make me smell, because even Pan doesn't smell and he's three-quarters goat. And I've got plenty of cheese, and bread baked on a spit, and white wine, and all that a peasant needs to make him rich. I haven't got a beard, but neither has Dionysus. I'm dark, but so are hyacinths—and Dionysus is superior to the Satyrs, and so are hyacinths to lilies. But this fellow's as red as a fox, and he's got a beard like a he-goat, and his skin's as white as a town-lady's. And if you have to kiss someone, you can kiss my mouth, but all you can kiss of him is the hair on his chin. And remember, dear girl, that you yourself were nursed by a sheep—and even so you're beautiful."

Chloë waited no longer but, partly because she was pleased by the compliment and partly because she had been wanting to kiss Daphnis for a long time, she jumped up and kissed him. It was an artless and inexperienced sort of kiss, but one which was quite capable of setting a heart on fire. So Dorcon ran off in dismay, and began to look for some other method of satisfying his love. But Daphnis reacted as if he had been stung rather than kissed. He suddenly looked almost indignant and shivered several times and tried to control his pounding heart; he wanted to look at Chloë, but when he did so he blushed all over. Then for the first time he saw with wonder that her hair was as golden as fire, that her eyes were as big as the eyes of an ox, and that her complexion was really even whiter than the milk of the goats. It was as if he had just got eyes for the first time, and had been blind all his life before.

So he stopped eating any food except for a mere taste, and if he had to drink he did no more than moisten his lips. Before, he had been more talkative than a locust; now he was taciturn. Before, he had been more active than a goat: now he sat idle. His flock was forgotten; even his Pan-pipe was thrown aside. His face was paler than grass at midsummer. The only person that he would talk to was Chloë; and if ever he was apart from her and alone, he would rave away to himself like this:

"Whatever is Chloë's kiss doing to me? Her lips are softer than roses and her mouth is sweeter than honey, but her kiss hurts more than the sting of a bee. I've often kissed kids, and I've often kissed newborn puppies and the calf that Dorcon gave her, but this kiss is something quite new. My breath's coming in gasps, my heart's jumping up and down, my soul's melting away—but all the same I want to kiss her again. Oh, what an unlucky victory! Oh, what a strange disease—I don't even know what to call it. Had Chloë drunk poison just before she kissed me? If so, how did she manage not to be killed? Hear how the nightingales are singing—and my pipe is silent. Look how the kids are frisking about—and I'm sitting still. Look how the flowers are blooming—and I'm not making any garlands. Yes, the violets and the hyacinths are in flower, but Daphnis is withering away. Is Dorcon going to seem better-looking than I am after all?"

That was how the worthy Daphnis suffered, and that was how he talked; for it was his first experience of love, and the language of love. . . .

ATHENAEUS (FL. CA. A.D. 200)
The Sophists at Dinner (ca. A.D. 230)

This remarkable, undisciplined celebration of classical Greek literature in fifteen books was known to the Greeks and Romans as *The Sophists at Dinner,* or the *Deipnosophistae.* Its sprawling exposition of matters of the palate, from "hairy bulbs" to the lettuce bed Aphrodite hid Adonis in to make sure he remained chaste between trysts, has absolutely none of the brilliant organizational precision of the golden age of classical Athens, and probably makes Aristotle turn over in his grave. Yet its vibrant *joie de vivre,* whether expressed in discussions of the quickest purgative or of the most pleasing mineral water to sip after pork, reminds us, in the decadence of the Pax Romana, of all that is most vital about Greek thought.

- *The Sophists at Dinner* is the earliest known surviving cookbook in western literature, though cooking had already become a refined science among the Greeks as early as fifth century B.C. Sicily, when Archestratus wrote, in hexameters, a book known as *Dainty Dishes.* Sicilian cooks spread the message of culinary refinement throughout the Greek Mediterranean, their philosophy of eating articulated in the most minute particulars, echoed in this century's French chef Brillat-Savarin or America's Julia Child.
- Written in imitation of the "banquet dialogue" made famous by Plato and Xenophon, *The Deipnosophistae* is a rambling, digressive, exceedingly fascinating and frequently tedious treatise on practical, theoretical, philosophical, and historical aspects of eating and everything imaginable associated with it.
- Born in Egypt, Athenaeus lived in Rome during the time of the Emperor Commodus. The feast of the Sophists supposedly took place in Rome, over a three-day period (one of its fictionalized guests is the physician Galen), although internal inconsistencies show that the author paid little attention to maintaining his structural purpose. Imagine *My Dinner with André* in an uncut seventy-two-hour version! Most of the time Athenaeus completely loses sight of all intentions except the culinary—which is exactly what makes him delicious reading.

. . . Pindar praises

Ancient wine and modern songs.

And Eubulus says—

Inconsistent it seems for a fair one to praise
   Old wine, and to say that such never can
     cloy;
But bring her a man who has seen his best days,
   And she'd rather put up with a whiskerless
     boy.

And Alexis says very nearly the same thing word for word; only using the word *little* instead of *never.* Though in reality old wine is not only more pleasant, but also better for health; for it aids digestion more; and being thinner it is itself more digestible; it also invigorates the body; and makes the blood red and fluid, and produces untroubled sleep. But Homer praises that wine most which will admit of a copious admixture of water; as the Maronean. And old wine will allow of more water being added to it, because its very age has added heat to it. And some men say that the flight of Bacchus to the sea is emblematic of the making of wine, as it was practiced long ago; because wine is very sweet when seawater is poured into it. And Homer praising dark-colored wine often calls it αἴθοψ. For the dark-colored wine is the strongest, and it remains in the system of the drinkers of it longer than any other. But Theopompus says that black wine was first made among the Chians; and that the Chians were the first people who imparted the knowledge of planting and tending vines to the rest

of mankind, having learned it from Oenopion the son of Bacchus, who was the original colonizer of their island. But white wine is weak and thin; but yellow wine is very digestible, being of a more drying nature.

Respecting the Italian wines, Galen is represented by this sophist as saying that the Falernian wine is fit to drink from the time that it is ten or fifteen years old, till it is twenty; but after that time it falls off, and is apt to give headaches, and affects the nervous system. . . .

. . . Antiphanes, that witty man, catalogs all the things which are peculiar to each city thus:

Cooks come from Elis, pots from Argos,
Corinth blankets sends in barges,
Phlius wine, and Sicyon fish;
While cheese is a Sicilian dish.
Aegium sends flute-playing maids;
Perfumers ply their dainty trades
At Athens, under Pallas' eye;
Boeotia sends us eels to fry.

And Hermippus says,

Tell me, ye Muses, who th' Olympic height
Cheer with your holy songs and presence
   bright;
Tell me what blessings Bacchus gave to man,
Since first his vessel o'er the waters ran.
Ox-hides from Libya's coasts, and juicy kail:
The narrow sea, still vocal with the wail
Of lost Leander's bride, the tunny sends,
And our first meal with kipper'd salmon
   mends.
Groats come from Italy, and ribs of beef;

"Hellenistic gold earrings, by Crispano, Taranto."
Copyright Archivi Alinari, 1992. By permission of Art
Resource.

While Thrace sends many a lie and many a
    thief.
Still do the Spartans scratch their sides in vain,
Mad with the itching of th' Odrysian pain.
Then Syracuse gives cheese and well-fed pigs;
Fair Athens olives sends, and luscious figs.
Cursed of all islands let Corcyra be,
Where no especial excellence we see.
Sails come from Egypt, and this paper too;
Incense from Syria; Crete upholds to view
The cypress tall; and, dear to mighty Jove,
In Paphlagonia grows the almond grove.
The elephant sends its teeth from Afric's sands;
Pears and fat sheep grow on Euboea's lands;
Rhodes sends us raisins, and beguiles the
    night
With figs that make our dreams and slumbers
    light;
From Phrygia slaves, allies from Arca's land;
The Pagasaean ports their hirelings brand;

Phoenicia sends us dates across the billows,
And Carthage, carpets rich, and well-stuff'd
    pillows. . . .

. . . It was a custom at feasts, that a guest
when he had lain down should have a paper
given to him, containing a bill of fare of what
there was for dinner, so that he might know
what the cook was going to serve up.

We find a fruit called Damascenes. Now
many of the ancient writers mention Damascus,
a city of great reputation and importance; and as
there is a great quantity of plum trees in the territory of the Damascenes, and as they are cultivated there with exceeding care, the tree itself has
got to be called a Damascene, as being a kind of
plum different from what is found in other countries. The fruit is more like prunes. And many
writers speak of them, and Hipponax says—

I have a garland of damascenes and mint.

And Alexis says—

A. And in my sleep I thought I saw a prize.
B. What was it?
                A. Listen.—There came up to me,
While still within th' arena's spacious bounds,
One of my rivals, bringing me a crown—
A ripe revolving crown of damascenes.
B. Oh Hercules! and were the damascenes
    ripe?

And again he says—

Did you e'er see a sausage toasted,
Or dish of tripe well stuff'd and roasted?

Or damascenes stew'd in rich confection?—
Such was that gentleman's complexion.

Nicander says—

The fruit they call a plum, the cuckoo's prize.

But Clearchus the Peripatetic says that the Rhodians and Sicilians call plums βράβυλα, and so Theocritus the Syracusan uses the word—

Heavy with plums, the branches swept the ground.

And again he says—

Far as the apple doth the plum surpass.

But the damascene is smaller in circumference than other plums, though in flavor it is very like them, except that it is a little sharper. Seleucus, in his Dictionary, says that βράβυλα, ἦλα, κοκκύμηλα, and μάδρυα are all different names for the same thing; and that plums are called βράβυλα, as being good for the stomach, and βορὰν ἐκ βάλλοντα, that is, assisting to remove the food; and ἦλα, which is the same word as μῆλα, meaning simply *fruit*, as Demetrius Ixion says in his Etymology. And Theophrastus says, κοκκύμηλα καὶ σποδιάς: σποδιάς being a kind of wild plum. And Araros calls the tree which bears the fruit κοκκυμηλέα, and the fruit itself κοκκύμηλον. And Diphilus of Siphnos pronounces plums to be juicy, digestible, and easily evacuated, but not very nutritious.

There is another fruit, called Cherries. Theophrastus says, in his book on Plants, that the Cherry tree is a tree of a peculiar character, and of large size, for it grows to a height of four-and-twenty cubits, and its leaf is like that of the medlar, but somewhat harder and thicker, and its bark like the linden; its flower is white, like that of the pear or the medlar, consisting of a number of small petals of a waxy nature; its fruit is red, like that of the lotus in appearance, and of the size of a bean; but the kernel of the lotus is hard, while that of the cherry is soft. And again he says, "The κράταιγος, which some call κραταίγων, has a spreading leaf like a medlar, only that is larger, and wider, and longer; and it has no deep grain in it as the medlar has. The tree is neither very tall nor very large; the wood is variegated, yellow, and strong: It has a smooth bark, like that of the medlar; and a single root, which goes down very deep into the earth; the fruit is round, of the size of an olive; when fully ripe it is of a yellow color, becoming gradually darker; and from its flavor and juice it might almost be taken for a wild medlar." By which description of the crataegus it appears to me that he means the tree which is now called the cherry.

Asclepiades of Myrlea speaks of a tree which he calls the Ground-cherry, and says, "In the land of the Bithynians there is found the ground-cherry, the root of which is not large, nor is the tree, but like a rosebush; in all other respects the fruit is like the common cherry; but it makes those who eat much of it feel heavy, as wine does, and it gives them head-aches." These are the words of Asclepiades. And it appears to me that he is speaking of the arbutus. For the tree which bears the arbutus-berry answers his description, and if a man eats more than six or seven of the berries he gets a headache. Aristophanes says—

And planted by no hand, the arbutus
Makes red the sunny hills.

Theopompus says—

The myrtle berries and red arbutus.

Crates says—

Beauteous the breast of tender maid,
As arbutus or apples red.

And Amphis—

Mulberries you see, my friend, are found
On the tree which we know as the mulberry;
So the oak bears the acorn round,
And the arbutus shines with its full berry.

And Theophrastus tells us, "The κόμαρος (as he calls it) is the tree which bears the arbutus berry."

There is question about the "Agen," a satyric drama, whether it was composed by Python (and if by him whether he was a native of Catana or of Byzantium), or by the king Alexander himself.

Then Laurentius says—"You, O Greeks, lay claim to a good many things, as either having given the names to them, or having been the original discoverers of them. But you do not know that Lucullus, the Roman general, who subdued Mithridates and Tigranes, was the first man who introduced this plant into Italy from Cerasus, a city of Pontus; and he it was who gave the fruit the Latin name of Cerasus, *cherry*, after the name of the city, as our historians relate."

Then Daphnis answers—"But there was a very celebrated man, Diphilus of Siphnos, many years more ancient than Lucullus, for he was born in the time of king Lysimachus (who was one of the successors of Alexander), and he speaks of cherries, saying, 'Cherries are good for the stomach, and juicy, but not very nutritious; if taken after drinking cold water they are especially wholesome; but the red and the Milesian are the best kinds, and are diuretic.' " . . .

But the white onions, called βόλβιναι, are fuller of good juice than the common onions; but they are not so good for the stomach, because the white portion of them has a certain thickness in it. Yet they are very tolerably wholesome, because they have a good deal of harshness in them, and because they promote the secretions. And Matron, in his Parodies, mentions the βολβίνη—

But sowthistles I will not even name,
Plants full of marrow, crown'd on th' heads
    with thorns;
Nor the white onions, minstrels of great Jove,
Which his dear Child, incessant rain, has
    nourish'd
Whiter than snowstorms, and like meal to
    view,
Which, when they first appeared, my stomach
    loved.

Nicander extols the onions of Megara. But Theophrastus, in the seventh book of his treatise on Plants, says—"In some places the onions are so sweet, that they are eaten raw, as they are in the Tauric Chersonesus." And Phaenias makes the same statement—"There is," says he, "a kind of onion which bears wool, according to Theophrastus; and it is produced on the seashore. And it has the wool underneath its first coat, so as to be between the outer eatable parts and the inner ones. And from this wool socks and stockings and other articles of clothing are woven." And Phaenias himself adopts the statement. "But the onion," he continues, "of the Indians is hairy." But concerning the dressing of onions, Philemon says—

Now if you want an onion, just consider
What great expense it takes to make it good:
You must have cheese, and honey, and sesame,
Oil, leeks, and vinegar, and assafoetida,
To dress it up with; for by itself the onion
Is bitter and unpleasant to the taste.

But Heraclides the Tarentine, limiting the use of onions at banquets, says—"One must set bounds to much eating, especially of such things as have anything glutinous or sticky about them; as, for instance, eggs, onions, calves' feet, snails, and such things as those, for they remain in the stomach a long time, and form a lump there, and check the natural moisture."

Thrushes, too, and crowds of other birds, formed part of the dishes in the propomata. Teleclides says—

But roasted thrushes with sweet cheesecakes
   served

Flew of their own accord down the guests'
   throats.

But the Syracusans call thrushes, not κίχλαι, but κίχηλαι. Epicharmus says—

The thrushes (κίχηλαι) fond of eating the
   olive. . . .

Now Heraclides the Tarentine asks this question; "Whether it is best to drink warm water or cold after the eating of figs?" And he says that those who recommend the drinking of cold water do so because they have an eye to such a fact as this, that warm water cleanses one's hands more quickly than cold; on which account it is reasonable to believe that food in the stomach will be quickly washed away by warm water. And with respect to figs which are not eaten, warm water dissolves their consistency and connection, and separates them into small pieces; but cold coagulates and consolidates them. But those who recommend the drinking of cold water say the taking of cold water bears down by its own weight the things which are heavy on the stomach (for figs do not do any extraordinary good to the stomach, since they heat it and destroy its tone; on which account some people always drink neat wine after them); and then too it quickly expels what is already in the stomach. But after eating figs, it is desirable to take an abundant and immediate draft of something or other; in order to prevent those things from remaining in the stomach, and to move them into the lower parts of the bowels.

Others however say that it is not a good thing to eat figs at midday; for that at that time

they are apt to engender diseases, as Phere-
crates has said in his Crapatalli. And Aristophanes, in his Proagon, says—

But once seeing him when he was sick in the
    summer,
In order to be sick too himself, eat figs at
    midday.

And Eubulus says, in his Sphingocarion—

No doubt it was; for I was sick, my friend,
From eating lately figs one day at noon.

And Nicophon says, in the Sirens—

But if a man should eat green figs at noon,
And then go off to sleep; immediately
A galloping fever comes on him, accursed,
And falling on him brings up much black bile.

Diphilus of Siphnos says that of figs some
are tender, and not very nutritious, but full of
bad juice, nevertheless easily secreted, and rising easily to the surface; and that these are
more easily managed than the dry figs; but that
those which are in season in the winter, being
ripened by artificial means, are very inferior;
but that the best are those which are ripe at the
height of the summer, as being ripened naturally; and these have a great deal of juice; and
those which are not so juicy are still good for
the stomach, though somewhat heavy. And the
figs of Tralles are like the Rhodian; and the
Chian, and all the rest, appear to be inferior to
these, both in the quality and quantity of their
juice. But Mnesitheus the Athenian, in his
treatise on Eatables, says—"But with respect to
whatever of these fruits are eaten raw, such as
pears, and figs, and Delphic apples, and such
fruits, one ought to watch the opportunity
when they will have the juice which they contain, neither unripe on the one hand, nor
tainted on the other; nor too much dried up by
the season." But Demetrius the Scepsian, in
the fifteenth book of the Trojan Preparation,
says that those who never eat figs have the best
voices. At all events, he says, that Hegesianax
the Alexandrian, who wrote the Histories, was
originally a man with a very weak voice, and
that he became a tragedian and a fine actor,
and a man with a fine voice, by abstaining from
figs for eighteen years together. And I know too
that there are some proverbs going about concerning figs, of which the following are samples:

Figs after fish, vegetables after meat.
Figs are agreeable to birds, but they do not
    choose to plant them. . . .

HELIODORUS (FL. A.D. 220–250)
Aethiopica

❦

*H*eliodorus, like Longus a predecessor of twentieth-century romance novelists, was born in Emesa, in Greek Phoenicia (Syria), and when he was younger may have been a sophist and a priest of Helios the sun god. He converted to Christianity, and became the bishop of Tricca in Thessaly.

Written at a time when upper-class leisure bred an insatiable appetite for romantic tales, the most popular of his three novels was the ten-book, picaresque *Aethiopica,* detailing the adventures of Chariclea, the white daughter of the king and queen of Ethiopia in the time of Alexander the Great, as she attempts to protect her virtue through one escapade after another "on the road" from Delphi to Meroe. Consistent with the tradition of comedy, the book ends happily with her marriage to the Thessalian prince Theagenes. Along the way, she encounters not only battles, kidnappings, torture, pirates, and imbroglios of every kind, but also fellow travelers, whose stories are fascinating enough to be recorded—like the one that follows.

- The *Aethiopica,* modeled structurally on Homer's *Odyssey,* is compelling for its clear presentation of character, its intricate yet masterfully interwoven plot, its adept handling of flashbacks, and its relentless tension and suspense, as well as for its elegant and straightforward Attic narrative style. Legend has it that when his youthful *Aethiopica* was condemned for leading the young astray, Heliodorus chose to resign his bishopric rather than have his book suppressed.
- Used as a model in medieval and Renaissance Europe, the *Aethiopica* influenced Torquato Tasso's *Jerusalem Delivered* as well as Miguel de Cervantes' *Don Quixote de la Mancha.*

. . . IX. But, as they persisted and begged Cnemon to tell his story, thinking that it would be a great consolation to them to hear of misfortunes equal to their own, he began as follows:

I am the son of Aristippus, an Athenian by birth, a man of considerable means, and a member of the Areopagus. After my mother's death, he married again; I was his only son, and he did not wish to be dependent upon my care alone in his old age. He married a lady, named Demaeneta, a most charming woman, but the cause of all my misfortunes. As soon as she entered the house, she endeavored to make herself absolute mistress, and easily persuaded the old man to do whatever she wanted, by the charm of her beauty and the obsequious attention which she bestowed upon him; more than any woman I have ever known, she possessed the art of inspiring passion, and a wonderful knack of seducing those of the opposite sex. When my father went out, she wept; when he returned, she ran to meet him, complained of his long absence, and declared that, if he had delayed longer, it would have killed her; she embraced him after every word, and moistened her kisses with her tears. Ensnared by her artifices, my father saw no one but her, and lived for her alone.

At first she pretended to look upon me as her own son, thereby strengthening her hold upon my father. Sometimes she would kiss me, and desired that I would give her the pleasure of my company. I permitted her caresses, in no way suspecting the purpose she had in view; my only surprise was that she showed such motherly affection toward me. But when she grew more wanton, and her kisses became hotter than decency permitted, and her looks immodest—all this aroused my suspicions, and I began to avoid and repel her advances. I omit the rest, why need I weary you with recalling it? the different ways in which she tempted me, the promises which she made; calling me her little boy, her darling, her heir, her life and soul, mingling with the tenderest names all that was most likely to win my affections; in more serious matters she played the part of a mother, but in dalliance clearly showed that she was in love.

X. At last, her passion declared itself. During the celebration of the great Panathenaic festival, the Athenians carry a ship through the streets in honor of Athena. I had just arrived at man's estate, and, after I had sung the usual hymn in honor of the goddess, and duly led the customary procession, I returned home, still wearing my ceremonial robes, my head still crowned with garlands. As soon as Demaeneta saw me, she lost her reason, and, no longer able to disguise her passion, ran toward me, calling me "her young Hippolytus, her darling Theseus." You can judge of my feelings at the time, seeing that the mere recollection of it makes me blush. That evening, my father supped in the Prytaneum; and, as was usual on the occasion of such meetings and public banquets, had arranged to pass the night there. During the night, Demaeneta entered my room, and endeavored to obtain the satisfaction of her unholy desires. When I firmly resisted all her caresses, promises, and threats, she sighed deeply and left me; and, when only one night had passed, the accursed woman plotted revenge.

At first, she kept her bed in the morning, and, when my father returned, and asked her what was the matter with her, she pretended that she was indisposed, and at first refused to answer him further; but at last, yielding to his pressing enquiries, she said: "That wonderful young man, that son of yours, whom I looked upon as my own, whom (as the gods can testify) I loved even more than you did, observing, from certain indications, that I was with child, (which I had concealed from you until I was certain of it) took advantage of your absence, while I was admonishing him, as I have always done, and exhorting him to be temperate, and avoid women and drinking (for I was aware of his irregularities, but I would not disclose them to you, for fear you might suspect me as his stepmother)—while, I say, I was discussing these matters with him alone, to spare his blushes, he burst forth into such abuse of both of us, that I should be ashamed to repeat it; after which, he kicked me in the belly, and reduced me to the condition in which you now see me."

XI. On hearing these words, my father, without saying anything to me, without questioning me or giving me time to defend myself, came to the conclusion that one who had shown such affection for me could not have accused me falsely. Chancing to meet me in the house, he attacked me with his fists, called his slaves and ordered them to scourge me, although I knew not for what I was being punished, a privilege usually granted to the greatest criminals. At length, when he had satisfied his anger, I said to him: "Now at least, my father, you ought to let me know for what crime I have been scourged, although you refused to tell me before." These words only provoked him more. "Deceitful wretch!" he cried, "is it from me that you would learn your infamies?" Then, turning away from me, he hastened to Demaeneta, whose rage, not yet satisfied, had laid a second plot to destroy me.

She had a maid called Thisbe, a handsome girl, who played admirably upon the lute. Demaeneta sent her to me with instructions to gain my affections. Without delay, she made advances to me; and she, who had oftentimes before rejected my suit, endeavored to attract me by looks, signs, and gestures. In my vanity, I believed that I had suddenly become an Adonis, and at last, one night, I admitted her to my arms; she visited me a second and a third time, and indeed, on several occasions. But, when I

exhorted her to take care that she was not surprised by her mistress, she said: "Oh, Cnemon, how simple you are! Do you think there is any danger for a slave such as I am, bought for a price, even if I am caught with you? if so, what punishment do you think my mistress deserves, a woman who boasts of noble birth, to whom the laws have assigned a husband, and who, although she well knows that death is the punishment of conjugal infidelity, is not afraid to commit adultery?" "Do not say so," I answered, "I cannot believe you." "Well, if you like, I will let you see her in the act." "If it is your wish," I said. "It is," she answered. "I desire for your sake, you have been so cruelly outraged by her, as well as for my own, who suffer terribly every day at her hands—the result of the bitter jealousy she feels against me. Therefore be a man, and surprise her with her paramour."

XII. I promised, and she retired. Three nights afterward, she came and woke me, telling me that Demaeneta was with her lover; that my father had been suddenly called into the country on business; and that the dishonorer of his bed had secretly, by appointment, entered his wife's room. She declared that it was my duty to prepare to avenge him and to arm myself with a sword, to prevent the villain's escape.

I did as she advised: I took a sword, and proceeded toward my father's room, while Thisbe carried a lighted torch in front. When I came to the door, I saw that there was a light burning inside; transported with rage, I broke upon the door, and rushed in, exclaiming, "Where is the wretch, the fine lover of this most virtuous woman?" With these words, I advanced, intending to run them both through with my sword. But, great heavens! my father leaped out of bed and fell on his knees before me, exclaiming: "Oh! my son, restrain yourself; pity your father; spare these gray hairs, that have brought you up. I have done you wrong, it is true; but death would be too cruel a vengeance. Do not abandon yourself to your rage, nor stain your hands with your father's blood."

Such were his piteous pleadings; for my part, as if smitten by a thunderbolt, I stood dumbfounded, unable to utter a word, looking for Thisbe, who had stealthily withdrawn. I gazed at the bed and round the room, not knowing what to say or do.

The sword fell from my hand; Demaeneta jumped out of bed, and seized it. When my father saw that he was out of danger, he laid hands upon me, and gave orders that I should be bound. Demaeneta, meanwhile, continued to exasperate him. "Did I not warn you of this?" she exclaimed; "did I not tell you to be on your guard against the youth, since he would seize the first opportunity of attacking you? I read his purpose in his eyes." "It is true," replied my father; "you warned me, but I refused to believe you." He then ordered me to be kept in chains, and refused to allow me to speak, or to tell him the real truth of the matter.

XIII. As soon as it was day, he took and led me, bound as I was, before the people; then, having poured ashes over his head, he thus addressed them: "Oh Athenians, it was not in expectation of this that I brought up my son; hoping that he would prove the support of my old age, I gave him, from his earliest years, a liberal education; after I had taught him the elements of letters, I introduced him among the members of his clan and family, registered his name among those who had reached the age of manhood, and secured him the standing of a citizen of our country, in conformity with the laws; in a word, my life's hopes were centered in him. But he, forgetting all this, first abused me and assaulted my lawful wife; and at last, with a naked sword in his hand, entered my chamber by night; if he is not guilty of the murder of his own father, he has only to thank Fortune, which inspired him with sudden terror, and caused the sword to fall from his hands. I now, therefore, have recourse to you, and formally denounce him. For although, according to the law, I might have slain him with my own hand, I did not wish to do so; I am content to leave the decision in your hands, for I am convinced that it is better that my son should be punished by the verdict of the law, rather than by death before a verdict has been pronounced." With these words, he began to shed tears.

Demaeneta also wept and pretended to be grieved at my sad lot. "Unhappy wretch!" she cried; "his death will be just, but premature; some avenging Deity has driven him to lift his hand against his parents." But her lamentations were not so much an indication of sorrow for me as a fresh evidence of the truth of the accusation.

In my turn, I asked permission to speak; but the clerk came forward and put the simple question to me: "Did you attack your father with a sword?" "I certainly did, but hear how that came to pass," I answered. Then all cried out that I had no right to ask to be heard in my defense. Some demanded that I should be stoned; others, that I should be handed over to the executioner; and others, that I should be thrust headlong into the Barathrum. As for my-self, while all this disturbance was taking place and they were deciding what should be my punishment, I kept crying out: "Oh, step-mother! I am destroyed by a stepmother! a stepmother is taking away my life without a trial!" My words attracted the attention of some of the judges, and made them suspect the truth; yet even then they refused to listen to me; for the mind of the people was preoccu-pied by the incessant disturbance.

XIV. When the votes were counted, 1,700 were found to be in favor of putting me to death, some voting that I should be stoned; others, that I should be flung headlong into the Barathrum. The rest, to the number of 1,000— and that no doubt because their suspicions of my stepmother inclined them to mercy—were for condemning me to perpetual banishment. Their opinion gained the day; for, although the others, taken together, were in an actual major-ity, yet, as there had been a difference of opin-ion among them in regard to my punishment, the 1,000 votes formed a relative majority. Thus I was driven from my father's hearth and my native land. However, the gods did not suf-fer the wickedness of Demaeneta to go unpun-ished. I will tell you afterward what happened to her. But now you must have some sleep; the night is far advanced and you need repose.

"By no means," said Theagenes; "you will only vex us still more, if you break off your story before telling us how this vilest of women was punished." "Listen, then," said Cnemon, "since such is your pleasure."

After the result of the trial I went down to the Piraeus, just as I was, and finding a ship there which was ready to set sail for Aegina, I embarked; for I remembered that some cousins of my mother lived there. On my arrival, I found those of whom I was in search, and at first I spent my time agreeably enough. About three weeks afterward, in the course of my usual walk, I found myself down at the harbor; at the same moment, a bark was putting in to shore; and I waited a little to see where it hailed from, and who were on board. Almost before the ladder was properly let down, someone leaped on shore, hurried toward me, and em-braced me. It turned out to be Charias, one of the friends of my youth. "I have good news for you, Cnemon," said he; "you are revenged upon your enemy. Demaeneta is dead." "Wel-come, Charias," I said; "but why hurry over this good news so rapidly, as if you were the bearer of evil tidings? Let me have further details; for I am very much afraid that she had died a nat-ural death, and has thus escaped the punish-ment she deserved." "Justice, to use the words of Hesiod, has not entirely deserted us; al-though she sometimes appears to wink at men's crimes, and to put off the day of punish-ment, nevertheless she casts her avenging eye upon such criminals; and it is she who has just punished the infamous Demaeneta. I know all that was said and done; you are aware of my re-lations with Thisbe; she told me everything. Af-ter the unjust sentence of banishment had been pronounced upon you, your unhappy fa-ther, regretting what he had done, retired into a lonely villa in the country, far from the haunts of men, and there he passed his days, 'eating his heart out,' in the words of the poet. As for Demaeneta, the Furies immediately began to torment her; your absence had only inflamed her passion for you; she never ceased to weep, apparently for your misfortunes, but in reality for her own unhappy fate; night and day she cried, 'Oh, Cnemon, my dear, my darling boy, my well-beloved!' The ladies of her acquaintance, when they came to visit her, were astonished, and loudly praised her, because, although only a stepmother, she showed a mother's affection. They endeavored to console her and restore her courage; but she answered that her sorrow was inconsolable, and that others did not know by what goads her heart was pierced." . . .

GREEK GODS/HEROES	ROMAN COUNTERPARTS
Aesclepios	Aesculapius
Aias	Ajax
Aphrodite	Venus
Apollo	Apollo
Ares	Mars
Artemis	Diana
Athena	Minerva
Demeter	Ceres
Dionysus	Bacchus
Eros	Cupid
Hades	Dis, Orcus
Hephaistos	Vulcan
Hera	Juno
Herakles	Hercules
Hermes	Mercury
Hypnos	Somnus
Kronos	Saturn
Odysseus	Ulysses
Persephone	Proserpina
Polydeuces	Pollux
Poseidon	Neptune
Thanatos	Mors
Zeus	Jupiter (Jove)

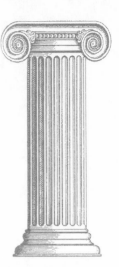

LANDMARKS OF GREEK HISTORY

3000 B.C.	End of the Neolithic Age, beginning of the Bronze Age

MINOAN OR HELLADIC

2000 B.C.	Middle Bronze Age
	Earthquakes ravage the Minoans
1800 B.C.	Construction of palace of Minos in Crete
	High point of Minoan civilization
1600 B.C.	Late Bronze Age
	First Greeks (Achaians from Ionia and Aeolia) arrive, with four-wheeled chariots, in the Peloponnesus
	Mycenean civilization centers in Pylos, Tiryns, and Mycenae
1500–1400 B.C.	Knossos and Minos' palace destroyed by tidal wave from volcano and earthquake on Thera
	Achaians invade Crete, capture Knossos

MYCENAEAN

1300 B.C.	Heroic Age begins
1193–1184 B.C.	The Trojan War: Mycenaeans gain control over the Bosphorus, which Troy previously commanded, and its access to Caucasus Black Sea metal mines.
	Agamemnon of Mycenae, king of the Argives; his brother Menelaos of Sparta, husband of Helen
1190 B.C.	Sea peoples invade Greece (Dorian Invasion)
	The "Dark Ages" begin
	Only Athens escapes destruction, as the Dorians occupy the Peloponnesus and the rest of Attica and Boeotia
	Surviving Mycenaeans flee to Ionia
	Beginning of "geometric" art
900 B.C.	Epic cycle sung by rhapsodes

9th century B.C.	**Homeric Hymns (800–600 B.C.)**
800 B.C.	Time of the bard named Homer?
	Iron Age begins
	Phoenicians arrive in Greece and restore literature, shipbuilding, and art
	End of Dark Age

PRECLASSICAL

8th century B.C.	**Greek towns begin to keep records and lists in prose**
	Archilochos, Hesiod
776 B.C.	Olympic Games founded
753 B.C.	Rome founded
734 B.C.	Syracuse founded
720 B.C.	Sparta conquers Messenia

7th century B.C.	**End of geometric art; education systematically emphasized**
	Alkman, Orpheus, Sappho, Solon, Terpandros, Thales, Tyrtaeus
680 B.C.	Gyges seizes throne of Lydia
675 B.C.	Sparta crushes first Messenian revolt
669 B.C.	Argive confederacy defeats Spartans at Hysiae
660 B.C.	Byzantium founded
650–40 B.C.	Spread of government by "tyrant"
640–30 B.C.	Standardized coinage begun in Lydia
638 B.C.	Solon born

630 B.C.	Messenia revolts against Sparta
625 B.C.	Periander rules Corinth
621 B.C.	Laws of Draco
612 B.C.	Sappho born in Mytilene

6th century B.C. **Doric and Ionic architecture**

Attic black-figure pottery replaced by red-figure

Aesop?, Alcaeus, Anacreon, Anaximander, Anaximenes, Pisistratus, Pythagoras, Simonides, Stesichoros, Theognis, Thespis, Xenophanes

595/594 B.C.	Solon, chief archon of Athens, legislates new reformed constitution
585 B.C.	Solar eclipse predicted by Thales
560 B.C.	Pisistratus abolishes Solon's constitution
556 B.C.	Simonides born on Ceos
550 B.C.	Peloponnesian League
546 B.C.	Death of Croesus
545 B.C.	Cyrus' Persians conquer Greeks in Asia Minor
540 B.C.	Persians attack Teos
	Anacreon flees to Abdera
	Polycrates becomes tyrant of Samos
	Theognis writes poetry in Megara
534 B.C.	Thespis wins tragedy festival in Athens, staged by the tyrant Pisistratus
531/529 B.C.	Pythagoras settles in Croton
528 B.C.	Hippias succeeds his faher Pisistratus as tyrant in Athens
525 B.C.	Aeschylus born
523 B.C.	Polycrates of Samos dies
518 B.C.	Pindar born in Boeotia
510 B.C.	Pisistratus' son Hippias dethroned in Athens
508 B.C.	Dithyrambic contests in Athens
507 B.C.	New constitution, based on reforms inspired by Clisthenes, makes Athens a democracy
505 B.C.	Early temple at Delphi completed by Athenians. Alcmaeonid family
504 B.C.	Pythagoras dies in Metapontum, of a hunger strike

CLASSICAL OR HELLENIC

500 B.C.	Statues become elaborate and lifelike. Art emphasizes composition
	Satyr plays added to the tragedy festival
5th century B.C.	**Aeschylus, Anaxagoras, Aristophanes, Democritus, Empedocles, Euripides, Heraclitus, Herodotus, Hippocrates, Korinna, Parmenides, Pericles, Pindar, Praxilla, Protagoras, Socrates, Sophocles, Telesilla, Thucydides, Zeno**
499 B.C.	Ionian revolt from Persia begins Persian War
	First recorded Dionysian Festival. Competitors: Aeschylus, Choirilos, and Pratinas
495 B.C.	Pericles, Sophocles born in Athens
494 B.C.	Revolt collapses, Ionians flee to Athens
493 B.C.	Persian fleet destroyed at Mt. Athos
490 B.C.	Darius leads first Persian invasion to quash Greek revolts, but is stopped at Marathon
	Phidias born
488/487 B.C.	Comedy introduced at the Greater Dionysia festival
487 B.C.	First use of ostracism in Athens, where public officials are elected now by lot
485 B.C.	Protagoras, Euripides born in Athens
484 B.C.	Aeschylus' first victory
483 B.C.	Themistocles directs the construction of a large naval fleet
480 B.C.	Xerxes returns for vengeance, destroys Athens
	Battle of Thermopylae
	Athenians destroy Persian fleet at Salamis, securing naval dominance
	Greeks defeat Persia at Platea (Mycale), in Asia Minor
	Sicilians defeat Carthage
478–76 B.C.	Fortification of Athens
477 B.C.	Delian League founded
476/472 B.C.	Pindar poet laureate of Hieron of Syracuse
476 B.C.	Pindar writes "First Olympian" ode
472 B.C.	Revolt of Naxos, Carystus, and Thasos from Delian League crushed by Athens
	Aeschylus stages *The Persians*
471 B.C.	Themistocles ostracized
469 B.C.	Socrates born
468 B.C.	Sophocles wins prize over Aeschylus

467 B.C.   Aeschylus stages *Seven Against Thebes*

465 B.C.   Darius and his son murdered; Artaxerxes I takes over

458 B.C.   Aeschylus produces the *Oresteia*

457 B.C.   Boeotian War begins

456 B.C.   Temple of Zeus at Olympia completed

              Aeschylus dies

455 B.C.   Euripides first competes in the Dionysia

454 B.C.   Delian League treasury moved from Delos to Athens

450 B.C.   Zeno studies with Parmenides in Athens

              Anaxagoras accused of impiety

449 B.C.   Peace made with Athens, Persia surrendering its Aegean and Asia
              Minor Greek colonies (end of Persian Wars)

447 B.C.   Parthenon begun under Pericles (designed by Phidias, Ictinus, and Cali-
              crates)

445 B.C.   Boeotian War ends

444 B.C.   Pericles' rule begins

441 B.C.   Euripides wins his first prize in tragedy

              Samos revolts against Athens

440 B.C.   Sophocles stages *Antigone*

              Pericles' first funeral oration

438 B.C.   Euripides' *Alcestis*

              Phidias' Athena dedicated

              Pindar dies

436 B.C.   Isocrates born in Athens

433 B.C.   Parthenon completed, the perfection of the Doric style

432–404 B.C. Peloponnesian War between Spartan League and Athens, Darius II of Persia
              allies with Sparta

              Euripides' *Medea*

430 B.C.   Pericles forced from office (dies of the plague in 429 B.C.)

              Cleon becomes major force in the assembly

429 B.C.   Plato born

              Sophocles' *Oedipus the King*

428 B.C.   Euripides stages *Hippolytus*

              Herodotus publishes *Histories.*

427 B.C.   Plague in Athens at its height, destroying sense of community

424 B.C.   Thucydides exiled when Spartan Brasidas captures Amphipolis

              Aristophanes stages *The Knights*

423 B.C.   Aristophanes' *The Clouds*

422 B.C.	Aristophanes' *Wasps*
421 B.C.	Erectheum begun on the Athenian Acropolis
	Peace of Nicias between Athens and Sparta
	Aristophanes' *Peace*
415 B.C.	Protagoras exiled from Athens because of his view of the gods
	Alcibiades flees
	Law passed against using names of real people in comedies
	Athenian expedition to Sicily
	Euripides' *Trojan Women*
414 B.C.	Aristophanes' *The Birds*
413 B.C.	New war between Sparta and Athens
	Athens expedition against Syracuse fails
411 B.C.	Aristophanes' *Lysistrata* performed
410 B.C.	Formation of the oligarchy
	Democracy restored
409 B.C.	Sophocles' *Philoctetes*
408 B.C.	Euripides' *Orestes*
406 B.C.	Euripides dies
	Sophocles dies in Athens
	Erectheum completed
405/404 B.C.	Euripides' *Bacchae, Iphigenia in Aulis*
	Aristophanes' *The Frogs*
	Dionysius I in Syracuse
	End of Peloponnesian War with fall of Athens to Sparta at Aegispotami
	Oligarchy established, the "Thirty Tyrants"
	Lysias and his brother Polemarchus arrested by "the Thirty"
	Polemarchus executed. Lysias flees
	Weak democracy restored by Thrasybulus
403 B.C.	Lysias returns to democratic Athens
401/399 B.C.	Xenophon's expedition under Cyrus, basis of *Anabasis*

POSTCLASSICAL OR HELLENISTIC

4th century B.C.	Community and idealism have dissolved in Athens
	Specialization sets in, along with the romantic novel for individual reading
	Art has become self-conscious, baroque
	Thucydides dies in Athens

Aeneas Tacticus, Aeschines, Aristotle, Demosthenes, Epicurus, Isocrates, Lysias, Menander, Plato, Praxiteles, Theophrastus, Xenophon

399 B.C.	Socrates accused of corrupting youth, not believing in the gods of the state. He is executed
	Plato leaves Athens
395 B.C.	Corinthian War (Sparta versus Corinth-Athenian confederacy) begins
394 B.C.	Battle of Coronea: Sparta forfeits all leadership in Greece
388 B.C.	Lysias' *Olympiacus* warns Greeks against dangers of disunity
387 B.C.	Plato returns to Athens, founds Academy
386 B.C.	The "King's Peace" ends Corinthian War
385? B.C.	Aristophanes dies
384 B.C.	Aristotle and Demosthenes born
382 B.C.	Philip of Macedon born
380 B.C.	Isocrates' *Panegyricus* urges Sparta and Athens to ally against Persia
375 B.C.	Xenophon's *Anabasis* appears
371 B.C.	Thebes defeats Sparta at Leuctra, end of Thebes' leadership in Greece
367 B.C.	Aristotle becomes Plato's student at Academy
366–365 B.C.	Plato in Syracuse, exposed to Pythagoreanism
362 B.C.	Thebes defeats Sparta at Mantineia
359 B.C.	Philip becomes king of Macedon
356 B.C.	Birth of Alexander
	Aeneas' *On the Defense of Fortified Positions*
355 B.C.	"Sacred War" between Philip and the Greek confederacy
351 b.c.	Demosthenes' *First Philippic*
348 B.C.	Philip of Macedon defeats Olynthus, Athens' ally
346 B.C.	End of Sacred War
347 B.C.	Plato dies
	Speusippus elected to succeed him as head of Academy
	Aristotle leaves Athens
346 B.C.	Philip presides at the Pythian Games
344 B.C.	Aristotle tutors Alexander
342 B.C.	Menander born in Athens
341 B.C.	Epicurus born on Samos
340 B.C.	Athens declares war on Macedon
338 B.C.	Philip defeats the Greeks at Chaeronea (Thebes)
	(Athens never again fully independent)
	Isocrates dies
336 B.C.	Alexander becomes king of Macedon

335 B.C.	Zeno born in Cyprus
	Destruction of Thebes
	Aristotle establishes the Lyceum in Athens
334 B.C.	Alexander, with 35,000 troops, invades Asia against Darius
331 B.C.	Alexander wins battles of Arbela and Gaugamela; burns and plunders Persepolis
	Founds Alexandria, in Egypt
330 B.C.	Lycurgus builds the first stone theater in Athens
	Demosthenes' "On the Crown"
	Temple at Delphi rebuilt
	Alexander declares himself Artaxerxes IV
327 B.C.	Alexander conquers Sogdiana, the remnant of the Persian Empire
326 B.C.	Alexander crosses the Indus
325 B.C.	Aristotle's *Poetics*
324 B.C.	Demosthenes exiled
323 B.C.	Alexander dies in Babylon
	His kingdom divided among his generals, founding new kingdoms in Egypt (Ptolemies), Syria (Seleucids), and Macedonia (Antigonids)
322 B.C.	Theophrastus becomes president of the Lyceum
314 B.C.	Zeno the Stoic arrives in Athens
316 B.C.	Menander's *Dyskolos* wins first prize
306 B.C.	Epicurus opens school in Athens
305 B.C.	Callimachus born in Cyrene
304 B.C.	Ptolemy declares himself king of Egypt
300 B.C.	Theocritus born in Sicily
3rd century B.C.	**Apollonius of Rhodes, Archimedes, Callimachus, Eratosthenes, Euclid, Leonidas, Theocritos**
297 B.C.	Library at Alexandria founded by Ptolemy I
295 B.C.	Apollonius born in Alexandria
280 B.C.	Pyrrhus invades Italy
	Achaian League reorganized for the last time
275 B.C.	Pyrrhus defeated in Italy
264–241 B.C.	First War between Rome and Carthage
263 B.C.	Zeno dies
260 B.C.	Theocritus dies
247 B.C.	Apollonius resigns as librarian in Alexandria

ROMAN

241 B.C.	Sicily becomes a Roman province
240 B.C.	Callimachus dies
214–205 B.C.	First War of Rome with Macedon
212 B.C.	Archimedes dies
200–197 B.C.	Second War

2nd century B.C.	**Bion, Meleager, Nicander, Polybius**
180 B.C.	Altar of Zeus at Pergamum
172–168 B.C.	Third War, Rome ends Macedonian kingdom
146 B.C.	Rome destroys Corinth, dissolving the Achaian League
	Rome destroys Carthage

1st century B.C.	**Dionysius of Halicarnassus, Dioscorides, Strabo**
88–85 B.C.	Greece conquered by Mithridates
	Greece conquered by Sulla
60 B.C.	End of Roman Republic, under Augustus
30 B.C.	Roman civil war between Augustus and Antony ends
20 B.C.	Strabo's *Geography*

1st century A.D.	**Dio Chrysostomos, Epictetus, "Longinus," Plutarch**

2nd century A.D.	**Apollodorus, Galen, Lucian, Pausanias, Ptolemy**
A.D. 170	Galen granted position in the Roman imperial court
A.D. 180	Marcus Aurelius dies

3rd century A.D.	**Athenaeus, Heliodorus, Longus, Plotinus**
A.D. 244	Plotinus begins teaching in Rome
A.D. 270	Plotinus dies

GLOSSARY

Abdera. Thracian coastal city, rich in corn, founded by Herakles and named for his faithful attendant Abderos. Though according to legend the city's air made its citizens stupid, so that "Abderite" became a put-down, Democritus and Protagoras are among its distinguished citizens.

Academy. The public grove of olive trees planted in honor of the hero Academus in the suburbs of Athens where Plato founded his school of philosophy about 385 B.C. It lasted as one of the west's first "universities" until Justinian closed it in A.D. 529.

Acastus. Brother of Alcestis and son of Pelias, king of Iolcus. He drove Jason and Medea into exile after Medea arranged the death of Pelias. He likewise exiled Peleus, who had fallen in love with his wife Hippolyta. In some stories, Peleus later returned to Iolcus, conquered it, and killed Acastus and his wife.

Achaia (Achaians; Achaea, Achaeans). Generic word for "Greeks" in the Homeric epics, referring to southeast Thessaly and the north coast of the Peloponnesian peninsula. Achaians, Argives, and Danaans are all used indiscriminately by Homer and the tragic dramatists to denote the people later called Hellenes.

Achelous. The longest and most celebrated river in Greece, rising on Mt. Pindus in central Epirus, flowing through Acarnania, and emptying into the Ionian Sea at the entrance to the Corinthian Gulf. Also the god of this river, who was one of the most important of the numerous river-gods.

Acheron. A river in southern Epirus, known for its wild gorge that was considered to be the entrance to Hades.

Achilles (Achilleus). King of the Myrmidons, son of the mortal Peleus and sea nymph Thetis, father of Neoptolemus, the greatest of the Greek warriors at Troy, and the principal hero of Homer's *Iliad*. Achilles, as was predicted to his mother Thetis, was slain by Paris the archer, whose arrow hit him in the one part of his body that she had not protected with magic: his "Achilles' tendon."

Acragas (Akragas, Agrigentum, Agrigento).

"Bas-relief: Gorgon's head"

A port city in southern Sicily, founded in 580 B.C. by colonists from Gela, famous for its riches and birthplace of Empedocles.

Acropolis. A plateau of rock about 200 feet high that served as the fortress of Athens, on which numerous temples, including the Parthenon, were located. In early times it was the residence of the kings of the city. The public treasury was also situated here, as were temples to the principal gods and goddesses.

Actaeon. Legendary hunter and grandson of Cadmus, who, witnessing Artemis and her nymphs bathing, was changed by the goddess into a stag and torn to pieces by his own dogs.

Admetus (Admetos). King of Pherae in Thessaly, husband of Alcestis, son of Pheres. The hero of Euripides' *Alcestis* was granted a new lease on life if he could find someone who loved him enough to die in his stead. Alcestis, his wife, agreed to the bargain, making him promise never to marry again. The result was grief for his entire kingdom, a situation remedied by the coming of Herakles.

Adonis. The beautiful youth so beloved by Aphrodite that after his death, from a boar's wound or by the arrow of Artemis, she was allowed to bring him back to earth for half of each year. He symbolizes the agricultural cycle. Annual festivals, the Adonia, were presided over by women in various parts of Greece.

Aegeus. Legendary early king of Athens, father of Theseus. When Theseus returned from slaying the Cretan minotaur, Aegeus awaited him on the promontory of Sunium (on the tip of the Attic peninsula). Theseus had forgotten to switch to white sails, the prearranged signal of success. When Aegeus saw the black sails of his son's ship he hurled himself, in despair, into the sea that has since borne his name: the Aegean.

aegis. The "goat-skin" banner of Zeus, from which lightning and thunder emanated, carried by his daughter Athena in Homer's *Iliad* to terrify the Trojans in the absence of Achilles. Fringed with golden tassels that dazzled the eyes of its beholders, its center depicted the blinding face of the Gorgon.

Aegisthus (Aigisthos). Son of Thyestes, and cousin of Agamemnon. When Agamemnon went to Troy, he became the lover of Queen Klytaimnestra; and, with her, slew the returning king, taking vengeance for Agamemnon's father Atreus's murder of Aegisthus' siblings.

Aeneas. Trojan hero in the *Iliad*, son of Aphrodite and the mortal Anchises, protected by her in battle. After the fall of Troy, according to the legend made famous by Virgil's *Aeneid*, he led a band of Trojan survivors to Italy, where his descendants founded Rome.

Aeolis (Aeolian, Aeolic, Aeolia; Aiolic, etc.). The northeastern Greek dialect used by Alcaeus and Sappho. Originally from Boeotia and Thessaly, the descendants of Aeolus moved to the western coast of Asia Minor, where they occupied territory near the Hellespont. Later they moved south to Lesbos and northward to Tenedos, as well as along the mainland coast as far as the Troad. The "Aeolian League" included Neonteichos, Pitane, Smyrna, Larissa, Temnos, Cille, and Myrina.

Aeolus. Ruler of the winds, described in Homer's *Odyssey* as living on a floating island with his intermarried sons and daughters; also, the first ruler of Thessaly, ancestor of the Aeolians.

Aetna (Etna). Volcanic mountain near Sicily's Catania, that erupted frequently in antiquity. Empedocles is said to have died by throwing himself into Aetna.

Aetolia. North of Achaia and Locris, and east of Acarnania, a wild and mountainous region in western Greece, the scene of many hunting legends including the famous Caledonian boar hunt. Its favorite gods were Artemis, Apollo, and Athena.

Agamemnon. Son of Atreus, brother of Menelaos, king of Mycenae, leader of the Greek forces against Troy. His insult to Achilles is the inciting incident of Homer's *Iliad*. Upon his return to Mycenae after the war, with Priam's daughter Cassandra in tow as his trophy-bride, Agamemnon was slain by his wife Klytaimnestra and her lover Aegisthus. The regicide, in turn, provoked vengeance by their children Orestes and Elektra.

Agatharcus. From Samos, fifth-century B.C. painter and the first known scene director (modern art director), who painted scenes for Aeschylean tragedy; was the first painter fully to develop perspective, and wrote a commentary on scene painting.

Agora. The "marketplace" in Athens, the forum where Socrates held his philosophical discussions with his followers.

Aias (Ajax). Son of Telamon of Salamis, a powerful hero in Homer's *Iliad*. Sophocles made his suicide the subject of his *Aias*.

Aiakos. Son of Zeus, father of Peleus and grandfather of Achilles. A judge in the underworld.

aídos. "Shame," "respect," or "reverence for authority," a primary restraining force in preclassical Greece. Because of *aídos*, Apollo refuses to fight with his elder, Poseidon.

Aietes. King of Colchis, father of Medea.

Alcestis. Daughter of Pelias, wife of Admetus of Pherae, heroine of Euripides' play *Alcestis*, which tells the story of her death on behalf of her husband.

Alcibiades. An Athenian, son of Clinias, known for his charismatic good looks; was born around 450 B.C. Socrates saved his life at the battle of Potidaea, in 432 B.C. Of a noble and wealthy family and raised in Pericles' household, Alcibiades was frustrated in his ambitions to become one of Athens' greatest leaders because his lack of self-discipline never allowed him to win the citizens' complete confidence.

Alexander III, "the Great" (Fourth-century B.C.). Son of Philip of Macedon, tutored by Aristotle, Alexander assumed the kingship at the age of twenty and proceeded, with intense determination served by charismatic brilliance and unique military genius, to bring under his sway all of Greece, the Persian empire of Darius, and most of the known world as far as the Indus River to the east and the head of the Nile to the south. In every country he conquered he founded cities and named them after himself, his lovers, and even his favorite horse, Bucephalus. His vision for Alexandria, in Egypt, led to the creation of the great library instrumental in preserving most of the surviving Greek texts. After Alexander's death from a fever, three of his generals partitioned the empire among them, giving rise to the dynasties called after them: Seleucid (eastern), Antigonid (Greek), and Ptolemid (Egypt).

Alexandria. City of Egypt founded by Alexander the Great and named for himself, center of "Alexandrian" culture from the third century B.C. Here Alexander's general Ptolemy I established his central government and the great library, containing in its heyday over half a million volumes. The library's "museum" was a residential center for writers, scientists, and scholars.

Alkmena. Wife of Amphitryon and mother of Herakles (by Zeus), daughter of Elektryon.

Alpheus. The largest river in the Peloponnesus, flowing through Arcadia and Elis, and into the Ionian Sea near Olympia. Alpheus the hunter pursued the nymph Arethusa and was transformed into a river, she into a tributary spring.

Amazons. A race of warlike women who lived without contact with men, according to mythology, in the far-off Caucasian lands, from which they led a number of invasions of Asia Minor and other countries. In the reign of Theseus they attacked Attica, and in the Trojan War played a late and ineffective part. Herakles led an attack on them.

ambrosia. The food that causes eternal life. Along with nectar, the honey-like food of the gods.

Amphitrite. Wife of Poseidon, daughter of Nereus.

Amphitryon. Grandson of Perseus, son of Alcaeus, husband of Alkmena. Herakles, though sired by Zeus, is called "Amphitryon's son."

anagkaí. "Necessity," "constraint," the inevitable workings of Fate. One of the primary paradoxes of Greek thought focuses on the futility of action to change necessity, while at the same time arguing that right-minded action is the only way to fulfill our best nature.

Anatolia. The peninsula of Asia Minor.

Anchises. Son of Capys, member of the royal house of Troy. His marriage to Aphrodite led to the birth of Aeneas, Trojan hero and founder of Rome.

Andromache. From Thebe, she is in Homer's *Iliad* the faithful wife of the Trojan warrior Hektor, who awaits him in vain on the wall as he goes out to a showdown with Achilles. Andromache, after her son Astyanax is killed, is taken into slavery by Neoptolemos, son of Achilles.

Andromeda. Daughter of Cepheus, king of Aethiopia, and Cassiope. Her mother bragged that her daughter was more beautiful than the Nereids, inspiring them to persuade Poseidon to dispatch a sea-monster to lay waste her country, which was to be saved only if Andromeda were sacrificed. She was chained to a rock, but Perseus, carrying the head of Medusa, which he had just captured, found her and rescued her by slaying the monster.

Andros. The northernmost island of the Cyclades.

antagonist. The "second actor" in Greek theater, who responded to the protagonist. Later evolved into the "villain."

Antigone. Daughter of Oedipus and Jocasta; sister of Ismene, Eteokles, and Polyneices; betrothed to Haemon, King Creon's son; and heroine of Sophocles' tragedy, who dies in defiance of Creon's order that her brother Polyneices be denied a proper burial.

Aphrodite. Goddess of love, procreation, the sea, and beauty, representing the irresistible powers of carnal attraction. Originally from Asia Minor, she is associated by the Greeks with the island of Cyprus ("Cyprian Aphrodite"), and with Cytherus, Corinth, and Paphos, where annual *Aphrodisia* festivals were held in her honor. She was born of the "sea foam" (*aphros*), the semen of Ouranos spilled when he was castrated by his son Kronos.

Apollo (Apollonian). Often called Phoebus, son of Zeus and Leto, brother of Artemis. In tragedy he is usually the god of healing, of prophecy, of archery, of civilization, and of music. He was worshiped throughout Greece, sometimes as a sun god, as the ideal of manhood, with his primary shrine being at Delphi where an oracle pronounced its wisdom to pilgrims from throughout the Mediterranean.

Apollodorus. Fifth-century B.C. Athenian painter, the first to represent appearance.

Known as the "shadow painter" because his pictures depicted gradations in color.

Arcadia (Arkadia; Arcady). The mountainous central region of the Peloponnesus, suited to raising cattle. The Arcadians considered themselves the most ancient of the Greeks. The god Pan was extensively worshiped there. Later romantic ages idealized the pastoral life of Arcadia.

Archelaos. King of Macedonia (413–399 B.C.), and patron of Euripides, Agathon, and other Greek writers and artists.

archon (archontes). One of nine Athenian officials governing Athens after the fall of royal rule. One of the archons was in charge of producing the Great Dionysian Festival. He chose the competitors, arranged the financing, engaged the actors, and appointed the *choregi* (choral producers).

Arcturus. A bright star near the constellation Orion, whose morning rising in September indicated the vintage season, and the time when the cattle came down from their upland pastures.

Areopagus ("Ares' hill"), in Athens, the seat of the first Athenian law court, where Ares was tried for murdering Poseidon's son. The oldest council in Athens.

Ares. Son of Zeus and Hera; god of war. Sometimes considered a spouse or lover of Aphrodite.

areté. "Excellence," the classical Greek ideal pursued in all realms of human experience: physical, mental, psychological, political, and spiritual.

Arethusa (Arethosia). A nymph in Ortygia who was changed into a fountain after avoiding the favors of the river god Alpheus.

Argos (Argolid; Argives). A city in the northeast corner of the Peloponnesus; the region in which this city was situated. This region was one of the centers of Achaian or Mycenaean civiliza-tion and plays a large role in mythological history. Also, the name of the builder of the ship Argo. Another Argos, son of Gaia, had one hundred eyes and was sent by Hera to watch over Io until he was slain by Hermes at the command of Zeus. His eyes were then transformed into the tail of a peacock.

Ariadne. Daughter of Minos and Pasiphae. She fell in love with Theseus and was deserted by him on the island of Naxos, where Dionysus found her.

Arion. Sixth-century B.C. poet thought to be the literary father of the choric dithyramb, from which tragedy evolved (according to Aristotle). He dressed the chorus in goatskin loincloths, representing satyrs, giving rise to the word "tragedy" (from *tragos*, goat; and *oide*, song).

Aristarchus (Aristarchos). Grammarian and critic (c. 217–145 B.C.).

Artemis. Daughter of Zeus and Leto, twin sister of Apollo, born at Delos, the virgin goddess of the hunt, also identified with the Moon; protectress of animals and especially of their young, she was also the patroness of childbirth.

Artemisia. The queen of Halicarnassus under Xerxes, who aided him in his expedition against Greece in 480 B.C. and fought bravely and not too intelligently at Salamis.

Artemisium. A promontory at the northern end of the island of Euboea; in 480 B.C. the Greek fleet won a naval battle against the Persians there.

Asclepios (Asclepius; Aesculapius;). A son of Apollo who learned to heal the sick and revive the dead. Slain by Zeus in envy, he was later deified and became the god of medicine.

Asopus. A river in Boeotia.

Aspasia. The mistress of Pericles, a charismatic and intelligent woman from Milesia.

Astyanax. Literally, "lord of the city." Son of Hektor and Andromache, frightened by his father's helmet plume when they bid farewell on the Trojan wall, in the famous scene in the *Iliad*, before Hektor goes out to be slain by Achilles.

Atalanta. Arcadian heroine, the mother of Parthenopaeus. She married Melanion because he beat her in a foot-race.

Até. "Blindness." Daughter of Eris and Zeus, an ancient goddess, who led men, heroes, and gods into rash actions.

Athena (Athene). Also called Pallas, virgin goddess, daughter of Zeus, and special protectress of Athens. Although regularly thought of as a warrior goddess, she was also the patroness of peaceful arts and of wisdom and the sciences. Her epithet *Polias* means "guardian of cities." Athens was named after her because it chose her gift of the olive over Poseidon's gift of water.

Athos. Mountain on the peninsula which projects from Chalcidice in Macedonia.

Atlas. Titan condemned to hold the heavens on his shoulders.

Atreus. Son of Pelops, husband of Aerope, father of Agamemnon, brother of Thyestes. The curse on his house began when he fed his brother's children to his brother for dinner, hoping to win the royal succession. He won the scepter, but also more pain than he could imagine when the curse on the house of Atreus led to the killing of his son Agamemnon by Klytaimnestra.

Atridae (Atreidai). "Sons of Atreus," patronymic referring to Agamemnon and Menelaos.

Attica (Attic). The central Greek peninsula bounded by the Corinthian and Saronic Gulfs to the west, the Aegean Sea to the south, and the strait of Euboea to the east; location of Athens and its port Piraeus. Many of the masterpieces of classical Greek are written in the Attic dialect.

Aulis. The harbor in Boeotia where the Greek fleet was assembled prior to sailing for Troy.

Aurora. Goddess of the dawn, her rosy fingers announcing each new day on the horizon.

Axios. River in Thrace.

Bacchus. Another name for Dionysus.

Bactria. A far-eastern province of the empires of the Persians and of Alexander.

Bellerophon. Rider of the winged steed Pegasus, by whose aid he slew the Chimera.

Boeotia (Boiotia). Fertile region northwest of Attica, allied with Sparta in the Peloponnesian War. Its natives included Plutarch, Korinna, and Hesiod.

Boreas. The North Wind.

Bosporus. The channel between the Propontis (Black Sea) and the Sea of Marmara.

boule. Athenian "senate," with 500 delegates chosen by lot, ten from each tribe. During their one-year term they functioned through rotating committees, *prytanes.*

Brasmas. Greatest Spartan general at the outset of the Peloponnesian War. He was killed at Amphipolis, just after winning a brilliant victory, in 422 B.C.

Byblos. Wine district in Thrace.

Byzantium. City on the European side of the Bosporus. Captured by the Athenian Cimon in 471 B.C.

Cadmus (Kadmos). Legendary founder of Thebes, son of Agenor of Tyre, brother of Europa.

caduceus (kerikeion). Staff carried by ambassadors in wartime, but particularly the wand carried by Hermes, entwined with two snakes and topped with feathers.

Calchas. Agamemnon's prophet, who advised him to sacrifice his daughter Iphigeneia to placate Artemis and restore the winds that would enable the Greek fleet, becalmed at Aulis, to sail for Troy.

Callicrates. Fifth-century B.C. Athenian architect, with Phidias one of the designers of the Parthenon.

Calypso. Nymph, daughter of Atlas, living on the island of Ogygia ("navel of the sea"). Odysseus dallied with her for seven years on his journey home from Troy.

Caria (Karia). District of southwestern Asia Minor, famous for its marble.

Carthage. Powerful Tunisian city on the northern coast of Africa, originally a Phoenician colony.

Cassandra. Daughter of Priam and Hekabe of Troy, taken as concubine to Mycenae by the conquering Agamemnon, she possessed the dubious gift of prophecy tempered by no one believing her (because she had turned down the affections of Apollo).

Castor. *See* **Dioscuri.**

Caucasus. A range of mountains between the Black Sea and the Caspian Sea.

Centaurs. Mythical race dwelling near the Black Sea with the heads and torsos of men and the bodies of horses, no doubt reflecting the Greeks' first view of the horse-riding Scythians.

Cerberus. Fifty-headed dog guarding the entrance to Hades.

Chalkis. Major settlement in Euboea.

Chaos. The yawning abyss out of which the Greeks believed all things developed.

Charites. The Graces, goddesses of charm and beauty.

Charon. The ferryman of the Styx, who conveyed the souls into Hades for the cost of an *obolus* (for which reason an *obolus* was placed in the mouth of the dead).

Charybdis. Whirlpool monster in the straits of Messina who swallowed down the waters of the sea thrice daily and thrice daily spewed them forth again; confronted by Odysseus. Off the coast of Sicily, opposite Scylla.

Cheiron. Wisest of the Centaurs, skilled in medicine, art, and gymnastics; son of Kronos and Philyra. Teacher of gods and heroes, including Achilles. Slain by accident by one of Herakles' poisoned arrows.

Chios (Keos). Large island south of Lesbos in the Aegean, known for its wine and marble and as the possible birthplace of Homer. Conquered by the Persians in 494 B.C., later one of the most powerful and loyal of Athens' allies.

choregos. Wealthy person whose duty it was to meet the expenses of the chorus in the dramatic and lyric spectacles of a given year. Appointed by the archon in charge of the festival, he was expected to entertain the poet and the members of the chorus after the performance.

chorepheus. Leader of the chorus in tragedy and comedy, occupying the middle position in the chorus line closest to the audience. He alone had solo lines, and responded to the actors on behalf of the chorus.

chorus. "Commentators" in Greek tragedy and comedy, who responded to the plight of the protagonist and often expressed the playwright's personal views.

Chronos. *See* **Kronos.**

Chrysa. Town in the Troad, south of the Hellespont.

Chryseis. Agamemnon's "spear-wife," trophy of war, whom he refused to return to her father Chryses; When he finally returned her, he claimed in her place the spear-wife of Achilles, Briseis, leading that hero to resign from the fighting.

Chryses. Father of Chryseis, and priest of Apollo, who brought the wrath of the god, in the form of a plague, down on the Achaians when Agamemnon refused to return Chryseis to him.

Cimmerians. Tribe, living near the Caspian Sea, which invaded Asia Minor in the eighth century B.C.

Circe. Daughter of Helios. In Homer's *Odyssey* she turned Odysseus' men into swine and enchanted Odysseus himself for years on her sacred island.

Cithaeron. Mountain range separating Boeotia from Megaris and Attica.

Cleomenes (Kleomenes). Sixth-century B.C. king of Sparta who twice invaded Attica.

Cleon. Most famous of Athenian demagogues, Pericles' successor as leader of Athenian democracy. A tanner by trade, he soon turned to politics, and from the death of Pericles in 429 B.C. to his own he was the most powerful man in Athens.

Cleophon. Athenian demagogue who violently opposed peace in the last years of the Peloponnesian War.

Clepsydra. The water-clock in Athens which measured the time allowed for speeches in the law courts.

Clisthenes. Reformer who inspired the formation of Athenian democracy based on the constitution of 507 B.C., following the dethronement of Pisistratus' son Hippias.

Cocytus. River in the underworld.

Colchis. Country east of the Black Sea, where Jason sought the Golden Fleece.

Colonus. Attic deme northwest of Athens, birthplace of Sophocles and site of the legendary tomb of Oedipus.

Colophon (Kolophon). Ionian city in Asia Minor, claiming to be the birthplace of Homer.

Conon of Samos. Third century B.C. astronomer and mathematician.

Corinth. Strategic city on the Isthmus, ally of Sparta during the Peloponnesian Wars.

Cos (Kos). Island of the Sporades, favorite of writers, birthplace of Hippocrates and home of Theocritus.

Cotyla. Cup. A liquid measure, about half a pint.

Cratinus (Kratinos). Playwright of Old Comedy, elder of Aristophanes; in 423 B.C. he won the first prize and vengeance on Aristo-

phanes, who had accused him of being over the hill.

Creon. Brother of Jocasta, king of Thebes after Oedipus; antagonist in Sophocles' *Antigone*.

Crete. The largest island south of the Aegean, seat of Minoan civilization, which was centered at Knossos.

Croesus (Kroisos). Son of Alyattes, and last king of Lydia (ca. 560–546 B.C.), famous for his wealth.

Cybele. Anatolian-Phrygian fertility goddess identified with Rhea, and associated with Attis. Her worship was wild and orgiastic in character.

Cyclades (Cycladic; Kyclades). Generic name for the islands of the central Aegean Sea circling Delos, and including Paros, Gyara, Andros, and Naxos.

Cyclopes. One-eyed giants, who lived a hermit-like existence as shepherds. One of them, Polyphemos, was blinded by Odysseus.

Cynic (-ism). Philosophical sect founded by Socrates' associate Antisthenes and/or Diogenes of Sinope (nicknamed *kuon*, "dog"), and centered at the Cynosarges gymnasium. Its primary belief was in immunity from life's pains by practicing independence from all worldly concerns.

Cypris. Another name for Aphrodite, because she was associated with Cyprus.

Cyprus. Large island in the Mediterranean, south of Cilicia.

Cyrus. Son of Cambyses, and founder of the Achaemenid Persian Empire in the sixth century B.C.

Cythera. Island off the southern tip of the Peloponnesus, famous for its worship of Aphrodite.

Daedalus (Daidalos). Legendary Athenian artisan who built wax wings so that he and his son Icarus (Ikaros) could escape from prison. His name is synonymous with expert craftsmanship.

daimon. "Inner god," later becoming the word "demon." Used by Socrates to describe the conscience-like entity within him that warned him when he was doing wrong, and commended him for doing right. Socrates was executed because he followed the voice of his inner daimon rather than blindly following the "gods of the state."

Damon. Fifth-century B.C. Athenian musician and Sophist, with whom Pericles and Socrates studied.

Danaë. Daughter of Acrisius, king of Argos, who confined her in a tower of bronze when an oracle predicted her son would kill him. Zeus impregnated her in a shaft of gold light and she bore the hero Perseus.

Danai (Danaans). Descendants of Danaos, another preclassical word for "Greeks."

Daphnis. Son of Hermes, a shepherd in Sicily credited with inventing bucolic poetry.

Dardanus (Dardanians). Mythical ancestor of the Trojans. Another term for "Trojans."

Darius. King of Persia, 521–485 B.C.; father of Xerxes. He began the Persian War with Greece.

Delos. Small island in the Aegean, the center of the Cyclades. Mythical birthplace of Apollo and Artemis, and the place where the Delian League initially held its treasury.

Delphi. Town in Phocis, on the lower slopes of Mt. Parnassus, site of the most important oracle of Apollo and the Pythian Games. Delphi was considered to be the "navel of the earth."

deme (demos). The smallest political division of Attica, equivalent of a modern ward or township, root of the term "democracy."

Demeter. Goddess of agriculture and corn; daughter of Kronos and Rhea; mother of Persephone.

Diagoras. Fifth-century B.C. philosopher-poet of Melos, famous for his atheism.

didaskolos (didascalia). "Teacher," the term applied to the directors of Greek tragedy hired by the *choregos* to stage the annual play contests.

"Altar for cereal offerings to Demeter, at Phaestum, Crete"

Because these plays taught mythology to the populace, they were called *didactic*.

dike. "Balance, justice." Also, the Attic word for "case" in Athenian jurisprudence.

Diomedes. Son of Tydeus and Deipyle, prominent Greek hero in the Trojan War.

Dionysian Festival, Great (Dionysia). Annual festival of the god Dionysius in which tragedies and satyr plays were performed.

Dionysius of Syracuse. Powerful fourth-century B.C. tyrant.

Dionysius (Dionysus). Son of Zeus and Semele, originally Thracian-Phrygian god of wine, wildlife, vegetation, and of the fertile power of nature, patron of drama at Athens. He was the god of the poor. His orgiastic worship, depicted in Euripides' *The Bacchae*, was strongly opposed by the powers that be for its savagery (involving the tearing of flesh and drinking of animal blood). He had an oracular shrine in Thrace. His cult celebrated the unity of all life, the cycle of death and rebirth, and the conception of the collective soul immanent in the community, which may transcend in its ecstatic ritual any individual's potential.

Dioscuri (Dioskouri). Literally, "sons of

Zeus," referring to Kastor and Polydeukes, who are variously sons of Leda and Tyndareus; brothers of Helen. Kastor was famed for his skill in dealing with horses, and Polydeukes for his skill in boxing. Both heroes, deified as the constellation Gemini, were regarded as protectors of sailors.

dithyramb, choral. A form of choral song in honor of Dionysius, dealing with a variety of heroes. Arion is credited with giving it formal dimensions in the sixth century B.C. Aristotle believed that drama arose from the choric dithyramb.

Dodona. Site of ancient oracle of Zeus in Epirus. The sounds made by the wind in the sacred oaks were interpreted by the priests.

Dorian (Doric). Greek dialect used in ancient Sparta and the Peloponnesus.

Dorus (Dorians). Son of Xuthus and Creusa, legendary founder of the race of Dorians and of the central Peloponnesian metropolis Doris.

Draco. Seventh-century B.C. Athenian lawmaker who wrote its earliest constitution.

Ecbatana (Ekbatana). Important city of Media, north of Persia, conquered by Alexander the Great.

Echidna. Half woman and half serpent, mate of Typhon, mother of Cerberus and the Hydra.

eiron. "Deflater," one who through apparent naiveté and simplicity deflates those who think they know. Applied to Socrates. The root of the modern word "ironic."

Elea. Laconian town, on the Tyrrhenian coast of southern Italy, where Parmenides founded the "Eleatic school" of philosophy.

Elektra (Electra). Daughter of Agamemnon and Klytaimnestra, who, so great was her love for her father in Euripides' version of the myth, conspired with her brother Orestes to kill their mother in revenge for her slaying of their father.

Elis. Country in the northern Peloponnesus where Olympia, site of the ancient games and temple of Zeus, was located. Famous for its horses.

Eleusinian Mysteries. Mystery cults of Demeter and Persephone, who celebrated their secret rituals in a town near Athens.

Eleven. Group of Athenian officials who had the function of a modern chief of police; they were also the executioners in cases of capital punishment.

Empusa. Specter haunting lonely places at night and associated with Hekate. The Empusa had the power of taking on any shape or likeness, and the reputation for eating her lovers.

Enceladus. One of the giants who made war on the gods. Zeus killed him and buried him under Mt. Aetna.

Eos. "Dawn," daughter of the Titan Hyperion and Thea, sister of Helios and Selene. Called "rosy-fingered" in Homer's epics.

Epeius. Builder, with Athena's help, of the wooden horse at Troy.

Ephesus (Ephesos). Major Ionian city on the west coast of Asia Minor.

Epidaurus. Peninsula town in Argolis on the Saronic gulf, site of the great theater and of a temple to Asclepios.

Epinikion. "Victory ode," poetic form used by Pindar, Bacchylides, and Simonides.

Erebus. The darkness surrounding the Underworld.

Erectheus. Legendary king of Athens, namesake of the Erectheum built on the Acropolis in his honor. The Athenians were called "Erechtheidae."

Erinyes. The punishing Furies. According to Heraclitus, "if the sun left its course, the Erinyes would find him."

Eros (Cupid). Associated with Aphrodite; god of violent sexual love.

Eteokles (Eteocles). Elder son of Oedipus and Jocasta, brother of Polyneices and Antigone.

One of the heroes in *Seven Against Thebes*, killed his brother, and was killed by him.

Euboea (Euboia). Largest island in the Aegean (called "Long Island," *Makris*), northeast of the Attic and Boeotian coasts, subject to Athens.

Eumenides. "Blessed spirits," as the patriarchal goddess Athena renamed the Erinyes (Furies) after she judged in favor of Orestes, giving them their own temple on the Acropolis of Athens to placate them for their failure to get vengeance on this man who slew his mother.

Eumolpus. Mythical founder of the Eleusinian mysteries, mentioned in the Homeric hymns. His descendants, the Eumolpidae, were priests of the mysteries.

Eupolis. One of the greatest comic poets before Aristophanes, his first play produced in 429 B.C.

Europa. Mother of Cretan King Minos, and of Rhadamanthys; Zeus, disguised as a bull, kidnaped her and took her to Mt. Ida in Crete.

Eurotas. Laconian river running through the ancient city of Sparta.

Eurysteus (Eurystheus). King of Argos, who made Herakles perform his "twelve labors."

Furies. *See* **Erinyes.**

Galateia. Sea nymph, daughter of Doris and Nereus, loved by the Cyclops Polyphemos.

gamos. Wedding. The celebratory culmination of most Greek comedies.

Ganymedes. Son of Tros; handsome Trojan youth whom Zeus abducted to Olympus to make cup-bearer to the gods.

Gela. City in southern Sicily, founded in 688 B.C. by colonists from Crete and Rhodes.

Geryon. Monster with three heads and three bodies whose cattle Herakles carried off.

Gorgias (Gorgios). Fifth-century B.C. Sophist and rhetorician from Leontini in Sicily. His Attic prose influenced Isocrates.

Gorgons. Along with her sisters Sthenno and Euryale, Gorgo had serpents on her head instead of hair, and was endowed with wings, claws, and enormous teeth. Anyone who looked at her turned to stone. Later confused with Medusa.

Gortyn. City in south-central Crete.

Greek Anthology (Palatine Anthology). Compiled in the tenth century A.D. by the Byzantine Constantinus Cephalas and finished by Planudes; contains the only surviving lyrics of Greek and Latin poets who otherwise would have come down to us in name only.

Gyges. Wealthy king of Lydia, 685–657 B.C.

Hades. Son of Kronos, brother of Zeus and Poseidon, husband of Persephone, god of the underworld.

Haemon. A Theban, the son of Creon, lover of Antigone.

Halikarnassos (Halicarnassus). Greek Asia Minor city, in Caria, where Herodotus was born.

Halirrhothius. Son of Poseidon, killed by Ares. Ares was tried for the murder on a hill in Athens, which hence was called the Areopagus.

Halys. Major river in Asia Minor (modern Kisihrmak) flowing into the Euxine.

hamartia. Tragic flaw, tragedy-proneness, or blind spot in the hero of classical tragedy.

harmonia. Being "in tune," or balance, a term used to describe the orderliness of the universe by Pythagoras.

Harmonia (Harmony). Daughter of Ares and Aphrodite, wife of Cadmus.

Harpies. Monstrous god-birds with heads of maidens, associated with the winds.

Hebe. Daughter of Zeus and Hera, goddess of youth, married to the deified Herakles.

Hebros. Thracian river associated with the worship of Dionysius.

Hekabe (Hecuba). Daughter of Phrygian Dimas, queen of Troy, wife of Priam, mother of Hektor and Paris.

Hekate (Hecate). Ancient earth goddess associated with the moon, magic, sorcery, and ghosts. Confused with Artemis and Persephone. Worshiped at crossroads.

Hektor. Son of Priam and Hekabe, brother of Paris, husband of Andromache, father of Astyanax; principal hero of the Trojans, killed by Achilles in revenge for Hektor's killing of Patroklos.

Helen. Daughter of Zeus and Leda, sister of the Dioscuri. Paris' abduction of her from Menelaos, at the behest of Aphrodite, instigated the Trojan War.

Helenus. Son of Priam and Hekabe, famous for his prophetic powers.

Heliaia (Heliasts). The democratic court of appeals of Athens, instituted by Solon. Jurors were chosen by lot from all classes, and paid three obols a day.

Helios. Sun god, whose 360 oxen were eaten by Odysseus' men in the *Odyssey*, loosing the god's wrath upon them.

Hellas (Hellenes). The Greeks' name for their country and for themselves; originally a small town in south Thessaly.

Hellespont. Modern straits of the Dardanelles, connecting the Black Sea and the Marmara with the Aegean.

Hellicon (Helikon). Largest mountain range of Boeotia, sacred to Apollo and the Muses.

Hephaestos (Hephaestus). Son of Hera; god of fire and metallurgy, associated with all volcanic places, particularly Lemnos and Aetna. Became crippled when Zeus, in jealousy, hurled him from Olympus. In Homer's *Iliad* he built palaces for the gods on Olympus and forged the shield of Achilles at the request of Thetis. In some stories married to Aphrodite, whom he catches in bed with Ares by weaving a golden net to catch them.

Hera. Sister and wife of Zeus; goddess associated with Argos, portrayed in Homer as jealous and hostile to all the women loved by Zeus. She

"Temple of Hephaestos, Athens"

is the goddess of power, the hearth, women's life, and marriage.

Herakles (Hercules). Popular hero, later deified, his name synonymous with strength; son of Zeus and Alkmena. Through the trickery of the jealous Hera, Eurystheus was given power over Herakles and ordered him to perform twelve labors.

Hermes (Mercury). Son of Zeus and Maia (daughter of Atlas), a god of various "angelic" attributes. Messenger and herald of the Olympians, he was also the guide of the souls of the dead and the patron of travelers, tricksters, and thieves. Associated with good luck. He carries the caduceus.

Hermione. Daughter of Helen and Menelaos.

hero. Half-god and half-human, ancient "heroes" included Achilles (son of the nymph Thetis and the mortal Peleus), the Dioscuri (sons of Zeus and Leda), Helen (daughter of Leda and Zeus), and Herakles (son of Zeus and Alkmena).

Hesperides. Daughters of Hesperis and Atlas (or Night and Erebus), goddess-guardians of the golden apples in the garden of the gods beyond the Atlas mountains at the western shore of the Ocean.

Hesperus. The evening star.

hexameter. Dactylic hexameter, the meter of Homeric epics as well as of didactic poets like Hesiod and pastoral poets like Theocritos; consisting of six poetic "feet" per line, the last of which must be a spondee. The line is often divided by a *caesura,* or pause.

Hieron (Hiero). Magnanimous fifth-century B.C. tyrant of Syracuse and Gela, in Sicily. Athletic champion and patron of Pindar, Aeschylus, and Simonides, among others.

Hippias. Tyrant of Athens 527–510 B.C., son of Pisistratus, whose forced abdication led to the formation of Athenian democracy. In 490 B.C. Hippias returned for revenge backed by a Persian expeditionary force, but was stopped at Marathon.

Hoplites. The heavily-armed foot soldiers in Greek armies.

hybris (hubris). Excess. The characteristic of the tragic hero is to allow his *hybris* to overcome his common sense, bringing him to the brink of self-destruction. Generally mistranslated as "pride," the characteristic of the tragic hero to go "over and beyond" what is normal. Hybris is an overstepping of boundaries and, depending on its results, is the worst of all sins man can be guilty of.

Hydra. Monster slain by Herakles whose blood Herakles used to poison his arrows.

Hymen (Hymenaeus). A legendary patron of marriage, after whom the songs sung at wedding feasts were named.

Hyperboreans (Hyperborean). Legendary race of people who lived in a land of perpetual sunshine, "beyond the North Wind," and worshiped Apollo.

Hyperion. Titan, son of Ouranos and Gaia; father by his sister Theia of Helios (sun), Selene (moon), and Eos (dawn).

Hypnos. Son of Nyx (night), with no mother; brother of Thanatos (death); god of sleep.

Ibykos (Ibycus). Choral lyric poet of the sixth century B.C., born at Rhegium in Italy. Erotic motifs seem to have played a large role in his works, which have not come down to us.

Icarian. The sea around the island of Icaria in the Aegean named after Icarus.

Icarus. Son of Daedalus, who ignored his father's warnings about flying too close to the sun on his wax wings and plunged to his death in the Icarian Sea.

Ictinus. One of the architects of the Parthenon, under the direction of Phidias.

Ida. A mountain in the Troad, the scene of the judgment of Paris. From its summit, the gods watched the Trojan War. A cave on Mt. Ida in Crete is said to have been where Zeus was hidden from his father Kronos.

Ilion (Ilium). Another name for Troy, subject of Homer's *Iliad;* from Ilios, the son of Tros, who founded Ilion; or Iliona, oldest of the daughters of Priam. In the seventh century B.C. a temple to Athena was founded by the Aeolian Greeks on the site of Troy and was known as Ilium.

Iolcus. Mycenaean town of Magnesia, in Thessaly, where Pelias and Jason lived.

Ion. Son of Apollo and Creusa, legendary ancestor of the Ionians. Also, a fifth-century B.C. playwright/poet.

Ionia. The fringe of settlements on the west coast of Asia Minor, from Miletus to Phocaea, originally colonized by Greeks fleeing from the Dorians. Here the earliest Greek philosophy and literature developed.

Ionic. The Ionic dialect was also spoken in the northern islands and in Euboea.

Ionian. The "Ionian Sea" is another name for the Adriatic, between the Balkan peninsula and Italy.

Iphigeneia. Daughter of Agamemnon and Klytaimnestra, sacrificed by her father at the suggestion of the prophet Calchas, at Aulis, so that the Greek expedition might sail for Troy.

Agamemnon convinced Klytaimnestra to send her to Aulis on the promise that she would be married to Achilles.

Iris. Messenger and rainbow goddess, wife of Zephyros, the west wind. In the *Iliad* she announces the will of Zeus to mortals.

Ismene. Daughter of Oedipus and Jocasta, sister of Polyneices and Eteokles, Antigone's confidant in Sophocles' *Antigone*.

Ister. The lower Danube.

Isthmian games. A great national festival, held every other year in honor of Poseidon at Corinth, respectively one and three years after the Olympics.

Isthmus (Isthmos). Narrow neck of land connecting the Peloponnesus with northern Greece. The principal city on the Isthmus was Corinth.

Ithaka (Ithaca). Island in the Ionian Sea, the home of Odysseus.

Ixion. King of the Lapithae, protected from his people's wrath by Zeus after he killed his father-in-law. Then he tried to seduce Hera. Zeus chained him to a wheel in Hades and set it revolving eternally: "Ixion's wheel."

Jason. Son of Aeson, leader of the Argonauts, husband of Medea, who set out, reluctantly, on the *Argo* to capture the Golden Fleece.

Jocasta. Wife of Laius, queen of Thebes; mother and wife of Oedipus.

Kastor. *See* **Dioscuri.**

katharsis. Purgation. Term used by Aristotle in his *Poetics* to refer to the overflow of pity and fear caused in the audience by a well-contrived drama.

kléos. "Fame, glory, honor" as verbal repute. Achilles and Hektor, in the *Iliad*, are both fighting for this, the fame they will leave behind after death.

Klytaimnestra (Clytemnestra). Daughter of Leda, sister of Helen; wife of Agamemnon, mother of Iphigeneia, Elektra, and Orestes. With her lover Aegisthos she killed Agamemnon

upon his return from Troy. She was, in turn, killed by her son Orestes.

Knossos. Capital of ancient Crete, principal city of Minoan civilization, where Minos had his court and built the labyrinth for the Minotaur. Near the present city of Iráklion.

komos. "Ritual merry-making," probably the origins of Old Comedy.

Kronos (Chronos). Son of Ouranos and Gaia, leader of his brother Titans. Castrated Ouranos at Gaia's advice, then married his sister Rhea by whom he conceived Zeus, Demeter, Hera, Poseidon, and Hades.

Kyrnos. Corsica.

Labdacus. King of Thebes, the father of Laius and grandfather of Oedipus.

Labyrinth. Elaborate maze built by Daedalus for King Minos to imprison the Minotaur, the monster born of his wife Pasiphae's infatuation with a bull.

Laertes. Father of Odysseus.

Laius. King of Thebes, the husband of Jocasta and father of Oedipus, by whom he was killed.

Lakedaimon (Lakedaimonians). Son of Zeus and Taygete, who married Sparta and named his city after her. Spartans were known as Lakedaimonians.

Lakonia. Region in the Peloponnesus, its capital Sparta.

Lamia. Fabulous monster, a shape-shifter like Proteus. Usually depicted as female, she had a vampire's appetite for blood.

Lampsakos (Lampsacus). Asia Minor city on the eastern entrance to the Hellespont, known for its wine and its worship of Priapus.

Laomedon. King of Troy, father of Priam.

Lapithae. Mythical Thessalian tribe. At the wedding of Peirithous, a bloody battle arose between the Lapithae and the Centaurs, a subject found frequently in Greek art.

Lasus. Sixth-century B.C. lyric poet who

wrote hymns and dithyrambs; rival of Simonides.

Laurium. The Attic deme near Cape Sunium famous for its silver mines. Coins made of its silver were known as "owls of Laurium" because they were stamped with Athena's totem animal.

Leda. Daughter of Thestius of Aetolia, wife of Tyndareus, king of Sparta, by whom or by Zeus (disguised as a swan) she became the mother of the Dioscuri, of Klytaimnestra, and of Helen.

Lemnos. Large volcanic island in the northeast Aegean, where Hephaistos landed when Zeus hurled him from heaven. According to myth the Lemnian women murdered all their husbands.

Lenaian festival (Lenaea). The annual theater festival for Athenians. Originally five plays were put on during the festival. Held west of the Acropolis in the winter month called Lenaeon (from the word for *maenad*; modern month of January). At this festival, originally, only comedies were staged, Aristophanes' plays among them.

Leonidas. Succeeded his brother Cleomenes to be king of Sparta 487–480 B.C., and was Spartan commander at Thermopylae, where he died in the battle against the Persians.

Lerna. District in Argolis where Herakles slew the Hydra.

Lesbos. Large island off the Asia Minor coast, birthplace of Sappho, Alcaeus, Terpandros, and Theophrastus. Its five cities included Mytilene, Antissa, and Pyrrha.

Lethe. River in Hades, from which the souls of the dead drank water that made them forget their lives.

Leto. Daughter of Coeus and Phoebe, lover of Zeus, mother of Apollo and Artemis.

Leukothea. "White goddess," a sea nymph, formerly Ino, daughter of Cadmus.

Libya. Greek name for Africa.

Linus. Personification of mourning song sung at the grape harvest (called the "Linus song").

logos. Word, reason, system. Used by the earliest Greek philosophers to describe the organizing force of the universe.

Loxias. Another name for Apollo.

Lycean. "Light-bringing," a title of Apollo's. Aristotle's Lyceum in Athens was near the temple of Lycean Apollo.

Lycia. Mountainous territory in southwest Asia Minor.

Lycurgus. Tyrant of Athens who ordered the transcription of the plays of Aeschylus, Sophocles, and Euripides to prevent further corruption from the fourth-century B.C. star system that was rewriting them freely in every new production. In 330 B.C. he built the first stone theater in Athens, large enough for 17,000 spectators. Also: the legendary lawgiver of Sparta, who established its first constitution.

Lydia. Wealthy district in southwestern Asia Minor, between Caria and Mysia. Its last king was Croesus.

Macedon (Macedonia). District of northern Greece connecting it with the Balkans, ruled most notably by Philip II and Alexander the Great.

Maenads. One of the names, along with Bacchae or Thyades, for the frenzied worshipers of Dionysus.

Magna Graecia. The Greek cities of southern Italy and Sicily, including Paestum, Cumae, Acragas, Elia, and Locri.

Magnesia. District in Thessaly.

Maia. Daughter of Atlas and Pleione, the oldest and most beautiful of the Pleiades; mother of Hermes by Zeus.

Marathon. Village and bay in an Attic plain northeast of Athens where a small Athenian army, aided only by Plataea, in 490 B.C. defeated the Persian expeditionary force led by the former Athenian tyrant Hippias and the Emperor Darius.

Medea. Colchian princess, daughter of Aeetes and Eidyia, niece of Circe, who, after aiding the Argonauts, returned with Jason to Greece as his wife. Later she killed their children in outrage at his infidelity.

Media (Medes). Mountainous territory south of the Caspian Sea inhabited by a separate Iranian people, frequently identified with the Persians. When Astyages was defeated by Cyrus, Media became part of the Persian Empire.

Medusa. Like the Gorgons, a female monster with snakes for hair. Her look was said to turn men into stone.

Megara. Greek city-state west of Attica and south of Boeotia on the isthmus of Corinth; prize fought over by Athens and Corinth. Pericles' Megarian Decree (432 B.C.) starved the city into submission, and was a primary cause of the Peloponnesian War.

Melissa. Nymph who discovered honey (*mele*). Used as a title by priestesses of Demeter.

Melos. Westernmost island in the Cyclades, near Thera, birthplace of Diagoras the atheist.

Memphis. Central city of lower Egypt.

Menelaos (Menelaus). King of Sparta, son of Atreus, brother of Agamemnon, husband of Helen, father of Hermione and Megapenthes.

Menippus. Third-century B.C. cynic philosopher educated by Metrocles, from Gadara in Syria. His seriocomic prose laced with verse came to be called "Menippean satire."

Merope. Wife of king Polybus of Corinth, foster-mother of Oedipus.

Messenia. Southwestern section of the Peloponnesus, rebellious subject of Sparta, defeated by Sparta three times in the seventh-century B.C. Messenian Wars.

Meton. Fifth-century B.C. Athenian mathematician, astronomer, calendar reformer, and town planner. Corrected the calendar to bring the sun's and moon's cycles into correlation.

Middle Comedy. Term designating the period, ca. 404 B.C.–ca. 321 B.C., between the Old Comedy of Aristophanes and the New Comedy of Menander. Though no entire Middle Comedy play survives, from titles and fragments we know that this was a transitional period during which concern for contemporary issues and everyday human behavior and the stock figures characteristic of New Comedy evolved from the more stylized, satirically oriented Old Comedy.

Miletus (Milesians). Southernmost Greek city on the coast of Asia Minor, birthplace of Anaximenes, Anaximander, and Thales. After the Persian Wars Miletus became subject to Athens.

Miltiades. Athenian general appointed by Callimachus at the battle of Marathon in 490 B.C.; credited with the victory.

mimesis. Imitation of a noble action in dramatic speech. The term is used by Aristotle in his *Poetics* to describe the mechanisms of theatrical effectiveness.

Minos. King of Crete, son of Zeus and Europa, husband of Pasiphae, father of Phaedra and Ariadne. His fabulous court was at Knossos, where he built the labyrinth to house Pasiphae's son, the Minotaur. After his death he was made a judge of the dead, with his brother Rhadamanthys.

Minotaur. Cretan monster, half man and half bull, born of the union between Queen Pasiphae and a bull. The Minotaur, to whom the Athenians and other Greeks had to make annual human sacrifice, was finally slain by Theseus.

Mnemosyne. Goddess of memory, lover of Zeus, mother of the Muses.

Moirai. From the Greek word for "share." The Fates (Roman *Parcae*).

Morpheus. One of the sons of Sleep, who sends visions of human forms (*morphai*) to men.

Musaeus. Legendary Thracian singer, associated with Orpheus.

Muses. Daughters of Zeus and Mnemosyne, patronesses of the arts and sciences, they lived on Mt. Helikon, where they appeared to Hesiod.

music. Modes of Greek music included the Lydian (sweet, effeminate), the Dorian (energetic, for military purposes), and the Phrygian (for Dionysian rituals).

Mykenai (Mycenae). Ancient city in northeast Argolis, famous for its "lions gate" and "Cyclopean walls"; center of Mycenaean civilization. Its king, Agamemnon, led the Achaians in the Trojan War to bring back his brother Menelaos' wife Helen.

Myrmidons. Followers of Achilles.

Myrtis. Fifth-century B.C. Boeotian poet. She was teacher of Korinna and Pindar.

Mystae. Initiates into the Mysteries.

mystery cults. Secret cults professing mystic ideas and practicing symbolic rituals witnessed only by initiates; usually associated with Demeter, Persephone, and/or Dionysius; the most famous were the Dionysian, Eleusinian, Pythagorean, and Orphic cults.

Mytilene (Mitylene). Principal city of Lesbos, home of Sappho and Alcaeus.

Narcissus. Son of the river Cephisus and the nymph Lirope, a beautiful young man who fell in love only when he saw his own image in the water.

Nauplia. Town on the Argolid coast, near the city of Argos.

Nausicaa. Daughter of Phaiakian King Alcinous and Queen Arete; she fell in love with Odysseus in Homer's *Odyssey*.

Naxos. Largest island in the Cyclades, known for its wine, citrus, figs, and worship of Dionysius. It was devastated by the Persians in 490 B.C. and conquered by Cimon in 471 B.C. Here Theseus, returning to Athens from having slain the Minotaur, abandoned Ariadne.

Nemea. Valley in the northern Argolis where Herakles killed the Nemean lion. Later famous for the "Nemean games," a counterpart to the Olympic games.

Nemesis. Goddess of retribution or righteous indignation for excess.

Neo-Platonism. Used to describe the third-century A.D. philosophical synthesis of Platonic thought with the thought of Pythagoras, Aristotle, and the Stoics.

Neoptolemos. Son of Achilles and Deidameia.

Nereids. Sea nymphs, the fifty daughters of the sea god Nereus and the Oceanid Doris.

Nereus. Aegean sea god, son of Pontus, father of the Nereids, ruler of the Aegean Sea.

Nestor. King of Pylos, son of Neleus, father of Antilochus, and oldest and wisest of the Greek chiefs in the Trojan War.

New Comedy. Its principal example: Menander. Starting around 320 B.C., New Comedy was of a completely different intellectual and artistic type from Old Comedy, reflecting how drastically conditions in Athens had changed under Macedonian rule. Alexander's conquests had opened up much of the world to Athens, making it much more cosmopolitan than it had been in the fifth century B.C. Citizens were more interested in affluence than politics, seeking delights of the mind and senses over the good of the state. Where Aristophanes' plots were flimsy, New Comedy insisted on "well-made" intricate plots. Other differences from Old Comedy:

- The chorus was no longer an integral part of the dramatic action.
- In place of Old Comedy's ferocious satire, New Comedy celebrated the everyday routines of the middle class.
- In place of the low comedy of Old Comedy, with its phalluses, bawdy jokes, and stag parties, New Comedy was a comedy of

manners and wit, preferring innuendo to ribaldry.

- Character delineation was essential, replacing the stereotypes of Old Comedy.
- In place of the illicit, profane love of Old Comedy, New Comedy dealt with love between young people.

Although only the plays of Menander survive, we know the names of sixty-four other New Comedy playwrights, including Diphilus (who wrote one hundred plays) and Philemon (ninety-seven).

Nike. Goddess of victory, daughter of the Titan Pallas and Styx.

Niobe. Daughter of Tantalus, wife of Amphion of Thebes, mother of fourteen children, because of which she boasted she was superior to Leto. Twelve of her children were killed by Apollo and Artemis, and Niobe herself turned by Zeus into a stone on Mt. Sipylus in Lydia, which shed tears for her lost children in the summer.

Notus. The south wind.

nous. "Mind," in its highest and most universal dimensions.

Nymphs. Minor female divinities of the field, stream, mountain, and forest.

Nyx. The goddess Night, daughter of Chaos.

Odysseus. King of Ithaca, son of Laertes, husband of Penelope, father of Telemachos, favorite of Athena. Made famous by Homer's *Odyssey* for his craftiness and versatility, he is the prototype of the modern hero.

Oedipus. Hero of Sophocles' *Oedipus the King* and *Oedipus at Colonus*. Son of Laius and Jocasta, father of Eteokles, Polyneices, Antigone, and Ismene. Lifted a plague on Thebes, and assumed kingship of the city, by solving the riddle of the Sphinx. But without knowing what he was doing, he had killed his father and was now married to his mother, bringing a new plague upon Thebes. When the overly confident Oedipus, filled with *hybris*, swears an oath to remove this plague as well by relentlessly tracking down its cause despite the warnings of his mother-wife Jocasta and the blind prophet Teiresias, he discovers the true identity of the father he slew and the truth of his incestuous situation. When he blinds himself in propitiation and resigns the kingship to Creon, Oedipus retires to Colonus. Sophocles' *Antigone* deals with the fate of Oedipus' daughter, Antigone, who dies defending her brothers' honor against Creon. His sons Polyneices and Eteokles' war against each other is the subject of *Seven Against Thebes*.

Okeanos (Oceanus). Son of Ouranos and Gaia; in the Ouranian pantheon preceding the Olympians, god of the ocean; replaced by Poseidon.

Old Comedy. The first form of Greek comedy, reaching its height in the fifth century B.C. Characterized by comic but biting and obscene comment on public institutions, events, and well-known figures. History records forty-two comic playwrights and 323 play titles. Only eleven survive—all by Aristophanes.

oligarchy. Rule by the few.

Olympia. Plain in Elis, in the Peloponnesus on the river Alpheus, where the Olympic games were celebrated every four years; citizens of every state in Greece took part. A famous sanctuary of Zeus was located there.

Olympus (Olympian). Mountain range between Macedonia and Thessaly. On its highest summit Hephaestos and Zeus built homes for all the "Olympian" gods.

omphalos. "Navel." Delphi was considered the *omphalos* of the earth, the place where easiest travel to the underworld and the heavens was accessible.

Orestes. Son of Agamemnon and Klytaimnestra, brother of Elektra and Iphigeneia.

At the urging of Apollo he murdered his mother to take vengeance for her murder of his father. He was hounded by the matriarchal Erinyes until he found refuge in Apollo's temple at Delphi. But the Furies found him there, so Apollo took him to Athens to Athena, who held a trial to decide whether he should be punished. When the jury she appointed tied, she broke the vote in his favor.

Orion. Mythic hunter, one of the Giants. After his death he was placed as a constellation among the stars.

Orpheus. Legendary student of Pythagoras, a musician, whose fifth-century B.C. cult shifted focus from the earth to heaven, practicing asceticism to release the soul from earthly desire and allow it to experience godhead.

Orphism. Orphics believed that all men are brothers, and in the unity of all living beings from the lowliest organism to God. The "sorrowful wheel" of reincarnation can be escaped only by initiation into the cult's purifications. Although rooted in Dionysian religion, Orphism believed that spiritual, not physical, rituals led to ecstasy. Orpheus has been called Dionysius "Apollonized."

Ortygia. Island near Syracuse, where Artemis was born. Also another name for Delos.

Ossa. Mountain in Magnesia in Thessaly, where the war of the Giants occurred.

ostracism. Banishment, usually for ten years; Athens' method of punishing unpopular wealthy citizens. The votes for ostracism were recorded on *ostraca* (potsherds).

Ouranos (Uranus). Father of Kronos, husband of Gaia; early sky god of the pantheon before Zeus' Olympian gods. His generation sometimes referred to as the "Ouranian" gods.

Paean. Ancient god of healing, later associated with Apollo, for whom it became another

"Temples at Paestum, Magna Graecia"

name. Also used for hymns of thanksgiving in his honor.

Paestum. Southern Italian coastal town, pilgrimage center of Magna Graecia from the seventh century B.C. Site of the best-preserved Doric temples.

Pallas. Title for Athena.

Palladium. A sacred image of Athena sent by Zeus to Dardanus, the founder of Troy. When it was stolen by Odysseus and Diomedes, Troy's doom was sealed.

Pan. Son of Hermes, originally Arcadian goat-footed god of flocks and shepherds. Sudden terror (panic) was caused by him, giving rise to "pandemonium." Since *pan* in Greek also means "all" or "whole," he later became a "universal" god.

Panathenaea (Panathenaean Festival). Fes-tival of Athena, celebrated annually in honor of her birthday. Accompanied by feasting and ritual processions and performances of all the arts.

Pandora. First woman on earth, whose curiosity loosed troubles upon humanity when she opened a forbidden box.

Paphlagonia. Country in northern Asia Minor; its inhabitants were reputedly coarse and backward.

Paphos. Town on the west coast of Cyprus, sacred to Aphrodite.

parasite (parasitos). Guest, "someone who sits next to," particularly at a banquet; originally without the negative connotations it accumulated by the time of Middle Comedy.

Paris (or **Alexander; Alexandros**). Trojan archer-prince, son of Hekabe and Priam, who carried off Helen, the wife of Menelaos. Aphrodite promised Helen to him if he gave her the award for beauty in her contest with Hera and Athena. Seeking revenge for the death of his brother Hektor, he killed Achilles.

Parnassos (Parnassus). Mountain of the Pindus range near Delphi, sacred to Apollo, Dionysius, and the Muses.

Parnes. Wooded mountain in Attica.

Parody (parodia). Exaggeration and incongruity used to criticize a poet or orator's subject.

Paros. One of the Cyclades, center for trade in the Aegean and birthplace of Archilochos.

Parthenica. Choral lyric poems designed to be sung by groups of virgins.

Parthenon. Temple of the virgin Athena, on the Acropolis of Athens, masterminded by Phidias. Begun in 447 B.C. and completed in 431 B.C.

Partheopaeus. Son of Atalanta, one of the seven champions who attacked Thebes.

Parthia (Parthians). Asian country known for its warlike inhabitants.

Pasiphae. Wife of Minos of Crete, whose passion for a bull led him to create an artificial cow-frame she could use to receive the animal's ministrations. As a result, she gave birth to the Minotaur.

Patroklos (Patroclus). Greek hero in the Trojan War; Achilles' closest friend, slain by Hektor—causing Achilles to rejoin the battle for vengeance.

Pegasus. Winged horse, son of Medusa, tamed by Bellerophon. Associated with Zeus' thunderbolt.

Pelasgus (Pelasgians). Mythical king of Argos. Greeks in general were often called Pelasgians because of a legend that Pelasgus was their earliest ancestor. Homer also uses the term to refer to a tribe allied with Troy.

Peleiades. Priestesses at the shrine to Zeus at Dodona, who interpreted his oracular utterances.

Peleus. Son of Aeacus and king of the Myrmidons of Thessalian Phthia, husband of Thetis, father of Achilles.

Pelias. King of Iolcus, son of Poseidon and Tyro, father of Alcestis and Acastus. He sent Jason on the quest for the Golden Fleece. On Jason's return, Medea manipulated Pelias' daughters into cutting him to pieces, saying it would restore his youth.

Pelion. Mountain in Magnesia in Thessaly where the Centaur Cheiron was born.

Pella. Capital of Macedon until 167 B.C.

Pellen. City in Achaea, allied with Sparta.

Peloponnesus (Peloponnesos). "Island of Pelops." Major southern Greek peninsula, connected with northern Greece and with Attica by the Isthmus of Corinth, the location of Olympia, Sparta, Pylos, Epidaurus, and Patras. The Peloponnesian League comprised Sparta and her allies. The Peloponnesian War, 431–404 B.C., was fought between Sparta, Corinth, and other city-states opposed to Athenian hegemony and Athens.

Pelops. Son of Tantalus, originally from Phrygia; husband of Hippodamia, daughter of Oenomaus; ancestor of the house of Atreus (Pelopidae). Tantalus cut him up and served him as food to the gods, but he was later restored to life by Zeus. Pelops' murder of his wife's lover, Myrtilos, caused his sons Atreus and Thyestes to be cursed. The Peloponnesus was named after him.

Penelope. Daughter of Icarius, wife of Odysseus, who faithfully awaited his return to Ithaca after the Trojan War.

Penthesilea. Daughter of Ares, queen of the Amazons, ally of Troy, slain by Achilles.

Pentheus. King of Thebes, son of Echion and Agave, grandson of Cadmus. Torn to pieces by the women of Thebes when he denied honor to Dionysius.

peplos. Woman's outer garment, a large rectangular piece of cloth, embroidered or decorated around its borders, and worn thrown around the shoulders and gathered up with the arms so that it fell in heavy folds. The Sacred Peplos, a huge piece of cloth woven by the maid-

"Archer"

ens of Athens with pictures of mythological events in which Athena took part, was presented to the goddess at the annual Panathenaea.

Periander. Powerful tyrant of Corinth, 625–585 B.C., and patron of the arts.

Pericles (Perikles). Leading Athenian statesman after the Persian Wars, member of the democratic faction as early as 469 B.C. He served as general and ruled Athens firmly under a democratic constitution. Pericles erected the Parthenon and the Propylaea. His policy was aggressive and imperialistic, in contrast to the pro-Spartan line of his conservative predecessors, and he recognized that this made a war sooner or later inevitable. In 432 B.C., with the outbreak of hostilities imminent, Pericles struck the first blow—with the Megarian Decree that placed an embargo on Megara.

Peripatetic School. Name given to Aristotle's philosophical institute, the Lyceum, because of the covered walk (*peripatos*) in the buildings constructed by Theophrastus to allow students to walk and talk without discomfort.

Persephone (Kore). Daughter of Zeus and Demeter, wife of Hades, queen of the underworld.

Perseus. Mythical hero, son of Zeus and Danaë, slayer of Medusa.

Persian Wars. From the Ionian revolt of 499 B.C. to the treaty negotiated by Callias in 449 B.C., these wars were fought to maintain Greek hegemony over the Aegean against the Persian Empire under Darius and his successors.

Phaedra. Daughter of Minos, sister of Ariadne, wife of Theseus.

Phaethon. Son of Helios and Clymene, who begged Helios to drive his chariot for one day but could not control the horses and was killed by Zeus' thunderbolt to prevent the earth from catching fire.

Phalaris. Sixty-century B.C. tyrant of Sicilian Acragas.

phallus. Image of the male sexual organ in a state of erection. Festivals of Dionysius, in which rites of fertility played a large part, always included a phallic procession featuring the phallus. Also, actors in Old Comedy wore enlarged phalluses as parts of their costume.

Phidias (Pheidias). Fifth-century B.C. Athenian sculptor, friend of Pericles, and chief designer of Periclean Athens, responsible for the Parthenon and the colossal gold and ivory statue of Athena that graced its primary sanctuary.

Philip II. King of Macedon, 359–336 B.C., father of Alexander the Great; united Macedonia and laid the foundation for his son's imperial expansion throughout the Mediterranean.

Philodemos. From Gadara, first-century B.C. Epicurean philosopher and poet in Roman Greece.

Philoktetes. Son of Poeas, a great archer; friend of Herakles, whose pyre he lighted; died of a snakebite in Lemnos.

Phocis. Country north of the Gulf of Corinth, site of Delphi.

Phoebus. Another name for Apollo.

Phoenicia (Phoenicians). Country on the extreme eastern shore of the Mediterranean (modern Lebanon). The Phoenicians were known for their prowess as traders, and for exporting the alphabet to Greece.

Phoenix. Son of Amyntor of Hellas, saved from his father's wrath by Peleus, who assigned him to be mentor of his son Achilles.

Phosphorus. The Morning Star.

phratry. Brotherhood, or "kinship group," a remnant of ancient Attic tribal organization.

Phrygia (Phrygian). Country in northwestern Asia Minor settled by Thracians, probably the origin of the cults of Dionysius and of Cybele. The Romans called Trojans "Phrygians."

Phrynichus. Most important tragedian before Aeschylus, and with Thespis one of the founders of the art; punished by the Athenians for producing *The Capture of Miletus* (ca. 494 B.C.) and reminding them of their failure to defend that city from the Persians. They voted to ban the play from all further production.

Phthia. Southeastern Thessaly, the home of Achilles.

Phyle. Attic deme at the foot of Mt. Parnes on the Boeotian border. In 404 B.C. Thrasybulus, at the head of an army of exiled democrats, captured Phyle and provided the leverage for expelling "the Thirty."

Pieria. District on the southeast coast of Macedonia, sacred to the Muses in preclassical times.

Piraeus. The port of Athens, four miles southwest of the city, fortified in the fifth century B.C. by Themistocles as a base for the Athenian fleet. Themistocles also built the "long walls" connecting Piraeus with Athens.

Pisistratus (Peisistratos). Benevolent tyrant of Athens off and on from 561 to 527 B.C., who began the temple of Olympian Zeus, ruled under the principles of Solon's constitution, and introduced the Great Dionysian Festival for the performance of tragedies.

Pittakos. Tyrant of Lesbos, whose court was in Mytilene, in the time of Sappho; one of the "Seven Sages."

Plataea. Southern Boeotian city near the Attic border. The sympathies of the inhabitants had always been with Athens, and they aided the Athenians at Marathon. In 479 B.C. the final defeat of the Persians on land took place near Plataea.

Pleiades. Constellation made of the seven daughters of Atlas and Pleione, who were turned into stars when Orion pursued them.

Pluto (Pluton). Supreme god of the underworld, another name for Hades.

Plutus. Son of Demeter and Iasius, god of wealth, personification of affluence, blinded by Zeus so he would distribute his abundance without vision.

polemarch. Originally the supreme commander of the Athenian military, one of the nine archons.

polis. "City-state," the characteristic form of Greek life. The *polis* was built around a fortified acropolis ("high-city"), where temples to the city's gods were built. City-states included Athens, Corinth, Megara, Mytilene, Sparta, and Thebes.

Polyclitus. Major fifth-century B.C. Argive sculptor, master of proportion.

Polycrates (Polykrates). Sixth-century B.C. tyrant of Samos, who built the great Temple of Hera, an aqueduct, and a powerful navy. He hosted Anacreon, Ibykus, and Theodorus in his court.

Polydeukes (Polydeuces; Pollux). One of the Dioscuri. Brother of Kastor, son of Zeus and Leda, or Leda and Tyndareus; brother of Helen.

Polygnotus. Fifth-century B.C. Athenian painter (although he was born on Thasos); friend of Sophocles and of Cimon.

Polyneices (Polynices). Son of Oedipus and Jocasta, expelled from Thebes by his brother Eteokles and returned as the Seven Against Thebes, only to die at his brother's hand. His sister Antigone buried him, which led to her own death under King Creon.

Polyphemos (Polyphemus). A one-eyed Cyclop, son of Poseidon and Thoösa. Blinded by Odysseus.

Polyxena. Daughter of Priam and Hekabe, sacrificed to appease the ghost of Achilles.

Poseidon. Son of Kronos and Rhea, brother of Zeus, father of the Cyclopes, god of the sea, his name literally "spouse of the rivers"; also the cause of earthquakes. Horse racing was under his patronage. After the fall of Minoan civilization through earthquakes and tidal waves, the predominant preclassical ocean god until his primacy was usurped by Zeus.

Potidaea. Corinthian colony on the Chalcidian peninsula of Pallene, in Macedon, subject to Athens until its revolt became one of the causes of the Peloponnesian War.

Praxiteles. Fourth-century B.C. Athenian sculptor, known for his Aphrodite and his Hermes.

preSocratics. Refers to philosophers who preceded Socrates, including Thales, Anaximander, Anaxagoras, Empedocles, Heraclitus, Zeno, and Leucippus and Democritus.

Priam. Son of Laomedon, last king of Troy during the Trojan War, husband of Hebake, father of fifty children, including Hektor, Cassandra, and Paris (Alexandros).

Priapus (Priapos). Son of Dionysius and Aphrodite, god of fertility and animal husbandry, usually represented with erect penis. The city of Priapus in Mysia was the center of his worship.

proagon. Dress parade held before the Great

Dionysian Festival. The chorus and actors marched through the city to the theater, carrying their masks. As they entered the theater, a crier announced the plays, playwrights, actors, and *choregi*.

Proclus. Fifth-century A.D. neo-Platonic educator, born in Byzantium.

Procustes. Legendary highway robber, who forced his victims to lie in beds of the wrong size. Those who were too large had their limbs lopped off, while those who were too short were stretched on the rack.

Prodicus. Sophist from Chios, contemporary of Socrates.

Prometheus. Titan, patron of mankind, who stole fire from heaven and brought it to earth. He educated humanity in the practical arts. Zeus punished him by chaining him to a rock in the Caucasus and sending an eagle to eat his liver until he was freed by Herakles.

Propontis. The Sea of Marmara, between the Aegean and the Euxine.

Propylaea. Monumental roofed marble gateway on the west of the Acropolis in Athens.

proskenion. Proscenium, the area below the *skené* in the Hellenistic theater.

protagonist. The "first actor" of Greek theater, who had the best parts and won the prizes.

Protesilaos. Thessalian commander, the first Greek to be killed in the Trojan War.

Proteus. A sea god and mythical king of Egypt, consulted by Menelaos on his way back to Sparta. Famous for changing shapes.

Proxenos. Citizen of Greek city-state appointed, because of family connections or other ties, to sponsor and protect resident aliens. Origin of "proxy."

Prytanes. The Athenian Council of 500 usually operated not as a whole but in tenths, each group of fifty representatives of a single tribe in charge of government for one tenth of the fiscal year. These fifty councilors, when in power, were called Prytanes (presidents).

Prytaneum. Building in which the Prytanes conducted their business, ate their meals, and entertained foreign ambassadors.

Prolemy II. Second-century B.C. king of Alexandrian Egypt, who expanded the great library of Alexandria, built the museum, and patronized the arts and sciences.

Pylos. City of Nestor, one of the Greek heroes at Troy, on the west coast of the Peloponnesus.

Pyrrha. Town on Lesbos.

Pythian. Epithet of Apollo, in whose honor musical contests and games were held at Delphi (Pythian Games) every third Olympiad.

Pytho. Ancient name for Delphi, where the python priestess gave oracular answers to pilgrims' prayers, before she was replaced by the Delphic Apollo.

Rhadamanthys. Son of Zeus and Europa, brother of Minos, ruler of Phaistos in Crete, who was appointed with his brother a judge of the dead.

rhapsode. A professional reciter of poetry, especially of the Homeric poems.

Rhea (Rheia). Fertility goddess, daughter of Gaia and Ouranos, wife of Kronos, and mother of Demeter, Hera, Hestia, Hades, Poseidon, and Zeus. Later identified with Cybele.

Rhodes. Easternmost Aegean island, ally of Athens that turned to the Spartan side during the Peloponnesian War.

Rhodopis. Famous courtesan of Naucratis, in Egypt, originally from Thrace. Sappho attacked her under the name of Doricha.

Sages, The Seven. Men of the seventh and sixth centuries B.C. known for their wise contributions to the laws of their city-states: Cleobulus (tyrant of Lindus on Rhodes), Periander (of Corinth), Pittakos (of Mytilene), Bias (of Caria),

Thales of Miletus, Chilon of Aparta, Solon of Athens.

Salamis. Island off the west coast of Attica, subject to Athens from the sixth century B.C., scene of the decisive defeat of the Persian navy in 480.

Samos. Ionian island southwest of the coast of Asia Minor.

Samothrace. Island near Ithaka off the coast of Thrace.

Sardis. Capital of Lydia in Asia Minor, known for being fabulously wealthy.

Saronic Gulf. Bay of the Aegean Sea between Attica and Argolis containing the island of Salamis, where the Greeks destroyed the Persian fleet in 480 B.C.

Sarpedon. Son of Zeus and Europa, brother of Minos and Rhadamanthys; a prince of Lycia, and ally of the Trojans during the war.

satyr play. The closing, fourth play in the tragic festival, providing Dionysian, profane, comic relief to the intensity of the preceding three tragedies. The leader of the satyric chorus was Papa-Silenus, father and mentor of Dionysius.

satyrs. Mythic race of beings, sons of Hermes and Iphthima, with goatlike characteristics, followers of Pan and/or Dionysius, who symbolized the animal vitality of human nature. On vases they are frequently painted with penis erect, attacking nymphs from behind.

Scamander (Skamandros). A famous river in the Troad, called "Xanthus" by the gods.

Scylla. Six-headed sea monster, who barked like a dog and had long necks and twelve feet, living in a cave on the Italian side of the straits between Italy and Sicily, across from the whirlpool Charybdis.

Scyros. Island of the Sporades off the coast of Euboea.

Scythians. Rude nomadic people dwelling northeast of Thrace, perhaps originally from the north shore of the Black Sea; the Athenians employed Scythian archers as policemen.

Semele. Daughter of Cadmus, mother of Dionysius.

sibyl. Divinely-inspired prophetess, usually of Apollo.

Sidon. Powerful city in Phoenicia, north of Tyre.

Sigeum. Northwestern promontory of the Troad, southern headland of the Hellespont, site of the Greek camp in the Trojan War.

Silenus. Known as "Papa-Silenus," the jolly old satyr who raised and taught the infant Dionysius.

Simoïs. River near Troy, son of Okeanos and Tethys.

Sirens. Sea-nymphs, daughters of Phorcys, who had the power of charming and luring to destruction all who heard their songs. Odysseus evades them by tying himself to his mast.

Sirius. The dog star.

Sisyphus. Son of Aeolus and Enarete; king of Corinth, and founder of the royal house there. For his avarice he was condemned to roll a stone uphill only for it to roll down again upon reaching the summit.

Smyrna. Coastal city of Asia Minor.

Sophists. "Adult education" itinerant teachers of rhetoric and philosophy, including Abdacus, Prodicus, and Protagoras, who were considered charlatans by Socrates and Plato because they pursued wisdom for practical purposes instead of for its own sake, and because they taught for money.

Sparta. The principal town in Lakonia, head of the Peloponnesian Confederacy and principal rival of Athens.

Sphinx. Monster with a winged lion's body and a woman's breast and head who proposed a riddle to the Thebans, killing all who could not solve it. When Oedipus answered correctly, she killed herself. The riddle: "What goes on four feet in the morning, two at noon, and three in the evening?" Answer: Man.

Sporades. Island group between Crete and Asia Minor.

stadium. Greek measure of length, about 600 feet. Appointed by Herakles as the course for the foot race at Olympia.

Stesichoros. Sixth- and fifth-century B.C. Sicilian poet, rival of Sappho and Alcaeus.

Stoa. "Colonnade." Usually roofed.

Stoicism. Stern and ascetic fourth-century B.C. philosophical school founded by Zeno of Citium in the Stoa of Athens. Its ideal is "perfect indifference" to all things.

strategos. Title usually translated as "general," referring to the ten influential Athenians elected each year by popular vote, one vote from each tribe, to take charge of the army and navy.

Styx. Daughter of Okeanos and Tethys, the principal river of Hades which flows around the underworld seven times and which souls of the dead had to cross to gain entrance.

Sunium. Promontory at the southern tip of Attica, famous for its temple of Poseidon/Athena, where Athena propitiated Poseidon to hold back the tidal wave from the explosion of Thera to keep it from deluging Athens.

Sybaris. Greek city in southern Italy, founded in the eighth century B.C. by Achaians. In the sixth century B.C., famous for the wealth and decadence of its citizens.

symposium Drinking party, banquet. Characterized by serious conversation, music, recitation, and dancing.

Syracusae. Wealthiest city of Sicily, on its southeast coast, known for its great theater.

Taenarus. Town in Lakonia, the southern-

"Stoa in the agora of Athens (reconstructed)"

most promontory of the Peloponnesus, near which was an entrance to Hades.

Tantalus. Son of Zeus and Pluto, father of Pelops, Broteas, and Niobe. Variously king of Lydia, Argos, or Corinth. For divulging secrets entrusted to him he was punished in Hades by reaching forever for the receding fruit of an overhanging tree.

Tarentum. Modern Taranto, city of Magna Graecia on the western coast of Calabria, important for its harbor.

Tartarus. Son of Aether and Gaia, father of the Giants. In Homer, Tartarus is the deepest pit of Hades; later synonymous with the underworld in general.

Tecmessa. Daughter of Phrygian Teleutas, spear-wife of Aias.

Teiresias. Blind Theban seer, famous for his role in *Oedipus the King*. Associated with the caduceus.

Telamon. Son of Aeacus, brother of Peleus, and father of Aias; one of the Argonauts.

Telemachos. Son of Odysseus and Penelope; his coming of age is celebrated in Homer's *Odyssey*.

Tenedos. Small island in the Aegean near the mouth of the Hellespont, to where the Greeks withdrew their fleet to make Troy believe they had left.

Teos. Ionian city on Asia Minor coast, birthplace of Anacreon.

Tethys. Daughter of Ouranos and Gaia, wife of Okeanos.

Teukros (Teucer). Son of Telamon, half-brother of Ajax; considered the best Greek archer at Troy.

Thamyris. Thracian bard blinded by the Muses because he challenged them to a singing contest.

Thanatos. Son of night, brother of sleep, god of death.

Thebe. City of Mysia ruled by King Eëtion,

whose daughter was Hektor's wife Andromache, who came to Troy to wed Hektor just before Achilles destroyed Thebes.

Thebes. Principal city in Boeotia, allied with Sparta. Birthplace of Korinna and Pindar. Here Oedipus and his father Laius ruled.

Themis. Daughter of Ouranos and Gaia, goddess of law and of custom.

Themiscyra. A district near the Sea of Azov, where the Amazons lived.

Themistocles. Distinguished Athenian statesman; in 493 B.C, he was responsible for Athens' naval supremacy and victory over the Persians at Salamis.

Theopompos. Playwright of Old Comedy, rival of Aristophanes.

Thera. Modern Thíra. The volcanic island of the Cyclades north of Crete thought to be a center of Minoan civilization, destroyed by massive earthquakes and volcanic eruptions.

Thermodon. River of Pontus (modern Thermeh) on whose banks the Amazons were supposed to have dwelt.

Thermopylae. The pass from Thessaly into Locris, gateway to southern Greece, where Leonidas and his Spartans made their famous suicidal stand against the invading Persians.

Thersites. Son of Agrios, portrayed as the ugliest of the Greeks, who in the *Iliad* serves as the voice of the commoner and critic of princes.

thesaurus. "Storehouse," "treasury."

Thesus. Legendary king of Attica, son of Aegeus and Aethra, father of Hippolytus, Demophoon, Acamas, and Melanippus. He volunteered to go to Knossos and destroy the Minotaur, which demanded annual tribute from the Greeks. After succeeding, with the help of Ariadne's golden thread, he abandoned her on Naxos.

Thesmophoria. Festival of Demeter and Persephone, held by the women of Athens each year at the beginning of November.

Thespis. Reputed founder of tragedy, victorious in the first recorded festival of tragedy, 534 B.C. Credited by Aristotle with:

- introducing the "first actor," the protagonist, who exchanged words with the chorus.
- inventing unpainted linen masks so an actor could play more than one role.
- organizing the first touring company, which traveled around Attica in wagons.

Thessaly. Large region in northern Greece, at the southern border of Macedonia, noted for its horses and its witchcraft; home of the Centaurs.

"The Thirty," or **"Thirty Tyrants."** Aristocratic committee charged by Sparta with administering Athens after the Peloponnesian War.

Thetis. Daughter of Nereus and Doris; a sea nymph, wife of Peleus, mother of Achilles.

Thrace. Northeastern province of Greece, known for its warlike populace, prophets, and harsh climate.

Thrasybulus. Leader of the democratic exiles in expelling "the Thirty" in 403 B.C.

Thurium (Thurii). Athenian colony in southern Italy, founded in 443 B.C. on the site of Sybaris.

Thyestes. Son of Pelops and Hippodamia, brother of Atreus, father of Aegisthos.

Timaeus. Fourth-century B.C. historian, born in Tauromenium, Sicily, and banished by Agathocles to Athens, where he wrote the history of Sicily.

timé. "Honor" in the sense of public recognition of one's value, the basis of heroic society. Because he had been deprived of his *timé* by Agamemnon, Achilles refused to fight.

Timocreon. Fifth-century B.C. lyric poet from Rhodes, rival of Simonides and Themistocles.

Timon. Third-century B.C. Skeptic philosopher.

Timotheus. Fifth- and fourth-century B.C. lyric poet, native of Miletus.

Tiryns. Ancient fortified city in Argos, sister-city to Agamemnon's Mycenae.

Titans. Twelve sons and daughters of Gaia and Ouranos—including Okeanos, Tethys, Hyperion, Kronos, Rhea, Themis, Phoebe, Mnemosyne, and Iapetus—who made war against the gods.

Tithonos. Son of Laomedon and Strymo, lover of Eos, the dawn, who abandoned him each morning. She requested eternal life for him, but neglected to add that this should be also eternal youth, and he continued aging but was unable to die.

Trachis. Town in the Malis district of Thessaly, sometime home of Herakles.

tragedy (tragodeia). Form of mythic drama dealing with major characters facing existential crisis, usually derived from their own flaws and heightened by the vagaries of fate. Its origins remain obscure despite theories that say it arose from religious rituals, from the choric dithyramb, and from hero-worship ceremonies performed at their tombs. Its parts:

- *Prologos*, opening image or speech
- *Parodos*, entrance of chorus to set the tone of the play
- *Epeisodion*, complicating episodes, alternating with
- *Stasimon*, chorus's response to each episode. Combination repeated from four to six times.
- *Exodos*, the chorus marches out.

trierarch. Title given to the wealthy persons in Athens who underwrote the outfitting of, and/or commanded, a warship (*trireme*).

trilogy (trilogia). Set of three tragedies, of which Aeschylus' *Oresteia* (*Agamemnon, Libation Bearers, Eumenides*) is the only surviving example, performed with a satyr play at the annual Dionysian Festival.

triobolus. Silver three-obol coin, half a *drachma*, with which citizens working for the city-state were compensated from the time of Pericles onward.

Triptolemos. Son of Celeus of Eleusis and Polyhymnia; hero who aided Demeter in her search for her daughter, as a reward for which she granted him knowledge of agriculture, which he handed down to humanity.

Triton. Sea god, son of Poseidon and Amphitrite, whose trumpet calmed the sea.

Trivia. Daughter of Demeter; sometimes called Hekate, and associated with Persephone. A *trivium* is a place where three roads meet, and Hekate has long been associated with crossroads.

Troad (Troas). Territory of Troy or Ilium, south of the Hellespont.

Troglodytes. Cave-dwellers, term used by geographers to describe uncivilized tribes.

Troizen (Troezen). Town in southeastern Argolis, on the Saronic Gulf. Birthplace of Theseus.

Trojan War. The Trojan War had its start at the wedding feast of Achilles' parents. Eris ("Discord") was the one grace not invited. In her anger, she dropped a golden apple onto the dance floor, inscribed "To the Fairest." Hera, Aphrodite, and Athena reached to pick it up simultaneously. The judgment of Paris was the aftermath, and the awarding of the apple to Aphrodite in exchange for the love of Helen. When Paris came to Menelaos' court, met and wooed her, then returned with her to Troy, Menelaos appealed to his brother Agamemnon, king of Mycenae and of the Achaian confederacy. Agamemnon led the Greek fleet against Troy to bring her back. Insulted in the ninth year of the war by Agamemnon, Achilles withdrew from the fighting only to return to battle to avenge the death of his best friend Patroklos, slain by Hektor. The death of Hektor at Achilles' hands virtually ended the Trojan War, returning Helen to her Achaean husband Menelaos.

Troy. Also known as Ilion or Ilium, fabled city of Priam and of Paris, whose abduction of Menelaos' wife Helen led to the Trojan War (1193–1184 B.C.). The city, on the Asian side of the Hellespont, commanded the approach to the Black Sea, rich in gold and breeding stock.

Tydeus. Son of Oeneus of Calydon and Perioboea, one of the seven champions who attacked Thebes; father of the Greek hero Diomedes.

Tyndareus. King of Sparta, husband of Leda, and at least the foster father of Kastor, Polydeukes, Helen, and Klytaimnestra.

Typhon. A fire-breathing, wind-blowing monster sometimes described as having one hundred heads, blazing eyes, and terrifying voices.

tyrannos. Ruler, or tyrant, though without the negative associations of the modern word. A tyrant drew his absolute power from all the disenfranchised.

Tyros (Tyre). Famous coastal city of Phoenicia.

Tyrtaeus. Seventh-century B.C. Athenian elegist. He introduced the Ionic elegy into Sparta.

Xanthos. River in Lycia, associated with Troy.

xenía. The institute of "guest-friendship," the strongest social bond in heroic Greece. The word *xeinos* means both "guest," "host," and "stranger." When Glaukos meets Diomedes on the Trojan battlefield, his life is spared by the Greek hero when Diomedes learns that his great-grandfather was *xeinos* to Glaukos' great-grandfather. One of the epithets of Zeus is "protector of *xeinoi*," as important a function as his protection of kings.

Xenocles. Fifth-century B.C. Athenian tragedian. He once defeated Euripides, but was ridiculed by Aristophanes; he introduced elaborate stage machinery.

Xenocrates. Fourth-century B.C. follower of Plato.

Xerxes. Persian king, 485–465 B.C., son of Darius and Atossa.

Zakynthos. Ionian island off the northwest corner fo the Peloponnesus, part of the Athenian empire at the time of the Peloponnesian War.

Zenobios. Second-century A.D. rhetorician and sophist from Antioch, who lived and taught in Rome.

Zenodotos (Zenodotus). Third-century B.C. Ephesian grammarian who served as superintendent of the library at Alexandria.

Zephyros. The west wind, son of Astraeus and Eos.

Zeus. Youngest son of Kronos and Rhea, hidden from his father in a cavern on Crete. Spouse of Metis and Hera, wielder of the thunderbolt and bearer of the aegis; "king of gods and men," ruler of Olympus, sky god, and head of the patriarchal Olympian pantheon whose governing and organizing power compares favorably with that of Fate itself. His worship, associated with his motherless daughter Athena's, replaced the worship of Poseidon in preclassical times.

Zeuxis. Fourth-century B.C. Ionic painter, who specialized in panels.

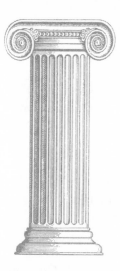

Sources & Recommendations

Atchity, Kenneth. *Homer's Iliad: The Shield of Memory*. Carbondale and Edwardsville: Southern Illinois University Press, 1978.

———. (with E.J.W. Barber). "Greek Princes and Aegean Princesses: The Role of Women in the Homeric Poems," in *Critical Essays on Homer*, ed. Kenneth Atchity. Boston: G. K. Hall & Company, 1987.

Auden, W. H. *The Portable Greek Reader*. New York: The Viking Press, 1948/67.

Barnstone, Willis. *Greek Lyric Poetry*. Bloomington and London: Indiana University Press, 1962/67.

Beye, Charles. *Ancient Greek Literature and Society*. Garden City, New York: Doubleday, 1975.

Boardman, John. *Greek Art*. New York: Oxford University Press, 1973.

Bowra, C. M. *The Greek Experience*. New York: New American Library, 1957/85.

Burnet, John. *Early Greek Philosophy*. London: A&C Black, 1930.

Cook, Arthur Bernard. *Zeus, A Study in Ancient Religion*. Cambridge: The University Press, 1914.

Cornford, Francis MacDonald. *Plato's Theory of Knowledge*. London: Routledge & Kegan Paul, 1973.

———. *From Religion to Philosophy*. New York: Harper & Row.

Dickinson, G. Lowes. *The Greek View of Life*. Ann Arbor: University of Michigan Press, 1958.

Dodds, E. R. *The Greeks and the Irrational*. Berkeley and Los Angeles: University of California Press, 1951.

Dover, Kenneth. *The Greeks*. Austin: University of Texas Press, 1980.

Ellis, Havelock. *Preface to Plato*. Cambridge, England: Grossett, 1963.

Encyclopaedia Britannica. 11th Edition. New York: The Encyclopaedia Britannica Company, 1910.

Fantham, Elaine, Helene Peet Foley, Natalie Boymel Kampen, et al. *Women in the Classical World*. New York: Oxford University Press, 1994.

Finley, M. I. *The World of Odysseus*. New York: The Viking Press, 1978.

Forsdyke, Sir Edgar John. *Greece before Homer*. New York: W. W. Norton & Company, 1957.

Forster, E. M. *The Greek View of Life*. Ann Arbor: University of Michigan Press, 1958/67.

Frankel, Hermann. *Early Greek Poetry and Philosophy*, trans. Moses Hadas and James Willis. New York: Harcourt, Brace, Jovanovich, 1973.

Frost, Frank J. *Greek Society*. Lexington, Mass.: Heath, 1971.

Gaster, Theodor H. *Thespis*. New York: Harper Torchbooks, 1950/61.

Glotz, G. *The Greek City and its Institutions*. London: Kegan Paul, Trench, Trubner & Company, Ltd., 1929.

Gouldner, Alvin W. *Enter Plato: Classical Greece and the Origins of Social Theory*. New York: Basic Books, 1965.

Grant, Michael. *Myths of the Greeks and Romans*. Cleveland: World Publishing Company, 1962.

Guthrie, W. C. *The Greeks and their Gods*. London: Methuen, 1950.

Hadas, Moses. *History of Greek Literature*. New York: Columbia University Press, 1950.

Hamilton, Edith. *The Greek Way*. New York: W. W. Norton & Company, 1930/58.

———. *The Echo of Greece*. New York: W. W. Norton & Company, 1957.

Hammond, N.G.L., and H. H. Scullard. *The Oxford Classical Dictionary*. Oxford: Clarendon Press, 1970.

Harriot, Rosemary. *Poetry and Criticism before Plato*. London: Methuen, 1969.

Harrison, J. E. *Prolegomena to the Study of Greek Religion*. Cambridge: The University Press, 1903.

Howe, George, and Gustave Adolphus Harrer, revised by Preston Herschel Epps. *Greek Literature in Translation*. New York: Harper & Row, 1924/48.

Jaeger, Werner. *Paideia: The Ideals of Greek Culture*, trans. Gilbert Highet. New York: Oxford University Press, 1939/65.

Kagan, Donald. *The Great Dialogue: History of Greek Political Thought from Homer to Polybus*. New York: The Free Press, 1965.

Kitto, H.D.F. *The Greeks*. Baltimore: Penguin Books, 1951.

Lang, D. M., and D. R. Dudley. *The Penguin Companion to Classical, Oriental & African Literature*. New York: McGraw-Hill Book Company, 1969.

Lattimore, Richmond. *Story Patterns in Greek Tragedy*. Ann Arbor: The University of Michigan Press, 1964/69.

Lesky, Albin. *A History of Greek Literature*. London: Methuen, 1966.

Lucas, Donald William. *The Greek Tragic Poets*. Boston: Beacon Press, 1952.

Murray, A. S. *A History of Greek Sculpture*. London: J. Murray, 1890.

Myres, John L. *Who Were the Greeks?* New York: Biblo and Tannen, 1967.

New Encyclopedia Britannica. 15th edition. Chicago: The University of Chicago Press, 1988.

Nietzsche, Friedrich. *The Birth of Tragedy* and *The Genealogy of Morals*, trans. Francis Golffing. Garden City, New York: Doubleday, 1956.

Nilsson. *A History of Greek Religion.* New York: W. W. Norton & Company, 1964.

North, Helen. *Sophrosyne: Self-Knowledge and Self-Restraint in Greek Literature.* Ithaca, New York: Cornell University Press, 1966.

Peck, Harry Thurston. *Harper's Dictionary of Classical Literature and Antiquities.* New York: Cooper Square Publishers, Inc., 1965.

Rose, H. J. *A Handbook of Greek Mythology.* London: Methuen, 1950.

———. *A Handbook of Greek Literature: From Homer to the Age of Lucian.* London: Methuen, 1934/48.

Sikes, E. E. *The Greek View of Poetry.* London: Methuen, 1931.

Slater, Philip E. *The Glory of Hera: Greek Mythology and The Greek Family.* Boston: Beacon Press, 1968.

Smith, F. Seymour. *The Classics in Translation.* New York and London: Charles Scribner's Sons, 1930.

Snell, Bruno. *The Discovery of the Mind.* New York: Harper & Row, 1960.

Starr, Chester G. *The Ancient Greeks.* New York: Oxford University Press, 1971.

Symonds, John Addington. *Studies of the Greek Poets.* 2 vols. New York: Harper & Brothers, 1880.

Thomson, George. *Aeschylus and Athens: A Study of the Social Origins of Drama.* New York: Grosset & Dunlap, 1968.

Toynbee, A. J. *Greek Historical Thought.* Boston: Beacon Press, 1950.

Voegelin, Eric. *The World of the Polis.* Baton Rouge: Louisiana State University Press, 1957.

Webster, T. L. *From Mycenae to Homer.* New York: W. W. Norton & Company, 1964.

Wedeck, Harry E. *Classics of Greek Literature.* London: Vision, 1963.

Whall, A. L. *The Greek Reader.* Garden City, New York: Doubleday, Doran & Company, Inc., 1943.

Whitman, Cedric Hubbell. *Homer and the Heroic Tradition.* Cambridge: Harvard University Press, 1958.

ACKNOWLEDGMENTS

Aeneas the Tactician. Reprinted by permission of the publishers and the Loeb Classical Library from *Aeneas Tacticus, Asclepiodotus, Onasander,* translated by Messrs. W. A. Oldfather and Pease, edited by E. Capps, W.H.D. Rouse, L. A. Post, and E. H. Warmington. Cambridge, Mass: Harvard University Press, 1923. Reprinted 1943.

Aeschines. Reprinted by permission of the publishers and the Loeb Classical Library from *The Speeches of Aeschines,* translated by Charles Darwin Adams, edited by E. H. Warmington. Cambridge, Mass: Harvard University Press, 1919. Reprinted 1948, 1958, 1968.

Aeschylus. *Eumenides,* translated by David Grene and Richmond Lattimore. Published by University of Chicago Press, 1942.

Aesop. First four translated by Kenneth Atchity, by his permission; others by S. A. Handford, *Aesop's Fables.* Baltimore: Penguin Books, 1954/69. ©S. A. Handford.

Alcaeus. Translated by Willis Barnstone, *Greek Lyric Poetry.* Bloomington and London: Indiana University Press by kind permission of Willis Barnstone and Indiana University Press.

Alkman. Translated by Willis Barnstone, *Greek Lyric Poetry.* Bloomington and London: Indiana University Press by kind permission of Willis Barnstone and Indiana University Press.

Anacreon. Translated by Willis Barnstone, *Greek Lyric Poetry.* Bloomington and London: Indiana University Press by kind permission of Willis Barnstone and Indiana University Press.

Anaxagoras. *The First Philosophers of Greece,* trans. Arthur Fairbanks. New York: Charles Scribner's Sons, 1898.

Anaximander. *The First Philosophers of Greece,* trans. Arthur Fairbanks. New York: Charles Scribner's Sons, 1898. Numbers mine.

Anaximenes. *The First Philosophers of Greece*, trans. Arthur Fairbanks. New York: Charles Scribner's Sons, 1898. Numbers mine.

Anonymous, *Hymn to Aphrodite*. Translated by Charles Boer. By kind permission of Swallow Press.

Apollodorus: The Library. Translated by Sir James George Frazer. London: William Heineman, 1921.

Apollonius of Rhodes' *The Voyage of Argo*. Translated by E. V. Rieu. Middlesex: Penguin Books, 1959.

Archilochos. ". . . but if you're in a hurry," translated by Martin Robertson. All others: Bloomington and London: Indiana University Press by kind permission of Willis Barnstone and Indiana University Press.

Archimedes. Translated by T. L. Heath. London: C. J. Clay and Sons, 1897.

Aristophanes. Translator anonymous, in *The Complete Greek Drama*, edited by Whitney J. Oates and Eugene O'Neill, Jr. 2 vols. Vol. 2. New York: Random House, 1938. © 1938 Random House.

Aristotle. Translated by Ingram Bywater, *Aristotle on the Art of Poetry*, Oxford: The Clarendon Press, 1909.

Athenaeus. *Atheneaeus: The Deipnosophists*, trans. Charles Burton Gulick. 7 vols. London: William Heinemann Ltd; New York: G. P. Putnam's Sons, 1928.

Bion. "Lament for Adonis," translated by Elizabeth Barrett Browning (1806–1861).

Demosthenes: *The Crown and Other Orations of Demosthenes*, translated with an introduction by Charles Rann-Kennedy, courtesy of "Everyman's Library," David Campbell Publishers Ltd.

Dio Chrysostomos. Translated by Moses Hadas. Bobbs-Merrill, Library of Liberal Arts.

Dionysius of Halicarnassus, *The Roman Antiquities*. Translated by Earnest Cary. Cambridge, Mass.: Harvard University Press, 1937.

Dioscorides. *The Greek Herbal of Dioscorides*, Englished by John Goodyer A.D. 1655, ed. Robert T. Gunther. New York: Hafner Publishing Company, 1959. Originally published 1934. "Illustrated by a Byzantine A.D. 512."

Empedocles. The first entry is translated by John Addington Symonds, from *Studies of the Greek Poets*. 2 vols. New York: Harper & Brothers, 1880. All the rest from *The First Philosophers of Greece*, trans. Arthur Fairbanks. New York: Charles Scribner's Sons, 1898.

Epictetus. George Long. *The Discourses; with the Encheiridion*, & fragments. London: Bohn's Popular Library. Bell, 1877.

Epicurus. As edited by Paul MacKendrick and Herbert M. Howe, in *Classics in Translation. Vol. I: Greek Literature*. Madison, Milwaukee, London: University of Wisconsin Press, 1966. Reprinted by permission of the publishers and the Loeb Classical Library from the text of R. D. Hicks, translated by Herbert M. Howe. Cambridge, Mass: Harvard University Press, 1931.

Euclid. Translated by Dionysius Lardner. London: Henry G. Bohn, 1855.

Euripides. From *Three Plays of Euripides: Alcestis, Medea, The Bacchae,* by Paul Roche. Translation copyright © 1974 by Paul Roche. Reprinted by permission of W. W. Norton & Company.

Galen. Translated by Arthur John Brock, M.D. Cambridge, Mass.: Harvard University Press.

Heliodorus. *The Aethiopica.* Athens: Privately Printed for the Athenian Society, 1907.

Heraclitus. *The First Philosophers of Greece,* trans. Arthur Fairbanks. New York: Charles Scribner's Sons, 1898. Numbers mine.

Herodotus. Translated by George Rawlinson (1859).

Hesiod's *Works and Days* and *Theogony.* Translated by Richmond Lattimore. Ann Arbor: University of Michigan Press, 1959.

Hippocrates. Translated by Francis Adams, in Lewis A. Richard, *Ancient Greek Literature in Translation.* San Francisco: Argonaut Press, 1966.

Homer, *The Iliad.* Translated by Richmond Lattimore. © 1962 University of Chicago Press (first published 1951). Reprinted with permission of the publisher.

Homer, *The Odyssey.* Translated by Robert Fitzgerald. Garden City, New York: Doubleday/Anchor, 1961/63. © 1961, 1963 by Robert Fitzgerald.

Isocrates. Translated by George Norlin. 3 vols. Cambridge, Mass.: Harvard University Press, 1928/80.

Korinna. Translated by Willis Barnstone, *Greek Lyric Poetry.* Bloomington and London: Indiana University Press by kind permission of Willis Barnstone and Indiana University Press.

Leonidas of Tarentum. *Selections from the Greek Anthology,* ed. Graham R. Tomsom (Mrs. Rosamund Marriott-Ball Watson). London: Walter Scott, 1889. Translations by, in order: William M. Hardinge, Charles Whibley, Richard Garnett, Garnett, C. Merivale, Garnett, C. Merivale, John Hermann Merivale, Hardinge, Andrew Lang, Lang, Alma Strettell.

Longinus. Translated by W. Hamilton Fyfe. Cambridge, Mass.: Harvard University Press, 1927.

Longus' *Daphnis and Chloë.* Translated by Paul Turner. New York: Penguin, 1968.

Lucian. *Selections from the Greek Anthology,* ed. Graham R. Tomsom (Mrs. Rosamund Marriott-Ball Watson). London: Walter Scott, 1889. Translations by, in order: Richard Garnett, Garnett, Garnett, Garnett, Thomas Farley, Garnett. "Dialogues" translated by H. Williams.

Lysias. Reprinted by permission of the publishers and the Loeb Classical Library from *Lysias,* translated by W.R.M. Lamb, edited by G. P. Goold. Cambridge, Mass.: Harvard University Press, 1930. Reprinted 1943, 1957, 1960, 1967, 1976.

Meleager. Translated by Willis Barnstone, *Greek Lyric Poetry.* Bloomington and London: Indiana University Press by kind permission of Willis Barnstone and Indiana University Press.

Menander. Translation, W. G. Arnott. University of London. Athlone Press, 1960. With permission of the Athlone Press.

Nicander. *The Poems and Poetical Fragments,* ed. and translated by A.S.F. Gow and A. F. Scholfield. Cambridge, Mass.: Harvard University Press, 1953.

Parmenides. Translated by John Burnet (1892).

Pausanias. *Descriptions of Greece,* translated by W.H.S. Jones. 4 vols. London: William Heinemann, 1918. Cambridge: Harvard University Press, 1964. Citation from volume 1.

Pericles. *The Complete Writings of Thucydides, The Peloponnesian War.* The unabridged Crawley translation with an introduction by Joseph Gavorse. © 1934 The Modern Library, Inc.

Pindar. *Pindar's Victory Songs.* Translation, introduction, and preface by Frank J. Nisetich. Copyright © 1980. Reprinted by permission of the Johns Hopkins University Press.

Plato. *The Republic of Plato, An Ideal Commonwealth.* Translated by Benjamin Jowett. Revised Edition. New York: Willey Book Company, 1901.

Plotinus. *The Essence of Plotinus: Extracts from the Six Enneads and Porphyry's Life of Plotinus,* ed. Grace H. Turnbull. Translation, Stephen Mackenna. © 1934 by Grace H. Turnbull. Oxford University Press, 1948.

Plutarch. *Against Going into Debt:* Translated by Smith and Goodwin, *Greek Literature in Translation,* ed. George Howe, Gustave Adolphus Harrer, and Preston Herschel Epps. New York: Harper & Row, 1924, 1948. *Parallel Lives:* Translated by Sir Thomas North, *Plutarch's Lives,* London: J. J. Dent and Company, 1899.

Polybius. *The General History of the Wars of the Romans,* London: J. Davis, 1812.

Praxilla. Translated by Willis Barnstone, *Greek Lyric Poetry.* Bloomington and London: Indiana University Press by kind permission of Willis Barnstone and Indiana University Press.

Ptolemy. *Ptolemy's Almagest,* trans. G. J. Toomer. London: Gerald Duckworth & Company, Ltd., 1984. © Copyright 1984 G. J. Toomer.

Pythagoras. Translated by John Burnet. Cambridge: Cambridge University Press.

Sappho. Translated by Willis Barnstone, *Sappho and the Greek Lyric Poets.* Bloomington and London: Indiana University Press by kind permission of Willis Barnstone and Indiana University Press. Also, "Hymn to Aphrodite," translated by John Addington Symonds, from *Studies of the Greek Poets.* A&C Black, 1893.

Simonides. Translations by, in order: Kenneth Atchity; John Adington Symonds (modernized); J. Sterling (modernized); Alma Strettel. All others by Willis Barnstone, *Greek Lyric Poetry.* Bloomington and London: Indiana University Press by kind permission of Willis Barnstone and Indiana University Press.

Socrates. Translated by Benjamin Jowett, *The Dialogues* [of Plato]. New York: O.U.P., Bigelow, Brown & Company, Charles Scribner's Sons, 1892.

Solon. Fragments translated by Kathleen Freeman. By courtesy of the University of Wales Press. "Ten Ages" translated by Willis Barnstone, *Greek Lyric Poetry.* Bloomington and London: Indiana University Press by kind permission of Willis Barnstone and Indiana University Press.

Sophocles. *The Antigone of Sophocles,* translated by H. R. Fairclough and A. T. Murray. San Francisco: Paul Elder and Morgan Shepard, 1902.

Stesichoros. Translated by Willis Barnstone, *Greek Lyric Poetry.* Bloomington and London: Indiana University Press by kind permission of Willis Barnstone and Indiana University Press.

Strabo. *The Geography of Strabo.* Translated by H. C. Hamilton and W. Falconer. Henry G. Bohen, 1854.

Telesilla. Translated by Willis Barnstone, *Greek Lyric Poetry.* Bloomington and London: Indiana University Press by kind permission of Willis Barnstone and Indiana University Press.

Terpandros. Translated by Willis Barnstone, *Greek Lyric Poetry.* Bloomington and London: Indiana University Press by kind permission of Willis Barnstone and Indiana University Press.

Theocritos. Translated by Thelma Sargent.

Theognis. Translation of "Morality and Manners" by J. H. Frere (1840). Others by Willis Barnstone, *Greek Lyric Poetry.* Bloomington and London: Indiana University Press by kind permission of Willis Barnstone and Indiana University Press.

Theophrastus: The Characters. Translated by Philip Vellacott. Harmondsworth, Middlesex, England: Penguin Books, 1967. © 1967 Philip Vellacott.

Thucydides, *The Complete Writings of.* Translated by R. Crawley. New York: Random House, 1934.

Xenophanes. *The First Philosophers of Greece,* philosophy translated by Arthur Fairbanks. New York: Charles Scribner's Sons, 1898. Lyrics translated by Willis Barnstone, *Greek Lyric Poetry.* Bloomington and London: Indiana University Press by kind permission of Willis Barnstone and Indiana University Press.

Xenophon. Translated by J. S. Watson.

Zeno. *The First Philosophers of Greece,* translated by Arthur Fairbanks. New York: Charles Scribner's Sons, 1898. Numbers mine.

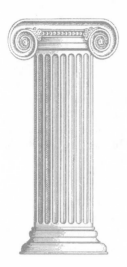
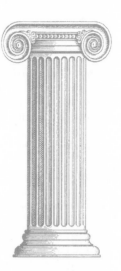

INDEX